D0981446

Drive & Hike

APPALACHIAN TRAIL

TIMOTHY MALCOLM

APPALACHIAN TRAIL
ROAD TRIP
WISCONSIN
Green Bay
Appleton
Sheboygan
Madison
Milwaukee
Rockford
Elgin
Chicago
Lake Michigan
Traverse City
Huron N.F.
Manistee N.F.
MICHIGAN
Sault Ste-Marie
Sudbury
Killarney P.P.
L. Nipissing
Manitoulin Island
Georgian Bay
Bruce Pen.
Parry Sound
Lake Huron
Saginaw Bay
Saginaw
Barrie
L. Simcoe
ONTARIO
Toronto
Hamilton
London
Grand Rapids
Flint
Lansing
Benton Harbor
Kalamazoo
South Bend
Detroit
Windsor
L. St. Clair
Ann Arbor
Buffalo
Lake Erie
Erie
Indiana Dunes N.L.
Toledo
ILLINOIS
INDIANA
Ft. Wayne
Cleveland
Allegheny N.F.
Lafayette
Urbana
Akron
Youngstown
Mansfield
PENNSYLVANIA
OHIO
Indianapolis
Columbus
Pittsburgh
Dayton
Wheeling
Cincinnati
Wayne N.F.
Morgantown
Hoosier N.F.
WEST VIRGINIA
Monongahela N.F.
Louisville
Frankfort
Huntington
Lexington
Charleston
KENTUCKY
Harrisonburg
Washington N.F.
New River Gorge N.R.
Waynesboro
Mammoth Cave N.P.
Daniel Boone N.F.
Beckley
Bowling Green
Nashville
Jefferson N.F.
Blacksburg
Roanoke
Lynchburg
Big South Fork N.R.
Murfreesboro
Kingsport
Damascus
Mt. Rogers
VIRGINIA
Shady Valley
Knoxville
TENNESSEE
Roan High Knob
Great Smoky Mountains N.P.
Mt. Guyot
Pisgah N.F.
Mt. Mitchell
Winston-Salem
Greensboro
Durham
Clingmans Dome
Chattanooga
Cherokee N.F.
Cherokee
Asheville
NORTH CAROLINA
Raleigh
Chattahoochee N.F.
Brasstown Bald
Uwharrie N.F.
Springer Mountain
Neels Gap
Greenville
Spartanburg
Charlotte
ALABAMA
Fayetteville
Birmingham
Sumter N.F.
Atlanta
Talladega N.F.
Columbia
GEORGIA
Augusta
SOUTH CAROLINA
Myrtle Beach
43
41
90
94
96
69
80
55
57
65
75
74
70
71
77
79
76
68
64
81
40
24
59
85
26
20
95
86
400
401

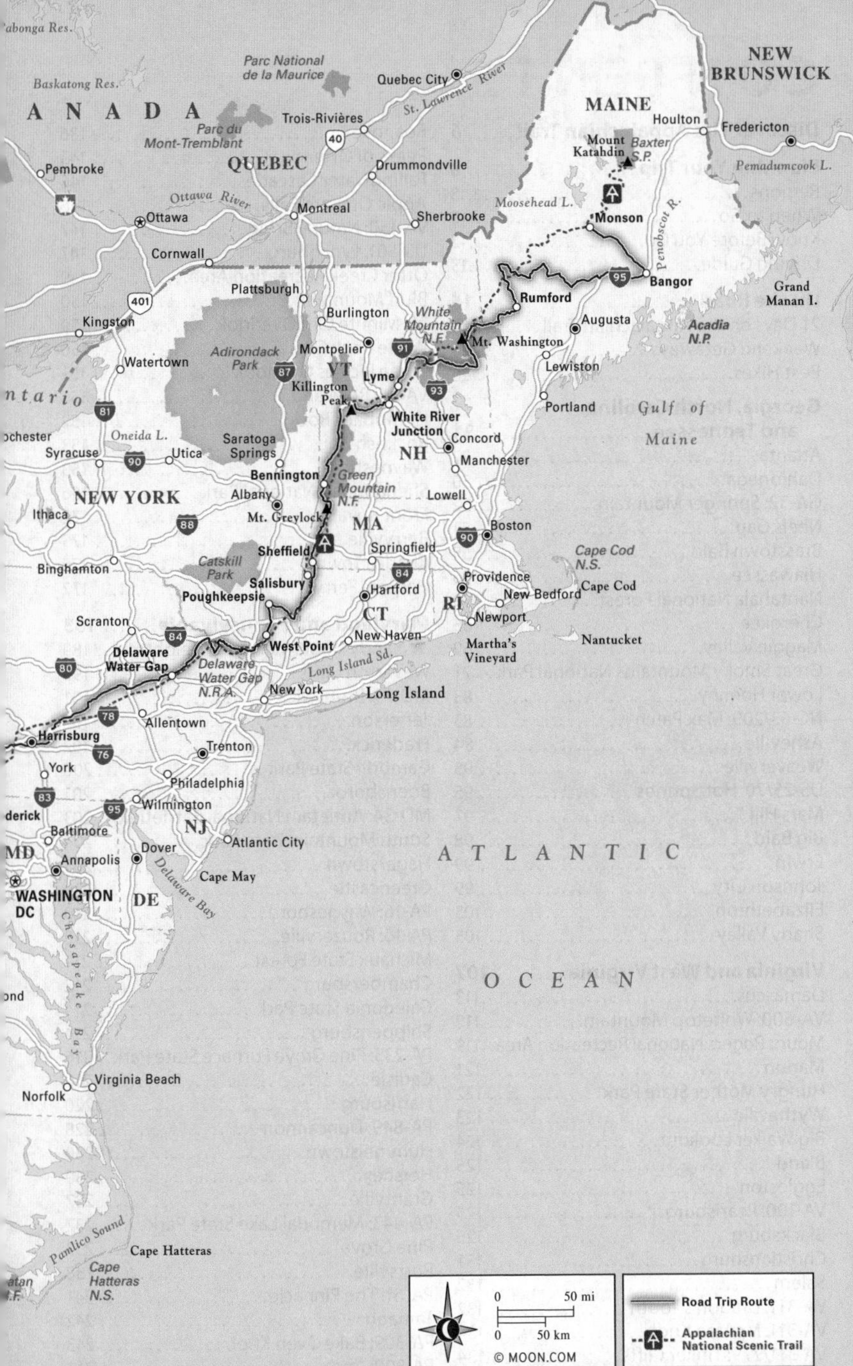

NEW BRUNSWICK
MAINE
QUEBEC
ANADA
Parc National de la Maurice
Quebec City
St. Lawrence River
Baskatong Res.
Trois-Rivières
Parc du Mont-Tremblant
Drummondville
Pembroke
Ottawa River
Ottawa
Montreal
Sherbrooke
Cornwall
Houlton
Fredericton
Pemadumcook L.
Mount Katahdin
Baxter S.P.
Moosehead L.
Monson
Penobscot R.
Bangor
Grand Manan I.
Rumford
Augusta
Acadia N.P.
White Mountain N.F.
Mt. Washington
Lewiston
Portland
Gulf of Maine
Plattsburgh
Burlington
Kingston
Adirondack Park
Montpelier
Watertown
VT
Killington Peak
Lyme
White River Junction
NH
Concord
Manchester
Oneida L.
Syracuse
Utica
Saratoga Springs
Bennington
Green Mountain N.F.
NEW YORK
Albany
Lowell
Ithaca
Mt. Greylock
MA
Boston
Sheffield
Springfield
Cape Cod N.S.
Binghamton
Catskill Park
Salisbury
Hartford
Providence
Cape Cod
Poughkeepsie
New Bedford
CT
RI
Newport
Scranton
New Haven
Martha's Vineyard
Nantucket
Delaware Water Gap
West Point
Long Island Sd.
Delaware Water Gap N.R.A.
New York
Long Island
Harrisburg
Allentown
Trenton
York
Philadelphia
Wilmington
Baltimore
NJ
Atlantic City
MD
Annapolis
Dover
Delaware Bay
Cape May
WASHINGTON DC
DE
Chesapeake Bay
ATLANTIC
OCEAN
Virginia Beach
Norfolk
Pamlico Sound
Cape Hatteras
Cape Hatteras N.S.
0
50 mi
0
50 km
© MOON.COM
Road Trip Route
Appalachian National Scenic Trail

CONTENTS

Discover The Appalachian Trail 6

Planning Your Trip 8
Regions 8
When to Go 10
Know Before You Go 12
Driving Guide 13

Hit the Road 15
21 Days on the Appalachian Trail 15
Weekend Getaways 23
Best Hikes 26

Georgia, North Carolina, and Tennessee 31
Atlanta 37
Dahlonega 50
GA-52: Springer Mountain 52
Neels Gap 53
Brasstown Bald 55
Hiawassee 56
Nantahala National Forest 59
Cherokee 66
Maggie Valley 69
Great Smoky Mountains National Park 71
Lower Hominy 83
NC-63/209: Max Patch 83
Asheville 84
Weaverville 95
US-25/70: Hot Springs 95
Mars Hill 97
Big Bald 98
Erwin 99
Johnson City 99
Elizabethton 103
Shady Valley 105

Virginia and West Virginia 107
Damascus 113
VA-600: Whitetop Mountain 118
Mount Rogers National Recreation Area 119
Marion 121
Hungry Mother State Park 122
Wytheville 123
Big Walker Lookout 124
Bland 125
Eggleston 125
VA-100: Pearisburg 125
Blacksburg 126
Christiansburg 131
Salem 132
VA-311: Dragon's Tooth 132
VA-311: McAfee Knob 134
VA-311/779: Tinker Cliffs 134
Roanoke 136
Peaks of Otter 143
Fallingwater Cascades 146
Apple Orchard Falls 146
VA-130: Natural Bridge 147
US-501: Lynchburg 147
Otter Creek Recreation Area 149
Bluff Mountain 150
20-Minute Cliff Overlook 150
White Rock Gap 150
Three Ridges Overlook 151
VA-56: Roseland 151
Humpback Rocks 152
Rockfish Gap 153
Waynesboro 153
Shenandoah National Park 156
Front Royal 172
Berryville 175
Charles Town 176
Harpers Ferry 177

Maryland and Pennsylvania 183
★ Sandy Hook: Maryland Heights 189
Weverton Cliffs 190
MD-79: Brunswick 191
Jefferson 192
Frederick 192
Gambrill State Park 200
Boonsboro 201
MD-34: Antietam National Battlefield 203
South Mountain State Park 204
Hagerstown 205
Greencastle 210
PA-16: Waynesboro 210
PA-16: Rouzerville 210
Michaux State Forest 211
Chambersburg 212
Caledonia State Park 214
Shippensburg 214
PA-233: Pine Grove Furnace State Park 216
Carlisle 218
Harrisburg 220
PA-849: Duncannon 228
Hummelstown 230
Hershey 230
Grantville 237
PA-443: Memorial Lake State Park 237
Pine Grove 237
Pottsville 238
PA-61: The Pinnacle 241
Tamaqua 242
PA-309: Bake Oven Knob 243
PA-309: Andreas 243

Lansford: No. 9 Coal Mine and Museum . . 244
★ Jim Thorpe . . . 244
Lehighton . . . 250
Beltzville State Park . . . 252
Brodheadsville . . . 252
Sciota: Eddie's Toy Museum . . . 253
PA-33: Wind Gap . . . 253
Stroudsburg . . . 254
Delaware Water Gap . . . 259
Delaware Water Gap National Recreation Area (Pennsylvania) . . . 259

New Jersey, New York, and Connecticut . . . 263

Delaware Water Gap National Recreation Area (New Jersey) . . . 270
NJ-94: Blairstown . . . 273
Branchville . . . 275
Stokes State Forest . . . 276
Sandyston . . . 277
US-6: Port Jervis, New York, to Tri-State Rock . . . 278
★ High Point State Park . . . 278
Sussex and Wantage . . . 280
Unionville: Wits End Tavern . . . 281
Pine Island . . . 281
NJ-517: Wawayanda State Park . . . 282
Warwick . . . 282
Greenwood Lake . . . 286
Sterling Forest State Park . . . 287
Bear Mountain State Park and Harriman State Park . . . 288
★ NY-9W: West Point . . . 295
Anthony's Nose . . . 299
Garrison . . . 299
Cold Spring . . . 301
Breakneck Ridge . . . 303
Beacon . . . 304
Poughkeepsie . . . 309
Pawling . . . 315
Kent . . . 316
Housatonic Meadows State Park . . . 321
West Cornwall . . . 321
Lakeville . . . 322
Salisbury . . . 322

Massachusetts and Vermont . . . 325

Mount Washington State Forest and Bash Bish Falls . . . 332
Sheffield . . . 334
MA-183: East Mountain State Forest . . . 336
Great Barrington . . . 337
Monument Mountain . . . 339
Stockbridge . . . 339
Lenox . . . 342
October Mountain State Forest . . . 345
Pittsfield . . . 346
MA-8A: Crane Museum of Papermaking . . 350
Cheshire: Ashuwillticook Rail Trail . . . 350
Adams: Susan B. Anthony Birthplace . . . 351
Mount Greylock State Reservation . . . 351
North Adams . . . 353
Clarksburg State Park . . . 358
Williamstown . . . 358
Bennington . . . 360
Shaftsbury: Robert Frost Stone House Museum . . . 364
Mount Equinox . . . 364
Manchester and Manchester Center . . . 365
Emerald Lake State Park . . . 370
Rutland . . . 370
Killington . . . 373
Woodstock . . . 378
Quechee . . . 381
Quechee State Park . . . 382
White River Junction . . . 384

New Hampshire and Maine . . . 387

Hanover . . . 393
Lyme . . . 397
NH-25: Polar Caves Park . . . 397
Mount Moosilauke . . . 398
Lost River Gorge and Boulder Caves . . . 398
White Mountain National Forest . . . 399
Gorham . . . 408
Shelburne . . . 409
ME-26: Grafton Notch State Park . . . 409
Rumford . . . 410
★ Angel Falls . . . 411
Rangeley . . . 413
Daggett Rock . . . 416
NH-25: ME-27: Sugarloaf Mountain . . . 416
Kingfield . . . 417
Norridgewock . . . 417
Skowhegan . . . 417
ME-15: Monson . . . 418
Gorman and Lyford . . . 419
ME-11: Baxter State Park . . . 421
Bangor . . . 423

Essentials . . . 431

Getting There . . . 432
Road Rules . . . 434
Hiking Basics . . . 436
Travel Tips . . . 436
Health and Safety . . . 437
Information and Services . . . 438
Suggested Reading . . . 438
Internet Resources . . . 439

Index . . . 441

List of Maps . . . 454

DISCOVER

The Appalachian Trail

The Appalachian Trail is the longest hiking-only footpath in the world, inspiring millions to test its presence and indulge in its beauty. Running continuously for 2,200 miles (3,540 km) from Maine to Georgia, it carves its way through wildflower fields, flowing rivers, and great peaks. Along the way, it tells the story of America.

The Appalachian Trail was conceptualized in 1921 as a way to connect city residents to American farms and wilderness. The Palisades Interstate Park Trail Conference—now the New York-New Jersey Trail Conference—created the first section of the trail, which opened in 1923 with a trailhead at the Bear Mountain Bridge in New York. Hiking or driving up to the bridge today, gazing at the rolling mountains on either side of the mighty Hudson River, you can understand the excitement the trail forefathers felt when completing their section.

Since its completion in 1937, the trail has been a monument to our connection to nature. Almost from the trail's creation, people have attempted to hike its entirety without interruption; today, some 3,000 people start thru-hikes each year, weathering the elements and pushing their minds and bodies to the very limits. Their journey wouldn't be the same without the small towns that punctuate the trail, made up of people who may prepare lunch, provide supplies, or offer shelter for the night.

It's this sense of community that has sustained the trail and its surrounding area for more than 80 years. Surprises await modern-day visitors at every step—whether in the delicious farm-to-table cuisine or the unique craft beer—but the best surprise may be the warm hospitality you'll find along the way.

To indulge in the Appalachian Trail is to experience the history of America itself, from the Civil War to Civil Rights. Every Appalachian Trail story is different, but each is distinctly American. Whether you're chasing it all the way from Georgia to Maine or connecting to it from a nearby city, you can blaze your own path on the Appalachian Trail.

PLANNING YOUR TRIP

Regions

Georgia, North Carolina, and Tennessee

The bustling metropolis of **Atlanta,** with its museums and eccentric neighborhoods, makes a perfect base for a trip through the lower Appalachian Mountains. This region features the wild **Nantahala National Forest,** home to Appalachian Trail town **Franklin, North Carolina,** plus the popular **Great Smoky Mountains National Park,** where millions annually visit to summit **Clingmans Dome,** the highest point on the Appalachian Trail. Bluegrass, beer, and art reign in exciting and young **Asheville, North Carolina.**

Virginia and West Virginia

The Appalachian Trail ambles along a constant ridge in Virginia and West Virginia, primarily through the **Blue Ridge Mountains** and **Shenandoah National Park.** Stopover cities include **Waynesboro,** with its laid-back outdoorsy vibe; **Front Royal** and its Civil War history; and **Roanoke,** where a **neon star** rises high above the skyline and beckons lovers of all stripes. Nearby

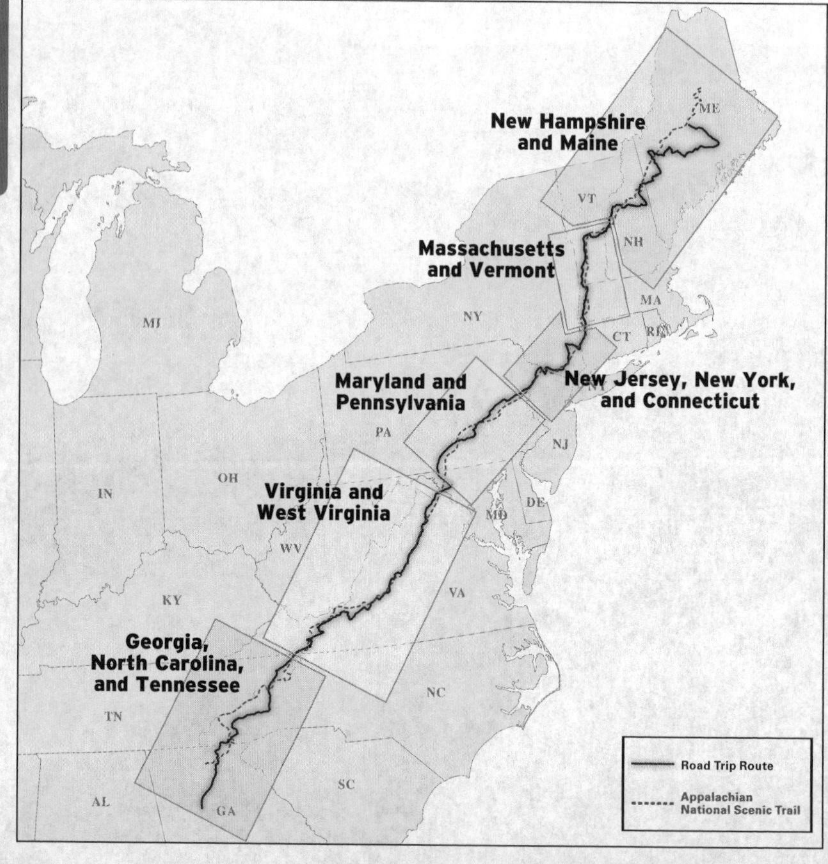

Clockwise from top left: a sign for the Appalachian Trail; Soco Falls near Maggie Valley in North Carolina; the Old Man of the Mountain Memorial in New Hampshire.

is iconic **McAfee Knob,** a necessary photo op, and every trail hiker should stop in **Harpers Ferry,** a historic community that's also home to the **Appalachian Trail Conservancy.**

Maryland and Pennsylvania

There isn't much of the Appalachian Trail in Maryland, but respites are welcome in **Hagerstown** and **Frederick,** the latter an artsy hub with fun dining and drinking spots. The Keystone State is known as **Rocksylvania** as the trail cuts through tenuous terrain. Hikers will find great backpacking opportunities at **Pine Grove Furnace State Park,** home to the **Appalachian Trail Museum.** In **Harrisburg,** visit the **National Civil War Museum** and dine at one of several fine restaurants. College town **East Stroudsburg** and trail towns **Duncannon** and **Delaware Water Gap** are not to be missed.

New Jersey, New York, and Connecticut

Visitors to **Delaware Water Gap National Recreation Area** can find marvelous **waterfalls** and the view from **Mount Tammany.** The **High Point Monument** towers above northern New Jersey, while in New York, hikers descend to the lowest point on the Appalachian Trail at the **Bear Mountain Bridge.** Stopover cities **Beacon** and **Poughkeepsie** offer artistic and gastronomical opportunities, and in Connecticut, the charming **Kent** and quaint **Salisbury** make excellent day-tripping destinations.

Massachusetts and Vermont

The Appalachian Trail climbs into the New England woods toward **Mount Greylock,** while along US-7, tourists enjoy the weekender charms of **Great Barrington, Stockbridge,** and **Lenox,** home to antiques centers and bistro dining. **North Adams** and **MASS MoCA** are necessary stops for art lovers, as are locations celebrating **Grandma Moses, Norman Rockwell,** and **Robert Frost.** In Vermont, scale the impressive **Mount Equinox** and daunting **Killington Peak** before visiting quintessential New England communities **Manchester Center** and **Woodstock.**

New Hampshire and Maine

Cooler with the chance of serious precipitation throughout most of the year, northern New England includes the alpine climate zones of **White Mountain National Forest,** anchored by the impressive **Mount Washington.** The trail is rugged and sometimes dangerous out here, especially through Maine's **100-Mile Wilderness.** Still, iconic moments can be stolen at **Height of Land** in quaint **Rangeley** and the great **Katahdin** inside **Baxter State Park.**

When to Go

Those who thru-hike the Appalachian Trail pack it from **March to October,** which is when you're best off as well. Spring can be wonderful south of Pennsylvania, when waterfalls are active and bugs aren't yet teeming, but north of the Mason-Dixon Line you're more likely to encounter snow or torrential rain through April. Summer is a fine time to visit the New England section of the trail, though mud is common in Vermont and bugs will attack throughout the season. If you want to hike parts of Great Smoky Mountains National Park and Shenandoah National Park, consider that traffic will be highest in summer and during fall weekends.

Speaking of **fall:** It gets busy everywhere. The leaves burst in oranges, yellows, and reds starting in late September in Maine and New Hampshire, and the color moves south through October. Mid-October is prime time for **leaf-peeping** in Connecticut, New York, and New Jersey, and the trail area will be packed. Fall colors reach the

Best Festivals

the popular hiker parade at Damascus Trail Days

From bluegrass to mountain biking to the AT itself, there's a great variety of festivals along the route.

- **Dahlonega Trailfest,** Dahlonega, GA (page 50): Breweries, wineries, craft vendors, and more set up booths at this southern AT stop in **September.**
- **Hot Springs Trailfest,** Hot Springs, NC (page 96): For a full weekend in **late April,** Hot Springs celebrates the AT with music, games, a duck race, and more.
- **Mountain Sports Festival,** Asheville, NC (page 91): With BMX mountain biking, disc golf, and other sports, this **May** event celebrates getting outside and getting in shape.
- **Damascus Trail Days,** Damascus, VA (page 114): The quintessential trail town celebrates the great outdoors with a **May** festival of speakers, live music, and a popular hiker parade.
- **Flip-Flop Festival,** Harpers Ferry, WV (page 180): This unique festival in **April** celebrates flip flop AT hikers with live music, food, and workshops.
- **Mason-Dixon Appalachian Trail Outdoor Festival,** Rouzerville, PA (page 210): Meet hikers at this small but festive **June** event that also includes music and a silent auction.
- **Duncannon Appalachian Trail Festival,** Duncannon, PA (page 228): Thru-hikers hit Duncannon around **June;** Duncannon celebrates with a morning hike, live music, crafts, and face painting for the kids.
- **Fresh Grass,** North Adams, MA (page 356): Hang out at MASS MoCA for this annual **September** celebration of bluegrass and folk music.
- **Skowhegan State Fair,** Skowhegan, ME (page 418): Enjoy a slice of country in **August** at this old-fashioned agricultural fair.

Virginias and southern Appalachians by late October, a fine time to visit the national parks because traffic is somewhat lighter.

From November to February, several roads are **subject to closure,** including Skyline Drive, Blue Ridge Parkway, Mount Washington Auto Road, and local roads at high elevations. Closures sometimes continue into March and April.

Know Before You Go

Weather

Considering the Appalachian Trail traverses nearly the entire Eastern Seaboard, weather can vary wildly from one location to the next. Areas south of Pennsylvania generally enjoy comfortable temperatures from April to October, though there's always the threat of snow in higher elevations in March and April, and even in October. In the summer average temperatures are 75-80°F (24-27°C), though conditions are cooler at higher elevations. Winter can be somewhat comfortable in the southern Appalachians, with temperatures in the 40s and 50s, but wind, rain, and snow are always possible.

North of the Mason-Dixon Line is another story. Between Connecticut and Pennsylvania the summers are hot and humid, while up in New England you can enjoy 65-75°F (18-24°C) days regularly from June to September. Spring and fall can bring a range of outcomes, with temperatures typically anywhere between 30 and 65°F (minus 1-18°C) with chances of torrential wind, rain, and snow. Only serious travelers enjoy tripping the north during winter, when temperatures routinely fall below freezing, and snow and ice are always possible.

Reservations and Passes

You'll need permits to camp at both **Great Smoky Mountains National Park** ($20) and **Shenandoah National Park** (free). Reservations are required to stay overnight in the Smokies, while all backcountry travelers need a permit at Shenandoah. Reservations are also required inside **Baxter State Park** in Maine, which has a quota for the number of permits it allots to long-distance hikers to climb **Katahdin.** If you're day-hiking Katahdin, you don't need a permit, but you'll need to follow day-use trails and it's advisable to making a parking reservation in advance. Also, only thru-hikers are permitted to camp overnight inside Pennsylvania state game lands. If you're planning on overnight camping at a campground, call ahead to make a reservation.

Camping

If hiking on or near the Appalachian Trail, you'll likely be close to either **shelters** or **campgrounds.** There are hundreds of manmade **lean-tos** (three-sided structures) along the trail, which are available to all hikers. Lean-tos can fit as many as a dozen campers, though no two lean-tos are the same. Hikers are asked to share lean-tos with others; if the structures are filled to capacity, typically you can camp nearby, or you may have to hike to the next lean-to.

Tent camping is also allowed along much of the Appalachian Trail, though there are some regulations and exclusions in specific areas. When camping, always follow **leave no trace** practices by taking all waste with you and sealed in a pack. Black bears are common in the backcountry and are attracted to scent. National parks and other designated areas will have bear-proof disposal containers; always keep food with you until you're able to dispose of waste safely in one of these containers.

Campfires are allowed throughout much of the trail, but there are exceptions depending on state or park regulations. Generally, campfires should be kept small and must always be extinguished before retiring for the night.

What to Pack

At the bare minimum, hikers should wear **breathable clothing** and **sturdy shoes**—preferably **boots** with good traction—and bring plenty of **water**. For day hikes of up to 10-12 miles (16-19.3 km), at least **two liters** of water is typically necessary. Backpacks that include **bladders** tend to work well for long-distance hikes, while experienced campers may bring **water filters,** which can be used to collect water. If collecting water in the backcountry, be sure to filter or boil it. Either way, anyone who hikes should pack water.

Hiking poles are useful in rocky areas, on steep hikes, and in potentially muddy or leaf-strewn areas that may be slippery. Most trails are well marked by **blazes** (the Appalachian Trail follows white blazes, and spur trails that lead to sights and campgrounds follow blue blazes), but bringing a **compass** is a good idea. Long-distance hikers should always leave contact information and hiking plans with friends and family members.

You should pack **food,** even if you're trekking a short distance. Granola is popular, as is small fruit (oranges, berries, grapes), meat and cheese sticks, and tidy sandwiches (think peanut butter and jelly or standard meat and cheese on bread). Always bring a plastic bag for food waste and trash, and store that bag in a backpack, taking it with you.

Long-distance and overnight hikers will pack equipment including but not limited to hammocks, tents, sleeping pads, blankets, skillets, pots, a camp stove, plates, silverware, cups, a utility knife, and dry foods such as rice and pasta. An **extra pair of clothing** is always a good idea when hiking, even for short distances, and dressing in layers that can be removed when warm is recommended. For areas where elevations can exceed 3,000 feet (915 m), keeping skin covered is a necessity—think gloves, hats, facial stockings, headbands, and jackets.

Driving Guide

Getting There and Back

The most convenient airport at the southern end of the route, especially for those wanting to visit or start a trek at Springer Mountain, Georgia, is **Hartsfield-Jackson Atlanta International Airport** (800/897-1910, www.atl.com, ATL), the world's busiest airport by passenger traffic. Maine's **Bangor International Airport** (207/992-4600, www.flybangor.com, BGR) is most convenient for those in the northern end of the route. Halfway through, **Harrisburg International Airport** (888/235-9442, www.flyhia.com, MDT) in Pennsylvania provides a wealth of connections to the East and Midwest.

Because the Appalachian Trail is a ribbon through America's eastern wilderness, there are more than a few places where you'll have to rely on state and county roads to get from one place to another. The most convenient interstate highways for travelers looking for quicker routes include **I-75,** which connects Atlanta travelers to the Blue Ridge; **I-81,** which runs alongside the Blue Ridge up through Pennsylvania; **I-84,** which cuts across New Jersey and New York to New England; and **I-91,** which runs up the middle of New England to **US-2,** the final stretch through Maine.

Rental Cars

Your best bet for car rentals is at **nearby airports,** as you'll be hard-pressed to find agencies in the more remote areas along the route. Note that much of the route is at higher elevations and has frequent twists and turns, sometimes-dangerous curves, and poor road conditions (especially in New Hampshire and Maine). That's to say, be careful with your rental.

Driving Tips

The Appalachian Trail brings city dwellers into wild countryside where forests thrive, wildlife roams, and GPS devices may not always work. Be sure to exercise caution when driving this route, handling curves at low speeds and observing all speed limits. While a black bear is unlikely to walk out onto the road (it has happened, though), squirrels, raccoons, and skunks are seen far more often. Still, the biggest wildlife threat to your car is the white-tailed deer, which is common to the eastern United States. **Deer pose the highest risk** around sunrise and sunset, and at night when visibility is low. Honk your horn if approaching deer by the road, brake slowly, and never swerve to avoid hitting one.

Finally, while in New Hampshire and Maine—especially on state and local roads—**be on the lookout for moose.** The highest collision risk is during late summer and early fall, during the fall breeding season, and at dusk or night. Drive slowly and use high beams whenever necessary.

As for GPS, you're bound to lose a connection with it (and your smartphone) at some point, especially if you're driving in the woods. **Plan each day's meal and rest stops ahead of time.**

Road Conditions

In higher elevations, roads will freeze or be heavily **snow-packed,** especially between **November and April.** These mountain roads are also subject to wind and rain damage. Sections of the Blue Ridge Parkway, plus Skyline Drive in Shenandoah National Park, and roads inside protected lands will close when conditions are unsafe for driving. Before setting out on your trip, inquire about road conditions with the appropriate parks and sites.

High-elevation roads may become extremely narrow and challenging to navigate. If you feel any trepidation about driving on a road, don't attempt it. When driving on a narrow road where traffic moves in both directions, proceed slowly and take note of areas where you can pull off to let oncoming traffic pass.

Mileposts

You'll only need to observe mileposts on the **Blue Ridge Parkway** and on **Skyline Drive** in Shenandoah National Park. The Blue Ridge Parkway counts down south to north, starting at Mile 469.1 at Great Smoky Mountains National Park and ending at Mile 0 at Shenandoah. Skyline Drive then begins at Mile 105 at the park's southern entrance, counting down to Mile 0 at the northern entrance in Front Royal.

Fueling Up

As a general rule, fill up the tank before starting a daily drive, or whenever you're below a half-tank and you've reached a town or city with at least one gas station. You'll encounter the greatest challenge in the area between **Chattahoochee-Oconee National Forest in Georgia and Asheville, North Carolina,** where stops include Hiawassee, Franklin, and Hot Springs; on the **Blue Ridge Parkway** and **Skyline Drive,** where nearby gas stations might be up to 30 miles east or west of an exit; and in **Maine,** where gas is harder to find north of US-2.

If you're pinching pennies, **avoid filling up too much in Pennsylvania and Connecticut,** where gas prices are historically well higher than the national average. **Tennessee and Virginia tend to have lower gas prices** than the national average.

HIT THE ROAD

This road trip follows the traditional thru-hiker's journey, which starts in Georgia and runs north to Maine. It begins in **Atlanta,** a major transportation hub, then follows Route 19 north to meet up with the Appalachian Trail as it weaves through wild Georgia, Tennessee, and North Carolina. From there, it follows a series of state routes, avoiding interstate highways to mirror the trail's purpose of connecting visitors to the countryside. At the northern portion of the route in Maine, it leaves the trail and extends to **Bangor,** the closest transportation hub to the end of the trail at Mount Katahdin.

While the route generally parallels the Appalachian Trail, in areas where accommodations near the trail are less frequent (such as parts of the Tennessee/North Carolina border, southern Pennsylvania and western/central Maine), the route separates from the trail and crosses small towns and cities such as Asheville, NC, and Hershey, PA.

Popular roads marked as part of the route include the **Blue Ridge Parkway** and **Skyline Drive** in Virginia, **Route 9** following the Hudson River in New York, and **Route 7,** which crosses many towns in Connecticut, Massachusetts, and Vermont. These roads typically feature plenty of nearby hikes and outstanding vistas.

21 Days on the Appalachian Trail

Day 1

ATLANTA

Spend a day learning about a couple of American legacies at the **Jimmy Carter Presidential Library and Museum** and the **Martin Luther King Jr. National Historic Site.** Spend your evening with the hip kids in **Cabbagetown** and **Reynoldstown.**

Day 2

ATLANTA TO CHEROKEE

161 miles/259 km, 3 hours

Leave early and take I-85 and US-23 north for two hours to reach **Nantahala National Forest**, a rather unheralded region of challenging peaks and wild trails. Hike **Wayah Bald** (7.2 miles/11.6 km, 4.5 hours), then stop in **Franklin** for a beer and a bite at **Lazy Hiker Brewing Co.** before spending the night in **Cherokee.**

Day 3

GREAT SMOKY MOUNTAINS NATIONAL PARK

108 miles/174 km, 3.75 hours

Start your day with breakfast at **Peter's Pancakes and Waffles** and a visit to the **Museum of the Cherokee Indian.** You'll spend the rest of the day inside **Great Smoky Mountains National Park**, the most visited national park in America. Drive up **Newfound Gap Road** to **Clingmans Dome,** the highest point along the Appalachian Trail. If you're up for a challenge, spend the rest of your afternoon hiking **Rocky Top Trail** (13.3 miles/21.4 km, 7 hours). After your drive or hike, continue on to **Gatlinburg** for dinner and to spend the night.

Day 4

GATLINBURG TO ASHEVILLE

81 miles/130 km, 1.75 hours

Wake up and head to **Asheville** via US-321 N and I-40 E. Mosey around downtown for a bit and visit the **Biltmore Estate.** Then check out the **River Arts district,** where you can peruse plenty of cool local art, before visiting **Wedge Brewing Company**. Be sure not to miss **Burial Beer Co.** while in the city. Finish the night with a nice meal at **The Admiral.**

Clockwise from top left: the Smokies as seen from an overlook on Newfound Gap Road; the Appalachian Mountains as seen from the Blue Ridge Parkway; downtown Atlanta.

Day 5

ASHEVILLE TO ELIZABETHTON

100 miles/161 km, 2.5 hours

Fuel up with some amazing biscuits at **Biscuit Head** before making the 40-minute trek via US-25 to **Hot Springs.** Hike **Lover's Leap Trail** (1.8 miles/2.9 km, 1 hour) and relax in the water at **Hot Springs Resort and Spa**. Then drive a little over an hour on US-208 and US-26 to **Johnson City.** Reward yourself with a beer at **Yee-Haw Brewing Company**. Before the day ends, drive the extra 10 miles (16.1 km) on US-321 to **Elizabethton.** Cool off in **Blue Hole Falls** and prepare for a heavenly plate at **Big Dan's BBQ.**

Day 6

ELIZABETHTON TO ROANOKE

180 miles/290 km, 3.5 hours

Start this trip by driving TN-91 north to **Damascus.** After an hour, you'll want to stretch your legs at the **Virginia Creeper Trail.** After another hour of driving on US-81 north, stop in **Wytheville** to honor Appalachia's first lady at the **Edith Bolling Wilson Birthplace and Museum.** Continue for another hour up US-81 to Christiansburg for a lip-smacking late lunch at **Due South BBQ.** Continue for another 45 minutes to reach **Roanoke** by evening. Hang out at **Center in the Square** and grab a bite at **Jack Brown's Beer and Burger Joint,** then finish the night at the **Roanoke Star.**

Day 7

ROANOKE TO WAYNESBORO

137 miles/221 km, 3 hours

Wake early to hike **McAfee Knob** (8.8 miles/14.2 km, 4.5 hours)—at sunrise, if you can—then take the **Blue Ridge Parkway** to high points like **Peaks of Otter** and **20-Minute Cliff Overlook.** Spend a night in **Waynesboro**, where you can feel like a thru-hiker on a much-needed zero day, grabbing a beer at **Basic City Beer Co.**

Day 8

WAYNESBORO TO BIG MEADOWS

60 miles/97 km, 2 hours

Be sure to spend this full day breathing in the air at **Shenandoah National Park.** If you're looking for a big hike, test the **Riprap-Wildcat Ridge Loop** (9.8 miles/15.8 km, 6 hours). If you'd rather take a shorter hike, visit **Blackrock Summit** (5.3 miles/8.5 km, 3 hours). Grab some picnic fare at **Loft Mountain Wayside** before ending the day on an easy but pretty note at **Dark Hollow Falls** (1.3 miles/2.1 km, 45 minutes). Set up camp just in time to watch the stars at **Big Meadows.**

Day 9

SHENANDOAH NATIONAL PARK

43 miles/69 km, 1.75 hours

Start with a real challenge by hiking the most popular trail in the park, **Old Rag** (9.1 miles/14.6 km, 5-8 hours), or go for the shorter but beautiful Pinnacles trail (2 miles/3.2 km, 1 hour), which is on the AT. Take US-211 west to **Luray** to grab a big lunch at **Triple Crown BBQ** before mingling with tourists at **Luray Caverns.** Spend the night in Luray.

Day 10

BIG MEADOWS TO FRONT ROYAL

53 miles/85 km, 1.5 hours

A Shenandoah experience isn't complete without a hike on **Hogback Mountain** (7 miles/11.3 km, 4 hours). After your hike, head to **Front Royal;** make a stop at the **Virginia Beer Museum** and drink off that sweat. If you're so inclined, take a detour to **Skyline Cavern** before your beer. Eat dinner at **Blue Wing Frog** and stay the night at **Mountain Home,** just 120 steps from the Appalachian Trail itself.

Day 11

FRONT ROYAL TO FREDERICK

65 miles/105 km, 1.5 hours

Drive an hour north on US-522 and US-340, because for anyone with even

Best Views

Harpers Ferry from Maryland Heights

From high summits to neon perches, these are some of the coolest places to check out fall colors, cityscapes, and long sunsets.

- **Rocky Top, TN** (page 76) is not only a Tennessee landmark, but also a place to catch outstanding views of the southern Appalachians.
- **Mount Rogers, VA** (page 119) stands at 5,728 feet (1,746 m) above sea level and gives hikers fantastic views of the Virginia highlands.
- **Roanoke Star, VA** (page 136), built with more than 2,000 feet (610 m) of neon tubing, offers a pretty nighttime view of Roanoke.
- **Maryland Heights, MD** (page 189) lets visitors peer down into iconic Harpers Ferry.
- **The Pinnacle, PA** (page 241) offers an impressive view of central Pennsylvania valleys, but only after a tough hike through Rocksylvania terrain.
- **High Point, NJ** (page 278) is not only a monument at the tip of New Jersey, it's also a slightly terrifying walk up a staircase. The views are nice, though.
- **Bear Mountain, CT** (page 323) is a worthy peak capped by an impressive rock pile. Sit atop and stare for a while.
- **Mount Greylock, MA** (page 352) stands at 3,491 feet (1,064 m), providing views of the Berkshires and the tiny towns below—for those who make it to the top.
- **Mount Moosilauke, NH** (page 398) is a challenging summit, but at the top you'll gaze upon the White Mountains and Adirondacks.
- **Height of Land, ME** (page 413) sits atop Spruce Mountain, offering an unbelievable view of wild Maine forests, lakes, and mountains.

Clockwise from top left: an Appalachian Trail sign in Harpers Ferry, West Virginia; High Point Monument in New Jersey; Abbott Lake and Peaks of Otter on the Blue Ridge Parkway.

Best Breweries

There is nothing better after a long hike than a cold beer (or three). Keep the following breweries in mind when you're planning your trip, because these are the ones that'll provide the quickest and coolest refreshment.

Long Trail Brewing Co. in Vermont

- **Lazy Hiker Brewing Co.,** Franklin, NC (page 63): Hey, it's made for hikers, with an outdoor space for kicking back. Great after hiking **Wayah Bald.**
- **Nantahala Brewing Taproom & Brewery,** Bryson City, NC (page 64): Enjoy a session IPA at this hiker-friendly brewery, especially after a hike to **Deep Creek.**
- **Hi-Wire Brewing,** Asheville, NC (page 89): Need a big beer or two, and want to chill out with a game, after hiking **Max Patch?** Head to this Asheville haunt.
- **Damascus Brewery,** Damascus, VA (page 116): All Appalachian Trail hikers should stop in Damascus, and this brewery is a prime spot for relaxing with a cold one. Head there after hiking **Mount Rogers.**
- **Devils Backbone Basecamp Brewpub,** Roseland, WV (page 151): This popular brewery in Western Virginia positions itself as a must-visit for hikers. It's also a must after hiking the strenuous **Three Ridges.**
- **Basic City Beer Co.,** Waynesboro, VA (page 154): Hikers can find a friend at this busy Waynesboro spot that has live music and food truck grub. Perfect after a **Humpback Rocks** hike.
- **Zeroday Brewing Co.,** Harrisburg, PA (page 224): Named for that very important rest day for thru-hikers the world over, this hangout has big Belgians and a great sense of humor. Hit it up after hiking to **Hawk Rock Overlook** over in Duncannon.
- **Hudson Valley Brewery,** Beacon, NY (page 306): A short hike from **Breakneck Ridge,** this innovative brewery is a bit off the trail but completely worth it.
- **Long Trail Brewing Co.,** Bridgewater Corners, VT (page 378): After taking on **Killington Peak,** book it to this brewing mecca and spend some time at its family friendly taproom.
- **Moat Mountain Smokehouse & Brewing Co.,** North Conway, NH (page 406): Chow down on a burger or some barbecue while downing a pint or two after hiking **Mount Washington.** You've earned it.

a passing interest in the Appalachian Trail, **Harpers Ferry** is a necessary stop. Visit the **Appalachian Trail Conservancy Headquarters** and pay respects at **Jefferson Rock.** Then make the quick jaunt to the lookout at **Maryland Heights,** which provides a premium view of Harpers Ferry. Continue on to **Frederick,** where you'll spend the night; be sure to walk downtown and glimpse the **Community Bridge Mural.**

Day 12

FREDERICK TO HARRISBURG

96 miles/155 km, 2 hours

Grab breakfast in Frederick, then drive to **Pine Grove Furnace State Park** to see the true halfway point of the trail at the **Appalachian Trail Museum.** Get to Harrisburg in time to visit the **National Civil War Museum,** then spend the evening walking its historic streets and enjoying a nice dinner at **Home 231.**

Day 13

HARRISBURG TO JIM THORPE

90 miles/145 km, 2 hours

After breakfast in Harrisburg, drive through the towns of Pennsylvania coal country via **I-81** and **US-209.** Stop to stretch your legs in the old mining city of **Pottsville,** taking a tour of **D.G. Yuengling & Son Brewery** and grabbing lunch at **Ruby's Kitchen.** Continue for another hour to the cozy town of **Jim Thorpe.** Visit the **Old Jail Museum** and, if you have time, hike **Glen Onoko Falls.** Enjoy dinner at **Moya.**

Day 14

JIM THORPE TO BLAIRSTOWN

55 miles/89 km, 1.5 hours

Head east on US-209 to **East Stroudsburg.** Grab breakfast at **The Cure Café.** Next, visit **Delaware Water Gap National Recreation Area** and hike the **Tumbling Waters Trail** (3 miles/4.8 km, 1.5 hours) or **Mount Tammany** via the **Loop Trail** (3.5 miles/5.6 km, 2.5 hours). Honor *Friday the 13th* with a meal at the **Blairstown Diner** and take a walk downtown by **Blair Academy.**

Day 15

BLAIRSTOWN TO BEACON

120 miles/193 km, 3 hours

You'll want to stop the car numerous times to view the scenic beauty of the rolling Hudson Valley on this trek. Drive CR-519 and NJ-23 north and stop to hike **High Point Trail** (4 miles/6.4 km, 2 hours) in **High Point State Park.** Continue onto **Warwick** for lunch at **Fetch,** and ice cream at **Bellvale Farms Creamery.** You'll end the day on another high note with a sunset hike to the top of **Bear Mountain** (4 miles/6.4 km, 2 hours), where the Appalachian Trail was born. Spend the night in **Beacon.**

Day 16

BEACON TO SALISBURY

97 miles/156 km, 2.75 hours

Drive 45 minutes to the **Franklin D. Roosevelt Presidential Library & Museum,** then head toward Connecticut and visit **Kent** for lunch at **Kingsley Tavern.** Be sure to see **Bull's Bridge** while you're there. **Caleb's Peak & St. John's Ledges** (4 miles/6.4 km, 2.5 hours) makes a great half-day hike, before spending the evening in **Salisbury.** Dine at **White Hart Restaurant & Inn;** maybe get a room there, too.

Day 17

SALISBURY TO PITTSFIELD

40 miles/64 km, 1 hour

Spend a leisurely day in Massachusetts, starting with a light hike on **Bash Bish Falls Trail** (1 mile/1.6 km, 30 minutes). Visit **Great Barrington** for a late breakfast at **Fuel Coffee Shop.** Then go bigger with a hike of **Monument Mountain.** Have a late lunch in **Stockbridge,** grabbing something quickly at **Elm Street Market,** before visiting the **Berkshire Botanical Garden.** Spend the evening in Lenox, maybe taking in a show at **Tanglewood Music Center.** Whatever you do, have

Trail Magic

Hiking the Appalachian Trail is a lot easier when there's some help out there. Thus enters "trail magic," in which a person helps a hiker out by leaving a care package at a key spot, giving out some free beer, or offering up a place for the night. You can do your part by volunteering officially or stopping by a trail town, where you can buy a thru-hiker a beer or drop off supplies at a shelter.

Volunteer Opportunities

- **Mount Rogers A.T. Club** (www.mratc.pbworks.com): Find out about opportunities to keep the trail clean and navigable in the Virginia highlands
- **New York-New Jersey Trail Conference** (www.nynjtc.org): Work to keep the northern portion of the AT in good shape.
- **AMC-Berkshire** (www.amcberkshire.org): Help crews work on the Appalachian Trail in western Massachusetts.
- **Appalachian Trail Conservancy** (www.appalachiantrail.org): Volunteer with the ATC to paint blazes, fix shelters, or clear trees.

Trail Communities

- **Hiawassee, GA** (page 56): This is an early stop for many thru-hikers for its modest food options and gear shop.
- **Franklin, NC** (page 63): This town in Nantahala National Forest has a must-stop brewery and an accommodating lodging community.
- **Hot Springs, NC** (page 95): The AT threads right through this small outpost, which has an AT festival in April.
- **Damascus, VA** (page 113): "Trail Town USA" is has multiple trail crossings, a huge festival every May, several gear shops, and a very hospitable brewery.
- **Waynesboro, VA** (page 153): Hikers love the Chinese buffet and brewery at this stop between the Blue Ridge and Shenandoah National Park.
- **Duncannon, PA** (page 228): Duncannon has a few inexpensive places for hikers to stay and a festival every June.
- **Delaware Water Gap, PA** (page 259): This hidden trail town has decent food and plenty of rest opportunities for tired feet.
- **Kent, CT** (page 316): In addition to shops, restaurants, and inexpensive accommodations, Kent also has showers in the middle of town specifically for thru-hikers.
- **Hanover, ME** (page 393): The AT runs through this college town with popular diners.
- **Monson, ME** (page 418): The last refuge before the 100-Mile Wilderness is a necessary stop for hikers.

a drink at **Brava** and stay overnight in **Pittsfield.**

Day 18

PITTSFIELD TO WOODSTOCK

120 miles/193 km, 2.5 hours

Drive scenic US-7 north toward **Rutland,** stopping along the way in **North Adams,** maybe to visit **MASS MoCA. Manchester Center** has plenty of lunch options. After Rutland, turn east on US-4. For a quick hike, **Thundering Brook Falls** (1 mile/1.6 km, 30 minutes) gets the legs moving, and **Long Trail Brewing Company** has the necessary provisions.

Day 19

WOODSTOCK TO LINCOLN

94 miles/151 km, 2.5 hours

On this day, drive on US-4 into **Hanover** and check out **Dartmouth College** and the **Hood Museum of Art.** Then run up US-5 to **Franconia** and **White Mountain National Forest.** Enjoy a late lunch at **Munroe's Family Restaurant** before visiting the **Old Man of the Mountain.** Hike **Arethusa Falls** (3 miles/4.8 km, 2 hours) and settle in for dinner in **Lincoln** at **Black Mtn. Burger Co.**

Day 20

LINCOLN TO RANGELEY

160 miles/258 km, 4 hours

Watch for moose on this trip. Start the day by driving up the **Mount Washington Auto Road** to the summit of **Mount Washington.** Then head east on US-2 to **Gorham** and grab some pub grub at **Mr. Pizza.** Take US-2 to ME-17 and enjoy the wild drive north to **Rangeley.** Be sure to stop at **Height of Land** and hike **Bald Mountain** (2.5 miles/4 km, 1.5 hours). Stay the night in Rangeley and dine at **The Shed.**

Day 21

RANGELEY TO BAXTER STATE PARK

185 miles/298 km, 4 hours

On this final day, your legs will get a workout from hitting the gas pedal. Start with breakfast at **The Gingerbread House Restaurant,** then drive ME-149, US-201, and ME-16 to **Monson.** Visit the **Appalachian Trail Visitor Center,** eat at **Spring Creek Bar-B-Q,** and continue on ME-6, then ME-11, past the 100-Mile Wilderness to **Millinocket** and **Baxter State Park.** Enjoy **Katahdin,** the northern end of the Appalachian Trail, whether you hike it or admire from a distance. From Katahdin, **Bangor** is 90 miles (144.8 km) and 2 hours away, primarily on US-95.

Weekend Getaways

So, you may not have 21 days to drive the entirety of the Appalachian Trail from Georgia to Maine. But, if you find yourself in a nearby city, you can always breathe it in for a weekend. Heck, that was Benton MacKaye's original purpose for the trail!

From Atlanta

Atlanta residents can escape the city by heading two hours north on US-19 and GA-75 into **Chattahoochee-Oconee National Forest. Brasstown Bald** is a great day hike, especially if you begin from the **Jacks Gap parking area.** After the hike, drive into **Hiawassee** for an evening of buffet-style grub and cool breezes. The next morning, take on **High Shoals Falls,** then reward yourself with some hush puppies and a beer at **The Happy Hawg.** Stroll it off at **Hamilton Gardens.** Take in one last view atop **Bell Mountain** before heading home.

From Charlotte

Drive west on US-74 and I-26 for about three hours to **Hot Springs,** the perfect miniature vacation for Charlotte residents. Hike nearby **Big Bald** in Tennessee for a real Appalachian Trail test, then rest your legs with a soak at **Hot Springs Resort and Spa.** Dine at **Iron Horse Station** before calling it a night. The

Clockwise from top left: historic row homes and shops in Jim Thorpe, Pennsylvania; driving around Mount Greylock State Reservation in autumn; the road to Brasstown Bald.

Small-Town Charm

Regardless of where you end up along the Appalachian Trail, you're bound to find yourself in a unique town that simply takes you by surprise. In addition to embracing the outdoors, these fun communities have great food and drink, modern art and music, and great people.

- **Dahlonega, GA** (page 50): The first major stop for thru-hikers, there's a museum (about gold!) and plenty of good food in this walkable downtown.
- **Asheville, NC** (page 84): One of the coolest small cities in America is home to breweries and restaurants galore, plus the historic Biltmore estate.
- **Roanoke, VA** (page 136): Great breweries and bars, plus an iconic neon landmark, make this an underappreciated city.
- **Waynesboro, VA** (page 153): For hikers, Waynesboro is hard to beat. An awesome outdoor shop, good breweries, and decent food options score this town high.
- **Frederick, MD** (page 192): A burgeoning arts scene, great restaurants, historic sites, and a cool little collegiate feel make this city a fun weekend trip.
- **Jim Thorpe, PA** (page 244): For families, this rail and coal town with a storied past has plenty to offer. Good bars, too.
- **Warwick, NY** (page 282): There's a great little food culture brewing in this hip town. Plenty of accessible hiking nearby, too.
- **Beacon, NY** (page 304): A renowned art museum, galleries, stores, delicious beer, cool dinner spots, and a mountain viewable from Main Street: What more can you want?
- **Great Barrington, MA** (page 337): This hip enclave has coffee shops, a historic theater, and nearby hiking trails.
- **North Adams, MA** (page 353): With festivals, a major art museum, funky restaurants and bars, and plenty of outdoor accessibility, this is a popular hangout.
- **Hanover, ME** (page 393): This community's Ivy League aura means pretty architecture, solid restaurants, and convivial drinking hangouts.
- **Rangeley, ME** (page 413): The incredible beauty of Maine is on full display here. Take in the fresh air while dining at a cool small-town restaurant.

next day, spend a morning at **Lover's Leap Trail.** Fill up after the workout at the **Smoky Mountain Diner.**

From Washington DC

Beltway residents are lucky to be pretty close to the Appalachian Trail. For instance, drive just one hour on I-270 north to **Frederick** for a fantastic day in a historic city. Hike to **Annapolis Rock,** visit **Everedy Square & Shab Row,** and reward yourself with a beer at one of the city's breweries. Get up early the next day for a hike of the **Big Red Trail** at **Greenbrier State Park** in **Boonsboro,** just 30 minutes away. Fuel up at **Dan's Restaurant & Tap House.** Finally, drive another 15 minutes west to visit

Antietam National Battlefield before heading back.

From Philadelphia

It's a mere 1.5 hours along I-476 north to **Jim Thorpe,** a fantastic home base for an overnight that includes a hike of **The Pinnacle.** While in Jim Thorpe, stop at the **Old Jail Museum** and shop the **Old Mauch Chunk Historic District.** Make it a full weekend with a hike to **Bake Oven Knob** and a beer at **Red Castle Brewpub,** plus a trip on the Lehigh River with **Jim Thorpe River Adventures.**

From New York City

There are plenty of easy escapes to the AT from New York, from **East Stroudsburg** to **Warwick** to **Bear Mountain State Park.** But my recommendation is to head two hours up I-87 and I-684 north to **Kent.** Spend some time shopping and dining, checking out Bull's Bridge, then hiking the **Macedonia Ridge**, which provides great views of nearby mountains. For a weekend, visit **Kent Falls State Park** with a picnic, then head north a bit to **West Cornwall.** See the **West Cornwall Covered Bridge** and score a table at **RSVP.**

From Boston

Drive MA-2 west three hours to **North Adams,** a perfect base camp for a hike of legendary **Mount Greylock,** a five-hour journey to one of the most famous summits along the AT. After your hike, grab a much-deserved meal at **Public Eat+Drink.** The following day, hit up **Renee's Diner** for breakfast before visiting **MASS MoCA.** Stop at **Natural Bridge State Park** to see the only natural white-marble arch in North America before heading home.

Best Hikes

Ready to get out and hit the dirt? Here are some of the best hikes along the Appalachian Trail, which offer a little bit of something for everyone.

Fall Foliage

SAM'S GAP TO BIG BALD (PAGE 98)

13 miles/20.9 km, 7 hours

Pigsah National Forest, North Carolina: This long ridge hike in the gives you all those Smoky Mountain views—without the carloads of tourists.

MCAFEE KNOB (PAGE 134)

8.8 miles/14.2 km, 5 hours

Salem, Virginia: With its iconic perch and widescreen views, McAfee Knob has everything you want for an October hike.

BEAR MOUNTAIN (PAGE 323)

6.7 miles/10.8 km, 4 hours

Mount Riga State Park, Connecticut: This fantastic hike through woods and dwarf pines reaches a large rock pile where you can view fall colors for days.

MOUNT GREYLOCK (PAGE 352)

6.2 miles/3.2 km, 5 hours

New Ashford, Massachusetts: Summit this iconic peak in October and you'll be rewarded with especially dazzling views.

History

SPRINGER MOUNTAIN LOOP (PAGE 53)

4.7 miles/7.6 km, 3 hours

Chattahoochee-Oconee National Forest, Georgia: The southern terminus of the AT is an emotional beginning (or end), and it's a doable climb for most.

BEAR MOUNTAIN (PAGE 290)

4 miles/6.4 km, 3 hours

Bear Mountain State Park, New York: This is where the Appalachian Trail was born. The views aren't bad either—you can see New York City on a clear day.

MOUNT GREYLOCK (PAGE 352)

6.2 miles/3.2 km, 5 hours

New Ashford, Massachusetts: This hike has great views and a rich history, having been summited by literary greats like Henry David Thoreau and Herman Melville.

Clockwise from top left: Buttermilk Falls at the Delaware Water Gap National Recreation Area; panoramic view from Brasstown Bald in Georgia; the iconic McAfee Knob in Virginia.

Historic Stopovers

History runs through much of the trail's surrounding area, with museums, sites, and other historical landmarks sprinkled throughout the region. With special focus on the Civil War, the Gilded Age, and the American Civil Rights movement, here are sites you'll want to visit while on and around the Appalachian Trail.

Antietam National Battlefield in Virginia

Civil War

- **Antietam National Battlefield,** Sharpsburg, VA (page 203): The single bloodiest battleground of the Civil War stands as a historic site and an enduring history lesson.
- **National Civil War Museum,** Harrisburg, PA (page 222): Spend hours learning the history of the war at this definitive museum.
- **Battle Monument,** West Point, NY (page 295): A Tuscan column dedicated to the men whose lives were lost for the Union is part of Trophy Point at West Point.

The Gilded Age

- **Biltmore Estate,** Asheville, NC (page 86): Built for the son of the wealthiest man in America, a Vanderbilt, this "little mountain escape" is a 178,000-square-foot mansion with its own village and winery.
- **Vanderbilt Mansion,** Hyde Park, NY (page 310): This Hudson River mansion with 54 rooms and Italianate gardens houses the other members of the Vanderbilt family. Bring a picnic!
- **Naumkeag,** Stockbridge, MA (page 340): Home to rapturous gardens that include the Blue Steps, this 44-room mansion symbolizes Berkshire elegance.

Civil Rights

- **Center for Civil and Human Rights,** Atlanta, GA (page 43): Spend at least a half-day at this museum and educational center. Stand in a recreated segregation-era lunch counter, and learn more about human rights leaders across the world.
- **Mast General Store,** Asheville, NC (page 91): This general store was once a lunch counter that was the site of a sit-in during the American Civil Rights movement.
- **W.E.B. DuBois National Historic Site,** Great Barrington, MA (page 337): Pay tribute to one of the pioneers of the Civil Rights movement at his birthplace. Nearby is the DuBois Center, which keeps documents written by the leader.

KATAHDIN (PAGE 422)
9.5 miles/15.3 km, 7 hours
Baxter State Park, Maine: The northern terminus of the Appalachian Trail is a great American peak with equal parts danger and excitement.

Waterfalls

TUMBLING WATERS TRAIL (PAGE 259)
3 miles/4.8 km, 2 hours
Delaware Water Gap National Recreation Area, Pennsylvania: This easy hike down steps leads to two simply beautiful falls.

BUTTERMILK FALLS TRAIL (PAGE 271)
2.8 miles/4.5 km, 2 hours
Delaware Water Gap National Recreation Area, New Jersey: Check out the tallest falls in New Jersey while ascending about 1,000 feet (305 m).

RACE BROOK FALLS (PAGE 335)
4.8 miles/7.7 km, 5 hours
Sheffield, Massachusetts: Climbing up these falls until you reach the summit of Mount Everett is quite the challenge.

THUNDERING BROOK FALLS (PAGE 374)
1 mile/1.6 km, 30 minutes
Killington, Vermont: Take a stroll on a boardwalk to a pretty waterfall tucked away in busy Killington.

Off the AT

BRASSTOWN BALD (PAGE 55)
6.5 miles/10.5 km, 4 hours
Chattahoochee-Oconee National Forest, Georgia: Start from Jack's Gap and make your way to this iconic lookout, the highest peak in Georgia.

MARYLAND HEIGHTS TRAIL (PAGE 190)
4.5 miles/7.2 km, 3 hours
Sandy Hook, Maryland: Outstanding views of Harpers Ferry and Civil War history await hikers on this moderate to strenuous climb.

MOUNT EQUINOX (PAGE 364)
7 miles/11.3 km, 4.5 hours
Manchester, Vermont: You'll test yourself up this heavy ascent, but the payoff is worth it: incredible views of Vermont, Massachusetts, and New York.

Georgia, North Carolina, and Tennessee

Georgia, North Carolina, and Tennessee

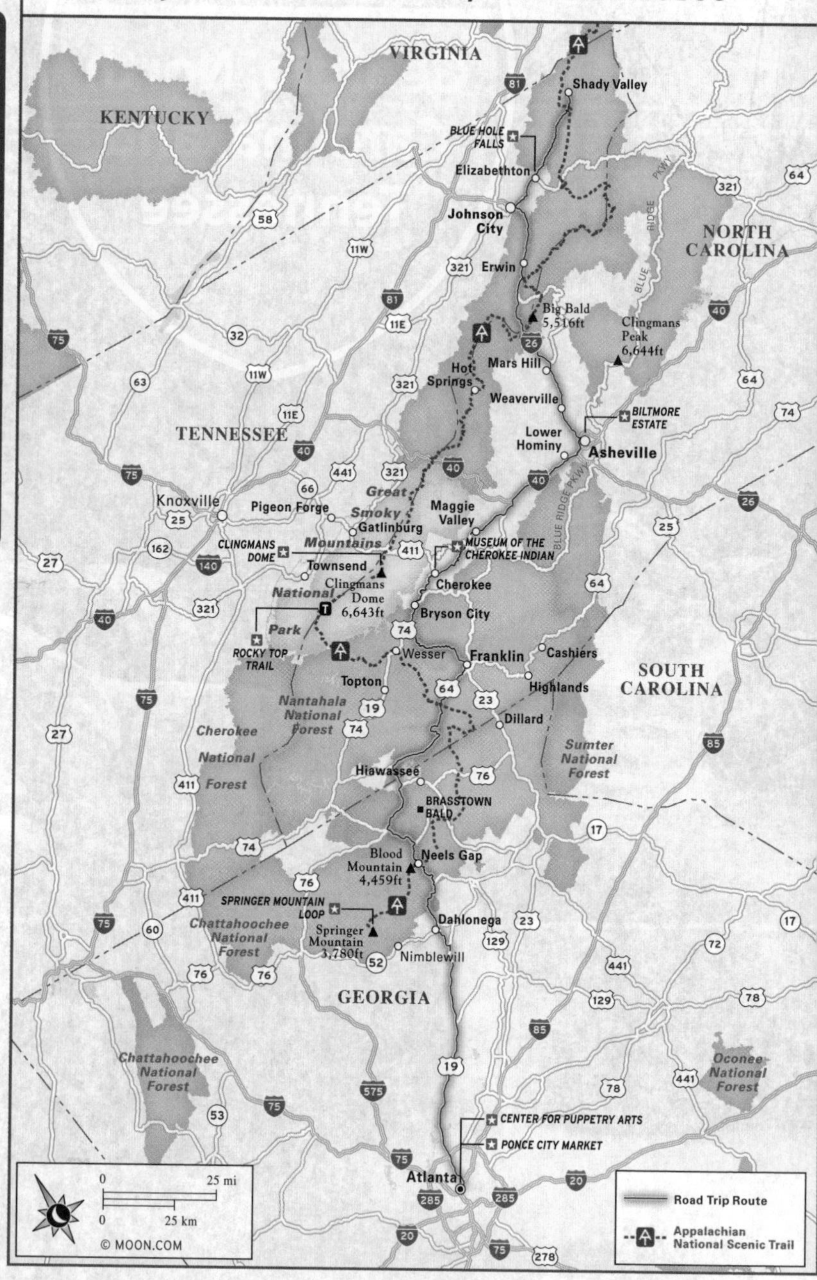

Highlights

★ **Center For Puppetry Arts:** This under-the-radar museum in Atlanta will take you on a trip through the history of puppetry, from ancient Egypt to the Muppets (page 42).

★ **Ponce City Market:** Shopping, eating, and playing are emphasized at this large-scale urban playground in Atlanta (page 43).

★ **Springer Mountain Loop:** Take on the southern terminus of the Appalachian Trail, the ultimate trailhead at 3,780 feet/1,152 meters (page 53).

★ **Museum of the Cherokee Indian:** Learn about the history of the Cherokee people through intense and immersive exhibits that include life-size models (page 66).

★ **Clingmans Dome:** The highest point on the Appalachian Trail offers 360-degree views of Great Smoky Mountains National Park (page 72).

★ **Rocky Top Trail:** Spend a day on this classic hike in Great Smoky Mountains National Park, summiting an unusual peak and taking in views of the North Carolina Blue Ridge (page 76).

★ **Biltmore Estate:** America's largest home is more than a Gilded Age wonder. Visitors can marvel at art, walk trails, and sip wine at this Asheville institution (page 86).

★ **Blue Hole Falls:** You'll be shocked by the color of this beautiful waterfall and swimming hole in Elizabethton (page 103).

Best AT Hikes

The first few hundred miles of the Appalachian Trail can be strenuous thanks to high elevations and rolling climbs. But many of the best day hikes in the Southern Appalachians can be done in just a few hours.

- **Springer Mountain Loop** (4.7 mi/7.6 km, Chattahoochee National Forest): Get to the trailhead of the AT and pay homage to the father of the trail with this sweet, even emotional hike (page 53).
- **Neels Gap to Blood Mountain** (4.3 mi/6.9 km, Blairsville): A great hike for people looking to take a step up from intermediate, it includes switchbacks, scrambling, and an awesome AT shelter (page 53).
- **Wayah Bald** (7.2 mi/11.6 km, Nantahala National Forest): The hike to Wayah Bald Tower gives you an opportunity to delight in rhododendrons, while the payoff includes 360-degree views of multiple mountain ranges (page 60).
- **Max Patch** (1.5 mi/2.4 km, Pisgah National Forest): Short, sweet, and necessary, Max Patch delivers everything a first-time Southern Appalachian hiker should want, including beautiful wildflowers and a grand overlook (page 83).
- **Sam's Gap to Big Bald** (13 mi/21 km, Pisgah National Forest): It'll take some time to complete this classic ridge hike, but it's worth the trip thanks to Big Bald's terrific Smoky Mountain views (page 98).

Just as the story of the Appalachian Trail begins with Springer Mountain in Georgia, the story of Southern Appalachia begins with the rolling Blue Ridge Mountains that crawl up this wild and wonderful region.

The first great frontier in America, Southern Appalachia is defined by the Blue Ridge, which begins in northern Georgia and continues north along the North Carolina-Tennessee border. It's here where self-sufficient Americans settled to live in mountain tranquility, and where an enterprising spirit and appreciation for nature's gifts are still celebrated today.

Before entering the mountains, you'll begin this trip in Atlanta, a major transportation hub and typical entry point for folks hoping to begin an Appalachian Trail trek. The city provides a fitting gateway to Appalachia: North of Atlanta, the roads climb into the Blue Ridge, and the trail snakes through untamed forest, scaling high peaks that climax with Clingmans Dome in Great Smoky Mountains National Park, the highest point on the AT.

Great Smoky Mountains National Park is the country's most popular national park, and its gateway towns of Gatlinburg and Pigeon Forge are teeming with tourists. You'll also find tourists east of the mountains in Asheville, a city in the midst of a major arts, music, and foodie renaissance. In this region you'll be reminded of the very first settlers of the area, the Cherokee Indians of North Carolina and Tennessee. They clashed frequently with European settlers through the early 19th century and still wield strong influence over this expanse of rolling hills and deep rhododendron forest.

Best Restaurants

★ **Home Grown, Atlanta:** This bright diner has no-nonsense southern home cookin' and smiling faces (page 48).

★ **Pop's Grits and Eggs, Maggie Valley, North Carolina:** The grits at this breakfast spot have been known to change people's lives (page 70).

★ **Little House of Pancakes, Gatlinburg, Tennessee:** Of all the pancake houses in the Smokies, this flips the most lids (page 79).

★ **Biscuit Head, Asheville, North Carolina:** You won't know what to do with yourself when you see the menu, but you'll know exactly what to do when you see the plate at your table (page 92).

★ **Curate, Asheville, North Carolina:** Welcome to flavor town, where Spanish tapas sing and reservations are necessary (page 92).

★ **Hawg N Dawg, Erwin, Tennessee:** Sometimes you just want a hot dog, and this little establishment makes some juicy ones (page 99).

Planning Your Time

The Southern Appalachia section of the trail covers a little more than 260 miles (418 km), so you'll need at least a full week for this area. You'll want to spend at least one day, if not two, in either Atlanta or Asheville, and the amazing national parks and forests here will take up the rest of your time.

Atlanta is a perfect starting point because of its outstanding access to all major American cities. It takes a bit longer to drive to the AT from Atlanta, but the city's convenient airport makes it worth it. If you're doing the whole region, note that Hiawassee, Asheville, Gatlinburg, and Johnson City have plentiful overnight options.

If you don't have time to do the entire region, pick Atlanta or Asheville as a base and spend a few days in either area. In Atlanta, spend a day exploring the city, one day hiking Springer Mountain, and maybe another day taking a side trip to Dahlonega or Hiawassee. In Asheville, spend some time in the city and then branch off to hike at Great Smoky Mountains National Park or Pisgah National Forest.

If you're planning on visiting this area after October, be aware that some roads in Great Smoky Mountains National Park close for the winter. It gets cold in high elevations, even in the Southeast.

Getting There

This region covers about **260 miles (418 km),** so there's a lot of driving, and much of it is in higher elevations on winding state routes. You'll start in Atlanta, Georgia (at 1,050 ft/320 m) and end in Shady Valley, Tennessee (at 2,785 ft/850 m).

Car

From Atlanta the route starts on **US-19** north toward Dahlonega and the Chattahoochee National Forest. Then it connects with **US-76, GA-69,** and then **US-64** east through Nantahala National Forest. Through the forest the route runs into **US-19,** which will continue east, though there's a lollipop on **US-441** into Great Smoky Mountains National Park. US-19 runs into **I-40,** which hits Asheville. Then it's up **I-26** through the suburbs and across the border into Tennessee. At Johnson City the route

Best Accommodations

★ **Peach House Bed & Breakfast, Atlanta:** The rooms at this pleasant little house call to mind Atlanta's history and culture with a dash of whimsy (page 49).

★ **Top of Georgia Hiking Center, Hiawassee, Georgia:** This is a perfect place for hikers to rest, meet some new friends, and gear up for the trek ahead (page 58).

★ **Old Edwards Inn and Spa, Highlands, North Carolina:** It's worth spending a little more on this resort getaway in Nantahala National Forest (page 66).

★ **Dancing Bear Lodge, Townsend, Tennessee:** These timber-built accommodations in an underrated town close to Great Smoky Mountains National Park provide a fine getaway (page 81).

★ **Bon Paul & Sharky's Hostel, Asheville, North Carolina:** This welcoming, funky hostel is perfect for those planning to spend bread on booze and food rather than lodging (page 93).

★ **Marshall House Inn, Marshall, North Carolina:** This boutique hotel near Weaverville is a rare find for the mountains, bringing a dash of New York style to Appalachia (page 95).

★ **Laughing Heart Lodge, Hot Springs, North Carolina:** A home for all hikers, this lodge doubles as a place to re-center yourself (page 96).

changes onto **US-321** into Elizabethton, and then takes **TN-91** up to Shady Valley toward Virginia.

All of this route switching is necessary because interstate highways tend to avoid mountains, a common theme you'll find throughout this road trip. Also, the state and federal routes are pretty fun and run into small towns that epitomize the region quite well. If you want a highway respite, **I-75** bypasses the north Georgia forest, and, in Chattanooga, runs north alongside the Blue Ridge Mountains. After Knoxville it meets **I-81**, which runs beside the western end of the mountains. On the east side, **I-85** and **I-77** parallel the mountains. Both **I-40** and **I-26** cut through the Blue Ridge and meet up in Asheville.

Air

Ten miles (16 km) south of downtown Atlanta, **Hartsfield-Jackson Atlanta International Airport** (800/897-1910, www.atl.com, ATL) is the world's busiest airport by passenger traffic, serving more than 260,000 passengers daily. It's a hub for Delta Airlines (800/221-1212) and a focus city for Frontier Airlines (801/401-9000), Southwest Airlines (800/435-9792), and Spirit Airlines (801/401-2222). It also services Alaska Airlines (800/252-7522), American Airlines (800/433-7300), Boutique Airlines (855/268-8478), JetBlue Airways (800/538-2583), and United Airlines (800/864-8331), plus several international carriers. Hartsfield-Jackson connects to Atlanta's MARTA public transportation system, with trains leaving every 10-15 minutes.

Asheville Regional Airport (61 Terminal Dr., 1, Fletcher, NC, 828/684-2226, www.flyavl.com, AVL) serves Allegiant (702/505-8888), American Airlines (800/535-5225), Delta (800/221-1212), Elite (877/393-2510), and United (800/864-8331). Nonstop destinations include Atlanta, Charlotte, Chicago, Dallas, Newark, New York, and Washington DC, plus multiple Florida cities. The airport is about 15 miles (24 km) south of downtown, and the S3 bus on Asheville's ART system provides rides from downtown.

Tri-Cities Regional Airport (2525 TN-75, Blountville, TN, 423/325-6000, www.triflight.com, TRI), is a 17-mile (27-km) drive north of Johnson City and services the area. Its carriers include Allegiant (702/505-8888), American Airlines (800/535-5225), and Delta (800/221-1212). Destinations serviced include Orlando, Tampa-St. Petersburg, Charlotte, and Atlanta.

Train

The small **Peachtree Station** (1688 Peachtree St. NW, 800/872-7245) is the main train station in Atlanta, servicing **Amtrak** (800/872-7245, www.amtrak.com) via its Crescent line, which connects New Orleans to New York City.

Bus

In Atlanta, **Greyhound** (6000 N. Terminal Pkwy., 404/765-9598, www.greyhound.com, 8am-1:30pm Mon.-Fri.) has a station at Hartsfield-Jackson airport, and another **downtown** (232 Forsyth St. SW, 404/584-1728, www.greyhound.com, noon-midnight daily). There's a **Greyhound station** (2 Tunnel Rd., 828/253-8451, www.greyhound.com, 7:30am-4:30pm, 8am-10pm Mon.-Fri., 7:30am-9:30am and 2:30pm-10pm Sat.-Sun.) in Asheville, connecting riders to Washington DC, Atlanta, and other locations. And there's a **Greyhound station** (137 W. Market St., 423/926-6181, 7:30am-3:30pm, 8am-10pm Mon.-Fri., 7:30am-9:30am and 1:30pm-10pm Sat.-Sun.) in Johnson City, with connections to Atlanta, Cincinnati, and other regional destinations.

Fuel and Services

Before driving into the mountains, make sure you have a full tank. There are a number of cities with numerous stations. If doing the whole trip, fill up first in Atlanta, then Dahlonega, Franklin, Cherokee or Gatlinburg, Asheville, and Erwin. Prices are generally below the national average in these areas.

For reports on road conditions when in Georgia, dial 511. In Tennessee, dial 511 or 877/244-0065 when out of state. In North Carolina, dial 511 or 877/511-4662 when out of state. For emergency assistance, call 911.

Atlanta

Atlanta (pop. 472,522) hasn't always been the sprawling metropolis that it is today. In the early 1800s the city was primarily a settlement for the Creek Indians, who largely stayed near the Chattahoochee River, the major (and nearly only) body of water in the city limits. European settlers forced the Creek Indians out of the area by the 1820s, kick-starting the city's first growth period. Atlanta became a rail hub connecting points on the Atlantic coast with the interior. The rails proved vital for the Confederate armies during the Civil War, but after a Union siege of the city in 1864, Confederate general John Bell Hood decided to retreat and called for the burning of all public buildings. After the war a rebuilt Atlanta, driven by its rail power, became the center of technology, commerce, and culture in the Southeast.

Since the turn of the 20th century, Atlanta has been a major hub of activity. It was the birthplace and childhood home of Martin Luther King Jr. and has been a key player in the fight for African American civil rights. It became a center for international commerce and conventions thanks to the 1976 opening of the Georgia World Congress Center, part of a large district of convention centers, sporting arenas, and museums. In 1996, the city hosted the Summer Olympics, and artifacts of that event can still be found throughout the city.

These days Atlanta both benefits from and bears the burden of its many

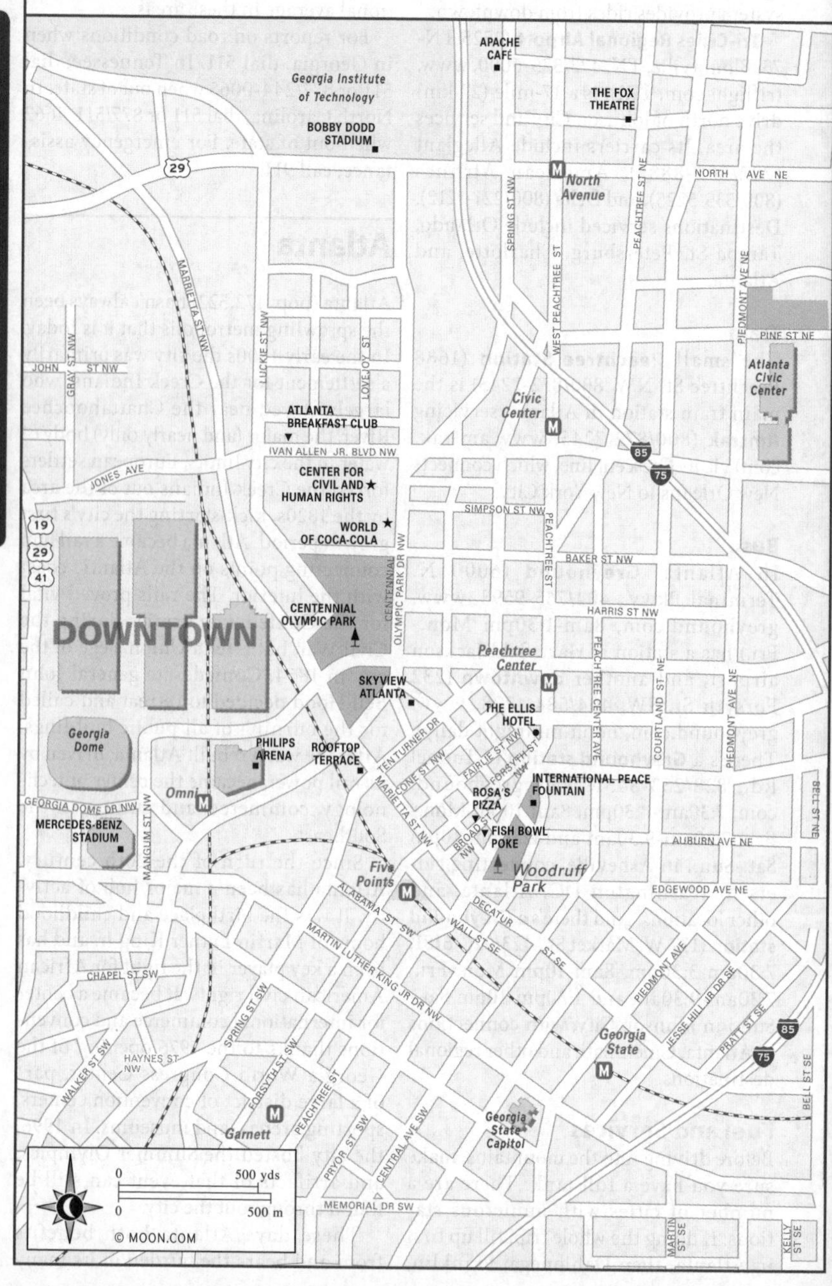
Atlanta
APACHE CAFÉ
THE FOX THEATRE
Georgia Institute of Technology
BOBBY DODD STADIUM
29
North Avenue
NORTH AVE NE
MARIETTA ST NW
LUCKIE ST NW
LOVEJOY ST
SPRING ST NW
WEST PEACHTREE ST
PEACHTREE ST NE
PIEDMONT AVE NE
PINE ST NE
Atlanta Civic Center
JOHN ST NW
GRAY ST NW
Civic Center
ATLANTA BREAKFAST CLUB
IVAN ALLEN JR. BLVD NW
85
75
JONES AVE
CENTER FOR CIVIL AND HUMAN RIGHTS
SIMPSON ST NW
PEACHTREE ST
19
29
41
WORLD OF COCA-COLA
CENTENNIAL OLYMPIC PARK DR NW
BAKER ST NW
HARRIS ST NW
CENTENNIAL OLYMPIC PARK
DOWNTOWN
Peachtree Center
PEACHTREE CENTER AVE
COURTLAND ST NE
PIEDMONT AVE NE
SKYVIEW ATLANTA
THE ELLIS HOTEL
Georgia Dome
PHILIPS ARENA
ROOFTOP TERRACE
TEN TURNER DR
CONE ST NW
FAIRLIE ST NW
FORSYTH ST NW
INTERNATIONAL PEACE FOUNTAIN
BELL ST NE
Omni
GEORGIA DOME DR NW
MANGUM ST NW
MARIETTA ST NW
ROSA'S PIZZA
BROAD ST NW
FISH BOWL POKE
MERCEDES-BENZ STADIUM
AUBURN AVE NE
Woodruff Park
Five Points
EDGEWOOD AVE NE
ALABAMA ST SW
DECATUR ST SE
WALL ST SE
MARTIN LUTHER KING JR DR NW
CHAPEL ST SW
PIEDMONT AVE
JESSE HILL JR DR SE
PRATT ST SE
85
75
Georgia State
SPRING ST NW
HAYNES ST NW
WALKER ST SW
FORSYTH ST SW
PEACHTREE ST
CENTRAL AVE SW
BELL ST SE
Garnett
PRYOR ST SW
Georgia State Capitol
0
500 yds
0
500 m
© MOON.COM
MEMORIAL DR SW
MARTIN ST SE
KELLY ST SE

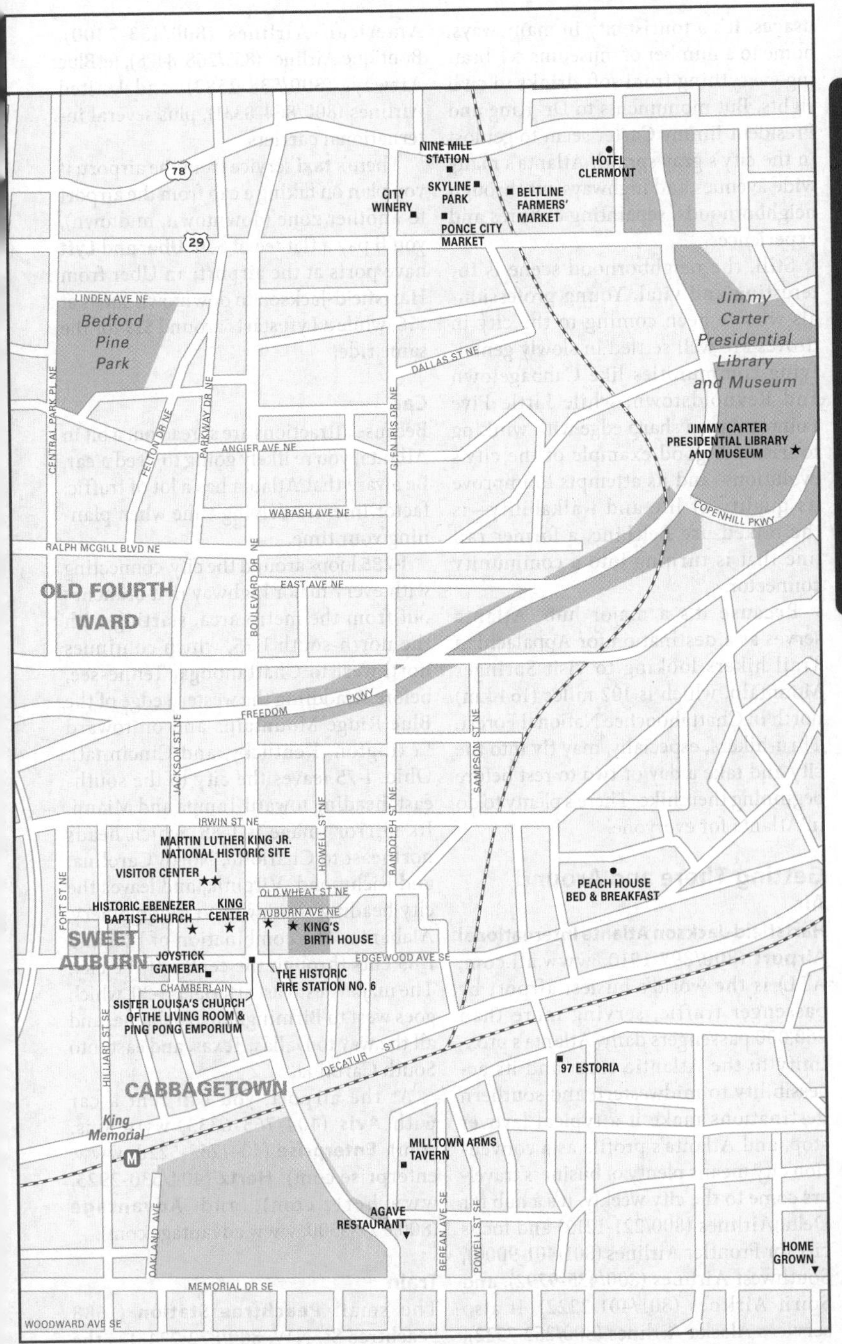
78
29
NINE MILE STATION
SKYLINE PARK
CITY WINERY
BELTLINE FARMERS' MARKET
PONCE CITY MARKET
HOTEL CLERMONT
LINDEN AVE NE
Bedford Pine Park
Jimmy Carter Presidential Library and Museum
DALLAS ST NE
CENTRAL PARK PL NE
FELTON DR NE
PARKWAY DR NE
GLEN IRIS DR NE
JIMMY CARTER PRESIDENTIAL LIBRARY AND MUSEUM
ANGIER AVE NE
WABASH AVE NE
COPENHILL PKWY
RALPH MCGILL BLVD NE
EAST AVE NE
OLD FOURTH WARD
BOULEVARD DR NE
FREEDOM PKWY
JACKSON ST NE
SAMPSON ST NE
HOWELL ST NE
RANDOLPH ST NE
IRWIN ST NE
MARTIN LUTHER KING JR. NATIONAL HISTORIC SITE
VISITOR CENTER
FORT ST NE
OLD WHEAT ST NE
PEACH HOUSE BED & BREAKFAST
HISTORIC EBENEZER BAPTIST CHURCH
KING CENTER
AUBURN AVE NE
KING'S BIRTH HOUSE
SWEET AUBURN
JOYSTICK GAMEBAR
EDGEWOOD AVE SE
THE HISTORIC FIRE STATION NO. 6
CHAMBERLAIN
SISTER LOUISA'S CHURCH OF THE LIVING ROOM & PING PONG EMPORIUM
HILLIARD ST SE
DECATUR ST
97 ESTORIA
CABBAGETOWN
King Memorial
M
MILLTOWN ARMS TAVERN
OAKLAND AVE
AGAVE RESTAURANT
BEREAN AVE SE
POWELL ST SE
HOME GROWN
MEMORIAL DR SE
WOODWARD AVE SE

usages. It's a tourist city in many ways, home to a number of museums celebrating everything from soft drinks to civil rights. But monuments to Dr. King and President Jimmy Carter seem to get lost in the city's gray sprawl: Atlanta's many wide avenues and highways cut through neighborhoods, separating cultures and experiences.

Still, the neighborhood scene is interesting and vital. Young professionals who've been coming to the city in droves are well settled in slowly gentrifying communities like Cabbagetown and Reynoldstown, while Little Five Points mixes a sharp edge with winking tourism. A good example of the city's evolution—and its attempts to improve its quality of life and walkability—is the mixed-use BeltLine, a former rail line that is turning into a community connector.

Because it's a major hub, Atlanta serves as a destination for Appalachian Trail hikers looking to visit Springer Mountain, which is 102 miles (164 km) north in Chattahoochee National Forest. Thru-hikers, especially, may fly into the city and take a day or two to rest before beginning their hike. There's plenty to do in Atlanta for everyone.

Getting There and Around

Air

Hartsfield-Jackson Atlanta International Airport (800/897-1910, www.atl.com, ATL) is the world's busiest airport by passenger traffic, serving more than 260,000 passengers daily. Atlanta's proximity to the Atlantic coast and its accessibility to midwestern and southern destinations make it a typical layover stop, and Atlanta's profile as a convention city means plenty of business travelers come to the city weekly. It's a hub for Delta Airlines (800/221-1212) and focus city for Frontier Airlines (801/401-9000), Southwest Airlines (800/435-9792), and Spirit Airlines (801/401-2222). It also services Alaska Airlines (800/252-7522), American Airlines (800/433-7300), Boutique Airlines (855/268-8478), JetBlue Airways (800/538-2583), and United Airlines (800/864-8331), plus several international carriers.

There's **taxi** service from the airport; if you plan on taking a cab from the airport to another zone (downtown, midtown), you'll pay a flat fee of $30. **Uber** and **Lyft** have ports at the airport; an Uber from Hartsfield-Jackson to downtown starts at $16, while a Lyft starts around $19 for the same ride.

Car

Because attractions are spread out a bit in Atlanta, you're likely going to need a car. Be aware that Atlanta has a lot of traffic; factor in extra driving time when planning your time.

I-285 loops around the city, connecting with every major highway that branches out from the metro area, starting with the north-south I-75, which continues northwest to Chattanooga, Tennessee, before straddling the western edge of the Blue Ridge Mountains and on toward Lexington, Kentucky, and Cincinnati, Ohio. I-75 leaves the city to the southeast, heading toward Tampa and Miami. Its mirror image is I-85, which heads northeast to Charlotte, North Carolina, and Richmond, Virginia, and leaves the city heading southwest to Montgomery, Alabama. The combination of I-75 and I-85 cuts through the center of the city. The major west-east arterial is I-20, which goes west to Birmingham, Alabama, and all the way to Dallas, Texas, and east into South Carolina.

At the airport, you can rent a car with **Avis** (404/763-6333, www.avis.com), **Enterprise** (404/763-5220, www.enterprise.com), **Hertz** (404/530-2925, www.hertz.com), and **Advantage** (800/777-5500, www.advantage.com).

Train

The small **Peachtree Station** (1688 Peachtree St. NW, 800/872-7245) is the

One Day in Atlanta

Morning

Wake up early and head to **Home Grown** for the best breakfast you're likely to have in a long time. After filling up, read up on our 38th president with an early-morning visit to the **Jimmy Carter Presidential Library and Museum.** Spend two hours or so at the Carter museum before driving over to the **Center For Puppetry Arts.** Spend another hour or so hanging out with the Muppets at this phenomenal facility.

Afternoon

Grab a light bar snack at **The Porter Beer Bar** before visiting the **Martin Luther King Jr. National Historic Site.** Spend time in the visitors center learning about the ongoing struggle for equality, then visit King's birthplace and final resting place. Take a break after visiting this heavy site, either with a quick nap at the hotel or with a drink nearby. Wait out rush hour traffic.

Evening

Dinner is at **The Optimist,** but don't fill up on booze. Your next stop is **The EARL** to take in some local music. After the show, take the party to **The Righteous Room,** pound for pound the best bar in the city. If you'd like, end your night here, but if you want the true Atlanta experience, finish the night with a can of cheap beer at the **Clermont Lounge.**

main train station in the city, servicing **Amtrak** (800/872-7245, www.amtrak.com) via its Crescent line, which connects New Orleans to New York City.

Take public transportation via **MARTA** (404/848-5000, www.itsmarta.com), which has four lines primarily inside the city's loop. All lines intersect at **Five Points** (30 Alabama St. SW); the north-south Red and Gold lines head to the airport and, going north, break off into the suburbs. The Green and Blue lines run west-east and provide connections to tourist attractions like the King Center, CNN Center, and Phillips Arena. The system operates 5am-2am weekdays and 6am-2am weekends; generally, trains arrive every 12-20 minutes.

You need to purchase a Breeze Card at a MARTA station vending machine. The card itself is $2, and it's an additional $2.50 for each fare.

Bus

There's a **Greyhound** (6000 N. Terminal Pkwy., 404/765-9598, www.greyhound.com, 8am-1:30pm Mon.-Fri.) station at Hartsfield-Jackson airport, and another **downtown** (232 Forsyth St. SW, 404/584-1728, www.greyhound.com, noon-midnight daily).

Inside the city MARTA has 91 routes. Breeze Cards are recommended if you're riding the bus on MARTA, but you can also insert coins or cash (up to $5) in a bus fare box.

Sights

Jimmy Carter Presidential Library and Museum

On 35 acres of a bubble relatively isolated from Atlanta's busy streets, the **Jimmy Carter Presidential Library and Museum** (441 Freedom Pkwy. NE, 404/865-7100, www.jimmycarterlibrary.gov, 9am-4:45pm Mon.-Sat., noon-4:45pm Sun., $8 adults, $6 seniors, military, and students, free age 16 and younger) immerses you in the life and times of the 38th president, with special attention paid to his major presidential accomplishments and his post-presidential civil rights leadership.

Visitors can enter a replica of Carter's Oval Office, which includes artifacts

like the chair, globe, and flag, and follow Carter through a day of his presidency. The center's archive contains more than 27 million pages of presidential papers; you can also view Carter's 2002 Nobel Peace Prize. Surrounding the center are landscaped gardens open to the public. The center also hosts concerts, workshops, and special author events.

★ Center For Puppetry Arts

After just three minutes in the Jim Henson Collection Gallery at the **Center For Puppetry Arts** (1404 Spring St. NW, 404/873-3391, www.puppet.org, 9am-5pm Tues.-Fri., 10am-5pm Sat., noon-5pm Sun., $12.50 museum ticket), I had to stop and clear my eyes. Anyone who's ever been affected by puppetry—whether through *Sesame Street* and Henson's Muppets or through puppets of all kinds across the world—should put this under-the-radar museum, theater, and workshop center on her or his list.

The center, devised by Atlanta businessman and puppeteer Vincent Anthony, runs constant educational programming where toddlers and big kids can learn puppetry and be wowed by the art form. It also hosts screenings of puppet-centric films and theatrical performances for all ages. It's also home to the Worlds of Puppetry Museum, which features the largest collection anywhere of Henson's puppets. The Henson exhibit takes visitors through his career, from producing commercials to singlehandedly changing children's entertainment. Real Muppets at displayed the center, including Miss Piggy, Gonzo, Big Bird, and Kermit the Frog. You can view Henson's early ideas scribbled on paper and sing along with videos presented as part of the exhibit.

The museum's Global Collection exhibit showcases puppets from across the

Top to bottom: downtown Atlanta; Martin Luther King Jr. National Historic Site; World of Coca-Cola.

world, some dating back several centuries. A special exhibit space changes annually, with the focus on Henson one year and the focus on international puppetry the next year.

Martin Luther King Jr. National Historic Site

The **Martin Luther King Jr. National Historic Site** spreads itself out over numerous city blocks, covering the enormous impact of Dr. Martin Luther King Jr. as an agent of global change. Here you'll find King's birthplace and final resting place, plus structures and exhibits that reveal his many accomplishments.

The site encompasses an L-shaped area of the historically black Sweet Auburn neighborhood. Start at the **visitors center** (450 Auburn Ave., 404/331-5190, ext. 5046, 9am-5pm daily), the departure point for free tours (10am daily, every 30 minutes) that go inside King's childhood home. Exhibits at the visitors center include *Courage To Lead,* which details King's journey from Atlanta to national prominence, along with the evolution of the American civil rights movement.

Across the street from the visitors center is the **King Center** (449 Auburn Ave., 404/526-8900, www.thekingcenter.org, 9am-6pm daily Memorial Day-Labor Day, 9am-5pm daily rest of year, free), which serves as a living memorial and holds nearly one million documents associated with King. It's also the home of King's Tomb, where both King and Coretta Scott King are buried. An eternal flame burns at the site. Neighboring the King Center is **Historic Ebenezer Baptist Church** (407-413 Auburn Ave., 770/435-2535), which was built between 1914 and 1922 and was King's childhood parish.

Cross Boulevard to visit **King's Birth House** (501 Auburn Ave.), where King spent the first 12 years of life. **The Historic Fire Station No. 6** (39 Boulevard), which served Sweet Auburn and illustrates King's impact in desegregating public institutions throughout Atlanta, is also part of the site. Visitors can take self-guided tours of the fire station.

World of Coca-Cola

If you're a soda lover, your Graceland may just be **World of Coca-Cola** (121 Baker St. NW, 404/676-5151, www.worldofcoca-cola.com, 10am-5pm Sun.-Thurs., 9am-5pm Fri.-Sat., $17 adults, $15 seniors, $13 ages 3-12). Celebrating America's preeminent soft drink, World of Coca-Cola runs through the history of the brand and blasts visitors with the full Coke experience through exhibits, movies, and interactive features. The *Milestones of Refreshment* exhibit is the history lesson, including items like a circa 1880s soda foundation and 1939 Argentine delivery truck. The Coca-Cola Theater is home to an extended commercial that makes you feel good about people, and maybe make you want a Coke, too. Then there's *Vault of the Secret Formula,* an entire exhibit devoted to the closely guarded formula for original Coca-Cola. Visitors can create their own soft drink formulas and put them up against "The Real Thing."

Center for Civil and Human Rights

It's recommended you spend up to two hours at the **Center for Civil and Human Rights** (100 Ivan Allen Jr. Blvd., 679/999-8990, www.civilandhumanrights.org, 10am-5pm Mon.-Sat., noon-5pm Sun., $21 adults, $19 seniors and students, $17 ages 7-12), but that may not be enough. The interactive experience at the facility includes a re-creation of a segregation-era lunch counter and an interactive glimpse into the lives of the Freedom Riders via oral histories and a short film. Also check out the *Spark of Conviction* exhibit, a gallery that showcases human rights leaders and efforts throughout the world.

Recreation

★ Ponce City Market

Close your eyes and imagine a large-scale, multi-zone playground for millennials devised and developed by advertising and marketing teams. In the grand tradition of San Antonio's Pearl Brewery complex, Atlanta's **Ponce City Market** (675 Ponce de Leon Ave. NE, 404/900-7900, www.poncecitymarket.com, 10am-9pm Mon.-Sat., noon-6pm Sun.) is a repurposed mecca of high-scale residential properties, curated food and drink, hangout areas like a rooftop park, a connection to a beltway, and copious shopping options. If you're in a rush and don't want to ask a local for a cool place to go, or if you just want the whole upcycled experience in one nifty package, probably with caramelized avocado or something, Ponce City Market will do.

The old Sears, Roebuck & Co. building, once the largest building in the South, opened as the market in 2014. It features a dizzying array of middle-class mall-style options across two levels with name brands like West Elm, Sephora, and J. Crew, plus plenty of specialty options: a hat shop, a stationery store, a Google Fiber store. There's a gourmet food court on the 1st floor, and on the 3rd floor, a connection to the 3-mile-long (4.8-km) Northeast Hiking Trail, part of the **BeltLine.** A weekly **farmers market** (BeltLine Shed, 4pm-8pm Tues. Apr.-Nov.) takes place in this area, while the market also hosts a number of daily events, from informational sessions with political leaders to artist talks and blood drives.

Arguably the biggest draw at Ponce City Market is **The Roof** (www.poncecityroof.com), an entertainment complex headlined by **Skyline Park** (www.skylineparkatlanta.com, 3pm-10pm Mon.-Wed., 3pm-11pm Thurs.-Fri., 5pm-11pm and 11am-11pm Sat., noon-9pm Sun., $10 adults, $7 ages 12 and younger, games and golf extra), contrived as an old-school carnival with midway games and mini-golf. The Roof also includes **Nine Mile Station** (770/999-1532, www.9milestation.com, 3pm-10pm Mon.-Wed., 3pm-11pm Thurs.-Fri., 11am-11pm Sat., noon-9pm Sun., under $50 dinner, under $35 brunch), a beer garden-and-shareable plate hot spot, and **Rooftop Terrace** (www.rooftopterraceatl.com), an event space.

Parks

Piedmont Park (1320 Monroe Dr. NE, www.piedmontpark.org, 6am-11pm daily) was forestland before it was purchased in 1834 and turned into farmland. In 1904 it was sold to the city, which turned it into a civic gathering place. The 189-acre park provides a refreshing wealth of green space where residents and visitors enjoy picnic areas, ballfields, Lake Clara Meer, and a variety of annual festivals. Piedmont is home to the **Atlanta Botanical Garden** (1345 Piedmont Ave. NE, 404/876-5859, www.atlantabg.org, 9am-5pm Tues.-Sun., $22 adults, $16 ages 3-12), whose grounds allow for a peaceful walk through an orchid house, an edible garden, a children's garden, and a popular Japanese garden with maples and rare bamboo.

Numerous parks are sprinkled throughout downtown Atlanta. The big one is **Centennial Olympic Park** (265 W Park Ave. NW), which was created as a gathering place for visitors to the 1996 Summer Olympics; it was also the site of the July 27 bombing during those Olympics. These days it's a sweeping stretch of green space between the midtown skyline and the landmarks that dot the park's west end. Check out the Fountain of Rings, which has an interactive foundation synchronized to music, or take a ride on **SkyView Atlanta** (168 Luckie St. NW, noon-11pm Sun.-Thurs., noon-midnight Fri., 10am-midnight Sat., $14 adults, $13 seniors, military, and students, $10 ages 3-11), a 20-story Ferris wheel that provides some high-quality views of the city.

Woodruff Park (91 Peachtree St. NW), previously Central City Park, is fully outfitted for the modern park lover. Amenities include a bocce ball court, table tennis, a children's play area, and plenty of green space on which to lie out. At the north end of the park is the **International Peace Fountain** (Auburn Ave. and Peachtree St.), an impressive water display built before the 1996 Olympics to honor Atlanta's place in the civil rights movement. It's a good place for a photo op. The park hosts meditation and yoga, plus a few festivals.

Spectator Sports

Atlanta is first and foremost a football city. Professionally, that means the Atlanta Falcons, who play at **Mercedes-Benz Stadium** (1414 Andrew Young International Blvd. NW, 470/341-5000, www.atlantafalcons.com), a space-age retractable-roof mega-stadium that opened in 2017. It's a Super Bowl venue, and it's also home to college football events like the Chick-fil-A Peach Bowl and, every so often, the College Football Playoff National Championship game.

Speaking of college football, the Georgia Tech Yellow Jackets (or the "Ramblin' Wreck") play at **Bobby Dodd Stadium** (177 North Ave. NW, www.ramblinwreck.com). Georgia Tech is part of the Atlantic Coast Conference. Sun Belt Conference members the Georgia State Panthers have taken over the Atlanta Braves' former Turner Field, now called **Georgia State Stadium** (755 Hank Aaron Dr. SE, www.stadium.gsu.edu). It's an enjoyable venue, even if seeing the right-field stands towering overhead is a bit jarring.

As for the Braves, the local baseball team now takes up residence well north of the city. **SunTrust Park** (755 Battery Ave. SE, www.braves.com) opened in 2017 and seats 41,149 for Braves home games. The park is attractive but pretty similar to other small, all-outdoor ballparks opened since 2000.

Back downtown, **Philips Arena** (1 Philips Dr., 404/878-3000, www.nba.com/hawks) is the home of the National Basketball Association's Atlanta Hawks. Philips also hosts the large touring concerts that come through Atlanta, from country music stars to the likes of Justin Timberlake and Elton John. The Women's National Basketball Association's Atlanta Dream also play their home games at Philips.

If you're looking for college hoops, the Georgia Tech men's and women's basketball teams play at **McCarnish Pavilion** (965 Fowler St. NW, 404/894-5400, www.ramblinwreck.com), which is also known as the "Thrillerdome."

Entertainment and Events

Bars and Clubs

Midtown

Next to the Plaza Theater, **The Righteous Room** (1051 Ponce de Leon Ave. NE, 404/874-0939, www.stayrighteous.com, 11:30am-3am Mon.-Sat., noon-midnight Sun., under $25) may be the perfect bar. The staff is friendly, the digs strike the perfect balance between stylish and dive, and the beer runs the gamut from Miller High Life to locals like SweetWater. Plus there's a beautiful jukebox, a brick-and-red-wallpaper motif that just sings, and awesome local art and photos on the walls. Add a menu of unusual pub grub (red-pepper hummus, onion straws, salmon quesadilla), and I'd actually move to the neighborhood to make this my local haunt. Righteous has a **sister location** (2143 Johnson Ferry Rd., Brookhaven, 11:30am-2am Mon.-Wed., 11:30am-3am Thurs.-Sat., 12:30pm-2am Sun., under $25), notable because it has a tree growing out of the bar.

A legend in its own right, **Manuel's Tavern** (602 North Highland Ave. NE, 404/525-3447, www.manuelstavern.com, 11am-midnight Mon., 11am-1am Tues.-Fri., 9:30am-1am Sat., 9:30am-midnight Sun., under $25) has played host to just about anyone with clout in Atlanta. In place since 1956, the tavern serves the city with a robust collection of liquor and a solid menu that includes sandwiches, burgers, and hot dogs, including its famous Ballpark Dog.

Downtown

Some people have absolutely had the greatest nights of their lives at **Sister Louisa's Church of the Living Room & Ping Pong Emporium** (466 Edgewood Ave. SE, 404/522-8276, www.sisterlouisaschurch.com, 5pm-3am Mon.-Sat., 5pm-midnight Sun., under $25). The church-cum-art gallery-cum-bar-cum-Ping-Pong hangout may offend the religious, as the bar has plenty of artwork and other goodies that range from lightly blasphemous to code red. It's worth a trip if you want to spend a cheap beer or two taking in neon-tinged sarcastic spirituality.

Drink some beer, or even a cocktail, while playing *Street Fighter* or *Mario Kart*. **Joystick Gamebar** (427 Edgewood Ave., 404/525-3002, www.joystickgamebar.com, 5pm-2:30am Mon.-Fri., noon-2:30am Sat., noon-midnight Sun., under $15) is an enjoyable arcade with a knowingly nerdy side and 1990s aesthetic. They serve cheap cans of Genesee Cream Ale along with house cocktails like the Arson Daly. Food includes street tacos and loaded fries.

Little Five Points

Scour a book to find the beer of your choice at **The Porter Beer Bar** (1156 Euclid Ave. NE, 404/223-0393, www.theporterbeerbar.com, 11:30am-midnight Mon.-Thurs., 11:30am-2:30am Fri., 11am-midnight Sun., under $25). In a cool, dimly lit bar with accommodating servers and bartenders, you'll get lost trying to find the perfect beer to accompany your buffalo shrimp po'boy or, if you're really cool, mussels and salt-and-vinegar popcorn.

Fun as heck, the **Euclid Avenue Yacht Club** (1136 Euclid Ave. NE, 404/688-2582, www.theeayc.com, noon-2:30am Tues.-Sat., noon-midnight Sun., 3pm-2am Mon., under $20) has been around for more than three decades and never disappoints. Let the name fool you, because it has the air of a yacht club with wood finishing and pastoral pictures. But beyond that it's a fun bar with tons of cheap and crazy drinks, a relaxed vibe, and fun events like a burlesque trivia night. Food includes the rawest in pub grub, from corn dogs to boiled peanuts.

Cabbagetown and Reynoldstown

Arguably the best pound-for-pound bar experience in Atlanta, **97 Estoria** (727 Wylie St. SE, 404/522-0966, 11am-3am Mon.-Fri., noon-3am Sat., 12:30pm-12:30am Sun., under $20) is half hipster hangout, half good ol' dive bar. Want proof? You'll have no idea whether the old Atlanta Braves logo is ironic or romantic. Either way, there's extremely cheap canned beer specials and a nice list of local micros, a cozy wood interior, and low-fi DJ nights. There's also an outdoor patio area.

With its classic light wood bar area and brick interior, **Milltown Arms Tavern** (180 Carroll St., 404/827-0434, www.milltownarmstavern.com, 11:30-2am Mon.-Thurs., 11:30am-3am Fri., noon-2am Sat., noon-midnight Sun., under $25) looks old-school, but you'd be surprised to learn it opened in 2005. Milltown Arms earns high marks for its friendly atmosphere, leaning Irish and soccer-mad, but welcoming to all with a menu of burgers and pub food.

East Point

Over in East Point, **Chairs Upstairs Bar and Restaurant** (2783 Main St., East Point, 404/768-0007, 11am-2am Mon.-Sat., 11am-midnight Sun., under $25) has a little of everything. Order a cocktail or a local beer at the long bar, or play billiards, foosball, or arcade games in the narrow seating area. There's outdoor seating, too. Chairs looks modern and hip, but it's very much a local haunt that doesn't take itself seriously.

Close to East Point is College Park, whose main drag is home to **Brake Pad** (3403 Main St., College Park, 404/766-1515, www.brakepadatlanta.com,

11am-midnight Sun.-Thurs., 11am-1am Fri.-Sat., under $25), part local bar, part snack bar, and fully a former auto garage. Food includes burgers, a mean brisket sandwich, and wings. The overhang allows for outdoor seating, so come on by for day drinking in your vintage Callahan Auto Parts T-shirt.

Live Music

Atlanta is bursting with live music venues. Young and hungry local bands vie for success at **529 Bar** (529 Flat Shoals Ave. SE, 404/228-6769, www.529atlanta.com, 2pm-3am Mon.-Sat., tickets under $20). Warm up with some jazz, R&B, blues, comedy, and world music at **Apache Café** (64 3rd St. NW, 404/876-5436, www.apachecafe.info, 7pm-midnight Sun.-Mon., 8pm-1am Tues., 8pm-1:30am Wed., 9pm-2am Thurs.-Sat., tickets under $30). Down in the southwest corner of the city, **St. James, Live!** (3220 Butner Rd., Ste. 240, 404/254-3561, www.stjamesliveatl.com, 7pm-midnight Thurs., 7pm-1am Fri.-Sat., 6pm-10pm Sun., tickets up to $60) is a jazzy, dimly lit venue with a Mediterranean vibe decorated in warm tones. **The EARL** (488 Flat Shoals Ave. SE, 404/522-3950, www.badearl.com, 11:30am-3am Mon.-Fri., 11:30am-midnight Sat.-Sun, tickets under $40) features unheralded acts, the kind you can throw around to look really cool, while serving up tasty burgers and snacks inside its intimate space.

Regional and national acts swing by **City Winery** (2718, 650 North Ave. NE, Ste. 201, 404/946-3791, 11am-10pm Sun.-Wed., 11am-11pm Thurs.-Sat., tickets up to $250), which is located inside Ponce City Market. A former iron smelting room inside an old plow factory, **Terminal West** (887 W. Marietta St. NW, Studio C, 404/876-5566, www.terminalwestatl.com, tickets up to $40) pulls in plenty of national acts with a focus on indie, including artists like Yo La Tengo and Guided By Voices. There's typically a greater range of shows, naturally, at the **Variety Playhouse** (1099 Euclid Ave. NE, 404/524-7354, www.variety-playhouse.com, tickets up to $100), which one night will feature Americana and the next a Beatles tribute band; seating is first come, first served. **Center Stage** (1374 W. Peachtree St., 404/885-1365, www.centerstage-atlanta.com) has three venues where it presents live concerts, comedy shows, and special events. The art deco **Buckhead Theatre** (3110 Roswell Rd. NE, 404/843-2825, www.thebuckheadtheatre.com, tickets up to $50) is a major concert venue, cycling in national acts and local favorites.

Performing Arts

The Fox Theatre (660 Peachtree St. NE, 404/881-2100, www.foxtheatre.org) opened in 1929 with an extravagant proscenium influenced by ancient Egyptian design. The former movie house glimmers and is one of Atlanta's theater landmarks; today it hosts live theater, comedy shows, and the occasional national touring band. **Alliance Theatre** (404/733-4650, www.alliancetheatre.org) produces and presents dynamic plays at numerous venues throughout the city. Its home venue is at the **Woodruff Arts Center** (1280 Peachtree St. NW). On the campus of Georgia Tech, the **Ferst Center for the Arts** (349 Ferst Dr. NW, 404/894-2787, www.arts.gatech.edu) presents dance shows, classical concerts, movies, and the occasional theatrical performance.

Festivals and Events

No festival in Atlanta is quite like the **Atlanta Dogwood Festival** (Piedmont Park, 1320 Monroe Dr. NE, Apr., www.dogwood.org, free). When the pretty white dogwoods begin to bloom, the city gathers at Piedmont Park to celebrate spring with live music, Frisbee dogs, rides and games, food, a 5K run, and artisans and crafters. **Music Midtown** (Piedmont Park, 1320 Monroe Dr. NE, Sept., www.musicmidtown.com, under $150) is the big, two-day aural festival in the city, which in the past has featured acts like Mumford & Sons and Bruno Mars. Also at Piedmont, the **Atlanta Jazz Festival** (Piedmont Park, 1320 Monroe Dr. NE, Memorial Day weekend, www.atlantafestivals.com, free) brings a host of local and notable musicians to the city. Finally, jam out to roots, Americana, and experimental rock at SweetWater Brewing Company's **420 Fest** (Centennial Olympic Park, 265 W Park Ave. NW). The brewery says it named it 420 Fest to honor Earth Day, but come on: previous headlining artists include Umphrey's McGee, 311, and Snoop Dogg.

Shopping

Part of the growing trend of all-in-one communities where high-end shopping mixes with high-end residential and dining, **Atlantic Station** (1380 Atlantic Dr. NW, www.atlanticstation.com) is an enticing open-air, walkable shopping area featuring stores like Banana Republic, H&M, and Ann Taylor Loft.

One step up from Atlantic Station is **Westside Provisions District** (1198 Howell Mill Rd., 404/872-7538, www.westsideprovisions.com, 10am-9pm daily)—whereas Atlantic has a Gap, Westside has a J. Crew. Its stores are spread out in brick buildings that once housed a meatpacking plant.

Food

Downtown

Get your New York-style pie at **Rosa's Pizza** (62 Broad St. NW, 404/521-2596, 11am-6pm Mon.-Fri., 11am-4pm Sat., under $25), a classic pizza joint with tile floors and little else. There's a few oddball toppings, but stalwarts like ground beef and mushroom can't be ignored. Calzones are available, too.

Just across the street, Hawaiian is served at **Fish Bowl Poke** (61 Broad St. NW, 404/343-2467, www.fishbowlpokeshop.com, 11am-5pm Mon.-Sat., under $15). Stand in line and order your custom poke bowl (fish with rice and toppings). Enjoy it in the clean, mod space or take it to go.

You'll get superb diner fare with a twist at **Atlanta Breakfast Club** (249 Ivan Allen Jr. Blvd. NW, 470/428-3825, www.atlantabreakfastclub.com, 6:30am-3pm daily, under $20). For breakfast there's shrimp and grits, maybe breakfast tacos, while lunch includes fried chicken and a shrimp po' boy.

Little Five Points

You'll need two hands and potentially an extra jaw to handle the burgers at **The Vortex** (438 Moreland Ave., 404/688-1828, www.thevortexatl.com, 11am-midnight Sun.-Thurs., 11am-2am Fri.-Sat., under $30). The specialty here is the Quadruple Coronary Bypass Burger, which features eight slices of Texas toast, 32 ounces of sirloin, 28 slices of cheese, 4 fried eggs, 27 strips of bacon, and 12 ounces of mayonnaise. The Vortex is a bar first, and an over-21 joint (you can smoke and curse here).

It's a good idea to make reservations for **Babette's Café** (573 North Highland Ave. NE, 404/523-9121, www.babettescafe.com, 5:30pm-10pm Tues.-Sat., 5pm-9pm Sun., under $50), which was inspired by the film *Babette's Feast* and showcases French and Italian cooking, with a sprinkling of Spanish. You'll want to pair a good bottle of wine with your dinner here.

Ask for more sauce, always, at **Nyamminz & Jamminz Jamaican Restaurant** (1083 Euclid Ave. NE, 404/730-3444, 11am-8pm Tues.-Sat., noon-6pm Sun., under $20). There's little concentration on the interior here, probably because the food does all the talking. Go for the oxtail or jerk ribs entrée, while a side of patty or rice and peas rounds out a good meal.

Cabbagetown and Reynoldstown

★ **Home Grown** (968 Memorial Dr. SE, 404/222-0455, www.homegrownga.com, 7am-3pm Mon.-Fri., 7am-2pm Sat.-Sun., under $20 breakfast and brunch, under $25 lunch) has no target demographic, only people who want good food. The happy, community-centric Home Grown serves up casual southern comfort food in a sunny diner. Breakfast is served all day, highlighted by the Comfy Chicken Biscuit (open-faced in sausage gravy), while lunch includes homemade pimento and fried green tomatoes (the Grant Stack) and a killer fried bologna sandwich on Texas toast. Music here darts from trap to Todd Rundgren, and the employees all seem to absolutely love the place.

Share southwestern tapas at the warm **Agave Restaurant** (242 Boulevard SE, 404/588-0006, www.agaverestaurant.com, 5pm-10pm Sun.-Thurs., 5pm-10pm Fri.-Sat., under $50). Agave specializes in soups, enchiladas, tostadas, and a famous dish of cayenne fried chicken. You may not want to share that last one.

Other Areas

Go deep into the Gulf coast without having to pop on a swimsuit at **The Optimist** (914 Howell Mill Rd., 404/477-6260, www.theoptimistrestaurant.com, 11:30am-2:30pm and 5pm-10pm Mon.-Thurs., 11:30am-2:30pm and 5pm-11pm Fri., 5pm-11pm Sat., 5pm-10pm Sun., under $50), located in the Georgia Tech area. With a raw bar, gumbo, mussels, and lobster rolls, the Optimist serves happy, hungry folks in a postindustrial dining room with rustic woods, clean blue and white linens, and subway tile.

The **Busy Bee Café** (810 Martin Luther King Dr. NW, 404/525-9212, www.thebusybeecafe.com, 11am-7pm Mon.-Fri., noon-7pm Sun, under $30) at Atlanta University City is certainly busy—its website lets you know the likely wait time. Come to this classic soul-food spot and order everything from a full Cajun fried turkey to fried fish, ham hocks, and black-eyed peas that will have you getting back in line.

Accommodations

$50-150

The **Highland Inn & Ballroom Lounge** (644 N. Highland Ave. NE, 404/874-5756, www.thehighlandinn.com, $60-120) is a fine option if you're on a budget. The 1920s-era building in the Poncey-Highland neighborhood is within walking distance of Ponce City Market and other midtown destinations, and while the rooms are on the smaller side, they're comfortable and manageable.

Want cooking classes with your stay? Try **Maison LaVigne** (3532 S. Fulton Ave., Hapeville, 404/754-5137, www.maisonlavigne.com, $100-140), which is close to the airport and 7 miles (11.3 km) south of downtown. This three-suite Victorian B&B has packages including a tea party and romantic dinner. And yes, you can also reserve culinary or wine courses with the innkeeper.

$150-250

Built in 1901, ★ **Peach House Bed & Breakfast** (88 Spruce St. NE, 404/908-0809, www.thepeach.house, $150-250) is a ridiculously cute peach-colored house with six ridiculously cute rooms. The Peach Blossom Suite is a lovely Victorian without the frilly additions, while the Sweet Auburn Room pays homage to the 1960s South; its green-yellow walls, mid-century furniture, and colorful bedding make it a stunning stay. The house has a front porch, workout equipment, and a seasonal hut tub.

Downtown, **The Ellis Hotel** (176 Peachtree St. NW, 404/523-5155, www.ellishotel.com, $140-200) is a high-rise boutique with 127 rooms and suites. Accommodations are simple and clean, and the hotel has a women's-only floor, a dog-friendly floor, and a fresh-air floor, where each room has a 24-hour air-filtering machine plus sealed mattresses and pillows.

The **Hotel Clermont** (789 Ponce De Leon Ave., 470/485-0485, www.hotelclermont.com, $210-250) has more than 90 rooms and suites plus a rooftop bar and restaurant. All rooms have king or queen beds, plus tiled bathrooms and lounge chairs. For entertainment, you can simply go to the basement: Yes, that's the iconic Clermont Lounge occupying the building's bottom floor.

Information and Services

For travel and tourism information, visit the **Atlanta Visitors Guide** (1075 Peachtree St. NW, 770/284-6388, www.atlantavisitorsguide.com) or the **Atlanta Convention & Visitors Bureau** (233 Peachtree St. NW, Ste. 1400, 404/521-6600, www.atlanta.net, 9am-5pm Mon.-Fri.)

On the radio, check out **WSB 95.5 FM** or **750 AM** for news and traffic, **WABE 90.1 FM** for public radio, and **WAMJ 107.5** (Majic 107.5) for urban contemporary.

Dahlonega

Take US-19 65 miles (105 km) north from Atlanta to reach the largest city close to the Appalachian trailhead. Dahlonega (pop. 6,437) gives hikers a golden opportunity to rest and relax before taking on the trail. And I really mean "golden"—in 1828 Dahlonega was the site of the first great gold discovery in America. Dahlonega is also an official Appalachian Trail community, with the **Dahlonega Trailfest** taking place in September.

Dahlonega is also a great place to catch some authentic Appalachian music. The free **Appalachian Jam sessions** (www.dahlonegadda.org) on Dahlonega's Public Square happen on Saturdays from late April to early October.

Gold Museum Historic Site

All the action in Dahlonega focuses on the town's public square, home to the **Dahlonega Gold Museum Historic Site** (1 Public Square N, 706/864-2257, 9am-4:45pm Mon.-Sat., 10am-4:45pm Sun., $7 adults, $6.50 seniors, $4.50 ages 6-17, $2 younger than 6). Set inside a historic 1836 courthouse building, the museum tells the story of America's first great gold rush. Visitors can see coins produced at the U.S. Mint branch that existed in the city and gold nuggets from the 19th century, plus get a full tour of the old courthouse, including the judge's chambers.

Dahlonega Trailfest

Toward the end of the hiking season, the city comes together at **Dahlonega Trailfest** (Sept., Public Square and Hancock Park, www.dahlonegatrailfest.org). The city was named an Appalachian Trail community in 2011, and the festival honors its essential presence as a pre-hike (or post-hike, for you southbound hikers) destination. Local craft vendors, hiking suppliers, brewers, winemakers, and restaurateurs all make it a point to be at this three-day event.

Food and Nightlife

One of the more fortunate gold discoverers was Capt. Frank Hall, and he practically fell into the stuff. According to legend, he was building his new residence in the late 1800s in Dahlonega when he struck gold. More than 100 years later, when the home was the **Smith House Inn & Restaurant** (84 S. Chestatee St., 706/725-8148, www.smithhouse.com, 11am-3pm Tues.-Thurs., 11am-7:30pm Fri.-Sun., under $25), a worker accidentally punched a hole that uncovered a mine shaft. That changed the entire direction of the inn, which today allows visitors to check out the 20-foot chute while enjoying country meals like fried chicken and baked ham.

It's the place with all the goofy stuff on the walls and the chicken fingers: **Shenanigans** (87 N. Chestatee St., 706/482-0114, www.theshenaniganspub.com, 11am-10pm Mon.-Tues., 11am-midnight Wed.-Sat., 11am-9pm Sun., under $30). This Irish haunt is extremely popular with the locals, and inexpensive food includes Irish fare, burgers, pizza, and nachos. And yes, they do have chicken fingers.

Prost! Get the full German experience at **Bratzeit** (77 Memorial Dr., 706/867-7741, www.bratzeit.com, 11am-2pm Wed., 11am-8pm Thurs.-Sat., noon-3pm Sun., under $25). Offerings include veal bratwurst, currywurst, potato pancakes, and spaetzle. German beer is on tap, and an outdoor patio opens for warm weather and Oktoberfest celebrations.

They sell "gold fingers" at **Foothill Grill** (995 Morrison Moore Pkwy. W, 706/864-0863, 7am-3pm Tues.-Sun., under $20), though don't be fooled: they're chicken fingers. Breakfast is served all day at this straightforward diner with booths, barstools, and laminated tables. Good eggs and bacon.

Grab a beer, and fill up for the night, at **Gold City Growlers** (10 Chestatee St., 706/864-4677, www.goldcitygrowlers.com, 11am-7pm Tues.-Wed., 11am-8pm Thurs., 11am-9pm Fri.-Sat., 1pm-6pm Sun., under $15). There are 20 taps and a small bar space for those hoping to try out some of the newest brews in northern Georgia; those in a hurry can fill up a growler and buy a snack, like beef jerky or beer bread.

Locals love to cavort at **Spirits Tavern** (19 E. Main St., Ste. D, 706/482-0580, www.spirits-tavern.com, 11am-11pm Sun.-Thurs., 11am-1am Fri., 11am-midnight Sat., under $20). Enjoy solid cocktails with juicy burgers and fresh salads and sandwiches. Their beef comes from Springer Mountain Farms up in northeast Georgia—not exactly on the mountain, but a nice reminder of where you've been.

Dahlonega is in the heart of a miniature wine country, with multiple wineries within 10 miles (16 km) of the city center. The best include **Cavender Creek Vineyards** (3610 Cavender

Top to bottom: Dahlonega Gold Museum Historic Site; Blood Mountain Shelter near Neels Gap; Brasstown Bald.

Creek Rd., 706/867-7700, www.cavendercreekvineyards.com, 12:30pm-5:30pm Sun. and Thurs., 12:30pm-7pm Fri., 11am-7pm Sat., under $20), which features frequent live music at a laid-back farm; **Wolf Mountain Vineyards** (180 Wolf Mountain Tr., 706/867-9862, www.wolfmountainvineyards.com, 11am-5pm Sat., 12:30pm-5pm Sun., under $30), where visitors can gather around a cedar-and-stone bar that recalls a beautiful mountain lodge; and **Three Sisters Vineyards & Winery** (439 Vineyard Way, 706/865-9463, www.threesistersvineyards.com, 11am-5pm Thurs.-Sat., 1pm-5pm Sun., under $25), which grows a variety of grapes at its small but friendly farm.

Accommodations

The **Smith House Inn & Restaurant** (84 S. Chestatee St., 706/725-8148, www.smithhouse.com, $100-215) has the fried chicken and the gold mine, but more importantly, it services visitors with Ritz-Carlton-style rooms. The sweet, unassuming rooms painted in earth tones are extremely comfortable, and the price is affordable for this tourist city.

Smack in the middle of the city is the **Dahlonega Square Hotel & Villas** (135 N. Chestatee St., 706/867-1313, www.dahlonegasquarevilla.com, $100-150), which offers six king rooms and six double-queen rooms, plus a separate suite. The spacious rooms are a cut above standard chain rooms, with some including vintage 19th-century-style furniture. The hotel also shuttles guests on local **winery tours** ($60) through its sister transportation company.

The **Park Place Hotel** (27 S. Park St., 706/864-0021, www.parkplacdahlonega.com, $120-250) is clearly the class of the city, featuring well-dressed farmhouse-chic guest rooms with hardwood floors, dark woods, and ample outdoor sitting space. Rooms are a little pricier than expected, but there's a lot of care in this unpretentious venue.

For a hostel experience, there's **Barefoot Hills** (7693 US-19, 470/788-8043, www.barefoothills.com/hikerhostel, $42). Barefoot Hills also has a **thru-hiking special** ($210), in which those about to begin a thru-hike can get a full-service room and shuttle to Springer Mountain.

GA-52: Springer Mountain

Welcome to the Appalachian Trail. From the trailhead, which is 1 mile (1.6 km) from the summit of **Springer Mountain,** you have about 2,200 miles (3,540 km) of trail ahead of you, finishing at Katahdin in Maine. Hundreds of thousands of dreams take flight at this very spot, part of Chattahoochee National Forest. While not everyone hikes it all the way through, every Appalachian Trail hiker contributes to the trail's special, shared journey.

Getting There and Around

Getting to Springer Mountain can take some work. The **trailhead** (Ellijay, 34.626648, -84.193993) is 96.9 miles (156 km) north of Atlanta by way of I-85, US-19, GA-136 and GA-52, and 20.5 miles (33 km) west of Dahlonega by way of GA-9 and GA-52. Near the Springer summit is a **parking lot** (34.637452, -84.195753). The Appalachian Trail Conservancy suggests that hikers park and start their hikes to Springer at **Amicalola Falls State Park,** where an 8-mile (12.9-km) **approach trail** (Ellijay, 34.599611, -84.223765) preludes the official AT trailhead. Why? It gets busy, especially in March and April when thru-hikers descend on Springer to begin their massive hikes.

You can drive to the Springer lot by turning right onto Nimblewill Church Road from GA-52. This uphill, at times rocky drive can be taxing for cars that aren't equipped to handle the terrain. It's a 10.7-mile (17.2-km) drive that typically takes 40-45 minutes. Thru-hikers will often call a shuttle that can pick them up from either Hartsdale-Jackson airport or the MARTA North Springs station in Atlanta. Most of these shuttles are driven by residents with personal cell numbers and email addresses. More official shuttle operators include **Survivor Dave** (www.atsurvivordave.com), who travels between North Springs and other locations. Also, **Barefoot Hills** (470/788-8043, www.barefoothills.com/hikerhostel) hostel in Dahlonega operates shuttles to and from Atlanta and its facility.

Hiking

You don't have to be a thru-hiker to do Springer. The following loop hike includes the summit and part of the AT. If you can, try to go either in midsummer or late in the year when the trail will be less crowded.

★ Springer Mountain Loop

Distance: 4.7 miles (7.6 km)
Duration: 2.5 hours
Elevation gain: 680 feet (207 m)
Difficulty: Moderate
Trailhead: Springer Mountain summit parking lot (34.637452, -84.195753)

Take the AT from the parking lot, going south toward the summit. Continue to the summit while passing the trailhead for the Benton MacKaye Trail, honoring the father of the AT. You'll ascend about half the climb on this mile-long (1.6-km) trek over relatively rocky terrain, after which you'll reach the summit, which provides views of the very southern Appalachians, bursting vividly during the fall. If you're there in the cool spring of April or likely colder November, you might catch some thru-hikers.

After taking in the summit, turn around and take the AT back until you connect again with the MacKaye Trail, identified by white diamond blazes. Turn right and take the MacKaye down the mountain and around to Ball Mountain. Near the Ball summit a spur trail with double white-diamond blazes leads to a scenic overlook of the area of Amicalola Falls State Park. There's also a memorial to MacKaye on the MacKaye Trail, plus stream crossings and abundant rhododendron, a regular sight in the Southern Appalachians. The MacKaye will run back into the AT after about 4 miles (6.4 km); turn left to take the AT back to the parking lot.

Accommodations

The closest place to stay to Springer is **Amicalola Falls Lodge** (418 Amicalola Falls Rd., Dawsonville, 800/573-9656, www.amicalolafallslodge.com, $30-250). The lodge has 24 campsites ($30-35), most with power and water, fire rings, and grills. There's also a number of cabins on-site, plus rooms in the lodge.

Information and Services

For more information about Springer Mountain, call **Chattahoochee-Oconee National Forest** (770/297-3000).

Neels Gap

From Dahlonega, take the winding US-19 north through the forest 31.2 miles (50 km) until you reach Neels Gap, an intersection with the Appalachian Trail. Here day hikers have an opportunity to taste the Southern Appalachian wilderness atop a pretty north Georgia summit.

Hiking

Neels Gap to Blood Mountain

Distance: 4.3 miles (6.9 km)
Duration: 2-2.5 hours
Elevation gain: 1,470 feet (448 m)
Difficulty: Moderate
Trailhead: Parking lot at Mountain Crossings at Walasi-yi (12471 Gainesville Hwy., Blairsville, 34.735098, -83.918053)

From the parking lot you'll cross US-19. Use caution: It's a curved road where cars may be coming quickly. On the other side of US-19, follow the white blazes of the Appalachian Trail southbound. Within 0.9 mile (1.4 km) you'll reach a junction

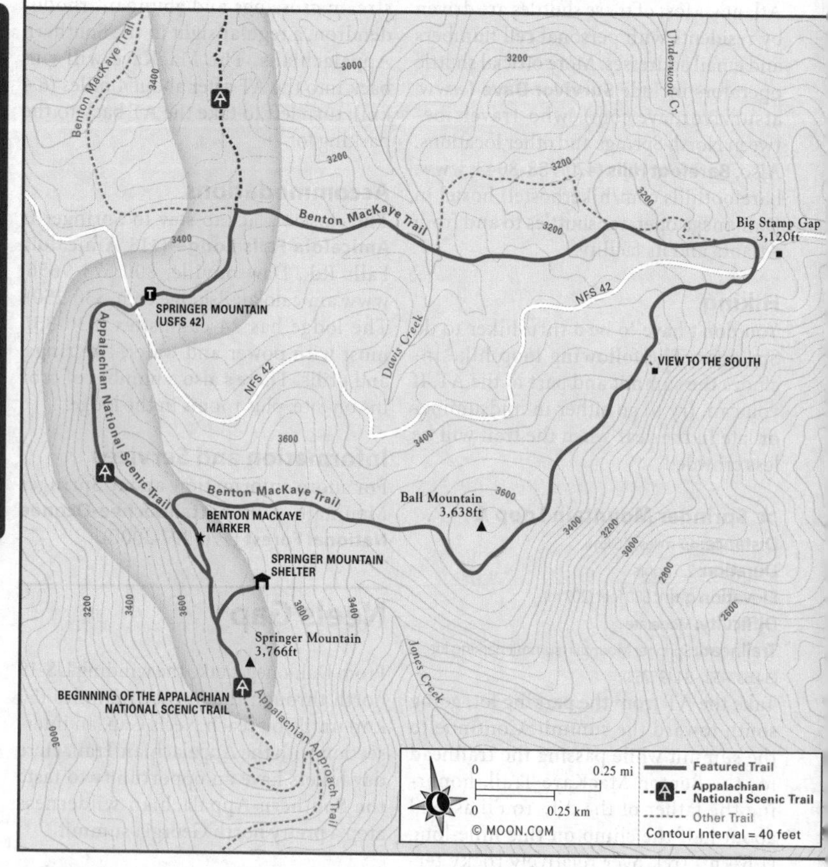

with the Byron Reece Memorial Trail; continue on the AT as it opens to some neat views. You'll begin to feel the climb at this point, as the trail begins ascending switchbacks. After 0.5 mile (0.8 km) you'll level out, but then you'll meet up with boulders, necessitating some work from the hands. After another 0.5 mile (0.8 km) you'll reach a pine forest, indicating you're close to the summit. It won't be long before you've reached the 4,460-foot (1,360-m) peak. At the summit is the **Blood Mountain Shelter** (34.739922, -83.937051), a stone building constructed in 1937. When finished, head back the way you came.

Shopping and Accommodations

At the parking lot at Neels Gap is **Mountain Crossings at Walasi-yi** (706/745-6095, www.mountaincrossings.com, 9am-5pm Mon.-Fri., 9am-6pm Sat.-Sun.), an outfitter/hostel on the trail where you can stock up on gear, food (pizza, ice cream), and AT gifts. This historic stone building has been around since the trail opened, and it marks the only covered portion of the trail. The **hiker's hostel** ($17) is first come, first served.

Brasstown Bald

To get here from Neels Gap, turn off US-19 at GA-180 and take that to Jacks Gap, about a 16-mile (26-km) drive.

It seems unfair that **Brasstown Bald,** the highest point in all of Georgia at 4,784 feet (1,458 m), is just a couple of cheap miles off the Appalachian Trail. Why not let AT hikers have the pleasure of 360-degree views of the Hiawassee Ridge, the Blue Ridge peaks to the north, and—on the clearest of days—the Atlanta skyline?

Brasstown Bald, and much of the area in this southern part of the Appalachian Trail, was originally Cherokee Indian land. The Cherokees settled throughout modern-day Appalachia well before the 1600s, expanding into various sub-tribes while making deep connections with their surroundings. The Brasstown Bald area was known as Itse'yi, meaning "place of fresh green," but early English settlers who traded with the Cherokee tribe misinterpreted the word as Untsaiyi, which means "brass." The settlement was called Brasstown by the English. The mountain was called Etonah by the Cherokee, a name that sticks today, though Brasstown Bald is the popular moniker.

The bald itself is also popular, as evidenced by a gigantic parking lot that can hold a few hundred vehicles. You can **drive to the lot** ($5) and hike the rest of the way, or you can hike one of a few trails that connect to the summit. At the summit is the **T. S. Candler Memorial** (March-October), a massive stone monument to a former Georgia Supreme Court judge who was an early supporter of Brasstown tourism. The memorial includes a visitors center, a theater showing a 15-minute movie on regional history and ecology, a **viewing tower** ($3 ages 16 and older), and plenty of viewing opportunities. On a clear day you can see downtown Atlanta, plus miles of rolling mountains. During the off-season you can walk about the memorial deck. There's also a picnic area at the summit.

There's the cheater's way to reach the summit (starting from the parking lot), or there are longer routes that start near the mountain's base. To be fair, the cheater's way is a good hike for all levels, with a decent 500-foot (152-m) ascent on paved road marked by placards revealing information about local flora, fauna, and history. For families, it's perfect.

Jacks Gap to Brasstown Bald

Distance: 6.5 miles (10.5 km)
Duration: 3.5-4 hours
Elevation gain: 1,900 feet (579 m)
Difficulty: Strenuous
Trailhead: Jacks Gap parking area at GA-180 (34.848279, -83.798707)

If you're hiking instead of driving to Brasstown Bald, you have two options. If you're really adventurous and have a full day, take the 10-mile (16-km) round-trip **Arkaquah Trail,** which starts at a crossing with Trackrock Gap Road. To reach the crossing, take GA-180 southwest, turn right onto Town Creek School Road, turn right on Track Rock Church Road, and turn right again on Trackrock Gap and go 0.7 mile (1.1 km).

If you have less time but want exercise, start at the Jacks Gap parking area. When at Jacks Gap, if you crossed GA-180 and continued south on the Jack's Knob Trail, you'd reach the Appalachian Trail in 2 miles (3.2 km), but for this hike you're staying on the **Jack's Knob Trail north.** Follow the blue blazes up on a relatively challenging stretch of incline totaling 1,400 feet (427 m) over 1.7 miles (2.8 km); there are switchbacks, which give you some time to rest. Keep an eye out for snakes, but also keep an eye out for quality views of surrounding Blue Ridge peaks.

When you feel about ready to give up,

you'll find yourself at picnic tables, signaling your arrival at the large parking area. Head toward the information center, where the trail continues on paved road to Brasstown Bald. Climb the 0.5-mile (0.8-km) summit access trail, reading about the local environment along the way, until getting to the enormous stone monument. Take in the views of the Blue Ridge, Georgia valleys, and maybe even Atlanta, before heading back on the summit access trail and Jacks Knob Trail. Pace yourself so your knees don't give out on the way down.

Hiawassee

From Jacks Gap, drive up GA-180 north to GA-75 north. That'll take you into Hiawassee (pop. 880), a small town with a big job: It's one of the first stops for Appalachian Trail hikers hoping for a little rest, a comfortable bed, and a lot of food. The trail intersects with US-76 about 10.5 miles (16.9 km) east of Hiawassee, which provides an opportunity to shuttle into town. There you'll find a few basic restaurants and a lot of southern charm. People here are extra courteous and happy to help hikers.

Sights

Georgia Mountain Fairgrounds

Hiawassee is home to the **Georgia Mountain Fairgrounds** (1311 Music Hall Rd., 706/896-4191, www.georgiamountainfairgrounds.com), which hosts multiple events each year, headlined by the **Georgia Mountain Fair** (July). A smaller version of a traditional county fair, the Georgia Mountain Fair has the usual carnival rides and food, plus arts and crafts, country and bluegrass music, and a 19th-century pioneer village with a general store and one-room schoolhouse.

Hamilton Gardens

Before reaching the Georgia Mountain

water mill at Georgia Mountain Fairgrounds in Hiawassee

Fairgrounds, make a quick right to go up to **Hamilton Gardens** (96 Pavilion Rd., 706/970-0011, www.hamiltongardens.org, 8am-8pm daily, donations appreciated, $5 guided tour). The gardens are named for Fred Hamilton, a Sears, Roebuck & Co. executive who spent years breeding plants. He moved his plants to this site off Lake Chatuge, which opened to the public in the 1980s and now maintains more than 1,500 rhododendrons and azaleas, plus other native trees and wildflowers, over 33 acres. The gardens are open year-round to the public and host frequent gatherings, such as plant sales and movie nights when the weather warms up.

Visitors can stroll on multiple easy trails at the gardens. The **Main Trail** (0.4 mi/0.6 km) offers plenty of rhododendron spotting, plus bare-tree views of the lake in colder months. Head down the **Lake View Trail** (0.16 mi/0.25 km) to get better lake views. Pets are not allowed at the site.

Bell Mountain

For many in Hiawassee, a longtime favorite peak has been **Bell Mountain** (220 Shake Rag Rd.), which provides exceptional views of the town below. The story behind it, however, reveals the complicated relationship between humans and nature.

Two men in the 1960s attempted to mine in Bell Mountain but didn't succeed; they left the peak scarred by a massive hole that remains today, which has become a popular spot to spray-paint graffiti on rock. Towns County, which now owns the mountain land, paved a road to a near-summit parking lot and put in a viewing platform at the peak. Visitors are now allowed to contribute their own graffiti. It's a point of controversy among locals, some of whom believe the graffiti is now part of the mountain's character, like the hole itself, while others see it as disrespectful to nature. You can decide for yourself.

Hiking

High Shoals Falls

Distance: 2.4 miles (3.9 km)
Duration: 1.5 hours
Elevation gain: 370 feet (113 m)
Difficulty: Easy
Trailhead: Indian Grave Gap Road (34.816021, -83.727107)

You'll feel as if you're walking through an enchanted land not meant for human discovery on the **High Shoals Trail,** which offers views of two distinctive waterfalls. From the trailhead, you'll descend a bit on a simple path marked by green blazes. Saunter past rhododendrons along High Shoals Creek before first reaching Blue Hole Falls, famous for its cobalt hue. Continue another 0.1 mile (0.16 km) or so to High Shoals Falls, which is more rambling and rollicking. There are observation decks for both falls, so take as many pictures as you'd like. Return the way you came.

Shopping

Northbound thru-hikers who may have forgotten something—and realized as such during those first few miles on the Appalachian Trail—rely on **Mountain Roots Southern Outfitters** (347 Town Pl., Ste. A, 706/896-1873, www.mountainrootsoutfitters.com, 11am-5pm Thurs.-Tues.). Mountain Roots has all the necessary hiking gear, plus T-shirts, hats, gifts, and jewelry.

Georgia's largest antiques mall is in Hiawassee, and it's suitably called the **Hiawassee Antique Mall** (518 N. Main St., 706/896-0587, www.hiawasseeantiquemall.com, 10am-5pm Mon.-Sat., noon-5pm Sun.). The mall boasts 40 dealers featuring everything from 1950s collectibles to vintage clothing. There's kind staff, clean aisles, and plenty to choose from here.

Food and Accommodations

Hikers find **Daniel's Steakhouse** (273 Big Sky Dr., 706/896-8008, 11am-8:30pm daily, under $25) an outstanding first stop for filling up, as it features an inexpensive buffet with country favorites like fried chicken and mashed potatoes. Don't expect white tablecloths here, just a bunch of food options and a laid-back atmosphere.

The popular place among locals is the **Deer Lodge** (7466 GA-17, 706/896-2726, 5pm-9pm Thurs.-Sun., closed in winter, under $30). Lines begin growing early (even before 5pm), probably so folks can be the first to taste breaded catfish, breaded rainbow trout, and all kinds of red meat.

The most tourist-packed of the local restaurants is probably **The Happy Hawg** (1586 US-76 W, 706/896-0012, www.thehappyhawg.com, 11am-7pm Wed.-Sat., 11am-3pm Sun. summer, 11am-7am Thurs-Sat. winter, under $20), and for good reason. Here you get lip-smacking barbecue from the smoker, plus hush puppies and fried corn, in a relaxed setting with checkerboard tables. There's plenty of seating on the deck overlooking Lake Chatuge, with televisions inviting patrons to hang out for a while.

For those wanting a morning pick-me-up, **McLain's on Main Café & Coffee Bar** (142 N. Main St., 706/970-3705, 7am-3pm Mon.-Fri., 8am-2pm Sat., under $10) is a cheery little coffee shop with outdoor seating, plus wraps and fresh salads.

Those staying in Hiawassee might get drawn in by **Lake Chatuge Lodge** (653 US-76, 706/896-5253, www.lakechatugelodge.com, $130-250), which is disguised as a resort-quality hotel on a lake but whose rooms are leaning more toward the motor lodge style. It's an old building, so be warned of minor structural issues that previous visitors have faced. Upper-floor rooms have balconies, but if you're not facing the lake, at least you can be outside.

One of the first major hiker havens on the AT is ★ **Top of Georgia Hiking Center** (7675 Hwy. 76 E, 706/982-3252, www.topofgeorgiahostel.com, $30-70). A hostel, gear outpost, and shuttle provider for AT hikers at mile 69, Top of Georgia has a reputation for being quite helpful. Its Yahoola Cottage has bunk rooms, a full kitchen, and a bathroom with hot shower. They don't supply sheets or pillows, however. Free shuttles go to the AT and into town.

Nantahala National Forest

Encompassing more than 530,000 acres in western North Carolina, Nantahala is the largest forest in the Tar Heel State, its name translating in Cherokee to "Land of the Noonday Sun" because sunlight can only hit some gorges when the sun is fully overhead. Nantahala is a sprawling forest with three districts, plenty of recreation opportunities, and outstanding hikes in the Blue Ridge Mountains.

The Appalachian Trail shoots up ridgeline and ascends balds blanketed by rhododendrons as it traverses Nantahala. It crosses US-74 at Wesser, where the Nantahala Outdoor Center provides a necessary outfitter and frequent overnight stay.

Getting There and Around

There are a few ways into Nantahala National Forest. The most convenient and accessible is Franklin, North Carolina. To reach Franklin from Hiawassee, Georgia, drive on US-76 west to GA-515, going north to US-64. Take US-64 east to Franklin, one of the ranger outposts of Nantahala National Forest. Other towns providing an outpost for Nantahala visitors include Dillard, Georgia, and Bryson City, Cashiers, Cowee, Highlands, Robbinsville, Topton, and Wesser in North Carolina.

US-64 runs north from near Hiawassee to Franklin, then continues east to Highlands and Cashiers. US-74 cuts through the western end of the park, moving through Topton, Wesser, and Bryson City before continuing east and connecting to I-40.

Sights

Gem Mines

Around 1870, men in Macon County, North Carolina, began mining for corundum, a mineral with two popular varieties: ruby and sapphire. No one has yet reached the source of these corundum mines, but there's always been an interest in the ruby and sapphire hunt in this part of Appalachia. So, along with the robust outdoor tourism in the area, there's a strong gem mining tourism industry. You'll find mines, shops, and museums all across the county, especially close to Franklin. These places will own a big chunk of land where you can dig a hole. Then you sift the hole for gems, washing away clay at the flume. This is a purely Appalachian experience costing little money and worth a high family fun factor.

Top choices include **Rose Creek Mine** (115 Terrace Ridge Dr., Franklin, NC, 828/349-3774, www.rosecreekmine.com, 9am-5pm Mon.-Sat. Apr.-Oct., starts at $10), **Mason Ruby & Sapphire Mine** (6961 Upper Burningtown Rd., Franklin, NC, 828/369-9742, www.masonsmine.com, 9am-5pm Mon.-Sat. Mar.-Oct., starts at $20), and **Jackson Hole Trading Post & Gem Mine** (9770 Highlands Rd., Highlands, NC, 828/524-5850, www.jacksonholegemmine.com, hours vary, starts at $10).

The Bascom

Highlands is attractive to art lovers, particularly for **The Bascom: Center for the Visual Arts** (323 Franklin Rd., Highlands, NC, 828/526-4949, www.thebascom.org, 10am-5pm Mon.-Sat., noon-5pm Sun.). With its six-acre campus of six buildings, the Bascom hosts exhibits in seven galleries, plus workshops and live events like receptions and annual festivals. The Horst Winkler Sculpture and Nature Trail winds through the countryside and past outdoor artwork, providing a connection to the **Highlands Plateau Greenway** (www.highlandsgreenway.com), which runs along Main Street to the west and east, and 4th and 5th Streets to the north and south.

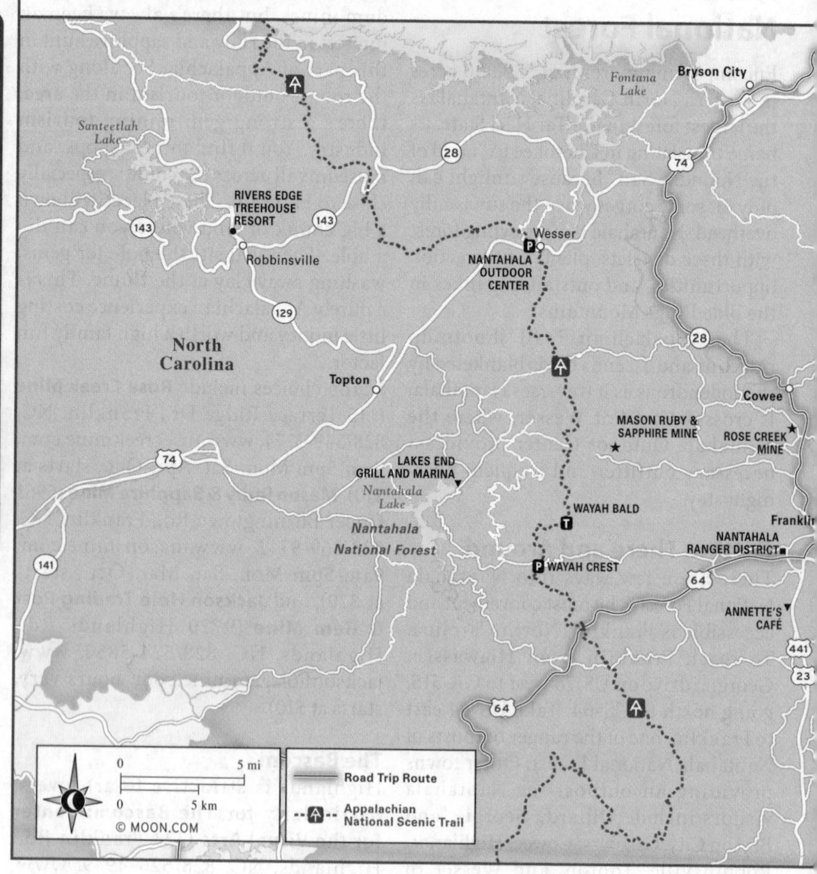

Hiking

Wayah Bald

Distance: 7.2 miles (11.6 km)
Duration: 4-4.5 hours
Elevation gain: 1,300 feet (396 m)
Difficulty: Moderate
Trailhead: Wayah Crest Picnic Area (35.153152, -83.581047)

If you had hiked Wayah Bald a few hundred years ago, you could have been accompanied by packs of red wolves. While the red wolves are no more, their spirit lives on at the mountain officially named "Wa ya," which is Cherokee for wolf. Today Wayah is also known for the **Wayah Bald Tower,** which sprouts above the tree line at 5,342 feet (1,628 m), marking one of the highest points in Nantahala National Forest. From the tower, which was built in 1937, you get 360-degree views from the Great Smoky Mountains in the north to hills far across Georgia to the south.

From the parking circle at the picnic area at Wayah Crest, walk to Wayah Road and turn right; at the AT crossing, turn left (or north) on the trail. You'll follow the AT for the entirety of this hike, cutting through lush forest with plenty of wild rhododendron. About 2.5 miles (4 km) into the hike, you'll see the yellow-blazed **Bartram Trail,** which you can also take to the bald.

The hike to the tower is about 3.6 miles (5.8 km). The ferocious forest fires that took out large portions of the Great Smoky Mountains and Nantahala National Forest in November 2016 left their mark on the wooden cab of the tower, but it has since been restored. Many trees on the bald were also destroyed, so you'll notice younger vegetation here. Take the AT back the same way to the crest.

Whiteside Mountain Trail

Distance: 2 miles (3.2 km)
Duration: 1-1.5 hours
Elevation gain: 490 feet (149 m)
Difficulty: Moderate
Trailhead: Cliffside Lake Recreation Area (13908 Highlands Rd., Highlands, NC, $4 per vehicle)

Whiteside Mountain, standing at 4,930 feet (1,503 m), is one of the most popular destinations at Nantahala and a ready-made tourist attraction. It's home to peregrine falcons, layers of cliffs, and outstanding 360-degree views. It's also a short but tough slog to the top, so be ready for that.

Start at the trailhead along a gravel road; you'll quickly reach an intersection and see blue blazes to the right. Go that way, and you'll begin ascending switchbacks featuring an item indicating a hike's popularity: stairs. Soon the views will emerge, but be careful, as the drop-off is extremely steep. Some overlooks have moderate cable protection. Keep heading up until you reach the summit, an outcrop with views of seemingly never-ending Blue Ridge peaks. Continue along the blue-blazed trail as it begins to descend, catching a few more overlooks

Top to bottom: Nantahala National Forest; view from the Wayah Bald Tower; the cliffs of Whiteside Mountain.

before heading into rhododendron city. You'll loop back to the gravel road; turn right and head back to the trailhead.

Ranger Falls Interpretive Trail

Distance: 3 miles (4.8 km)
Duration: 1.5 hours
Elevation gain: 600 feet (183 m)
Difficulty: Easy
Trailhead: Cliffside Lake Recreation Area (13908 Highlands Rd., Highlands, NC, $4)

This 3-mile (4.8-km) loop informs visitors of the abundant flora and fauna within Nantahala National Forest. The big attraction on this trail is Ranger Falls, which cascades 35 feet (11 m) along gneissic rock. The cliffside beach and picnic areas make a nice spot to park the family for a spell. You'll start with a mile-long (1.6 km) trek over a regularly used dirt path through woods. At the first fork, stay left, then begin a descent while following signs to the falls. Soon you'll be on the floor at Skitty Creek, and 0.2 miles (0.3 km) away are the falls. After enjoying the falls, continue on the Ranger Falls Trail to an intersection, where you'll turn right. After 0.2 miles (0.3 km), turn right onto a road, and in another 0.2 miles (0.3 km), turn left at a clearing. Soon you'll descend just a little to the trailhead.

Recreation

Fishing

Fishing is permitted at several locations in Nantahala, including Balsam Lake, Cherokee Lake, and Cheoah Work Center Pond out in the forest's west end. Brown, rainbow, and native brook trout are regulars in the Nantahala waters.

Horseback Riding

Two camps in the forest offer horseback riding on trails: **Hurricane Creek** (Franklin, 828/524-6441) and **Wine Spring Campground** (Franklin, 828/524-6441).

Boating

You can take a nonmotorized boat out on several bodies of water in Nantahala. Some of the most popular include Balsam Lake (NC-1756, Tuckasegee, Apr.-Oct., free), Jackrabbit Mountain Recreation Area (465 Jack Rabbit Rd., Hayesville, 828/837-5152, free), and the Fingerlake Day Use Area (NC-28 at Almond Boat Park Rd., Bryson City, Apr.-Oct., free).

Food and Nightlife

Dillard

The Dillard family has been part of the Appalachian landscape since the late 1700s, when Capt. John Dillard purchased land that would become the town of Dillard, Georgia. His descendants, Carrie and Arthur Dillard, had a stone house in town, and in 1917 they opened it to boarders. Today **The Dillard House** (768 Franklin St., Dillard, GA, 706/746-5348, www.dillardhouse.com, 8am-8pm daily, under $30) is a working inn and restaurant that still accommodates travelers and feeds everyone, focusing on good old-fashioned southern cuisine served family style. There's no need to order, though you'll need to specially request the country-style ham, and for breakfast, the country ham and red-eye gravy.

Feel right at home at **Annette's Café** (6798 US-441, Dillard, GA, 706/746-2688, 7am-3pm Mon. and Wed.-Fri., 7am-4pm Sat., under $15). Ridiculously inexpensive, the breakfast at Annette's is top-quality and includes eggs, sandwiches, and pancakes. Lunch is just as good, delivering on southern staples like catfish and okra. Spring extra for a piece of chocolate or red velvet cake while you're at it. There's an informal dining area with a lunch counter.

Highlands

Grab an IPA at **Satulah Mountain Brewing Company** (454 Carolina Way, Highlands, NC, 828/482-9794, www.satulahmountainbrewing.com, 2pm-9pm Thurs., 2pm-10pm Fri.-Sat., under $20), which also offers beer from nonlocal breweries inside its taproom. It's a comfy spot with a beautiful wood bar and picnic tables outside. No food is served.

Locals grab seats at the bar at **Ugly Dog Public House** (294 S. 4th St., Highlands, NC, 828/526-8364, www.theuglydogpub.com, 4pm-11pm Mon., 11:30am-11pm Tues. and Sun., 11:30am-midnight Wed.-Sat., under $30), which carries a small menu of pub favorites including burgers and pizza. Be sure to peruse the photos of very good dogs on the walls. (You can bring your own photo, too!)

For an all-in-one experience, check out **Mountain Fresh Grocery** (521 Main St., Highlands, NC, 828/526-2400, www.mfgro.com, 7am-8pm Mon.-Sat., 8am-6pm Sun., under $20), which is a full-service gourmet market, burger joint, pizza parlor, and café with cakes and espresso. Locals will tell you to go for the pizza, cooked in a hickory wood-fired oven.

Those wanting something more formal can get a nice meal at **Wild Thyme Gourmet** (343 Main St., Highlands, NC, 828/526-4035, 11am-4pm Thurs.-Tues., 5:30pm-9pm Thurs.-Sat. and Mon.-Tues., under $40 dinner, under $20 lunch). Wild Thyme claims classic American with an Asian influence, though only a few dishes that would qualify, such as its waterfall beef, a stir-fry with some spice. Sit at leather booths inside, or at tables outside when the weather is warm.

Cashiers

Cashiers has the second location of Ugly Dog, this being the **Ugly Dog Pub** (25 Frank Allen Rd., Cashiers, NC, 828/743-3000, www.uglydogpub.com, 11:30am-11pm Sun.-Mon., 11:30am-midnight Wed.-Sat., under $30). It has the same menu as in Highlands, with wings, guacamole, burgers, and pizza.

There's a fun Mexican spot in Cashiers: **Chile Loco Authentic Mexican Restaurant** (45 Slab Town Rd., Cashiers, NC, 828/743-1160, 11am-8pm Mon.-Wed., 11am-9pm Thurs.-Fri., 11am-8:30pm Sat., under $20), which from the outside might resemble an insurance agency. Inside you'll spot Mexican pottery, a small bar, and colorful décor. The enchiladas are popular here. Try the chilaquiles (tortilla chips in green tomatillo sauce with cheese and meat).

Lie back in some rustic farmhouse seating and enjoy a cup of coffee at **Bucks Coffee Café** (6 NC-107, Cashiers, NC, 828/743-9997, 7am-6pm daily), or enjoy a big breakfast meal at **Randevu Restaurant** (18 Chestnut Sq., Cashiers, NC, 828/743-0910, www.randevunc.com, 8am-3pm Wed.-Mon., 5pm-9pm Wed.-Sat. and Mon. Mar.-Oct., under $20 breakfast and lunch, under $50 dinner). Randevu does three-egg omelets and country Benedicts in the morning, sandwiches for lunch, and for dinner a whole lot of surf-and-turf like Carolina trout and red snapper from the Gulf.

Franklin

Why is Franklin popular with hikers? One clear reason is the brewery scene, with two in this relatively small town. Famous among the outdoor crowd, **Lazy Hiker Brewing Co.** (188 W. Main St., Franklin, NC, 828/349-2337, www.lazyhikerbrewing.com, noon-9pm Mon.-Thurs., noon-11pm Fri.-Sat., noon-8pm Sun., under $20) features a wide range of styles in a modern taproom with plenty of wood tables and bar space. Lazy Hiker also has a substantial outdoor seating area. There's a food truck on the premises.

Also in town is **Currahee Brewing Company** (100 Lakeside Dr., Franklin, NC, 828/634-0078, www.curraheebrew.com, noon-9pm Mon.-Thurs., noon-10pm Fri.-Sat., noon-8pm Sun., under $20), which was named after the Cherokee word that roughly translates to "stand alone," and is also the nickname of the 506th Infantry Regiment, which dates to World War II. Currahee offers a few sessionable beers in a large modernist space along the Cullasaja River. Like at Lazy Hiker, there's a food truck on the Currahee property.

Folks stopping in Franklin for a quick bite will find **Caffe Rel** (459 E. Main St., Franklin, NC, 828/369-9446, 11am-9pm Wed.-Sat., under $25) a fantastic option. It's casual, but in a bistro style with tin ceilings and plenty of household decorations on the walls and atop shelves. Caffe Rel leans on European with southeastern influence, so move toward the Louisiana-style crawfish tails and Charleston-style shrimp and grits.

For both coffee and beer check out **Rathskeller** (58 Stewart St., Franklin, NC, 828/369-6796, www.rathskellerfranklin.com, 8am-7pm Tues.-Thurs., 8am-11pm Fri.-Sat., under $20). Small bites are available inside this fun public house with live music every weekend.

Topton

Over along Lake Nantahala, **Lakes End Grill and Marina** (17838 Wayah Rd., Topton, NC, 828/321-3000, www.visitlakesend.com, 7:30am-2pm Mon.-Wed., 7:30am-8pm Thurs.-Sat., 8am-4pm Sun., under $30) serves up yummy casual fare with a pretty view. Coffee is available for breakfast. Lunch has sandwiches and popular burgers, while you should make a point to attend the Friday-night fish fry, with all-you-can-eat local catches.

Bryson City

You can spot up at the timber bar of **Nantahala Brewing Taproom & Brewery** (61 Depot St., Bryson City, NC, 828/488-2337, www.nantahalabrewing.com, 3pm-10pm Mon.-Thurs., noon-11pm Fri.-Sat., noon-10pm Sun., seasonal, under $20), where crowds gather in the evenings and on weekends, especially on college football Saturdays. Nantahala produces a full range of beer, with its flagships including an easy-drinking IPA.

Drive down US-19 east to **Nabers Drive-In** (1245 Main St., Bryson City, NC, 828/488-2877, 8am-8pm Mon.-Sat., under $15). Yup, we're talking about an old-school drive-in here. Pull up, order your grilled cheese, chicken strips, or hot dogs, or maybe a breakfast plate of egg, toast, and jelly, and get served at the car with a view of the river. Stay for a dessert sundae; heck, go inside and sit down at a table if you need to. Prices are extremely low. Experiences tend to be hit-or-miss, but you have to try it once.

The **Everett Street Diner** (126 Everett St., Bryson City, NC, 828/488-0123, 7am-2pm Mon.-Sat., 7:30am-2pm Sun., under $15) is more of a sit-down eatery, with home-like accommodations and very friendly staff. The plates will fill you up, like biscuits and gravy for breakfast, catfish for lunch, and blackberry cobbler for dessert.

Accommodations

Under $100

Hikers taking a zero day in Franklin can post up at the **Gooder Grove Adventure Hostel** (130 Hayes Cir., Franklin, NC, 828/332-0228, www.goodergrove.com, 8am-9pm Mon.-Sat., 11am-7pm Sun., $13-30). Private rooms, bunkhouses and tent space are available. **Baltimore Jack's Place** (7 E. Palmer St., Franklin, NC, 828/524-2064, www.baltimorejacksplace.com, $15-30) has a private room and bunk area and is named for an eight-time AT thru-hiker who spent the end of his life in Franklin.

Up north in Bryson City, you're in good hands at the **Nantahala Outdoor Center** (13077 W. Hwy. 19, Bryson City, NC, 828/785-5082, www.noc.com, 10am-4pm Sun.-Thurs., 10am-5pm Fri.-Sat., $40-400). The NOC has a range of options: platform tents, hostel-quality bunks, an eight-room "motel" called the Dogwood, and deluxe cabins for more relaxed getaways. **River's End** (828/488-7172, 11am-6pm Tues.-Sun., under $25) is the good eating option on property.

If you're on a budget but don't want the hostel experience, Franklin is your best bet, as it's home to all the chain hotels with lower rates, like the **Rodeway Inn** (1320 E. Main St., Franklin, NC, 828/349-0600, $40-80), the **Hampton Inn** (244 Cunningham Rd., Franklin, NC, 828/369-0600, $80-120), and the **Microtel Inn & Suites** (81 Allman Dr., Franklin, NC, 828/349-9000, $60-100). There's also the **Carolina Motel** (2601 Georgia Rd., Franklin, NC, 828/524-3380, www.carolinamotel.com, $70-120), which offers solid, comfortable rooms in a basic motor lodge setting. There's an outdoor pool here, and you can rent a small or large log cabin.

$100-150

Oak Hill Country Inn (1689 Old Murphy Rd., Franklin, NC, 828/349-9194, www.oakhillcountryinn.com, $120-200) is just off the highway in Franklin and has four pastel-colored rooms and a rustic cottage. All rooms, named after gemstones, have fireplaces, and the cottage includes a full kitchen and living room and is good for families or groups.

The rooms at **Franklin Terrace Bed and Breakfast** (159 Harrison Ave., Franklin, NC, 828/369-8888, www.franklinterrace.com, $100-150) are also named after gemstones, and are more muted and elegant than the basic Victorian B&B. This antebellum house has served as a hotel since 1915. It's in the heart of the town and is a best bet for travelers wanting a B&B experience.

There's affordable lodging in Highlands. **Mitchell's Lodge & Cottages** (264 Dillard Rd., Highlands, NC, 828/526-2267, www.mitchellslodge.com, $70-180) has perfectly fine rooms in its log lodge and cottages, but know that the aesthetics hearken to the 1990s.

$150-250

Highlands Inn (420 Main St., Highlands NC, 828/526-9380, www.highlandsinn-nc.com, $120-250) dates to the late 19th century, making it the oldest accommodations in the hotel-happy Highlands. The hotel's 31 country cottage rooms are comfortable but look like they haven't been updated since the 1990s.

Main Street Inn (270 Main St., Highlands, NC, 828/526-2590, www.mainstreet-inn.com, $150-315) mixes in a bunch of room types, including cozy standard rooms with exposed brick walls and guesthouse accommodations with balconies. Beige walls and clean white linens mean simple, unthreatening designs, perfect for the everyday traveler.

In downtown Highlands, **200 Main** (200 Main St., Highlands, NC, 855/271-2809, www.200main.com, $150-300) is a more affordable choice in this relatively expensive town. Warm guest rooms with fireplaces can be had for less than $200. Lawn games, a fire pit, and a rustic patio are available for guests.

Atop Flat Mountain, the **Skyline Lodge** (470 Skyline Lodge Rd., Highlands, 828/526-2121, www.skyline-lodge.com, $140-220) is affordable for Highlands, though rooms aren't exactly designed fashionably. Think your aunt's carpeted basement hangout, but with hotel amenities and nice views.

Looks may be deceiving with **Calhoun House Inn & Suites** (110 Bryson Ave., Bryson City, NC, 828/788-0505, www.calhounhouse.com, $170-215). From the outside it's a basic two-story hotel with a balcony, but step inside these rooms and you'll find understated suites with hardwood floors dating to the 1920s and updated décor that fits distinct themes. Renovated in 2006, the delightful hotel includes Jacuzzi tubs in each room.

Not unlike an urban boutique hotel, **The Everett Hotel** (16 Everett St., Bryson City, NC, 828/488-1976, www.theeveretthotel.com, $200-300) features cool interiors with wood ceilings and sharp lines. The rooftop terrace with fire pit is a draw here.

The **McKinley Edwards Inn** (208 Arlington Ave., Bryson City, NC, 828/488-9626, www.mckinleyedwardsinn.com, $140-180) calls itself "shabby chic." Some pieces of furniture will look shabbily out of place in these rooms, but McKinley Edwards looks great for the price point. Pros include plenty of decks and a wonderful staff.

For something different, check out **Rivers Edge Treehouse Resort** (195 Old US-129, Robbinsville, NC, 828/735-2228, April-Oct., $150-250), a collection of cabins so named because trees come right through the decks. Interiors are pretty similar, with spacious rooms tastefully dressed floor to ceiling in timber. There's a barbecue pit and Adirondack chairs accessible to all.

Over $250

Looking to spend your Nantahala vacation in style? ★ **Old Edwards Inn and Spa** (445 Main St., Highlands, NC, 866/526-8008, www.oldedwardsinn.com, $200-550) is impossibly acclaimed and the perfect destination for honeymooners, couples seeking a romantic getaway, or travelers who want the most elegant experience in the mountains. Guests receive champagne upon arrival and complimentary valet parking. Guest accommodations, which include suites and cottages, strike a balance between proper English design and comfortable mountain chic. Imagine a *Country Living* magazine come to life: that's every room here. Old Edwards owns several businesses in Highlands, including restaurants and multiple inns, plus an 18-hole golf course. The **Spa at Old Edwards** (16 Church St., Highlands, NC, 828/526-9887, www.oldedwardsinn.com/spa, 9am-6pm daily, seasonal) has saunas, whirlpools, steam rooms, and Swiss showers, and offers facials, massages, mud masks, and acupuncture treatments. You can even stay in a spa suite, which includes a private elevator to the spa.

Dog lover? Do I have the luxury hotel for you. **The Park on Main** (205 Main St., Highlands, NC, 800/221-5078, www.theparkonmain.com, $250-400) is jam-packed with canine paintings, both in the lobby and in the hotel's 24 guest suites. The rooms are black and white with beautiful rugs over dark hardwood floors. And yes, dogs are not only allowed here but embraced, with dog beds and water dishes.

Camping

There are a few campgrounds in the forest, including **Hurricane Creek** (Franklin, 828/524-6441, $6, first come, first serve) and **Wine Spring Campground** (Franklin, 828/524-6441, free, reservations required).

Information and Services

The folks at the **Nantahala Ranger District** (90 Sloan Rd., Franklin, NC, 828/524-6441, 8am-4:30pm Mon.-Fri.) are very helpful.

Cherokee

The Cherokee Indians, specifically the Eastern Band of the Cherokee Nation, were the first settlers of Southern Appalachia. While much of their land was taken from them in the early 19th century, the tribe's presence remains strong, especially in the community of **Cherokee** (pop. 2,138). Home to a large casino and museum, and on the outskirts of an entrance to Great Smoky Mountains National Park, Cherokee is driven primarily by tourism but is still an important location for understanding the history of the region.

It's a 34.6-mile (55.7-km) drive from the middle of Nantahala to Cherokee. To reach Cherokee from Franklin, North Carolina, drive north on US-23 to an intersection with US-74. Take that west to US-441, which winds north into the community.

★ Museum of the Cherokee Indian

A walk through the **Museum of the Cherokee Indian** (589 Tsali Blvd., 828/497-3481, www.cherokeemuseum.

Bluegrass Music of Appalachia

Bluegrass is a classic American style of music. Irish and Scottish immigrants who moved into Appalachia in the late 18th century and early 19th century brought their balladeering and fiddle-playing with them, and they became influenced by the rich storytelling of the southern blues tradition and the improvisation of jazz. As the genre coalesced, it grew out of the hills and into the mainstream, becoming a recognized radio genre in the 1940s.

You'll find traces of Appalachian music along the entire AT route, but it's especially prominent in the South where it originated. Asheville is obviously a great choice if you want to hear some authentic Appalachian bluegrass, but check out a few of these other great options as well:

- **Marianna Black Library** (Academy and Rector Sts., Bryson City, NC, 828/488-3030): On the first and third Thursdays of each month, the library welcomes anyone with an unplugged instrument to perform in a community jam. Then, on the second and fourth Thursdays of each month from June to August, the library hosts a music series with local performers in bluegrass, Celtic, and blues.

- **Bluegrass with Blue** (Nantahala Outdoor Center, 13077 Hwy. 19, Bryson City, NC, 828/785-5082): Every Friday during the summer, the Nantahala Outdoor Center hosts a traditional bluegrass concert by the river featuring Blue, a local musician and paddling instructor.

- **Great Smoky Mountains Railroad** (45 Mitchell St., Bryson City, NC, www.gsmr.com, weekends Jan.-Mar., daily Apr.-Dec. with some off days in Nov., $55-110): This passenger train rides along the Nantahala River toward the Nantahala Gorge. You'll see gorgeous Smoky Mountain views while hearing authentic bluegrass and Appalachian stories.

- **Music of the Mountains** (Sugarlands Visitor Center and Townsend, TN, Sept.): This festival features local and regional acts in folk, bluegrass, country, and Celtic music over two days, with free Saturday concerts at Sugarlands.

- **Dahlonega Jam Sessions** (1 Public Square, Dahlonega, GA, www.dahlonegadda.org): You'll find plenty of Appalachian music in this little gem of a town, but be sure to check out the free jam sessions on Dahlonega's Public Square every Saturday from late April to early October.

org, 9am-7pm daily summer, 9am-5pm daily off-season, $6-10) reveals a multi-textured history that both surprises and educates. Its main exhibit, *Story of the Cherokees: 13,000 Years*, won an award from the National Association for Interpretation and is an absolute must-see. Artifacts and informative signage help tell the story, but most impressive are the several life-sized dioramas displaying key moments and people in Cherokee history. There are also life-sized figures in *Emissaries of Peace: The 1762 Cherokee & British Delegations*, a detailing of Henry Timberlake's dealings with the Cherokees in an attempt at brokering peace with the British.

The museum sponsors various events throughout the year, including performances by the Warriors of Anikituhwa, who are the official cultural ambassadors of the Tribal Council of the Eastern Band of Cherokee Indians. They occasionally perform the Cherokee War Dance, plus social dances like the Bear Dance and Hunting Dance. The museum also hosts

workshops and storytelling programs for groups.

Harrah's Cherokee Casino Resort

Rising above the valley between Nantahala National Forest and the Great Smoky Mountains, **Harrah's Cherokee Casino Resort** (777 Casino Dr., 828/497-7777, www.caesars.com/harrahs-cherokee) is a major economic driver for the Cherokee tribe. For visitors, it's an all-in-one entertainment and vacation experience, evolving several times since its 1997 opening to now include more than 100 table games, a poker room with 20 tables, a 15,000-square-foot conference center, a food court, brand-name restaurants, and a 1,108-room hotel. It's also the only game in town for an adult beverage: Cherokee is a dry town aside from the casino, which serves 7am-2am Monday-Saturday and noon-2am Sunday. The resort also includes a 3,000-seat event center that plays host to country stars and touring comedians.

Unto These Hills

Every year during the high tourism season, the Cherokee Indians perform the historical drama ***Unto These Hills*** at the **Mountainside Theatre** (564 Tsali Blvd., 828/497-2111, www.visitcherokeenc.com, 8pm Mon.-Sat. June-Aug., $25 adults, $15 ages 6-12). The play tells the story of the Eastern Cherokees from their original settlement in Southern Appalachia until they were driven out of the area via the Trail of Tears. More than six million people have watched *Unto These Hills*, which is a gripping and informative, but entertaining, way to spend a summer evening in Cherokee.

Top to bottom: inside the Museum of the Cherokee Indian; Harrah's Cherokee Casino Resort; a display at the Wheels Through Time museum in Maggie Valley.

Food

Cherokee leans hard on fast food and chain restaurants, but there are three superior options among the fray. For breakfast, I recommend **Peter's Pancakes and Waffles** (1384 Tsali Blvd., 828/497-5116, 6:30am-2pm daily, under $20). Known for its smiling service and massive portions, Peter's packs 'em in for fluffy pancakes, biscuits and gravy, and steak and eggs. The backpacker pancakes special puts a blend of nuts into the batter. If you can, opt for the window in the back that overlooks the rushing Oconaluftee River.

BJ's Diner (840 Tsali Blvd., 828/497-4303, 7am-2pm Mon.-Fri., under $10) is a tiny roadside stop with picnic tables, and it specializes in picnic-style burgers, plus quick sandwiches and chicken tenders. The Buddy Burger is the bite to get here: a beef patty with a metric ton of vegetables, bacon, and cheese. The old-school dining car with Cherokee signage is worth it, if only for the riverside dining option. The diner may close if the weather is poor.

One of the true local food hangouts in Cherokee is **Sassy Sunflowers Bakery & Café** (1655 Acquoni Rd., 828/497-2539, 9am-4pm Mon.-Fri., 10am-4pm Sat., under $15), a cheery and expansive café with glowing yellow walls and plenty of seating. People go nuts about the chicken salad, but don't sleep on the cupcakes, muffins, and slices of red velvet cake. For fresh food in the area, it's hard to beat.

Accommodations

You'll find more than a few chain motels in Cherokee, along with a lion's share of unfussy budget inns named after some aspect of the Cherokee or Smokies experience. For the most part you can't go wrong with the cheaper options; because there's so much tourism, innkeepers have to run tidy accommodations or else they'll get snuffed out.

The best of the bunch include the **Stonebrook Lodge** (436 Paint Town Rd., 828/497-2222, www.stonebrooklodge.com, $120-180), which has basic economy-style rooms; **Pink Motel** (1306 Tsali Blvd., 828/497-3530, $100-160), a hipster motor lodge with a fairy mascot and carnation-hued rooms; **River's Edge Motel** (1026 Tsali Blvd., 828/497-7995, $100-180), a two-story lodge with kind accommodations, river views, and a dash of style with patterned bedspreads; and **Great Smokies Inn** (1636 Acquoni Rd., 828/497-2020, $60-120), which has a lobby that gives off a Cracker Barrel vibe, and rooms that are spacious and unpretentious.

Maggie Valley

It's a 15.2-mile (24.5-km) drive east on US-19 to **Maggie Valley** (pop. 1,290), a quaint stretch of land outside Great Smoky Mountains National Park that hasn't been completely overdeveloped by tourism. Named for the daughter of the man who founded the local post office, Maggie Valley was the birthplace of famous moonshiner Marvin "Popcorn" Sutton. If you were around Maggie Valley about 20 years ago, you would've seen Sutton selling his autobiography, *Me and My Likker*. He ran into trouble a few too many times, and after being sentenced to 18 months in prison for illegally distilling spirits, he committed suicide.

Sutton's spirit lives on through corporate whiskey made in his name and with his recipe. As for Maggie Valley, there may yet be moonshine in these hills. If you decide to go on your own 'shine search, be sure to grab a nice southern meal here, and maybe check out some motorcycles.

Sights

Even if you're not the biggest motorcycle fan in America, you'll enjoy **Wheels Through Time** (62 Vintage Lane, 828/926-6266, www.wheelsthroughtime.com, 9am-5pm Thurs.-Mon. Apr.-Nov., $15 adults, $12 seniors, $7 ages 6-14) , which packs in thousands of moving machines, from restored automobiles to rows upon rows of motorcycles spanning the machine's history in America.

The collection comes from Dale Walksler, founder of the museum, who moved his pieces to Maggie Valley in 2002. Some of the most interesting exhibits include the Chopper Graveyard, which showcases old-school bikes of the 1950s and 60s, and America's Rarest, home to a 1912 Thor and a Traub that was found behind a brick wall in an apartment building. The museum also has a gift shop and an annual raffle where the prize is a restored and storied bike.

While the "hike" to **Soco Falls** (35.492852, -83.169741) takes less than 10 minutes, this double waterfall shouldn't be missed when in Maggie Valley. Keep an eagle eye out for the parking area, which is on US-19 north between Cherokee and Maggie Valley. Spot the turnoff for NC-412, then get ready to park. After a blue sign pointing toward the waterfall, park in the area along the side of the road. Then, from the parking area, walk through the gap in the guardrail to go down to the waterfall. You'll arrive at a viewing platform where you can take in the breathtaking falls cascading down jagged rock. Exercise caution, as always.

Food

You might spot motorcycles outside **Country Vittles Family Style Restaurant** (3589 Soco Rd., 828/926-1820, www.countryvittlesrestaurant.com, 7am-2pm Wed.-Mon., under $20), a low-slung shack of a restaurant that serves up an all-you-can-eat smorgasbord of down-home favorites. There's plenty of eggs and pancakes for breakfast, and burgers, chicken platters, and soups are among the highlights for lunch.

The food does all the talking at ★ **Pop's Grits and Eggs** (3253 Soco Rd., 828/944-0677, 7am-2pm daily, under $15). If you're up for it, get the shrimp and grits, which includes chorizo and asiago cheese and may just change your entire perception of the dish. Some have said it's the best breakfast they've ever had. If you'd rather stay safe (but why would you?), Pop's has plenty of egg-centric plates, pancakes, waffles, French toast, and a deep lunch menu.

Get some darn good pizza at **Brickhouse Burgers & Pizza** (3914 Soco Rd., 828/944-0909, www.brickhouseburgersandpizza.com, 11am-9pm Tues.-Sat., under $25). Brickhouse carries several burgers, headlined by a bourbon-sauce concoction. The pizza steals the show, however, with a range of topping ideas and specialties. Eat in the clean dining area or take it outside under umbrellas or in Adirondack chairs.

The Maggie Valley Sandwich Shop (2507 Soco Rd., 828/944-0620, www.maggievalleysandwichshop.com, 11am-5pm Tues.-Sat., under $15) is a local favorite. Owners Jim and Tammy put together some killer sandwiches here, including a savory barbecue beef and cheddar, plus flatbread pizzas, salads, and hot dogs. There are picnic tables outside if you want to enjoy the mountain air.

Accommodations

Inexpensive and solid motor lodges dot US-19 as it runs through Maggie Valley; like with Cherokee, it's hard to go wrong with most choices here. **A Holiday Motel** (3289 Soco Rd., 828/926-1186, www.holidaymotel.net, $60-120) features standard and spacious rooms that have everything you'll need. **Alamo Motel and Cottages** (1485 Soco Rd., 828/926-8750, www.alamomotel.com, $60-120) packs dorm room-style furniture into its funky, country-fried rooms; it also has one- and two-bedroom cottages available. **Smoky Falls Lodge** (2550 Soco Rd., 828/926-7440, www.smokyfallslodge.com, $80-160) matches its scenery with a log-cabin exterior, while inside the guest rooms are outfitted with plenty of timber. If you're here for the woodsy experience, this is your place.

For an enhanced experience, try **Cabins at Twinbrook Resorts** (230 Twinbrook Lane, 828/926-1388, www.twinbrookresort.com, $150-300). The cabins, which are available with one, two, three, and four bedrooms, are outfitted in typical timber-heavy décor with some dated furniture. That said, they have working full kitchens, and the property includes an indoor pool. It's a nice getaway, even if you have to hang out with a velvet chair.

Great Smoky Mountains National Park

Great Smoky Mountains National Park is America's most popular national park, taking in more than 11 million visitors annually. Resting between Nantahala National Forest and Cherokee National Forest, the Smokies is an enchanted wonderland of deciduous forest. You'll find eastern hemlock trees, plenty of pine and oak in the western end of the park, and spruce and fir up in the high elevations past 4,500 feet (1,372 m). But all of this is exposed quite regularly to smog. There's the original blue mist that hovers in places throughout the park, but beyond that the park is often choked by air pollution caused primarily by car traffic. The park is extremely busy during the summer and fall, so if you're coming around these times, be prepared to drive slowly and see a lot of smog.

The park can be sliced into three distinct sections. The western end of the park, which includes the Cades Cove area, doesn't have the extreme peaks found in the middle of the park, making it a good introduction to the Smokies experience. The bulk of Smokies tourism occurs in that middle area, where US-441 (Newfound Gap Road) cuts through the Tennessee-North Carolina border, taking visitors from the tourist-friendly Gatlinburg and Pigeon Forge area down to Cherokee. The eastern end of the park, which includes Cataloochee and Cosby, is relatively underdeveloped and doesn't see nearly as much tourism.

The Appalachian Trail cuts through all three sections, arriving from the southwest at the Tennessee-North Carolina border at Fontana Dam. It moves along the Thunderhead Mountain ridge until meeting Clingmans Dome, the most popular park attraction and, at 6,643 feet (2,025 m), the highest point in both the park and the entire AT. After crossing Newfound Gap Road the trail enters the wild eastern end of the park, where shelters are fewer, before leaving at Big Creek.

Pets are allowed in the park, but on a leash, and they're not permitted on trails.

Getting There

From Maggie Valley the closest entrance is the Oconaluftee Visitor Center outside Cherokee. Drive west on US-19 to US-441, then head north to the visitors center.

Visiting the Park

Entrances

The Sugarlands and Oconaluftee Visitor Centers are the most typical gateways to the park, as both are on Newfound Gap Road, which is the only road that vehicles can use to bisect the park. Otherwise you can enter in Townsend, Tennessee, on Rich Mountain Road, which connects to Cades Cove. From Cades Cove, visitors can take Laurel Creek Road east toward Newfound Gap Road, or continue southwest on Parson Branch Road to US-129.

Park Passes and Fees

Great Smoky Mountains National Park is a rarity among national parks: It's free.

Visitors Centers

There are four visitors centers at the park. They are **Oconaluftee Visitor Center** (1194 Newfound Gap Rd., Cherokee, NC, 828/497-1904, 8am-sunset daily summer,

9am-sunset daily Dec.-Feb.), **Sugarlands Visitor Center** (1420 Fighting Creek Gap Rd., Gatlinburg, TN, 865/436-1200, 8am-7pm daily June-Aug., 8am-6pm daily Apr.-May and Sept.-Oct., 8am-5pm daily Mar. and Nov., 8am-4:30pm Dec.-Feb.), **Cades Cove Visitor Center** (686 Cades Cove Loop Rd., Townsend, TN, 865/436-7318, 9am-7pm April-Aug., 9am-6:30pm Mar. and Sept.-Oct., 9am-5:30pm Nov., 9am-4:30pm Dec.-Jan., 9am-5pm Feb.), and **Clingmans Dome Visitor Center** (Clingmans Dome Road, Bryson City, NC, 35.556784, -83.495985, 865/436-1200, 9:30am-6pm daily summer; off-season hours vary).

Information and Services

The visitors centers provide plenty of information, whether you want to take 20 minutes gazing at a map with a ranger, or you're hoping to acquire a national park passport stamp.

For more information, contact the **park headquarters** (107 Park Headquarters Rd., Gatlinburg, TN, 865/436-1200, www.nps.gov/grsm).

Getting Around

The best way to get around in the Smokies is by driving Newfound Gap Road, which is open year-round and connects the Sugarlands Visitor Center and the Oconaluftee Visitor Center. Laurel Creek Road, also open year-round, brings visitors from Sugarland to Cades Cove. The best approach for tackling the Smokies is having a home base relatively close to either Sugarlands or Oconaluftee, which means staying in either Gatlinburg or Cherokee. For those willing to drive a bit, Townsend, Tennessee, makes a good base, as Cades Cove offers opportunities to see historic structures and hike the Thunderhead Mountain ridge.

A number of roads in the park close for the winter. They include:

- Balsam Mountain Road (open May-Oct.)
- Clingmans Dome Road (open Apr.-Nov.)
- Forge Creek Road (open Mar.-Dec.)
- Heintooga Ridge Road (open May-Oct.)
- Little Greenbrier Road (open Apr.-Nov.)
- Parson Branch Road (open Apr.-Nov.)
- Rich Mountain Road (open Apr.-Nov.)
- Roundbottom/Straight Fork (open Mar.-Oct.)

Sights

★ Clingmans Dome

Welcome to the highest point of the Appalachian Trail: the 6,643-foot (2,025-m) **Clingmans Dome.** The AT meets up with the main walkway that leads to the concrete observation tower—which resembles a mushroom with an arm—but it doesn't actually go up to the tower. That you can do on your own, ascending the arm to get 360-degree views of the entire

Great Smoky Mountains. Of course, it's more likely your view is obstructed by pollution, that unfortunate character trait of the park.

If you're not hiking the AT to Clingmans Dome, you might be driving up Clingmans Dome Road to the large parking area. From there it's a 0.5-mile (0.8-km) slog up a paved walkway, and in the summer you'll be among thousands of tourists in all kinds of footwear. Know that temperatures at the dome can be 10-20 degrees cooler than down in the valleys nearby, so add a layer at least. Also know that while the observation tower is always open, Clingmans Dome Road closes in the winter and during bad weather.

Newfound Gap Road

The way to see the park without ever getting out of your car is by taking the leisurely drive on Newfound Gap Road. You'll be driving a maximum of 30 mph on the 31-mile (49.9-km) Newfound Gap Road, which starts in the north at the Sugarlands Visitor Center in Gatlinburg and ends in the south at the Oconaluftee Visitor Center in Cherokee. The drive is completely worth it, and you'll want to stop numerous times to catch splendid views of the sloping Blue Ridge. After climbing to the top of Newfound Gap (5,048 ft/1,539 m), which is surrounded by spruce forest, you can park the car, stretch the legs, and visit a rest stop.

Hiking

Newfound Gap to Clingmans Dome

Distance: 9 miles (14.5 km)
Duration: 8 hours
Elevation gain: 3,000 feet (914.4 m)
Difficulty: Strenuous
Trailhead: Newfound Gap parking area (35.611257, -83.425526)

If you want to do the true hike to Clingmans Dome, you should make arrangements with someone to shuttle you

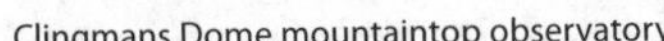

Clingmans Dome mountaintop observatory

Great Smoky Mountains National Park

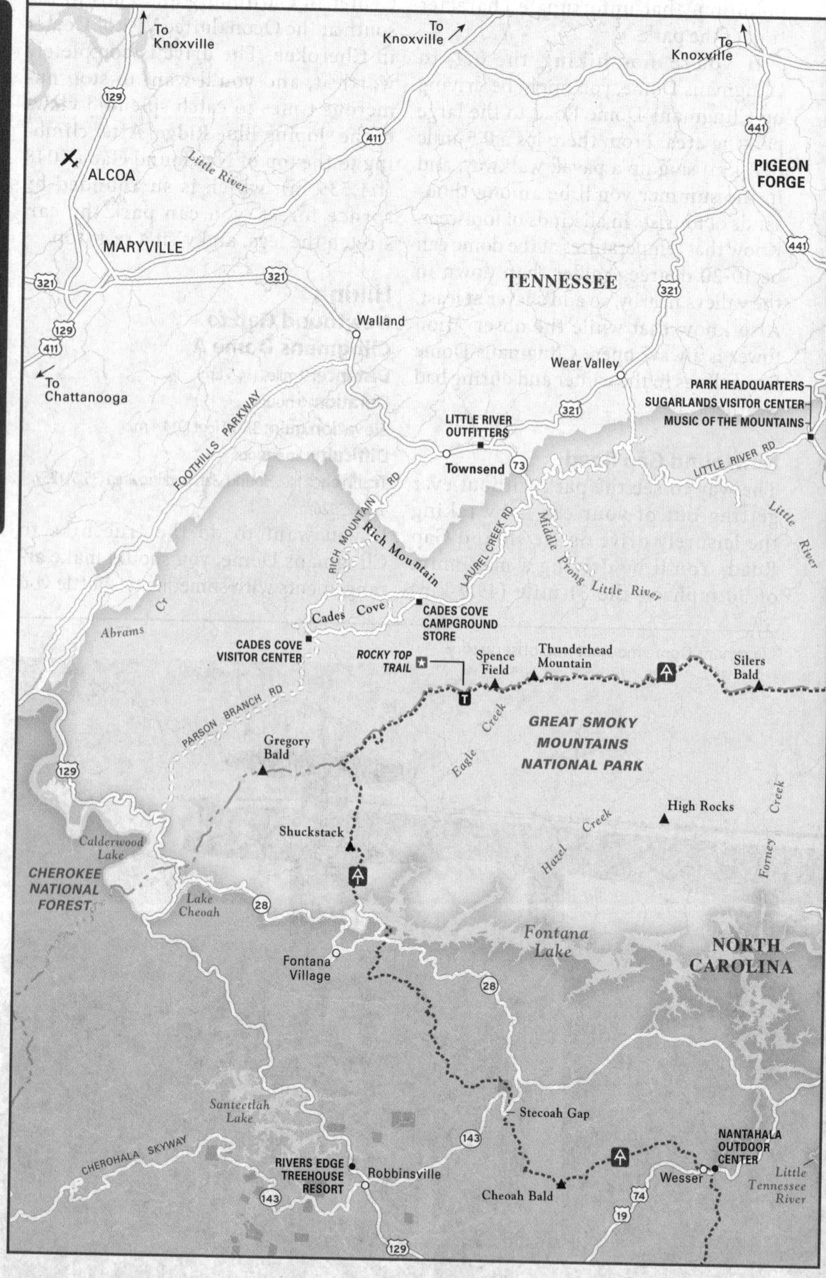

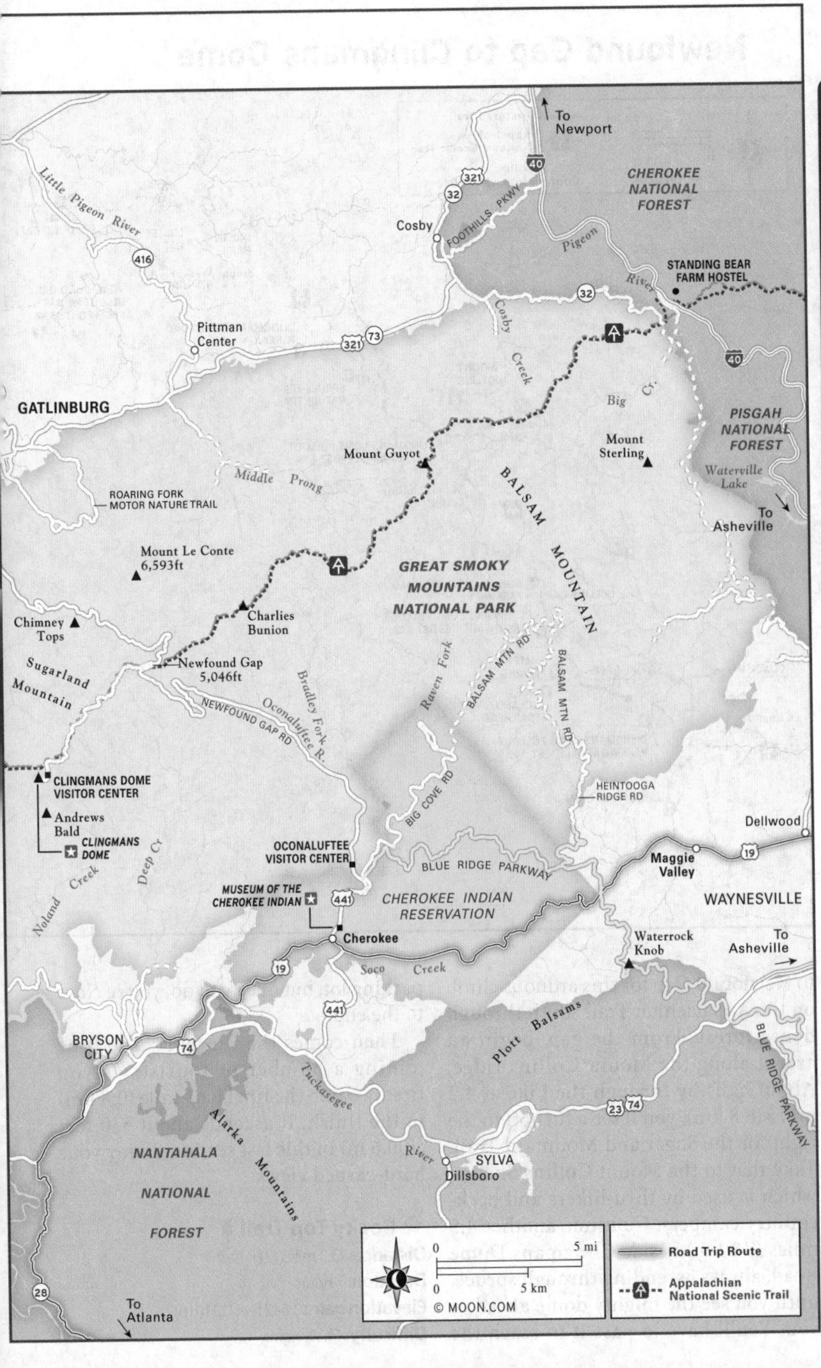
To Newport
40
321
32
CHEROKEE NATIONAL FOREST
Little Pigeon River
Cosby
FOOTHILLS PKWY
Pigeon River
416
STANDING BEAR FARM HOSTEL
32
Pittman Center
321
73
Cosby Creek
40
GATLINBURG
Big Cr.
PISGAH NATIONAL FOREST
Mount Sterling
Mount Guyot
Middle Prong
BALSAM MOUNTAIN
Waterville Lake
ROARING FORK MOTOR NATURE TRAIL
To Asheville
Mount Le Conte 6,593ft
GREAT SMOKY MOUNTAINS NATIONAL PARK
Charlies Bunion
Chimney Tops
Sugarland Mountain
Newfound Gap 5,046ft
Bradley Fork
Raven Fork
BALSAM MTN RD
BALSAM MTN RD
NEWFOUND GAP RD
Oconaluftee R.
CLINGMANS DOME VISITOR CENTER
Andrews Bald
CLINGMANS DOME
BIG COVE RD
HEINTOOGA RIDGE RD
Dellwood
Deep Cr.
Noland Creek
OCONALUFTEE VISITOR CENTER
BLUE RIDGE PARKWAY
Maggie Valley
19
MUSEUM OF THE CHEROKEE INDIAN
441
CHEROKEE INDIAN RESERVATION
WAYNESVILLE
Cherokee
Waterrock Knob
To Asheville
19
Soco Creek
441
Plott Balsams
BRYSON CITY
74
Tuckasegee River
BLUE RIDGE PARKWAY
Alarka Mountains
23
74
NANTAHALA NATIONAL FOREST
SYLVA
Dillsboro
0
5 mi
0
5 km
© MOON.COM
Road Trip Route
Appalachian National Scenic Trail
28
To Atlanta

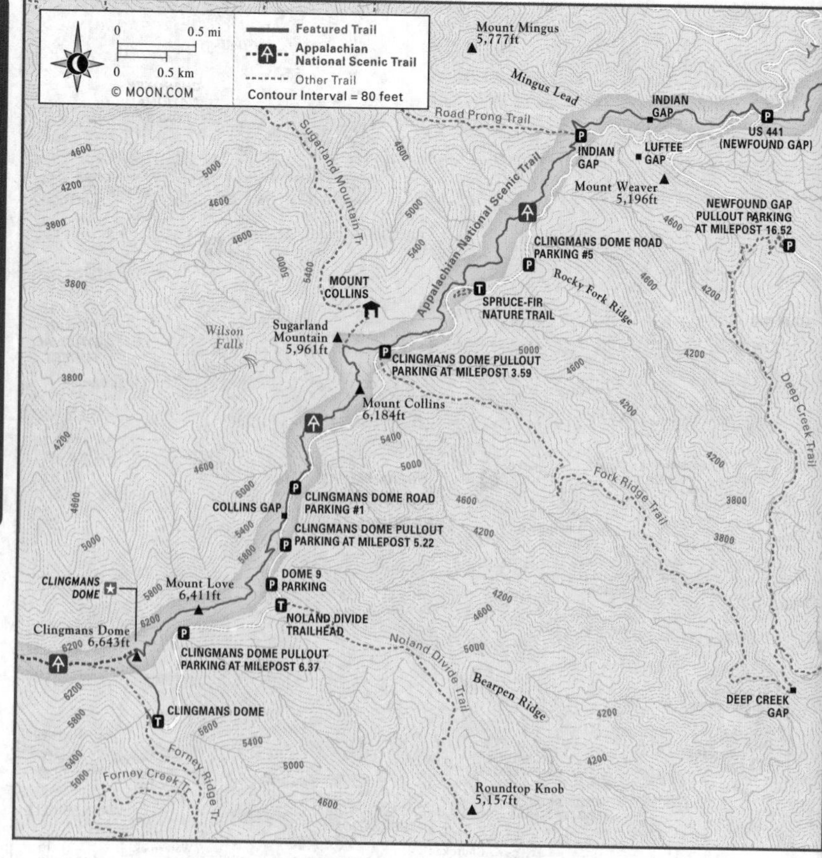

to Newfound Gap for this arduous climb on the Appalachian Trail south through dense forest. From the gap, begin an ascent along the Mount Collins ridge. About halfway through the hike at 4.2 miles (6.8 km), you'll see a turnoff to the right for the Sugarland Mountain Trail. Take that to the Mount Collins Shelter, which is used by thru-hikers and backcountry campers. Continue another 4.5 miles (7.2 km) beside Clingmans Dome Road, always ascending through spruce, until you see the mighty dome ahead of you. You'll have to pass it to reach the parking lot, but once you do, you're close to the end.

Then comes the fun part. You'll be joining a number of tourists as you tiredly climb the final half-mile (0.8 km) to the finish. It ascends about 330 feet (100.6 m) in this last section. Enjoy your hard-earned views!

★ Rocky Top Trail

Distance: 13.3 miles (21.4 km)
Duration: 7 hours
Elevation gain: 3,642 feet (1,110 m)
Difficulty: Challenging

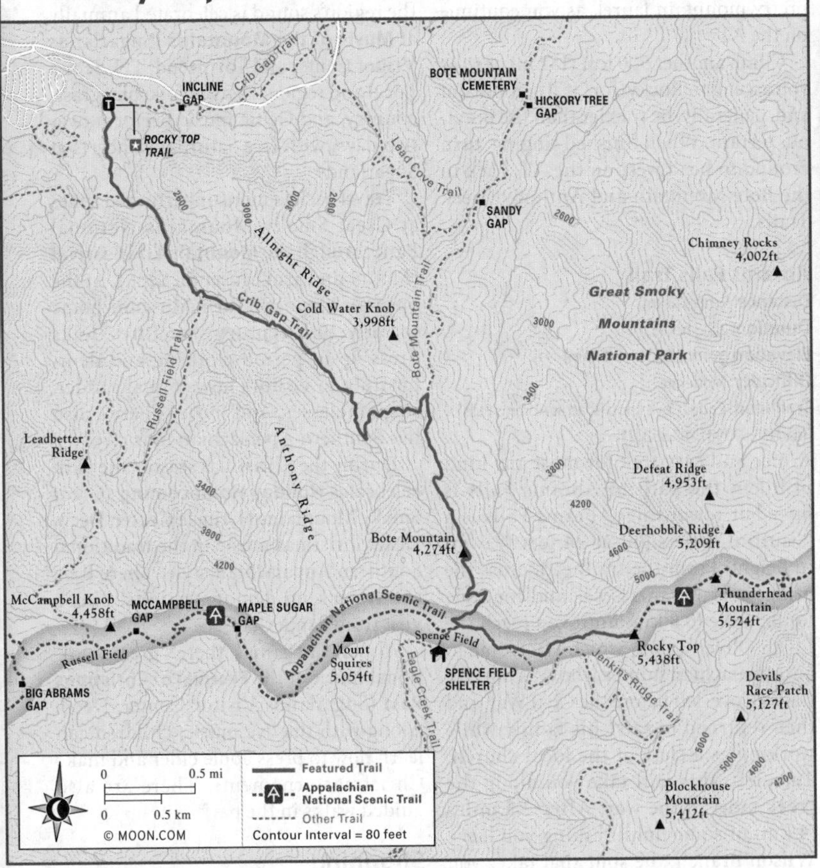

Trailhead: Anthony Creek trailhead at Cades Cove Visitor Center (35.604958, -83.770213)

People sometimes can't help but sing the University of Tennessee fight song, "Rocky Top," when they reach the climax of this long but rewarding trail. The song, written by bluegrass band the Osborne Brothers in 1967, was possibly inspired by the 5,440-foot (1,658-m) summit of the same name. It's classic Tennessee with its jagged terrain, abundant flora, and sweeping views.

For access to Rocky Top, start at the Cades Cove Visitor Center parking lot and head to the Anthony Creek trailhead. You'll be on the Anthony Creek Trail for about 3.5 miles (5.6 km), passing rhododendron and a horse farm. The trail will hit a dead end at the Bote Mountain Trail; take this to the right as the elevation begins to pick up. Here the rhododendron climbs and arches overhead, and after another 1.5 miles (2.4 km) or so you'll reach the Appalachian Trail. This is Spence Field, once a grazing area and home to a cabin built in the 19th century by James Spence. If you turn right the path opens up into meadow, and you can take Eagle Creek Trail to the **Spence**

Field Shelter; go left and find incredible south- and southeast-facing views, plus pretty mountain laurel, as you continue on the AT.

Climb another 500 feet (152 m) or so as you ascend to Rocky Top. It'll smooth out and, generally, be rockier than the previous terrain. When finished singing, turn around to head west on the AT, back to the Bote Mountain and Anthony Creek Trails.

Abrams Falls Trail

Distance: 5 miles (8 km)
Duration: 2.5-3 hours
Elevation gain: 1,800 feet (549 m)
Difficulty: Moderate
Trailhead: Cades Cove Loop Road at Abrams Falls Road (35.590981, -83.852071)

A nice and easy trek for most any kind of hiker, the path to Abrams Falls is busy but rewarding: Abrams Falls is a beautiful little sight at 24 feet (7.3 m) in height. From the trailhead, cross the bridge over Abrams Creek and continue for 0.5 mile (0.8 km) until you reach the Elijah Oliver Cabin, which was home to an Appalachian hunter who was born in Cades Cove, left before the Civil War, and then returned to raise his family while working as a clerk at the local church. Turn left; this will take you along the creek most of the way. After 2.5 miles (4 km) of some uphill hiking you'll see Wilson Branch, the spur that takes you down to the falls. When you get there, enjoy the mist spraying off the falls. Take a dip in the water if it's warm. When you're finished, head back the way you came to the lot.

Entertainment and Events

You may be surprised to learn that the roots of Southern Appalachian music are found partly in Ireland, as immigrants from the Emerald Isle brought their traditional Celtic music to the hills, where it felt right at home. Combining Celtic with gospel and blues from the South created a sound that lives today: sometimes yearning, sometimes rollicking, always heartfelt and enjoyable. The tradition of the region's sound is celebrated annually at **Music of the Mountains** (Sugarlands Visitor Center and Townsend, TN, Sept.). Local and regional acts in folk, bluegrass, country, and Celtic music perform over two days, with free Saturday concerts at Sugarlands.

Travel back to more unperturbed times at Great Smoky Mountains National Park through the **Mountain Life Festival** (Mountain Farm Museum, Sept.). At the open-air Mountain Farm Museum, home to early 20th-century structures, folks dress up in period clothing and demonstrate to visitors how to make cider, soap, molasses, and more. There's also live Southern Appalachian music.

During the Christmas season, the park celebrates **Holiday Homecoming** (Great Smoky Mountains Heritage Center, Dec.). Hear Christmas music in the traditional Southern Appalachian style. There'll be candy-making demonstrations, plus a visit from Santa Claus.

Also at Christmas, there's great traditional music at the **Festival of Christmas Past** (Sugarlands Visitor Center, Dec.). Along with the live music, children can learn how to press apple cider and make Christmas ornaments. There are also guided walks in the park.

Shopping

Oh, is there shopping around Great Smoky Mountains National Park. Especially in Gatlinburg, you'll find gifts and odd, kitschy treats for just about any mountain man or woman. There are a lot of options, from stores that sell decorative signs to chocolate shops. I'll highlight some of the things more pertinent to your journey.

For a great gift in Gatlinburg, check out **Alewine Pottery** (623 Glades Rd., Ste. 10, Gatlinburg, TN, 865/430-7828, 9am-6pm Mon.-Sat., 9am-5pm Sun.), which sells striking handmade pieces and offers live music. For a little foodstuff,

Smoky Mountain Farms Jelly Store (458 Brookside Village Way, 865/436-4049, 9am-5pm daily) has a dizzying selection of jellies, jams, pickles, and more. Finally, **Day Hiker** (634 Parkway Ste. 1, Gatlinburg, TN, 865/430-0970, 9am-5pm Mon.-Fri.) caters to the visiting hiker with poles, backpacks, sunglasses, water bottles, and apparel.

For those staying in Townsend, **Little River Outfitters** (106 Town Square Dr., Townsend, TN, 865/448-9459, 9am-5pm Sun.-Thurs., 9am-6pm Fri.-Sat.) looks out for the local fly fishers with a wide variety of rods, waders, and ties.

Food

Inside the Park

There's only one manageable food option within Great Smoky Mountains National Park. The **Cades Cove Campground Store** (10035 Campground Dr., Townsend, TN, 865/448-9034, 9am-5pm daily, under $10) has a snack bar with breakfast food, sandwiches, soup, and ice cream, making for a decent last-minute option.

Outside the Park

Gatlinburg

Breakfast is big business in Gatlinburg, and the currency is pancakes. The popular place is probably **Pancake Pantry** (628 Parkway, Gatlinburg, TN, 865/436-4724, 7am-3pm daily, under $15), the oldest pancake house in town (it dates to 1960). In an old European-style building that recalls Willy Wonka's chocolate factory, Pancake Pantry offers 24 varieties of pancake, crepe, and blintz. Those seeking a challenge may opt for the Morning Star: hash browns drenched in cheese and topped with a fried egg, then covered with vegetables and served with, of course, a pancake (or toast). Make sure to bring cash, and get ready for a decent wait, as everybody lines up first for the Pantry.

You can spot **Log Cabin Pancake House** (327 Historic Nature Trail, Gatlinburg, TN, 865/436-7894, 7am-2pm daily, under $15) by the covered wagon standing atop the restaurant. There's probably a wagon's worth of pancakes available at the Log Cabin, like Caribbean pancakes and the Pancake Royale, featuring four hearty cakes with banana and cream cheese sauce. It serves sandwiches for lunch, but a buffet is also available after 11am.

★ **Little House of Pancakes** (807 East Parkway, Gatlinburg, TN, 865/436-8784, 7am-2pm daily, under $15) doesn't have the rustic flash of Log Cabin, and it's a little farther out from the high-tourism area of the town, but it earns high marks on what matters most. There are plenty of specialty pancakes available, but the ambitious will go for the all-you-can-eat cakes, which are 16 inches in diameter and are served on a pizza tray.

You can also get your pancake meal, plus the usual southern breakfast fare, at **Crockett's Breakfast Camp** (1103 Parkway, Gatlinburg, TN, 865/325-1403, 7am-1pm daily, under $15), which is good if you want the themed Davy Crockett experience.

For dinner, you can't go wrong with **Bennett's Pit Bar-B-Que** (714 River Rd., Gatlinburg, TN, 865/436-2400, www.bennetts-bbq.com, 8am-8pm Sun.-Thurs., 8am-9pm Fri.-Sat., under $30 lunch and dinner, under $15 breakfast). Dig into ribs, brisket, and shoulder that's been smoking over hickory for more than half the day. Sauce, naturally, comes on the side. For breakfast there's an all-you-can-eat bar as well as regular dishes, but you're here for the barbecue.

Big ol' steak dinners are enjoyed at **The Peddler Steakhouse** (820 River Rd., Gatlinburg, TN, 865/436-5794, www.peddlergatlinburg.com, 5pm-9pm Sun.-Fri., 4:30pm-10pm Sat., under $40). You can do steak (cut tableside), potato, and salad bar, or you can do everything from fried dill pickles to rainbow trout. Surroundings are timber-heavy but not formal, so you won't feel out of place in non-smelly hiking gear.

Speaking of trout, the **Smoky**

Mountain Trout House (410 Parkway, Gatlinburg, TN, 865/436-5416, 5pm-9pm daily, under $30) is all about it. They prepare trout in a variety of ways, most popularly the Eisenhower, breaded with cornmeal and bacon, then served with bacon and butter sauce. The smoked mountain trout is also a specialty for the area. The digs are old and a bit lodge-like, but that's typical for the area.

No Way Jose's Mexican Cantina (555 Parkway, Gatlinburg, TN, 865/430-5673, 11am-9pm Sun.-Thurs., 11am-10pm Fri.-Sat., under $30) has a lot going for it: fresh Mexican food—which is hard to find in the Smokies—a fun atmosphere, and a waterside location giving diners the opportunity to enjoy the view.

Pigeon Forge

Pigeon Forge isn't the breakfast mecca of Gatlinburg, but there are options. The best is **Sawyer's Farmhouse Breakfast** (2831 Parkway, Pigeon Forge, TN, 865/366-1090, www.sawyersbreakfast.com, 8am-2pm daily, under $15), one of the more modern eateries you'll find around these parts, with fresh timber walls and cool lighting. Big appetites prepare for the Forge: two eggs with potatoes, biscuit and gravy, and meat. Lunch and dinner are also served.

It's a whole lot of everything at the **Old Mill Restaurant** (164 Old Mill Ave., Pigeon Forge, TN, 865/429-3463, www.old-mill.com, 8am-8pm Mon.-Thurs., 8am-8:30pm Fri.-Sat., under $15 breakfast and lunch, under $40 dinner). Lunch and dinner offer an inexpensive base price for meals like catfish and "city" ham, served with corn chowder, fritters, mashed potatoes, and green beans. It's a fun, family-friendly place made of post and beam.

J.T. Hannah's Kitchen (3214 Parkway, Pigeon Forge, 865/428-4200, www.jthannahs.com, 11am-9pm Sun.-Thurs., 11am-10pm Fri.-Sat., under $25) is a big, stuffed Smokies experience. Sit in the ramshackle, barn-like dining room with garage signage everywhere. There's a big menu with tons of variety, from burgers to pasta to seafood.

Get a day's worth of meals at **Mama's Farmhouse** (208 Pickel St., Pigeon Forge, 865/908-4646, 8am-8pm Sun.-Thurs., 8am-9pm Fri.-Sat., under $25). Good buttermilk biscuits and a hash brown casserole are breakfast staples, while at lunch and dinner Mama's has a limited menu with family-style eats: country-fried pork for dinner Friday, while on Sunday there's turkey and stuffing.

Townsend

Townsend isn't nearly as crowded as Gatlinburg and Pigeon Forge, so it's easier to snag a table.

The laid-back **Black Bear Café** (7621 E. Lamar Alexander Pkwy., Townsend, TN, 865/448-8887, 11am-8pm daily, under $15) has all the good stuff: trout, fried bologna, hush puppies, and steak and potatoes in beige digs with a fun Smokies mural on the wall. Save room for chocolate cake.

Also on the relaxed side is the **Misty Morning Café** (8125 E. Lamar Alexander Pkwy., Townsend, TN, 865/738-3213, 10am-7pm Mon.-Sat., 10am-4pm Sun., under $15), which offers surprises. Lunch includes sandwiches plus nontraditional fare for the area, like a Philly cheesesteak; you can even order brisket here. It's a friendly place you'll want to visit twice.

Burger Master Drive In (8439 TN-73, Townsend, TN, 865/448-8408, 11am-8pm Thurs.-Sun. spring and fall, 11am-9pm daily summer, under $15) has been in Townsend for more than 50 years, a place where visitors and residents alike can enjoy juicy burgers and tasty soft-serve cones. Order a burger, some fries, and a milk shake, and sit out on the picnic tables to end a perfect day on the trail.

For a more formal experience, **Dancing Bear Appalachian Bistro** (7140 E. Lamar Alexander Pkwy., Townsend, TN, 5pm-9pm Wed.-Sun., under $50) is where you want to eat. Forget big plates of chicken-fried this: Dancing Bear—part of the Dancing Bear Lodge—has a menu of farm-to-table for the Appalachian set. Get cute with the Appalachian Lunchable, which has bacon, ham, gouda, and deviled eggs, or go deep with the sourced whole-roasted trout. Native wood and stone inform the décor here.

Accommodations

Outside the Park

Gatlinburg

There's no shortage of places to stay in Gatlinburg, Pigeon Forge, and Townsend. The main roads are clogged with motels, inns, and resorts, and in summer it can be impossible to lock down a room. Reserve early if you're going to stay in one of the big tourist towns. In the summer the rates for most discount and moderate accommodations will increase to $120-150 per night, but offseason rooms are typically less than $100 per night.

The famous **Gatlinburg Inn** (755 Parkway, Gatlinburg, TN, 865/436-5133, $120-220 summer) dates to 1937 and boasts past guests like Lady Bird Johnson and Liberace. It's also where the Osborne Brothers wrote "Rocky Top." Some of the tidy rooms here have balconies, while some rooms are large enough for families.

Jack Huff's (204 Cherokee Orchard Rd., Gatlinburg, TN, 800/322-1817, $110-160 summer) has been in the same family since 1959, and the care is still present. You're not getting a lavish room here, but the spaces are big. An outdoor pool includes a waterslide.

Zoder's Inn & Suites (402 Parkway, Gatlinburg, TN, 865/436-5681, $120-200) is right on Cliff Branch, with balconies overlooking the creek. Zoder's is family friendly with an outdoor pool and spacious rooms on par with the moderately priced chains.

Crossroads Inn & Suites (440 Parkway, Gatlinburg, TN, 865/436-5661, $100-150) is perfect for large groups, with a ton of rooms over multiple levels with balconies. There are queen and king beds in all rooms, plus whirlpool suites just slightly more expensive than the kings. It's a good value.

Tucked a few blocks from the main drag, **Mountain House Inn** (247 Newton Lane, Gatlinburg, TN, 865/436-6626, $40-100) has extremely affordable rates, even during summer. Rooms are basic and have what most people need, including a clothes iron, refrigerator, and Wi-Fi.

Pigeon Forge

In Pigeon Forge, the **Black Fox Lodge** (3171 Parkway, Pigeon Forge, TN, 865/774-4000, $180-260 summer) is an expansive hotel where visitors can spot up at the bar for a drink, grab a bite at an on-site restaurant, and swim in the substantial outdoor pool. Rooms have a clean, contemporary feel and are loaded with Bluetooth alarm clocks, Wi-Fi, and charging stations.

Tennessee Mountain Lodge (3571 Parkway, Pigeon Forge, TN, 865/453-4784, $40-100) is very affordable with queen and king rooms, but you'll have to get past the tacky wood treatment of the walls.

In the heart of town, **Riverside Motor Lodge** (3575 Parkway, Pigeon Forge, TN, 865/453-5555, $60-180) is a good choice for groups, featuring two-room packages and Jacuzzi suites, plus larger suites with a fireplace and flat-screen TV outfitted with streaming services.

Townsend

The best lodging option in Townsend may be the ★ **Dancing Bear Lodge** (7140 E. Lamar Alexander Pkwy., Townsend, TN, 800/369-0111, $180-300 summer), offering cottages, cabins, and villas made of timber and outfitted in luxury furnishings. Most accommodations have fireplaces and hot tubs, while some have full kitchens.

Go halfway between camping out and glamping at the **Wright Cabins** (136 Black Mash Hollow Rd., Townsend, TN,

865/448-9090, $80-200). There are 13 cabins on the property, many of them rented out well in advance, which include full kitchens, porches or decks, grills, and fireplaces.

Cabin rentals are a pretty normal practice in the Smokies. Other properties with cabins available include **Pioneer Cabins & Guest Farms** (288 Boat Gunnel Rd., Townsend, TN, 865/448-6100, $125-200), **Mountain Mist Cabins** (345 Boat Gunnel Rd., Townsend, TN, 865/448-6650, $130-300), and **Smoky Mountain Getaway Cabins** (247 Boat Gunnel Rd., Townsend, TN, 865/448-6027, $100-420).

Hartford

Standing Bear Farm Hostel (4255 Green Corner Rd., Hartford, TN, 423/487-0014, $15) has bunkhouse, cabin, tent, and tepee camping options with showers, laundry, mail drop, shuttle service, and fire pits.

Camping

Inside the Park

Front-country sites all have running water and flush toilets, plus picnic tables and fire grates:

- **Abrams Creek** (Tallassee, TN, Apr.-Oct., $17.50, reservations required)
- **Balsam Mountain** (Cherokee, NC, 865/436-1200, May-Oct., $17.50, reservations required)
- **Big Creek** (Newport, NC, 865/436-1261, Apr.-Oct., $17.50, reservations required)
- **Cades Cove** (10042 Campground Drive, Townsend, TN, 865/448-2472, year-round, $21-25)
- **Cataloochee** (Waynesville, NC, Mar.-Oct., $25, reservations required)
- **Cosby** (127 Cosby Entrance Rd., Cosby, TN, 423/487-2683, Mar.-Oct., $17.50)
- **Deep Creek** (1090 W. Deep Creek Rd., Bryson City, NC, 828/488-6055, Apr.-Oct., $21)
- **Elkmont** (434 Elkmont Rd., Gatlinburg, TN, Mar.-Nov., $21-27)
- **Smokemont** (Cherokee, NC, 828/497-9270, year-round, $21-25)

If you plan on **backcountry camping,** you must have a permit ($20) and advance reservations (www.smokiespermits.nps.gov). Appalachian Trail thru-hikers (qualified by the park as AT-only hikers who begin and end their hikes at least 50 miles/81 kilometers outside the park boundaries) can receive their permit up to 30 days before entering the park, must travel through the park within eight days, and can visit nearby towns like Gatlinburg. There's a three-night limit on backcountry camping, and fire is only permitted at designated campsites and shelters. Hikers must camp at established shelters when in the backcountry.

Shelters on the AT in the Smokies include **Mollies Ridge Shelter** (35.545635, -83.794923), **Russell Field Shelter** (35.561589, -83.766878), **Spence Field Shelter** (35.563701, -83.732481), **Derrick Knob Shelter** (35.566385, -83.642190), **Silers Bald Shelter** (35.564238, -83.568526), **Double Spring Gap Shelter** (35.565211, -83.542939), **Mount Collins Shelter** (35.594001, -83.471613), **Icewater Spring Shelter** (35.629975, -83.386707), **Pecks Corner Shelter** (35.651180, -83.309181), **Tricorner Knob Shelter** (35.693922, -83.257146), **Cosby Knob Shelter** (35.728367, -83.182688), and **Davenport Gap Shelter** (35.769292, -83.122284).

Outside the Park

There are several good options for camping outside the park. **Smoky Bear Campground and RV Park** (4857 E. Parkway, Gatlinburg, TN, 865/436-8372, $22-120) has tent sites, cabins, and 30- or 50-amp service for RVs. There's also an on-site pool and hot tub. Also check out the **Pigeon Forge/Gatlinburg KOA Holiday Campground** (3122 Veterans Blvd., Pigeon Forge, TN, 800/562-7703,

$38-200), which offers 30- or 50-amp service for RVs, cable TV, paved patios, and cabin (with utilities) and tent camping. The same holds true in Townsend at the **Great Smokies KOA Holiday Campground** (8533 TN-73, Townsend, TN, 865/448-2241, $34-150). For something more rustic on the AT, the **Walters Picnic Shelter** (35.781617, -83.103144) is just 0.7 mile (1.1 km) northeast of the AT's exit from the park in Big Creek.

Lower Hominy

50 miles (80.5 km) east of Cherokee via US-19 and US-40 is **Lower Hominy,** a township that doesn't have much, but is a popular stopover for weary travelers looking for a cheaper alternative to Asheville, just 10 miles west.

Accommodations

Most of the lodging here is of the chain variety, with options including the **Sleep Inn** (1918 Old Haywood Rd., Asheville, 828/670-7600, $60-200), the **Holiday Inn** (435 Smokey Park Hwy., Asheville, 828/665-2161, $80-180), the **Red Roof Inn** (16 Crowell Rd., Asheville, 828/667-9803, $50-120), and the **Comfort Inn** (15 Crowell Rd., Asheville, 828/665-6500, $60-180). Stick to the chains, because the few independently owned motels in town are of poor quality.

NC-63/209: Max Patch

Max Patch is one of the great sights of the Appalachian Trail, an enormous bald on which you can spend hours (as long as the wind isn't bad). Come on a calm, warm day and you'll find folks lying out, tossing the Frisbee, and admiring panoramic views of the Blue Ridge and Asheville valley. If the weather is bad, or looking bad, don't risk the hike. Max Patch is completely exposed, and at 4,630 feet (1,411 m), it's up there. You don't want to be caught in treacherous conditions here.

Getting There

While driving on US-19 north, watch for the turnoff for NC-63. Turn left onto NC-63 to head back toward the Appalachian Trail, which at this point is rising and falling through Cherokee National Forest and Pisgah National Forest. Follow NC-63 until it merges with NC-209, and continue on the latter as it heads north toward Hot Springs. At Meadow Fork Road (NC-1175) you'll see a sign that points toward Max Patch. Follow that sign (a left turn) and stay on Meadow Fork for 5.3 miles (8.5 km) to Little Creek Road. Turn right and drive until an intersection with Max Patch Road; turn right to the trailhead. In all it's a 37.4-mile (60-km) drive.

Hiking

Max Patch

Distance: 1.5 miles (2.4 km)
Duration: 1 hour
Elevation gain: 430 feet (131 m)
Difficulty: Easy
Trailhead: Max Patch Road, Hot Springs (35.796174, -82.962521)

The traditional hike to Max Patch is simple, which is one reason it's so popular. From the lot, walk on the Appalachian Trail south toward the gravel road that leads to Max Patch. The road, also on the AT, runs alongside the summit, then begins to climb quickly. It won't last very long, but appreciate the wildflowers growing around you before you emerge from the greenery and find yourself at the beginning of the bald. Continue to climb to the very top as views open around you. The ground is covered in grass and wildflowers during summer. Enjoy the connection here with the grand Blue Ridge sky, as if you can touch the clouds, before turning around and heading back on the AT.

For a longer and more moderate hike, you can continue on the AT north to

Lemon Gap. That hike, counting the return trip, will run a total of 12.4 miles (20 km). Or you can stop at the **Roaring Fork Shelter** (35.805232, -82.949544), which is just 1.8 miles (2.9 km) beyond the summit of Max Patch.

Asheville

Everyone who's been to **Asheville** (pop. 89,121), the 12th-largest city in North Carolina and gateway to the Blue Ridge Mountains, will tell you, "Oh man. You're gonna love it." Well, they're right.

Asheville is a miniature version of Austin, Texas, a quietly loud city that expresses itself in bold colors. With a thriving local music scene, a growing list of craft breweries, and a strong connection to the outdoors thanks primarily to those booming Blue Ridge peaks a short drive from downtown, Asheville has become a destination for young professionals to work, play, and settle.

Asheville is also home to the Biltmore Estate, the largest privately owned house in America, and a site that sees more than one million visitors annually. The chateau-style mansion is just a sliver of the city's outstanding architectural profile. Exciting buildings in the city include city hall and the S&W Cafeteria, both fine examples of the use of art deco in Asheville; the Grove Park Inn, with its arts-and-crafts interior; and Biltmore Village, which looks straight out of 19th-century Britain.

Getting There and Around

From Lower Hominy and the west, it's a quick 8-mile (12.9-km) drive east on US-74 ALT or I-40 into downtown Asheville. I-40 is the main west-east highway in the city, while I-26 slashes north to south, even though it's a west-east arterial.

Top to bottom: Biltmore Estate; Thomas Wolfe Memorial; Botanical Gardens at Asheville.

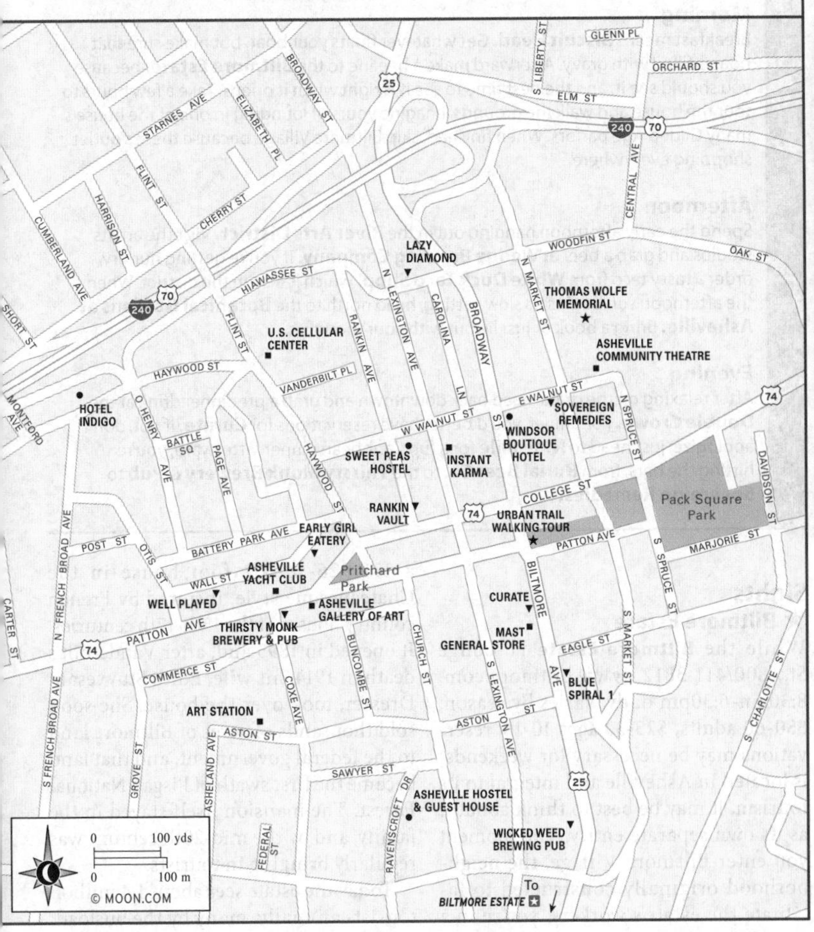

You can fly into **Asheville Regional Airport** (61 Terminal Dr., Ste. 1, Fletcher, 828/684-2226, www.flyavl.com, AVL), which serves **Allegiant** (702/505-8888), **American Airlines** (800/535-5225), **Delta** (800/221-1212), **Elite** (877/393-2510), and **United** (800/864-8331). Nonstop destinations include Atlanta, Charlotte, Chicago, Dallas, Newark, New York, and Washington DC, plus multiple Florida stops.

Greyhound (2 Tunnel Rd., 828/253-8451, www.greyhound.com, 7:30am-4:30pm and 8pm-10pm Mon.-Fri., 7:30am-9:30am and 2:30pm-10pm Sat.-Sun.) operates to and from Asheville, connecting to destinations like Atlanta and Washington DC.

Around Asheville, you can take **Asheville Regional Transit** (www.ashevillenc.gov), or ART, which has nearly 20 routes. Bus fare is $1. The main bus station is **ART Station** (49 Coxe Ave., 828/253-5691, 6am-9:30pm Mon.-Fri., 7am-9:30pm Sat., 8:30am-6pm Sun.).

One Day in Asheville

Morning

Breakfast means **Biscuit Head.** Get whatever floats your boat, but make sure that boat is filled with gravy. Afterward make a beeline to the **Biltmore Estate,** because you should see it, and the best time to see it is right when it opens. Take a few hours to tour the house and walk the grounds. Imagine yourself lounging in one of the house's many Gilded Age parlors. When finished, skip Biltmore Village because there's outlet shopping everywhere.

Afternoon

Spend the early afternoon hanging out in the **River Arts District.** Visit the artists' studios and grab a beer at **Wedge Brewing Company.** If you're getting hungry, order a tasty taco from **White Duck Taco Shop,** which is also in the district. When the afternoon sun begins its slow setting, head north to the **Botanical Gardens at Asheville.** Bring a book or just lie out with your thoughts.

Evening

After relaxing on the grass, head back downtown and grab a predinner drink at the **Double Crown.** For dinner, you'd better have reservations for **Curate.** If not, don't apologize; just head to **Nine Mile** for a fun Caribbean dinner. Afterward, you're hitting the bars, from **Burial Beer Co.** to the **Thirsty Monk Brewery & Pub** to **Sovereign Remedies.**

Sights

★ Biltmore Estate

While the **Biltmore Estate** (1 Lodge St., 800/411-3812, www.biltmore.com, 8:30am-6:30pm daily, varies by season, $50-60 adults, $25-30 ages 10-16, reservations may be necessary for weekends) is located in Asheville and integral to its tourism, it may be best to think about it as its own separate entity. The moment you enter Biltmore Village, the neighborhood originally constructed to facilitate the estate's workers, you're in a completely different world. Biltmore is immaculately planned and designed, gorgeous in many ways, and so robust in its offerings that it begs for its own day of indulging.

During the Gilded Age of the late 1800s, George Washington Vanderbilt II, son of America's richest man, William Henry Vanderbilt, wanted a "little mountain escape" in Asheville, a place he had visited numerous times. Vanderbilt bought 700 parcels of land and, in 1889, started construction of a 178,926-square-foot house in the Chateauesque style, inspired by French country houses of the 15th-17th centuries. It opened in 1895 and, after Vanderbilt's death in 1914, his wife, Edith Stuyvesant Dresser, took over the house. She soon sold thousands of acres of Biltmore land to the federal government, and that land became the first swath of Pisgah National Forest. The mansion itself stayed in the family, and by the mid-20th century was regularly bringing in tourists.

Today the estate sees about 1.4 million tourists annually, many by the busload. The mansion includes original art by Pierre-Auguste Renoir and John Singer Sargent, plus a library with 10,000 volumes, a bowling alley, an indoor pool, and 65 fireplaces, and is the largest house in America. There's plenty to take in outside the mansion, however. Walk the rose garden with more than 250 varieties, or amble about through the shrub garden or spring garden. You can do a 0.5-mile (0.8-km) loop on the Bass Pond Path, too.

Also on the property is the **Biltmore**

Winery (11am-8pm Sun.-Fri., 10am-8pm Sat., varies by season), which is home to 20 varieties of locally made wine. Complimentary tastings are offered daily with Biltmore admission, while premium tastings and tours are add-ons. The **Farm in Antler Hill Village** (11am-6pm daily, varies by season) is home to animals, farm demonstrations, and the Smokehouse, which offers Carolina barbecue. Other dining options include **Village Social** (828/257-5968, 7am-11am daily breakfast, 11:30am-4pm daily lunch, 4pm-10pm Sun.-Thurs. and 4pm-11pm Fri.-Sat. dinner, under $20 breakfast, under $35 lunch, under $50 dinner), a seafood-heavy farm-to-table eatery; **Bistro** (828/225-6230, noon-8pm Sun.-Thurs., 11:30am-9pm Fri.-Sat., under $25 lunch, $50 dinner), a bright, blue-tablecloth European spot with prix fixe dinner; and **Cedric's Tavern** (828/225-1320, 11:30am-9pm Sun.-Thurs., 11:30am-10pm Fri.-Sat., under $35 lunch, under $50 dinner), a tavern with craft beer, Biltmore wine, live music, and hearty fare from Ireland and beyond.

You can also take a **trolley tour** of the entire estate (price varies), which lasts an hour and allows visitors to get off and back on at their own leisure.

Thomas Wolfe Memorial

Author Thomas Wolfe was known for his realistic depictions of people in and around his life. And because Wolfe grew up in Asheville, his stories read like windows into the past of this Blue Ridge city. It's only fitting that his childhood home stands today as its own glimpse into the past. Named "Old Kentucky Home," the boardinghouse run by Wolfe's mother is now the **Thomas Wolfe Memorial** (52 N. Market St., 828/253-8304, www.wolfememorial.com, 9am-5pm Tues.-Sat., $5 adults, $2 ages 7-17). Depicted in Wolfe's 1929 novel *Look Homeward, Angel,* the house was damaged in a 1998 fire but reopened to the public in 2004. Guided tours are offered daily of the house, painted in its original "dirty yellow," while a visitors center educates on the life and times of one of Asheville's most famous native sons.

Urban Trail

Get the quick and dirty overview of Asheville's culture and history through the **Urban Trail Walking Tour** (start at 80 Court Plaza, www.exploreasheville.com). The trail takes guests through the city's evolution, starting with philanthropist George Willis Pack, who established the public library, then backtracking to the frontier period of early settlers and farmers, before moving into the present day with monuments that illustrate the city's ever-changing population. Visit the Explore Asheville website for an interactive map so you can follow the trail on your phone.

The website also has information on the **Architecture Trail** (start at 5 Oak St., www.exploreasheville.com), which leads guests to 14 sites primarily stylized in art deco. They illustrate how Asheville grew exponentially during the 1920s, just before the Great Depression struck and put the city in severe debt.

Botanical Gardens at Asheville

On 10 acres on the campus of the University of North Carolina at Asheville, the **Botanical Gardens at Asheville** (151 W. T. Weaver Blvd., 828/252-5190, www.ashevillebotanicalgardens.org, daily during daylight, free) traces its origins to the early 1960s and provides a lovely setting for relaxation. It's home to beautiful spring wildflowers, from thousands of trilliums to the crested dwarf iris and wild geraniums. A second peak comes in late summer. You can take a 0.5-mile (0.8-km) loop around the gardens, bring a picnic, wade in streams, or just bring a good book and find a shady spot to hang out. Since it's free, you're likely to be joined by college students studying a bit.

Recreation

Hiking

Asheville is still in the process of connecting a network of walking trails. The most developed is the French Broad River Greenway (West 1), which begins at **Hominy Creek Park** (195 Hominy Creek Rd.) and continues 3 miles (4.8 km) along the river to **French Broad River Park** (508 Riverview Dr.).

Parks

Carrier Park (220 Amboy Rd., 6am-8pm daily) sits along the French Broad River and offers a connection to the French Broad River Greenway, plus ballfields, a roller hockey rink, and a lawn bowling field. The Greenway ends at **French Broad River Park** (508 Riverview Dr.), which includes a popular dog park and a scenic vista of the river.

Spectator Sports

As Asheville is a tourist center, it makes perfect sense that the city's minor league baseball team is called the Asheville Tourists. The single-A affiliate of the Colorado Rockies, the Tourists play at **McCormick Field** (30 Buchanan Pl., 828/258-0428), 1 mile (1.6 km) south of downtown. You may remember the Tourists from the movie *Bull Durham*, as the team protagonist Crash Davis plays for at the end of his career; in 2018 Asheville celebrated the film with a special jersey.

The University of North Carolina at Asheville Bulldogs play Division I NCAA basketball at the 3,400-seat **Kimmel Arena** (227 Campus Dr., www.uncabulldogs.com). The men's and women's teams play in the Big South Conference against colleges such as Winthrop and High Point.

Entertainment and Events

Nightlife

In North Carolina, establishments that serve alcohol but whose food sales are not at least 30 percent of revenue are considered "membership clubs," or private clubs. If someone goes to a membership bar for the first time, they may have to fill out a short application and/or pay a small fee (typically under $10).

Breweries

Asheville packs in a tremendous number of craft breweries—so much so that in 2009 it was named Beer City U.S.A. by The Brewers Association. It annually collects honors for being one of the country's premier beer-drinking cities.

Start at **Burial Beer Co.** (40 Collier Ave., 828/475-2739, www.burialbeer.com, 2pm-10pm Mon.-Thurs., noon-10pm Fri.-Sun., under $15), occupying a house in the South Slope District but making the most of itself. Relying on its rustic mysticism, Burial is set in a postindustrial movie-set-looking facility. The bar is typically busy, while a side room up a wooden ramp is good for groups. The beer here is pretty tremendous, and they're always trying crazy things to keep you guessing. Come in spring for their annual **Sharpen the Blades saison festival** (April).

Anchoring the hoppin' West Asheville neighborhood, **Archetype Brewing** (265 Haywood Rd., 828/505-4177, www.archetypebrewing.com, 3pm-10pm Mon.-Thurs., 1pm-midnight Fri.-Sat., 1pm-9pm Sun.) mixes American and Belgian styles in an expansive, light-wood taproom and brewery space. The super-friendly Archetype is a busy place but isn't as hyped as some of the other local joints. Small bites are available as well.

Wicked Weed Brewing Pub (91 Biltmore Ave., 828/575-9599, www.wickedweedbrewing.com, 11:30am-11pm Mon.-Thurs., 11:30am-1am Fri.-Sat., noon-11pm Sun., under $20) has been among the top dogs in Asheville, making both fresh IPAs and distinctive Belgians. In 2017 the brewery entered into a partnership with Anheuser-Busch, which to many beer lovers is a death knell, but Wicked Weed still independently brews. Wherever you land on this issue, Wicked Weed still draws the crowds at its cool postindustrial space with exposed beams, brick walls, and long tables. A restaurant at its location serves elevated farm-to-table. Wicked Weed's sour beer offerings are served at **The Funkatorium** (147 Coxe Ave., 828/552-3203, 2pm-10pm Mon.-Thurs., noon-midnight Fri.-Sat., 11am-10pm Sun., under $20). Both places, with their massive size and loads of merchandise, feel more corporate than the typical brewery.

Also pretty popular, **Green Man Brewery** (27 Buxton Ave., 828/252-5502, www.greenmanbrewery.com, 2pm-10pm Mon.-Thurs., noon-11pm Fri.-Sat., noon-10pm Sun., under $20) has been around since 1997. Green Man offers a range of brews but has long focused on old English styles. Still, you almost have to do 'em all these days, and its Rainmaker double IPA is outstanding. In keeping with the English theme, the brewery space is rowdy like a British bar.

Hit up **Wedge Brewing Company** (37 Paynes Way, 828/505-2792, www.wedgebrewing.com, noon-10pm daily, under $20), which has two locations in the River Arts District and exemplifies the neighborhood's spirit. Metal artist John Payne converted a 100-year-old warehouse into studio space, then leased out the remaining studio spaces to working artists. Payne died in 2008, but artists still live in the building, and Wedge is there on the dock level to give them—and the River Arts District—the (good) beer it wants and needs. It also provides space for community events and brings in food trucks.

Hi-Wire Brewing (24 Huntsman Pl., 828/738-2448, www.hiwirebrewing.com, 4pm-10pm Mon.-Thurs., 3pm-midnight Fri., noon-midnight Sat., under $20) is a fun place. The South Slope location has a beer garden, plenty of games (including vintage video game systems), and a convivial atmosphere. Hi-Wire likes sessionable beers and prefers lagers, so you're here to have a couple nice hours with friends.

Finally, cider fans, this one's for you: **Urban Orchard Cider Co. and Bar** (210 Haywood Rd., 828/774-5151, www.urbanorchardcider.com, 2pm-10pm Mon.-Thurs., noon-11pm Fri.-Sat., noon-10pm Sun., under $20). This family-owned cidery offers a range of flavors, from the bone-dry Hopped to the semi-sweet Sidra Del Diablo. A food menu has light bites, sandwiches, and charcuterie.

Bars

Want a local beer and gas for your car? **The Brew Pump** (760 Haywood Rd., 828/774-5550, www.thebrewpump.com, 4am-11pm Mon.-Thurs., 2pm-midnight Fri.-Sat., 2pm-11pm Sun., under $15) is half gas station convenience store, half bar. Walk in, grab a seat at the bar, have a drink, and then be on your way. Or hang later, as Brew Pump has a beer garden with picnic tables and games.

For a good Belgian beer bar, try **Thirsty Monk Brewery & Pub** (92 Patton Ave., 828/254-5470, 4pm-midnight Mon.-Thurs., noon-1:30am Fri.-Sat., noon-10pm Sun., under $20). Walk downstairs for the Belgian stuff in traditionally quiet digs, while the ground-floor bar does a whole lot of everything and the upper level is more of a cocktail bar.

For a dynamite bourbon selection, fun karaoke, and a wonderful vibe, check out **The Double Crown** (375 Haywood Rd., 828/412-5491, www.thedoublecrown.com, 5pm-2:30am Mon.-Sat., 5pm-midnight Sun., under $20).

Under the low ceiling at the divey **Lazy Diamond** (4 Woodfin St., 828/575-9676, 5pm-2am daily, under $15), you can play pinball, write on the wall, or find a new friend while enjoying cheap lagers. It's a membership bar.

Really popular and still humming after all these years, the **Asheville Yacht Club** (87 Patton Ave., 828/255-8454, 4pm-2am daily, under $20) loves its crazy tiki-bar drinks. It has fun cocktails (try the Painkiller), a lively environment, and cheap beer.

You'll get just about any kind of drink you want at the wonderful, multilevel **Sovereign Remedies** (29 N. Market St., Ste. 105, 828/919-9518, www.sovereignremedies.com, 4pm-2am Mon.-Fri., 10am-2pm Sat.-Sun., under $20). **Rankin Vault** (7 Rankin Ave., 828/254-4993, noon-2am daily, under $20) is another solid cocktail bar. Rest on a nice chair or sofa and let the night linger with a stiff drink.

And for something completely different, go to **Well Played** (58 Wall St., 828/232-7375, www.wellplayedasheville.com, noon-10pm Sun.-Thurs., noon-1am Fri.-Sat., under $20), the first board game café in North Carolina. Appetizers and small sandwiches are on the menu, plus a bunch of mostly canned beer (works well with the games), wine, and nonalcoholic beverages. They carry more than 500 board games of all eras and types, and host weekly gamer events.

Live Music

The big game in town is the **U.S. Cellular Center** (87 Haywood St., 828/259-5736, www.uscellularcenterasheville.com). The 7,654-seat arena hosts regular concerts featuring national and regional acts, from the National to the Asheville Symphony.

You'll catch awesome indie and rock artists, and established heroes of your teenage years at **The Orange Peel** (101 Biltmore Ave., 828/398-1837, www.theorangepeel.net), considered a top live music venue since it opened in 2002. For those who'd rather chill out during a concert with a cocktail, its downstairs bar **Pulp** (a membership club) shows a live feed of all concerts and hosts separate comedy nights.

A former movie theater and now one of the premier music spots in the city, the **Isis Music Hall** (743 Haywood Rd., 828/575-2737, www.isisasheville.com) features primarily local and regional talent in rock, bluegrass, indie, and Americana. Its restaurant **Kitchen 743** (5pm-midnight Tues.-Sun., 10am-2pm Sat.-Sun., under $30 dinner, under $20 brunch) serves elevated new American with more than a few vegetarian and vegan options.

Metal and punk bands, comedians, and burlesque performers all play at the **Odditorium** (1045 Haywood Rd., 828/575-9299, www.ashevilleodditorium.com, 5pm-2am Mon.-Thurs., 3pm-2am Fri.-Sat., noon-2am Sun., under $20). There are a couple shows a week here; otherwise, this is one of the members-only bars in Asheville ($1 plus a drink) that has a lot of cool things to see: candles, skeletons, an old cigarette machine, mounted animals. You know, the usual.

The Mothlight at Mr. Freds (701 Haywood Rd., 828/666-6666, www.themothlight.com, under $20) epitomizes the Austin-light eccentricity of the city. Always putting on interesting shows, from rock and Americana concerts to comedy shows to dance parties, it doubles as a funky bar with brick backdrop and plenty of drink specials.

Performing Arts

Asheville has a small but vibrant theater scene that isn't afraid to take on obscure or previously unknown shows. **The Magnetic Theatre** (375 Depot St., 828/239-9250, www.themagnetictheatre.org) puts on relatively new plays, many written by Asheville residents. It also hosts regular comedy nights. **Asheville Community Theatre** (35 E. Walnut St., 828/254-1320, www.ashevilletheatre.org) is the oldest continuously operating theater in the city, putting on popular and under-the-radar shows. It also hosts workshops and special events like holiday shows. In summer, the **Montford Park Players** (92 Gay St., 828/254-5146, www.montfordparkplayers.org, 7:30pm Sat.-Sun. summer, donations suggested) dazzle with Shakespeare in the park. It's a fine opportunity to bring a picnic and lie out in the warmth.

Festivals

Asheville's great outdoors and great music scene come together over Memorial Day weekend at the **Mountain Sports Festival** (www.mountainsportsfestival.com, May). Competitions in disc golf, running, and BMX mountain biking join up with continuous live music at Carrier Park (220 Amboy Rd.). Enjoy food, beer, cider, and wine from local vendors, too.

For more than 15 years, the **Asheville Fringe Festival** (www.ashevillefringe.org, Jan.) has banded together arts organizations in an effort to demonstrate the power of art at every angle. There are more than 45 performances spread throughout the city, each designed to push boundaries and spark conversation.

Shopping

Want the full Biltmore experience? Just outside the estate is **Historic Biltmore Village** (10 Brook St., 828/398-6062, www.historicbiltmorevillage.com), which is really an outdoor outlet mall but disguised in the buildings originally constructed for grounds workers. The stores are what you'll find in most any mid- to upper-market mall (Brooks Brothers, J. Jill, Talbots), but the original English village backdrop makes for an inviting atmosphere. The village includes a range of both chain and local restaurants, making this a popular daylong excursion.

Since the 1940s, the building that's home to the **Mast General Store** (15 Biltmore Ave., 828/232-1883, www.mastgeneralstore.com, 11am-6pm Mon.-Thurs., 10am-9pm Fri.-Sat., noon-6pm Sun.) has been instrumental in community evolution. Once the site of a sit-in at the lunch counter during the nascent days of the civil rights movement, and later a place that sold hot tubs, Mast has seen quite a lot. These days it sells a bunch of necessary items for the mountain traveler, including outdoor gear and local foods like beef jerky, churro nuggets, cookies, and lots of candy.

Hoping to score some incense? **Instant Karma** (36 N. Lexington Ave., 828/301-8187, 10am-7pm Mon.-Thurs., 9am-9pm Fri.-Sat., 9am-7pm Sun.) will get you stocked up on everything hippie, from Hacky Sacks to bohemian wear.

Art Galleries

Asheville has two distinct hotbeds of visual arts: the downtown Asheville Art District, which tends to showcase veteran artists and regional fare, and the River Arts District, which leans more adventurous and younger.

The downtown scene lives by the monthly or every-other-month exhibit turnover. Plenty of focus is on the **Asheville Gallery of Art** (82 Patton Ave., 828/251-5796, www.ashevillegallery-of-art.com, 11am-6pm Mon.-Sat., 1pm-4pm Sun.), showing off the work of 31 local member artists in various media. Exhibits run monthly and feature either the work of a single artist or of the entire group. Over at **Blue Spiral 1** (38 Biltmore Ave., 828/251-0202, www.bluespiral1.com, 10am-6pm Mon.-Sat., noon-5pm Sun.), three levels showcase the work of more than 100 regional artists ranging from encaustic to black-and-white photography. It also keeps the estate of Will Henry Stevens, a famous modernist painter of the Appalachian highlands and southern landscape. The wild and pop-friendly **ZaPow Gallery** (150 Coxe Ave., Ste. 101, 828/575-9112, www.zapow.com, noon-8pm Sun.-Thurs., noon-10pm Fri.-Sat.) hosts fun exhibits for the ultramodern art lover, like one devoted to the world of Harry Potter. There are affordable pieces, too. A lot of everything is at **Momentum Gallery** (24 N. Lexington Ave., 828/505-8550, www.momentumgallery.com, 10am-6pm Mon.-Sat., noon-5pm Sun.), which highlights mid-career artists in the contemporary style. Exhibits typically change every two months.

Down in River Arts, individual artists open their studios to the public. First off, you must visit **St. Claire Art Studio & Gallery** (344 Depot St., 104, 828/505-3329, www.stclaireart.com, 10am-5pm Mon.-Sat.). Stephen St. Claire's studio shows off his radiant, often haunting landscapes, challenging your perception of the Blue Ridge and existence in the outdoors. It takes patience and a keen eye for beauty to create a long-lasting basket for the home, but that's what Matt Tommey does at **Sculptural Art Baskets by Matt Tommey** (191 Lyman St., 404/538-5173, www.matttommey.com, 10am-4pm Mon.-Sat.). A basket weaver since the 1990s, Tommey crafts one-of-a-kind pieces that seem to embody the wildness of Appalachia. A sought-after acrylic artist influenced by Afro-Cuban and Moroccan tribal music, Jonas Gerard works on stunning paintings in his studio, **Jonas Gerard Fine Art** (240 Clingman Ave. Ext., 828/350-7711, www.jonasgerard.com, 10am-6pm daily). Gerard's abstracts are playful but challenging to the eye; you can get lost looking at his work while in his studio.

Food

Breakfast and Brunch

Two Words: ★ **Biscuit Head** (733 Haywood Rd., 828/333-5145, www.biscuitheads.com, 7am-2pm Mon.-Fri., 8am-3pm Sat.-Sun., under $20). Go to the original location of this Asheville classic for one of several dozen biscuit options. You could do the traditional biscuit and gravy, or maybe a gravy flight (your choice of three), a special like the mimosa fried chicken biscuit or brisket biscuit, or fried catfish with your biscuit. As for the gravies, there are several, including a sweet potato coconut gravy. It's a big, wide-open place with sunlight streaming in and everyone in a great mood, because biscuits.

Don't miss out on **Early Girl Eatery** (8 Wall St., 828/259-9292, www.earlygirleatery.com, 7:30am-3pm Mon.-Wed., 7:30am-9pm Thurs.-Fri., 8am-9pm Sat.-Sun., under $20 breakfast, under $25 lunch and dinner). Authentic, honest, and true, this lovely southern comfort café is pretty packed but for good reason: It makes great breakfast. Go for shrimp and grits, the black bean and cheddar omelet, or the Porky breakfast bowl, which has just about everything with avocado relish on top. Everything is fresh as heck.

American

The Admiral (400 Haywood Rd., 828/252-2541, www.theadmiralasheville.com, 5pm-9:30pm Sun.-Thurs., 5pm-10pm Fri.-Sat., under $50) is considered by many one of the top food experiences in the city. And it is. Nothing here is truly innovative; instead, the Admiral does locally sourced New American pretty well, and it makes some cool cocktails. People go gaga for beef tartare and the arugula salad. Dark wood, dim lighting, and an open kitchen fascinate the regular diner; to the foodie, it's another pretty darn good New American restaurant.

For more New American, there's **Jargon** (715 Haywood Rd., 828/785-1761, www.jargonrestaurant.com, 5pm-9pm Mon.-Sat., 10am-2:30pm and 5pm-9pm Sun, under $40 dinner, under $20 brunch). They call brunch "blunch" here, and the cuisine is "continental social." That feels like a bit much, but the food is darn good and the cocktails are inventive. It's a foodie's paradise in an exciting spot.

Spanish

★ **Curate** (13 Biltmore Ave., 828/239-2946, 11:30am-10:30pm Tues.-Thurs., 11:30am-11pm Fri., 10am-11pm Sat., 10am-10:30pm Sun., under $60) is pronounced *coo-rah-tay.* It's also busy all the time because it's arguably the best restaurant in Asheville. Spanish tapas are done with full flavor and care by a kitchen you can watch in real time, and you'll want to talk to your server about what's in everything. A soft fried eggplant is the star of the *berenjenas con miel.* A paella is perfectly cooked. They have mussels, but they're cooked in a fragrant fish sauce.

Every dish is an adventure. Snag a reservation—it's a must.

Caribbean

Nine Mile (751 Haywood Rd., 828/575-9903, www.ninemileasheville.com, 11:30am-10pm daily, under $30) serves up Caribbean specialties with a side of natty bread. Entrees have outstanding names, like the Ambush in the Night (jerk-rubbed mahi tuna with coconut-lime cream, basmati rice, black beans, and asparagus). Some dishes are hot and can be made hotter. Lime-green walls and warm lighting add excitement to the meal. The **original location** (233 Montford Ave., 828/505-3121, 11:30am-10pm daily, under $30) is north of downtown Asheville.

Mexican Fusion

If you'd rather grab something small—say, a taco—head to **White Duck Taco Shop** (1 Roberts St., 828/258-1660, www.whiteducktacoshop.com, 11:30am-9pm Mon.-Sat., 10:30am-3pm Sun., under $20). The menu changes from time to time, but regardless of what's there, you're going to love it. Not afraid to change up the definition of the dish, White Duck's tacos have simple ingredients but full flavor (Korean beef bulgogi, jerk chicken, bahn mi tofu, Thai peanut chicken). Chips and queso are available, too.

Accommodations

Under $100

A character all its own, ★ **Bon Paul & Sharky's Hostel** (816 Haywood Rd., 828/775-3283, www.bonpaulandsharkys.com, under $35) catches the eye immediately with its red-and-white-striped exterior. Friendly to all, especially hikers, Bon Paul & Sharky's, which is named after the owner's late pet goldfish, has private rooms and a bunkhouse next to the back deck. There's a shared kitchen and a couple of bathrooms, and with the location in West Asheville, it's perfect if you're open for a night of barhopping.

Above Lexington Avenue Brewery is **Sweet Peas Hostel** (23 Rankin Ave., 828/285-8488, www.sweetpeashostel.com, $32-100), which offers coed bunks, an area of "pod" bedding (you have an alcove with a curtain), private rooms, and a studio. Guests share a living room and kitchen. This is really close to downtown if you want to be in the mix there.

Also in the downtown area is **Asheville Hostel & Guest House** (16 Ravenscroft Dr., www.avlhostel.com, $65-85), a youth hostel with an age range of 18-40. There are two bedrooms here, plus a tiny house with its own bathroom. There's a shared kitchen. Guests typically check in and head out, meaning less social interaction most times.

As for standard budget motels, the **Mountaineer Inn** (155 Tunnel Road, 828/254-5331, $60-100) does the trick, with an outdoor pool and basic motor lodge rooms.

$100-150

You'll get an experience akin to a decent chain at **Brookstone Lodge** (4 Roberts Rd., 828/398-5888, $120-200). Rooms are comfortable, even a little colorful, and there's an indoor pool and decent breakfast.

You'll find many of the chain economy motels in this range, including the **Days Inn** (201 Tunnel Rd., 828/782-3933, $100-170), the **Quality Inn & Suites** (1340 Tunnel Rd., 828/298-5519, $60-150), the **Comfort Inn** (15 Rockwood Rd., 828/687-9199, $70-150), and the **Clarion Inn Biltmore Village** (234 Hendersonville Rd., 828/274-0101, $70-150)

$150-250

For more than 125 years, the **Cedar Crest Inn** (674 Biltmore Ave., 828/252-1389, www.cedarcrestinn.com, $150-250) has been serving guests with distinct, elevated Victorian accommodations. There are some real stunners here, including the Tower Bedroom with its turret bathroom, the Serenity Suite that offers a private veranda, and the Queen Anne and its pillowed, draped ceiling. A separate cottage has two rooms, while the carriage house has a few rooms along with a garden-level suite.

Beaufort House Inn (61 N. Liberty St., 828/254-8334, www.beauforthouse.com, $150-260) is a tucked-away 1894 Queen Anne Victorian within walking distance from downtown Asheville. Rooms are Victorian-lite, in that the décor is never stuffy and much more practical. The separate Savannah Cottage is beautiful with a canopy bed in white linens, plus there's a Jacuzzi tub. Some rooms have a private balcony or separate entrance.

For chains, you can stay at the **Holiday Inn** (1450 Tunnel Rd., 828/298-5611, $100-220), the **Hilton** (43 Town Square Blvd., 828/209-2700, $150-240), and the **Sleep Inn** (1918 Old Haywood Rd., 828/670-7600, $80-200).

Over $250

There are quite a few four-star options in Asheville. The **Omni Grove Park Inn** (290 Macon Ave., 800/438-5800, www.omnihotels.com, $260-450) is a gorgeous stone estate that's worth every penny of the pricey stay. Its 531 guest rooms include several suites plus an adults-only level. Guests can unwind at a subterranean spa that winds through rock formations or put in a round or two at the 18-hole golf course designed by Donald Ross. In the evening, sit on a patio gazing at the mountains for a lovely sunset or hang by the fireplace with a glass of wine.

White Gate Inn (828/253-2553, www.whitegate.net, $225-385) is a traditional bed-and-breakfast specializing in large quarters, many that include fireplaces. Some rooms also have canopy beds, suggesting romantic getaways. There's also a carriage house, plus a 1905 bungalow with two suites offering multiple rooms and jetted tubs. White Gate has an on-site spa in which guests can get full-body massages and a range of treatments.

The uber-contemporary **Hotel Indigo** (151 Haywood St., 828/239-0239, $140-330) has beautiful rooms with high ceilings, comfortable chairs, funky local art, and prized views of the Blue Ridge Mountains. Suites have fireplaces and balconies, with some kings offering an immersive experience thanks to large floor-to-ceiling windows with only the mountains ahead of you. There's an on-site farm-to-table restaurant serving small plates.

Very modern and posh, the **Windsor Boutique Hotel** (36 Broadway, 844/494-6376, www.windsorasheville.com, $300-500) combines contemporary bachelor with farmhouse chic décor with amenities like in-room massages, restaurant deliveries, and passes to the local YMCA.

At Biltmore itself is **Inn on Biltmore Estate** (1 Antler Hill Rd., 828/225-1600, www.biltmore.com, $300-500). There's nothing but king rooms and suites here, and the suites are absolutely jaw-dropping: At a minimum of 700 square feet, they include living quarters and separate bedrooms, plasma televisions, pretty mountain views, and breakfast in the private dining room. Stays include 24-hour concierge and room service, access to the spa, a heated outdoor pool, and complimentary shuttle service to downtown Asheville.

Information and Services

Get to know Asheville at the **Asheville Visitor Center** (36 Montford Ave., 828/258-6129, www.exploreasheville.com, 8:30am-5:30pm Mon.-Fri., 9am-5pm Sat.-Sun.). There's also a visitor pavilion at **Pack Square Park** (80 Court Plaza).

Weaverville

Weaverville (pop. 3,981) is an exurb of Asheville 9.5 miles (15.3 km) north of the city. Weaverville is part of the Dry Ridge—and it does get pretty dry in these parts. A family community with a delightful Main Street, Weaverville has good restaurants and a few hospitable places to stay. It makes for an alternative base for folks looking to visit both Asheville and the mountains over a few days. For the scenic route take US-19 Business north; the quicker route is I-26 west.

Food

The always-bustling **Glass Onion** (18 N. Main St., 828/645-8866, www.glassonionasheville.com, 11:30am-3pm and 5pm-9pm daily, under $40, under $20 brunch and lunch) serves affordable and delightful "global Italian," which means northern Italian style using local ingredients. The space, with hardwood floors, patterned ceiling, and a cool gray template, is inviting for both a romantic dinner or a fun group meal.

Also bustling, but with families grabbing pies for the night, is **Blue Mountain Pizza and Brewpub** (55 N. Main St., 828/658-8777, www.bluemountainpizza.com, 11am-9pm Sun. and Tues.-Thurs., 11am-10pm Fri.-Sat., under $30). Blue Mountain brews its own beer, which is hit or miss, but it doesn't matter because the place is friendly with good grub, regular live music, and even outdoor seating. You'll find the usual sandwiches and salads here, along with quesadillas, pasta dishes, and customizable pizzas.

For dessert, head to the **Creperie and Café** (113 N. Main St., 828/484-9448, www.creperieandcafe.com, 8am-8pm Mon.-Thurs., 8am-9pm Fri.-Sat., 9am-3pm Sun., under $15). Somewhere between French bistro and takeout pizza joint with a nice outdoor seating area, the Creperie has a small but effective list of savory breakfast, lunch, and dinner crepes, plus traditional sweet crepes. The Presley crepe (Nutella, bacon, and peanut butter) is a good choice.

Competing for your sweet tooth is **Well-Bred Bakery & Café** (26 N. Main St., 828/645-9300, under $20), which is bound to draw you in with its case of lovely scented baked treats and savory lunch items. The café menu has gourmet sandwiches like curry chicken salad on croissant, plus breakfast fare like quiche and strata. It's a friendly place with plenty of local traffic. Don't forget to walk out with a pastry.

Accommodations

The kitchen of the **Dry Ridge Inn** (26 Brown St., 800/839-3899, www.dryridgeinn.com, $130-180 Mar.-Nov., $150-200 Oct.) dates to 1849; that plus the rest of the house serves as a bed-and-breakfast with pastel-colored rooms, each with private bathroom. Innkeeper Kristen cooks a full breakfast that may include eggs, French toast, waffles, and fresh fruit, while co-innkeeper Howard may serve you while wearing a kilt—all for a history lesson.

Up US-25 in the nearby town of Marshall is the ★ **Marshall House Inn** (100 Hill St., Marshall, 828/649-6445, www.marshallhouseinn.com, $130-150), a gorgeous historic home remodeled by a friendly couple to serve as a bed-and-breakfast with four guest rooms. The cute modern rooms overlook either the downtown or the French Broad River. There's subway tile in some bathrooms, local art on the walls, and king beds abound. This place is great.

US-25/70: Hot Springs

Stay on US-25 as it combines with US-70. From Weaverville it's a 27.3-mile (44-km) drive to **Hot Springs** (pop. 567). This is one of the most serious trail towns, especially because the Appalachian Trail is a sidewalk here. As the trail enters town, it meets with Lance Avenue; hikers have to walk down Lance as it becomes Bridge Street, then over the French Broad River, before returning to the woods.

Because the trail comes into town, and the town has become so hospitable to hikers, Hot Springs is a frequent stopover for either overnight staying or a sit-down bite. Some hikers even rest up in one of the town's legendary tubs, filled with water from the natural springs generated by Spring Creek. Hot Springs gets busy early in the hiking season, and it responds every April with a festival to celebrate its unique profile.

Hiking

Lover's Leap Trail

Distance: 1.8 miles (2.9 km)
Duration: 1 hour
Elevation gain: 1,000 feet (305 m)
Difficulty: Moderate
Trailhead: 138 Silver Mine Road

The famous Lover's Leap Trail is named such because of a Cherokee legend. According to the story, Mist-On-The-Mountain, the daughter of a powerful chief, fell in love with a common visitor. Her father rejected this and instead pushed upon her an old brave. One night Mist-On-The-Mountain climbed to the ridge to meet her lover, but the brave found them, killed the commoner, and cornered her. Feeling the spirit of her lover, Mist-On-The-Mountain jumped to her death. Thus, Lover's Leap.

From the trailhead, hook up with the Appalachian Trail northbound as it skirts the French Broad River. Soon it'll go up into the woods, ascending switchbacks, before leveling out at the Lover's Leap Ridge. You'll spot the orange-blazed Lover's Leap Trail to the left, and that's what you want. Admire the views of the French Broad from the high perch. Soon, you'll start back down, past the Pump Gap Trail and to the parking lot where you began.

Entertainment and Events

When the thru-hikers begin showing up in Hot Springs, it's time for **Trailfest** (April). The weekend is filled with action, starting with a big spaghetti dinner and guest speaker on Friday evening, followed by yoga, giveaways, and live music on Saturday, then a duck race and free hiker feed for dinner. On Sunday morning, there's a pancake breakfast.

Shopping

It's necessary that Hot Springs has an outpost for hikers needing supplies, food, or a kind face, and that place is **Bluff Mountain Outfitters** (152 Bridge St., 828/622-7162, www.bluffmountain.com, 9am-5pm Sun.-Thurs., 9am-6pm Fri.-Sat.). Bluff Mountain has just about everything: maps, clothes, shoes, poles, books, and toys, plus a separate grocery section. Hikers can stock up on granola, jerky, crackers, noodles, pasta, and a whole lot more. They leave the door open during peak hiking season, so there's typically someone there to help out. They also provide a shuttle service.

Food and Accommodations

★ **Laughing Heart Lodge** (289 US-25, 828/622-0165, 828/206-8487 hostel, www.laughingheartlodge.com, $100-160 lodge, $20-45 hostel) serves as an inn that hosts healing therapy sessions designed to help visitors de-stress, clear out noise, and recover. Guests routinely seek the lodge's therapy sessions; at the very least, they connect either with other visitors or with themselves. Retreats are popular here, and the lodge specializes in hosting groups with special needs.

The seven rooms in the main lodge are modestly decorated with pine floors, and most are of ample size. Also on the property is a **hostel** that is widely recognized as one of the top overnight draws along the Appalachian Trail. It can accommodate up to 35 people in shared bunks and private spaces. The common area has a game room, refrigerator, hot plate, coffeemaker, toaster, and microwave, plus Wi-Fi and a DVD player. There are three bathrooms.

Commanding the area between the French Broad River and Spring Creek, **Hot Springs Resort and Spa** (315 Bridge St., 828/622-7676, www.nchotsprings.com, $100-150) offers the hot spring experience at its most luxurious. The 100-acre resort and spa has **mineral baths** (noon-10pm Mon.-Thurs., 10am-midnight Fri.-Sun., $42-60) outside by the river, plus four luxury suites and a separate deluxe cabin with mineral-water Jacuzzis. For those wanting the hot spring life without spending too much on accommodations, Hot Springs Resort runs the **Hot Springs Campground** ($30-50), which offers more than 100 tent sites, eight primitive cabins, and RV hookups. The resort also has spa services that include massage, mud wraps, and hot stone treatments.

Holding a wide piece of real estate on the edge of downtown, **Iron Horse Station** (24 S. Andrew Ave., 828/622-0022, www.theironhorsestation.com, $85-160) has four types of rooms, all relaxed with beige walls and hardwood floors, some with exposed brick. Standard rooms have doubles or queens, while the rest have either queens or kings. There are no TVs, telephones, or refrigerators in any room.

The **restaurant at Iron Horse Station** (24 S. Andrew Ave., 828/622-0022, www.theironhorsestation.com, 11:30am-9pm Sun.-Thurs., 11:30am-10pm Fri.-Sat., under $30 dinner, under $20 lunch) specializes in elevated southern food, like fried catfish po'boy for lunch or bourbon-glazed salmon for dinner. It has casual seating with brick facing, plus a nice bar with local beer and wine. There's local music every weekend.

Hikers can bank on a big meal at **Smoky Mountain Diner** (70 Lance Ave., 828/622-7571, 6am-8pm Mon.-Thurs., 6:30am-8pm Fri.-Sat., 6:30am-2pm Sun., under $20). They'll also get a whole lot of hospitality. The awesome AT murals on the wall are welcoming, but so are the kind servers, who bring out giant plates of greasy goodness. The breakfast biscuit sandwiches are great here, as is the skillet breakfast; later in the day, you can't go wrong with a country dinner of meatloaf or honey-stung chicken.

Mars Hill

It's a quick 10-mile (16-km) drive up I-26 west from Weaverville to **Mars Hill** (pop. 2,197), home to **Mars Hill University** (100 Athletic St.), a private liberal arts university with an enrollment of around 1,400. It's a good place to fill up.

Food

If you need a quick bite, you can't go wrong with **Stackhouse Restaurant** (37 S. Main St., 828/680-1213, 11am-10pm Mon.-Sat., under $30), which has tasty grub and brews served by good people. Spot up at the bar, order a local beer, and get yourself some fried pickles. Maybe make it two orders of fried pickles. Their "Landfills" (enormous plates of fries) include the Trail Boss, made up of jerk sweet fries, pulled pork, and grilled pineapple.

The Original Papa Nick's (2 S. Main St., 828/689-8566, www.theoriginalpapanicks.com, 11am-8pm Wed.-Sat., 1pm-8pm Sun., under $30) is an institution in Mars Hill. The brick corner spot has a large dining room and good pizza, with the cheese being a throwback favorite. Delicious pasta dishes, too.

The university students help **Black Sheep Burritos** (14 S. Main St., 828/689-8899, www.blacksheepburritos.com, 11am-8pm Mon.-Sat., under $15) rake in the dough. This casual hangout offers a range of flavors, from the popular California with cilantro avocado cream sauce and french fries to the Mongolian beef with marinated steak and red peppers.

Trail Tale

Every year, thousands of people attempt to hike the entire 2,200 miles (3,540 km) of the Appalachian Trail, usually northbound from Springer Mountain in Georgia to Katahdin in Maine. The arduous journey typically takes between six and seven months. Every year, more and more people are doing it.

So, **how many thru-hikers are there?** According to the Appalachian Trail Conservancy, in the 1970s, when only a select few rugged mountaineers attempted the thru-hike, 785 people finished 2,000 miles (3,220 km) of the AT, which is a suitable way to measure thru-hiker totals. A decade later, in the 1980s, a total of 1,430 people logged 2,000, almost doubling the previous decade's total. That number jumped to more than 3,300 in the 1990s, to nearly 6,000 over the 2000s, and, from 2010 to 2017, nearly 7,000. In 2017, 3,839 people started thru-hikes at Springer Mountain, while 1,723 people checked in at Harpers Ferry, West Virginia, and just 685 completed the journey at Katahdin.

How many people go south from Katahdin to Springer? Per the ATC, in 2017, 497 people started the trek in Maine and an estimated 95 people reached Georgia. The numbers are so low because hiking south from Maine to Georgia is generally a rougher trip with a narrower window of completion, starting in the arduous terrain in midsummer and ending in the high elevations of the Blue Ridge in the cold months of November and December.

Big Bald

After leaving Great Smoky Mountains National Park, the Appalachian Trail holds the Tennessee-North Carolina border, dancing between two national forests: Cherokee National Forest in Tennessee and Pisgah National Forest in North Carolina. Comprising more than 500,000 acres, the vast Pisgah covers the section of the Blue Ridge Mountains that surrounds Asheville.

Part of both Pisgah and Cherokee, the hike from **Sam's Gap** (4460 Flag Pond Rd., Mars Hill) to Big Bald, a 5,516-foot (1,681-m) summit looking down at its neighbors, is a fantastic starter kit for the AT wannabe who wants to burn some daylight. You get outstanding views of the Smokies and Black Mountains on a special summit, while ascending at a doable pace with just enough of a workout.

To get to Sam's Gap from downtown Mars Hill, take I-26 west 12 miles (19.3 km), as this is the most efficient way to cut through some of the forest.

Hiking

Sam's Gap to Big Bald

Distance: 13 miles (21 km)

Duration: 6-7 hours

Elevation gain: 3,270 feet (997 m)

Difficulty: Strenuous

Trailhead: Sam's Gap Trailhead at Pisgah National Forest, 4460 Flag Pond Road, Mars Hill (35.952869, -82.560892)

This is a straight walk on the AT starting at Sam's Gap. Go north as you enter deep forest. You'll climb about 600 feet (183 m) in a mile, then level off for a bit before a moderate descent on switchbacks. About 4 miles (6.4 km) in you'll pass a trail that's part of Wolf Laurel, a gated community started in 1965 and populated primarily with part-time residents wanting a luxurious mountain getaway. Keep moving and you'll spot a blue-blazed spur trail used to circumnavigate Big Bald when the weather is poor. If the weather is good, stay on the AT another 0.5 mile (0.8 km) to Big Bald. Stand in awe at the 360-degree panoramic view of the Smokies. If it's really nice, munch on a picnic. When you're done, head back on the AT south to Sam's Gap.

Erwin

The trail heads east as you continue up I-26 west. You'll run into the trail one more time on the highway before reaching Erwin (pop. 6,097), the county seat of Unicoi County, Tennessee. It's a 20-mile (32-km) drive from Sam's Gap to **Erwin,** where there's a couple of revered eateries.

Stop at the ★ **Hawg N Dawg** (202 Union St., 423/743-9600, 10:30am-7:30pm Mon.-Fri., under $10) if you're looking for some cheap piggy goodness. The pork sliders are killer, and Friday is rib day. They carry a ton of sauces to sweeten up your barbecue, too. Also, grab a Coney dog to go; I recommend the Dawg. For dessert—or heck, for breakfast—check out **Dari Ace** (1105 Jackson Love Hwy., 423/743-7050, 8am-9pm Tues.-Sat., under $10). Inside this wistful little diner with checkerboard floors are burgers, fries, shakes, and ice cream—all you need on a summer day. Also, the restaurant will have you know that it allows no profanity whatsoever.

Johnson City

Just on the outskirts of the Blue Ridge Mountains, cradling them from the west, is **Johnson City** (pop. 66,027), the ninth-largest city in Tennessee and home to East Tennessee State University. It was once known as "Little Chicago" thanks to its reputation as a southern satellite for big-city crime in the 1920s. Legend has it Al Capone would roam the streets of Johnson City, while bootleggers brought their products down the mountain to be included in a comprehensive network of criminal activity.

Maybe all that crime did a number on Johnson City, because its population receded just a little during the mid-20th century. But thanks to the college, plus profitable medical centers, the city has come back to life over the past few decades. The downtown still contains old, cheap haunts and has a sparse feel, but there are some great little bars here, plus the college's presence lends the city a constant vibrancy.

Getting There and Around

I-26 is the main highway cutting through the city en route to nearby Kingsport. You can fly into **Tri-Cities Regional Airport** (2525 TN-75, Blountville, 423/325-6000, www.triflight.com, TRI), whose carriers include **Allegiant** (702/505-8888), **American Airlines** (800/535-5225), and **Delta** (800/221-1212). Destinations serviced include Orlando, Tampa-St. Petersburg, Charlotte, and Atlanta. There's also a **Greyhound station** (137 W. Market St., 423/926-6181, 7:30am-3:30pm and 8pm-10pm Mon.-Fri., 7:30-9:30am and 1:30pm-10pm Sat.-Sun.) in Johnson City, connecting riders to Atlanta, Cincinnati, and other regional destinations.

You can get around by bus via **Johnson City Transit** (137 W. Market St., Ste. A, 423/929-7119, www.johnsoncitytransit.org), which operates eight routes. Fares are $1 for adults, $0.50 for seniors and elementary students.

Sights

East Tennessee State University

With an enrollment of 15,250, **East Tennessee State University** (1276 Gilbreth Dr., www.etsu.edu) increases the population of Johnson City by nearly 25 percent. The public university founded in 1911 is home to the James H. Quillen College of Medicine, and it's also known for having an accredited program in bluegrass, old-time, and country music.

ETSU also has a robust Appalachian storytelling program, with the **Reece Museum** (363 Stout Dr., 423/439-4392, 9am-4:30pm Mon.-Fri., free) acting as a stunning campus resource. The Reece specializes in Appalachian history and culture. It has three galleries and rotates

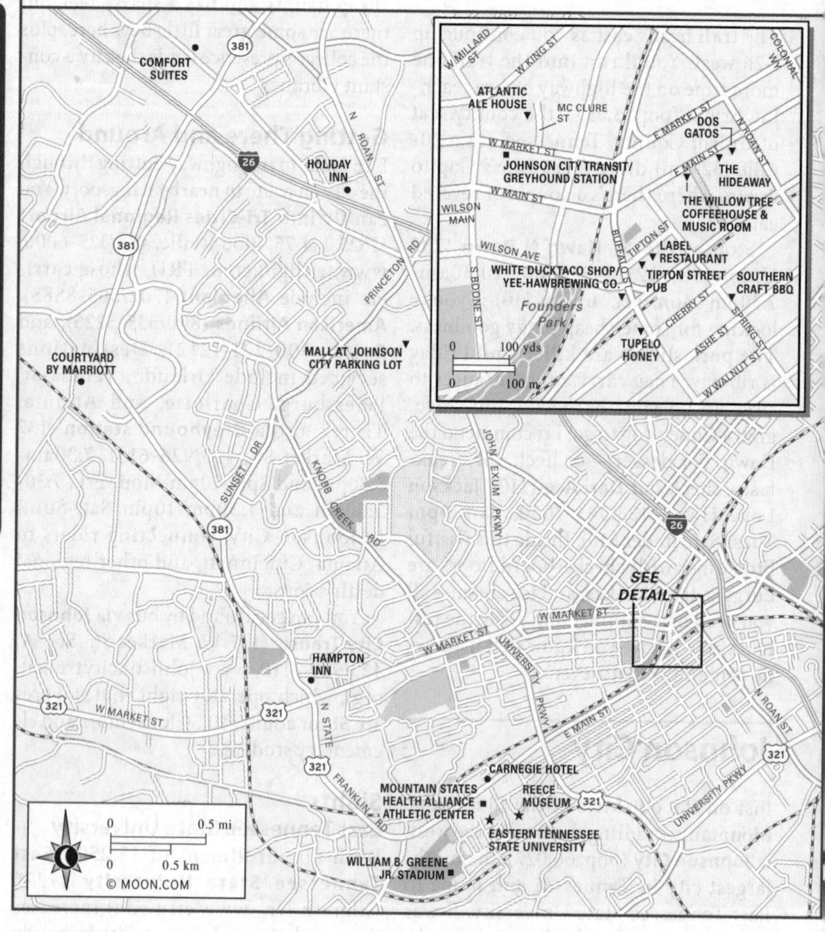

exhibits, often focusing on local artists and photographers.

Hands On! Regional Museum

If you have kids and you're in Johnson City, **Hands On! Regional Museum** (315 E. Main St., 423/434-4263, www.handsonmuseum.org, 9am-5pm Tues.-Fri., 9am-6pm Sat., 1pm-5pm Sun., $9, free ages 2 and younger) is probably on your list. There are two floors of interactive exhibits at Hands On! including a children's grocery area, television studio, coal mine, Tesla coil, and model airplane. The center runs monthly special programs and is available for party rentals.

Recreation

Spectator Sports

The ETSU Buccaneers play Division I NCAA basketball out of the Southern Conference. Both the men's and women's teams play at **Mountain States Health Alliance Athletic Center** (1081 John

Robert Bell Dr., www.etsubucs.com), which is also known as the "Mini-Dome."

The Bucs also field a football team, which had been disbanded from 2003 to 2014, that plays in in the FCS-level Southern Conference. They play at **William B. Greene Jr. Stadium** (1300 Jack Vest Dr., www.etsubucs.com).

Entertainment and Events

Bars and Clubs

You can't miss the enormous tank exclaiming "YEE HAW" once you enter Johnson City. That's **Yee-Haw Brewing Co.** (126 Buffalo St., 423/328-9192, www.yeehawbrewing.com, 11:30am-9pm Sun.-Wed., 11:30am-midnight Thurs.-Sat., under $20). The beers are fine, with maybe just the dunkel a standout, but the atmosphere is killer here: arcade games like Skee-Ball, bubble hockey, and basketball toss, plus plenty of televisions. There's a long bar and outdoor seating with fire pits. There's also a **White Duck Taco Shop** (126 Buffalo St., 423/328-9193, www.whiteducktacoshop.com, 11:30am-9pm daily, under $15) connected to the brewery.

The popular bar in Johnson City is the **Tipton Street Pub** (110 Tipton St., 423/434-0306, www.tiptonstreetpub.com, 11-3am Mon.-Fri., noon-3am Sat.-Sun., under $20). There are brick walls and low lighting in this bar that packs 'em in during the weekends—especially the college crowd—and offers plenty of cheap drinks.

The Hideaway (235 E. Main St., 423/926-3896, 8pm-3am daily, under $20) has been called "dicey," but that can also mean pretty darn fun, and it is. First, it's the first name in local music, a rock venue that's been hosting new and established bands for more than a decade. Second, the people are cool, there's a lot

Top to bottom: Hot Springs in North Carolina; Yee-Haw Brewing Co. in Johnson City; Blue Hole Falls in Elizabethton.

of cool art to gaze upon, and the beer is cheap.

The **Atlantic Ale House** (111 McClure St., 4pm-10pm Tues.-Thurs., 4pm-11pm Fri.-Sat., 3pm-8pm Sun., under $20) is nowhere near the Atlantic Ocean, but I forgive them because they're a nice, clean establishment with 16 craft taps, plus outdoor seating and local food trucks spotting up regularly.

Events

While bootlegging isn't a thing anymore in Johnson City (I think), the music of the Windy City remains at the **Little Chicago Downtown Music & Arts Festival** (Aug., www.littlechicagofestival.com). There's plenty of family fun, a ghost tour, art exhibits, vendors, and a large slate of live music echoing the region's bluegrass, country, and blues sound.

Food

Johnson City has some great food trucks, including **Let's Taco Bout It** (423/773-8226), which is self-explanatory indulgent Mexican; **Caribbean Grill** (423/218-5184), serving up phenomenal plates of meat and rice; **Foodie Fiction** (423/967-4891) with yummy burgers and fries; and **Street Eats** (423/300-6364), a good hot dog vendor. The food trucks typically gather for Food Truck Junction, which takes place every few months at the **Mall at Johnson City parking lot** (2011 N. Roan St., www.mallatjohnsoncity.com).

Tupelo Honey (300 Buffalo St., 423/202-9740, www.tupelohoneycafe.com, 11am-9pm Mon.-Thurs., 11am-10pm Fri., 9am-10pm Sat., 9am-9pm Sun., under $35) is thought by many to be the best game in Johnson City. It serves good slow comfort food restaurant in rustic digs. It's not mind-blowing, but the fried pickle burger is great and the train depot layout is cute.

Meanwhile, up the road, **Label Restaurant** (112 Tipton St., 423/631-0505, www.labelrestaurant.com, 11:30am-9pm Mon., 11:30am-10pm Tues.-Thurs., 11:30am-11pm Fri.-Sat., 11am-2:30pm and 3:30pm-9pm Sun., under $20 brunch, lunch, under $35 dinner) specializes in meat and features a long whiskey list. There's also sushi, but I recommend sticking to meat; either spring for the dry-aged rib eye or get any number of burgers (the Privilege features the dry-aged rib eye as well). Label gets busy, so be prepared to wait on the weekends.

The portions are huge at **Southern Craft BBQ** (601 Spring St., 101, 423/232-8845, www.southerncraftbbq.com, 11am-9pm Sun.-Tues., 11am-10pm Wed.-Thurs., 11am-11pm Fri.-Sat., under $30), which all started with a father and son at a smoker along Watauga Lake. Now it's owned by the same folks as Label, and it's pretty popular with customers ordering brisket and burnt ends. Like the other restaurants in Johnson City, it feels a little cold and overly warehouse-like. But the food is good.

Casual options include **Dos Gatos** (238 E. Main St., 423/630-0120, 7am-6pm Mon.-Thurs., 7am-9pm Fri., 9am-9pm Sat., noon-6pm Sun., under $10), a pleasant, slightly hip joint with light wood floors, plenty of tables, and good Stumptown coffee; and the **Willow Tree Coffeehouse & Music Room** (216 E. Main St., www.thewillowtreejc.com, 8am-8pm Mon.-Tues. and Thurs.-Sat., 8am-9pm Wed., 9am-6pm Sun., under $20), a café-slash-performance space that pulls in local and regional musicians a few times each week. There's comfortable seating on sofas, in recliners, and at standard café tables. Food includes quiche and grilled cheese, and the coffee and chai are quite popular.

Accommodations

There are a number of chain hotels at the intersection of I-26 and TN-381, but that said, Johnson City is an Airbnb city. If you want to stay in the downtown and enjoy yourself, your best bet is to check the web. But there is one notable downtown property: the **Carnegie Hotel** (1216

W. State of Franklin Rd., 423/979-6400, www.carnegiehotel.com, $140-300). The Carnegie has queens and kings, plus a few suites, and fills its rooms with classic wood furniture. Bathrooms have granite countertops. Plenty of care is shown here.

The chain hotels in the city include the **Hampton Inn** (508 N. State of Franklin Rd., 423/929-8000, $80-180), **Comfort Suites** (3118 Browns Mill Rd., 423/610-0010, $80-150), **Courtyard by Marriott** (4025 Hamilton Place Dr., 423/262-0275, $120-200), and **Holiday Inn** (101 W. Springbrook Dr., 423/282-4611, $90-160).

Elizabethton

From Johnson City, it's a hop of 10 miles (16 km) east on US-321 to **Elizabethton** (pop. 13,854), one of the more historic locations in Tennessee. At Sycamore Shoals State Historic Park you can learn about the struggle between the Cherokees who long lived in the region and the European settlers who sought their own piece of the land—in some ways the beginning of Tennessee as we know it. Along with the history are some really beautiful sights, including one of the most picturesque tiny waterfalls you'll ever come across.

Sycamore Shoals State Historic Park

The Cherokee Indians had been living in this part of modern-day eastern Tennessee for centuries when European settlers made their way into the Blue Ridge Mountains. In 1772 these settlers established a community in the area around Sycamore Shoals, which is defined by rapids along the Watauga River. Three years later the settlers, led by Daniel Boone, purchased the land from the Cherokee, but the agreement violated a British proclamation.

Tensions increased when the British armed the Cherokee as condition of their support during the American Revolution. Thus, the settlers built Fort Watauga in 1775 to defend themselves, and the Cherokee invaded shortly after. Four years later, after defending the fort, the settlers welcomed the Overmountain Men, who gathered at Sycamore Shoals before defeating British loyalists at the Battle of Kings Mountain in modern-day South Carolina.

While the original Fort Watauga is no more, a replica stands at **Sycamore Shoals State Historic Park** (1651 W. Elk Ave., 423/543-5808, 9am-4pm Mon.-Sat., 1pm-4:30pm Sun., free). You can walk the Mountain River Trail along the Watauga River to learn more about the region's history, and every July there's an event held at the park's amphitheater called "Liberty!" which tells the story of the settlers, the Cherokee, and the American Revolution.

The Carter Mansion

The oldest frame house in Tennessee, the **Carter Mansion** (1031 Broad St., 423/543-5808) has withstood the test of time and stands today as a window into the 18th century. Built between 1775 and 1780 for European settler John Carter and his family, the home turned over to his son Landon soon after. Landon fought the Cherokee Indians at Fort Watauga, then later served in politics while raising a family with wife, Elizabeth. The county, Carter, is named after him, while Elizabethton is named after the matriarch.

The home, meanwhile, stayed in the Carter family until 1877, then was passed around a bit before ending up in state hands by 1973. The house has been restored and preserved, with original art and fireplaces, and hosts occasional events and programs. The public can view the house's exterior, but public tours aren't frequent.

★ Blue Hole Falls

Blue Hole Falls (36.436135, -82.075995) is a must-visit, a breathtaking natural hole with an incredible blue color that will make you audibly gasp (at least I did).

To get there, hop on TN-91 north and drive 10 miles (16 km) north from Elizabethton's downtown. Hang a left on Panhandle Road and drive through the neighborhood for about a mile. You'll see a parking area to the left. From there it's a swift 0.2-mile (0.3-km) jaunt down to the hole—just watch where you're walking. When you get there you'll see the gorgeous waterfall spilling into a pool of honestly blue water. It's as if you took a quick vacation to the Caribbean, even if for 10 minutes.

There are two other accessible falls here, one above Blue Hole and another back a bit. Each are beautiful individually but not very tall. Blue Hole is a popular place in the summer, with swimmers and daredevils alike doing what they do. Just be respectful of the place, because few are like this east of the Mississippi.

Elizabethton Covered Bridge

It's usual to see covered bridges up in New England, but there are only four left in Tennessee, which makes the **Elizabethton Covered Bridge** (Hattie Ave. and 3rd St.) a unique sight. The 154-foot (47-m) bridge was built in 1882 by slightly inexperienced contractor E. E. Hunter—as in, he was a doctor. But, hey, he must've done well, because this bridge that spans the Doe River has outlived almost all of its contemporaries.

The bridge is in the spotlight each year for **Elizabethton Covered Bridge Days** (June), which includes live music, a car show, and vendors by the bridge.

Food

In the never-ending quest for mouth-smacking barbecue in Tennessee, **Big Dan's BBQ** (256 TN-91, 423/542-2272, 11am-8pm Tues.-Sat., under $10) checks out, and I'm not just talking about the University of Tennessee-colored checkerboard ceiling. Stop by for lunch and pick up a pulled pork sandwich—gooey but balanced with a hearty topping of coleslaw (Wednesdays those sandwiches are buy one, get one free). Popular meat entrees include burnt ends and "pig wings." If you're feeling extra adventurous, the Touchdown Club packs in sliced pork, sliced beef, turkey and bacon.

Jiggy Rays Downtown Pizza (610 E. Elk Ave., 423/518-1500, www.jiggyrays.com, 9am-10:30pm Mon.-Thurs., 11am-11pm Fri.-Sat., noon-5pm Sun., under $25) gets pretty crowded on the weekends, with live music and throngs of people swallowing down pies. The Original Jiggyrita is a favorite—a margherita pizza with feta, bacon, and peppercorn parmesan sauce. The Hillbilly Pit Pie must be great after a long hike: pulled pork, bacon, and coleslaw, but in a pizza. Jiggy Ray's has a fun vibe with a cool bar and kind servers.

You have to go out of the way a little to eat at **Country Diner** (411 E. 4th Ave., Watauga, 423/434-0090, 7am-6pm Tues.-Fri., 7am-noon Sat., under $20), but you won't be let down. Small and straightforward, Country Diner has some booths, a little outdoor seating, and a lot of good food. Burgers, eggs and bacon, fresh fish—everything's a hit.

Step away from the big country dinners for a moment and head into **Red Chili** (435 E. Elk Ave., 423/213-2104, 11am-4pm Wed.-Thurs. and Sat., 11am-9:30pm Fri., under $30). It isn't open often, it only accepts cash, and it's BYOB, but this is very good Korean food. There are few post-hiking meals better than a big dish of bibimbap, and Red Chili can deliver on that with savory meats, salty broth, crunchy vegetables, and the appropriate egg on top.

Shady Valley

Head north up TN-91 22.7 miles (36.5 km) from Elizabethton and you might pass **Shady Valley** without even batting an eye, but it's an important location because of its environmental impact. At an elevation of 2,785 feet (849 m), the unincorporated town has cranberry peat bogs, rare for the Appalachians or any high-elevation area. East Tennessee University runs the bog, which is owned by the Nature Conservancy, who also owns preserves and hundreds of acres in the town. Its unique and fragile land makes it an environment suitable for dozens of rare plants and animals like the bog turtle and golden eagle.

It's also home to the **Shady Valley Cranberry Festival** (second weekend in Oct.), which encompasses the whole town and lasts the entire weekend. It includes a parade through Shady Valley with floats, horses, and marching bands, plus tours of the cranberry bog.

Before leaving Tennessee, grab a bite at the sweet **Raceway Restaurant** (5342, 2864 TN-91, 423/739-2499, 8am-7pm Mon.-Tues. and Thurs.-Fri., 8am-2pm Wed., 7am-7pm Sat., under $10 breakfast and lunch, under $15 dinner). Surrounded by NASCAR posters and memorabilia, you'll gladly indulge in Raceway's extensive biscuit menu for breakfast, sandwiches and burgers for lunch, and plates like rib eye steak and jumbo shrimp for dinner. This comfortable, down-home community restaurant takes either cash or checks.

If you need to grab something for the road, the **Shady Valley Country Store** (110 TN-133, 423/739-2325, 7am-8pm Mon.-Sat., 9am-6pm Sun. April-Nov.) has plenty of options, from beverages to sandwiches to cold remedies. Just know it's the "Home of the Snake," and what does that mean? Well, the store is along a storied stretch of road that includes US-421, which has 489 quick curves and is a bucket-list ride for motorcyclists. The Shady Valley Country Store has awesome biker lore aplenty. Buy a "Snake" shirt while you're here.

Virginia
and West
Virginia

Virginia and West Virginia

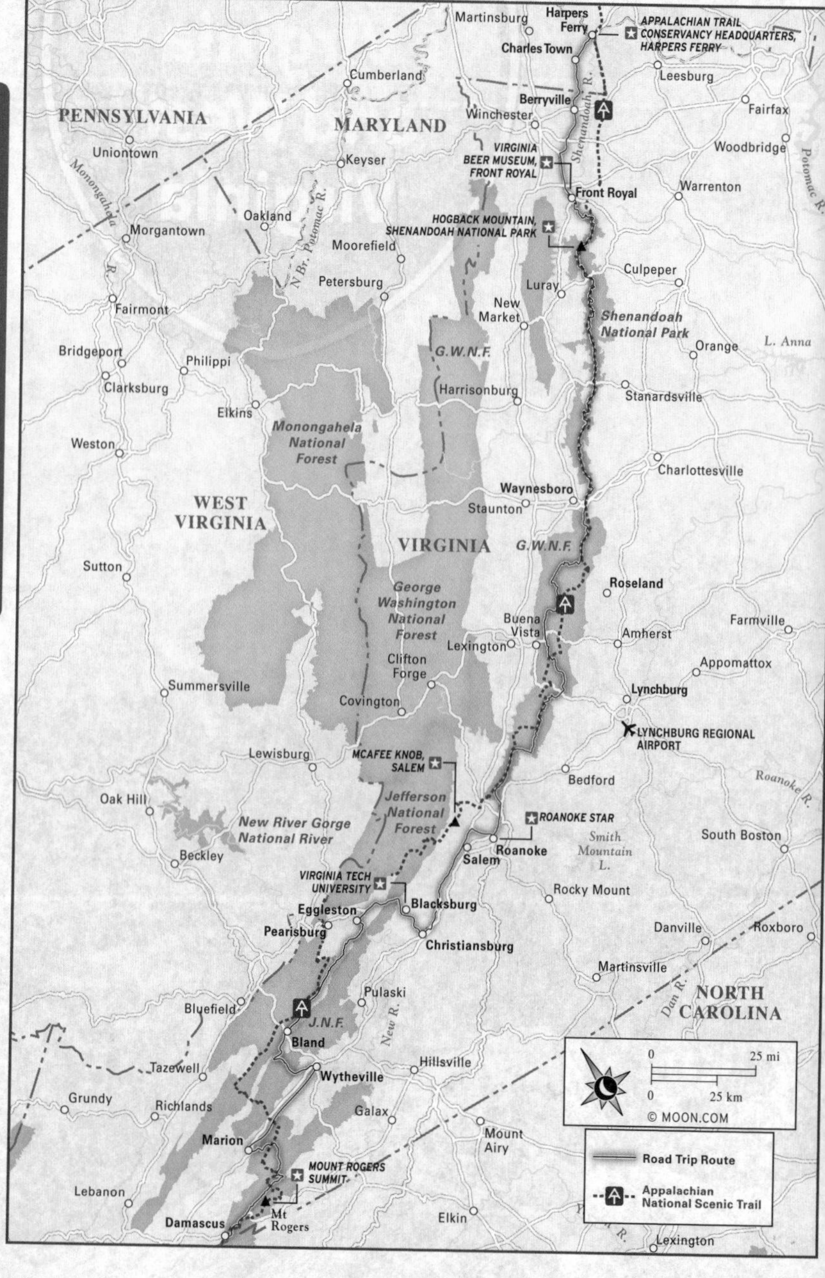

Highlights

★ **Mount Rogers Summit:** Not only does this 1,300-foot (396 m) hike lead you to the highest point in Virginia, it's also home to more than a few wild ponies (page 119).

★ **Virginia Tech University:** This beautiful campus in Blacksburg makes for a nice stroll. The military drills at Drillfield are especially neat to watch (page 126).

★ **McAfee Knob, Salem:** One of the most iconic spots on the entire AT, this perch is accessed by a superb day hike up to a ridge (page 134).

★ **Roanoke Star:** Drive to the top of this peak and find romance underneath a beaming 88-foot-tall (27-m) light display (page 136).

★ **Hogback Mountain, Shenandoah National Park:** This moderate day hike on the AT offers summits of two Shenandoah peaks with fantastic views (page 168).

★ **Virginia Beer Museum, Front Royal:** Sip brews from across the commonwealth while getting a history lesson (page 172).

★ **Appalachian Trail Conservancy Headquarters, Harpers Ferry:** The emotional midpoint of the AT is also a great resting spot with books, gear, and a wealth of trail history (page 178).

The ribbon of Appalachian Trail that slinks up the Virginias rises and drips with the curves of the Blue Ridge Mountains, creating a skywalk across a deciduous landscape that changes daily.

It's a 558-mile (892-km) walk through the Virginias for AT hikers, primarily through the swath of mountains that define the western part of Virginia. That portion includes George Washington and Jefferson National Forests and Shenandoah National Park, where hikers will compete for space with the constant crawl of cars along the Blue Ridge Parkway and Skyline Drive. In spring the waterfalls flow as the chill gives way to a refreshing sunshine, while in summer the forests maintain a brilliant green amid the sweltering heat. Of course, it's autumn when folks most flock to the Virginias, breathing in the crisp air while stopping at overlooks to stretch legs and gaze upon the fireworks of foliage beyond.

The Virginias are a popular destination for sure, as Blue Ridge visitors opt to spend time in vibrant and accessible cities like Roanoke, Waynesboro, and Front Royal. Roanoke is beginning to prove exciting with younger tourists diving into its food-and-drink scene, while Waynesboro and Front Royal provide gateways to Shenandoah and are perfect day trips for the outdoorsy visitor. The college town of Blacksburg gets really busy on fall weekends, when all eyes are on the Virginia Tech Hokies' football game.

For those looking for the true hiker experience, the Virginias are bookended by two incredible communities. Down south in Damascus, multiple trails converge, and the town celebrates the Appalachian Trail with the most popular festival of thru-hiking season. Meanwhile in Harpers Ferry, West Virginia, flip-floppers mark their beginnings and ends, and thru-hikers take a moment to appreciate getting halfway, at least on an emotional level. These towns include fun escapes for all, from cool breweries and restaurants to smaller trails and on-the-water experiences. Most of all, the people here are tremendous, inviting you to their corner of Appalachia with a story and a smile.

Planning Your Time

Because there's 558 miles (898 km) of Appalachian Trail in the Virginias, distilling a trip into a few days isn't optimal. You'll want at least one week to explore the Virginias, and possibly more—you can spend an entire week exploring Shenandoah National Park alone. With so many small cities and large towns surrounding the parks and forests, there are plentiful opportunities to hang back in higher-populated areas.

Damascus, which is minutes from Virginia's border with Tennessee and provides a connection to **US-58,** is a good place to start your trip if you want to devote the majority of your time to hiking or cycling. You'll have your pick of inns, hostels, and campgrounds, plus access to the AT, Virginia Creeper Trail, and Whitetop Laurel Creek. Wytheville, which is at the intersection of **I-77** and **I-81,** is a southerly hub an hour north of Damascus and 90 minutes south of Roanoke. As for Roanoke, it has the largest airport in western Virginia and works as a hub for travels north and south.

North from Roanoke, you'll want to take the Blue Ridge Parkway up to Waynesboro, which has accommodations and restaurants where you can refuel before Shenandoah. When in Shenandoah you can stay in the park, but Luray serves as an outside-the-park option accessible from **US-211,** which cuts through the Blue Ridge. North of the park, Front Royal is always a fine option because of its wealth

Best AT Hikes

You may think it's all about the views when hiking the Appalachian Trail in the Virginias, but there's much more to the experience than summiting. Enjoy vistas, waterfalls, and dense forests on this portion of the trail.

- **Mount Rogers Summit** (8.5 mi/13.7 km, Mount Rogers National Recreation Area): Not simply a summit hike, Mount Rogers is home to a pony population that you'll very likely come in contact with while adventuring (page 119).
- **McAfee Knob** (8.8 mi/14.2 km, Salem): This is a must-hike if you're an AT fan. The payoff is an iconic view of the Blue Ridge (page 134).
- **Riprap-Wildcat Ridge Loop** (9.8 mi/15.8 km, Shenandoah National Park): This is a good day hike with challenging climbs, a pine forest, and a swimming hole (page 160).
- **Little Hogback and Hogback Mountain Loop** (7 mi/11.3 km, Shenandoah National Park): This half-day hike fits just about any kind of hiker, with vistas, nice climbs, and a walk through a lush forest (page 168).

of hotels and motels, and just a bit farther north, Charles Town, West Virginia, provides a secondary option.

Getting There

If you're starting this leg of the trip in Damascus, you could either be arriving from Tennessee via Shady Avenue, or from the west or east via US-58, which spans the length of Virginia from Virginia Beach west to Cumberland Gap, Tennessee. **US-58** connects to **I-81, I-77, I-85, I-95,** and **I-64.** Driving (or cycling or walking) is the only way to Damascus, as the town has no air, train, or bus service.

Car

From Damascus you'll take **US-58** east until it splits at **VA-603;** stay on VA-603 and take that to **VA-16** north to Marion. VA-16 ends at **US-11,** which you'll take north toward Wytheville. At Wytheville, turn onto **US-52** north to Big Walker Lookout and Bland. There US-52 intersects with **VA-42,** and you'll take that to **VA-100** and **VA-622** to Eggleston. Further on **VA-730** you'll reach **US-460,** which snakes east into Blacksburg, then Christiansburg (also via US-11). US-460 continues toward Roanoke. After Roanoke, you'll hop on the **Blue Ridge Parkway** to Waynesboro, then onto **Skyline Drive** at Shenandoah National Park. Skyline Drive drops you off at Front Royal, where you'll start on **US-522** before forking onto **US-340** toward Charles Town and, finally, Harpers Ferry.

When driving the Virginias, it's especially important to consider potential road closures. The Blue Ridge Parkway closes for poor winter weather, and sections of the drive might be closed for improvement projects. Check with the National Park Service for the most up-to-date information. Also, while Shenandoah is always open, Skyline Drive (the only road through the park) will close when weather is treacherous or conditions are dangerous.

Air

Public airports in the region include **Roanoke-Blacksburg Regional Airport** (5202 Aviation Dr. NW, 540/362-1999, www.roanokeairport.com, ROA), which has service to eastern and midwestern hubs like Atlanta, Philadelphia, Charlotte, and Chicago via Allegiant

Best Restaurants

★ **Palisades Restaurant, Eggleston:** Adventurous and meticulous farm-to-fork plates are served in an old general store (page 125).

★ **Fatback Soul Shack, Christiansburg:** Southern food is served with sass in a casual space with truck beds as booths (page 131).

★ **Lucky, Roanoke:** Terrific locally sourced food is served in a perfect Manhattan-meets-Appalachia setting (page 141).

★ **Blue Wing Frog, Front Royal:** You won't find a healthier restaurant than this. It's a fun place with a happy staff (page 173).

★ **Spelunker's, Front Royal:** Sure it's "fast food," but this is nostalgia heaven, with juicy burgers and rich shakes (page 173).

(702/505-8888), American Airlines (800/433-7300), Delta (800/221-1212), and United (800/864-8331). Rental car companies are stationed at the airport, and there's a bus stop 150 feet (46 m) east of the terminal building for Smart Way (540/982-6622), which runs throughout the Roanoke region.

Lynchburg Regional Airport (350 Terminal Dr. 100, 434/455-6090, www.lynchburgva.gov, LYH) has four arriving and departing flights each per day, and they all go to and from Charlotte via American Airlines. There are four on-site rental agencies at the airport, plus taxi services and a bus stop for the Greater Lynchburg Transit Company (434/455-5080, www.gltconline.com).

Shenandoah Valley Regional Airport (77 Aviation Circle, Weyers Cave, 540/234-8304, www.flyshd.com, SHD) provides connections to Washington DC and Chicago via United. Four car rental companies service the airport, and you can reserve a shuttle to take you to Staunton or Waynesboro ($40-60).

Train

The closest **Amtrak** (800/872-7245, www.amtrak.com) line to this area is the Crescent, which starts in New York City and runs south past Washington DC to Charlottesville and Lynchburg. It continues south toward Charlotte, Atlanta, and New Orleans. A branch of Amtrak's Northeast Regional, which starts in Boston, extends into Lynchburg and Roanoke.

If your trip includes Harpers Ferry, you can hop on a **MARC** (Mon.-Fri., www.mta.maryland.gov) train on the Brunswick Line toward Washington DC.

Bus

The closest **Greyhound** bus stations to Damascus are in Bristol, Tennessee (827 Shelby St., 423/764-6161), and in Marion (141 Dabny Drive, 276/783-7114). There are also Greyhound stations in Roanoke (26 Salem Ave. SW, 540/343-5436), Lynchburg (800 Kemper St., 434/846-6614), and Charlottesville (310 W. Main St., 434/295-5131).

Roanoke is home to Valley Metro, which runs the **Smart Way Bus** (800/388-7005, www.smartwaybus.com, $4 one-way). Smart Way has one line that connects downtown Roanoke to Salem and Blacksburg, including a stop at Roanoke-Blacksburg Regional Airport.

The **Greater Lynchburg Transportation Company** (434/455-5080, www.gltconline.com) runs 10 main lines with several variations, each starting at Kemper Street Station (825 Kemper St.).

Best Accommodations

★ **Crazy Larry's Hostel, Damascus:** This hostel is popular in the AT community and includes breakfast in the price (page 117).

★ **Clay Corner Inn, Blacksburg:** This thoughtful inn with modern-rustic rooms also has a spa and hot breakfasts (page 131).

★ **Black Lantern Inn, Roanoke:** There's nothing extravagant about this inn, but it does everything very well. It has private rooms and pretty outdoor spaces (page 143).

★ **Loft Mountain Campground, Shenandoah National Park:** Not as crowded as Big Meadows, Loft Mountain is accessible and quiet (page 162).

★ **Mountain Home, Front Royal:** A couple runs this hostel a stone's throw from the AT; breakfast is included (page 174).

★ **Hillbrook Inn, Berryville:** A great romantic getaway awaits at this first-class accommodation—located on land first purchased by George Washington (page 176).

In the Shenandoah Valley, you can hop on a **BRITE Bus** (www.britebus.org), which connects Waynesboro to Staunton and Harrisonburg. Most lines run Monday-Friday, but there's a Saturday-evening trolley that runs throughout Staunton.

Fuel and Services

Make sure you have a full tank of gas before driving the long stretches of highway. Damascus has three gas stations, and the bigger towns in southwestern Virginia like Marion and Wytheville have a few as well. Don't drive the Blue Ridge or Skyline without first filling up; you'll have chances in Roanoke, Waynesboro, and Front Royal. If you're low while on the Blue Ridge, you'll have to jump off the Parkway at a route that cuts through, then drive another 20-30 minutes to the closest community (such as Lexington or Lynchburg). The same is true for Skyline Drive (towns include Harrisonburg, Elkton, and Luray).

Dial 511 for reports on road conditions when in Virginia and West Virginia. For emergency assistance, call 911.

Damascus

Take TN-133, or Shady Avenue, 13.5 miles (21.7 km) through the hinterlands of Cherokee National Forest, cross the Tennessee border with Virginia, and enter **Damascus** (pop. 797), a small town with a big reputation in the outdoor community. Damascus is known as "Trail Town U.S.A.," because quite a few trails either start in or run through the community. The Appalachian Trail runs right through town, while the 34-mile (55-km) Virginia Creeper Trail, a walking and cycling route from Abingdon to Whitetop, has its midpoint here. Also, Damascus is in the middle of the Iron Mountain Trail, which extends 24 miles (39 km) north to Iron Mountain Gap and 23 miles (37 km) south to TN-91. Finally, the TransAmerica Bicycle Trail crosses through Damascus on its way to Yorktown. Thus, tiny Damascus is pretty important.

Many of the businesses in town cater to the outdoor community, whether they sell hiking gear or provide bike rentals, or serve up enormous plates stacked with proteins and carbohydrates. There are a couple of hostels and inexpensive inns, and Laurel Creek—which runs right through town—provides opportunities for kayaking and fly fishing. Damascus is also home to the annual Trail Days, two days focused on the Appalachian Trail with music, food, vendors, exhibits, workshops, and—of course—guided hikes. If you're hoping to hike the AT in Virginia or Tennessee, make a point to visit Damascus.

Damascus Trail Days

Arguably the premier celebration of the Appalachian Trail and trail life, **Damascus Trail Days** (May, www.trailday.us) unites hikers, cyclists, and outdoor enthusiasts at a time when northbound thru-hikers are expected to be entering town. Over a weekend, typically in mid-May, Damascus rolls out featured speakers, raffles, craft tents, live music, a pole-throwing contest, a talent show, food, and foraging demonstrations, plus helping-hand initiatives like foot massages, gear shakedowns, and repair. The weekend climaxes with the annual hiker parade, in which attendees and marchers are encouraged to bring water guns for spraying one another. Shuttles run throughout town to take people to and from designated stops. Hikers and attendees can camp at a designated quiet **campground** (1004 S. Shady Ave., $5, $20 parking).

Recreation

The big trail in Virginia (besides the AT) is the **Virginia Creeper Trail** (www.vacreepertrail.org), which begins in Abingdon and heads southeast to Damascus before heading up into Jefferson National Forest, then down to Whitetop. The 34-mile (55-km) trail is popular with cyclists and horseback riders and also serves as a nice warmup (or alternative) to the AT. There are 47 trestle bridges on the trail, plus restrooms, picnic shelters, and informational kiosks. Always pass to the left on this trail, which can be mighty popular in the warmer months.

For those looking for just a taste of the Creeper Trail, try starting at **Alvarado Station** (21198 Alvarado Road, Abingdon) and jaunting five miles east to **Damascus Town Park** (301 S. Beaver Ave., Damascus). The elevation changes only about 200 feet on this easy section.

Damascus is also home to the **Iron Mountain Trail** (access at US-58, Douglas Dr.), a yellow-blazed path that starts at Iron Mountain Gap 24 miles (39 km) northeast of the town. The trail sees a suitable number of visitors during the summer and fall, especially mountain bikers, as it leads through verdant forest to Damascus, then south on decidedly rockier terrain to TN-91. Fun bit of trivia: Before 1972 the Iron Mountain Trail was part of the Appalachian Trail, but the AT was moved a little farther south.

The **TransAmerica Bicycle Trail** (access at US-58, Douglas Dr.) also zips through Damascus. The trail is 4,228 miles (6,800 km) long and connects Astoria, Oregon, to Yorktown, Virginia. It takes a cyclist between two and three months to finish the entire trek.

Damascus is also a popular fishing town. The Whitetop Laurel Creek is a popular spot for small-stream fly fishing. The **Commonwealth of Virginia's Department of Game & Inland Fisheries** (www.dgif.virginia.gov) has designated special-regulation sections of the creek for fly fishing; there is a 12-inch minimum size limit and six-fish-per-day creel limit. A statewide freshwater license ($8 for one day, up to $47 annually) is necessary to fish. Between October and mid-June the commonwealth stocks the creek with trout. Trout fishing in trout-stocked waters is free with a trout-fishing permit June 16-September 30.

Outfitters

Damascus has a host of outdoor and adventure shops that double as rental

Damascus to Roanoke

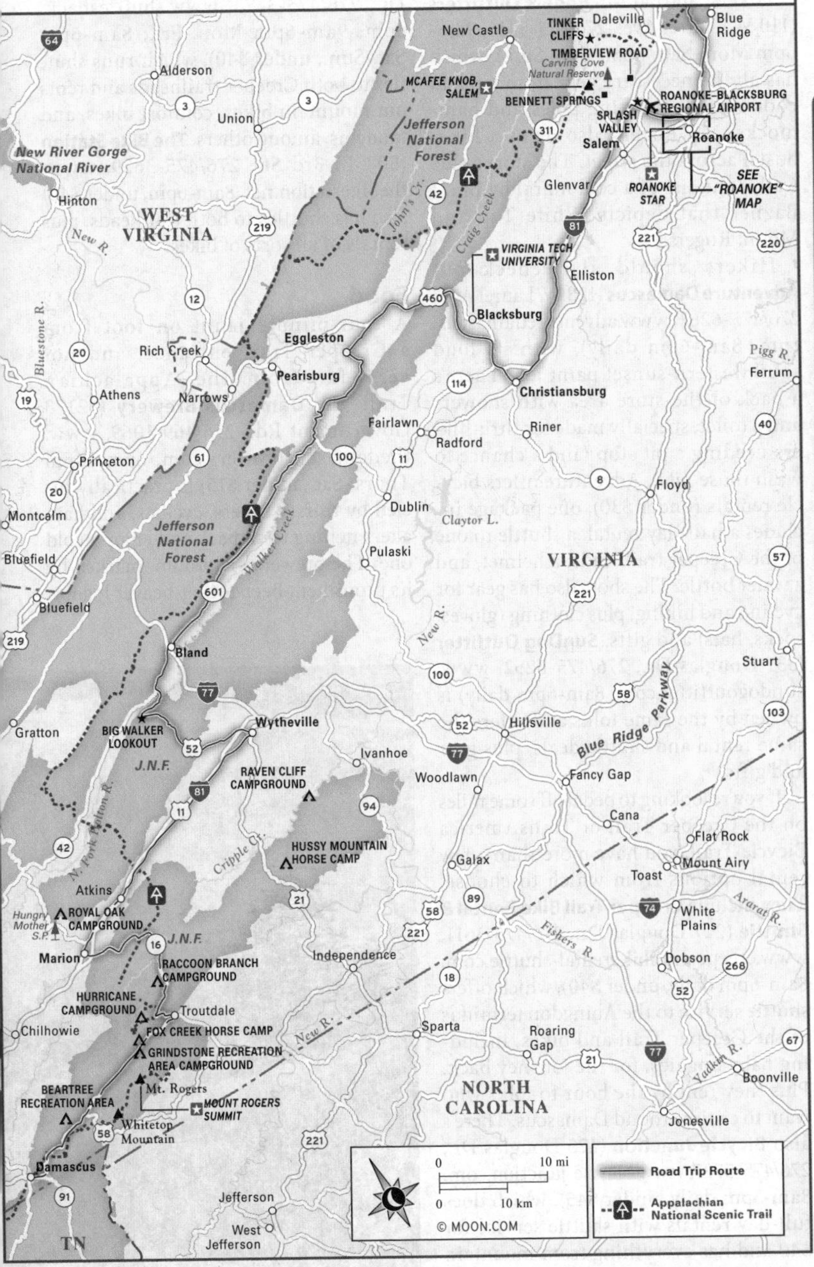

64
New Castle
TINKER CLIFFS
Daleville
Blue Ridge
Alderson
MCAFEE KNOB, SALEM
TIMBERVIEW ROAD
Carvins Cove Natural Reserve
3
3
BENNETT SPRINGS
ROANOKE-BLACKSBURG REGIONAL AIRPORT
Union
Jefferson National Forest
SPLASH VALLEY
311
Salem
Roanoke
New River Gorge National River
Glenvar
ROANOKE STAR
SEE "ROANOKE" MAP
Hinton
42
John's Cr.
Craig Creek
WEST VIRGINIA
219
81
221
220
New R.
VIRGINIA TECH UNIVERSITY
Elliston
12
460
Blacksburg
Bluestone R.
Eggleston
Rich Creek
20
Pigg R.
Pearisburg
Ferrum
114
Christiansburg
19
Athens
Narrows
Fairlawn
Riner
Radford
40
61
100
11
Princeton
8
Floyd
20
Dublin
Montcalm
Jefferson National Forest
Walker Creek
Claytor L.
Pulaski
Bluefield
VIRGINIA
57
601
221
Bluefield
New R.
219
Bland
Stuart
100
Blue Ridge Parkway
77
58
103
Gratton
BIG WALKER LOOKOUT
Wytheville
52
Hillsville
52
77
Ivanhoe
J.N.F.
RAVEN CLIFF CAMPGROUND
Woodlawn
Fancy Gap
81
N. Fork Holston R.
11
94
Cana
Cripple Cr.
HUSSY MOUNTAIN HORSE CAMP
Flat Rock
42
Galax
Mount Airy
Toast
Atkins
21
89
Ararat R.
Hungry Mother S.P.
ROYAL OAK CAMPGROUND
58
74
White Plains
221
Fishers R.
16
J.N.F.
Marion
Independence
Dobson
268
RACCOON BRANCH CAMPGROUND
18
52
HURRICANE CAMPGROUND
Troutdale
Chilhowie
FOX CREEK HORSE CAMP
Sparta
Roaring Gap
67
GRINDSTONE RECREATION AREA CAMPGROUND
New R.
21
Yadkin R.
77
Boonville
Mt. Rogers
BEARTREE RECREATION AREA
MOUNT ROGERS SUMMIT
NORTH CAROLINA
Jonesville
58
Whitetop Mountain
221
Damascus
91
Jefferson
West Jefferson
TN

0 — 10 mi
0 — 10 km
© MOON.COM

Road Trip Route
Appalachian National Scenic Trail

facilities, so you can buy equipment and get trail help all in one package.

Hikers: Start at **Mt. Rogers Outfitters** (110 W. Laurel Ave., 276/475-5416, 9am-6pm Mon.-Sat., noon-6pm Sun.), which has all the necessary gear from tents to cookware to trekking poles and hammocks. Mt. Rogers also owns a hiker hostel across the street. The store's side wall is the site of a cool mural by Brant Bazner that depicts White Top and Mount Rogers.

Hikers should also check out **Adventure Damascus** (128 W. Laurel Ave., 276/475-6262, www.adventuredamascus.com, 8am-6pm daily), with its loud southwestern-sunset paint job. There's a back-of-the-store area with showers and a toilet, specially made for thru-hikers needing a pit stop (and a chance to wash those pits). Adventure offers bicycle rentals (under $30); one package includes a half-day rental, a shuttle to one of the Creeper trailheads, a helmet, and a water bottle. The shop also has gear for cycling and hiking, plus clothing (gloves, socks, hats) and gifts. **SunDog Outfitter** (331 Douglas Dr., 276/475-6252, www.sundogoutfitter.com, 8am-6pm daily) is owned by the same folks and offers the same rental and shuttle deals, plus gear and gifts.

If you're looking to pedal off some miles on the Creeper Trail or TransAmerica Bicycle Trail, you have more than a few rental options from which to choose. They include **Creeper Trail Bike Rental & Shuttle** (227 Douglas Dr., 276/475-3611, www.creepertrailbikerental-shuttle.com, 8am-6pm daily, under $40), which offers shuttle service to the Abingdon terminus of the Creeper Trail and bikes, including baby buggies, for the journey back. Plus they rent by the hour to folks who want to cruise around Damascus. There's also **Bicycle Junction** (425 Douglas Dr., 276/475-5727, www.bicycle-junction.com, 8am-5pm daily, under $45), which does full-day rentals with shuttle service for $40 and has everything from mountain bikes to cruisers. Brothers Gary and Jerry Camper own **ShuttleShack** (112 Douglas Dr., 276/475-3773, www.shuttleshack.com, 9am-6pm Mon.-Fri., 8am-6pm Sat.-Sun., under $40), which runs shuttles to both Creeper trailheads and rents out mountain bikes, comfort bikes, and tandems, among others. **The Bike Station** (504 E. 3rd St., 276/475-3629, www.thebikestation.net, 8am-6pm, under $40) also has shuttles to both trailheads, plus rentals of all sorts of bikes.

Food

A four-minute jaunt on foot from a Creeper Trail entrance, and not very far from the Appalachian Trail, the **Damascus Brewery** (32173 Government Rd., 276/469-1069, www.thedamascusbrewery.com, 6pm-10pm Thurs.-Sat., under $15) is practically fueled by thirsty hikers, cyclists, and kayakers itching to sit back and enjoy a cold one. The brewery's taproom, marked by its prominent beer-toting-beaver logo, is

a cozy garage with hardwood and stools by a bar. When the weather cooperates, people flock outside for lawn games. It's always rotating the taps, and it cans 32-ounce beers, so if you're going to be thirsty later, grab one to go.

As far as food, there aren't a ton of good options in Damascus. **Mojo's Trailside Café & Coffee** (331 Douglas Dr., 276/475-5505, www.mojostrailsidecafe.com, 7am-5pm Sun.-Wed., 7am-9pm Thurs.-Sat., under $15) is solid, however, and it feels somewhere in between a chic coffeehouse and a lived-in diner. It has inexpensive breakfasts and lunches, though I'd shell out for "The Serial" bagel. The English Joe (egg, cheese, and bacon on an English muffin) is a steal.

Accommodations

As Trail Town U.S.A., Damascus has plenty of hiker hostels. The **Mt. Rogers Outfitters Hostel** (110 Laurel Ave., 276/475-5416, www.mtrogersoutfitters.com, $21) is a small house on the main drag with four rooms available, each with two bunks. Each bunk, which is made of wood, has a Therm-a-rest sleeping pad. Showers and towels are available.

★ **Crazy Larry's Hostel** (209 Douglas Dr., 276/475-7130, www.crazylarryshostel.business.site, $40) is popular and centrally located. It has comfortable rooms, showers are available, and you can do your laundry and have breakfast, which is included in the price. Tenting is also available. Crazy Larry also has **Crazy Larry's B&B and Cottage** (209 Douglas Dr., 276/475-7130, www.crazylarryshostel.business.site, $300), which is a standalone rental that sleeps up to 12.

Hiker's Inn (216 E. Laurel Ave., 276/475-3788, www.hikersinndamascus.com, $25-75) has bunk-bed rooms, plus a twin room, two queen rooms, a king room, and an Airstream. There's a miniature kitchen area, outdoor patio, and barbecue grill. Dogs are allowed.

The Broken Fiddle Hostel and Inn (104

view of the Appalachian Mountains from the Whitetop Mountain summit

Damascus Dr., 276/608-6220, $10-45) has a cute and fixed-up bunk area, plus private rooms and tent space. Laundry and continental breakfasts are available.

Woodchuck Hostel (533 Docie St., 406/407-1272, www.woodchuckhostel.com, $12-45) is a clean and bright spot with comfortable beds with memory foam mattresses. There are cabin options as well. Some resupply is available, as is breakfast. For those who just need a hammock hanger or tepee, that's available too.

The Place (203 E. Creepers Way, 276/475-3441, donations requested) is a church hostel meant for long-distance Appalachian Trail hikers and cyclists on the TransAmerica Bicycle Trail. The Place has bunks that can sleep up to 30, plus tent space and hammock hangers. Showers are available with towels.

VA-600: Whitetop Mountain

The Appalachian Trail heads east from Damascus through Mount Rogers National Recreation Area, while US-58 (also known as the Jeb Stuart Highway) parallels it for a bit before turning right at Konnarock Road. Stay on Konnarock Road for 2.4 miles (3.9 km), then turn right onto Whitetop Road, which will take you to a trailhead for a hike of this underappreciated peak.

Mount Rogers seems to get all the attention in this area of Virginia, but **Whitetop Mountain** shouldn't be overlooked. At 5,518 feet (1,682 m), it's the second-highest peak in the state to Mount Rogers and has a classic bald, perfect for enjoying views of the surrounding highlands and picnicking.

There are two good ways to reach the summit of Whitetop Mountain, both via the Appalachian Trail. The "easy" way is from Mount Rogers, but that's only easy because the hike from Rogers to Whitetop is simple. You still have to hike to the summit of Rogers to get there, and that's a longer and more challenging hike. The second way to reach Whitetop's summit is from the mountain base, using the AT.

Hiking

Whitetop Mountain Summit and Buzzard Rock

Distance: 7 miles (11.3 km)

Duration: 4 hours

Elevation gain: 1,085 feet (331 m)

Difficulty: Moderate

Trailhead: Parking area at Elk Garden (36.646783, -81.582831)

From the parking lot, follow the Appalachian Trail as it heads south through the woods. You'll begin a moderate climb on the AT past a stream and campsites. After about 2.5 miles (4 km) you'll reach Whitetop Road, which leads to a trailhead closer to the summit. Stay on the AT and you'll meet a spring at which you can collect good water. After a short descent you'll climb once more on the trail until the trees fade and the sky opens. There are radio towers on the Whitetop summit, which can be disappointing, but there are a few spots to spread out and enjoy the sunlight.

But we're not finished! Continue on the AT for another 0.2 mile (0.3 km), and you'll reach Buzzard Rock, an outcropping that has even better views of the highlands. Find a sturdy spot and contemplate. When you've taken it all in, turn around and take the AT north down the mountain until you reach the Elk Garden lot.

Mount Rogers National Recreation Area

From Damascus the Appalachian Trail stretches through **Mount Rogers National Recreation Area** (NRA) for about 60 miles (97 km), mostly up and down peaks of more than 4,000 feet (1,219 m). Overall there are about 500 miles (805 km) of trails inside the area, a 200,000-acre piece of land managed by the U.S. Forest Service that also offers horseback riding, camping, fishing, hunting, and swimming.

Hiking

★ Mount Rogers Summit

Distance: 8.5 miles (13.7 km)

Duration: 6-7 hours

Elevation gain: 1,300 feet (396 m)

Difficulty: Strenuous

Trailhead: Parking area at Massie Gap (36.634485, -81.509457)

The Mount Rogers summit stands 5,728 feet (1,746 m) high, but luckily this classic hike starting at Massie Gap begins some 4,000 feet (1,219 m) above sea level, so you don't have a slog ahead of you. Instead, the hike of about 4 miles (6.4 km) each way moderately climbs the highest natural point in Virginia, so this is a great introduction for amateurs to half-day hiking. Plus—and this is maybe the best thing about Mount Rogers—there are ponies. Mount Rogers is home to feral ponies whose grazing helps prevent forest fires. In exchange for their grazing, the National Park Service takes care of the ponies. You'll undoubtedly spot these wild, untamed creatures while hiking the peak; pictures are welcome, but don't feed the ponies.

From the parking area, take the Rhododendron Gap Trail until a junction with the Appalachian Trail. You'll hike

Top to bottom: bricks marking the work of Appalachian Trail hikers; along the trail on Mount Rogers; Hungry Mother Lake.

south on the trail toward Mount Rogers. After 1.5 miles (2.4 km) you'll reach a junction with Wilburn Ridge, but stick with the AT as it climbs toward the summit. The Thomas Knob Shelter comes in 3.5 miles (5.6 km) up the trail, and it's a beauty: two stories and recently renovated with a nearby water source. From here you're less than a mile (1.6 km) from the summit. Soon you'll reach the Mount Rogers Spur Trail, whose blue blazes you should follow to the top. This final stretch is an incredible journey through a wet forest of tall pines. The summit is forested but there's a marker there acknowledging the highest point in the commonwealth. Celebrate your small victory before heading back down on the spur trail and AT.

Recreation

Fishing is permitted in streams and lakes throughout the NRA, but the best trout inventory you'll find is at **Whitetop Laurel Creek** (east of Damascus off Creek Junction Rd.). The trout are plentiful here, and anything smaller than a foot must be released. **Big Wilson Creek** (VA-613 south of VA-603) is another popular trout-catching spot. **Hale Lake** (Hales Lake Rd. and Blue Springs Rd.) is good, too, as is Cripple Creek in the eastern end of the NRA. Swimming is permitted in Hale Lake.

Horseback riding is popular in the NRA, with several trails specifically made for hooves. The **Taylors Valley Loop** (12.5 mi/20.1 km) includes the Virginia Creeper Trail and time along Whitetop Laurel Creek. The trailhead of the **Fox Creek Loop** (7.8 mi/12.6 km) is at **Fox Creek Horse Camp** (3078 Fairwood Rd., Troutdale); from there it meets with the Iron Mountain Trail and comes back around on two quieter trails. The **Horse Heaven Loop** (8.5 mi/13.7 km) is best accessed from **Hussy Mountain Horse Camp** (1195 CC Camp Rd., Speedwell) and promises beautiful open views and the pine trees of the East Fork Trail.

Camping

The **Grindstone Recreation Area Campground** (1946 Laurel Valley Rd., Troutdale, 276/388-3983, $24-32) is a well-regarded spot inside the NRA. Grindstone has 53 sites for tent and RV camping, plus flush toilets, showers, fire rings, and picnic tables. The campground also has an amphitheater, playground, and water play area.

Beartree Recreation Area (20993 Beartree Gap Rd., 276/388-3642, $24-55) is another larger spot with 55 single and 29 double sites, plus flush toilets, showers, and tables. It's 9.2 miles (14.8 km) east of downtown Damascus, with shuttle service from Adventure Damascus, so those wanting to hang in town will find it accessible. There's also a 12-acre lake onsite for swimming and fishing.

With 30 campsites, **Hurricane Campground** (2021 Hurricane Campground Rd., Sugar Grove, 276/783-5196, Apr.-Oct., $15-25) is a little more relaxed, tucked within an oak and hemlock forest with rhododendron. Flush toilets, showers, and a playing field are among the amenities.

The 20-site **Raccoon Branch Campground** (6416 Sugar Grove Hwy., Sugar Grove, 276/783-5196, $15-25) is close to the AT and Dickey Knob, which offers a stunning vista.

Raven Cliff Campground (544 Raven Cliff Lane, Ivanhoe, 276/783-5196, $5) has 20 primitive units with picnic tables and grills, plus access to a Cripple Creek, good for fishing and wading. Look for the 1810 iron ore furnace on-site.

Comers Rock Campground and Picnic Area (3703 Hales Lake Rd., Elk Creek, 276/783-5196, Apr.-Oct., $5) is a smaller, primitive campground offering a connection to Comers Rock Overlook and the Unaka Nature Trail.

For people bringing horses to ride, check out **Hussy Mountain Horse Camp** (1195 CC Camp Rd., Speedwell, 276/783-5196, Apr.-Oct., $7) and **Fox Creek Horse Camp** (3078 Fairwood Rd., Troutdale,

276/783-5196, Apr.-Nov., $5). Coggins test paperwork is required to govern horses in Virginia.

Marion

Marion (pop. 6,117) is a cozy town with a quintessential American main street anchored by a hotel and an art deco theater. On a warm evening the breeze whispers softly through the town, drawing visitors for monthly arts events, while locals are found frequenting the several restaurants in the downtown, bringing kids to the drive-in theater and buying groceries at the weekly farmers market.

Getting There and Around

Take VA-603 through Mount Rogers National Recreation Area until it runs into VA-16. Turn left at the junction, through Troutdale, and head north, then northwest, 18 miles (29 km) up the Sugar Grove Highway to Marion. Marion is home to a **Greyhound station** (141 Dabny Dr., 276/783-7114), which is in the same building as a heating-and-cooling business. The station has will-call availability.

The Lincoln Theatre

Opening in 1929, **The Lincoln Theatre** (117 E. Main St., 276/783-6092, www.thelincoln.org) has a similar history to other theaters in small cities and towns across the eastern part of America. Closed in the 1970s and left to rot, the theater was saved with an extensive restoration that ended in 2004. Today it's a beautiful venue whose interior recalls a gilded Mayan temple. It's home to tapings of the syndicated television program *Song of the Mountains,* which features bluegrass acts from Appalachia, and also hosts frequent bluegrass and country acts trying to make that next step to stardom.

Food and Accommodations

You'll find a mix of ultra-casual and ultra-curated things at **Wooden Pickle Food & Spirits** (120 E. Main St., 276/783-2300, 4pm-9pm Mon.-Thurs., 4pm-10pm Fri.-Sat., under $30), which features a small L-shaped bar and a dining area against exposed brick. Lots of wine bottles are visible to the naked eye; no doubt your drink will pair well with a specialty pizza or Atlantic salmon.

There were originally 27 lions painted on the ceiling of **27 Lions** (111 E. Main St., 276/378-0844, www.27lions.com, 4pm-9pm Mon.-Thurs., 4pm-midnight Fri.-Sat., under $40). The restaurant and tap house serves burgers, brick-oven pizza, sandwiches, and a grub-friendly late-night menu on the weekends inside a toned-down space that feels like an old Irish tavern. There are 27 beers on tap, and they rotate among popular national brands and regional flavors. Look for the carousel lion statue inside the restaurant, a perfect photo op for kids.

The understated **Wolfe's BBQ Restaurant and Catering** (138 E. Main St., 276/387-0823, 11am-8pm Tues.-Thurs., 11am-9pm Fri.-Sat., 11am-4pm Sun., under $25) is totally worth it. There's plenty of space to spread out and enjoy a heaping plate of ribs or brisket, given a special dry-rub treatment and accompanied by sauces. Sides include what's usual for around here: fried okra, hush puppies, and barbecue beans. Don't skip the banana pudding for dessert.

Once in a while you find a place that seems to know exactly what people want in a hangout. **Sisters' Café & Gifts** (212 E. Main St., 276/783-9080, 7:30am-5pm Mon.-Fri., 10am-1pm Sat.) is just that, offering all-day breakfast, lunch, coffee, wine, housewares, clothing, and small gifts with an emphasis on local makers. Breakfast includes a biscuit bar where you can load up on whatever you'd like, while lunch has salads and sandwiches. There's plenty of seating here, with some living room furniture for those wanting to stay. You probably will.

Headspace Brewing Company (120 N. Chestnut St., 276/780-8860,

5pm-midnight Fri.-Sat., under $15) is a funky little newbie inside an industrial structure. It offers lighter fare while hosting plenty of regular events, from trivia nights to weekly beer-pong tournaments and live music.

Three doors down from the Lincoln Theatre, the **General Francis Marion Hotel** (107 E. Main St., 276/783-4800, www.gfmhotel.com, $100-150) was built in 1927 and retains some of its Prohibition-era charm, but its authenticity is questionable. The main ballroom is dressed in gold curtains, dark wood paneling, and chandeliers. Rooms with full, queen, king, and connector queen beds have period-looking furniture, though it's certainly nice and sleek. An on-site restaurant called **The Speakeasy** (107 E. Main St., 276/783-4800, 3pm-9pm Tues.-Thurs., 4pm-10pm Fri.-Sat., 8am-2pm Sun., under $40 dinner, under $20 brunch) doesn't quite give off that vibe: It's more or less a straight-up bar with some dining space.

Hungry Mother State Park

It's a quick 3-mile (4.8-km) drive from Marion up VA-16 north to **Hungry Mother State Park** (2854 Park Blvd., Marion, 276/781-7400, 6am-10pm daily), which is named after a local legend. According to the story, a woman named Molly Marley escaped a Native American ambush with her child in tow. Molly collapsed, and the child searched for help. Upon finding help, the child could only say "hungry mother." Molly was reportedly found dead at the foot of a mountain now known as Molly's Knob. Hungry Mother Stream is nearby, which flows into the narrow Hungry Mother Lake, a site for boating, swimming, and fishing.

Hungry Mother State Park also has campgrounds, 17 miles (27 km) of hiking and biking trails, and—atypical for parks—a chapel, a restaurant, and a conference center. While the Appalachian Trail runs parallel to the park to the south, Hungry Mother is an extremely accessible playground, and the lake offers an opportunity to refresh.

Hiking

Molly's Knob Loop

Distance: 6.5 miles (10.5 km)
Duration: 3-4 hours
Elevation gain: 1,320 feet (402 m)
Difficulty: Moderate
Trailhead: Molly's Knob trailhead (36.885216, -81.521842)

You'll get the greatest hits of Hungry Mother on this perfect day hike. There's an immediate and sweat-inducing climb off the bat, as you follow the white blazes of the Molly's Knob Trail for about 1.3 miles (2.1 km). Along the way you'll reach an observation deck, and this offers a view of the knob; either way, continue up until you reach the purple-blazed Molly's Vista Trail. This ventures to the top, where you'll get sumptuous Blue Ridge views—especially in fall—plus benches for resting or picnicking.

Head back the way you came on the Vista Trail until meeting back up with the Molly's Knob Trail. Go left to continue for another 0.5 mile (0.8 km). You'll meet up with the orange-blazed CCC Trail, which you'll want to take to the left. That will keep heading down the ridge until landing at the blue-blazed Lake Trail Loop. Turn right to coast along the lake for a while (nearly 3 mi/4.8 km). There are a few switchbacks that veer from the lake, but otherwise you'll be admiring this body of water surrounded by what seems to be endless forest.

Recreation

Swimming (11am-6pm Mon.-Fri., 11am-7pm Sat.-Sun., Memorial Day-Labor Day, $5-8) is permitted at Hungry Mother Lake from a lifeguard-manned beach. You can fish for bass, catfish, walleye, and sunfish among other species on Hungry Mother Lake, and kayaking, canoeing, paddleboarding, and electric-powered johnboats (fishing boats with a flat bottom) are allowed.

Accommodations and Camping

There are 81 campsites total at Hungry Mother, spread out across four campgrounds. **Creekside Campground** (VA-348, 0.1 mi/0.2 km north of Lake Dr., $35) has 20 sites plus electricity and water hookups. **Camp Burson** (VA-16, 0.5 mi/0.8 km north of CR-617, $35-39) has 30 sites with electric, water, and sewer hookups and 20 without sewer hookups. Both sites allow RVs up to 35 feet (11 m). **Royal Oak Campground** (Cabin Fever Dr., 0.1 mi/0.2 km north of VA-348, $24) has 11 tent-only sites and a bathhouse. There are no hookups here.

You can also stay in a **cabin** (1800/933-7275, $448-794 weekly in season, $374-595 weekly off-season) at Hungry Mother, though between Memorial Day and Labor Day cabins are rented by the week. The park offers 20 standard cabins of varying size and style, from three one-bedroom cabins (some made solely of logs) that sleep two to two-bedroom cinder block cabins that sleep up to six. The **Hemlock Haven cabins** (1800/933-7275, $675-794 weekly in season, $506-595 weekly off-season) are generally split into two types: two-bedroom cinder block cabins with full kitchens and living rooms with sofas, and two-bedroom cabins without full kitchens but with utensils. Some even have wet bars. Each is unique, so your best bet is to contact the park to find your perfect match. Also available is the **Hungry Mother Lodge** (1800/933-7275, $1,896-2,479 weekly in season, $1,580-1,859 weekly off-season), which was built by the Civilian Conservation Corps in the 1930s. It has six bedrooms, a full kitchen, a gas grill, gas fireplace, porch, and picnic shelter, and is best for large groups.

Wytheville

From Marion it's a 27-mile (43-km) drive north on US-11 to **Wytheville** (pop. 8,211), the seat of Wythe County, which is named for George Wythe, the first of seven men from Virginia who signed the Declaration of Independence. Raided somewhat successfully in July 1863 by Union soldiers, who retreated mere hours after claiming the town, Wytheville later was the site of Virginia's last lynching, part of a sullied history as a hotbed for white supremacy.

These days Wytheville is home to the **Chautauqua Festival** (Elizabeth Brown Memorial Park, June, www.wythe-arts.org), a weeklong celebration of arts and community. The night before the festival there's a prelude with a hot-air balloon glow, illuminating the night sky in an impressive display of color and enormity. The festival includes daily art displays and exhibits, live music and theatrical performances, food vendors, and a craft fair.

For those driving through, the **Great Lakes to Florida Highway Museum** (975 Tazewell St., 276/223-3330) offers a neat look at some American nostalgia. The museum, an old Texaco gas station, celebrates US-21, which stretches from Ohio to Florida and passes through Wytheville.

Wytheville is the home of Edith Bolling Wilson, second wife of President Woodrow Wilson and the only Appalachian-born first lady. Her life is immortalized at the **Edith Bolling Wilson Birthplace and Museum** (145 E. Main St., 276/223-3484, www.edithbollingwilson.org, 10am-4pm Tues.-Fri., 10am-2pm Sat., free, $5 for house tour), which features rotating exhibits that touch on World War I life, the Girl Scouts, and other topics related to Bolling Wilson's life. You can see photographs, household items, and the Bolling family Bible as part of the standing collection.

If you're looking for a night out, your best bet is to check out **Wohlfahrt Haus Dinner Theatre** (170 Main Dr., 888/950-3382, www.wohlfahrthaus.com, $44 adults, $42 seniors, $31 students, $27 ages 11 and younger). Wohlfahrt presents community-style musical theater while serving a four-course dinner. Its Matterhorn Lounge (11am-2pm Mon.-Fri., 4pm-10pm Tues.-Sat., under $30) serves lunch and dinner, including German staples like schnitzel and braten, and is also home to a beer garden.

Food and Accommodations

Wytheville has a variety of fast-food restaurants spread across town, along with a few smaller independent joints without pretense. **Virginia Heights Restaurant** (790 W. Spiller St., 276/228-6133, 6am-2:30pm Mon.-Wed., 6am-7pm Thurs.-Sat., 8am-2pm Sun., under $25) is where much of the community comes to chow down. Big breakfasts of southern favorites like biscuits and gravy stand up well, while dinner is all about burgers, rib eye, and other meaty goodness. Folks are warm and friendly here, naturally.

A few blocks from the major downtown intersection of Main and 4th Streets is **Trinkle Mansion Bed & Breakfast** (525 W. Main St., 276/625-0625, www.trinklemansion.com, $120-170). The mansion is more than 100 years old, a Classical Revival home built by gentleman farmer William Trinkle for his family. Now the mansion has four warm guest rooms with queen beds and, depending on the room, everything from claw-foot tubs to four-poster beds to fireplaces. If you're on a romantic getaway, a guest cottage has a bit more space, plus a front porch for relaxing.

Right in the heart of town, and directly across from the Edith Bolling Wilson Birthplace and Museum, is the **Bolling Wilson Hotel** (170 E. Main St., 276/233-2333, $100-200), an Ascend property that's part of the Choice family. The hotel has basic and comfortable king and queen rooms, and is on par with, say, a Hampton Inn. Speaking of which, the **Hampton Inn** (950 Pepper's Ferry Rd., 276/228-6090, $100-200) is just outside the downtown near the junction of I-77 and I-81. Also nearby is a **Best Western** (355 Nye Rd., 276/228-7300, $60-120), a **Holiday Inn Express** (165 Main Dr., 276/335-2222, $120-200), and a **La Quinta Inn & Suites** (1800 E. Main St., 276/228-7400, $100-150).

Big Walker Lookout

US-52 runs right through Wytheville; take that north 13.3 miles (21.4 km) to **Big Walker Lookout** (8711 Stoney Fork Rd., Wytheville, 276/663-4016, 10am-5pm daily, $5), a 100-foot (30-m) observation tower that promises views of mountain peaks in five states. But, you know, you must climb the thing first, and as it's not protected by walls, it's not for the faint of heart. Built in 1953, the tower is atop a mountain pass that was used to warn locals about potential Union raids during the Civil War. For those willing to climb the tower, there's a small fee; otherwise, there's a country store that sometimes hosts bluegrass bands.

Bland

Stay on scenic US-52 as it winds down the mountains on switchbacks, after which it hooks up with VA-42. Continue on this road into **Bland** (pop. 409), a tiny unincorporated community that happens to also be the seat of Bland County, which is unique for having no incorporated communities within its boundaries.

Bland is a stopover for truckers and travelers driving I-77. And the place to stay is the **Big Walker Motel** (70 Skyview Lane, 276/688-3331, $50-100), an inexpensive and friendly accommodation where hikers especially feel welcome. Renovations were done over the last five years. Within walking distance to the motel are a convenience store and a few chain food options, but you should take advantage of the motel's picnic tables and gazebo. Hikers may be able to arrange shuttle service to the motel.

Eggleston

The drive on VA-42 east is lonely but worth taking some time, as you'll be surrounded by mountain ridges on both sides while gently ascending and descending and passing brooks that otherwise twist around you. The Appalachian Trail continues to your left while going east, and it begins to peel more northward as you continue on VA-100 north, then VA-730 before entering **Eggleston** (pop. 254).

Eggleston was a tourist destination in the 1800s because of its New River hot springs (Eggleston's original name was Gunpowder Springs because of the sulfur smell coming off the springs). The resorts have long been closed, but the New River is still a hot topic. There's constant debate among geologists about whether the New River is one of the world's oldest rivers, but the fact that it cuts through the mountains—and doesn't simply flow along their base—makes it unique.

If you're hankering for a bite while approaching Eggleston, you must stop at the ★ **Palisades Restaurant** (168 Village St., 540/626-2828, www.thepalisadesrestaurant.com, 4:30pm-8:30pm Tues.-Thurs., 4:30pm-10pm Fri.-Sat., 10:30am-2pm and 3pm-8:30pm Sun., under $40 dinner, under $20 brunch), a hidden gem that's a few steps from making someone a culinary star. Set up in a former general store with an entire wall of shelves filled with all sorts of items, the Palisades sources locally and takes care in everything it plates. You'll get creative, Southern-inspired dishes with well-prepared meats and fish; though some may say the best items on the menu are the delicious stone-oven pizzas. Palisades offers a prix fixe Sunday brunch with staples like biscuits and gravy and eggs Benedict.

VA-100: Pearisburg

Instead of taking VA-730 into Eggleston, stay on VA-100 north to **Pearisburg** (pop. 2,786), which puts you back on the Appalachian Trail. The trail comes off the mountain from Angels Rest, a popular overlook at 3,600 feet (1,097 m) above sea level, and enters the Wilburn Valley just west of downtown. The valley—and the town of Pearisburg—is shaped by the New River cutting through the mountains. This town gets more than a few overnight and zero-day stays as hikers head north into Hemlock Ridge.

Hiker staying in Pearisburg will be happy at **Angels Rest Hiker's Haven** (204 Douglas Lane, 540/787-4076, www.angelsresthikershaven.com, $12-55). Offering tent sites, a bunkhouse option, and single and double rooms, Angels Rest also offers acupuncture services at its hiker health clinic. Those wanting that zero day should get a day pass ($7), which includes use of the bathhouse, a hot shower, common area use, laundry and detergent, loaner clothes, and a free local shuttle and Wi-Fi service.

The **Holy Family Hostel** (516 Mason Ct. Dr., 540/921-3547, www.holyfamilypearisburg.org, contributions suggested) is on the property of Holy Family Catholic Church, about 1.5 miles (2.4 km) from the center of town. The hostel includes a hot shower, a kitchen for meals, and lawn space for tents.

Hiking

Angels Rest and Wilburn Valley Overlook

Distance: 4.6 miles (7.4 km)
Duration: 3 hours
Elevation gain: 1,600 feet (488 m)
Difficulty: Strenuous
Trailhead: Cross Avenue at Appalachian Trail crossing (37.329281, -80.751663)

The directions for this hike are simple: You're on the white-blazed Appalachian Trail the entire way, except for the blue-blazed spur trail you take off the AT to reach Angels Rest, which is a boulder overlooking the valley. That view is nice but can be crowded with trees and people, so you'll want to hike an extra 0.6 mile (1 km) south to the Wilburn Valley Overlook, which gives you a really nice widescreen look at the New River and the surrounding area.

There is a catch: After a relatively easy first half mile (0.8 km) or so, the hike starts really climbing. You'll be stopping every few minutes while trudging up switchbacks to make up about 1,000 feet (305 m). Bring your water and prepare to be patient. The payoff, including those views, lush forest, and some beautiful mountain laurel, is worth it. Plus, the way down goes a lot quicker (just don't go too fast).

Blacksburg

VA-730 merges with US-460, so stay east on that road as it slinks back into Jefferson National Forest. After an 18-mile (29-km) drive, you'll come out of the forest and into **Blacksburg** (pop. 42,620), home to Virginia Tech University. Blacksburg was established in 1798 by William Black, who planned a grid of streets that created 16 square blocks, a layout that is now a part of Blacksburg's logo. The town has grown as Virginia Tech has grown, from a small agricultural school to a major university with Division I athletics.

Blacksburg is a university town for sure, packed with bars and restaurants that fill up in accordance with student schedules. For Appalachian Trail hikers it's a bit off the beaten path (24 mi/39 km southeast of Pearisburg), but for day hikers and outdoorsy folks wanting a slightly larger locale to hang their clothes and sit back with a beer (among thousands of people), Blacksburg has a lot to offer.

★ Virginia Tech University

The population of Blacksburg is approximately 42,000, give or take. About 25,000 of those people are students at **Virginia Tech University** (www.vt.edu). A large agricultural, technical, and military institute, Virginia Tech has for nearly 150 years been the engine of Blacksburg and its surrounding areas.

In 1872, the commonwealth purchased a Methodist school named Preston and Olin Institute and farmland in Montgomery County. On that land Virginia incorporated the Virginia Agricultural and Mechanical College, which after several name changes became Virginia Polytechnic Institute and State University (Virginia Tech for short) in the early 1990s. Its mascot is the Hokie, an evolved and snarling version of a maroon-colored turkey, while burnt orange is the school's secondary color. Its impressive campus is populated by buildings made of Hokie Stone, which is a cut of gray dolomite limestone that can also show hues of pink and brown. The gray, pink, and brown combine to show a more muted palette of the Virginia Tech colors, making it easy to understand why it's a treat to walk the Blacksburg campus.

Many buildings crowd around the **Drillfield,** a massive oval field that is used by the Virginia Tech Corps of Cadets for military drills. Members of the Corps of Cadets may also stand guard at War Memorial Court. The court is on the upper level of War Memorial Chapel, and features eight Indiana limestone pylons representing brotherhood, honor, leadership, sacrifice, service, loyalty, duty, and *ut prosim* ("That I may serve"). At the center of the court is a cenotaph memorializing Virginia Tech's Medal of Honor recipients. The court is a stirring symbol of university pride and national sacrifice. War Memorial Chapel, underneath the court, seats 260 and hosts religious services throughout the year.

Also overlooking the Drillfield is the **April 16 Memorial,** which marks the darkest day in the university's history, when in 2007 a gunman shot 49 people on campus, killing 32 and wounding 17. The powerful memorial includes 32 Hokie Stones representing each of the dead, plus a larger reviewing stand of Hokie Stone that overlooks the configuration. At night, ground lighting shines on the 32 stones.

Formerly the Virginia Tech Horticulture Garden, the **Peggy Lee Hahn Horticulture Garden** (200 Garden Lane, 540/231-5970, www.hort.vt.edu, 7am-9pm daily, free) is both a resource for learning about plant species and a beautiful place to relax and revel in nature. Highlights at the nearly six-acre site include the shade gardens, which are approached through outstretched maple branches and host a sandstone rendition of Frank Lloyd Wright's *Maid in the Mud;* a display of dwarf evergreen conifers; and the Jane Andrews Memorial Stream Garden, anchored by

Top to bottom: General Francis Marion Hotel in Marion; Virginia Tech University in Blacksburg; Due South BBQ in Christiansburg.

a 10-foot (3-m) waterfall and 200-foot-long (61-m) waterway. Visitors can view the waterfall and reflect at a bridge made of Hokie Stone. If you're visiting the garden between 8am and 5pm on a weekday, pick up a visitors pass from the **Virginia Tech Visitor Center** (925 Prices Fork Rd., 540/231-3548, 7:30am-6pm Mon.-Fri., 8:30am-2:30pm Sat., 1pm-5pm Sun.); otherwise, you'll get a parking ticket at the garden.

Smithfield Plantation

Forty-two slaves and indentured servants constructed the house at **Smithfield Plantation** (1000 Smithfield Plantation Rd., 540/231-3947, www.historicsmithfield.org, 10am-5pm Mon.-Tues. and Thurs.-Sat., 1pm-5pm Sun.), which became the social center of the area that eventually became Blacksburg. Settlers heading west through the mountains would visit the house of William Preston before continuing their journey. Political discourse was also standard at Smithfield, where Preston hosted notable guests and formal dances.

You can visit the home at Smithfield, plus tour the gardens, grounds, and cabins on-site, to get a sense of formal Appalachian life in the late 1700s. There have been attempts in recent years to illuminate visitors on Smithfield's large slave population and the realities of slave life during that time, including the opening of an interpretive slave garden, but the bulk of Smithfield clearly focuses on Preston.

Recreation

Spectator Sports

Often a major bowl contender, the Virginia Tech Hokies football team plays at **Lane Stadium** (185 Beamer Way, 540/231-6731, www.hokiesports.com). If the Hokies are home (Thursday or Friday nights or Saturday afternoons Sept.-Nov.), it's hard to find parking and a place to eat in Blacksburg. But of all towns on or near the Appalachian Trail, Blacksburg might be the most enticing for college football fans.

Cassel Coliseum (675 Washington St. SW, www.hokiesports.com) is home to the Virginia Tech men's basketball team, which has spotty success historically but regularly plays some of the top programs in the country (Duke, North Carolina). The women's team, which also plays in Cassel, also plays stiff conference competition like Duke and Notre Dame, and they historically fare slightly better than their male counterparts.

If you want baseball, the Hokies set up shop at **English Field** (260 Duck Pond Dr., www.hokiesports.com). The softball team plays at **Tech Softball Park** (240 Beamer Way, www.hokiesports.com).

Entertainment and Events

Nightlife

Top of the Stairs (217 College Ave., 540/953-2837, www.topofthestairs.com, 3pm-2am daily, under $20) is the most popular student hangout (called TOTS by everyone) and home to the TOTS Rail, which is the drink you might make if you were moving and had to dump everything you own into a glass (vodka, rum, triple sec, bourbon, whiskey, cranberry juice, Sprite). It gets packed on weekend nights and game days. They also serve sandwiches, salads, and ribs.

Sharkey's (220 N. Main St., 540/552-2030, www.sharkeysswinganddribjoint.com, 11am-2am daily, under $30) also has wings and ribs, but the long bar is perfect for spotting up for Hokies game day, or whenever you have time to have a few beers. There's a lot of standard drink fare, but there are a few locals featured here.

PK's Bar & Grill (432 N. Main St. B, 540/552-3278, 11am-2am daily, under $25) has all the pub grub you could want, from scores of specialty pizzas to wings, wings, and more wings. But folks come here for the convivial nature: a jukebox, plenty of TVs, pool tables, darts, and lots of weekly specials. Thursday night is Tijuana Toss: Order an extra-large pizza, and when you're finished, someone will come to your table and flip a coin. If you call it right, the pizza is on the house.

Looking for a top-quality beer selection? You'll be able to session some good offerings at **Blacksburg Taphouse** (607 N. Main St., 540/552-3023, www.blacksburgtaphouse.com, 11am-10pm daily). There are loads of regional favorites and specialties here, plus burgers and other craft American food. Patio seating is available, and if you're a cigar smoker, Joe's Cigar Bar ($10) is a members-only 2nd-floor lounge that allows day visitors for a fee.

Seeking something less collegian? **622 North Restaurant and Wine Bar** (622 N. Main St., 540/951-1022, www.622north.com, 11am-2am Tues.-Fri., 10am-2am Sat.-Sun., 2pm-2am Mon., under $40 dinner, under $20 lunch, brunch) has one of the best pound-for-pound drink selections in Blacksburg, with interesting craft beer from across the country and a deep specialty cocktail list (plus wine, of course). The food is classic formal American at this sleek contemporary spot with a sofa-filled lounge area.

Performing Arts

Standing in the middle of the Virginia Tech campus, the **Moss Arts Center** (190 Alumni Mall, 540/231-5300, www.artscenter.vt.edu, 10am-5:30pm Mon.-Fri., 10am-4pm Sat. galleries and business) provides both a home for university arts programs and larger regional entertainment. Onstage at its Anne and Ellen Fife Theatre, well-known acts like Ben Folds and Bela Fleck bring crowds to their feet, while three art galleries showcase a variety of exhibits and installations. Also on-site is the Cube, a four-story experimental space for performance and installations. Its annual **Cube Fest** (Aug.) is a special music festival with public performances with a focus on music technology and sound evolution.

A Depression-era art deco structure, the **Lyric Theatre** (135 College Ave., 540/951-0604, www.thelyric.com) has always been a movie house, though its configuration has shifted with the times. After a closure from 1989 to 1996, the venue reopened and underwent full-scale renovations. Today it shows independent films daily and hosts infrequent special events like concerts and dance parties accompanying famous movie musicals. Note the comedy and tragedy masks that adorn the top of the building; the originals, which stood from 1930 to 1950, are said by some to be in the bottom of a nearby lake.

Shopping

Walkabout Outfitter (1560 S. Main St., 540/739-3263, www.walkaboutoutfitter.com, 10am-8pm Mon.-Sat., noon-6pm Sun.) is owned by an Appalachian Trail thru-hiker named Kirk, and he wants to make sure hikers have place to both shop and enjoy. There are plenty of clothes here, plus hiking gear and camping supplies. There are six locations throughout the region.

If you're hoping to fish while in the area, check out **Matt Hagan Outdoors** (1540 S. Main St. #120, 540/739-3403, www.matthaganoutdoors.com, 10am-9pm Mon.-Sat., 11am-7pm Sun.), which sells rods and reels in addition to general outdoors and hunting supplies. Owner Matt Hagan is a two-time NHRA world champion race car driver from nearby Christiansburg.

Food

The dining scene in Blacksburg reflects two things: the desires of a hungry lot of students, and the global diversity that comes to learn at Virginia Tech.

What's popular? **Preston's Restaurant** (901 Prices Fork Rd., 540/231-0120, 5pm-9pm Mon.-Thurs., 5pm-10pm Fri.-Sat., 11:30am-1:30pm Sun., under $50 dinner, under $30 brunch) offers formal dining and Sunday brunch inside the Inn at Virginia Tech. The menu focuses on farm American, from duck breast to scallops. There is daily breakfast (7am-9:30am

Mon.-Fri., 7am-10am Sat.-Sun., $13) and weekday lunch (11:30am-1:30pm Mon.-Fri., $14), both of which are buffet-style, so hungry hikers may find this a pretty good deal. Each day lunch includes a different theme, from "New York Deli Classic" to "Virginia Farm Day."

If you happen to own a spangled leather poncho, wear it to **Gaucho Brazilian Grille** (880 University City Blvd., #201, 540/922-2854, 5:30pm-9:30pm Tues.-Sat., under $40). This authentic Brazilian restaurant is a huge favorite for hearty meals like *bagual* (steak topped with a cauliflower-gorgonzola cheese sauce), *moqeuca* (shrimp and chicken stew), and *panchola* (steak with a side of pineapple and potato salad). Moreover, it has big, bold sandwiches packed with grilled ingredients and melted cheese, tapas for days, crock meals, and sweet desserts. Gaucho is very popular, so reserve if necessary, and don't be put off by not knowing Brazilian cuisine, because the servers are extra helpful at this fun place.

Strut into **Cabo Fish Taco** (117 S. Main St., 540/552-0950, 11am-10pm Sun.-Thurs., 11am-1am Fri.-Sat., under $30) while flashing a "gnarly" hand gesture, because this busy spot is close to being Sammy Hagar's favorite mountain retreat. Cabo does good interpretations of street tacos (whitefish, chicken, steak, grouper), along with fajitas, bowls, and burritos. There's plenty of margaritas and tequila-fueled cocktails here, too.

The best single bite in Blacksburg might be at **Marco and Luca** (725 University City Blvd., 540/552-0028, 10:30am-8:30pm Mon.-Sat., under $15). That bite is dumplings. Marco and Luna has a popular one to which it adds a special sauce, which is quite wonderful. They also do noodles and pork buns, but go wild on the dumplings.

The Cellar (302 N. Main St., 540/953-0651, 11am-2am daily, under $30) mixes Mediterranean favorites like pizza, pasta, and gyros with a laid-back sports bar feel. There's a six-pack store next to the Cellar, and there are a couple of nice selections in the restaurant beer list, but for the most part it's the same choices as you'll find in a standard taproom.

For a more traditional Italian experience, **Avellino's Italian Restaurant & Pizzeria** (1440 S. Main St., #110, 540/953-4040, www.avellinosrestaurant.com, 11am-9pm Sun.-Thurs., 11am-10pm Fri.-Sat., under $40) delivers with rich and heaping pasta dishes, plus pretty traditional pizza. It's like a localized, more refined Olive Garden.

Finally, the **Black Hen & Bar Blue** (126 Jackson St. NW, 540/951-3000, www.theblackhenrestaurant.com, 5pm-10pm Tues.-Sat., 11:30am-2pm Thurs.-Sat., under $50) features creative American fare with a local twist, from North Carolina Cajun swordfish to Berkshire pork chops with green tomato-bacon sauté. White brick and black leather make this a popular contemporary spot for a nice dinner.

Accommodations

$100-150

Guests give high marks to the **Inn at Virginia Tech** (901 Prices Fork Rd., 540/231-8000, www.innatvirginiatech.com, $100-180), which features double and king rooms adorned in Virginia Tech colors. Rooms also have foam and feather pillows, Wi-Fi connections, and executive work desks, and many have views of the Cumberland Mountains to the west.

Within walking distance of downtown Blacksburg, the **Main Street Inn** (205 S. Main St., 540/552-6246, www.hotelblacksburg.com, $100-150) is an affordable and accessible stay with 34 suites. The bright suites have sitting rooms with refrigerators and microwaves, plus bathrooms with granite countertops, and either king or queen beds.

Since this is a college town, you can stay at any number of chain hotels that fill up during orientation, parents weekend, graduation, and home-game weekends. Those hotels include the **Courtyard**

by Marriott (105 Southpark Dr., 540/552-5222, $120-180), the **Hilton Garden Inn** (900 Plantation Rd., 540/552-5005, $120-200), and the **Holiday Inn Express & Suites** (1020 Plantation Rd., 540/552-5636, $120-180).

$150-250

If you don't mind paying a couple of extra bucks, ★ **Clay Corner Inn** (401 Clay St. SW, 540/552-4030, www.claycorner.com, $150-200) is a gem. Its main house, built in 1929, has a queen suite called the Appalachian Room, complete with forest-chic threads and a map of the Appalachian Trail. The main house also has a relaxing living room with leather couches and a European breakfast room. Two other on-site houses provide additional accommodations with colorful walls and dramatic lighting. Clay Corner also has a spa providing reiki, yoga, meditation, and a pool. A hot entrée is served for breakfast each day, along with a standard buffet of fruit, granola, baked goods, and yogurt.

Information and Services

The **Montgomery County Regional Tourism Office** (149 College Ave., 540/951-0454) offers tourist information and a connection to organizations throughout Blacksburg and nearby Christiansburg.

Christiansburg

From Blacksburg, it's a mere 7.7-mile (12.4-km) cruise down US-460 Business east—with a minute on US-460 east thrown in—to **Christiansburg** (pop. 21,041), a primarily residential town close to I-81 that was incorporated in 1833, though it was established as a tiny settlement with taverns and rest stops in 1792. That's pretty much what it remains today. Between larger Blacksburg and Roanoke, Christiansburg is a quieter overnight stay with fun food options.

Food

Look for the big pig statue. That's when you'll know you're at **Due South BBQ** (1465 Roanoke St., 540/381-2922, www.duesouthbbq.com, 8:30am-9pm Mon.-Sat., 9:30am-8pm Sun., under $30), an off-the-avenue spot with ample seating (plus a covered outdoor area) and big hocks of pork. From local pigs by way of Salem and Smithfield, Due South heats up and serves up pork sandwiches and rib plates. Dinners like "Big Slop" include a jumbo sandwich and three sides. Due South also makes its own sauces—which can be bought in its store—that lead with loads of vinegar and brown sugar.

★ **Fatback Soul Shack** (2440 Roanoke St., 540/251-3182, 10:30am-9pm Sun.-Thurs., 10:30am-11pm Fri.-Sat., under $30) lives by a motto of "It ain't easy bein' greasy!" Here you have hush puppies, frog legs, gator, fried oysters, chicken wings, macaroni and cheese, corn on the cob, and everything else you'd find on your southern fantasy menu list. There's live music on weekends, truck beds as booths, and a breezy, friendly atmosphere. Now don't be shy, get on over there.

Accommodations

The intersection of I-81 and US-460 means plenty of short stays for long-distance drivers, so there's enough hotel to go around in Christiansburg. All are chains and include the **Quality Inn** (50 Hampton Blvd. NE, 520/505-2289, $50-100), the **Super 8** (2780 Roanoke St., 540/251-2238, $50-100), the **Holiday Inn Express** (2725 Roanoke St., 540/382-6500, $100-150), the **Homewood Suites** (2657 Roanoke St., 540/838-1742, $100-180), the **Fairfield Inn & Suites** (2659 Roanoke St., 540/381-9596, $120-180), and the **Hampton Inn** (380 Arbor Dr. NE, 540/381-5874, $120-180).

Salem

From Christiansburg, drive up US-11 north a quick 25 miles (40 km) to **Salem** (pop. 25,432), an independent city southwest of Roanoke that is in some ways an extension of Roanoke. An early settlement on US-11, founded in the early 19th century when that was the Wilderness Road and travelers sought a passage to Kentucky from the East, Salem is now another crucial location for rest and refueling.

Hikers taking a zero day can take in a ballgame in Salem. The Salem Red Sox, a minor-league affiliate of the Boston Red Sox, play at **Salem Memorial Ballpark** (1004 Texas St., 540/389-3333, www.salemsox.com). The Sox play in the Class-A advanced Carolina League.

Putting on regular events, the **Salem Civic Center** (1001 Roanoke Blvd., 540/375-3004, www.salemciviccenter.com) can seat 7,000 people. It's home to concerts by artists like Michael McDonald and Lynyrd Skynyrd.

Food

Blue Apron (210 E. Main St., 540/375-0055, www.blueapronredrooster.com, 11:30am-2pm and 5pm-9pm Tues.-Sat., under $40) and its sister bar Red Rooster are the consummate New American experiences in Salem. Salmon, roast chicken, and a foie gras from the Hudson Valley of New York are among the very fine offerings inside this brick bistro with wide windows.

Bob Rotanz and Jim "Mac" McEnerney, native New Yorkers who attended Roanoke College in Salem, decided in 1980 to open their own sub shop in town. Mac left in 1980, but Bob hung around and slowly expanded the place into a full-blown restaurant. Today, **Mac and Bob's** (316 E. Main St., 540/389-5999, www.macandbobs.com, 11am-midnight Mon.-Thurs., 11am-2am Fri., 9am-2am Sat., 10am-11pm Sun., under $40) is the heartbeat of the community and specializes in no-frills American food, plus calzones, breakfast, and a full bar.

Accommodations

If you're shut out of accommodations in Roanoke or you need a place to stay before taking on the Blue Ridge Mountains, there are several chain hotels just off I-81 in Salem. These chains include the **Comfort Suites** (100 Wildwood Rd., 540/389-7171, $60-100), the **Comfort Suites Inn at Ridgewood Farm** (2898 Keagy Rd., 540/375-4800, $80-120), the **La Quinta Inn** (140 Sheraton Dr., 540/404-9659, $80-130), the **Fairfield Inn & Suites by Marriott** (121 Sheraton Dr., 540/302-4005, $100-150), the **Hampton Inn** (450 Litchell Rd., 540/389-2424, $100-180), and the **Holiday Inn Express & Suites** (991 Russell Rd., 540/562-3229, $150-250).

VA-311: Dragon's Tooth

The "triple crown" of Virginia hiking includes McAfee Knob, Tinker Cliffs, and this hike, Dragon's Tooth. And, boy, is Dragon's Tooth the sharpest point of the crown—this hike is tough. The actual tooth in question is a monolith made of Tuscarora quartz that protrudes from the summit of Cove Mountain just a few miles west of McAfee Knob. Folks carefully, and maybe dangerously, scale the tooth to get the coolest picture ever.

Dragon's Tooth

Distance: 5.7 miles (9.2 km)
Duration: 3-4 hours
Elevation gain: 1,500 feet (457 m)
Difficulty: Strenuous
Trailhead: VA-311 0.6 mile/1 kilometer north of VA-624 (37.378760, -80.156109)

For the first part of this hike you'll be on the blue-blazed Dragon's Tooth Trail, which gets packed in the warm season, so be patient and pick up after yourself.

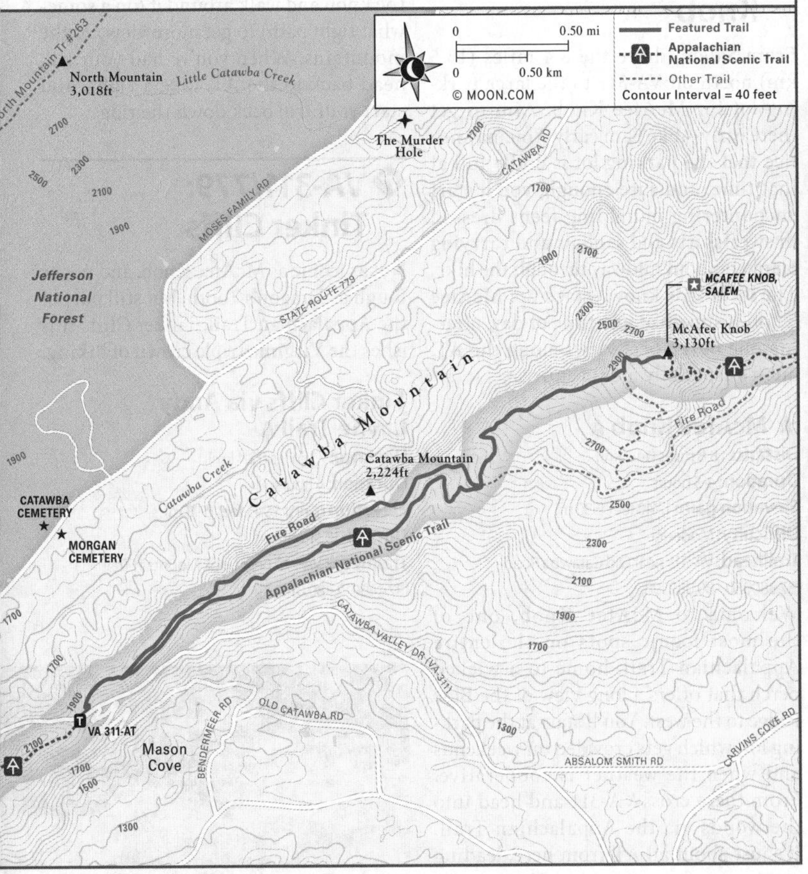

You'll soon be ascending, passing a yellow-blazed trail to the left while crossing and hiking alongside a creek. The ascent here isn't too bad, but the slope worsens once you reach the Appalachian Trail.

Heading to the right on the AT, the hike becomes a match against your nerves. You'll be nearly climbing rock, a few times confronting iron bars made to support a lift up, while finishing the steep ascent. Once at the top you'll have an easy glide to the Dragon's Tooth spur, which takes you to the quartz formation. Admire the pretty views and debate climbing the rocks.

When finished, get back onto the AT and turn right, heading north back down Cove Mountain. When the trail splits, stay with the AT and continue down for some scenic vistas. Toward the bottom you'll confront that yellow-blazed trail again; turn left to take that trail, which hooks back up with the original Dragon's Tooth Trail. Turn right onto the blue-blazed trail to reach the parking area.

VA-311: McAfee Knob

From Salem, drive the 8.4 miles (13.5 km) north on VA-311 to the large parking lot for McAfee Knob. Aim to get there early—like 5am early. You may notice that the parking lot is oddly full at that time, and sure enough, you'll start encountering mumbling teens dressed in sweatshirts and sandals and carrying blankets about midway through the hike. The local kids know what's up: McAfee Knob is superb at any time of day, offering one of the best views along the AT, but it's especially nice at sunrise.

★ McAfee Knob

Distance: 8.8 miles (14.2 km)
Duration: 4-5 hours
Elevation gain: 1,740 feet (530 m)
Difficulty: Moderate
Trailhead: VA-311 near Old Catawba Road (37.380060, -80.089398)

Welcome to McAfee Knob, one of the most iconic spots on the entire Appalachian Trail, home to a wicked perch that offers a long view of the Blue Ridge to the west. You'll start at the parking lot, which gets crowded on weekends and when the weather is cooperative. From there cross VA-311 and head into the woods via the Appalachian Trail. It's just about all AT from here, leading you to an information kiosk just 0.3 mile (0.5 km) up, then past the Johns Spring Shelter and Catawba Mountain Shelter.

The hike is a steady ascent that rides along a narrow woods path for a while, then passes a spring before turning left and heading up a bit more. After about 3.5 miles (5.6 km) you'll reach a clearing with power lines, which is how you'll know you're close. A bit farther up is the McAfee Knob Spur Trail, which you want to follow to reach the knob, where an area of wrinkled rock clears and a cliff protrudes into the sky. Folks regularly take daring photos at the cliff's edge, and some just dangle their legs. Either way, be extremely careful. You can also pass the knob and walk around it (on a somewhat tight path) to get more views of the mountains. When you've had your fill, head back to the AT, take a right, and start your trip back down the ridge.

VA-311/779: Tinker Cliffs

Not as iconic as McAfee Knob, and not as tough as Dragon's Tooth, but still part of the Appalachian Trail, Tinker Cliffs finishes the Virginia triple crown of hiking.

Tinker Cliffs via Andy Layne Trail

Distance: 7.7 miles (12.4 km)
Duration: 4 hours
Elevation gain: 1,945 feet (593 m)
Difficulty: Strenuous
Trailhead: VA-779 near Cook Mountain Trail (37.446012, -80.014278)

Take the Andy Layne Trail, marked by yellow blazes, up to the Appalachian Trail, while passing such gothic-sounding places as Scorched Earth Gap and the Murder Hole. The former is named after a hiker's vulgarity-laden response to being misdirected into a thick bushwhacking expedition, while the latter has quite a history, including the true story of a cave climber who suffered a fatal fall into the 234-foot (71-m) depression. You'll be able to see Murder Hole from a perch.

Hike from the parking area along the Andy Layne, crossing two bridges over Catawba Creek within the first mile (1.6 km). You'll soon encounter the gates of the Roanoke Cement Co., but it's OK to continue: the company allows hikers to trespass. From here you'll ascend a challenging 1.8 miles (2.9 km) of nearly 1,000 feet (305 m) before reaching the AT. Go right on the AT to Scorched Earth Gap. Continue on with awesome views of nearby Broad Run Mountain and other Jefferson National Forest peaks. After about 3.8 miles (6.1 km) you'll reach a viewing area with room to rest. When finished, turn around on the AT and follow it back to the Andy Layne, then head back to the parking area.

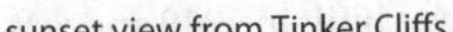

sunset view from Tinker Cliffs

Roanoke

Stay on US-1 for 7 miles (11.3 km) and you'll find yourself in **Roanoke** (pop 97,032), the major metro area in southwestern Virginia, a hub of the Blue Ridge Mountains, and the largest city within 20 miles (32 km) in either direction of the Appalachian Trail. Originally Roanoke's salt licks attracted animals like buffalo and elk, and they were so distinctive that the city's original name was Big Lick. By the 1880s that name was changed to Roanoke, and the city began to reshape itself as a railroad hub. Both the Norfolk & Western Railway and Virginian Railway ran through the city, bringing manufacturing jobs and servicing a booming bituminous coal industry.

The railroads went by the wayside, mostly, but today scores of young professionals are moving into Roanoke, bringing a renewed energy to the city. Adding to that is the diversity of the city—you'll see folks of all races and ethnicities hanging out in the same places, from breweries to markets to burger joints. This is a scrappy city where residents don't seem to be very afraid of speaking their minds and being creative. It's a fun place, one worthy of exploring regardless of if you're hiking through or staying a little while.

Getting There and Around

If you're driving to Roanoke, US-581 (connecting to I-81) runs through the center of the city, as do US-460/11 and US-220. If need a cab, the best service is **City Cab** (2817 Lansing Dr. SW, 540/815-5050).

You can get to Roanoke by air thanks to the **Roanoke-Blacksburg Regional Airport** (5202 Aviation Dr. NW, 540/362-1999, www.roanokeairport.com, ROA), which has service to eastern and midwestern hubs like Atlanta, Philadelphia, Charlotte, and Chicago via Allegiant (702/505-8888), American Airlines (800/433-7300), Delta (800/221-1212), and United (800/864-8331). Rental car companies are stationed at the airport, and there's a bus stop 150 feet (46 m) east of the terminal building for Smart Way (540/982-6622), which runs throughout the Roanoke region.

Roanoke is home to Valley Metro, which runs the **Smart Way Bus** (800/388-7005, www.smartwaybus.com, $4 one-way). Smart Way has one line that connects downtown Roanoke to Salem and Blacksburg, including a stop at Roanoke-Blacksburg Regional Airport.

Sights

★ Roanoke Star

Newcomers to Roanoke may look up at the sky and wonder where the heck that star is coming from, and what exactly it means. Well, it's the **Roanoke Star** (2000 J. B. Fishburn Pkwy., 540/853-2000, 7am-11pm daily), a brilliant piece of civic art that stands atop Mill Mountain, 1,045 feet (319 m) above sea level, and symbolizes the city's bright spirit. Actually three stars formed by 2,000 feet (610 m) of neon tubing, the star was built in 1949 and was first used to cheer up the city during the holidays. The city quickly realized the star's power goes far beyond Christmas and decided to light it up every night.

You can drive up to the base of the star by following Mill Mountain Road on switchbacks to a parking area. At night you'll be joined by locals and tourists alike, folks kissing and taking selfies, all pretty darn happy to be towering above Roanoke with the star hovering overhead. If you can't make it yourself, you can check out the **Mill Mountain StarCam** (www.roanokeva.gov) to see the view from the structure.

Center in the Square

Smack in the heart of downtown, the popular **Center in the Square** (1 Market St., 540/342-5700, 10am-5pm Tues.-Sat., 1pm-5pm Sun.) is home to four museums, a green rooftop, and an 8,000-square-foot aquarium—all in one building.

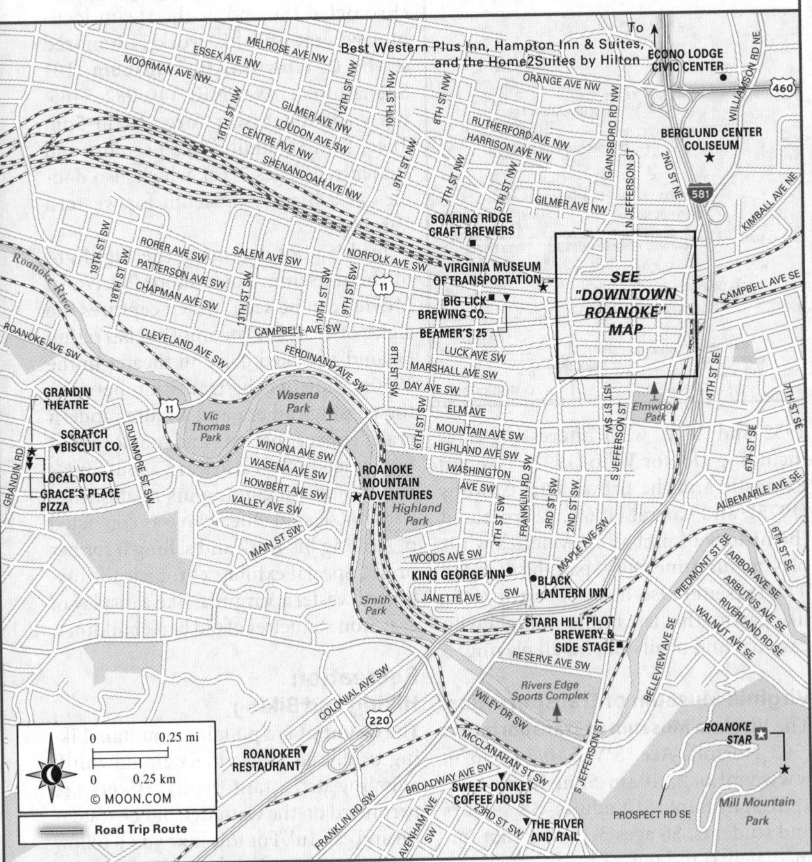

Taubman Museum of Art

Designed by the late architect Randall Stout, who was mentored by Frank Gehry, the **Taubman Museum of Art** (110 Salem Ave. SE, 540/342-5760, www.taubmanmuseum.org, 10am-5pm Wed.-Sat., noon-5pm Sun., free) is itself a work of modern art, its jagged glass piercing the sky while an extension shaped like a rocket stands next to it. The Taubman features a mix of long-term exhibits and rotating affairs. Everything from social justice and addiction to classic cars have a place at the Taubman. Its interactive space for children and family members is Art Venture ($5), which allows kids to create art and solve problems in a fun, constructive way.

Roanoke Pinball Museum

You've never been so amazed by pinball machines. The **Roanoke Pinball Museum** (One Market Sq. SE, 2nd Fl., 540/342-5746, www.roanokepinball.com, 11am-8pm Tues.-Fri., 10am-8pm Sat., 1pm-6pm Sun., $12.50 adults, $9 ages 10 and younger) opened in 2015 with more than 50 machines dated between

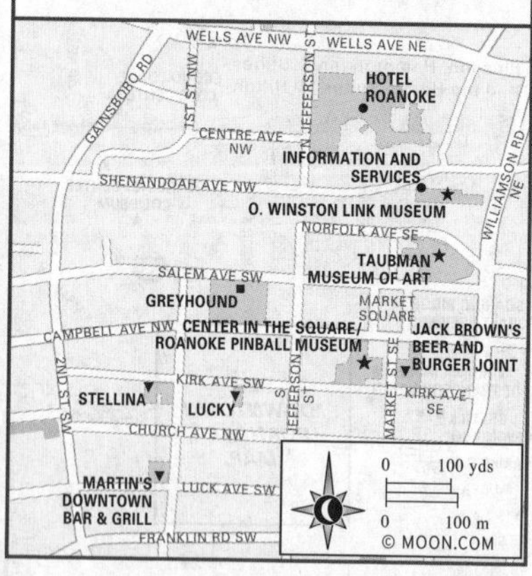

1932 and 2016, with interesting ones including Doctor Who (1992), Captain Fantastic and the Brown Dirt Cowboy (1975), and Corral (1961). Learn about the history of pinball in America while playing machines that span the decades. The museum also hosts special events, like parties that last until midnight with cash bar and plenty of pinball playing.

Virginia Museum of Transportation

The **Virginia Museum of Transportation** (303 Norfolk Ave. SW, 540/342-5670, www.vmt.org, 10am-5pm Mon.-Sat., 1pm-5pm Sun., $10 adults, $8 seniors and students, $6 ages 3-12) may not immediately stand out, as it encompasses a 45,000-square-foot brick building that once was the Norfolk & Western Railway train station. But that building houses an impressive collection of more than 2,500 objects including vintage train cars, freight trucks, and a recently rebuilt exhibit on Virginia air travel and transportation history. Outside in its rail yard the museum has a deeper collection, with the showstopper being famous steam locomotives the Norfolk & Western Class J-611 and Class A-1218.

O. Winston Link Museum

Being a rail hub, Roanoke has a robust history of train transport. O. Winston Link was one of the photographers who chronicled the end of the steam locomotive era, and his work is honored at the **O. Winston Link Museum** (101 Shenandoah Ave. NE, 540/982-5465, www.roanokehistory.org, 10am-5pm Tues.-Sat., $6 adults, $5.50 seniors and students, $5 ages 3-12), which also doubles as a history museum for western Virginia.

Link's photos remain the highlight of the museum. His famous "Drive-In Movie" can be seen, which captures the sight of a steam locomotive barreling beyond a packed drive-in theater in the 1950s, showing the transition between the passing rail era and a more modern era of convertible cars and movies about fighter jets. You'll also learn about Link's tribulations, including his relationship with his second wife, who was convicted of stealing his work and selling it for her profit. Special exhibits chronicle the history of western Virginia, like a display of cast-iron statuettes of old bank buildings.

Recreation

Hiking and Biking

The Gauntlet is a popular mountain biking trail, and most riders zip downhill enjoying its instant thrills. Hikers are permitted on the Gauntlet, but be watchful and careful. For this hike you'll follow the cyclists by going down the Gauntlet. Step lightly and never too quickly.

The Gauntlet Loop

Distance: 7 miles (11.3 km)
Duration: 3-4 hours
Elevation gain: 1,180 feet (360 m)
Difficulty: Difficult
Trailhead: Timberview parking area (3399 Timberview Road, 37.363500, -79.977628)

Start by following the easy Horse Pen Trail for a moment before turning left onto the Trough, a challenging 1.08-mile (1.7-km) trail that leads uphill to the ridge of Brushy Mountain. At the end of the Trough you'll reach an intersection with the Brushy Mountain Trail, a gentler ride on a fire road with moderate climbs and descents along the Brushy ridge. After about 2 miles (3.2 km), and after passing the Royalty Trail, you'll reach an intersection with the Hi-Dee-Hoe and Gauntlet trails. Turn right to take the Gauntlet downhill. From here it's 2 miles (3.2 km) of constant knee soreness. Watch for mountain bikers. At the base of the trail is the extremely easy Horse Pen Trail again. Turn right and walk the final 1.2 miles (1.9 km) on very little elevation until you reach the parking lot.

Parks

Spanning 13.6 miles (21.9 km), the **Roanoke River Greenway** (Bridge Street and Railroad Avenue SW) hugs the river and provides an enjoyable paved trail for walkers and cyclists. There are plenty of places to pick it up in the city, including at Wasena Park (1119 Wiley Dr. SW), Rivers Edge Sports Complex (302 Wiley Dr. SW), and Piedmont Park (Piedmont St. and Arbor Ave. SE).

Rivers Edge Sports Complex (302 Wiley Dr. SW, 540/853-2236) is one of the larger patches of green in the city, a park with two baseball diamonds, 16 tennis courts, and football and soccer fields. It's also a popular special event space.

Wasena Park (1119 Wiley Dr. SE, 540/853-2236) is on the Roanoke River providing access to the greenway, plus it has fields, pavilions, and playgrounds. Check out the truss footbridge over the river providing more parkland connection.

Elmwood Park (706 S. Jefferson St., 540/853-2236) is smack in the middle of Roanoke and has an amphitheater. In the winter Elmwood becomes an ice-skating rink.

Drive to **Mill Mountain Park** (2000 J. B. Fishburn Pkwy., 540/853-2236) and

Top to bottom: McAfee Knob overlook; the Roanoke farmers market at Center in the Square; Virginia Museum of Transportation in Roanoke.

experience a full day of Roanoke fun. The park is home to the Roanoke Star, but it's also where you can get face to face (or at least close enough) with a red panda, lynx, or Burmese python thanks to the **Mill Mountain Zoo** (540/343-3241, www.mmzoo.org, 10am-5pm daily, $9 adults, $7 ages 3-11). Also at the park is the **Discovery Center** (540/853-1236, 10am-4pm Tues.-Sat., noon-4pm Sun. April-Oct., noon-4pm Tues.-Sun. Nov.-March), which hosts educational workshops and is home to a black snake, beehive, corn snake, and box turtle. Atop Mill Mountain is a beautiful 0.5-acre wildflower garden cared for by volunteers.

The second-largest municipal park in the nation, **Carvins Cove Natural Reserve** (Carvins Cove Rd., Salem, 540/853-2236, 6am-11pm daily, $3) is a sublime 12,700 acres of hiking, water sports, cycling, and more. There are three parking lots: **Boat Dock** (9644 Reservoir Rd.), **Bennett Springs** (4300 Carvins Cove Rd., Salem), and **Timberview Road** (3399 Timberview Rd). Each offers a distinct experience. Those wanting to drop a kayak, canoe, or paddleboat into the Carvins Cove Reservoir should head to Boat Dock, which also provides access to the peaceful Happy Valley Trail; Bennett Springs is best for mountain biking (especially on the Gauntlet) and more difficult hiking trails; and Timberview has access to the easy Horse Pen Trail and the south end of the reservoir.

Water Sports

Splash Valley (7415 Wood Haven Rd., 540/777-6300, 11am-7pm Mon.-Thurs., 11am-8pm Fri., 10am-7pm weekends and holidays Memorial Day-Labor Day, $6-10) is a small city-run water park with two 34-foot (10-m) waterslides, a children's area, and a lazy river. No outside food or drink is permitted; Splash Valley has a concession stand.

Hugely popular in the summer, **Smith Mountain Lake** (1235 State Park Rd., Huddleston, 540/297-6066) is a 40-mile-long, 20,600-acre man-made pool dating to 1963 and designed to manage the flow of the Roanoke River. Smith Mountain Lake State Park borders a small chunk of the lake and hosts an amphitheater, hiking trails, and cabins. Independent boat rental operators surrounding the lake are stocked with kayaks, canoes, paddleboards, and more. Fishing for bass, catfish, crappie, and muskellunge is permitted at the lake.

Outfitters

Need a personal guide to help you explore the Blue Ridge? You can find one at **Roanoke Mountain Adventures** (806 Wasena Ave., 540/525-8295, www.roanokemountainadventures.com, 9am-5:30pm Mon.-Tues. and Thurs.-Sat., 10am-5:30pm Sun.). With an impressive facility, Roanoke Mountain Adventures has gear and clothing for hikers, cyclists, and water enthusiasts. They also do shuttles and tours, plus rentals of mountain bikes, road bikes, paddleboards, kayaks, and tubes ($12-55); call ahead if you want to reserve craft.

Entertainment and Events

Breweries

Roanoke hasn't approached Asheville's brewing status, but there's a certain adventurous spirit that percolates in the air here. There aren't many breweries in the city, but they are relatively young and hopeful about the scene's future.

Soaring Ridge Craft Brewers (523 Shenandoah Ave. NW, 540/339-9776, www.soaringridge.com, 4pm-9pm Wed.-Fri., 2pm-9pm Sat., 1pm-7pm Sun., under $20) opened in 2014 and is the first downtown brewery in the city. There's live music on the weekends at this impressively large space with televisions, picnic tables, and garage doors that open when the weather cooperates.

With its large outdoor beer garden, **Big Lick Brewing Co.** (409 Salem Ave., 540/562-8383, www.biglickbrewingco.com, 4pm-9pm Wed.-Thurs., 4pm-10pm

Fri., 1pm-10pm Sat., noon-6pm Sun., under $15) is a fun spot in the downtown. The inside is nice too: an industrial building redone with light woods and high ceiling fans. There's lots of live music, especially on the weekends, and a good variety of beer choices.

Starr Hill Brewery is based in tiny Crozet, about 100 miles (161 km) up the Blue Ridge Parkway. You can get its bottles throughout the area, but you can also stop by **Starr Hill Pilot Brewery & Side Stage** (6 Old Whitmore Ave., 540/685-2012, www.starrhill.com, 3pm-9pm Mon.-Thurs., noon-10pm Fri., 11am-10pm Sat., noon-7pm Sun., under $15), the brewery's satellite in Roanoke. The cute tasting room with twinkling lights and picnic tables hosts trivia and other live events.

Bars

I'd put money on **Stellina** (104 Kirk Ave. SW, 5pm-11:30pm Wed.-Sat., under $30) as the best bar not simply in Roanoke, but in all of western Virginia. To get there, walk into the Italian restaurant Fortunato and head toward the restrooms. Seriously. Half speakeasy, half good time had by all, Stellina is all about ambitious and lovely cocktails served in a classy, cozy wood space. Stellina can't hold too many at a time, so you may be shut out.

There's live music every night at **Martin's Downtown Bar & Grill** (413 1st St. SW, 540/985-6278, www.martinsdowntown.com, 11am-2am Mon.-Fri., 3pm-2am Sat., under $30), from bluegrass to classic rock to louder stuff. Martin's also offers a huge menu with barbecue, sandwiches, a couple kinds of mac-and-cheese, and snacks, plus a full bar with several taps.

Performing Arts

When national acts drop into Roanoke, they typically head to the **Berglund Center Coliseum** (710 Williamson Rd. NE, 540/853-2241, www.theberglundcenter.com), which hosts country stars and big-ticket children's shows. The smaller, 2,440-seat Berglund Performing Arts Theatre adjacent to the coliseum specializes in regional fare, tribute shows, and major local events. Even smaller still and in the same complex, Berglund Hall highlights small-scale acts and trade shows.

Built in the 1930s and saved over the last 20 years with a recent renovation, the nonprofit **Grandin Theatre** (1310 Grandin Rd. SW, 540/345-6177, www.grandintheatre.com) is a fine place to catch an old flick or something completely new. Indie films and documentaries are on the regular slate here, as well as a classic film series that runs monthly.

Festivals and Events

For more than 50 years, the **Roanoke Festival in the Park** (May, www.roanokefestival.com) has brought together the community during Memorial Day weekend. Dig local and national acts playing rock, bluegrass, and country at the Elmwood Park Amphitheater, while three other stages host local acts and family entertainment. There's also craft vendors, food, and kids' activities.

Food

Even if you can't grab a seat at **Jack Brown's Beer and Burger Joint** (210 Market St. SE, 540/342-0328, 11am-2am daily, under $30), order something to go. Jack Brown's is well known in the Blue Ridge as a chain with 11 locations, including its original some 115 miles (185 km) north in Harrisonburg. The packed bar with lived-in charm has more than 70 beers in bottle or can, with offerings ranging from St. Bernardus Abt 12 to Stella Artois, plus plenty of local suds. Burgers are made with wagyu beef and run the gamut of flavor combinations. I'm a sucker for the Jalapeno Popper, which is of course topped with hots and cream cheese. Giddy up.

★ **Lucky** (18 Kirk Ave. SW,

540/982-1249, www.eatlucky.com, 5pm-9pm Mon.-Wed., 5pm-11pm Thurs-Sat., under $40) is considered by many to be the class of Roanoke, serving up meticulously curated craft cocktails and southern-inspired entrees (fried chicken, rib eye) and small plates (corn dogs, terrine) under a tin ceiling with perfectly dimmed lighting. Lucky is the perfect mix of Manhattan and western Virginia.

Similar and arguably as good, **The River and Rail** (2201 Crystal Spring Ave. SW, 540/400-6830, www.riverandrailrestaurant.com, 11am-2pm and 5pm-10pm Tues.-Fri., 11am-2pm and 5pm-11pm Sat., 11am-2pm Sun., under $50 dinner, under $30 lunch, brunch) has a beautiful modern formal flair with casual patio seating, along with the standard dark-floored dining room. Menus change daily and include selections like softshell crab and beef hanger steak with Tennessee blue cheese and wild mushrooms. It's also good for craft cocktails and some "me" time with the raw bar.

In case the name **Local Roots** (1314 Grandin Rd. SW, 540/206-2610, www.localrootsrestaurant.com, 11:30am-2pm and 5pm-10pm Tues.-Sat., 11am-2:30pm and 5pm-9pm Sun., under $50 dinner, under $25 lunch, brunch) wasn't enough of a hint, this is a farm-to-table restaurant. A menu with ingredients from nearby farms changes daily, but expect dishes like Carolina bison flank steak and Virginia day-boat scallops. Wood tables and a small bar characterize this cute place where reservations are harder to attain than in other Roanoke joints.

If you want the high-ceiling, New American treatment on burgers and pizza, you have **Beamer's 25** (357 Salem Ave. SW, 540/904-6233, www.beamers25.com, 11am-10pm Sun.-Thurs., 11am-midnight Fri.-Sat., under $40). Part of the Parry Restaurant Group, which owns a dozen western Virginia restaurants, Beamer's 25 has solid burgers and big ol' Vidalia rings, plus a bunch of pie options and a decent tap list with a formidable collection of local brands.

Want to forget the New American buzzwords and industrial chic dining room? The **Roanoker Restaurant** (2522 Colonial Ave. SW, 540/344-7746, www.theroanokerrestaurant.com, 7am-9pm Tues.-Sat., 8am-9pm Sun., under $30) is without pretense. A longtime city staple, the Roanoker cooks Virginia favorites like country ham and red-eye gravy in a diner-style setting. Service is good, and you're sure to be full afterward.

Good Cuban food in Roanoke? Heck yeah. Head to **Cuban Island Restaurant** (3150 Williamson Rd., 540/529-7762, 11am-8:30pm Tues.-Sat., under $20), a bright little walk-in where you can indulge in affordable dinner plates like chicken steak and fried pork or grab some Cuban tacos. The service is friendly, and you'll definitely have enough to eat. You can exercise the full belly off late at night (10pm-2am Fri.-Sat.) when the restaurant becomes a Latin dance club.

In the Grandin Village section of the city, **Grace's Place Pizza** (1316 Grandin Rd., 540/981-1340, www.gracesplacepizzeria.com, 11am-9pm Sun.-Thurs., 11am-10pm Fri.-Sat., under $25) is arguably the best pizza in Roanoke. Slices are cheesy and packed without falling apart, while those hankering for something else can find pasta, sandwiches, and other pizza-shop fare.

You'll be standing in a nice little line to order your meal at **Scratch Biscuit Company** (1820 Memorial Ave. SW, 540/855-0882, www.scratchbiscuit.com, 6am-1pm Mon.-Fri., 7am-2pm Sat., 10am-2pm Sun., under $15), which breaks up its body-warming biscuit menu items by price. You can get the $2 Sling Blade (mustard on a biscuit) or the $4 Bless Your Heart (biscuit with fried green tomato topped with bacon and chipotle). There's coffee and a fast-food-style seating section.

Sweet Donkey Coffee House (2108

Broadway Ave. SW, 540/491-0004, www.sweetdonkeycoffee.com, 6am-9pm Mon.-Fri., 7am-9pm Sat., 7am-7pm Sun., under $15) is just that … no, not a sweet donkey, but a house. Walk into this old three-story brick building and find budding writers and students, young families, and locals grabbing to-go cups after invigorating workouts. There's plenty of seating both downstairs and up, plus a patio and yard space. Food offerings include waffles and quiches, while the coffee is highly beloved.

Accommodations

Under $100

The better discount chains in Roanoke include the **Econo Lodge Civic Center** (308 Orange Ave. NE, 540/343-2413, $50-80), the **Quality Inn Roanoke Airport** (6626 Thirlane Road NW, 540/366-8861, $50-80), and the **Motel 6** (6621 Thirlane Rd. NW, 540/265-2600, $50-80).

$100-150

Good chains at this price point are northwest of downtown in the Valley View Mall area. They include the **Hampton Inn & Suites Roanoke Airport** (5033 Valley View Blvd. NW, 540/366-6300, $110-150), **the Home2Suites by Hilton** (4830 Valley View Blvd. NW, 581/581-1000, $110-150), and the **Best Western Plus Inn at Valley View** (5050 Valley View Blvd. NW, 540/362-2400, $110-150).

$150-250

Enjoy local chocolate and wine while settling into a room at the ★ **Black Lantern Inn** (1526 Franklin Rd. SW, 540/206-3441, www.blacklanterninn.com, $140-200), a private home purchased and completely renovated by its beloved previous owner. The new owners are a couple that has traveled the world and keeps up the inn superbly. The Black Lantern has three understated rooms with king beds, including a loft space that truly feels private. A covered outdoor seating area on the property makes for a romantic dinner setting. Black Lantern is the best bet for an inn-style experience in Roanoke.

A circa 1900 Colonial Revival bed-and-breakfast, the **King George Inn** (315 King George Ave. SW, 757/675-4034, www.kinggeorgeinnbandb.com, $140-170) has four modest rooms—two queens and two kings—plus a quiet reading area and daily farm-fresh breakfast.

For an equally historical stay, but with updates thanks to a mega-chain, the **Hotel Roanoke** (110 Shenandoah Ave., 540/985-5900, $180-350) is a part of the Curio Collection of hotels by Hilton and centrally located. The Hotel Roanoke was built in 1882 as a grand, Tudor-style accommodation. It's gorgeous, as are its stately rooms with classic 1930s-inspired touches like patterned rugs and gold bathroom mirrors. The hotel also has two grand ballrooms, a fitness center, outdoor pool, and in-room spa services.

Information and Services

For more information about Roanoke, head to the **Roanoke Visitor Information Center** (101 Shenandoah Ave. NE, 540/342-6025, www.visitroanokeeva.com, 9am-5pm daily).

Peaks of Otter

From downtown Roanoke you'll want to hop on Orange Avenue heading north, also known as Alternate US-220. That will become US-460, which heads north about 6 miles (9.7 km) from Bonsack to the Blue Ridge Parkway exit. Hop off US-460 and hop on the Blue Ridge Parkway north. For the next 105 miles (169 km) you'll be cruising this iconic American road to its northern entrance outside Waynesboro.

The 469-mile (755-km) Blue Ridge Parkway conveniently lists mile markers along the way, and since this guide works its way north, the markers count down in that direction (the Parkway's southern terminus is in Cherokee, NC). Therefore, you'll be entering at Mile 105 and heading toward Mile 0.

You'll pass several overlooks upon entering the Parkway, including Mills Gap, which offers some of the most splendid sunrise and sunset views you'll get, and Pine Tree Overlook, opening to a lush James River valley backdrop. About 19 miles (31 km) up the drive you'll reach **Peaks of Otter** (MM 86), which is named for the trio of summits surrounding the area and overlooking the town of Bedford. Called Sharp Top, Flat Top, and Harkening Hill, the Peaks of Otter have been key in the westward movement of settlers. For about 8,000 years Native Americans visited the area to hunt and rest, and early European settlers came to the area in the mid- and late 1700s, soon opening inns and farmsteads to take advantage of the gorgeous scenery.

Today Peaks of Otter is a notable Blue Ridge area with campgrounds, a visitors center, and a famous lodge. There's also some good hiking in this region, of course, with opportunities to get a closer view of the summits.

Hiking

There are multiple trails in the Peaks of Otter area, each relatively short with big payoffs and some crowds during the high season.

Sharp Top Trail

Distance: 3 miles (4.8 km)
Duration: 2-2.5 hours
Elevation gain: 1,340 feet (408 m)
Difficulty: Strenuous
Trailhead: Across the Parkway from the visitor center (37.443568, -79.609404)

The most popular of the Peaks of Otter trails is this challenging little ditty that climbs more than 1,000 feet (305 m) to the summit of Sharp Top, whose stone was used in the construction of the Washington Monument. Sharp Top was once thought to be the tallest peak in Virginia (it's not even close).

You'll stick to the Sharp Top Trail for

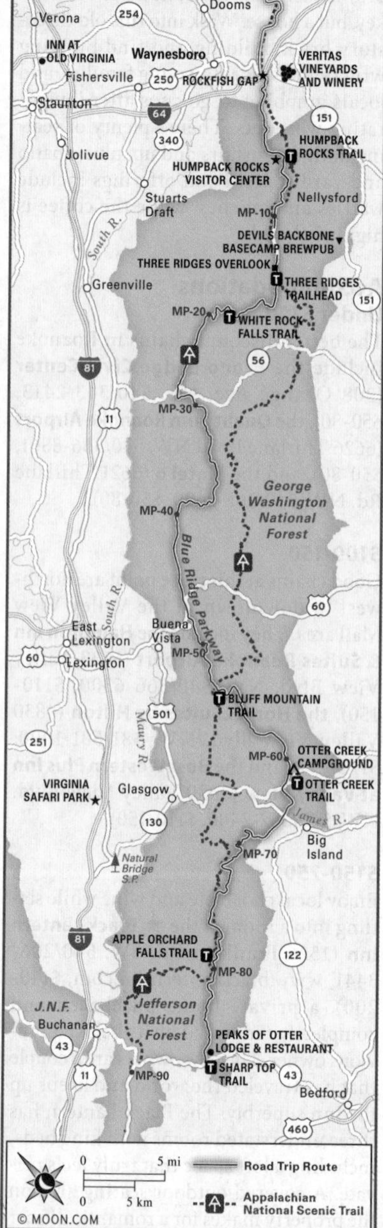

the entirety of this hike, which might be packed with tourists, especially those who aren't necessarily ready for the ascent. You'll climb on dirt, then on stairs, for about a mile (1.6 km). The hike gets a bit more strenuous in this section, as you quickly head up hundreds of feet. After 1.5 miles (2.4 km) you'll reach a cabin, which invites you to the summit. There are numerous places to view the world from the summit, and stairs will take you to each, but go for the one with the smallest crowds. One such place is Turtle Rock, accessible by scrambling a bit behind the cabin. You can continue on the trail an additional 0.2 mile (0.3 km) to reach Buzzards Roost, an area with large boulders you can scramble that are perfect for summit scouting; either way, your way back is the way you came.

Food and Accommodations

The one and only hotel on the Blue Ridge Parkway, **Peaks of Otter Lodge** (85554 Blue Ridge Pkwy., Bedford, 866/387-9905, www.peaksofotter.com, $160-250) is more affordable than you might think. All of the double and king rooms have wide windows that look out to Abbott Lake and Sharp Top, and you'll want to plan on taking in those views, because there's limited Wi-Fi access and no cell access whatsoever. Most rooms also have balconies or patios, though traditional rooms with two doubles may not.

Part of the complex, **Peaks of Otter Restaurant** (7:30-10:30am, 11:30am-3:30pm, and 4:30pm-9pm Mon.-Sat., 11:30am-3:30pm and 4:30pm-9pm Sun., under $25 lunch and dinner, under $15 breakfast and brunch) offers commanding lake views and good, traditional American for a quick sit-down bite. I'd go for the 1/2 Peaks fried chicken with cinnamon apples. When finished, jaunt around the gift shop (9am-8pm

Top to bottom: Abbott Lake and Sharp Top Mountain, one of the Peaks of Otter; lower falls, Fallingwater Cascades; Apple Orchard Falls.

Mon.-Fri., 7am-8pm Sat.-Sun.) and country store (10am-4pm Sat.-Sun. April-May, 10am-4pm daily Memorial Day-Nov.) for local wares and a souvenir sweatshirt. For hikers and campers, the **Sharp Top Store** (9am-5pm Sat.-Sun. April-May, 9am-5pm daily Memorial Day-Nov.) offers groceries, camping supplies, and cinnamon rolls. Get the cinnamon rolls.

Fallingwater Cascades

A quick 3 miles (4.8 km) up the Blue Ridge Parkway is the parking area for **Fallingwater Cascades** (MM 83.1). From here you can hike down some 360 feet (110 m) to Fallingwater Cascades, a small but easy-to-access waterfall that drops 100 feet (30 m).

Fallingwater Cascades Trail

Distance: 1.7 miles (2.7 km)
Duration: 1-1.5 hours
Elevation gain: 360 feet (110 m)
Difficulty: Moderate
Trailhead: Fallingwater Cascades parking area (37.472987, -79.580383)

Nowhere near as popular as the nearby Peaks of Otter trails and activities, Fallingwater Cascades provides a peaceful respite and some water, something you don't see right away while on the Blue Ridge. You'll start by crossing the Parkway and entering the woods on the loop trail. Turn right to head to the top of the waterfall. You'll roll alongside the Parkway for the first stretch of the hike, then separate as you head deeper into the woods. Soon you'll get to a stream crossing, which is Fallingwater Creek. A bridge gets you across (though it's not very wide) and then you'll continue down along the stream on stairs. At the bottom is a large boulder scene with the cascades falling along its face. When finished taking in the cascades, cross the creek once more and head up some stairs to ascend back to the parking area. If you wanted to, you could continue on the trail, part of the Flat Top National Recreation Trail, to get to Flat Top. Otherwise, watch for the parking area signs and head to the car.

Apple Orchard Falls

Drive another 5 miles (8 km) up the parkway and stop at **Apple Orchard Falls** (MM 78.4). Fallingwater Creek is nice, but Apple Orchard Falls is much more substantial, totaling 200 feet (61 m) and careening around boulders in such a way that you may get a spraying if you're close enough. Apple Orchard Falls is arguably the finest waterfall in Virginia, and it's absolutely worth the half-day hike to its floor and back.

Hiking

Apple Orchard Falls Trail

Distance: 5.6 miles (9 km)
Duration: 4-4.5 hours
Elevation gain: 1,680 feet (512 m)
Difficulty: Moderate
Trailhead: Apple Orchard Falls parking area (37.507802, -79.523994)

At the parking area, following the Apple Orchard Falls Trail to the left, then head right at the first intersection. Follow the trail's blue blazes up a gradually tougher ascent for about 2 miles (3.2 km), passing two campsites along the way. After 2 more miles (3.2 km) you'll meet the falls, which tumble ferociously when there's enough water, splitting at a boulder close to the bottom. The National Forest Service constructed a timber viewing platform at the falls, which is a good place to snap some photos.

From the bottom, climb stairs up to the top of the falls, where you'll reach a bridge and another waterfall. Continue on the trail another 0.6 mile (1 km) until you reach an intersection with a woods road. This is Apple Orchard Falls Road; turn right and follow it for 1 mile (1.6 km) before it forks with the blue-blazed Cornelius Creek Trail. Take the

Cornelius Creek Trail the rest of the way, heading downhill and passing a couple of swimming holes, plus more cascades and stream crossings. Beware of stinging nettles, those prickly plants that can be found in the damper low areas by the stream.

VA-130: Natural Bridge

As the Blue Ridge Parkway approaches the James River, it intersects with US-501, which runs south toward Lynchburg and north to Buena Vista. Turn left on US-501 to head north, and wind through the mountains until an intersection with VA-130, or the Wert Faulkner Highway. Turn onto the Faulkner and within 2 miles (3.2 km) you'll be in Natural Bridge, which is home to a 215-foot (66-m) high arched monster: the remains of a cave or tunnel called, well, Natural Bridge.

The community of **Natural Bridge** is a fun little excursion off the Blue Ridge, and if anything, you'll want to check out the bridge. If you have small children who want a change from the mountain overlooks, there's a great little safari park in the area.

Natural Bridge of Virginia

Eerie and awe-inspiring, Natural Bridge was called by Thomas Jefferson "the most sublime of nature's works." It was allegedly surveyed by George Washington, considered a sacred site of the Monacan tribe of Native Americans, has been depicted by painter Frederic Church, and was referenced in Herman Melville's *Moby-Dick*. There are few natural sights as incredible in all of America.

You can get up close to the 215-foot (66-m) limestone arch known as Natural Bridge through **Natural Bridge State Park** (6477 S. Lee Highway, 540/291-1326, 8am-7pm daily, $8 adults, $6 ages 6-12). The park has 6 miles (9.7 km) of hiking trails, including the **Cedar Creek Trail** (2 mi/3.2 km, easy) which includes the bridge.

Virginia Safari Park

There are a couple of ways to spot animals in Natural Bridge, and the best by far is at **Virginia Safari Park** (229 Safari Lane, 540/291-3205, www.virginiasafaripark.com, 9am-4pm Mon.-Fri., 9am-5pm Sat.-Sun., $20-25 adults, $14 ages 2-12), which offers a 180-acre drive-through experience of viewing animals in the open air. Visitors are encouraged to feed deer, llamas, and other animals with the park's specialty feed, but be ready for a good car wash afterward. There's also a walk-through area where visitors can feed giraffes, pet pigs and goats, see tigers (from a safe distance) and hang out with reptiles. An on-site café serves up pizza, ice cream, and hot dogs, and there's a gift shop with kitschy animal-themed gifts. The best time to visit is in the morning when the animals are most active and the traffic isn't too bad.

US-501: Lynchburg

At the James River head right onto US-501 south to **Lynchburg** (pop. 80,212), the "City of Seven Hills" and a long-time center for industry and commerce in Virginia. From its railroad past when tobacco barons made a fortune off slave labor in the downtown, to its designation as capital of Virginia during the Civil War, Lynchburg has changed its profile numerous times. Since the 1970s Lynchburg has been known as the home of Liberty University, Jerry Falwell's Christian research school. As for travelers of the Appalachian Trail, Lynchburg is an early respite after about 30 miles (48 km) of the Blue Ridge Parkway.

Point of Honor

One of them, in the Daniels Hill Historic District, is **Point of Honor** (112 Cabell St., 434/455-6226, www.pointofhonor.org,

10am-4pm Mon.-Sat., noon-4pm Sun., $6 adults, $5 seniors, $4 students, $3 ages 6-17), an 1815 Federal-style house of red brick with a white balcony and porch. Point of Honor reflects the Era of Good Feelings of the early 1800s and includes more than 25,000 objects, many dating back to the Civil War and beyond. Tours are available on a first-come, first-served basis and last 45 minutes.

Food and Accommodations

There's pretty good food and drink in Lynchburg. Head to **El Jefe Taqueria Garaje** (1214 Commerce St., 434/333-4317, www.eljefetaqueriagaraje.com, 11am-10pm Sun.-Wed., 11am-1am Thurs.-Sat., under $25), one of those Parry Group restaurants along with Beamers 25, to pair a taco or two with some tequila. Nearby is **Bootleggers** (50 13th St., 434/333-4273, www.bootleggersburger.com, 4pm-10pm Mon.-Thurs., 4pm-11pm Fri., 11am-11pm Sat., 11am-9pm Sun., under $30), yet another Parry joint, which serves burgers and pub grub with craft beer and whiskey. The uber-cool **Benny Scarpetta's** (1019 Main St., 434/528-5111, www.bennysva.com, 11am-midnight Sun.-Thurs., 11am-2:30am Fri.-Sat., under $20) has a tiger mural on the wall, thin-crust pizza bigger than your head, and a boisterous college vibe.

The **Craddock Terry Hotel** (1312 Commerce St., 434/455-1500, www.craddockterryhotel.com, $150-220) is set inside an old shoe factory with exposed brick and modern touches like bright golds and double vanities. Also in the city is the **Carriage House Inn Bed and Breakfast** (404 Cabell St., 434/846-1388, www.thecarriagehouseinnbandb.com, $170-300), offering four rooms in the main house with fireplaces and clawfoot tubs peppering otherwise tepid design with one-dimensional colors and a slightly dated aesthetic. The same goes for the carriage house of the Carriage House, with rooms feeling more vintage

downtown Lynchburg at dusk

than refreshing. Hot breakfasts and massages are available here, which is great.

Otter Creek Recreation Area

At 348 miles (565 km) long, the James River is the longest in Virginia, successfully cutting through the Blue Ridge Mountains of George Washington National Forest as it flows toward the Chesapeake Bay. In the mountains, Otter Creek ambles into the James River, and this confluence is recognized by the National Parks Service at **Otter Creek Recreation Area** (MM 60.9). You'll pass Thunder Ridge Overlook and a couple of other leg stretchers before reaching Otter Creek, which is part of the lowest-elevation stretch of Parkway at about 650 feet (198 m) above sea level.

The **Otter Creek Campground** (85919 Blue Ridge Pkwy., Bedford, MM 60.9, 434/299-5125, $20) has space for 42 tents and 26 RVs. There are no showers here, but there are flush toilets and water.

Hiking

Otter Creek Trail

Distance: 7.4 miles (11.9 km)
Duration: 4 hours
Elevation gain: 640 feet (195 m)
Difficulty: Moderate
Trailhead: Otter Creek Campground (37.575895, -79.337461)

This trail hugs the Parkway as it descends to the James River, but it's a lengthy descent, so plan some time to do this hike. From the campground head south toward the James. Within the first mile (1.6 km) you'll go through two tunnels, then after another mile (1.6 km) you'll meet the Lower Otter Creek Overlook. Keep on the Otter Creek Trail and pass the Otter Creek Dam, then be careful on some concrete steps that get you across the creek. Soon you'll reach the James River Visitor Center. Awaiting you another 0.2 mile (0.3 km) ahead is Big Rocky Row, a neat series of outcrops accessible from the Appalachian Trail. Pass Big Rocky Row and you'll get to the Trail of Trees, an opportunity to view birds like broad-winged hawks and wood thrushes.

Finally you'll be at the James River and, specifically, the James River Bridge. Step up to the pedestrian bridge and cross the river. On the other side are restored, mid-19th-century locks in the river that allowed boats to travel through tough terrain. Plaques by the locks tell the story of boat travel in the 1800s. The hike ends by going up the way you came down; it's not a terribly hard ascent.

Bluff Mountain

Park off the Blue Ridge Parkway at the **Punchbowl Mountain Overlook** (MM 51.7). The Appalachian Trail crosses the road here and, once you take it south, leads to the pretty awesome summit of **Bluff Mountain**—and some spooky history.

Hiking

Bluff Mountain Trail

Distance: 3.6 miles (5.8 km)
Duration: 2.5-3 hours
Elevation gain: 1,306 feet (398 m)
Difficulty: Moderate
Trailhead: Punchbowl Mountain Overlook (37.674098, -79.334268)

From the parking area at Punchbowl, head south on the Appalachian Trail. If after 0.5 mile (0.8 km) you see a blue-blazed spur trail directing you toward Punchbowl Shelter, you're going the right way. The shelter, by the way, is a cozy covered and raised building with a picnic table—your basic AT shelter near a pond.

Continue on the AT and you'll head up to the summit of Punchbowl, not the star attraction today. You'll descend after that and then, just as quickly, begin an ascent surrounded by mountain laurel and rhododendron to the summit of Bluff Mountain. Another half mile (0.8 km) or so later and you'll reach the gorgeous peak with valley views, marked by a concrete slab that is a memorial to one Ottie Powell. Ottie was a four-year-old boy, full name Emmett Cline Powell, who got lost after straying from his school group on November 9, 1890. His body was found five months later at the exact spot of the concrete slab.

When you're finished paying respects to little Ottie, turn around and head back on the AT.

20-Minute Cliff Overlook

A leg-stretcher on the Blue Ridge, **20-Minute Cliff Overlook** (MM 19) is unique in that you're seeing the saddle view of mountains instead of a sheer horizon of mountains, which is more frequent at overlooks. But the fun of 20-Minute Overlook is the origin of its name: Residents of the valley below would know it was 20 minutes until sunset when the sun hit the cliffs of those mountains from their vantage point.

White Rock Gap

There are worthy stops between Bluff Mountain and **White Rock Gap** (MM 18.5), such as Big Spy Mountain Overlook (MM 26.4) and Bald Mountain (MM 22). But I'll focus on White Rock Gap, a parking area that offers several trails.

Hiking

The most popular trail at White Rock Gap is for White Rock Falls, a 35-foot (11-m) cascade tumbling down boulders, tucked just a mile (1.6 km) from the Blue Ridge Parkway.

White Rock Falls Trail

Distance: 5 miles (8 km)
Duration: 2.5 hours
Elevation gain: 850 feet (259 m)
Difficulty: Moderate
Trailhead: White Rock Gap parking area (MM 18.5) (37.895809, -79.044543)

You can get to the falls from either the White Rock Gap parking area or the Slacks parking area (MM 20), but give yourself a slightly more challenging hike by starting from the former. You'll look for a yellow-blazed trail at the parking area; when you spot it, head into the woods. After 1.4 miles (2.3 km) you'll cross

White Rock Creek on rocks, then ascend on switchbacks to the top of the falls, one of the prettier sights in the Blue Ridge thanks to its moss-covered boulders and jagged rock walls forming the boundary for a pool. Soon you'll reach the Parkway again at Slacks; cross into Slacks and take the blue-blazed Slacks Overlook Trail until it hits the White Rock Gap Trail. Make a right here, which after 0.5 mile (0.8 km) will get you back at the parking area.

Three Ridges Overlook

There's some false information in the name **Three Ridges Overlook** (MM 13.6). Well, it is an overlook, but you don't see three ridges from this spot. What you do get here, however, is a good full-day or two-day hike on the Appalachian Trail that requires planning and stamina.

Hiking

Three Ridges

Distance: 14.4 miles (23.2 km)
Duration: 9-10 hours
Elevation gain: 3,960 feet (1,207 m)
Difficulty: Strenuous
Trailhead: Three Ridges parking area (13.6 MM) (37.907083, -78.979412)

This is a terrific hike exploring the Three Ridges Wilderness and getting farther out from the Parkway than typical. You'll start on the AT and head south, beginning a climb of Meadow Mountain, which skirts the border of Augusta and Nelson Counties. Once at the ridge you'll descend a bit, passing a spur trail that leads to the Maupin Field Shelter, plus a few other trails that head to and surround a campground. There's more climbing from here, including Bee Mountain and the beginning of the Three Ridges. A beautiful vista awaits, depicting the clear Shenandoah Valley as it spreads for miles. Continue through woods and pass even more minor trails, including one that leads to the picturesque Chimney Rock Overlook (5.1 mi/8.2 km). At 7.1 miles (11.4 km) you'll reach the Harpers Creek Shelter on the other side of the Three Ridges; if you're breaking up the hike into two days, this is a good place to stop for the night.

After the shelter you'll cross Harpers Creek and climb to the Mau-Har Trail, a blue-blazed path that you'll take back to the trailhead. Turn right and follow the trail on a descent to Campbell Creek and another camping area. Then you'll head back uphill for a good 2 miles (3.2 km) before hitting Maupin Field Shelter once more. This means you're back at the AT, on which you'll turn left to head back to Meadow Mountain and, soon, the trailhead.

VA-56: Roseland

VA-664 appears at the Three Ridges trailhead (MM 13.6), which is also part of Reeds Gap and the Appalachian Trail. This crossing is a popular one for weary thru-hikers. During the high season, the Devil's Backbone shuttle trucks up VA-664 and picks up hikers, taking them back down the 10-minute drive to **Roseland.**

Devils Backbone Basecamp Brewpub

In Roseland, you'll find the **Devils Backbone Basecamp Brewpub** (200 Mosbys Run, 434/361-1001, www.dbbrewingcompany.com, 11:30am-9pm Mon.-Thurs., 11:30am-10pm Fri.-Sat., under $20). The stone lodge outpost of this popular brewery has 16 taps and a "test kitchen" concept regarding food, but it will gladly put some burgers on the grill for thru-hikers. Devils Backbone also has a **campground** ($20-60) on site with 25 full RV sites, 25 dry RV sites, and 25 primitive tent sites, plus a bathhouse, showers, and laundry.

After a full-night's rest, hikers can resupply for breakfast at **The Summit** (540/602-6026), the brewery's on-site café

The Brew Ridge Trail

The self-guided **Brew Ridge Trail** (www.blueridgetrail.com) includes six breweries between the Charlottesville and Roseland areas, emphasizing the comforts of a big cold drink after a long day of hiking or spending time on the water. The trail launched in 2009 and features both large and small operations.

- ♦ **Blue Mountain Barrel House** (495 Cooperative Way, Arrington, 434/263-4002)
- ♦ **Blue Mountain Brewery** (9519 Critzers Shop Road, Afton, 540/456-8020)
- ♦ **Devils Backbone Brewing Company:** (200 Mosbys Run, Roseland, 434/361-1001)
- ♦ **South Street Brewery** (106 South Street, Charlottesville, 434/293-6550)
- ♦ **Starr Hill Brewery** (5391 Three Notched Road, Crozet, 434/823-5671)
- ♦ **Wild Wolf Brewing Company** (2461 Rockfish Valley Highway, Nellysford, 434/361-0088)

that serves eggs, pancakes, breakfast burritos, and a wide variety of coffee drinks.

Humpback Rocks

Closing in on the northern end of the Blue Ridge Parkway, you'll get to the pull-off for the Humpback Gap Overlook and **Humpback Rocks Trail** (MM 6). Because of its proximity to the **Humpback Rocks Visitors Center** (MM 5.8), this is a well-traveled area where you'll encounter plenty of hikers and tourists.

Hiking

Humpback Rocks Trail

Distance: 2 miles (3.2 km)
Duration: 1 hour
Elevation gain: 750 feet (229 m)
Difficulty: Moderate
Trailhead: Humpback Gap Overlook (37.969163, -78.897476)

You're better off starting this hike from the parking area at MM 6, not the visitors center at MM 5.8, though you can start there and walk through a historic farm where a collection of 1890s timber buildings inform travelers about the cozy solitude of 19th-century Appalachian life. If you do this route may be somewhat confused; cross the Parkway and continue alongside it until you reach the parking area at MM 6. That's where most people are parking.

From the parking area, you can either take the quick way to the overlook or attempt the mile-long (1.6-km) ascent. Do the latter, though the first part of this hike is an annoying uphill slog with and past tourists who probably aren't wearing hiking gear. Soon you'll encounter some stairs, which is a nice respite from the slanted dirt road, and that'll take you to rock faces you'll have to navigate. Again, slower tourists may not be happy to maneuver these rocks, but if you're experienced, amble as you wish upwards and you'll soon find yourself on a more level trail. This is the final section, leading you to one last outcrop. That's Humpback Rocks, where folks gather to take pictures and possibly propose marriage, which I saw one morning here.

It's here you realize that nature is a shared bond, and no matter how we hike, we're all trying to feel something similar. Humpback Rocks offers 360-degree views of Shenandoah National Park, the southern Blue Ridge riding through

George Washington National Forest, and faraway valleys on both sides. It's a pretty cool perch, and it's pretty great that it's so accessible.

When finished, start a quicker journey back to the trailhead. Be careful if it's slippery.

Rockfish Gap

The Blue Ridge Parkway descends from the Humpback area, slowly depositing cars into **Rockfish Gap** (MM 0). This is the northern entrance of the Parkway and the gateway to Waynesboro, the closest city between the Blue Ridge and Shenandoah National Park.

The Appalachian Trail meets the Blue Ridge at its entrance and walks along what's now Skyline Drive—over US-64, which zips underneath—until it heads back into the woods. While here, park your butt at a picnic table at **King's Gourmet Popcorn** (130 Afton Overlook, Afton, www.kingsgourmetpopcorn.com, 9am-7pm Mon.-Thurs., 9am-8pm Fri., 8am-8pm Sat.-Sun., under $10), a funny yellow truck that makes insanely good kettle corn in a variety of flavors. King's also sells a robust collection of pork rings.

Waynesboro

It gets confusing when coming off the Blue Ridge Parkway, but immediately look for the signs for US-250 west to **Waynesboro** (pop. 21,491), an important location for Appalachian Trail thru-hikers and anyone wanting to check out either the Blue Ridge Parkway or Shenandoah National Park. Waynesboro acts as a terrific zero day for thru-hikers, as its community is extremely giving toward its random visitors.

Get to know Waynesboro at the **Waynesboro Heritage Museum** (420 W. Main St., 540/943-3943, www.waynesboroheritagefoundation.com, 9am-5pm Tues.-Sat., free), an easy way to pass the time, especially on a cold or rainy day. Easy-to-follow and pretty exhibits take visitors through the evolution of the city, from its settling to its role in a bustling manufacturing age to modern-day changes. A postcard gallery adds a dash of residential nostalgia to the experience. The museum features rotating special exhibits, as well.

Recreation

The **Waynesboro Water Trail** (www.visitwaynesboro.net) gives any kayaker an opportunity to see the town from a new vantage point. The trail begins at **Ridgeview Park** (700 S. Magnolia Ave.) as you launch your kayak into the South River. The river has novice rapids (Class II+ being the most challenging) as it flows 4 miles (6.4 km) to **Basic Park** (1405 Genicom Dr.) at the northern end of town. You can take out at numerous access points along the river, including **Constitution Park** (105 W. Main St.) and **North Park** (800 Bridge Ave.).

Fishing is allowed in the South River, but in some spots you must have a Virginia trout-fishing permit (free in trout-stocked waters June 16-Sept. 30.), which you can acquire from the **Commonwealth of Virginia's Department of Game & Inland Fisheries** (www.dgif.virginia.gov).

Owned by the appropriately named Chuck Walker, **Rockfish Gap Outfitters** (1461 E. Main St., 540/943-1461, www.rockfishgapoutfitters.com, 10am-6pm Mon.-Sat., noon-5pm Sun.) is immensely important for hikers of all stripes, especially those coming off the Blue Ridge and preparing for Shenandoah. Staff here knows everything about the area and offers suggestions and necessary contacts. Cyclists can get bikes fixed here, and those wanting to kayak or paddle can rent for the day ($35-60, reservations appreciated). Rockfish does not provide shuttle service.

Entertainment and Events

Nightlife

Basic City Beer Co. (1010 E. Main St., 540/943-1010, www.basiccitybeer.com, 3pm-10pm Tues.-Fri., noon-10pm Sat., noon-8pm Sun., under $25) is a bright and fun brewery and taproom with tons of room for live music and hanging out. Basic City brews adventurous beer and hosts live music inside its production space, where there's a few picnic tables. Pool tables and a large TV in an adjacent space are made for watching big games. Basic City partners with a food truck called Hops Kitchen, which serves craft sandwiches and sharables like pork sliders and chicken satay.

In its large bar-and-grill-style space, **Seven Arrows Brewing Company** (2508 Jefferson Hwy. 1, 540/221-6968, www.sevenarrowsbrewing.com, 11am-9pm Sun.-Mon., 11am-10pm Wed.-Thurs., 11am-11pm Fri.-Sat., under $30) is the perfect place to watch the ball game, hang with a big group, or just get a sense of the town. Seven Arrows was founded by a couple of ultra-marathoners, so you know their goal is to deliver beer that'll quench some serious thirsts. Their partner kitchen, Nobos, serves up pub bites, sandwiches, and build-your-own burgers, among other sharable foods.

For some local beer, good pub grub, and a spirited bar scene, head to **Heritage on Main Street** (309 W. Main St., 540/946-6166, www.heritageonmainstreet.com, 11am-midnight Sun.-Thurs., 11am-1am Fri.-Sat., under $30). Heritage has a big ol' menu, including chicken wings where you can split your order by flavor, plus a ton of fun appetizers and small plates, from poutine to stroganoff. There's a basic beer list with some local favorites, plus good craft cocktails, a nice stage with weekend local music, and shuffleboard.

Enjoy a glass of wine with a pristine view at **Veritas Vineyards and Winery** (151 Veritas Lane, Afton, 540/456-8000, 9:30am-5:30pm Mon.-Fri., 11am-5pm Sat.-Sun., under $40). With more than 50 acres set beneath the Blue Ridge, this family winery producing reds, whites, rosés, and sparkling wines has an impressive tasting room with leather couches and chairs, a large stone fireplace, and a truly warm décor. Better yet is the winery's wide deck and stunning Blue Ridge vistas, which can be enjoyed on Adirondack chairs. Light food is available on the weekends, and you can order a cheese plate any time. It's hard to beat this kind of wine-tasting experience east of Napa Valley, and folks know this, so get there early or on a weekday if you're interested.

Performing Arts

The stately redbrick **Wayne Theatre & Ross Performing Arts Center** (533 W. Main St., 540/943-9999, www.waynetheatre.org) is a 1926 vaudeville venue gutted by fire in 1980 and renovated recently to host live music, movies, and theater in multiple spaces. Don't expect megastars to visit the Wayne; instead, you'll see a mix of regionally famous musicians, popular musical theater runs, and plenty of movie nights, from documentaries to feel-good family flicks. A 100-seat cabaret space hosts intimate performances, while a gallery space inside the center rotates shows by local artists.

Food

Few eateries along and near the Appalachian Trail carry the reputation of **Ming Garden Buffet** (316 Federal St., 540/942-8800, www.minggardenwbo.com, 11am-10pm Tues.-Sun., under $20). Thru-hikers swear by Ming Garden's lunch and dinner buffets, which are stocked with proteins like fried chicken dishes and greasy beef, and plenty of fish, sushi, shrimp, and pastries. Ming's looks like the Google stock image for "Japanese restaurant inside a casino" with its fish tanks, koi pond (complete with a wooden walking bridge), and several televisions.

The Green Leaf Grill (415 W. Main St.,

540/949-4416, www.thegreenleafgrill.com, 11am-9pm Sun.-Thurs., 11am-10pm Fri.-Sat., under $40) jams some Cajun cooking into an otherwise American craft menu. You'll find gumbo, fried alligator, po'boys and a Bourbon Street sirloin steak (it has a honey-bourbon glaze) inside this brick-walled pseudo-bistro that the locals seem to love.

Silk Road (2040 Rosser Ave., 540/949-9097, www.silkroadcuisineva.com, 11am-10pm Sun.-Thurs., 11am-11pm Fri.-Sat., under $30) offers the usual range of sushi and sashimi, as well as a ridiculous selection of "fusion" dishes, from Thai to Chinese to hibachi. Stick to the sushi—it's pretty darn good. The cool restaurant has ice-blue lighting and a large ovular bar with plenty of televisions.

Accommodations

If you need an inexpensive bed in Waynesboro, the **Quality Inn** (640 W. Broad St., 540/942-1171, $50-100) does the trick. It's an older building but it's kempt, and it's close to anything you'd want downtown. Otherwise there are more than a handful of chain motels and hotels populating the area around US-64.

Thru-hikers can grab a free night of camping and a hot shower at the **Waynesboro Family YMCA** (648 S. Wayne Ave., 540/943-9622, www.waynesborofamilyymca.org, 5:15am-10pm Mon.-Fri., 7am-7pm Sat., noon-7pm Sun., free for thru-hikers), which also has solar chargers and poles for hammocks.

Also for hikers, **Stanimal's 328 Hostel & Shuttle Service** (1333 W. Main St., 540/290-4002, www.staminals328.com, $30-50) is owned by a thru-hiker who supplies his guests with lounge chairs (including a massage chair), sofas, Netflix, clean linens, bunks, and a full kitchen with free coffee. Stanimal's also has shuttles that cover all of Virginia, plus breakfast ($7) and dinner ($10).

For a more traditional inn experience, **Belle Hearth Bed & Breakfast** (320 S. Wayne Ave., 540/943-1910, www.bellehearth.com, $120-200) is a quiet and lovely little spot south of the downtown area. This is a Victorian B&B with floral wallpaper and linens, but in no way is it stuffy or forced. Amenities, depending on the room, include fireplaces, four-poster beds, and large antique tubs. Breakfast is served daily.

Get the luxury cabin experience at the **Iris Inn** (191 Chinquapin Dr., 540/943-1991, www.irisinn.com, $150-400, rates change by season), which offers six ultramodern cabins with fireplaces and kitchens decorated in dark woods, whites, and blacks. The Iris also has four cottages made for romantic getaways, plus various rooms in the main building with porch access. Wine lovers will enjoy the range of packages the Iris offers, like two-night weekends ($215 additional per couple) that include a light dinner, wine-tasting passes for local vineyards, and a meal at a wine festival. Three-night weekends include a day of equestrian—with wine, of course.

Information and Services

Find information on Waynesboro through the **Waynesboro Department of Tourism** (301 W. Main St., 540/942-6512, www.visitwaynesboro.net).

Wildlife in Shenandoah

Shenandoah has thousands of acres of wilderness, including pine forests and vast displays of wildflowers from geraniums and poisonous mountain laurel in the spring and early summer to goldenrods at the tail end of the growing season. Of course, the plant to know most is the pink azalea (part of the genus rhododendron), which blooms in May and colors the trails with brilliant beauty. Various other rhododendrons are found throughout the park.

You may spot, if you're lucky, coyote, bobcat, muskrat, and gray fox at Shenandoah, along with various frogs, newts, turtles, rattlesnakes, birds, and fish. But two animals in particular are of interest. First is the vulnerable Shenandoah salamander, which measures about 3-4 inches in length and can be striped or unstriped. It is found in north-facing talus slopes in forests, so don't expect to spot them when on Skyline Drive. The other animal is the Shenandoah mascot: the black bear. The NPS estimates a few hundred black bears live in the park, so the chances of spotting one aren't zero. If you do spot one, keep a safe distance (at least 50 yards); if you're too close, loudly talk and make noise at the bear, slowly move away if possible but don't turn your back on it, and make sure all food is properly disposed of. As always: leave no trace.

Shenandoah National Park

You don't need to get off the Blue Ridge Parkway, but if you do in Waynesboro, take US-250 east 5 miles (8 km) from downtown to the cacophonous intersection that includes the Parkway, US-64, and Skyline Drive. You're getting on Skyline Drive and entering **Shenandoah National Park** (www.nps.gov/shen), a 200,000-acre ribbon of deciduous wonderland flanked on either side by rolling, pastoral Appalachian hills. To the west is the Shenandoah Valley, George Washington National Forest, and the Monongahela National Forest. To the east is the Virginia Piedmont slowly resting near the Potomac River and Chesapeake Bay.

Shenandoah was established in 1935 after President Calvin Coolidge authorized the National Park Service to acquire acreage in the Appalachians for a park. The park opened in 1936 on July 4 weekend with a visit from President Franklin D. Roosevelt. Today, visitors can learn about the history of the mountains, from their first Native American settlers to their modern-day development as a tourist attraction.

Shenandoah is an accessible getaway for residents of Washington DC and Baltimore to the north and Richmond and Norfolk to the south. Hiking opportunities are plentiful, with more than 500 miles (805 km) of trails at your disposal,

and the waterfalls and vistas are splendid. The most popular way to experience Shenandoah by far is **Skyline Drive,** the 105-mile (169-km) thruway that winds south to north from Waynesboro to Front Royal; during the summer and fall it's crowded with tourists and getaway hikers. (Note that Skyline Drive is like the Blue Ridge Parkway in that stops along the drive are assigned mile markers, counting down from 105, south to north.) Meanwhile the Appalachian Trail dips and dives through the park, crossing Skyline Drive several times. Drivers are encouraged to be patient and drive slowly.

Getting There

There are four ways to enter Shenandoah National Park.

From the south I-64 is the closest interstate to Waynesboro, and you would exit at the Blue Ridge Parkway north to Skyline Drive at **Rockfish Gap** (Skyline Drive at US-250, 38.033777, -78.85902). From the north I-66 skirts the park, and you would exit at US-522 south toward Skyline Drive South into **Front Royal** (Skyline Drive at US-340, 38.905729, -78.198624).

From east and west there are two entrances. The southern of the two is at **Swift Run Gap** (MM 65.7, 22591 Spotswood Trail, Elkton, 38.366176, -78.578864). US-33 is the way into the park from both the east and west sides, and it connects to Ruckersville to the east and Harrisonburg to the west. The northern of the two east-west entrances is **Thornton Gap** (MM 31.6, Skyline Drive at US-211, 38.660959, -78.320761), which is accessible from US-211, which connects to Luray to the west and Sperryville to the east.

The closest airport to the park is **Shenandoah Valley Regional Airport** (77 Aviation Cir., Weyers Cave, 540/234-8304, www.flyshd.com, SHD), which provides connections to Washington DC and Chicago via United. Four car

Shenandoah National Park

One Day in Shenandoah National Park

Morning

What else should you do but start the day with a hike? Let's say you're starting in the Southern District; if so, drive to the **Blackrock Summit** trailhead and knock out this three-hour hike as the sun climbs above the Blue Ridge. You should have time to breakfast, so drive out of the park and head to **Staunton.** Visit **Farmhouse Kitchen & Wares** for a big egg breakfast, then clean up and head back into the park.

Afternoon

Spend the first part of the afternoon driving leisurely up **Skyline Drive.** Be sure to stop at the **Loft Mountain Wayside** to pick up snacks for your predinner hunger pangs. Stretch your legs once or twice, but make sure you stop the car at **Dark Hollow Falls** to check out this iconic waterfall. Munch on some snacks while continuing the drive north toward Front Royal and stop at **Pinnacles Overlook** to soak in one of the finest views in the park. If you have time, do the one-hour hike to get a little closer to that splendid view.

Evening

Grab some picnic grub at **Elkwallow Wayside,** then drive back toward the Central District of Shenandoah on Skyline Drive. Your destination is **Big Meadows,** where you can spread out a blanket and enjoy your dinner before lying back and gazing at the starry spectacle of the night sky. It's the perfect capper to a fulfilling day at Shenandoah.

rental companies service the airport, and you can reserve a shuttle to take you to Staunton or Waynesboro ($40-60).

Getting Around

You don't have a lot of options for getting around at Shenandoah. Skyline Drive is the only access to the entire park, and it sees heavy use between June and October. The park doesn't operate its own bus system, like some other national parks, so driving your own car is nearly the only option. If you're without a car, visit a park office, which has a list of **independent shuttle drivers** who will come to the park. Also, a **taxi service** in Front Royal or Waynesboro may head into the park to shuttle you to lodging.

If you stay at Skyland you pay additional for its **shuttle service** (877/847-1919, $40 per person).

Visiting the Park

Shenandoah gets pretty crowded in the summer and fall, though nowhere near as busy as Great Smoky Mountains National Park. Still, with one major road running through the park, you'll want to strategize the appropriate time to visit Shenandoah. Skyline Drive can be closed at times between November and April, so the best time to visit is right when spring arrives in May, plus early June before schools let out. You'll get blooming rhododendron and other spring flowers, plenty of waterfall activity, and a decidedly less crowded Skyline Drive.

You can absolutely visit in winter, and it can be simply gorgeous, but you're taking chances with snowfall at higher elevations and road conditions being less than ideal. If there are any road worries, the NPS will close sections of Skyline Drive.

Most visitors opt to stay in either Front Royal or Waynesboro, as those towns bookend the park and provide the best home bases with plenty of restaurants, accommodations, and entertainment options. I recommend Staunton, which is 14 miles (23 km) west of Waynesboro and has a quaint Main Street charm.

Park Passes and Fees

National park entry prices may seem hefty, but they go a long way. According to the National Park Service, 80 percent of all entrance fees go toward "projects that directly benefit visitors," while the remaining 20 percent goes to parks that don't charge fees (such as Great Smoky Mountains National Park).

Each vehicle is $25, and passes are good for seven consecutive days. So if you leave Shenandoah after two days, drive up to Harpers Ferry for a day, then return to Shenandoah on the fourth day, your pass is still valid. Motorcycles (with up to one passenger) are $30, also for seven consecutive days, and individuals arriving by bicycle, limousine, commercial buses not doing a tour, or taxi are $10 each. You can also buy an annual pass to Shenandoah, which includes up to three more adults, for $50.

A great deal for seniors is the lifetime senior pass, which at $80 is a one-time payment that provides entrance to all federal lands for the rest of the buyer's life. If a lifetime senior pass holder is in a vehicle, the other members of that vehicle are free visitors to the park.

Those looking to camp at Shenandoah have to pay a separate $15-20 per night, depending on the campground. Appalachian Trail thru-hikers must have a permit, which can be acquired for free at a Shenandoah visitors center.

Visitors Centers

There are two visitors centers at Shenandoah National Park. The **Harry F. Byrd Visitor Center** (Skyline Drive MM51, 9am-5pm daily March-Nov.) takes care of backcountry permits and has a bookstore, videos, restrooms, and an information desk. The **Dickey Ridge Visitor Center** (Skyline Drive MM 4.6, 9am-5pm daily Apr.-Nov.) has the same amenities as the Byrd Visitor Center, plus a cozy lounge area by a fireplace. Both centers also have cancellations for park passports. Rangers are happy to suggest hikes and activities in the park, but if lines are long at the visitor center, be courteous and don't take up too much time when seeking information.

Reservations

There are two large lodges in Shenandoah: **Big Meadows Lodge** (Skyline Drive MM 51, 877/247-9261) and **Skyland** (Skyline Drive MM 41.7, 877/247-9261). Reservations are recommended for both accommodations. You can also stay at **Lewis Mountain Cabins** (Skyline Drive MM 57.5, 877/247-9261), which has rustic cabins with private baths and outdoor grill areas. The Potomac Appalachian Trail Club oversees six primitive cabins in the park; to reserve one, call 703/242-0693.

Campgrounds will make some sites available for reservations ahead of time, but the majority of their sites can be booked on a walk-up basis.

Information and Services

You can get plenty of information from the park rangers at Shenandoah's visitors centers, who are happy to point out places to visit on their maps. Be aware that the visitors centers are constantly busy, so try to keep your conversations with rangers quick while folks wait in line behind you.

For general questions, you can call the **Shenandoah National Park information line** (540/999-3500), and when camping, call the **backcountry line** (540/999-3500, ext. 3720, Mon. and Thurs. only).

Southern District

The **Southern District of Shenandoah National Park** (Skyline Drive MM 105 to Skyline Drive MM 65.5) is the least crowded area, away from the bustle of Front Royal and home to just one campground. If you're hoping to avoid tourists and explore wilderness, the south is the way to go.

Sights

If there's a sight that epitomizes the rocky

landscape of the park's Southern District, it's **Blackrock Summit** (Skyline Drive MM 83). A popular summit accessible both from a 0.5-mile (0.8-km) walk from a parking area and a more challenging 5.3-mile (8.5-km) out-and-back hike, this spot on the Appalachian Trail includes a distinctive pile of black rocks that invites both serious backpackers and kids eager to hop around on boulders.

Hiking

Riprap-Wildcat Ridge Loop

Distance: 9.8 miles (15.8 km)
Duration: 6 hours
Elevation gain: 2,635 feet (803 m)
Difficulty: Strenuous
Trailhead: Riprap parking area (Skyline Drive MM 90, 38.177738, -78.764895)

One of the more challenging attempts in Shenandoah, the Riprap-Wildcat Ridge Loop is for the serious hiker who has a day to burn. From the Riprap parking area, hook up with the Appalachian Trail and head north until you reach the Riprap Trail. Turn left onto the Riprap and follow its blue blazes toward Chimney Rock. Flat at the top like the chimney of a caldera home, Chimney Rock is a fun formation of rocks surrounded by pines and opening to glorious views of the Blue Ridge.

Continue on Riprap downhill to a stream, into a gorge, and past a swimming hole. Take a dip if you'd like, but dry yourself quickly because there's a lot more to go. Next up is an intersection with the Wildcat Ridge Trail, which you'll take to the left. You'll head uphill and get tired on switchbacks until the trail hits the AT. Turn left here to head back toward the Riprap parking area.

Blackrock Summit

Distance: 5.3 miles (8.5 km)
Duration: 2.5-3 hours
Elevation gain: 650 feet (198 m)
Difficulty: Easy
Trailhead: Brown Gap parking area (Skyline Drive MM 83, 38.240327, -78.710460)

You can always start this hike at the Blackrock parking area, but that feels like cheating. Allow yourself some time in the woods and start this hike at the Browns Gap parking area. From here, it's a hike on the Appalachian Trail southbound toward Blackrock. It's a really nice, easy hike with extremely moderate elevation changes at the beginning and climax of the journey. And the climax is special: a collection of black rocks jutting out every which way. Amble onto whatever rock you'd like to catch a great view of the valley below.

Big Run Loop

Distance: 5.9 miles (9.5 km)
Duration: 2.5-3 hours
Elevation gain: 1,405 feet (428 m)
Difficulty: Moderate
Trailhead: Doyle's River parking area (Skyline Drive MM 81.1, 38.254260, -78.683082)

Looking for some quiet time away from the crowds? Want both sweet views and some time alone with Virginia flora? Big Run Loop has you covered. From the Doyle's River parking area head south toward Big Run Overlook, then follow the marker noting the Big Run Loop. You'll descend more than 1,000 feet (305 m) on the blue-blazed Big Run Loop Trail, along the way encountering more than a few wildflowers. After more than 2 miles (3.2 km) you'll hit an intersection with a yellow-blazed trail. Follow that yellow trail to the left, which begins a moderate climb of 1,000 feet (305 m). After the climb, hook up with the Appalachian Trail and walk it back to the Doyle's River parking area.

Recreation

Fly fishers swear by **Big Run** (Skyline Drive MM 81), the longest stream in Shenandoah. Brook trout are plentiful in early spring and late fall. In Virginia, nonresidents hoping to go freshwater fishing must purchase a **state license** ($8 for one day, up to $47 annually), while those hoping to go trout fishing between

Shenandoah National Park (Southern District)

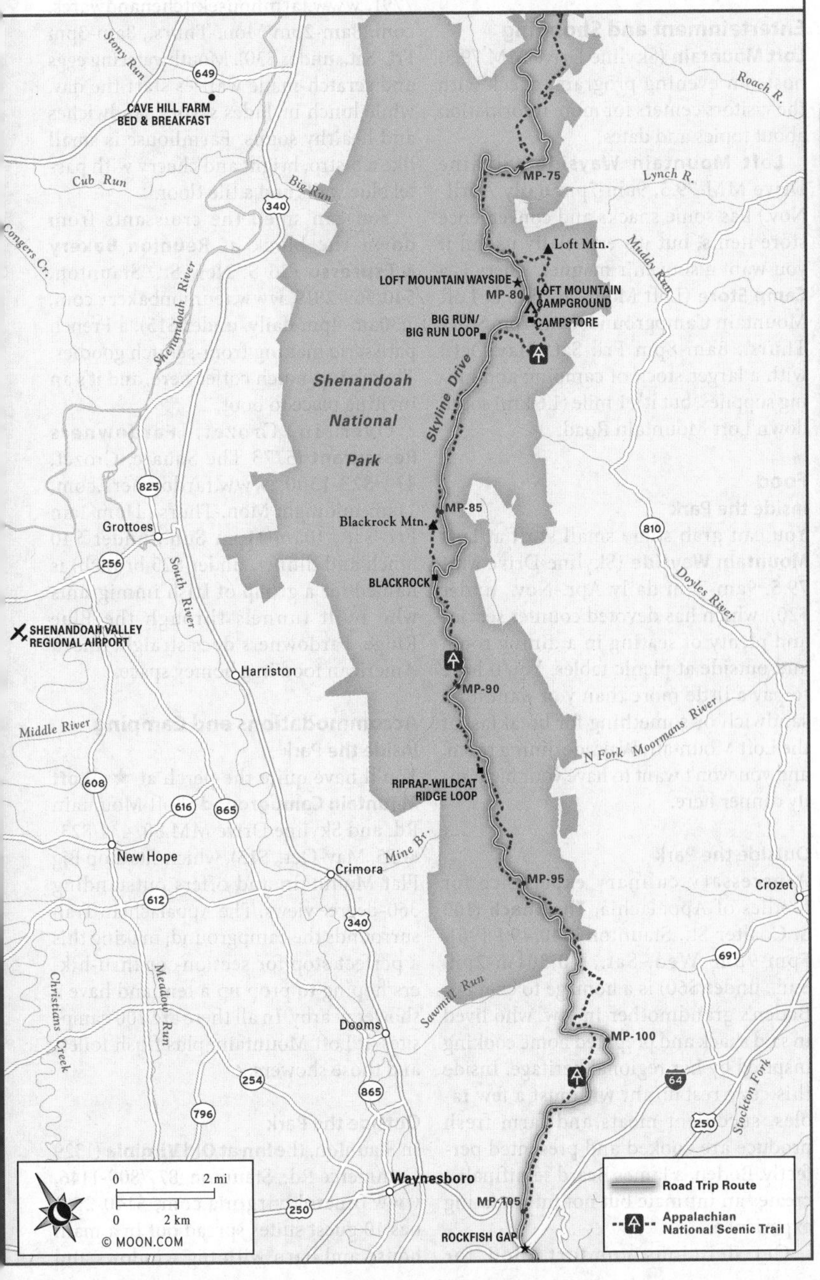

October 1 and June 15 must purchase a special **trout fishing license** ($47).

Entertainment and Shopping

Loft Mountain (Skyline Drive MM 79.5) hosts an evening program; check with the visitors centers for more information about topics and dates.

Loft Mountain Wayside (Skyline Drive MM 79.5, 9am-7pm daily April-Nov.) has some snacks and convenience store items, but it's especially useful if you want a souvenir magnet. There is a **Camp Store** (Loft Mountain Rd. at Loft Mountain Campground, 8am-7pm Sun.-Thurs., 8am-8pm Fri.-Sat. May-Oct.) with a larger stock of camping and hiking supplies, but it's 1 mile (1.6 km) south down Loft Mountain Road.

Food

Inside the Park

You can grab some small stuff at **Loft Mountain Wayside** (Skyline Drive MM 79.5, 9am-7pm daily Apr.-Nov., under $20), which has devoted counter service and plenty of seating in a dining room and outside at picnic tables. You'll have to pay a little more than you want for a sandwich or something for breakfast at the Loft Mountain Wayside dining room, and you won't want to have your big family dinner here.

Outside the Park

A necessary culinary experience for foodies of Appalachia, **The Shack** (105 S. Coalter St., Staunton, 540/490-1961, 5pm-9pm Wed.-Sat., 10:30am-2pm Sun., under $60) is a homage to chef Ian Boden's grandmother-in-law, who lived in said shack and prepared home cooking inspired by her regional heritage. Inside this cozy restaurant with just a few tables, succulent meats and farm-fresh produce are cooked and presented perfectly. Boden, a James Beard semifinalist creates an intimate but not intimidating experience.

Get delicious comfort food for breakfast at **Farmhouse Kitchen & Wares** (101 W. Beverley St., Staunton, 540/712-7791, www.farmhousekitchenandwares.com, 8am-2pm Mon.-Thurs., 8am-3pm Fri.-Sat., under $30). Mouthwatering eggs and scratch-made waffles start the day, while lunch includes savory sandwiches and healthy soups. Farmhouse is small like a bistro, bright and cheery with pastel blue walls and a tile floor.

You can smell the croissants from down the block at **Reunion Bakery & Espresso** (26 S. New St., Staunton, 540/569-2819, www.reunionbakery.com, 7:30am-4pm daily, under $15), a French patisserie making from-scratch goodies. There's top-notch coffee here, and it's an inviting place to boot.

Over in Crozet, **Fardowners Restaurant** (5773 The Square, Crozet, 434/823-1300, www.fardowners.com, 11am-midnight Mon.-Thurs., 11am-1am Fri.-Sat., 10am-11pm Sun., under $40 lunch and dinner, under $25 brunch) is named for a group of Irish immigrants who built tunnels through the Blue Ridge. Fardowners does straight-ahead American food in a homey space.

Accommodations and Camping

Inside the Park

You'll have quite the perch at ★ **Loft Mountain Campground** (Loft Mountain Rd. and Skyline Drive MM 80, 434/823-4675, May-Oct., $15), which sits atop Big Flat Mountain and offers outstanding 360-degree views. The Appalachian Trail surrounds the campground, making this a perfect stop for section- or thru-hikers hoping to prop up a tent and have a shower nearby. In all there are 200 campsites at Loft Mountain, plus flush toilets and those showers.

Outside the Park

In Staunton, the **Inn at Old Virginia** (1329 Commerce Rd., Staunton, 877/809-1146, www.innatoldvirginia.com, $140-250) has 10 guest suites spread out in a main house and barn with big windows and plenty of space. Hot daily breakfast is served inside a glass conservatory.

Also in Staunton is the historic **Stonewall Jackson Hotel** (24 S. Market St., Staunton, 540/885-4848, www.stonewalljacksonhotel.com, $130-220), built in 1924 and restored in 2005 with kings and queens. The hotel has a heated indoor pool and whirlpool, a lounge made for sipping predinner cocktails, and outdoor space to enjoy a drink with friends.

Affordable and quaint, **Cave Hill Farm Bed and Breakfast** (9875 Cave Hill Rd., McGaheysville, 540/289-7441, www.cavehillfarmbandb.com, $120-250) is set in an 1830 manor and surrounded by acreage that was once home to a vineyard and later a dairy farm. It's a little overly Victorian and antique, but Cave Hill Farm gets high marks for service and cleanliness.

Central District

The **Central District of Shenandoah National Park** (Skyline Drive MM 65.5 to Skyline Drive MM 31.6) has it all: exceptional views from overlooks, high peaks, family-friendly campgrounds and hotels, and the bulk of the park's tourism. If you only have a weekend to spend in Shenandoah, you'll get everything you need by hanging out in the Central District.

Sights

Inside the Park

Existing for more than 12,000 years, **Big Meadows** (MM 51) provides the setting for a quintessential Shenandoah experience: lying on a blanket and watching the stars at night. Multiple trails run through Big Meadows, a 136-acre area that each year is mowed, burned, and left fallow by the National Park Service as a way of maintaining and preserving

Top to bottom: Blackrock Summit; the popular Old Rag trail; Little Stony Man Cliffs from Stony Man Mountain trail.

the land. In the evenings Big Meadows is especially dramatic, with the sun coloring sprays of clouds just overhead. Once the sun sets, find a bare spot and look up to the stars for an immersive and peaceful experience.

Outside the Park

The most popular of the age-old caverns in the Shenandoah Valley, **Luray Caverns** (101 Cave Hill Rd., Luray, 540/743-6551, www.luraycaverns.com, 9am-6pm daily, $28 adults, $15 ages 6-12) is not just stalagmites and stalactites. Luray is the mall food court of tourist attractions, combining a car and carriage museum, Native American exhibits, a humongous display of model trains, and yes, those caves, for an immersive all-day experience that draws tons of tourists. Yes, this could be described as a trap, but everything at Luray Caverns is well executed, from the tours down to the cavern where formations look like miniature cities rising from floor and ceiling, to the historical documents on display at the 19th-century farming community turned museum at the site.

Hiking

Old Rag

Distance: 9.1 miles (14.6 km)
Duration: 6 hours
Elevation gain: 2,415 feet (736 m)
Difficulty: Strenuous
Trailhead: VA-600 near Rivers Song Lane (38.570783, -78.286428)

Welcome to Old Rag, the most popular single hike at Shenandoah National Park. It's also the toughest one in many ways, due to its length and intense scrambling. Be prepared for a full day out here; take plenty of water, wear sturdy shoes, and be patient with less experienced people on the trail.

Most people start outside the park in Nethers, a community 1 mile (1.6 km) east of the park, because it offers the most accessibility. From there, walk along Nethers Road back toward the park (west) until you reach the Old Rag upper parking area. Follow the blue blazes into the woods and start climbing switchbacks. After 2 miles (3.2 km) of this, the trail becomes far rockier with scramble opportunities and tight fits. Use hands and knees if necessary in this part, then emerge after another mile (1.6 km) and continue to Byrd's Nest Shelter. You'll soon also pass the Old Rag Shelter, then a pair of fire roads. Turn right onto the yellow-blazed Weakley Hollow Fire Road, which comes in at about 6 miles (9.7 km). The Weakley Hollow Fire Road leads to the upper parking area, and from there you can take Nethers Road back to the lower parking area. After more than 9 miles (14.5 km), you'll want to have a beer and air out those feet.

Dark Hollow Falls

Distance: 1.3 miles (2.1 km)
Duration: 45 minutes
Elevation gain: 425 feet (130 m)
Difficulty: Easy
Trailhead: Dark Hollow Falls parking area (Skyline Drive MM 50.7, 38.519722, -78.430897)

Eminently popular, Dark Hollow Falls isn't the best waterfall hike in the park, but people love this one because it's easy work for a nice payoff. Take the Dark Hollow Falls Trail from the parking area, following a creek that runs into Hogcamp Branch. At Hogcamp follow the trail down to the base of the upper falls. It's definitely beautiful when the water is plentiful, and especially in the fall when the leaves are strewn about. Continue down to the lower falls, where you'll see a connection to the Rose River Trail. Don't take that; instead, head back up. If you're new to Shenandoah and the type who needs to do all the popular hikes, you can take the hour for this, but otherwise you're not missing out.

Entertainment and Shopping

Events

Lewis Mountain (Skyline Drive MM 57.2) hosts a weekly evening program from its

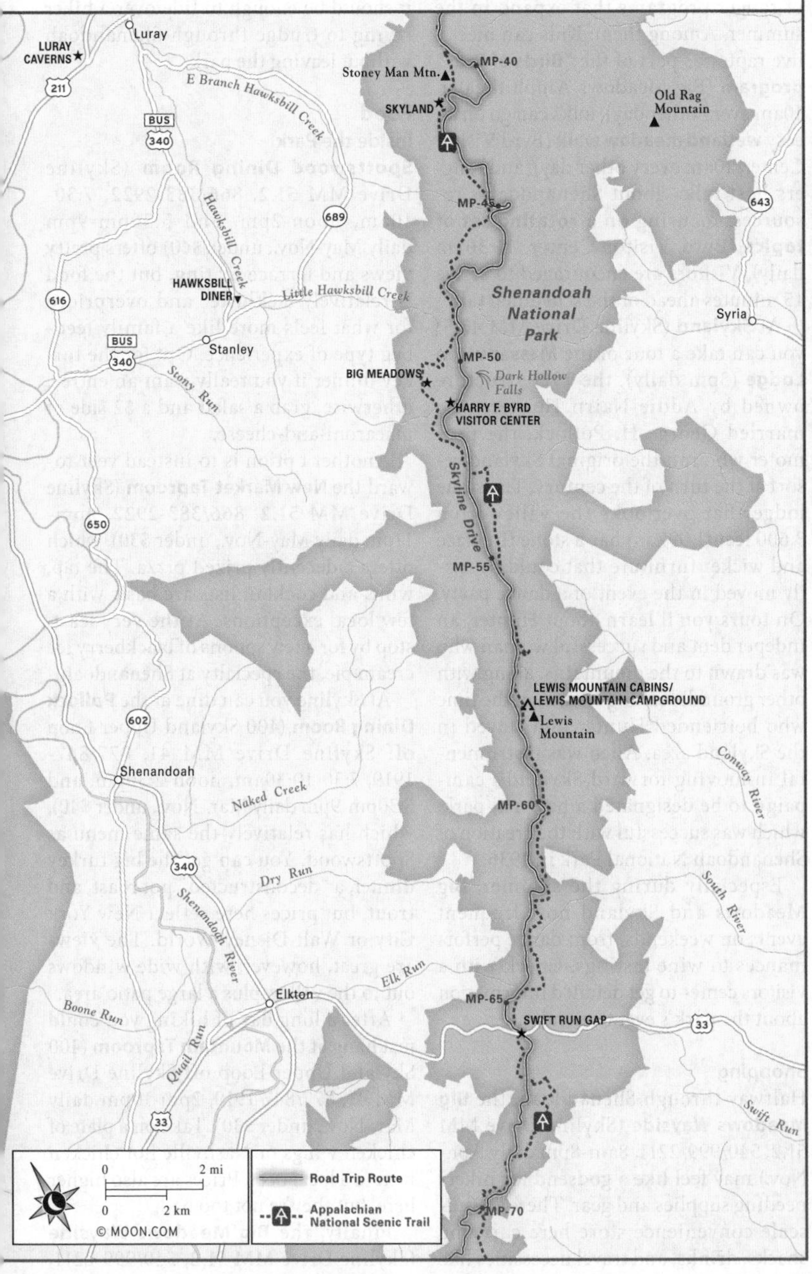
Shenandoah National Park (Central District)
Luray
LURAY CAVERNS
211
E Branch Hawksbill Creek
BUS 340
Hawksbill Creek
689
Stoney Man Mtn.
MP-40
SKYLAND
Old Rag Mountain
MP-45
643
HAWKSBILL DINER
Little Hawksbill Creek
616
Shenandoah National Park
Syria
Stanley
BUS 340
Stony Run
MP-50
BIG MEADOWS
Dark Hollow Falls
HARRY F. BYRD VISITOR CENTER
Skyline Drive
650
MP-55
LEWIS MOUNTAIN CABINS/ LEWIS MOUNTAIN CAMPGROUND
Lewis Mountain
602
Conway River
Shenandoah
Naked Creek
MP-60
340
Dry Run
Shenandoah River
South River
Elk Run
Elkton
Boone Run
MP-65
SWIFT RUN GAP
33
Quail Run
33
Swift Run
MP-70
0 2 mi
0 2 km
© MOON.COM
Road Trip Route
Appalachian National Scenic Trail

picnic grounds. At **Big Meadows** (Skyline Drive MM 51) the park features a range of ranger programs that expand in the summer. Among them: Kids can meet a live raptor as part of the **"Birds of Prey" program** (Big Meadows Amphitheater, 10am every other day), folks can go on an easy **wetland meadow walk** (Byrd Visitor Center, 10am every other day), and rangers host talks about Shenandoah's resources, focusing on a **rotating set of topics** (Byrd Visitor Center, 11:30am daily). Visitors are encouraged to arrive 15 minutes ahead of the scheduled talk.

At **Skyland** (Skyline Drive MM 42.5) you can take a tour of the **Massanutten Lodge** (3pm daily), the 1911 structure owned by Addie Nairn Hunter, who married George H. Pollock, the promoter who ran the original Skyland resort at the turn of the century. The stone lodge that overlooks the valley from 3,600 feet (1,097 m) has a stone fireplace and wicker furniture that could be easily moved in the event of a dance party. On tours you'll learn about Hunter, an independent and successful woman who was drawn to the mountains, along with other groundbreaking women of the time who befriended Hunter and stayed in the Skyland area. Allen was instrumental in moving forward Skyland's campaign to be designated a national park, which was successful with the creation of Shenandoah National Park in 1936.

Especially during the summer, Big Meadows and Skyland host frequent events on weekends, from dance performances to wine tastings. Check with a visitors center to get detailed information about the park's event calendar.

Shopping

Halfway through Shenandoah, the **Big Meadows Wayside** (Skyline Drive MM 51.2, 540/999-2211, 8am-8pm daily Apr.-Nov.) may feel like a godsend for hikers needing supplies and gear. There's a full-scale convenience store here carrying snacks, drinks, and travel necessities like sunblock and bug spray. The camp store has some gear but a lot more apparel, and it should be enough to tide over a hiker trying to trudge through Shenandoah without leaving the park.

Food

Inside the Park

Spottswood Dining Room (Skyline Drive MM 51.2, 866/383-2922, 7:30-10am, noon-2pm, and 5:30pm-9pm daily May-Nov., under $40) offers pretty views and terrace seating, but the food is relatively lackluster and overpriced for what feels more like a family feedbag type of experience. Opt for the turkey dinner if you really want an entrée; otherwise, grab a salad and a $2 side of macaroni-and-cheese.

Another option is to instead veer toward the **New Market Taproom** (Skyline Drive MM 51.2, 866/383-2922, 4pm-11pm daily May-Nov., under $30), which offers a decently prized pizza. The tap, wine, and cocktail lists are basic with a few local exceptions. At the very least, stop by for a few spoons of blackberry ice cream pie, the specialty at Shenandoah.

At Skyline you can dine at the **Pollock Dining Room** (400 Skyland Upper Loop off Skyline Drive MM 41, 877/847-1919, 7:30-10:30am, noon-2:30pm, and 5:30pm-9pm daily Mar.-Nov., under $40), which has relatively the same menu as Spottswood. You can get the big turkey dinner, a "deconstructed" pot roast, and trout, but prices here reflect New York City or Walt Disney World. The views are great, however, with wide windows out to the valley, plus a large patio area.

After a long day of hiking you could just hang at the **Mountain Taproom** (400 Skyland Upper Loop off Skyline Drive MM 41, 877/847-1919, 2pm-10pm daily Mar.-Nov., under $30). Take on a plate of chicken wings or Nashville hot chicken next to a local beer. Prices are also higher here, but they're not too bad.

Finally, the **Big Meadows Wayside** (Skyline Drive MM 51.2, 540/999-2211,

8am-8pm daily Apr.-Nov., under $20) has its own menu with eggs and pancakes for breakfast, and chili, salad, fried chicken, and other "local" favorites for lunch and dinner. Again, you're not getting meticulous and innovative here, just quick carry-out-style food made for your hungry hiker appetite. It's just fine.

Outside the Park

Skip all pretense and get some grub at **Hawksbill Diner** (1388 E. Main St., Stanley, 540/778-2006, 6am-8pm Sun.-Thurs., 6am-9pm Fri.-Sat., under $25). Big ol' portions and little dent in the wallet make this place a winner. Its friendly digs include counter seating.

A family-run business if there ever was, the small but potent **Triple Crown BBQ** (1079 US-211 West, Luray, 540/743-5311, www.shenandoahsmokehouse.com, 11:30am-6:30pm Fri.-Sun. Apr.-Nov., under $30) does Virginia-style pulled pork, smoked sausage, ribs, and smoked chicken. You may see the four Coleman children hanging around at Triple Crown, a trailer kitchen whose outdoor deck has ample seating.

Accommodations and Camping

Inside the Park

The smallest campground at Shenandoah is **Lewis Campground** (Skyline Drive MM 51.2, 540/999-3500, Mar.-Oct., $15), whose 31 sites are first come, first served. The plus side of this is Lewis is generally pretty quiet, so if you're looking for solitude, this is your place. There's a central bathhouse here, and all sites have picnic tables and fire rings.

You could hop inside at **Lewis Mountain Cabins** (Skyline Drive MM 57.5, 540/999-2255, Mar.-Nov., $40-170), which are either one- or two-bedroom domiciles with bathrooms, electric lighting, heat, ceiling fans, linens, and towels. Pets are allowed, but there's a two-per-cabin maximum.

Centrally and conveniently located, **Big Meadows Campground** (Skyline Drive MM 51.0, 540/999-3500, Mar.-Nov., $20) packs more than 200 campsites and picnic areas into its secluded, woodsy environs. Big Meadows has flush toilets, showers, and dump stations, plus a firewood vendor. The Appalachian Trail runs right behind the campground, while multiple trails are accessible from the area. Nearby are the Harry F. Byrd Visitor Center and Big Meadows Wayside general store, making Big Meadows a popular and accessible site for your Shenandoah experience.

If you want to rest in a room with windows and doors, the **Big Meadows Lodge** (Skyline Drive MM 51.0, 877/847-1919, May-Nov., $120-200) is calling your name. Wood-walled rooms have comfortable beds and standard motel amenities like a coffee maker and hair dryer, but there's no air-conditioning and no cell service. There are five two-room cabins on-site, as well, which have the same amenities plus wood-burning fireplaces.

Then there's **Skyland** (Skylands Upper Loop off Skyline Drive MM 41, 877/847-1919, Mar.-Nov., $115-365), a 20th-century imagining of George F. Pollock's vision for this in-the-clouds retreat, standing at the highest part of Skyline Drive (3,680 ft/1,122 m). Somewhere between a hotel and a woods lodge, Skyland has comfortable rooms with coffee makers and hair dryers. Suites and premium and preferred rooms have air-conditioning and televisions; cabins have just ceiling fans; and traditional rooms may have TVs and ceiling fans, but not every room does.

Outside the Park

Inexpensive and comfortable, **Luray Caverns Motel** (831 W. Main St., Luray, 540/743-5661, www.luraycaverns.com, $100-160) is perfect for families who want access to Big Meadows and Skyland plus time to hang in Luray. Rooms are suitable if a little dated, but everything is clean and kind.

Also in Luray, **Woodruff House**

Bed & Breakfast (330 Mechanic St., Luray, 540/244-7588, www.woodruffhousebandb.com, $140-170) is good for couples getaways: there's a Jacuzzi in every room, plus a hot tub on-site. Rooms are big enough and clean.

Northern District

Folks staying in Front Royal are closest to the **Northern District of Shenandoah National Park** (Skyline Drive MM 31.6 to Skyline Drive MM 0). There's certainly variety in the Northern District, from waterfalls to challenging peaks, but traffic can be heavy here during the high season.

Hiking

Little Devils Stairs

Distance: 6 miles (9.7 km)
Duration: 4 hours
Elevation gain: 1,480 feet (451 m)
Difficulty: Strenuous
Trailhead: Keyser Run Road, 2 miles/3.2 kilometers north of Pullins Bluff Road (38.730479, -78.258345)

Little Devils Stairs is a fun, semi-iconic hike in Shenandoah, notable for the way its intense scrambling can knock the wind out of you. It also has a few great waterfalls, and it's best accessed from outside of the park, so with all of these things in mind, hike Little Devils Stairs in the winter or spring. From the parking area at the end of Keyser Run Road, start to the right and head up the blue-blazed Little Devils Stairs Trail. Nearly 1 mile (1.6 km) into the hike, the trail gets tough. You'll need to scramble, and in some places really think about where those hands are going. You'll also encounter small waterfalls, so be careful about slipping on the way up. Either way, be sure to stop and appreciate the gorge around you, and how insignificant you may feel in this impressive, rocky expanse. When finished the scrambling you'll be on switchbacks until you reach the yellow-blazed Keyser Run Fire Road. Turn left and take that the rest of the way. You'll get enveloped by a hemlock forest and spot an old cemetery before heading down the steep mountain toward the parking lot.

★ Little Hogback and Hogback Mountain Loop

Distance: 7 miles (11.3 km)
Duration: 4 hours
Elevation gain: 1,200 feet (366 m)
Difficulty: Moderate
Trailhead: Hogback Trail parking area (Skyline Drive MM 20.8, 38.761467, -78.282368)

Want the perfect half-day hike at Shenandoah? This is the one, bringing you through woods to the summits of both Little Hogback and Hogback Mountains. You'll start it on the Appalachian Trail, turning left to head north. Soon you'll cross Skyline Drive (be careful, because it's relatively close to a curve), then continue until an intersection with the Piney Brook Trail. Head left on that trail, which provides some pleasing forest scenes and will a mile (1.6 km) later have you crossing the tiny Piney River. Then you'll go left on the Pole Bridge Link Trail and, 0.8 mile (0.5 km) later, left on the Keyser Fire Road. You'll cross Skyline Drive once more, then hook back up with the AT to the left. Get a load of the views from Little Hogback at this time, and from here you'll see the slope of earth between you and Hogback. You'll be going from here to there, by way of some switchbacks that cause a little strain, but keep your eyes on the prize (and the rhododendrons). Dig the views whenever possible, which show everything from expansive valley to power lines. Now descend on the AT until you cross Skyline Drive, and that's your car staring at you.

Stony Man Mountain

Distance: 3.2 miles (5.1 km)
Duration: 2.5 hours
Elevation gain: 770 feet (235 m)
Difficulty: Moderate
Trailhead: Little Stony Man Cliffs parking area (Skyline Drive MM 38.9, 38.605689, -78.366851)

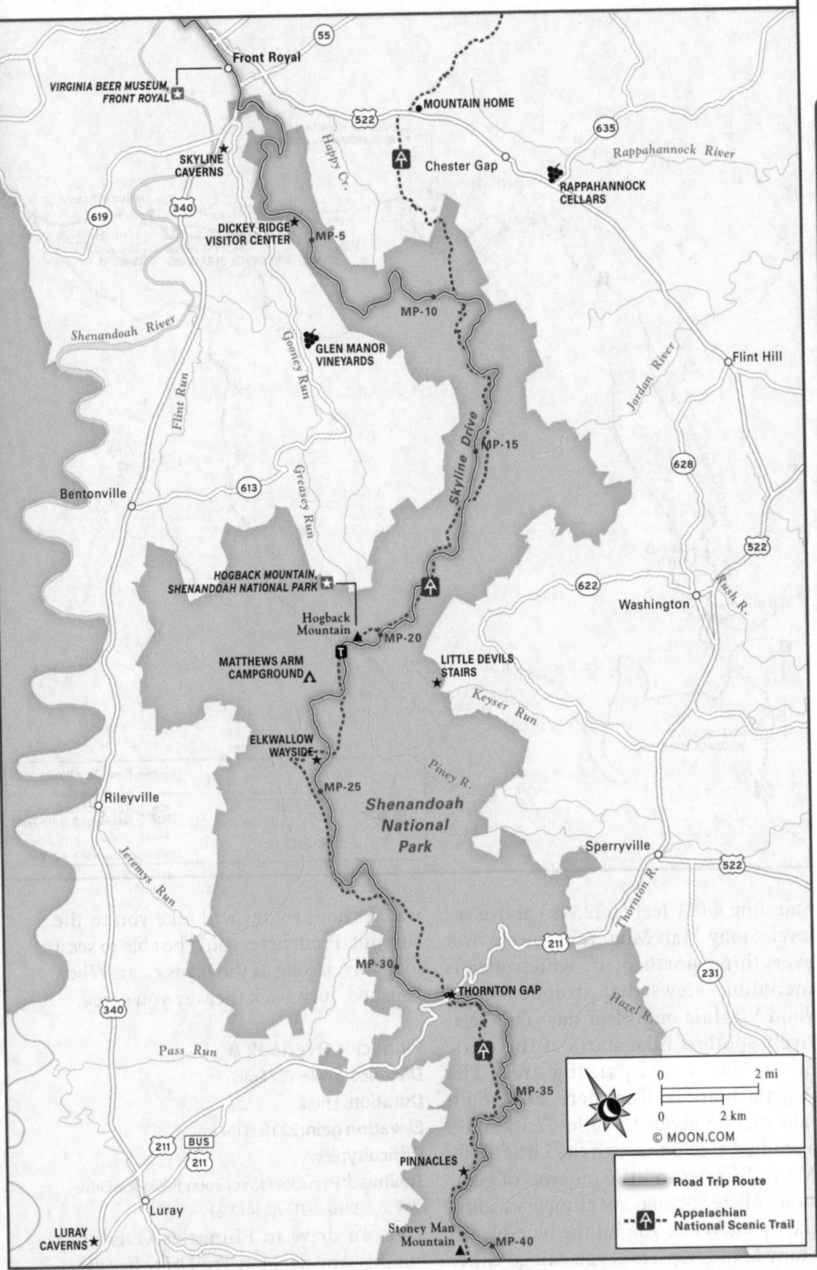
Shenandoah National Park (Northern District)
Front Royal
VIRGINIA BEER MUSEUM, FRONT ROYAL
MOUNTAIN HOME
SKYLINE CAVERNS
Happy Cr.
Chester Gap
Rappahannock River
RAPPAHANNOCK CELLARS
DICKEY RIDGE VISITOR CENTER
MP-5
MP-10
Shenandoah River
GLEN MANOR VINEYARDS
Gooney Run
Flint Run
Jordan River
Flint Hill
Skyline Drive
MP-15
Bentonville
Greasey Run
HOGBACK MOUNTAIN, SHENANDOAH NATIONAL PARK
Hogback Mountain
MP-20
Washington
Rush R.
MATTHEWS ARM CAMPGROUND
LITTLE DEVILS STAIRS
Keyser Run
ELKWALLOW WAYSIDE
Piney R.
MP-25
Rileyville
Shenandoah National Park
Sperryville
Jeremys Run
Thornton R.
MP-30
THORNTON GAP
Hazel R.
Pass Run
MP-35
PINNACLES
Stoney Man Mountain
MP-40
Luray
LURAY CAVERNS
55
522
635
619
340
613
628
622
211
231
BUS
0
2 mi
2 km
© MOON.COM
Road Trip Route
Appalachian National Scenic Trail

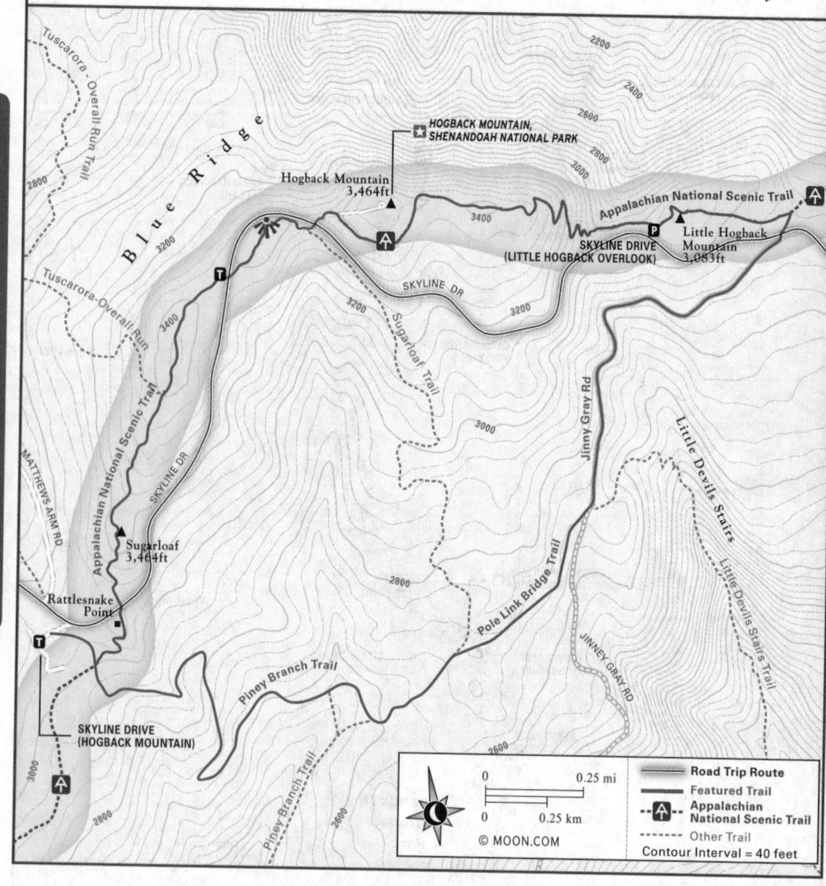

Standing 4,011 feet (1,223 m) above sea level, Stony Man Mountain towers over everything north of it, which means incredible views that stretch far beyond Virginia on a clear day. This relatively spotless hike starts at the Little Stony Man Cliffs parking area. The Appalachian Trail is there, and you'll take that for about 1.3 miles (2.1 km) on a gradual ascent through the Little Stony Man Cliffs, a fun little outcrop of gemstone where you may see climbers scaling the rocks. When you hit the blue-blazed Stony Man Loop Trail, you can go either way, as both routes will take you to the summit. From here, you'll be able to see a long way, as long as the sky is clear. When finished, turn back the way you came.

Pinnacles Overlook

Distance: 2 miles (3.2 km)
Duration: 1 hour
Elevation gain: 220 feet (67 m)
Difficulty: Easy
Trailhead: Pinnacles Picnic Grounds (Skyline Drive MM 36.7, 38.625091, -78.341085)

You can drive to Pinnacles Overlook, but this Appalachian Trail hike has great views and only takes an hour. Head toward the restrooms at the picnic grounds and start by turning left onto the AT. You'll pass two cliffs to the left, providing fabulous views of sloping mountains that look especially incredible when grown out in midsummer or decked out in the whirlwind of fall foliage. After 0.9 mile (1.4 km) the trail turns right, and you'll encounter a rock that opens to views of Old Rag. Continue another few minutes to the Corbin Cabin Parking Area, where you can turn around to complete a 2-mile (3.2-km) hike.

Entertainment and Shopping

Ranger Programs

There's a frequent educational program about bears at **Elkwallow Wayside** (Skyline Drive MM 24, 2pm daily), while the **Matthews Arm Campground** (Skyline Drive MM 22.2) hosts a weekly ranger talk about Shenandoah; topics change. Check with the visitors centers for topics and dates.

Park rangers host frequent talks about resources preserved and protected at Shenandoah (Dickey Ridge Visitor Center, Skyline Drive MM 4.6, 11am daily). Visitors are encouraged to arrive 15 minutes ahead of the scheduled talk.

Shopping

You should know about Route 11 Potato Chips. Based in Mount Jackson, which is about 30 miles (48 km) west of Shenandoah via US-211, Route 11 makes some tasty chips, including fun flavors like Chesapeake crab, dill pickle, and Mama Zuma's Revenge, a habanero-hot style sure to burn your tongue. You can find Route 11 Potato Chips at the **Elkwallow Wayside** (Skyline Drive MM 24.1, 9am-6pm Sun.-Fri., 9am-7pm Sat. Apr.-Nov.), which like the other waysides has a basic collection of foodstuffs for the

Top to bottom: Old Rag from Pinnacles Overlook; Front Royal; the Virginia Beer Museum.

car, plus a gift shop with magnets, mugs, and apparel.

Food

Inside the Park

The final wayside driving north, **Elkwallow Wayside** (Skyline Drive MM 24.1, 9am-6pm Sun.-Fri., 9am-7pm Sat. Apr.-Nov.) has sandwiches and grilled food you can pick up at the counter. There are picnic tables outside—just watch for black bears!

Accommodations and Camping

Inside the Park

The **Matthews Arm Campground** (Matthews Arm Rd. off Skyline Drive MM 22, 540/999-3132, May-Oct., $15) has more than 150 campsites for tents and RVs, plus fire rings and picnic areas, flush toilets, and drinking water. Most spots are first come, first served, and Saturdays in the summer and fall get hectic quickly. Prepare in advance for Matthews Arm.

Front Royal

Once you exit Shenandoah National Park via Skyline Drive, you'll be entering **Front Royal** (pop. 15,153), the gateway to the park once called "Helltown" because livestock wranglers and other working-class folks during the late 1700s visited the town's many taverns after a hard day's work. The drinking scene isn't what it used to be in town—officially named Front Royal in 1788 reportedly because of a famous royal oak tree in the center of the community—but it's still a popular place with some nice restaurants and a hip, outdoorsy vibe. Patagonia is a big deal here, as are bicyclists and runners taking to the streets every morning.

Sights

Warren Rifles Confederate Museum

The **Warren Rifles Confederate Museum** (95 Chester St., 540/635-3463, www.vaudc.org/museum, 9am-4pm Mon.-Sat., noon-4pm Sun. Apr.-Oct., $5, free ages 11 and younger) includes authentic items from the war, including arms, battle flags, cavalry equipment, documents, and pictures. Some of the memorabilia belonged to Confederate generals such as Robert E. Lee and Stonewall Jackson. While the bulk of the museum is a large room filled with stuff, docents at the museum are knowledgeable and connect pieces to moments in history.

Belle Boyd Cottage

Belle Boyd was a spy for the South during the Civil War, extracting information from Union soldiers and delivering it to Confederate forces. In May 1862 she relayed important news about a Union retreat to Gen. Stonewall Jackson, leading to his successful occupation of Front Royal. This feat started at a cottage her family was staying at inside the town, known today as the **Belle Boyd Cottage** (101 Chester St., 540/636-1446, 10am-4pm Mon.-Sat. Apr.-Oct., $3, free ages 10 and younger). You can visit and take a tour of the cottage, whose rooms are reproduced with authentic items from the Civil War era.

★ Virginia Beer Museum

You can drink and get an education at the whimsical **Virginia Beer Museum** (16 Chester St., 540/313-1441, 4pm-8pm Mon.-Thurs., 4pm-10pm Fri., noon-11pm Sat., noon-5pm Sun., under $20). Part taproom, part history museum, the relatively new venue is set in an old house with a porch and ample outdoor seating space. You can prop up at the old bar inside its "Hell Town Saloon" and feel like you've been dropped into a time capsule while sipping on modern Virginia beer (special stuff is shipped all the time from breweries statewide), which is always on tap. The museum has a cool collection of vintage cans, glassware, beer memorabilia, and plaques that inform about the history of the state's brewing scene. There's live music on weekends, plus special events like beer lectures and celebrations for days like Cinco de Mayo and Guy Fawkes Day, as well as the day that George Washington became a Master Mason.

Skyline Caverns

If you're going to see one cavern, Luray Caverns is probably the one you want. But if you're the kind of person that wants to see two caverns—and you're out there—then **Skyline Caverns** (10344 Stonewall Jackson Hwy., 540/635-4545, www.skylinecaverns.com, 9am-5pm Mon.-Fri., 9am-6pm Sat.-Sun. mid-Mar.-mid-June, 9am-6pm daily mid-June-Labor Day, 9am-5pm daily Labor Day-mid-Nov., 9am-4pm daily mid-Nov.-mid-March, $22 adults, $11 ages 7-13, free ages 6 and younger) is a good choice. Skyline was discovered in 1937 and opened in 1939, and has since provided folks with an opportunity to view millions-years-old formations through one-hour tours. As is customary at these caverns, there's other stuff to do, like a miniature train ($6 ages 3 and above) and a dragon mirror maze ($6 ages 5 and above).

Wineries

The Blue Ridge is overflowing with wineries, with nearly a dozen located within 20 miles (32 km) of Front Royal. One of the finest is **Rappahannock Cellars** (14437 Hume Road, Huntly, 540/635-9398, www.rappahannockcellars.com, 11:30am-5pm Sun.-Fri., 11:30am-6pm Sat., under $30), founded by a winemaker who was producing in Northern California before moving his entire family (of 12 kids) to Virginia. Tastings ARE available for all, while visitors can reserve tours of the cellar, production pad, and barrel room. Also on site is **Dida's Distillery** (11:30am-5pm Fri. and Sun.-Tues., 11:30am-6pm Sat.), which produces clear spirits and conducts tastings.

Glen Manor Vineyards (2244 Browntown Rd., 540/635-6324, www.glenmanorvineyards.com, 11am-5pm Mon. and Wed.-Sat., noon-5pm Sun., under $30) is a 17-acre swath of rolling hillside on the much larger White family farm. The vineyards were established in 1995 and grow a lot of Bordeaux varieties, which are used to produce a range of reds and whites, plus a rosé. The smaller facility is open for tastings by the glass and cozy moments.

Shopping

The staff is fun and knowledgeable at **Mountain Trails** (120 E. Main St., 540/749-2470, www.mountain-trails.com, 10am-7pm Mon.-Thurs., 10am-8pm Fri.-Sat., noon-5pm Sun.), which sells Patagonia, Kuhl, Osprey, and more.

Do you like books? Do you like cats? If you answered yes to both questions, then head to **Royal Oak Bookshop** (207 South Royal Ave., 540/635-7070, www.royaloakbookshop.com, 10am-6pm Mon.-Sat., noon-5pm Sun.), You may get dizzy looking at all the used books because the store is shaped like a horseshoe, but luckily the store has tour guides—a few cats that lounge and walk about.

Food

If there's only one place you visit in Front Royal, make it ★ **Blue Wing Frog** (219 Chester St., 540/622-6175, www.bluewingfrog.wordpress.com, 11am-9pm Mon.-Thurs., 11am-10pm Fri.-Sat., 10am-9pm Sun., under $30). Not so much a restaurant as a food place, Blue Wing Frog knows where all of its ingredients originated (it even makes its own condiments) and won't rush you to make a hasty decision. If you're just wanting some picnic food for Shenandoah, the staff will put together something amazing for you. People can't get enough of the "skrimps" (grilled shrimp), and there's a good selection of local beer and wine.

In a drive-thru burger world dominated by fast-food titans, ★ **Spelunker's** (116 South St., 540/631-0300, 11am-10pm daily, under $15) is a throwback with a lot of charm and flavor-packed food. Their burgers are juicy and fresh, their fries are crispy, and their shakes are rich and satisfying. It's some of the best "fast food" you'll ever enjoy.

Element (317 E. Main St., 540/535-1695, 11am-3pm, 5pm-9pm Tues.-Sat., under $40 dinner, under $30 lunch) is the New American joint in town, leaving room on the menu for trout, grilled pork loin, sea scallops, and ricotta gnocchi. Lunch has sandwiches, salads, and pub grub like a burger and fish-and-chips. The space feels a little more office space than warm, cozy restaurant, but the food is worth it if you want a nice dinner.

If you see the gas-station-looking property with a bunch of wood underneath the pavilion, don't just drive past thinking it's someone's weird art experiment. This is **PaveMint Taphouse and Grill** (9 S. Commerce Ave., 540/252-4707, www.pavemintaphouse.com, 11am-9pm Sun.-Thurs., 11am-10pm Fri.-Sat., under $30), a fun, funky beer joint at a converted gas station. They call their style "farm to street," showcasing street food like crab balls, queso fries, poutine, and okra poppers, but you're going to smell the smoker (the reason for all that wood) and want barbecue. Good choice. Pulled pork and brisket sandwiches are popular. There's a big tap list, cans are available, and craft cocktails are made daily.

Thanks to Satya Ben, Front Royal has acceptable Thai cuisine. **Ben's Family Cuisines** (654 W. 11th St., 540/551-3147, www.bensfamilycuisines.com, 11am-9pm Tues.-Thurs., 11am-10pm Fri.-Sat., noon-8pm Sun., under $20) has staples like pad thai and drunken noodle, and meals are cooked to order, typically by Ben herself. The family-run restaurant is unassuming, maybe a little boring inside, but the service is great and the food is roundly praised.

Grab your coffee (or tea) at **Happy Creek Coffee & Tea** (18 High St., 540/660-2133, www.happycreekcoffee.com, 7:30am-8pm Mon.-Sat., 8am-7pm Sun., under $10), an expansive, woodsy stop that brings in plenty of community folk. There's plenty of seating, including areas for kids to play around.

Accommodations

Under $100

As you enter Front Royal you'll be bombarded by cheap motor lodges extolling "great rates" and "televisions." Some of them aren't worth your time, but a few are very suitable for some quick rest before heading in or out of Shenandoah. The best include **Relax Inn** (1525 N. Shenandoah Ave., 540/635-4101, www.relaxinnfrontroyal.us, $50-80), where guests enjoy quick and smiling service; the **Royal Inn Motel** (533 S. Royal Ave., 540/636-6168, $50-80), whose rooms feel more spacious than the typical motor lodge; and the **Twi-Lite Motel** (53 W. 14th St., 540/635-4148, $50-80), which has clean rooms and a swimming pool.

Hikers appreciate the amenities provided by Lisa and thru-hiker Scott at ★ **Mountain Home** (3471 Remount Rd., 540/692-6198, $28), a "cabbin" in a renovated building measured to be 120 steps from the Appalachian Trail. Mountain Home has six beds, a bathroom, a library, and a small kitchen. Breakfast is included with your stay. Guests can also rent the entire cabin ($155). You can also park your car at the house for a small fee, and Mountain Home runs shuttles into town for its guests.

$150-250

In a beautiful 1869 Italianate lodge, **Lackawanna Bed & Breakfast** (236 Riverside Dr., 540/636-7945, www.lackawannabb.com, $150-200) has two rooms that can sleep two and one suite that can sleep up to four. The Charles Suite has a sitting room, two televisions, and an additional futon. The gems of this stay are the 40-foot-long (12-m) front porch that faces the Shenandoah River and the in-ground swimming pool. With so few accommodations here, you'll feel

Strange Happenings at Mount Weather

Standing in Bluemont, Virginia, just 23 miles (37 km) northeast of Front Royal, is Mount Weather, elevation 2,000 feet (610 m). But this isn't some hiking summit; instead, Mount Weather is an emergency operations center used primarily by the Federal Emergency Management Agency (FEMA). A bunker for government officials during the Cuban Missile Crisis, Mount Weather has been occupied by FEMA since 1979.

America first learned about Mount Weather in 1974, when TWA Flight 514 crashed near Mount Weather, killing 92 people and leaving debris across the mountain. But camera crews weren't originally allowed on the mountain, as it holds quite a few secrets. Among them:

- Mount Weather has its own leaders, emergency response officials, and laws.
- According to a 1991 *Time* magazine article, Mount Weather has its own underground complex where the president can give an address in the event of a nuclear disaster.
- Mount Weather was reportedly used as a bunker for federal officials during the September 11, 2001, attacks on America. According to one witness at the time, the mountain opened and swallowed a craft similar to Air Force One.

as if you're staying at your own private retreat.

Information and Services

The folks at the **Front Royal Town Tourism Office** (414 E. Main St., 540/635-5788, 9am-5pm daily) are helpful and can provide detailed information about what's happening in town.

Berryville

Take US-522 North to US-340 North, a 22.6-mile (36.4-km) drive in all, to get from Front Royal to **Berryville** (pop. 4,185), the seat of Clarke County and just minutes from the West Virginia border. There are a few places to eat and stay here, a good option for those wanting to step away from the summertime bustle of Front Royal.

Santorini Grill (108 S. Buckmarsh St., 540/955-8135, www.santorini-grill.com, 9am-9pm Mon.-Fri., 8am-9pm Sat.-Sun., under $30) is a favorite with the locals for its big portions of popular Greek street food like gyro and souvlaki. There's inexpensive moussaka and pastitsio here, and because why not, full breakfast daily with egg dishes, pancakes, and (an oddity outside of the mid-Atlantic) creamed chipped beef. The interior is approximate to any fast-food eatery.

You can stop at **The Berryville Grille** (9 E. Main St., 540/955-4317, www.theberryvillegrille.com, 9am-4pm Tues., 9am-9pm Wed.-Sat., 9am-8pm Sun., under $30) for a quick bite. Set in a historic 19th-century building that once was an inn, the Berryville Grille has inexpensive egg breakfasts and well-portioned country cooking, from chicken-fried steak to homemade meat loaf.

Those seeking a place to stay in Berryville should look up **Waypoint House** (211 S. Church St., 540/955-8218, www.waypointhouse.com, $125-200), run by a kind couple who own a singing cat. Waypoint has three rooms, including one that looks like a shore house bedroom with starfish, seashells, and that pastel Cape May blue. A daily home-cooked breakfast is included, as is a pretty garden with crocus, tulips, and vegetables.

Charles Town

Charles Town, which is just 13.4 miles (21.6 km) up US-340 from Berryville, was founded by Charles Washington, brother of George, in 1787. It brings the trip into West Virginia, where just 4 miles (3.2 km) of Appalachian Trail exist. The trail is 9 miles (14.5 km) east of the town, straddling the West Virginia border with Virginia in Keys Gap before creeping into Harpers Ferry. For people wanting to visit Harpers Ferry but not wishing to stay there, Charles Town is a fine option with a substantial number of spots to eat and rest.

Food and Nightlife

The 1787 Tiffin House between the oldest two sycamore trees in Charles Town is where you'll find **Paddy's** (210 W. Liberty St., 304/725-4999, 11am-11pm Mon.-Sat., 10am-9pm Sun., under $30). This is a classic half-Irish, half-sports-bar joint where you can have Irish favorites like bangers and mash, shepherd's pie, and pot-o-gold fritters (crispy potato fritters). There's a lot of seating here, including a nice patio area and a renovated bar.

A couple of brothers started **Abolitionist Ale Works** (129 W. Washington St., 681/252-1548, www.abolitionstaleworks.com, 3pm-10pm Mon.-Thurs., 3pm-midnight Fri., 11am-midnight Sat., noon-8pm Sun., under $20), which is named in honor of Charles Town's unique place in American history. A fun staff serves visitors a range of beer varieties at the narrow taproom with a long bar. The abbreviated food menu includes pizza, hummus, and pretzel rods. Outdoor seating is available.

For a good home-cooked meal, head to the very basic **Grandma's Diner** (227 W. Washington St., 304/724-9960, www.grandmasdinernc.com, 7am-3pm Mon.-Sat., 8am-2pm Sun., under $20), home of some the most inexpensive meals you'll ever enjoy in this day and age. How's a $4 hamburger? Or two eggs with toast, home fries, and a meat for $8? You can really load up here.

Mad Monks Coffee Shop (109 W. Washington St., 681/252-1239, www.madmonkscoffeeshop.com, 8am-3pm Mon.-Fri., 9am-1pm Sat., under $15) isn't just a kitschy name. Actual monks brew the coffee here. I'm talking about the Canons Regular of the New Jerusalem, who live in Charles Town and opened a coffee shop because they felt it could fulfill a need. And how: Everyone loves the coffee, and the small breakfast and lunch dishes (like egg soufflé or an apple-brie open-faced sandwich) are sublime. The homey, living room-style shop is marked by hardwood and brick.

It's hard to find authentic New York-style bagels in the Blue Ridge, but **Royalicious** (126 Patrick Henry Way, 304/728-4663, 6am-8pm Mon.-Fri., 7am-8pm Sat., 7am-4pm Sun., under $20) does a nice job. Go for breakfast and be sure to get an Italian cookie for later.

Accommodations

Those needing a quick stay can rely on **Abolitionist Ale Works** (129 W. Washington St., 681/252-1548, www.abolitionstaleworks.com, $100), which has a two-bedroom condo available for rent on the 2nd floor of its building.

There's a wealth of Civil War history at your fingertips at **Carriage Inn Bed and Breakfast** (417 E. Washington St., 304/728-8003, www.carriageinn.com, $120-250). Its Mary Rutherford Room once was the hiding spot for Stonewall Jackson's battle flag, and soldiers hid out in the attic, now the Robin's Nest Suite. Two suites have Jacuzzi tubs and every room has at least a queen bed. Breakfast is served daily in the formal dining room of this stately structure.

Pricey but fitting for a romantic getaway, ★ **Hillbrook Inn** (4490 Summit Point Rd., 304/725-4223, www.hillbrookinn.com, $200-350) sits on the very first patch of land purchased by George Washington. You can stay in the main house's gorgeous period-style rooms, where you'll feel as if you're staying in an early 19th-century story (though with completely updated amenities), or in a cottage where furniture is decidedly more vintage but still extremely tasteful. Hillbrook also has gatehouse suites, fresher and more modern accommodations that feel like home, which occupy the same building as its spa. Eggs Benedict and other brunchy breakfast items are served daily. There's also the **Redbook Restaurant** (4486 Summit Point Road, 304/728-8858, www.redbookrestaurant.com, $60-100), which specializes in gourmet and charges by the course.

Harpers Ferry

While he wasn't the first ferry owner in the lowland at the confluence of the Potomac and Shenandoah Rivers, Robert Harper was the man who purchased the land from Lord Fairfax and thus gets the name recognition today with **Harpers Ferry** (pop. 286), the historic community where the Civil War comes alive, where folks visit to bask in nature's delights, and where hikers every year feel overwhelming happiness upon arriving on its narrow streets.

Harpers Ferry is primarily a national historical park, designated as such in 1944 because of its unique significance in American history. It was the site of an important U.S. armory and arsenal, where workers manufactured more than 600,000 muskets, rifles, and pistols. In 1859 abolitionist John Brown led 21 men into Harpers Ferry to raid the arsenal in an attempt at causing a slave uprising throughout the South. He was defeated by U.S. Marines and later hanged after a guilty verdict. Harpers Ferry was also crucial during the Civil War, thanks to its strategic placement near waterways and surrounded by mountains, and both the Union and Confederacy held the town multiple times.

The historical park area of Harpers Ferry is closest to the rivers, and rangers host daily tours of the town. The Harpers Ferry Historic District includes a higher residential concentration with beautiful old homes. That area is home to the **Appalachian Trail Conservancy,** which keeps a shop and rest spot for hikers. For many thru-hikers, Harpers Ferry represents a halfway point of sorts, even if the real halfway spot on the trail is in Pine Grove Furnace State Park in Pennsylvania. Either way, Harpers Ferry is a celebrated and important community full of history and trail magic. As the "halfway" mark it is a common start or finish for flip-floppers, who split the AT into two slightly more manageable section hikes.

Getting There and Around

Staying in Washington DC, Pittsburgh, Cleveland, or Chicago? Harpers Ferry is a train ride away with **Amtrak** (Potomac and Shenandoah Sts., 800/872-7245, www.amtrak.com). Harpers Ferry is on the Capitol Limited Line, which runs from Washington DC to Chicago. A train heading west daily from Washington stops in Harpers Ferry at 5:16pm, while a train heading east daily from Chicago stops there at 11:31am.

You can also get to Harpers Ferry on **MARC** (www.mta.maryland.gov/marc-train). The commuter-friendly Brunswick Line runs through the town. The eastbound trains toward Washington DC stop in Harpers Ferry three times per day Monday-Friday (5:25am-6:50am), while the westbound trains toward Martinsburg stop five times per day Monday-Friday (after 5pm).

You can drive into Harpers Ferry and park at the train station's public lot, but once spots are taken there's really nowhere else to go, as there's no parking allowed on the streets in the Lower Town. The better bet, especially on weekends

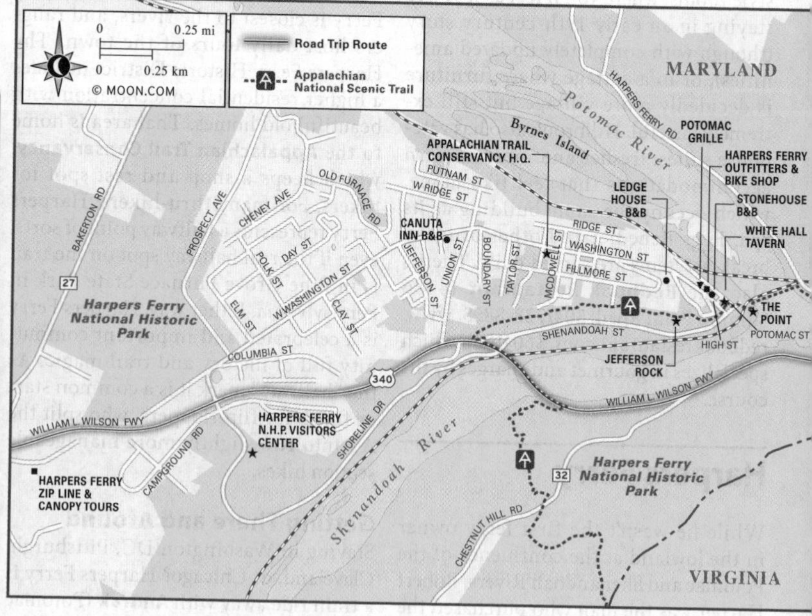

and really anytime in the summer or fall, is to park at the main parking lot at the **visitors center** (171 Shoreline Dr.) and step onto a shuttle bus (free) that gets to the Lower Town within 10 minutes. Shuttle buses run every 10 minutes from the visitors center.

Sights

The Point

The point where the Potomac and Shenandoah Rivers meet is called, appropriately enough, **The Point** (39.323016, -77.728427). A viewing area with a bench is at the Point. You can also gaze up at Maryland Heights and maybe spot some hikers looking down at you from that perch.

Jefferson Rock

"The passage of the Patowmac through the Blue Ridge is perhaps one of the most stupendous scenes in nature," wrote Thomas Jefferson in 1785. He was talking about a raised area near the Point at Harpers Ferry. A formation of Harpers shale stands at this area, and it's called **Jefferson Rock** (Appalachian Trail south from Church St., 39.322627, -77.733231). At one point a popular place to sit or stand, Jefferson Rock is now off-limits to climbers and sitters, as it's extremely unstable.

White Hall Tavern

Maybe the coolest part of the Harpers Ferry guided tour is the **White Hall Tavern** (39 Potomac St., 304/535-6029, 9am-5pm daily), which dates back to the 1830s and was a fulcrum in the community, full of boisterous politicians and high-profile visitors drinking more than their share. Today, you can get a glimpse of the preserved space.

★ Appalachian Trail Conservancy Headquarters

Technically this isn't the midpoint of

the Appalachian Trail, and that's something you'll be reminded of if you walk into the **Appalachian Trail Conservancy Headquarters** (799 Washington St., 304/535-6331, www.appalachiantrail.org, 9am-5pm daily). Still, thousands of thru-hikers annually feel jubilation upon reaching the ATC, a 15-minute walk uphill from the Point at Harpers Ferry, because it's the symbolic halfway mark for so many. After trekking the dense, remote forests of Georgia, North Carolina, Tennessee, and Virginia, the ATC is a godsend.

Inside you'll find a valuable resource, whether you're a thru-hiker or day-tripper. Pick up maps or AT-themed books, talk to staffers, and splurge on a trail gift like a pin or compass. There's also a little bit of trail memorabilia here, like an original Katahdin sign and all the thru-hiker photos you can handle. Hikers can rest up in the back, go through a gear shakedown, and write about their trail experiences in a big hikers binder.

Hiking

Four State Challenge

Whether or not you're a thru-hiker, you might want to dig in for the **Four State Challenge** (42.9 mi/69 km), a strenuous one-day hike starting in Waynesboro, Pennsylvania, and heading south through Maryland and into Harpers Ferry and Virginia, all on the Appalachian Trail. The intense 24-hour hike is only doable because Maryland is pretty flat (comparatively speaking). Also called "the Death March" by hikers, the Four State Challenge is actually best when hiking north to south, not south to north.

Recreation

Care to zip through air while being surrounded by river? Through River

Top to bottom: Charles Town; Jefferson Rock in Harpers Ferry; the Appalachian Trail Conservancy Headquarters.

Trail Tale

In October 2017, **Dale "Grey Beard" Sanders** reached the Appalachian Trail Conservancy to close his **flip-flop hike.** He started in the spring, hiking from Harpers Ferry to Springer Mountain in Georgia, and then, in midsummer, began a hike at Katahdin that he finished back in Harpers Ferry. Sanders isn't unique for doing the flip-flop, but he is unique for his age when completing the hike: 82. Sanders is the oldest person to hike the entire Appalachian Trail in one year. He broke the previous eldest-hiker record of 81 years, accomplished in 2004 by Lee Barry. So what did Sanders do after finishing his flip-flop at the ATC headquarters? With family, friends, and two dogs, he sipped sparkling cider and danced.

Riders, **Harpers Ferry Zip Line & Canopy Tours** (408 Alstadts Hill Rd., 304/535-2663, www.riverriders.com, 9am-5pm daily, $60-120) offers lines of up to 800 feet (244 m) high, just tall enough to get some neat bird's-eye views of the community. River Riders also runs rafting, kayaking, and tubing experiences ($25-75) on the Shenandoah and Potomac Rivers.

River & Trail Outfitters (1332, 604 Valley Rd., Knoxville, MD, 301/834-9950, www.rivertrail.com, $25-75) hosts white-water rafting and tubing excursions and rents kayaks and canoes.

Entertainment and Events

Flip-Flop Festival

A celebration of new beginnings and vanquished foes, plus a way to get to know Harpers Ferry, the **Flip-Flop Festival** (April, www.flipflopfestival.com) is the highlight event of the year in the small community. Those splitting the AT into two hikes—one north from Harpers Ferry to Katahdin, and one south from Harpers Ferry to Springer Mountain—find the Flip-Flop Festival exactly their cup of tea. There's live music, food, and vendors, plus workshops on safety, etiquette, and hacks in the backcountry.

Shopping

Hikers can trust **Harpers Ferry Outfitters & Bike Shop** (106 Potomac St., 304/535-2087, 10am-6pm daily), which has gear aplenty, plus bicycles for those hoping to pedal around town.

Food

Harpers Ferry has a lukewarm dining scene with most places existing to pull in tourist dollars. The order of the day is New American and old-time tavern, with the best of the bunch being **Potomac Grille** (186 High St., 304/535-1900, 11:45am-5pm daily). Serving burgers and pub fare, Potomac is just

the place for sitting on an outdoor deck with a craft beer.

Accommodations

$100-150

An amateur historian and Peruvian poet and chef run **Cantuta Inn B&B** (1117 Washington St., 304/535-9978, www.cantutainn.com, $110-160), which has four quiet rooms. The highlight of the house may be the Peruvian art and décor strewn about the hallways.

$150-250

Stay in a suite with a deck overlooking Harpers Ferry at the **Ledge House Bed and Breakfast** (280 Henry Clay St., 877/468-4236, www.theledgehouse.com, $140-200). This house with three suites has king or queen beds, incredible views, and clean, comfortable rooms. It's a nice, romantic spot.

Stonehouse B&B (156 High St., 304/460-9550, www.hfstonehouse.com, $130-170) dates to 1839 and is called a "doily-free" zone. You'll know why when you visit this modern, chic bed-and-breakfast that still plays cozy and rural. One room has walls of exposed stone, while an upstairs suite is a loft-like space with dark woods and a creative person's vibe. It's a fun place to stay.

Information and Services

For more information about Harpers Ferry, visit the **Harpers Ferry-Bolivar Historic Town Foundation** (www.historicharpersferry.com).

Harpers Ferry National Historical Park

Maryland
and
Pennsylvania

Maryland and Pennsylvania

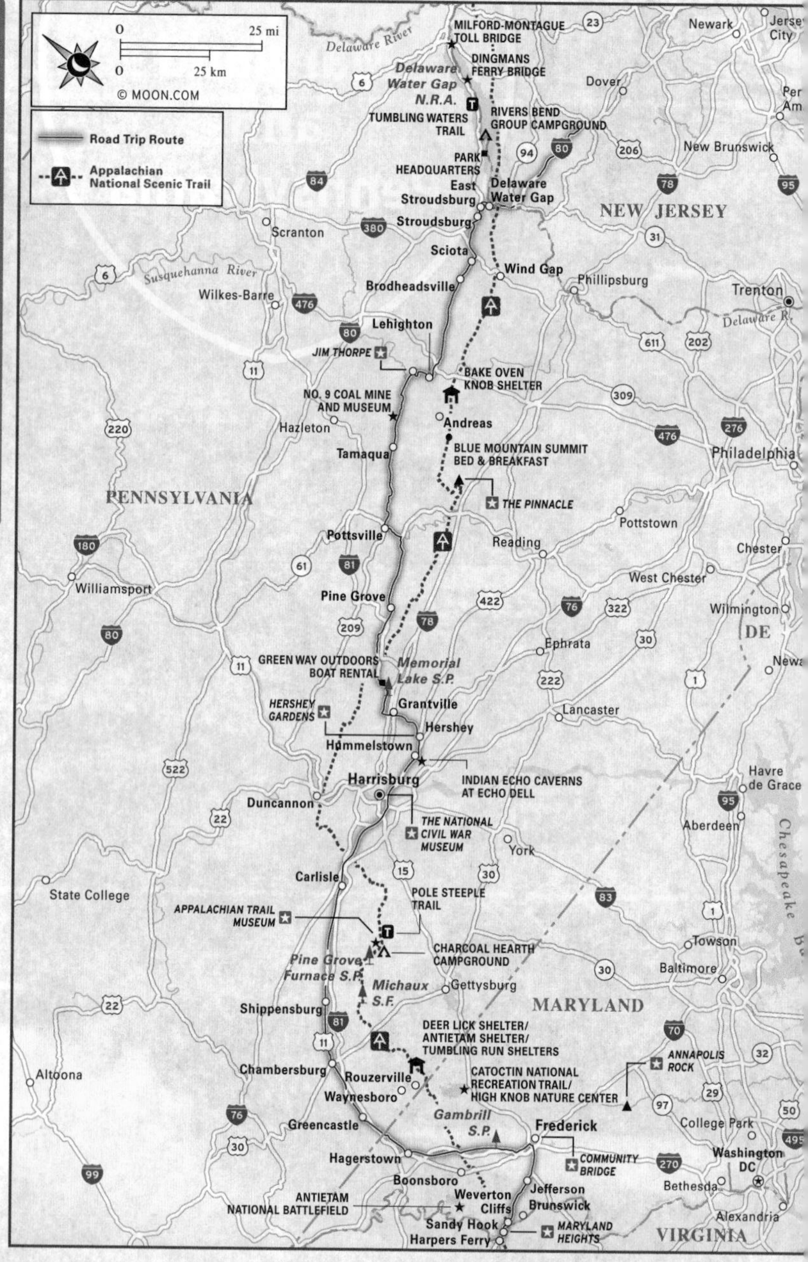

Highlights

★ **Maryland Heights:** Visit an old Union battery site before catching an outstanding view of Harpers Ferry on this excellent half-day hike in Sandy Hook (page 189).

★ **Community Bridge Mural:** This beautiful mural in Frederick is a testament to community as well as an illusory feast for the eyes (page 194).

★ **Annapolis Rock:** This moderate hike in South Mountain State Park leads to a splendid view of the Cumberland Valley among a bed of boulders (page 204).

★ **Appalachian Trail Museum:** Celebrate the midpoint of the AT with this venue in Pine Grove Furnace State Park that pays tribute to thru-hikers, volunteers, trail angels, and pioneers (page 216).

★ **National Civil War Museum:** This Harrisburg museum preserves the memory of the Civil War through a large collection of manuscripts, photographs, and soldier apparel and weaponry (page 222).

★ **Hershey Gardens:** Set on 23 acres atop a community built on chocolate, this renowned botanical garden offers hours of pleasure for the senses (page 231).

★ **The Pinnacle:** This moderate AT hike near Potsville offers the best overlook in Rocksylvania (page 241).

★ **Jim Thorpe:** This picturesque town has great museums, restaurants, and a nearby waterfall (page 244).

Leaving Harpers Ferry and entering Maryland, Appalachian Trail hikers can bid adieu to the South and prepare for a much rockier existence.

For the next 270 miles (435 km), the trail rides along the Ridge and Valley area, where unbroken ridges stretch for miles and gaps provide just enough room for highways to pass through, connecting otherwise disparate communities. Rivers cut through the mountains, allowing for larger cities and towns like Harrisburg, Jim Thorpe, and Stroudsburg to grow. Some cities and large towns, like Frederick, Hagerstown, and Hershey, are just beyond the ridges. Visitors to this region will find these locations perfect for longer stops.

But the heart of the Appalachian Trail's journey through Maryland and Pennsylvania are the tiny communities providing quick respite. Thru-hikers gulp down scoops of ice cream once they reach the trail's midpoint, marked by the Appalachian Trail Museum, and they eat pancakes aplenty and celebrate the trail with a festival in Duncannon. Farther north, hikers stop at Wind Gap for sandwiches and an opportunity to rest tired feet. Pennsylvania is known among the trail community as "Rocksylvania" thanks to its laughably rocky ridges, slowing down speedsters and forcing more than a few hikers to the nearest outfitter for a new pair of boots. Luckily, as hikers leave Rocksylvania, they receive complete hospitality in Delaware Water Gap, a trail town with all the necessary resources.

While much of the trail here hides in state forests, there are plenty of nearby towns worthy of day trips, or just a quick bite to eat. The region is particularly noted for its wealth of Civil War history, from battlefields to towns ripped apart during the conflict. Plus, the area's strong German influence shines in its food. You'll want all the pretzels and cured meats you can handle when trekking through Maryland and Pennsylvania.

Planning Your Time

You could spend a long weekend seeing the best of Maryland and Pennsylvania, but that would be cheating the 270 miles (435 km) of Appalachian Trail that runs through this area. Five days is sufficient here, and families especially can stretch the trip to a week or more.

The southern terminus of this route is aside the Potomac River in Sandy Hook, accessible via **US-340,** which runs beside Harpers Ferry en route to Maryland. Frederick is the closest city to the starting point, providing a good hub in which to grab a hotel room. I-70 connects Frederick to Baltimore, while I-270 runs from the city to Washington DC. Farther north, Harrisburg and Hershey are both solid options for a base while exploring the entire area in both directions. Harrisburg is home to an international airport, while Hershey has plenty of family-friendly attractions; make sure to reserve hotel rooms for Hershey far in advance, especially if you want to visit during the summer.

Jim Thorpe is worth a full day but is plenty crowded, so you may want to stay in nearby Pottsville, especially during the fall season. And if you're thinking about Stroudsburg in the early fall, remember that school goes back in session and parents nab hotel rooms early.

Getting There

Uniquely, you can start this route by walking from the northern terminus of the previous route. From Harpers Ferry, walk across the footbridge to the C&O Canal and Maryland Heights—or to be more succinct, take the Appalachian Trail. While the trail continues toward

Best AT Hikes

Because the Appalachian Trail in Maryland and Pennsylvania rides the ridge, getting a bird's-eye view of the action isn't hard. These hikes have tremendous overlooks, and some challenge those wanting the authentic rock-stepping experience.

- **Weverton Cliffs Trail (3 mi/4.8 km, Knoxville):** A short but rewarding hike on switchbacks to a scenic overlook of the Potomac River and the northern end of the Blue Ridge (page 190).
- **Appalachian Trail to Annapolis Rock (5 mi/8km, Boonsboro):** You'll need to hike under a highway, but soon the noise fades along a peaceful amble to a superb lookout (page 205).
- **Hawk Rock Trail (2 mi/3.2 km, Duncannon):** Short but sweet, this goes up a mountain to a couple of impressive vistas (page 229).
- **The Pinnacle (8.7 mi/14 km, Hamburg):** There's plenty of variance on this popular hike, which combines some tough Rocksylvania scrambling with a climax that brings clear-day views that can't be beat (page 241).
- **Totts Gap to Wolf Rocks (8.7 mi/14 km, Bangor):** Get a real taste of Rocksylvania with this long hike to a couple of great vistas, a trail shelter ... and did we mention rocks (page 256)?

the right once across the Potomac River, the trailhead for Maryland Heights is to the left.

You can drive to Maryland Heights by exiting US-340 just after the Potomac and turning onto Sandy Hook Road, which hugs the riverside and leads you to the trailhead. Or you can take a train: the **Amtrak Capitol Limited** (800/872-7245, www.amtrak.com) service stops in Harpers Ferry, as does **MARC's commuter rail** (Mon.-Fri., www.mta.maryland.gov), both originating in Washington DC.

Car

You'll spend the first part of the trip on **US-340** in Maryland heading toward Frederick, then on **US-40** toward Hagerstown. After that, you'll primarily follow **US-11** into Harrisburg before taking **US-322** and **US-422** through the Hershey area. **PA-443** and **PA-61** link that stretch with towns closer to the Appalachian Trail. From here it's a drive along **US-209** north, through Pennsylvania's anthracite coal country, all the way to Stroudsburg. **PA-611** finishes the trip, connecting US-209 with **I-80,** which is the route over the Delaware River.

Much of the route parallels the north-south **I-81,** which passes through Hagerstown and Harrisburg before angling farther north toward the Pocono Mountains. Other major highways include the east-west **I-70,** which connects Hagerstown and Frederick to Washington DC via I-270; the east-west **I-76 (Pennsylvania Turnpike),** which passes south of Harrisburg and provides a connection to Philadelphia; its auxiliary **I-476,** which meets the route in Lehighton and also runs to Philadelphia; and east-west **I-80,** which blasts through the Poconos before hitting Stroudsburg and providing a connection to New Jersey.

Air

Harrisburg International Airport (1 Terminal Dr., Middletown, 888/235-9442,

Best Restaurants

★ **Volt, Frederick:** A *Top Chef* finalist owns this New American resto where seasonal produce and fish become inventive meals inside a 19th-century mansion (page 198).

★ **Krumpe's Do-Nut Shop, Hagerstown:** People line up early to bag a couple of these moist, fresh doughnuts. Here's the catch: it opens at night (page 209).

★ **Home 231, Harrisburg:** This hip little scratch kitchen fills up fast with foodies seeking comfort food with flavorful twists (page 227).

★ **Goodies Restaurant, Duncannon:** Authentic as can be, this little diner frequently serves breakfast to hikers and challenges patrons to a pancake-eating extravaganza (page 229).

★ **Moya, Jim Thorpe:** This intimate date-night spot is known for bold flavors and a small but rewarding menu (page 249).

★ **Café on Broadway, Wind Gap:** This family-run, do-it-all kitchenette has burgers, sandwiches, eggs, and fresh-baked goodies, all perfect for hungry hikers (page 253).

www.flyhia.com, MDT) is 9 miles (14.5 km) southeast of Harrisburg. It provides nonstop service on Air Canada (888/247-2262), Allegiant (702/505-8888), American Airlines (800/433-7300), Delta (800/221-1212), United (800/864-8331), and Southern Airways Express (800/329-0485) to 13 cities, including Washington DC, Philadelphia, Atlanta, Boston, Charlotte, Chicago, Detroit, Pittsburgh, and Toronto. Many of the hotels along Eisenhower Drive in Harrisburg provide airport shuttle service.

Hagerstown Regional Airport (18434 Showalter Rd., 240/313-2777, www.flyhagerstown.com, HGR) offers flights to Pittsburgh on Southern Airways Express, and to Florida destinations on Allegiant. There's free parking at the airport.

Lehigh Valley International Airport (3311 Airport Rd., Allentown, 610/266-6000, www.flylvia.com, ABE) is a 40-minute drive south from Lehighton. Carriers include Allegiant, American Airlines, Delta, and United, offering nonstop flights to Chicago, Newark, Philadelphia, Detroit, and Atlanta, among other locations.

Train

You can take **Amtrak** (800/872-7245, www.amtrak.com) or **MARC** (Mon.-Fri., www.mta.maryland.gov) trains to Harpers Ferry and walk to Maryland Heights; a few other locations on this route are also accessible by train. MARC's Brunswick Line travels to Brunswick and Frederick, though only on weekdays.

Amtrak's Keystone Service connects New York City to the **Harrisburg Transportation Center** (4th and Chestnut Sts., 800/872-7245, www.amtrak.com) via Philadelphia.

Bus

In Frederick, **Greyhound** (214/849-8966, www.greyhound.com) departs from the **MARC station** (100 S. East St., 301/663-3311) and offers connections to Washington DC, Baltimore, Philadelphia, and New York City.

Hagerstown is home to the **Bayrunner Station** (123 W. Franklin St.,

Best Accommodations

★ **Inn Boonsboro, Boonsboro:** A restored 1790 hotel themes its rooms after literary couples, a nod to the inn's co-owners, author Nora Roberts and her husband Bruce Wilder (page 203).

★ **Burgundy Lane Bed & Breakfast, Waynesboro:** Hikers stay at this warm 19th-century town house whose owners can arrange transportation (page 210).

★ **White Rose Motel, Hershey:** The best bang for the buck in Chocolate Town, U.S.A. has clean rooms and a couple of single-family cottages (page 236).

★ **The Hotel Hershey, Hershey:** This magnificent five-star resort hotel features beds with Egyptian cotton linens, as well as a full-service spa (page 236).

★ **Red Umbrella Bed & Breakfast, Grantville:** This perfect little Victorian B&B inside an 1845 Federal home is outside the bustle of Hershey (page 237).

★ **The Maid's Quarters Bed, Breakfast and Tearoom, Pottsville:** A lovingly kept B&B in an old stone home doesn't overdo it with the Victorian design aesthetic (page 240).

★ **Times House, Jim Thorpe:** There are beautiful, understated accommodations and breakfast in your room at this moderately priced inn housed in a historic brick building (page 250).

301/898-2571), from which Greyhound runs a bus to Washington DC.

From the **Harrisburg Bus Station** (411 Market St., 717/255-6970), you can get to quite a few hubs including Washington DC, Baltimore, Philadelphia, New York City, Boston, and Pittsburgh. If you're in Hershey, you can get to Harrisburg via **Capital Area Transit** (717/238-8304).

The **Schuylkill Transportation System** (300 S. Center St., 800/942-8287) in Pottsville provides Greyhound service to Philadelphia and New York City.

Greyhound also leaves for Philly from the **Stroudsburg Bus Station** (102 Foxtown Rd., 570/421-3040).

Fuel and Services

You don't have to worry about running out of gas on this trip, with plenty of small towns and cities with at least one station dotting the route.

Dial 511 for reports on road conditions when in Maryland and Pennsylvania. For emergency assistance, call 911.

★ Sandy Hook: Maryland Heights

Take US-340 over the bridge from Harpers Ferry to the first exit at Keep Tryst Road. Stay right, then turn right at Sandy Hook Road. That road hugs the Potomac River and dips under the railroad bridges before becoming Harpers Ferry Road. After 0.5 mile (0.8 km), the first parking area to **Maryland Heights** will be to your right.

Rising above Harpers Ferry, Maryland Heights was always known as a spectacular and important overlook. In the early days of the Civil War, Union troops scrambled to build a battery at Maryland Heights to help ward off the Confederate forces of Lt. Gen. T. J. "Stonewall" Jackson, as the peak offered outstanding coverage of Harpers Ferry and the surrounding area. The Union was unsuccessful in protecting the armory and arsenal against Jackson, and the Battle of Harpers Ferry resulted in 12,419 U.S. troops being captured, the largest surrender of Union troops on one Civil War stage.

The Union soon reclaimed Harpers Ferry and took bigger steps to fortifying Maryland Heights. To this day hikers can see evidence of the Union's occupation of the mountain, including the original battery just off the main Maryland Heights Trail. The most impressive remnant is the 1862 stone fort erected by Union troops. Rock walls descending 500 feet (152 m) helped secure this structure, from which 30-pounder Parrott rifles shot across the valley at oncoming Confederate soldiers. You can also visit the main overlook on the mountain, a clearing where you can read the faces of Harpers Ferry tourists strolling through the town.

Maryland Heights Trail

Distance: 4.5 miles (7.2 km)
Duration: 3 hours
Elevation gain: 1,125 feet (343 m)
Difficulty: Strenuous
Trailhead: Parking area on Harpers Ferry Road (39.330839, -77.734674)

History isn't hard to find at Maryland Heights, even if the trailhead is trickier to spot. Park at one of two parking areas along Harpers Ferry Road that can handle eight cars each (get here early to avoid being shut out of a spot). Walk southeast toward the confluence of the Potomac and Shenandoah Rivers to find the trailhead, which immediately bends up into the mountain. An easy climb becomes a harder climb on a green-blazed trail. After ascending about 300 feet (91 m) you'll reach the ridge, which is a steadier uphill toward the lookout. A side trail leads to remnants of a naval battery. Come back and soon turn left onto the blue-blazed Stone Fort Trail for the full Maryland Heights experience.

The Stone Fort Trail continues to ascend as it reaches the site of the Union stone fort built in 1862. After exploring the stone walls and campgrounds, continue the blue loop downhill toward the 100- and 30-pound batteries, the latter the first constructed by the Union on the mountain. When you reach the red-blazed Overlook Cliff Trail, turn left and take that downhill and through rocky ground until there's nothing ahead of you but Harpers Ferry. Take all the pictures here, then return on the Overlook Cliff Trail until it meets back up with the green blazes, which is your way back to the parking area.

Weverton Cliffs

Appalachian Trail hikers start their Maryland trek straddling the Potomac River but soon have to get back in the woods. Luckily **Weverton Cliffs** welcomes them, a scenic overlook that shows off the river cutting and winding through the Blue Ridge. Hop off US-340 at MD-67, and take that north to the first right, which is Weverton Cliff Road. The parking lot is 0.2 mile (0.3 km) to the right.

Weverton Cliffs Trail

Distance: 3 miles (4.8 km)
Duration: 2 hours
Elevation gain: 360 feet (110 m)
Difficulty: Moderate
Trailhead: Parking area on Weverton Cliff Road, Knoxville (39.333078, -77.683310)

Maryland's elevation doesn't get too nasty, so enjoy the ease of this 360-foot (110-m) climb toward Weverton Cliffs. The Appalachian Trail is at the parking lot, so head north and begin the ascent on a mind-numbing number of switchbacks. At the ridge you'll reach a junction. Instead of staying on the AT, take the blue-blazed side trail to the overlook. Come back the way you came on this up-and-back. You can also hang on the AT north, as the first shelter (the Ed Garvey Shelter) is just 2.2 miles (3.5 km) north, though it's also another 320 feet (98 m) uphill. Constructed in 2001 with the help of students from the Maryland School for the Deaf, the shelter is named after the former president of the Potomac AT Club and is made of pine and oak. There's a privy near the shelter.

MD-79: Brunswick

Take US-340 east from the Weverton Cliffs exit 4.4 miles (7.1 km) to MD-17. Exit the highway there and drive south to reach **Brunswick** (pop. 5,870), a former B&O Railroad hub with a quaint commercial district. Home to a rail yard from 1891 to 1912, Brunswick saw a population increase at the turn of the 20th century. These days it remains a railroad town, but with commuter service, while the celebrated downtown area is home to a museum, boutique shopping, and the annual Railroad Days festival, making for a fun little side trip for hikers.

Getting There and Around

MARC Train Service (Mon.-Fri., www.mta.maryland.gov) out of Washington DC provides a commuter line, called the Brunswick Line, which stops here and continues west to Harpers Ferry and Martinsburg.

Sights

Brunswick Main Street

There isn't an actual Main Street in Brunswick. **Brunswick Main Street** is instead an especially devoted and active community presence, part of a statewide effort called Main Street Maryland that was created in 1998 to promote downtown revitalization. Brunswick Main Street, created in 2004, keeps the heart of the town humming with a plethora of events, the biggest being **Brunswick Railroad Days** (Oct.), a street fair with train rides, children's activities, two music stages, and a beer tent.

Brunswick Heritage Museum

Kids and lovers of train sets will marvel at the model railroad that occupies the 3rd floor of the **Brunswick Heritage Museum** (40 W. Potomac St., 301/834-7100, www.brunswickmuseum.org, 10am-2pm Fri., 10am-4pm Sat., 1pm-4pm Sun., $7 adults, $4 ages 4-12), which details the importance the railroad played in western Maryland life during the first half of the 20th century. While the museum includes exhibits on Victorian-era life and medical history, the highlight is most definitely the model railroad. The enormous set showcases the B&O Railroad line as it threads through Brunswick, including the 5-mile-long (8-km) train yard that employed thousands.

Recreation

C&O Canal Trail

Boats began traveling the C&O Canal in 1828, paralleling the Potomac River as it ventured from Washington DC west to Cumberland, Maryland. While flood damage eventually rendered the canal inoperable, its towpath was saved and in 1971 became a national historic park. Hikers, runners, and cyclists can travel the full 184.5 miles (297 km) of the towpath, now called the **C&O Canal Trail**, though the clay-packed and stony ground is rough in some spots.

In Brunswick, hop onto the trail with a bike from **Three Points Cycle** (5 W. Potomac St., 301/834-7199, www.threepointscycle.net, 11am-5pm Mon. and Fri.-Sat., 11am-2:30pm Sun., hours vary seasonally). The shop is just 150 feet (46 m) from the C&O Canal Trail. The **Brunswick Visitors Center** (40 W. Potomac St., 301/834-7100, 10am-2pm Thurs.-Fri., 10am-2pm Sat., 1pm-4pm Sun., hours vary seasonally) is in the same building as the Brunswick Heritage Museum.

Food and Drink

The "Main Street" area is home to a church-turned-coffee shop called **Beans in the Belfry** (122 W. Potomac St., 301/834-7178, www.beansinthebelfry.com, 8am-9pm Mon.-Thurs., 8am-10pm

Fri.-Sat., 8am-7pm Sun., under $15), which serves café staples plus chili, sandwiches, and beer and wine. Also check out the former firehouse-turned-brewery called **Smoketown Brewing Station** (223 W. Potomac St., 301/834-4828, www.smoketownbrewing.com, 5pm-9pm Wed., 5pm-10pm Thurs., noon-10pm Fri.-Sat., noon-7pm Sun., under $15). In bare bones but sizable digs, Smoketown offers several beer styles, of which the darker seem to be better.

Jefferson

Head east on US-340 13 miles (21 km) from Weverton Cliffs, or 6.5 miles (10.5 km) from MD-17, and exit the highway at Lander Road for **Jefferson** (pop. 2,111), an unincorporated community serving as a midway point between Harpers Ferry and Frederick. Because of its placement, Jefferson had more than a few taverns for weary travelers; thus, it was for a time called Trap Town.

If you're spending summer days hiking the Harpers Ferry area, there's no better trap-town remedy than old-fashioned soft serve from the **Little Red Barn Ice Cream Café** (4610 Lander Rd., 301/378-8100, www.littleredbarnicecream.com, 11am-9pm Mon.-Sat., 1pm-6pm Sun., under $15). The Little Red Barn doesn't make its own ice cream, handing those duties to Hershey's, but you can't beat the country store atmosphere. There are also "barn dogs" and sandwiches like the Trap Town Turkey.

Frederick

From Jefferson, continue east on US-340 for 8.5 miles (13.7 km); you might glance at the various churches rising in proximity to one another in **Frederick** (pop. 65,239) and think "Boy! This is a city of clustered spires!" Well, you've just shouted out the city's motto. The second-largest incorporated city in Maryland, Frederick is known for its myriad churches, including the Gothic Revival-style **All Saints Episcopal Church** (106 W. Church St., 301/663-5625) and the imposing **Evangelical Lutheran Church** (31 E. Church St., 301/663-6361), which both date to the late 18th century.

Frederick is also known for a downtown with funny, narrow streets that resemble alleys more than actual roadways. If you've spent any time in the Back Bay or Beacon Hill sections of Boston, or even in Baltimore, you'll know what I'm talking about. In short: Proceed carefully when you walk these streets.

The downtown is a sparkling little nook for date nights and weekend trips. A vibrant restaurant scene and plenty of funky shops populate much of this area, and most of the crowd is in the over-29 range. **Hood College** (401 Rosemont Ave., 301/663-3131) is the college nearby, but with an enrollment of less than 2,000, there isn't much student spillover into the city.

Getting There and Around

Frederick is conveniently accessible by both federal and state highways. US-340 merges with US-15, which meets I-70 outside the city, then US-40 for a more direct route. US-15 continues north toward Pennsylvania.

The best way to park downtown in Frederick is by using the public parking garages, which charge $1 per hour 24 hours per day, seven days per week.

The **MARC Train Station** (100 S. East St.) is the end of an extension of the Brunswick Line that runs to Washington DC; rides typically last 100-110 minutes.

The **Greyhound Bus Terminal at the MARC station** (100 S. East St., 301/663-3311) offers connections to Washington DC, Baltimore, Philadelphia, and New York City. Within the city limits, Frederick operates the **TransIT program** (301/600-2065, $1.50 per trip, $0.75 seniors), which includes about a

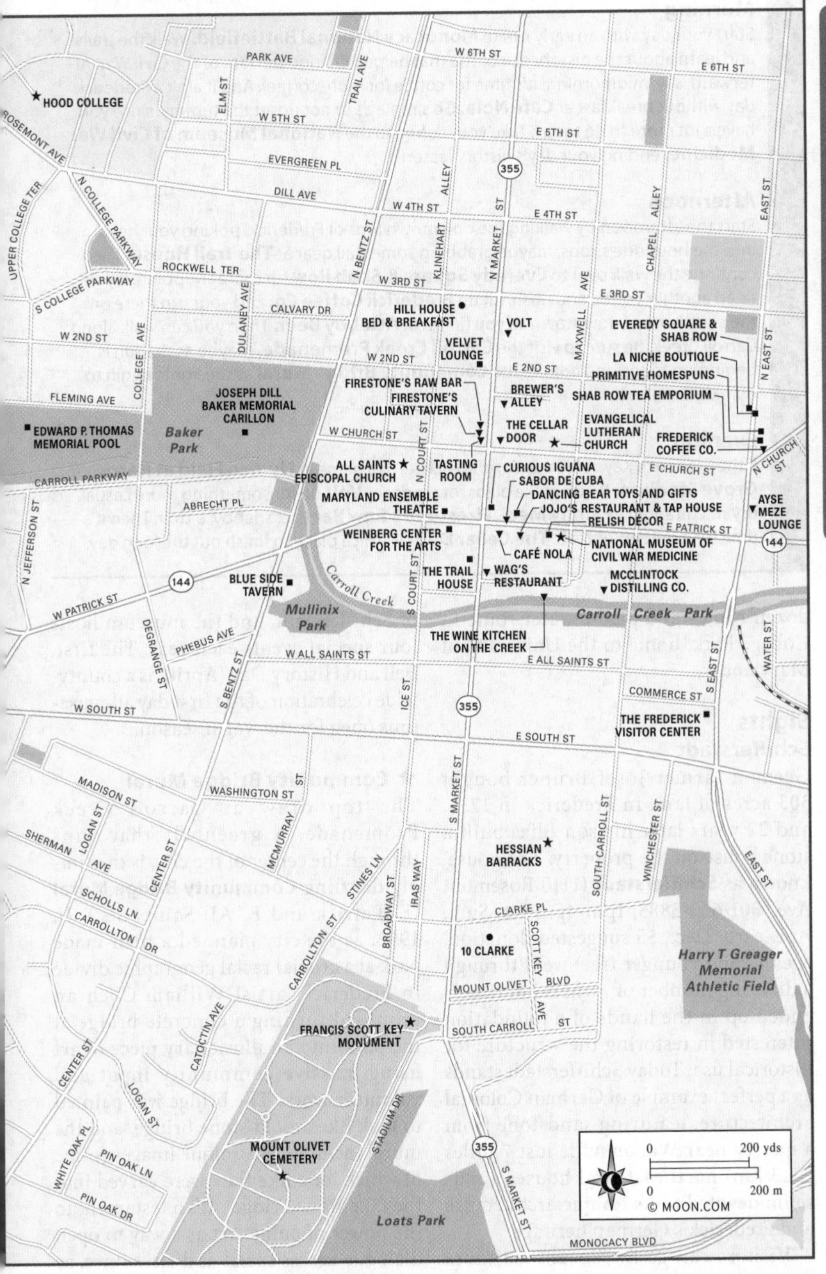

Frederick, MD
HOOD COLLEGE
PARK AVE
W 6TH ST
E 6TH ST
W 5TH ST
E 5TH ST
ELM ST
TRAIL AVE
ROSEMONT AVE
EVERGREEN PL
DILL AVE
W 4TH ST
E 4TH ST
N COLLEGE PARKWAY
UPPER COLLEGE TER
ROCKWELL TER
S COLLEGE PARKWAY
W 3RD ST
E 3RD ST
N BENTZ ST
KLINEHART ALLEY
ALLEY
N MARKET ST
CHAPEL ALLEY
EAST ST
MAXWELL AVE
HILL HOUSE BED & BREAKFAST
VOLT
CALVARY DR
DULANEY AVE
W 2ND ST
E 2ND ST
COLLEGE AVE
VELVET LOUNGE
EVEREDY SQUARE & SHAB ROW
LA NICHE BOUTIQUE
PRIMITIVE HOMESPUNS
SHAB ROW TEA EMPORIUM
N EAST ST
FIRESTONE'S RAW BAR
FIRESTONE'S CULINARY TAVERN
BREWER'S ALLEY
JOSEPH DILL BAKER MEMORIAL CARILLON
FLEMING AVE
EDWARD P. THOMAS MEMORIAL POOL
Baker Park
W CHURCH ST
THE CELLAR DOOR
EVANGELICAL LUTHERAN CHURCH
FREDERICK COFFEE CO.
N CHURCH ST
E CHURCH ST
N COURT ST
ALL SAINTS EPISCOPAL CHURCH
TASTING ROOM
CURIOUS IGUANA
SABOR DE CUBA
DANCING BEAR TOYS AND GIFTS
JOJO'S RESTAURANT & TAP HOUSE
RELISH DÉCOR
CARROLL PARKWAY
ABRECHT PL
MARYLAND ENSEMBLE THEATRE
WEINBERG CENTER FOR THE ARTS
E PATRICK ST
AYSE MEZE LOUNGE
CAFÉ NOLA
NATIONAL MUSEUM OF CIVIL WAR MEDICINE
N JEFFERSON ST
144
W PATRICK ST
BLUE SIDE TAVERN
Carroll Creek
THE TRAIL HOUSE
WAG'S RESTAURANT
MCCLINTOCK DISTILLING CO.
S COURT ST
Mullinix Park
Carroll Creek Park
PHEBUS AVE
DEGRANGE ST
S BENTZ ST
W ALL SAINTS ST
THE WINE KITCHEN ON THE CREEK
E ALL SAINTS ST
WATER ST
S EAST ST
COMMERCE ST
355
ICE ST
W SOUTH ST
THE FREDERICK VISITOR CENTER
E SOUTH ST
MADISON ST
WASHINGTON ST
S MARKET ST
SOUTH CARROLL ST
WINCHESTER ST
LOGAN ST
SHERMAN AVE
MCMURRAY ST
CENTER ST
STINES LN
HESSIAN BARRACKS
EAST ST
SCHOLLS LN
CARROLLTON DR
CARROLLTON ST
BROADWAY ST
IRAS WAY
CLARKE PL
SCOTT KEY AVE
10 CLARKE
BLVD
Harry T Greager Memorial Athletic Field
MOUNT OLIVET
CATOCTIN AVE
FRANCIS SCOTT KEY MONUMENT
SOUTH CARROLL
ST
CENTER ST
LOGAN ST
STADIUM DR
WHITE OAK PL
PIN OAK LN
MOUNT OLIVET CEMETERY
PIN OAK DR
Loats Park
0
200 yds
0
200 m
© MOON.COM
MONOCACY BLVD

One Day in Frederick

Morning

Start your day with an early run to **Monocacy National Battlefield.** Walk the trails and learn about the history of a battle that helped change the fate of the Civil War. Afterward, say, midmorning, it's time for coffee (or more coffee). And it ain't a Frederick day without breakfast at **Café Nola.** Go simple as to not upset the tummy, since you have a lot more to do today. Take your coffee to the **National Museum of Civil War Medicine,** ending your day's history lesson.

Afternoon

Start the afternoon by walking the downtown area of Frederick, poking your head into the boutique shops, maybe grabbing some trail gear at **The Trail House.** Then continue the walk over to **Everedy Square & Shab Row** for more shopping. If you need another coffee and nosh, hit up **Frederick Coffee Co.** End your trip there on the south end of downtown so you first visit **Attaboy Beer.** Then you can walk along Carroll Creek. Be sure to visit the **Carroll Creek Promenade,** maybe as the sun is beginning to set, and admire the **Community Bridge Mural** as the lights begin to twinkle overhead.

Evening

If the Frederick Keys are in town, grab tickets to a game at **Nymeo Field at Harry Grove Stadium.** If not, make plans for dinner at **Volt** or, for something more casual, Bryan Voltaggio's **Family Meal. Firestone's Raw Bar** isn't shabby, either. Then it's time for a quick nightcap; **The Cellar Door** is a nice place to finish out the long day.

dozen routes and a commuter route to College Park, home to the University of Maryland.

Sights

Schifferstadt

German farmer Josef Bruner bought 303 acres of land in Frederick in 1736, and 22 years later his son Elias built a stone house on the property. The house, known as **Schifferstadt** (1110 Rosemont Ave., 301/663-3885, 1pm-4pm Sat.-Sun., Apr.-early Dec., $5 suggested donation, ages 12 and younger free) went through a dizzying number of owners but finally ended up in the hands of a foundation interested in restoring the structure for historical use. Today Schifferstadt stands as a perfect example of German Colonial architecture, featuring sandstone from a quarry near Walkersville just 7 miles (11.3 km) northeast, and houses a museum devoted to its unique architecture and Frederick's German heritage.

Visitors can go for docent-led tours of Schifferstadt, and the museum hosts four special events each year. The first, Bell and History Day (April), is a countywide celebration of the first day all museums open for the warm season.

★ Community Bridge Mural

The top draw at Carroll Creek Promenade, a greenbelt that runs through the center of the city, is the simply dazzling **Community Bridge Mural** (E. Patrick and E. All Saints Sts.). In 1993, as the city planned a man-made park at a crucial racial geographic divide in Frederick, artist William Cochran proposed turning a concrete bridge at the park into an illusionary piece of art using massive community input and volunteer work. The bridge was painted to look like an old stone bridge, and the mural includes 180 unique images (some of which look like they were carved into the fake stone bridge). It's a testament to the power of public art as a way to open dialogue across racial and class lines, as well as unify people across man-made constructs. The bridge is the artistic centerpiece of Frederick. Be sure to find the hauntingly gorgeous "Archangel," the bridge's quintessential illusion.

National Museum of Civil War Medicine

Opening in 1990, the **National Museum of Civil War Medicine** (48 E. Patrick St., 301/695-1864, 10am-5pm Mon.-Sat., 11am-5pm Sun., $9.50 adults, $8.50 seniors, $7 students, free ages 9 and younger) is one of a kind. It's the only museum in America devoted solely to medicine of the Civil War, featuring an inventory of more than 5,000 artifacts including the only known surviving war-era surgeon's tent, and a preserved human arm found at Antietam. Exhibits re-create medical scenes from the war, including a military hospital ward. Not entirely suitable for small children.

Hessian Barracks

It's unknown exactly when the **Hessian Barracks** (242 S. Market St., 301/600-4047, hours vary by season) were constructed, but one account states British general Edward Braddock likely stayed in them during his Braddock Expedition during the French and Indian War in 1755. More accepted accounts date the barracks to the 1770s, when they held prisoners during the Revolutionary War and, later, the War of 1812. Much later they were a silkworm production site, a Civil War hospital, and the original Maryland Institution for the Deaf. You can learn about the barracks' role in Frederick and American history when it opens the second Saturday of the month, from May to December. It's also open by appointment.

Top to bottom: Carroll Creek Linear Park in Frederick; Hessian Barracks; Francis Scott Key Monument at Mount Olivet Cemetery.

Francis Scott Key Monument

Frederick is the birthplace of Francis Scott Key, author of "The Star-Spangled Banner." A monument is at **Mount Olivet Cemetery** (515 S. Market St., 301/662-1164, 8:30am-5pm daily), which explains its daily hours begin "by the dawn's early light" and end at "twilight's last gleaming." The Key monument depicts the lawyer and poet proudly proclaiming his iconic lyric sheet atop a high pedestal. His gravestone is beneath. The cemetery has 8 miles (12.9 km) of paved roadway, which can be used by walkers, runners, and cyclists.

Hiking

The best hiking in or near the city limits is at **Monocacy National Battlefield** (5201 Urbana Pike, 301/662-3515, 7am-sunset daily, free), the site of a July 1864 Civil War battle that delayed the Confederate march toward Washington DC by one day, just enough for Union forces to fend off the attack. Visitors can take a self-guided tour of Monocacy, and they can veer off the route and go on one of six marked trails. The hardest among them is the 1.9-mile (3-km) **Brooks Hill Loop Trail,** which starts at a farmhouse and ascends the titular hill before returning.

Recreation

Parks

Occupying a narrow strip of floodplain south of downtown, **Carroll Creek Linear Park** (N. Market St. and Carroll Creek Way) puts its funny locale and size to exceptional use. Walkers, joggers, strollers, and shoppers can meander the park, which is home to the Community Bridge Mural, and gaze out at the luxury condominiums being built nearby.

Baker Park (N. Bentz St. and Carroll Pkwy.), which stretches out along Carroll Creek west of downtown, has more space for family gatherings, plus a covered bridge and the **Edward P. Thomas Memorial Pool** (500 Fleming Ave., 301/663-5666, 12:30pm-6pm Mon.-Fri., 12:30pm-8pm Sat.-Sun. Memorial Day-Labor Day, $3-6 nonresidents, $3-5 residents). Baker Park is also home to the **Joseph Dill Baker Memorial Carillon** (200 Carroll Pkwy.), a 1941 tower of 49 bells. A recital takes place at 12:30pm on the third Sunday of each month.

Spectator Sports

Frederick has a minor-league baseball team in the Frederick Keys, who play at **Nymeo Field at Harry Grove Stadium** (21 Stadium Dr., 301/662-0088). The Keys are a Class-A affiliate of the Baltimore Orioles, playing a season that starts in April and wraps up in September.

Entertainment and Events

Nightlife

Frederick has a robust brewing industry in which regional breweries coexist with smaller, garage-to-growler enterprises. If you're looking for a beer scene similar to Asheville without the dizzying sense that you could be missing something, Frederick is the place for you.

You should probably start your Frederick beer tour at the place whose offerings most people have seen in stores. While it didn't start in Frederick, **Flying Dog Brewery** (4607 Wedgewood Blvd., 301/694-7899, www.flyingdogbrewery.com, 9am-5pm Tues., 9am-8pm Wed.-Fri., noon-8pm Sat., noon-6pm Sun., under $20) calls the city its home today. It's known primarily for its Raging Bitch Belgian IPA, and its label art by Ralph Steadman, who worked for decades with writer Hunter S. Thompson. Flying Dog has a large plant, but its tasting room is cozy and isn't very different from your regular, everyday luncheonette.

For the local joint that's been doing it since 1996, head to **Brewer's Alley** (124 N. Market St., 301/631-0089, www.brewers-alley.com, 11:30am-11:30pm Mon.-Tues., 11:30am-midnight Wed.-Thurs., 11:30am-12:30am Fri.-Sat., 11:30am-8pm Sun., under $30). This brewpub that makes its own beer, plus serves lunch and dinner from burgers to pizza, is a solid all-in-one place for the family.

Along with having an exceptional name, **Attaboy Beer** (400 Sagner Ave., Ste. 400, 301/338-8229, www.attaboy.com, 4pm-10pm Wed.-Thurs., noon-10pm Fri.-Sat., under $20) is a great place to hang with a beer. Specializing in pales but unafraid to experiment with wild fermentation, Attaboy is a family enterprise with long tables, an industrial look, and a busier nighttime crowd. Food trucks are on-site.

Uptown, **Monocacy Brewing Company** (1781 N. Market St., 240/457-4232, www.monocacybrewing.com, 4pm-9pm Thurs.-Fri., noon-9pm Sat., noon-6pm Sun., under $20) strikes one as a bit more mature, with clean lines and tall wooden chairs at the bar.

The freewheeling **Midnight Run Brewing** (912 N. East St., www.midnightrunbrewing.com, 6pm-10pm Thurs., 5pm-10pm Fri., 1pm-9pm Sat., under $20) does whatever it feels like in its small space. There's no food here.

Want cocktails? **The Cellar Door** (5 E. Church St., 301/695-8460, 3pm-midnight Tues.-Thurs., 3pm-1:30am Fri., 11am-1:30am Sat., 11am-10pm Sun., under $40) pours chic martinis and other drinks inside its lounge and restaurant, with pillows and comfortable seating for those so inclined. It gets loud on weekend nights.

Somewhere between casual hang and sports bar is **JoJo's Restaurant & Tap House** (16-18 E. Patrick St., 301/732-5197, 11:30am-2am Tues.-Fri., 11am-2am Sat.-Sun., under $40). JoJo's has taco specials, fish, and burgers, along with a convivial bar vibe.

Or you can go straight to the source. Plenty of local bars use gin from **McClintock Distilling Co.** (35 S. Carroll St., 240/815-5259, www.mcclintockdistilling.com, 4pm-8pm Thurs.-Fri., noon-8pm Sat., noon-6pm Sun., under $10), which also produces white whiskey and vodka. Tours are free, and tastings are $5.

Performing Arts

As is common for theaters of its size, the **Weinberg Center for the Arts** (20 W. Patrick St., 301/600-2828, www.weinbergcenter.org) was built in the early 20th century. The building originally showed movies. As its ownership changed hands in mid-century it began to deteriorate, and, in June 1976, a massive flood signaled doom for the theater. It was saved by local companies and individuals, then restored to its current look, with some later renovations. The Weinberg is a presenting space, with acts such as Darlene Love and Colin Mochrie and Brad Sherwood of *Whose Line Is It Anyway?*

Pound for pound, **Maryland Ensemble Theatre** (31 W. Patrick St., 301/694-4744, www.marylandensemble.org) delivers some of the best theater in the Free State. The main-stage slate includes challenging and lesser-known works, but there's also plenty of family fare throughout the year.

Get your live music fix at the **Blue Side Tavern** (6 S. Bentz St., 301/663-0200, www.thebluesidetavern.com, 3pm-2am Mon., 3pm-midnight Tues.-Thurs., 11:30am-2am Fri., 10am-2am Sat., 11am-midnight Sun., under $40), which offers primarily bluegrass, including a Monday-night jam. Blue Side also serves Southern comfort fare like red-eye country biscuits and jambalaya.

Festivals and Events

The highlight of the city's calendar year, the **Frederick Festival of the Arts** (June, www.frederickartscouncil.org) unites local arts organizations with a massive fair along Carroll Creek, plus live music performances, children's entertainment, and more at Carroll Creek Linear Park.

Also at the park, the **Maryland Craft Beer Festival** (May, www.mdcraftbeerfestival.com) brings the craft hounds out. And guess what? This beer festival is not saturated with the usual national brands; this is all local.

Shopping

Downtown

Clyde and Gerry Hicks have been running **The Trail House** (17 S. Market St., 301/694-8448, www.trailhouse.com, 10am-7pm Mon.-Thurs., 10am-8pm Fri., 9:30am-5:30pm Sat., noon-5pm Sun.) since 1984, selling gear, clothing, tents, and bags to ready hikers and climbers across western Maryland. The Trail House also keeps guidebooks and maps, and the staff is happy to chat about where to go locally.

Looking a skate shop? **Pitcrew** (880 N. East St., 301/698-1813, 10am-8pm Mon.-Sat., noon-5pm Sun.) is a paradise for skateboarders, offering a dizzying selection of boards, gear, and apparel.

Few women's clothing boutiques hold such a high reputation as **Velvet Lounge** (203 N. Market St., 301/695-5700, 10am-8pm Mon.-Thurs., 10am-9pm Fri.-Sat., 11am-6pm Sun.), which cycles through a range of hot and classic brands, including Obey, Steve Madden, AG Jeans, and Toms. It's fun but never imposing.

You'll want to outfit your house with a bunch of accessories from **Relish Décor** (38 E. Patrick St., 301/698-7360, noon-5pm Mon. and Thurs.-Fri., 11am-5pm Sat.-Sun.). Dishes and kitchenware are popular here.

Dancing Bear Toys and Gifts (15 E. Patrick St., 301/631-9300, 10am-8pm Mon.-Sat., 11am-6pm Sun.) is the local toy emporium, specializing in constructive pieces for small children, plus summer camps and programs for early childhood visitors.

Curious Iguana (12 N. Market St., 301/695-2500, 10am-6pm Mon.-Wed., 10am-8pm Thurs.-Sat., 11am-5pm Sun.) is a comfy and whimsical bookstore, packing tons of new releases and fresh finds into its casually colorful corners.

Everedy Square & Shab Row

Back in the 1970s, local businessman Bert Anderson bought an area of former artisan dwellings and manufacturing warehouses, restored them, and brought in a collection of small businesses and restaurants. **Everedy Square & Shab Row** (301/662-4140) together comprise a three-block stretch in downtown Frederick, offering a full day's worth of shopping.

Highlights of the area include **Primitive Homespuns** (120 N. East St., 301/663-1852, 11:30am-5pm Mon. and Wed.-Fri., 11am-5pm Sat., noon-5pm Sun.), a depot for folk art, wool, and needlework; **La Niche Boutique** (130 N. East St., 240/529-7305, 11am-5pm Wed.-Fri., 11am-6pm Sat., 11am-4pm Sun.), a stop for funky and fresh home décor options like wall signs and comforters; and the **Shab Row Tea Emporium** (112 N. East St., 301/378-8537, 10am-6pm daily), a one-stop shop for loose and bagged tea, cups, and accessories. It holds tastings, too.

Food

Downtown

Frederick has a lion's share of shiny New American restaurants, headlined by ★ **Volt** (228 N. Market St., 301/696-8658, www.voltrestaurant.com, 5:30pm-9:30pm Tues.-Fri., 11:30am-2pm and 5:30pm-9:30pm Sat.-Sun., under $60), owned by Frederick-born chef Bryan Voltaggio, runner-up on season six of *Top Chef* (to his brother Michael, no less). He sticks to local ingredients, specializing in fresh fish and seasonal produce, while offering three- and six-course meals plus brunch. Volt is set up inside a 19th-century mansion; its dining room is a crisp white on white, while the lounge is dark woods and amber with leather couches and a peppy bar.

Voltaggio owns a second restaurant in Frederick: **Family Meal** (882 N. East St., 301/378-2895, 7am-10pm daily, under $30), a new-age diner inside an old car dealership. Imagine elevated diner food (both in taste and price) with a vintage 1950s aesthetic.

Feel like a 1920s socialite at **Firestone's Culinary Tavern** (105 N. Market St.,

301/663-0330, 11am-1:30am Tues.-Sat., 10am-1am Sun., under $50), which fills a large space with a tin ceiling in the heart of downtown. Firestone's has brunch, lunch, and dinner, specializing in elevated American gastro cuisine. Firestone's also owns **Firestone's Raw Bar** (109 N. Market St., 301/663-0330, 11am-10pm Tues.-Thurs., 11am-11pm Fri.-Sat., 11am-9pm Sun., under $40), which fascinates seafood lovers with tuna tartare, oysters, and lobster in a postindustrial space with subway tile and leather seating.

Wine drinkers should check out the **Tasting Room** (101 N. Market St., 240/379-7772, www.trrestaurant.com, 11am-10pm Mon.-Thurs., 11am-11pm Fri.-Sat., 11am-8pm Sun., under $70 dinner, under $30 lunch and brunch). Wines are paired with American surf-and-turf, plus a dash of French influence.

Also pairing wine with New American, **The Wine Kitchen on the Creek** (50 Carroll Creek Way, 301/663-6968, www.thewinekitchen.com, 11:30am-9pm Sun. and Tues.-Thurs., 11:30am-10pm Fri.-Sat., under $50 dinner, under $30 lunch and brunch) is part of a franchise, serving steak, fish, and small plates in a large wood-toned space.

The fun local joint is **Wag's Restaurant** (24 S. Market St., 301/694-8451, www.eatatwags.com, 11am-2am Mon.-Sat., under $20) which delivers burgers the way nature intended, plus sandwiches, salads, and the like. Its long bar with actual barstools is a happening place during happy hour ... or really most any night.

The colors of **Sabor De Cuba** (9 E. Patrick St., 301/663-1036, www.sabordecubarestaurant.com, 11:30am-8:30pm Mon.-Thurs., 11:30am-10pm Fri.-Sat., noon-8pm Sun., under $30) shine almost as much as the food. Inside this blue, white, and yellow building are authentic dishes like *vaca frita* and *camarones enchilados*.

For a quick cup of coffee or a nosh in the morning, then a drink at the full bar at night, hang out at **Café Nola** (4 E. Patrick St., 301/694-6652, www.cafe-nola.com, 7am-2am Mon. and Wed.-Fri., 7am-3pm Tues., 9am-2am Sat.-Sun., under $20). There are happy hour specials every day. Try the Texas-style *migas* or the GraNola, a cranberry granola treat with toasted coconut and bee pollen, for a healthy breakfast.

Everedy Square & Shab Row

The shopping and dining mall of Everedy Square & Shab Row includes **Ayse Meze Lounge** (6 N. East St., 240/651-5155, www.aysemeze.com, 11:30am-9:30pm Tues.-Thurs., 11:30am-10pm Fri.-Sat., 11:30am-8:30pm Sun., under $20), which cooks traditional Greek and Mediterranean dishes, and **Frederick Coffee Co.** (100 East St., 301/698-0039, www.fredcoffeeco.com, 6am-10pm Mon.-Thurs., 6am-11pm Fri., 6:30am-11pm Sat., 7am-9pm Sun., under $15), which pairs coffee with sandwiches and egg dishes.

Accommodations

Under $100

The highways on Frederick's perimeter are populated with economy hotels and motels. The **Super 8** (20 Monocacy Blvd., 301/228-0672) and **Econo Lodge** (6021 Francis Scott Key Dr., 301/698-0555) are off I-70, while down the road and off I-270 are the **Sleep Inn** (5631 Spectrum Dr., 301/668-2003) and **Days Inn** (5646 Buckeystown Pike, 301/228-0784).

$100-150

A couple of hotels off US-270 fall into the family-friendly range. Those are the **Hampton Inn** (5311 Buckeystown Pike, 301/698-2500, $110-150) and **Extended Stay America** (5240 Westview Dr., 301/668-0808, $90-150).

$150-250

Frederick's downtown has a couple of bed-and-breakfasts, tops among them **10 Clarke** (10 Clarke Pl., 301/660-6707, www.10clarke.com, $150-225), a restored

Victorian that combines traditional comforts like patterned rugs and antique lamps with ultra-chic design choices like clean wallpaper and subway tile in the bathrooms.

A few blocks north, **Hill House Bed & Breakfast** (12 W. 3rd St., 301/682-4111, www.hillhousefrederick.com, $145-200) features four rooms in a circa 1870 town house. It's a bit more old-fashioned, with a premium on Victorian antiques, but it's right in the middle of the downtown hubbub.

South of downtown, off I-270, those wanting the chain hotel experience can stay at the **Courtyard by Marriott** (5225 Westview Dr., 301/631-9030, $150-200), **Residence Inn by Marriott** (5230 Westview Dr., 301/360-0010, $170-220), or **Hilton Garden Inn** (7226 Corporate Ct., 240/566-1500, $175-225)

Information and Services

The **Frederick Visitor Center** (151 S. East St., 301/600-4047, 9am-5:30pm daily) offers recommendations, plus has a map showing its **Frederick History Bicycle Loop,** which stops at numerous points of interest.

Gambrill State Park

A popular getaway for camp-seeking Washington DC refugees, **Gambrill State Park** (8602 Gambrill Park Rd., 301/271-7574) is 7.6 miles (12.2 km) north of Frederick on US-40. It sits 1,400 feet (427 m) up the ridge of Catoctin Mountain, which has long been a resource for the Monocacy River valley. The first Catoctin iron furnace was built a few miles north of the park, near iron ore and limestone deposits on the mountain, and whiskey stills were constructed on the peak after George Washington levied the whiskey tax on Appalachian producers in 1791. The whiskey production of those backwoods stills were integral during Prohibition.

Gambrill State Park provides a connection to the furnace and an old whiskey still, which are north at Catoctin Mountain Park (along with Camp David), through the **Catoctin National Recreation Trail.** The south trailhead is here, beginning a 26.6-mile (43-km) marathon-plus through Catoctin and running parallel to the Appalachian Trail. Visitors to Gambrill State Park can also hike, bike, and ride on up to 16 miles (26 km) of trails and visit an old tea room that is available for events. The **High Knob Nature Center** has information on the wildlife found in the park, from blue jays and tufted titmice to rattlesnakes and black bears.

Hiking

Black Locust Trail

Distance: 3.3 miles (5.3 km)
Duration: 2-2.5 hours
Elevation gain: 1,000 feet (305 m)
Difficulty: Moderate
Trailhead: Parking area at High Knob Nature Center (39.461981, -77.495382)

This trek is easy for experienced hikers, but some may consider it moderate to challenging. It really depends on your skill level. Just know that there's some gradual rise leading to scenic overlooks of the Appalachian ridge, and the rocky terrain can be tricky for the unequipped.

Start at the parking lot and look for the black-on-white blazes north of the High Knob Nature Center. The trail hangs with the Yellow Poplar Trail until breaking off on its own, then meeting up with the Green Ash Trail and, finally, the Catoctin NRT. You'll be ambling up and down much of the way on this loop.

Fishing

Just as you enter the park, a small pond is off to the left. That's the fishing pond. Park at the campground and take the short walk down to the pond to draw largemouth bass, bluegill, and channel catfish. No license is needed, but no swimming allowed.

Trail Tale

While hiking the Appalachian Trail near Boonsboro, about 1,038 miles (1,670 km) north of Springer Mountain, hikers encounter a giant stone stub with a door. It looks like a thumb. It's actually the very first **Washington Monument.**

In the first decades of the 19th century, there was a substantial trend of people building monuments to America's first president. He died in 1799, and by the beginning of the Era of Good Feelings, Americans felt it was time to begin honoring those who helped create their promising future. A monument was commissioned for Baltimore in 1815, but it was slow going. Fast-forward to 7am on July 4, 1827, when the citizens of Boonsboro united at the town square and marched 2.8 miles (4.5 km) to a site outside town. They began constructing a stone tower of 15 feet (4.6 m) high, finishing before dusk. Later in the year workers finished the tower, topping it at 30 feet (9 m).

The monument would be destroyed time and again, and finally a restoration project in 1882 set to fix it. It did, but the tower fell apart 10 years later. Finally, in 1936, the Civilian Conservation Corps rebuilt the tower. It hasn't changed since. The monument is accessible via a short uphill walk from a nearby **parking lot** (6620 Zittlestown Rd., Middletown). You can climb to the top of the monument for a great view that includes Antietam National Battlefield.

Camping

The **main campground** (8002 Gambrill Park Rd., $18.49-$50.49) is located at the park's Rock Run area, which is at the south end off of Gambrill Park Road. The campground has 13 basic sites (for RVs and tents), 9 tent-only sites, and 8 with electric capabilities. Fire rings are at every site. A bathhouse has showers and flush-toilets. There are also two group sites that can fit up to 20 people; those are open from April to October.

Also at Rock Run are four camper cabins with electricity, so you can turn on a cooling fan or charge your smartphone. Reservations are recommended for the cabins.

Boonsboro

Don't miss the quick left turn after the Appalachian Trail trailhead off the Baltimore National Pike (US-40). Seriously, it comes really fast. Turn onto Boonsboro Mountain Road and head down to **Boonsboro** (pop. 3,336). While not an official trail town, Boonsboro is a small community steeped in Civil War history and perfect for a bite to eat.

It's also the absolute best place to go if you're really into the works of Nora Roberts. The best-selling author of more than 200 romance novels has invested plenty in Boonsboro, with her family behind four businesses in town, including the inn and two restaurants. Her husband, Bruce Wilder, owns the local bookstore. You may even get to see Roberts about town, since she famously despises flying.

Boonsboro Museum of History

Find rarities from the Civil War era at the **Boonsboro Museum of History** (113 N. Main St., 301/432-6969, www.boonsboromuseum.org, 1pm-5pm Sun. May-Sept., nominal fee), including a vast collection of carved bullets. Buttons, thimbles, bottle stoppers, and other ephemera from the mid-1800s are also on display. Also learn about abolitionist John Brown, who raided Harpers Ferry and was later hanged after being convicted of murder for the deaths of five men during the raid.

Greenbrier State Park

Appalachian Trail hikers will pass through **Greenbrier State Park** (21843 National Pike, Boonsboro, 301/791-4767, 8am-sunset daily, $3-$7 per person during summer season) on the way to Annapolis Rock, but only slightly. The park is known most for Greenbrier Lake, a 42-acre man-made body of water used for swimming, fishing, and boating. The park also has campgrounds and 10 internal hiking trails.

Lifeguards are on duty at the Greenbrier Lake beach from Memorial Day to Labor Day (11am-6pm daily) for swimming. Anglers need a license to fish at the lake, which is stocked with largemouth bass and bluegill. Patrons can bring their own boats with electric trolling motors, or they can rent rowboats and paddleboats ($10-$14) at the far end of the beach. There's a sand volleyball court at the opposite end of the beach.

From April to October, Greenbrier operates its **main campground** ($21.49-$27.49), which includes 165 sites with hot showers in bathhouses. There are fire rings and parking areas at all campsites.

Big Red Trail

Distance: 4.7 miles (7.6 km)

Duration: 2.5-3 hours

Elevation gain: 710 feet (216 m)

Difficulty: Moderate

Trailhead: Beside Greenbrier Lake (39.541808, -77.617511)

A few ascents and descents await you on the Big Red Trail, the longest among the network of paths at Greenbrier State Park. Start alongside Greenbrier Lake and pass the short Copperhead Trail as you begin moving downhill. About 0.7 mile (1.1 km) into the hike you'll cross the Rock Oak Fire Trail at a switchback. Soon you'll begin the big uphill climb of 400 feet (122 m), then level off on the Short Hill ridge before going back downhill. One last uphill push comes just before reaching the Camp Loop Trail at about the 4-mile (6.4-km) mark. The final bit includes a decline before leveling off.

Shopping

Missing a Nora Roberts (or J. D. Robb) book? **Turn the Page Bookstore** (18 N. Main St., 301/432-4588, www.ttpbooks.com, 10am-6pm Mon.-Sat., 11am-4pm Sun.) has all of them. Roberts's husband, Bruce Wilder, owns the sprawling bookstore that offers a full variety of titles, not just romance. The bookstore also sells fits like soy candles, local soap, and Roberts merchandise, and serves coffee from a Frederick coffee roaster. Turn the Page hosts author events, and Roberts frequently participates in signings.

Food and Nightlife

The **Old South Mountain Inn** (6132 Old National Pike, 301/432-6155, 5pm-close Tues.-Fri., 4pm-close Sat., 10:30am-1:30pm and 2pm-close Sun.) has been a favorite stop of politicians since the 18th century and was headquarters of a Confederate general during the battle of South Mountain. Now it's a pub serving upscale, traditional American fare like pâté, crab imperial, lobster tail, and beef Wellington. Hardwood floors, fireplaces, and paintings of war leaders adorn this renovated venue.

For a quick slice, **Rasco NY Pizza** (280 N. Main St., 301/799-5080, 10:30am-10pm Mon.-Thurs., Sat., 10:30am-11pm Fri., 11am-9pm Sun., under $15) makes some of the better ones south of the New York City area. It serves traditional Italian dishes to-go, as well.

The local tap is **Dan's Restaurant & Tap House** (3 S. Main St., 301/432-5224, www.drnth.com, 11am-close Mon.-Sat., noon-close Sun., under $30 lunch, under $40 dinner), which offers a solid tap list plus wings, burgers, salads, sandwiches, and hearty entrees. For you Roberts fans, Dan is one of her sons. The low-profile bar in town is **Yellow House** (8005 Old National Pike, 301/432-5227, noon-midnight Mon.-Fri., 9am-2am Sat., noon-10pm Sun., under $20), which is a yellow house. Don't get stuffy with your drink order here. There are plenty of bar games to keep you occupied, though the conversation is lively.

For a coffee and pastry, head to **Stone Werks Coffee + Sweets** (7 N. Main St., 678/749-2158, www.stonewerkssweets.com, 7am-4pm Mon.-Sat., under $15). Owned by the friendly and fun August and Elisabeth Stone, Stone Werks sells quiches, cupcakes, cookies, and macarons inside a cool brick space with comfy leather seating.

Accommodations

Right at the main intersection of town, the ★ **Inn Boonsboro** (1 N. Main St., 301/432-1188, www.innboonsboro.com, $225-310) has almost always been a hotel since its construction in 1790. It sat dormant at the end of the 20th century until author Nora Roberts and her husband Bruce Wilder became owners of the property. Before opening, the building caught fire, destroying all but the original masonry, but the inn still reopened in 2009. Seven of the eight luxury guest rooms are named for famous literary couples, their décor sprung from the pages of their associated novels. For example, the Titania and Oberon (*A Midsummer Night's Dream*) includes splashes of Shakespearean romance with a four-poster bed, calm blue walls, and his-and-her sinks. Wine, soft drinks, and cheese are served in the evenings.

An inn and retreat center set on a large farm property, **Stoney Creek Farm** (19223 Manor Church Rd., 301/432-6272, $220-265) has four luxurious rooms combining bed-and-breakfast charm with rustic modernity. We're talking beautiful hardwood floors, exposed brick, a commanding central fireplace, and claw-foot tubs in some rooms.

MD-34: Antietam National Battlefield

From Boonsboro, drive 7.4 miles (11.9 km) west on MD-34 to Sharpsburg, then turn right on MD-65 to reach **Antietam National Battlefield** (4831 Dunker Church Rd., Sharpsburg, 301/432-5124, 9am-5pm daily, $5 per person, $10 per vehicle).

On Sept. 17, 1862, Union forces led by Maj. Gen. George B. McClellan waged a morning attack on Confederate general Robert E. Lee's army in a field by the Antietam Creek near Sharpsburg. The fighting lasted through the afternoon and included more than 120,000 soldiers, including a late arrival by Gen. A. P. Hill's contingent from Harpers Ferry that saved the Confederates from defeat. In total more than 3,600 soldiers died and another 17,000 were wounded, making the Battle of Antietam the bloodiest single day of the Civil War.

The battlefield has been immaculately preserved, looking very nearly the way it did the morning of that fateful day. Visitors can walk the battlefield, read more than 300 informational tablets, view 96 monuments built by battle veterans, and see the whole field from an observation tower.

Visitors can also walk through Antietam National Cemetery, which was dedicated five years after the battle and is where thousands of Union soldiers are buried. Many unknown soldiers are buried there, their graves marked with numbers. A plot separate from the main cemetery contains graves of black soldiers from World War I.

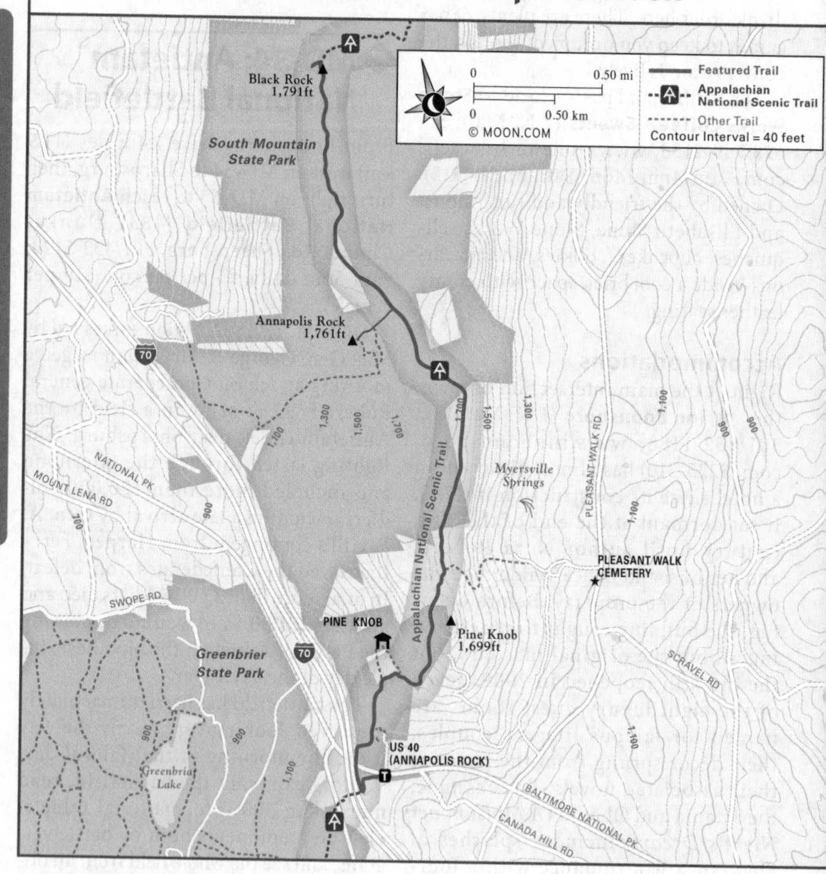

South Mountain State Park

It's a quick 4.5-mile (7.2-km) drive east on the Boonsboro Mountain Road to US-40, where just to the right, beyond the highway underpass, you'll see a trailhead taking folks into the 40-mile-long (64-km) **South Mountain State Park** (21843 National Pike, Boonsboro, 301/791-4767). The park spreads out to the north and takes the Appalachian Trail with it. AT hikers here will come across Annapolis Rock, a scenic overlook providing sweeping views atop white cliffs. The park has no maintained trails other than the AT; otherwise, hunters typically descend upon South Mountain to pursue white-tailed deer.

★ Annapolis Rock

The views from Annapolis Rock are spectacular, giving hikers a clear shot of Greenbrier Lake and the valley looking south toward Harpers Ferry. That said, when you go may determine the kind of experience you have here. You will want to get here early enough in the day, or

Trail Tale

If, when enduring a long day on the trail, you happen to spot a winged dragon diving down from the sky to steal children, you actually may not be hallucinating. When German immigrants settled in Frederick County in the 1730s, they brought with them **the legend of the Snallygaster.** Translating loosely to "quick spirit" in German, the ghastly Snallygaster lived in the caves of South Mountain, then would quietly swoop onto farms, swiping cows, kids...you name it, all while screeching out a sound akin to a train whistle.

Cute story, right? Well in 1909, a local man claimed he was captured by the Snallygaster. His neck was wounded by the beast, who then threw him back onto farmland. Somehow he survived to tell the tale—to the local newspaper, nonetheless, which published the story. Proving this may be one of the greatest viral stories of all time, then-President Theodore Roosevelt even acknowledged the Snallygaster.

Soon three men apparently fought back against the Snallygaster, sending him away...almost for good. Years later more people said they saw the beast, or maybe a child of the beast, and reportedly revenue agents found it dead in a vat of moonshine. The Snallygaster may be dead, but you never know: Look around while hiking in South Mountain State Park. You may just encounter the quick spirit.

later in the evening, to avoid being shut out of a spot.

Appalachian Trail to Annapolis Rock

Distance: 5 miles (8 km)
Duration: 2.5-3 hours
Elevation gain: 800 feet (244 m)
Difficulty: Moderate
Trailhead: Appalachian Trail trailhead at Baltimore National Pike (39.535583, -77.604219)

Pull off to the left before the curve and park in the relatively large parking area. The trailhead is easy to spot, and from there it's a jaunt on the AT until you get near Annapolis Rock. You'll first encounter a bridge over I-70; continue north on the AT and don't cross the bridge. Continue on the trail and hike a gentle fall and rise for the next 2 miles (3.2 km). At 2.3 miles (3.7 km), a blue spur trail will emerge directing you to Annapolis Rock. Take that trail for 0.2 mile (0.3 km) until it leads you right to the view. Amble on the rocks a bit, and be careful as you scope out the best place to take it in. When finished, turn around and head back to the AT and the trailhead.

While leaving early means avoiding the crowds, it also means you may have to grapple with fog. Rest assured, once the fog starts clearing, the view will have you saying "This is cool" repeatedly.

Hagerstown

Originally named Hager's Fancy by its founder, German immigrant Jonathan Hager, **Hagerstown** (pop. 39,662) is the seat of Washington County, the sixth-largest incorporated city in Maryland, and the closest major Maryland city to the Appalachian Trail.

The German roots of Hagerstown still play a part in the city's culture, as does a visible Swedish heritage (Hagerstown is home to a Volvo plant). Hagerstown played a prominent role in the Civil War and was the backdrop for multiple engagements, including an 1864 invasion by Lt. Gen. Jubal Early and his 1,500 Confederate troops. The city was also a railroad hub. Remnants of this history are found throughout the city, while its present shows a growing community with a mix of retail and manufacturing.

Hagerstown has enough amenities and dining options for a half day off, if you're hiking a lot. It could be a zero day

option, but you're better off waiting until Harrisburg for that. Still, you might regret not biting into one of Hagerstown's famous local doughnuts.

Getting There and Around

The AT trailhead for Annapolis Rock is 10 miles (16 km) from downtown, a quick car ride northwest on US-40, and local trail angels are known to give rides into town to hikers needing a bite or rest from time to time.

Hagerstown is home to the **Bayrunner Station** (123 W. Franklin St., 301/898-2571), from which Greyhound runs a bus to Washington DC. Locally, the **Washington County Commuter** departs from the **Washington County Transit Center** (1000 W. Washington St., 240/313-2750) and shuttles folks on about a dozen routes.

Sights

Miller House

Home to the Washington County Historical Society, the **Miller House** (135 W. Washington St., 301/797-8782, 1pm-4pm Wed.-Fri., 9am-4pm Sat., $5) is the kind of small brick town house that's common in old American cities like Philadelphia and Baltimore. Built in 1825 by William Price, the house changed hands a few times before Dr. Victor Miller Jr. purchased it in 1911, turning a piece of the house into physicians' offices. Since donated to the historical society, the house, which is sometimes called the Price-Miller House, is decorated primarily to resemble its state in the early 19th century. Tours are available year-round.

Hagerstown Roundhouse Museum

Hagerstown has a long railroad history, including being the hub of the Western Maryland Railway and being a vital

Top to bottom: Antietam National Battlefield; looking out from Annapolis Rock; Caledonia State Park.

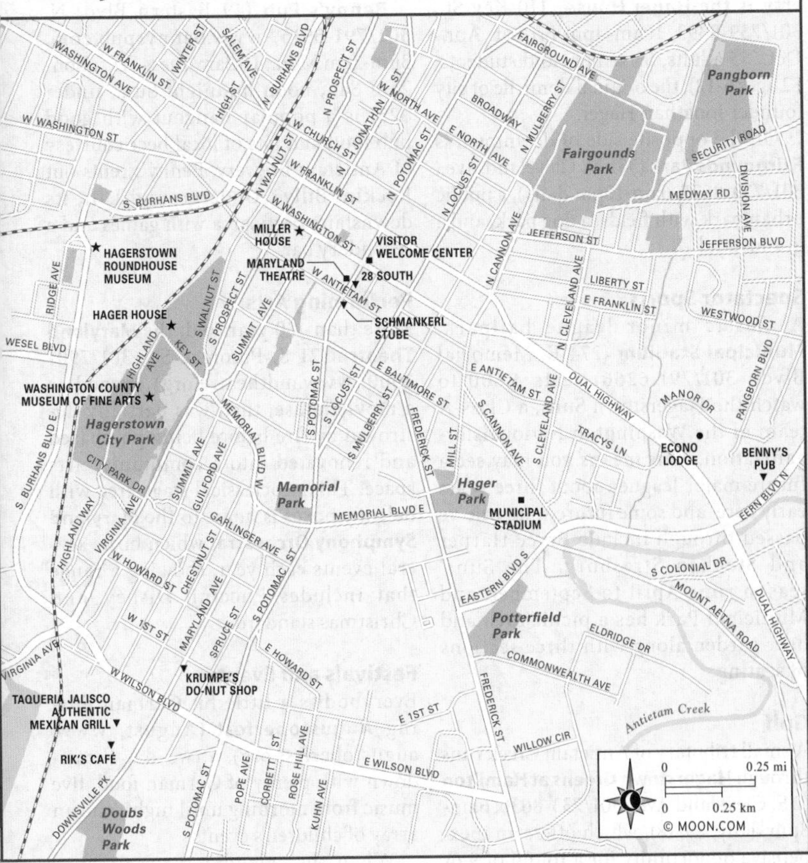

connection for rail lines heading up and down the East Coast. The primary maintenance facility for locomotives in Hagerstown was called the Roundhouse, which is no longer standing. Marking its legacy is the **Hagerstown Roundhouse Museum** (296 S. Burhans Blvd., 301/739-4665, www.roundhouse.org, 1pm-5pm Fri.-Sun., $6 adults, $1 ages 4-15), which serves as a portal to the city's railroad past. The Roundhouse Museum has an outdoor train yard, indoor model train layouts, and artifacts including bells, lights, and more.

Recreation

Parks

Commanding the southwestern section of the city, **Hagerstown City Park** (501 Virginia Ave., 301/739-8577) is its own lost world of willow trees and starry skies. The park is home to three man-made lakes, walking trails, picnic areas, and the **Washington County Museum of Fine Arts** (401 Museum Dr., 301/739-5727, 9am-5pm Tues.-Fri., 9am-4pm Sat., 1pm-5pm Sun., free), which showcases a permanent collection of more than 7,000 pieces ranging from old master paintings to Hudson River School work to contemporary sculpture. Also on the park property is the **Hager House** (110 Key St., 301/739-8393, 10am-4pm Fri-Sat. Apr.-Oct., $5 adults, $3 seniors and students, $2 ages 6-12), the original domicile of city founder Jonathan Hager.

On the opposite side of downtown is **Fairgounds Park** (351 N. Cleveland Ave., 301/739-8577, 6am-10pm daily), a public urban park with fields, a dog park, and a grandstand.

Spectator Sports

A classic minor league ballpark, **Municipal Stadium** (274 E. Memorial Blvd., 301/791-6266) seats 4,600 to watch the Hagerstown Suns, a Class-A team in the Washington Nationals organization. This means you may see a future major leaguer about three years early here, and some future stars who've passed through include Bryce Harper and Stephen Strasburg. The Suns' season runs April to September, and Municipal Park has a picnic area and beer garden along with three sections of seating.

Golf

A small tributary of Antietam Creek runs through **Hagerstown Greens at Hamilton** (2 S. Cleveland Ave., 301/733-8630, 6am-8pm daily, $9-18), which offers an inexpensive opportunity for a round of 9 or 18 holes. The nine-hole course with multiple tee boxes is moderately challenging for beginners, with one par-5 with a few hazards.

Entertainment and Events

Nightlife

The city brewery (and the very first one in western Maryland) is **Antietam Brewery** (140 Western Maryland Pkwy., 240/513-4490, www.antietambrewery.com, 3pm-10pm Thurs.-Fri., noon-10pm Sat., noon-6pm Sun., under $15). Antietam has a deep catalog of brews, all of them extremely sessionable at between 5 and 7 percent ABV. There's a beautiful wood bar at its new taproom.

Benny's Pub (49 Eastern Blvd. N, 301/791-5915, www.bennyspub.com, 3pm-2am Mon., 11-2am Tues.-Fri., noon-2am Sat., noon-midnight Sun., under $25) is a popular hangout with good pub food and lots of local beer courtesy of Antietam Brewery. Benny's rents out Rockin' Billy's Underground Lair, its downstairs party area with games and a secondary bar.

Performing Arts

More than 100 years old, the **Maryland Theatre** (21 S. Potomac St., 301/790-2000, www.mdtheatre.org) opened as a movie house, then was partially destroyed by fire before being purchased and renovated into a community arts space. This neoclassical stage area with balcony boxes is home to the **Maryland Symphony Orchestra,** which hosts several events each year, showing a range that includes Puccini, Disney, and Christmas standards.

Festivals and Events

Everybody's a little bit German during **Augustoberfest** (August, www.augustoberfest.org), a two-day throwdown with plenty of German food, live music from morning until night, and an array of children's events.

When the calendar turns to summer, it's time for the **Western Maryland Blues Fest** (June, www.blues-fest.org, free Fri., $25-35 Sat.) at Hagerstown City Park. Local and regional blues musicians play over a Friday evening and all day Saturday.

Shopping

Hagerstown Premium Outlets (495 Premium Outlets Blvd., 301/790-0300, 10am-7pm Sun.-Thurs., 10am-9pm Fri.-Sat.) has about everything you're looking for in the traditional outdoor outlet mall space. Get a taste of regional flair at the **Pennsylvania Dutch Market** (1583

Potomac Ave., 240/420-8555, 10am-5pm Wed., 9am-6pm Thurs., 9am-7pm Fri., 8am-4pm Sat.). Buy an Amish-made piece of furniture, or bite into some homemade pretzels, barbecue, and doughnuts.

Food

If there's one food that you'll forever associate with Hagerstown, it's the doughnut…or rather, do-nut. ★ **Krumpe's Do-Nut Shop** (912 Maryland Ave., 301/733-6103, www.krumpesdonuts.com, 7pm-2am Sun.-Fri.) does doughnuts for dessert *and* post-drinking carb loading, and boy do people show up for these fresh, warm, moist treats. Get there before 7pm, or else you'll be in a line dozens deep, even on weeknights. Krumpe's was founded by Rudolf Krumpe, a German immigrant who arrived in Hagerstown in 1936.

There's plenty of German heritage on display at **Schmankerl Stube** (58 S. Potomac St., 301/797-3354, http://schmankerlstube.com, 11am-10pm Tues.-Sat., 11am-9pm Sun., under $40 dinner, under $20 lunch, $25 brunch). Women in dirndls wait on customers at this ultra-authentic spot, which serves schnitzel and *knusprige schweinshaxe* (pork shank with mushroom cream sauce) for lunch and dinner, and brunch includes traditional staples like bratwurst in curry sauce and Bavarian meatballs.

Just up the block, **28 South** (28 S. Potomac St., 240/347-4932, www.28south.net, 11am-midnight Tues.-Thurs., 11am-1am Fri.-Sat., 11am-9pm Sun., under $40 dinner, under $25 lunch) has New American dishes like country chicken and seared scallops, plus a focus on pizza and hot dogs, tacos, and burgers. The space features wood floors, high-top tables, and booths in earth tones.

It may be odd that a single strip mall has possibly the two best restaurants in Hagerstown, but that's the reality here. **Taqueria Jalisco Authentic Mexican Grill** (1037 Maryland Ave., 301/797-8202, 10:30am-9pm daily, under $20) has bright orange and lime walls and retro diner-style tables, but better yet, it serves cheap street tacos and warm chips, like only the best taquerias.

A few doors down is **Rik's Café** (1065 Maryland Ave., 301/302-7541, www.rikscafeexperience.com, 11am-8:30pm Sun.-Tues., 11am-9:30pm Wed.-Sat., under $40), which unabashedly features cuisine from all corners of the globe. Have a Chinese rice bowl one day, the next enjoy Hawaiian wasabi alfredo, then return for Maryland-style crab cakes. There's a big dining area and a separate bar area with high tops, a long bar, and sofas.

Accommodations

Under $100

Hagerstown isn't a place for boutique and independent hotels; instead, it's populated by low- and mid-budget hotels on the periphery. That said, they all generally score well with patrons. Good bets at the lower price point include the **Econo Lodge** (900 Dual Hwy., 301/739-9051, $50-80), the **Comfort Suites** (1801 Dual Hwy., 301/791-8100, $70-100), and the **Baymont Inn & Suites** (431 Dual Hwy., 301/660-3883, $60-110).

$100-150

Moderately priced hotels in Hagerstown include the **Sleep Inn & Suites** (18216 Col. Henry K. Douglas Dr., 301/766-9449, $90-140), the **Hampton Inn** (1716 Dual Hwy., 301/739-6100, $90-140), the **Homewood Suites** (1650 Pullman Lane, 301/665-3816, $100-150), and the **Ramada Plaza** (1718 Underpass Way, 301/797-2500, $80-130)

Information and Services

The **Visitor Welcome Center** (16 Public Square, 301/791-3246, www.visithagerstown.com, 9am-5pm Mon.-Fri., 10am-4pm Sat.) is a pretty welcoming place; they'll give you all the information you need about Hagerstown and Washington County sights, dining options, lodging, and more.

Greencastle

Take US-11 north from Hagerstown until you cross the Mason-Dixon Line and enter Pennsylvania, the Keystone State and birthplace of the nation. Five miles (8 km) from the border is **Greencastle** (pop. 3,996), a tiny borough that was once a settlement of Rigdonite Mormons founded by Latter-Day Saints leader Sidney Rigdon. It was also taken over by the Confederacy during the early days of the Gettysburg Campaign of the Civil War in 1863, but two months later it was retaken by Union forces.

These days it's less stressful in Greencastle, thanks in part to the delicious treats at **Mikie's Ice Cream & Green Cow** (179 S. Antrim Way, 717/597-4011, 11am-10pm daily, under $10). Go for summer fare like burgers and sandwiches, and stay for soft serve and homemade waffle cones. A game room has a menagerie of arcade games, while the attached Green Cow Gift Shop sells toys, housewares, and bath and body goods.

PA-16: Waynesboro

Officially becoming a trail town in 2014, **Waynesboro** (pop. 10,568) is just 5 miles (8 km) west of the Appalachian Trail's crossing at PA-16, and it's 8.6 miles (13.8 km) east of Greencastle, also via PA-16. It's a cute little town that thru-hikers enjoy for the hearty food options.

Food and Accommodations

Food options in Waynesboro are headlined by the fast-casual burger joint the **Waynesburger** (100 W. Main St., 717/749-0074, 11am-9pm Mon., 10:30am-9pm Tues.-Sat., 11am-8pm Sun., under $10), whose sunny interior and several dozen milk shake options brighten everyone's day.

Speaking of brightening days, **Parlor House** (724 S. Potomac St., 717/762-5415, 6am-8pm Mon.-Thurs., 6am-8:30pm Fri.-Sat., 10:45am-2:30pm Sun., under $30) keeps people happy with its diner charm of checkered floor and cherry-red stools, and its versatile menu featuring specials like slippery beef pot pie on Wednesdays and salmon cakes every Friday.

Terrific diner food is also available at **Main Street Diner** (91 W. Main St., 717/749-7000, www.mainstreetdinerpa.com, 8am-2pm Wed.-Sat., under $15). Breakfast is served all day, and there's just one lunch entrée: fish-and-chips.

Hikers are known to stay at ★ **Burgundy Lane Bed & Breakfast** (128 W. Main St., 717-762-8112, www.burgundylane.biz, $90-120), which has six guest rooms set in a well-kept 19th-century brick town house. Rooms are thematic, from the Magnolia with understated southern charm, to the Out of Africa room painted in searing gold and crimson and with a bed dressed in African prints. Innkeepers Dave and Margaret Schmelzer can arrange transportation for hikers who wish to stay at the Burgundy.

Those wanting to keep on the trail may head 2 miles (3.2 km) from the PA-16 crossing to stay at the two **Deer Lick Shelter** buildings. Another 2.4 miles (3.9 km) from there is the older **Antietam Shelter**, and just 1.2 miles (1.9 km) more are the two **Tumbling Run Shelters**, one of which is conveniently marked "snoring."

PA-16: Rouzerville

A little farther east on PA-16 from Waynesboro, and 11.2 miles (18 km) east of Greencastle, is **Rouzerville** (pop. 917), a teensy community that plays host to the **Mason-Dixon Appalachian Trail Outdoor Festival** (June, Red Run Park, 12143 Buchanan Tr. East, free). Timed to occur when northbound thru-hikers should be ambling through the area, the festival has an area where locals can "meet the hikers" as they refuel and rest. There's also live music, food vendors, children's activities, a silent auction, and yoga in the park.

Four miles (6.4 km) east of Rouzerville is the community of **Blue Ridge Summit,** which is literally a summit. Located on South Mountain, the community peaks at 1,345 feet (410 m) but quickly dips to as low as half that height. Hikers seeking supplies like shampoo, deodorant, granola bars, and first-aid items can find the trail hiker's box at the **Blue Ridge Summit Post Office** (14959 Buchanan Tr. East, 800/275-8777, 8am-4pm Mon.-Fri., 9am-11:30am Sat.), also home to a logbook signed by thru-hikers.

Michaux State Forest

After crossing PA-16, the Appalachian Trail enters **Michaux State Forest** (40 Rocky Mountain Rd., park headquarters located at 10099 US-30, Fayetteville, open 6am-8pm daily). Comprising more than 85,000 acres, Michaux is the site of the country's first forestry school, the Pennsylvania State Forest Academy, which is now incorporated into Penn State Mont Alto.

Michaux is also home to the **Flat Rock Trail System,** which begins north of US-30 and runs up to Shippensburg Road. It contains 38 miles (61 km) of multiuse trails for hiking, mountain biking, ATVs, and horseback riding. Some of the trails cross the Appalachian Trail as it slogs north through the rocks. Early in the park the trail runs past **Chimney Rocks,** a collection of jagged rocks atop Buzzard Peak. They offer sweeping views of the Cumberland Valley.

Hiking

Chimney Rocks Loop

Distance: 4.4 miles (7.1 km)
Duration: 2-2.5 hours
Elevation gain: 1,000 feet (305 m)
Difficulty: Moderate
Trailhead: Old Forge Picnic Area (39.795774, -77.483433)

From the picnic area, find the AT blazes and begin a hike north on the trail. After passing a junction with the blue-blazed Tumbling Run Trail, you'll pass a stream, then start crawling up a steep grade of 900 feet (274 m). After 2 miles (3.2 km) on the AT be on the lookout for the blue-blazed spur trail leading you to Chimney Rocks. Head over and enjoy the view. With more time you can continue on the AT toward the peak of Snowy Mountain and reach the mountain's fire tower. If not, come back on gravel and rocks and make your way down to the car.

Fishing

Cold-water fishing for trout is permitted in the east branch of the Conococheague Creek, the east and west branches of the Antietam Creek, Mountain Creek, Laurel Lake, Fuller Lake, and Waynesboro Reservoir. Warm-water fishing is available at **Long Pine Run Reservoir,** Waynesboro Reservoir, and Carbaugh Dam.

Accommodations

There are several lean-tos on the Appalachian Trail in Michaux State Forest, including Tumbling Run, Rocky Mountain, Quarry Gap, Birch Run, Tom Run, and James Fry (or Tagg Run). Primitive camping is also permitted in the park. Primitive campers don't need a **state camping permit** (free) unless they're staying more than one night.

Chambersburg

Go north from Greencastle 11.4 miles (18.3 km) and find the only northern community burned by Confederate soldiers during the Civil War. That would be **Chambersburg** (pop. 20,268), which was destroyed in 1864 but rebuilt shortly afterward; the burning is memorialized at a fountain in the borough's **Memorial Square** (East McKinley St. at Memorial Dr.). A farming and manufacturing community with nearby Amish and Mennonite populations, Chambersburg is definitively blue-collar, in the most traditional sense of the term. Folks here value hard work and know everyone in the community. Consider Chambersburg an opportunity to grab some food or a place to stay if you're looking to hike in Michaux State Forest or Caledonia State Park.

Sights

The house where abolitionist John Brown stayed in 1859 in preparation for his raid on Harpers Ferry still stands today as the **John Brown House** (225 E. King St., 717/264-1667, 10am-4pm Tues.-Sat. May-Oct., 10am-4pm Nov.-Apr., $4 adults, $3 children). Then called the Ritner Boarding House, the structure today is filled with period furniture. Call ahead for a tour.

In 1912, the very early days of the automobile, an Indiana entrepreneur and car lover named Carl G. Fisher aimed to roll out a transcontinental highway. Opened in 1913 and spanning from New York City to San Francisco, the Lincoln Highway follows a variety of American roads, among them US-30. In Chambersburg, the Lincoln Highway is US-30, and there's a **Memorial Marker** (201 Lincoln Way W.) to find and photograph.

The marker is a small post branded with the highway's "L" logo. Nearby,

autumn color at Long Pine Run Reservoir in Michaux State Forest

across from the Historic Texas Lunch, is an old gasoline pump branded with the logo. Considering this is one of two places on the Appalachian Trail road trip crossing the Lincoln Highway (the actual AT crosses the highway in Michaux State Forest), it's a fun roadside spot to mark.

Food

American

The restaurants of Chambersburg value food over fireworks. **The Cottage Pub & Restaurant** (572 Wayne Ave., 717/264-8543, www.cottagepubandrestaurant.com, 11am-midnight Mon., 11am-1am Tues.-Sun., under $30), creator of wings and burgers, sandwiches and seafood dishes in a neighborhood haunt everybody has visited since 1933.

The Historic Texas Lunch (108 Lincoln Way West, 717/264-4439, 5am-9pm Mon.-Sat., 6am-8pm Sun., under $25), which has booths, counter seating, hot dogs for lunch (among other things), and omelets for breakfast (also among other things).

EJ's Grill (346 Lincoln Way East, 717/263-1137, 4pm-9pm Tues.-Thurs., 4pm-10pm Sat.-Sun., under $40), a no-frills local dinner hangout serving seafood, including a slew of seafood specials. The crab cakes are well beloved.

And finally, arguably the best breakfast in Chambersburg is at **Molly Pitcher Waffle Shop** (109 S. Main St., 717/261-0067, 8am-3pm Tues.-Sat., 8am-2pm Sun., under $15). This old-fashioned breakfast counter with a superb neon sign serves great omelets and chicken-and-waffles, among other waffle treats.

Latin American

Authentic Peruvian is found at **Inka Kitchen** (1228 Lincoln Way East, 717/491-1833, 11am-9pm Tues.-Sat., 11am-8pm Sun., under $30), a colorful spot with tangerine walls.

For rarely found Guatemalan cuisine, hit up the bare-bones but pastel-cute **Las Palmeras** (209 Southgate Mall, 717/446-0857, 11am-9pm Sun.-Thurs., 10am-10pm Fri.-Sat., under $25).

Asian

Really good sushi, plus other cuisine from East Asia, is on the menu at **Kenzo Japanese & Asian Fusion** (1495 Lincoln Way East, 717/263-0076, 11am-9:30pm Tues.-Thurs., 11am-10pm Fri., noon-10pm Sat., noon-9:30pm Sun., under $30), which with its wall-to-wall wood is one of the few sushi restaurants embracing a "rustic" design.

More stylish, with a nightclub-style bar area, is **Volcano Japanese Restaurant** (955 Wayne Ave., 717/504-8989, 11am-3pm and 4:30pm-10pm Mon.-Fri., noon-10:30pm Sat., noon-10pm Sun., under $30). There's plenty of sushi and hand rolls here, plus a hibachi feature.

Dive into exceptional Korean at **Korean Bulgogi House** (408 W. Loudon St., 717/263-0419, 11am-9pm Mon. and Wed.-Sat., under $25). Enjoy bibimbap in, again, a no-frills atmosphere of white walls and wood furniture.

Accommodations

Chambersburg has a few bed-and-breakfasts. Among them is the massive 1880 Victorian house built by John Watson Craig, called the **Craig Victorian Bed & Breakfast** (756 Philadelphia Ave., 717/977-7107, www.craigvictorian.com, $65-125). The kind and romantic rooms are inexpensive and aren't overly dramatic. Two suites have whirlpool tubs, while one also has an en suite kitchen.

Lillie's Garden B&B (65 Norland Ave., 717-261-6593, www.lilliesgarden.com, $105-$159) is set in an everyday residence a little beyond downtown. There are four rooms in total, all resembling a slightly elevated guest room at your friend's house, while two of the rooms have optional private bathrooms.

Chambersburg has several chain hotels, most of them sprinkled beside I-81. The **Best Western** (211 Walker Rd., 717/262-4994, $70-120) is a solid choice and has an outdoor pool. Nearby is the **Country Inn & Suites** (399 Beddington Dr., 771/261-0900, $70-120), which features an indoor pool and uninspiring but comfortable rooms. **The La Quinta Inn & Suites** ($80-130) is similar to the others with a bit more flair, but that's if you want psychedelic colors on your walls.

Caledonia State Park

After a 13-mile (21-km) drive east on US-30 from Chambersburg, you'll find **Caledonia State Park** (101 Pine Grove Rd., Fayetteville, 717/352-2161) wedged inside Michaux State Forest. Caledonia is 1,125 acres of parkland for families and casual hikers, with some overnight accommodations.

There are 10 miles (16 km) of trails at Caledonia, with the most enjoyable being the **Raccoon Run Trail,** an old section of the Appalachian Trail that rises nearly 800 feet (244 m) over 5 miles (8 km). Spot the remains of an old AT shelter here. You can hook up with the AT via Raccoon Run about 4 miles (6.4 km) from the trailhead.

Caledonia is home to **Caledonia Public Golf Course** (9515 Golf Course Rd., Fayetteville, 717/352-7271, www.caledoniagc.com, $10-35), which offers 18 countryside holes with tree-lined fairways. Nearby is the **Totem Hole Playhouse** (9555 Golf Course Rd., 717/352-2164, www.totempoleplayhouse.org), a small summer stock theater where popular musicals entertain. Its second artistic director, who served for 30 years, was William H. Putch, husband of *All in the Family* actress Jean Stapleton.

The park also has a public swimming pool (Sat.-Sun. May-June and Aug.-Sept., daily June-Aug., $6 adults, $5 seniors) and **two campgrounds** ($15-41) with tent and trailer sites, plus unique houses for rent ($15-165).

Shippensburg

Continue north from Chambersburg on US-11 another 11.2 miles (18 km) to **Shippensburg** (pop. 5,575), which has nothing to do with shipping but with Edward Shippen III, a former mayor of Philadelphia who acquired this rugged land just beyond the Blue Ridge from heirs of William Penn. Shippen's granddaughter Peggy would go on the marry an army general named Benedict Arnold, becoming a high-paid spy while helping her husband.

Today Shippensburg is known for its school, **Shippensburg University** (1871 Old Main Dr., 717/477-7447, www.ship.edu), whose nearly 7,000 undergraduates pack into the campus north of downtown. On campus is the **Fashion Archives and Museum of Shippensburg University** (501 N. Earl St., noon-4pm Mon.-Thurs., $5 adults, $4 seniors, free under age 12), which hosts regular exhibits using the woman's dress as a tool for studying history. Also visit the **H. Ric Luhrs Performing Arts Center** (475

Lancaster Dr., 717/477-7469, www.luhrscenter.org). Its Grove Theatre seats about 1,500 and plays host to national touring acts like the Beach Boys and Jay Leno, plus musicals and children's entertainment.

Shippensburg also shuts down each year for the **Shippensburg Corn Festival** (Aug., www.shippensburgcornfestival.net, free). More than 250 food and craft vendors set up, as families enjoy an antique car show, live music and entertainment, and a corn-eating contest.

This is a fun town, and a good stop for a bite to eat, especially if you're a night-owl or looking to fill up without emptying your wallet. For those staying overnight, **Capital Area Transit** (bus stop 100 S. Conestoga Dr., Mon.-Fri.) provides bus service to Shippensburg, connecting to Harrisburg.

Food and Nightlife

Pizza

Take a bite of the piping-hot stuff at **Pizza Man** (201 N. Seneca St., 717/530-1607, www.shippizzaman.com, 11am-11:30pm Sun.-Mon. and Wed.-Thurs., 11am-12:30am Fri.-Sat., under $20), whose booths and tables get good traction.

Alfredo's Pizza (397 Baltimore Rd., 717/532-5542, www.alfredospizzarestaurant.com, 10:30am-10pm Sun.-Thurs., 10:30am-11pm Fri.-Sat., under $20) serves a range of unique pies, like the cowboy pizza (steak, bacon, and barbecue sauce), in a sitting area with murals.

Then there's **Pizza 'n Stuff** (85 W. King St., 717/532-3431, www.pizzanstuff-ship.com, 10:30am-10pm Sun. and Tues.-Thurs., 10:30am-11pm Fri.-Sat., under $20), whose "stuff" is Mexican food. Order a cheap burrito to pair with your pie.

Finally, **Big Richards** (39 Richard Ave., 717/300-3737, www.bigrichardspizza.com, 11am-9:30pm Sun.-Wed., 11am-1am Thurs.-Sat., under $20) is really close to campus and open really late on party nights. Stop into what locals call "the shop on Richard" for the usual pizzeria fare.

American

Inside the Shippen Place Hotel, **University Grille** (32 King St., 717/530-1148, www.ugrille.com, 11am-2am Mon.-Sat., under $35) spotlights burgers, sandwiches, and pub favorites like fried tacos and fried pickles. It has a convivial bar area and kind staff.

CJ's American Pub & Grill (487 King St., 717/532-5612, www.cjspubgrill.com, 11am-9pm Tues.-Thurs., 11am-10pm Fri.-Sat., 11am-8pm Sun., under $35) is a friendly, wood-toned hangout with steaks and seafood dishes, along with the usual pub fare.

Arooga's (105 W. King St., 717/221-9464, www.aroogas.com, 11am-2am daily, under $30) has an active sports bar area and serves items like wings and fajitas.

Asian

For something not breaded or fried, try **Pho Uy-Vu** (300 S. Fayette St., 717/300-7926, 10am-8pm daily, under $15), which brings Vietnamese street dishes like pho, plus cultural variations, inside a mint-green spot with plenty of floor-to-ceiling windows.

Asian Taste (825A W. King St., 717/530-1118, www.asiantasteshippensburg.com, 11am-10pm Mon.-Thurs., 11am-11pm Fri.-Sat., noon-9:30pm Sun., under $15) is basic, no-frills Americanized Chinese food. There's also hibachi.

Accommodations

The **Quality Inn & Suites Shippen Place Hotel** (32 E. King St., 717/532-4141, $50-100)—more casually known as the Shippen Place Hotel—is the only choice for lodging in downtown Shippensburg. The 57 simple rooms with bright yellow walls won't immediately draw you in, but the price point is cheap and there's a bar and restaurant in the lobby, plus a coffee bar, and all the young staff members are courteous.

Closer to the university is the **Courtyard by Marriott** (503 Newburg Rd., 717/477-0680, $100-180), with its airy rooms and vibrant food-and-drink area. The **Holiday Inn Express & Suites** (120 Walnut Bottom Rd., 717/532-1100, $90-150) is a mile (1.6 km) from downtown and offers a similar experience to the Courtyard. The **Best Western** (125 Walnut Bottom Rd., 717/532-5200, $70-120) is quite suitable and affordable, and it has an indoor pool.

PA-233: Pine Grove Furnace State Park

Pine Grove Furnace State Park (1100 Pine Grove Rd., Gardners, 717/486-7174, 8am-9pm daily), accessible by taking US-11 north to PA-233 east, is an important patch of land on the Appalachian Trail. Within its 696 acres is the midpoint of the AT: About 1,100 miles (1,770 km) done, another 1,100 miles to go. The Appalachian Trail Museum stands by this marker, a necessary visit for all thru-hikers, section hikers…heck, anyone who's ever even walked a foot on the trail.

The park is on land that was once the Pine Grove Iron Works, a charcoal-fired facility in the 1800s that smelted iron ore to make wagon wheel iron and locomotive parts, among other items. An enormous furnace stack still stands at the park, just around the corner from the Appalachian Trail Museum.

★ Appalachian Trail Museum

Opening in a former gristmill in 2010, the **Appalachian Trail Museum** (1120 Pine Grove Rd., Gardners, 717/486-8126, www.atmuseum.org, April-October, free) celebrates the experience of the trail, highlighting the stories of thru-hikers and trail pioneers like Grandma Gatewood, Gene Espy, and Ed Garvey. The museum also maintains the Appalachian Trail Hall of Fame, which honors important hikers, volunteers, pioneers, trail angels, and administrators spanning the more than 75 years of the trail's existence.

Across the way from the museum is the **Pine Grove Furnace General Store** (1 Bendersville Rd., Gardners, 717/486-4920, Mar.-Nov.), which sells hiker and camper supplies and food like sandwiches, chips, and drinks. Oh, and then there's the ice cream. The general store is home to the **Half-Gallon Challenge,** in which thru-hikers mark the halfway point of their trips by taking a spoon to a carton of ice cream. (Note: Ice cream no longer comes in half-gallon cartons, so the actual size is 1.5 quarts, or .375 gallons. Sorry!) Either way, it's a delicious challenge, one thru-hikers take seriously. Outside seating is available.

Hiking

Buck Ridge Trail

Distance: 12 miles (19.3 km)

Duration: 7 hours

Elevation gain: 942 feet (287 m)
Difficulty: Moderate
Trailhead: Parking area across from park office (40.033199, -77.303403)

There's a small network of trails at Pine Grove Furnace State Park; the longest trail quickly leaves the park and runs mostly through Michaux State Forest. From the trailhead, you're practically on level ground following yellow blazes for the first mile (1.6 km), but you'll start a gradual, easy climb on craggy trail, plus former logging roads. The trail ends at the Kings Gap Environmental Education Center, a 2,531-acre forest that's home to the Cameron-Masland Mansion, plus programs increasing awareness of natural resources. This an up-and-back hike and could take a bit longer than seven hours if you're stopping for food, drink, and occasional rest.

Pole Steeple Trail

Distance: 1.5 miles (2.4 km)
Duration: 1-1.5 hours
Elevation gain: 535 feet (163 m)
Difficulty: Moderate
Trailhead: Old Railroad Bed Road at Laurel Lake (40.038273, -77.270141)

According to the park, the quartzite rock outcropping at Pole Steeple was created at the Pangaea, when North America collided with Africa. That alone makes it worth seeing this marvel, which also provides magnificent views of the park. From the shore of Laurel Lake you'll be stepping up rocks all the way up Piney Mountain to the top. It gets dicey, especially if you dislike exposure. The last section of the hike is a scramble using hands, but the payoff is worth the work. After imagining exactly how it would feel to experience the collision of two continents, start your careful trek down.

Recreation

Swimming and Boating

Both Fuller and Laurel Lakes have swimming beaches (8am-sunset May-Sept.,

Pine Grove Furnace State Park

free), though Laurel doesn't have lifeguards. Both beaches have snack bars.

Boating is permitted only on Laurel Lake, which offers a boat launch. Registration is necessary for motorboats, and either registration or a launching permit is required for nonmotorized boats.

Fishing

Drop in a line in search of pickerel, perch, bass, and trout in either Fuller or Laurel Lake. Mountain Creek has cool-water species of trout. Ice fishing is also permitted on Laurel Lake, but not in the designated ice-skating area. State fishing licenses are required.

Ice-Skating

Near the boat launch at Laurel Lake, the park opens a spot when it's icy to lace up and glide.

Accommodations

Shack up at the park's **Charcoal Hearth Campground** (101 Bendersville Rd., Gardners, March-December, $15-56), which includes 70 tent and trailer sites with picnic tables and fire rings. Flush toilets, warm showers, and some electrical hookups are available. You can also stay at the Paymaster's Cabin, a two-story historic home with electric heat, a full kitchen, showers, and an outdoor area with picnic table and fire ring.

Carlisle

Carlisle (pop. 37,695), a 20.2-mile (32.5-km) ride up US-11 from Shippensburg, may be best known as the city that turned a young Native American named Jim Thorpe into arguably the finest athlete in American history. Thorpe moved from his Oklahoma Sac and Fox Nation to Pennsylvania to attend Carlisle Indian Industrial School, which ran as a pseudo social engineering experiment aimed at assimilating Native Americans into white Euro-American culture. Thorpe excelled, especially as a sports star. He won Olympic gold medals in the pentathlon and decathlon in 1912, then played baseball for the New York Giants and football for the Canton Bulldogs. The site of the Carlisle Indian Industrial School is now the U.S. Army War College, a major instructional facility for senior military officers and civilians along the city outskirts.

Carlisle provides plenty of decent food and drink options, plus spillover hotel choices for those hoping to stay around the Harrisburg area. **Capital Area Transit** (bus stop 1 Courthouse Square, Mon.-Fri.) provides bus service to Carlisle, connecting to Harrisburg.

Dickinson College

In the heart of the city is **Dickinson College** (28 N. College St.), founded in 1783 by Declaration of Independence signer Benjamin Rush, and whose most famous alum is former president James Buchanan. Its walkable campus includes numerous old limestone buildings like the 1886 Bosler Hall. The **Weis Center for the Performing Arts** (1 Dent Dr., 570/577-3727) hosts approximately 30 shows each year, mixing in world music, dance, and theater, sometimes featuring students.

U.S. Army Heritage and Education Center

The comprehensive history of the U.S. Army is available at the **U.S. Army Heritage and Education Center** (950 Soldiers Dr., 717/245-3972, www.ahec.armywarcollege.edu, 10am-5pm Mon.-Sat., noon-5pm Sun., free). Across the street from the U.S. Army War College, it houses 16 million military items and 350,000 military volumes, while telling the story of the American foot soldier. Military and history buffs will be floored with the sheer scope of material here and would enjoy a full day taking in the exhibits and exploring the sources.

Guests can experience firsthand

the turbulence of war with the Soldier Experience Gallery, where dog tags unlock an interactive series of stories running through American military history. Outdoors is the Army Heritage Trail, a 1-mile (1.6-km) walking path that goes through a trench and past antique tanks and helicopters. Ridgway Hall is a public research facility that features an exhibit called *Enter the War on Terrorism*. The center hosts **Army Heritage Days** (May) over Armed Forces Weekend, during which reenactors engage the public and speakers discuss Army history.

Food and Nightlife

Good ol' elevated American is served at **1794 the Whiskey Rebellion** (10 S. Hanover St., 800/704-1188, 4pm-10pm Mon.-Sat., under $40). Bite into steak or colonial chicken pot pie while ordering a cocktail. The fireplace, warm tones, and wood treatments make 1794 feel like an old colonial tavern.

For a taste of Belgium, try **Café Bruges** (16 N. Pitt St., 717/960-0223, www.cafebruges.com, 11:30am-9:30pm Sun.-Thurs., 11:30am-10:30pm Fri.-Sat., under $40). A deep Belgian beer list means you're enjoying yeasty and farm-fresh brews alongside mussels and frites. Totally worth it.

For beer with English fare, check out **Market Cross Pub & Brewery** (113 N. Hanover St., 717/258-1234, www.marketcrosspub.com, 11am-11pm Mon.-Tues., 11am-midnight Wed.-Thurs., 11am-1am Fri.-Sat., 11am-10pm Sun., under $30). Market Cross brews a couple of its own creations and features more than a dozen beers on its guest list. Food includes real English fare like cottage pie and beef 'n' Guinness, and fake English food like Ye Old BLT.

Drinks abound at **Gingerbread Man**

Top to bottom: Dickinson College; U.S. Army Heritage and Education Center; National Civil War Museum in Harrisburg.

(5 S. Court House Ave., 717/249-6970, 11am-2am daily, under $30), which serves pub food but is known for its lively drinking scene, pool tables, and jukebox. **Alibi's** (10 N. Pitt St., 717/462-4629, 11am-midnight Mon.-Wed., 11am-2am Thurs.-Sat., noon-midnight Sun., under $25) is also a hit with the legal-age college crowd. The large tavern-style building can fill up; food here includes bar shareables.

Chow down on chili and cheese hot dogs at **Hamilton Restaurant** (55 W. High St., 717/249-4410, 6am-9:30pm Mon.-Sat., under $20). But that's not all at this standard diner: Breakfast is popular, especially Pennsylvania favorites scrapple (fatty "meat" product) and chipped beef (take my word for it).

It's breakfast with a smile at **Fay's Country Kitchen** (203 S. Hanover St., 717/243-5510, 6am-2pm Mon.-Sat., 7am-2pm Sun., under $15). Try a skillet at this cozy diner with Coca-Cola signage and red trim. And please get scrapple.

If you don't want scrapple, **Spoons Café** (57 W. Pomfret St., 717/793-1048, www.spoonscafe.net, 10am-4pm Mon.-Fri., 11am-3pm Sat., under $10) lovingly crafts healthy salads and sandwiches with plenty of vegan and gluten-free options. Sit inside its extremely green quarters (we're not just talking about the food).

Accommodations

Because Carlisle is at the intersection of the Pennsylvania Turnpike (I-76) and I-81, there are more than several chain hotels standing near off-ramps. The one outlier is **Carlisle House Bed & Breakfast** (148 S. Hanover St., 717/249-0350, $150-200), which encompasses two buildings, one dating to 1826 and the second to 1884. The guest rooms have queen or king beds and are very comfortable and bright with a mix of solid and floral design touches. Be sure to introduce yourself to the innkeepers, a couple with the last name Carlisle. Must've been fate.

Harrisburg

The ninth-largest city in Pennsylvania and its capital city since 1812, **Harrisburg** (49,528) is a pretty cosmopolitan town, but it's taken a while to get there. A farming town into the mid-1850s, Harrisburg grew as a training camp for Union soldiers during the Civil War, then as a major railroad hub connecting Pittsburgh to the east, becoming key in the rise of the steel industry. As steel declined in the 20th century, so did Harrisburg's importance, driven home by suburban flight and environmental problems. You may have heard of Three Mile Island, the site of a partial nuclear meltdown in 1979 that left minimal damage but caused more than 140,000 people to temporarily flee the Harrisburg area.

The city has since had fits and starts, but you'll see plenty of inventive small businesses and restaurants, parkland highlighting the city's unique geography on the river and proximity to mountains, and young energy fueling the downtown district and nearby neighborhoods. Appalachian Trail hikers walk parallel to Harrisburg about 20 miles (32 km) west before crossing the Susquehanna River in the northern town of Duncannon, but for many, the food, nightlife, accommodations, and sights of the capital of Pennsylvania provides an intriguing option for a zero day. A few places in the city have figured this out, too.

Getting There and Around

Drive 22.8 miles (37 km) east from Carlisle on US-11, over the Susquehanna River and into Harrisburg. The Pennsylvania Turnpike (I-76), I-81, and I-83 also run through the city, providing connections to most nearby metropolitan areas, including Baltimore, Philadelphia, and New York City.

The **Harrisburg International Airport** (1 Terminal Dr., 888/235-9442, www.flyhia.com, MDT) is 9 miles (14.5

Harrisburg

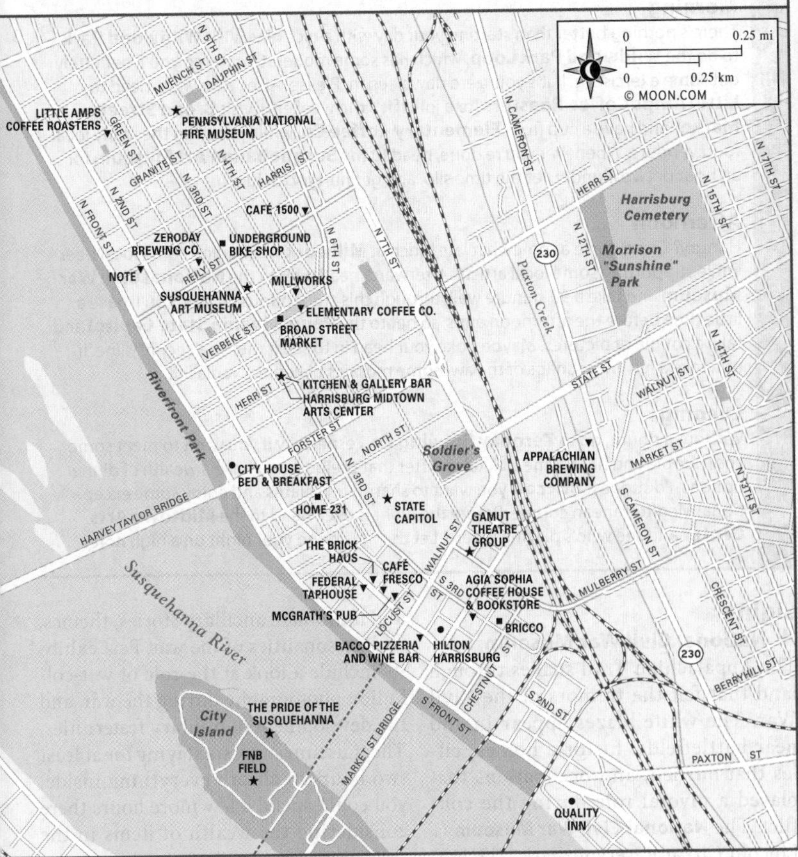

km) southeast of Harrisburg. It provides nonstop service on Air Canada (888/247-2262), Allegiant (702/505-8888), American Airlines (800/433-7300), Delta (800/221-1212), United (800/864-8331), and Southern Airways Express (800/329-0485) to 13 cities, including Washington DC, Philadelphia, Atlanta, Boston, Charlotte, Chicago, Detroit, Pittsburgh, and Toronto. Many of the hotels along Eisenhower Drive in Harrisburg provide airport shuttle service.

Keystone Service from Amtrak (800/872-7245, www.amtrak.com) connects New York City to the **Harrisburg Transportation Center** (4th and Chestnut Sts., 800/872-7245, www.amtrak.com) via Philadelphia.

You can take a **Greyhound** (214/849-8966, www.greyhound.com) from most major East Coast hubs to the **Harrisburg Bus Station** (411 Market St., 717/255-6970). In the city limits, **Capital Area Transit** (901 N. Cameron St., 717/238-8304) has several dozen routes with daily schedules. Some of the routes extend to suburban areas and nearby hubs like Hershey and Carlisle.

One Day in Harrisburg

Morning

There's nothing better than starting your day with a nice hike. Visit **Wildwood Park** to do the **Wildwood Park Loop**, which has some moderate parts so you'll definitely get some exercise in. If it's your zero day, sleep in. Please. After your walk, head to **Little Amps Coffee Roasters** for a jolt. If it's the weekend, visit **Broad Street Market** and have a cup from **Elementary Coffee Co.** while perusing the many local food vendors. Whenever you're done, head to the **Susquehanna Art Museum** for an hour or two. Ponder, let the time slip, and get hungry for lunch.

Afternoon

Hungry? Good. Have a somewhat late lunch at **Millworks,** sampling some local beer while supporting some local artists. Afterward, head over to the **National Civil War Museum** and take a 90-minute walk through this stupendous facility. You'll have a little time before the afternoon ends, so get to the **Pennsylvania State Capitol** and take a couple of pictures. Maybe poke your head in to see if there's a security line. If not, take a few more snaps of the awesome mosaics of Pennsylvania life.

Evening

Without a doubt, go to **Zeroday Brewing Co.,** especially if you want to meet some cool people and hear some trail tales. After that prelude, you have a wealth of dinner options. I'd suggest **Bricco** if you want to share a few plates and enjoy some exceptional Mediterranean cuisine. Before the night is over, head to the **Midtown Arts Center** and see who's playing where. Let the music end your night on a high note.

Sights

★ National Civil War Museum

The Appalachian Trail snakes through land that felt the tremors of the Civil War. The white blazes appear in and near battlefields, historic homes, cities that burned, and occupations that played a pivotal role during the conflict. The **National Civil War Museum** (1 Lincoln Cir. at Reservoir Park, 717/260-1861, www.nationalcivilwarmuseum.org, 10am-5pm Mon.-Tues. and Thurs.-Sat., 10am-8pm Wed., noon-5pm Sun., $12 adults, $11 seniors, $10 students) pulls together the disparate stories to craft a narrative of the Civil War that's unbiased and unflinching.

The museum showcases artifacts from both famous names associated with the war and the everyday soldier fighting for his cause. You'll find uniforms, weapons, and tools used by soldiers more than 150 years ago. There's also an impressive collection of manuscripts and photographs. Exhibits typically last for a year and illuminate ancillary stories, themes, and personalities of the war. Past exhibits include a look at the role of wet-collodion photography during the war, and the development of military fraternities. The museum suggests staying for at least two hours to absorb everything inside; you could spend a few more hours there considering the wealth of items in the collection.

Pennsylvania State Capitol

When in Harrisburg, a visit to the **State Capitol** (501 N. 3rd St., www.pacapitol.com, 7am-6pm Mon.-Fri., 9am-3pm Sat.-Sun.) isn't a bad idea. This beaux-arts building made of Vermont granite and topped by a 94-foot-diameter (29-m) dome opened in 1906 after a ceremony attended by President Theodore Roosevelt. Inside, the rotunda is decorated with local tile depicting Pennsylvania iconography, from animals and artifacts to workers and industries. Other sculptures, windows, and murals around the capitol depict life in Pennsylvania. As state capitols go, this is a beauty.

Visitors can take a guided 30-minute tour of the Capitol (8:30am-4pm Mon.-Fri., 9am-3pm Sat.-Sun.). Self-guided tours are also permitted, and brochures are available at the welcome center, accessible from the east wing of the building. Visitors can also sit in on House or Senate proceedings at their respective chambers.

Susquehanna Art Museum

The **Susquehanna Art Museum** (1401 N. 3rd St., 717/233-8668, www.sqart.com, 10am-5pm Tues. and Thurs.-Sat., 10am-7pm Wed., noon-5pm Sun., $8 adults, $5 seniors, students, and military) is the only art museum in central Pennsylvania, spotlighting a range of art while serving as a home for new artists to be discovered. For that it's unique—it's not simply satisfied with putting the past on a pedestal, so to speak. Past exhibits include early works by Ansel Adams, African American art since 1950, and a look at Pennsylvania impressionist art. The museum does regular calls for entries from artists near and far, while also hosting workshops and providing other educational opportunities. For a couple of hours and not the usual art museum experience, this is an affordable and exciting option.

Pennsylvania National Fire Museum

A 1935 ladder truck is the highlight at the **Pennsylvania National Fire Museum** (1820 N. 4th St., 717/232-8915, www.pnfm.org, 10am-4pm Tues.-Sat., 1pm-4pm Sun., $6 adults, $5 seniors and students), though there are plenty of interesting artifacts inside this 1899 Victorian firehouse that once housed Reily Hose Co. No. 10. The museum details the evolution of firefighting in the Keystone State, from hand to horse to current-day trucks. The museum also has a stirring collection of helmets honoring the firefighters lost on September 11, 2001. Free parking is available in a lot across the street from the museum.

Recreation

Biking

For those wanting to get around town on their own volition, the **Underground Bike Shop** (1519 N. 3rd St., 717/979-7341, www.theundergroundbikeshop.com, 9am-6pm Mon.-Tues. and Thurs.-Fri., 9am-4pm Sat., 11am-2pm Sun.) might have something for you. Ian at the shop specializes in turning used bikes into like-new wonders that need a good home.

City Island

City Island (accessed via Market Street Bridge or, to pedestrians, by Walnut Street Bridge) is a 63-acre patch of land in the middle of the Susquehanna River whose park includes playgrounds, a carousel, a Civil-War themed train, and **miniature golf** (600 Riverside Dr., City Island, 717/232-8533, 11am-8pm daily, $7 adults, $6 children).

From City Island, visitors can hop on **The Pride of the Susquehanna** (1 Riverside Dr., City Island, 717/234-6500, www.harrisburgboat.com, noon-3pm daily summer, noon-1:30pm fall, $11 adults, $9 seniors, $6 ages 3-12), a paddle wheeler that ventures onto the Susquehanna River on 45-minute sightseeing tours. The boat can hold up to 120 passengers and often hosts special events like jazz nights and wine-and-cheese cruises.

Also on City Island is **FNB Field** (245 Championship Way, City Island, 717/231-4444), home to the Harrisburg Senators (Apr.-Sept., $9-$38), the Class-AA minor league baseball affiliate of the Washington Nationals. Here at this capacity 6,187 ballpark you're bound to see a few future major leaguers, plus a few former major leaguers.

Riverfront Park

Walkers, runners, and bicyclists find **Riverfront Park** (North Front St. from

Vaughn St. to Paxton St.) a leisurely change of pace. The park includes a pedestrian walkway and a stage area where the city hosts many of its festivals.

Wildwood Park

A 4.3-mile (6.9-km) drive north from the State Capitol, **Wildwood Park** invites locals and tourists to get away from the city. Anchored by Wildwood Lake, the park features trails, bird-watching opportunities, and the 12,000-square-foot **Benjamin Olewine III Nature Center** (100 Wildwood Way, 717/221-0292, 10am-4pm Tues.-Sun.), which also serves as the park office. The nature center is an indoor habitat of sorts, with interactive, hands-on exhibits allowing kids to learn more about the creatures found in the park. Fishing is permitted in Wildwood Lake during regular park hours.

Wildwood Park Loop

Distance: 3.1 miles (5 km)
Duration: 1-1.5 hours
Elevation gain: N/A
Difficulty: Moderate
Trailhead: Nature Center Lot

For a nice loop around the park, do this three-miler that'll take you past marshland, then beside the lake and along a canal. From the trailhead hike north on the Wildwood Way Trail toward Paxton Creek as it winds around the park, often up and down some moderate hills. After a mile (1.6 km) you'll pass a small marsh area. Continue on, and after about 1.5 miles (2.4 km) you'll make a sharp left turn. Soon you'll be on the orange-blazed Towpath Trail. Take that south as it skirts the lake and runs along the remnants of the Pennsylvania Canal. After a mile (1.6 km) on the Towpath, the Wildwood Way comes back, and you'll finish the hike on this trail for another 0.3 mile (0.5 km).

Entertainment and Events

Nightlife

Attention hikers: Here is your brewery. **Zeroday Brewing Co.** (250 Reily St.,

a boardwalk trail at Wildwood Park

717/745-6218, www.zerodaybrewing.com, 4pm-11pm Tues.-Thurs., 4pm-midnight Fri., noon-midnight Sat., noon-8pm Sun., under $15) is co-owned by Theo Armstrong, who thru-hiked the Appalachian Trail in 2005. His idea was to create a brewery and taproom experience worthy of a hiker's zero day, a casual place where folks can get to know one another. Beers include a Belgian wit named Wit's End, which may or may not be inspired by a dive bar on the AT in New York, and Milksteak IPA, which was definitely inspired by the TV show *It's Always Sunny in Philadelphia*. A collaboration beer is called Marketing Gimmick.

Also tapping into the hiker crowd, the **Appalachian Brewing Company** (50 N. Cameron St., 717/221-1080, www.abcbrew.com, 11am-11pm Sun.-Thurs., 11am-midnight Fri.-Sat., under $30) has been around since 1997 inside an early 20th-century building. Beers call out to aspects of the outdoors, like Hoppy Trails IPA and Mountain Lager, while the kitchen serves "trail burgers," its biggest draw being the Fire Jumper, combining pepper jack cheese, jalapenos, and chipotle sauce. Yowza.

Down on the Restaurant Row section of the city, **The Brick Haus** (229 N. 2nd St., 717/233-4287, 4:30pm-2am Mon.-Fri., 5pm-2am Sat., 4pm-2am Sun., under $15) is a two-tier, smoky, great little bar. It has a drink called the Lumberjack with whiskey, Bailey's, Yukon Jack, and...wait for it...a strip of bacon. The bartenders describe is as "breakfast in a shot." Patrons are a mix of devout locals and kids trying to be cool.

Also at the Row is **McGrath's Pub** (202 Locust St., 717/232-9914, www.mcgrathspub.net, 11am-2am daily, under $35), the definitive Irish pub around these parts. Walk into a dimly light, vintage brown interior with a friendly barkeep and narrow hallway. The diverse beer list goes beyond Irish favorites, with locals like Troegs and Victory getting their due. The kitchen serves burgers, sandwiches, and native-themed fare like Irish meatloaf with Guinness gravy, and good ol' shepherd's pie, also with Guinness gravy.

Performing Arts

The multiuse **Harrisburg Midtown Arts Center** (1110 N. 3rd St., 717/412-4342, www.harrisburgarts.com) showcases performances across three distinct venues. The Stage on Herr holds 200 visitors and hosts small concerts, arts exhibits, DJ nights, and theatrical performances. The Capitol Room is a former art deco ballroom reimagined to host concerts and theatrical events. Its ground-floor **Kitchen & Gallery Bar** (11am-2am Mon.-Sat., 10am-2am Sun., under $40) hosts local and regional artists while serving fast-casual fare like smoked barbecue ribs and crab cakes.

Gamut Theatre Group (15 N. 4th St., 771/238-4111, www.gamuttheatre.org) is a combined children's theater company and a Shakespearean theater company, and its aim is to present intriguing theater in new ways to children and adults through mainstage performances, classes, and residencies. Gamut Theatre Group presents its shows inside a former church.

Festivals and Events

Harrisburg's art community gathers for the three-day **Artsfest** (Riverfront Park, Memorial Day weekend, www.jumpstreet.org, free), during which more than 250 artists showcase their creations for a jury. More than 40,000 people come out for the festival to peruse leather, jewelry, ceramics, paintings, photography, and sculpture. There's live music, a children's festival, and a small film festival, plus food vendors.

One of the biggest bashes in Pennsylvania, **Kipona** (Riverfront Park and City Island, Labor Day weekend, free) is a celebration of the Susquehanna River. There's music on three stages, including two at Riverfront Park, plus a biergarten, children's activities, cultural festivals, and fireworks over the river. On City Island is a Native American powwow featuring members of the Iroquois tribe.

Food

Farmers Market

Since 1860, **Broad Street Market** (1233 N. 3rd St., 717/236-7923, www.broadstreetmarket.org, 7am-6pm Thurs.-Fri., 7am-4pm Sat.) has stood strong as Harrisburg's quintessential marketplace. In the vein of a traditional farmers market, it features more than 40 vendors with produce, meats, cheeses, baked goods, and prepared meals. Eat everything from Indian to Spanish to Greek to barbecue, or buy artisan popcorn, distilled spirits, gourmet doughnuts, or old-fashioned deli meats. Sometimes there's live music on Saturdays. If being in a cramped building searching for produce isn't your thing, you can pass, but this is a solid opportunity to get to know more than a few local food producers.

Midtown

Part brewery, part farm-to-table cuisine, part art gallery, **Millworks** (3409 Verbeke St., 717/695-4888, www.millworksharrisburg.com, 11:30am-10pm Tues.-Thurs., 11:30am-midnight Fri.-Sat., 10am-10pm Sun., under $40 dinner, under $25 lunch and brunch) goes all in on supporting local. Order the stout gravy fries or go big with a grass-fed hanger steak with crispy smashed potatoes. The large space has a wall of cut timber, stylish booths, outdoor garden seating, and a rooftop beer garden for enjoying their saisons or a boozy barleywine.

Café 1500 (1500 N. 6th St., 717/831-8322, www.cafe-1500.com, 11am-2pm and 5pm-10pm Mon.-Sat., 10am-2pm Sun., under $40 dinner, under $20 lunch and brunch) does casual really well. Inside a warm bistro (despite exposed industrial ceilings), plates are simply gorgeous and the food is even better. They specialize in dinner bowls, but check out the blackened chicken and brie with "Zeroday" cranberry jam. They're thinking of you, dear hiker.

Set in a funky Victorian, **Note** (1530 N. 2nd St., 717/412-7415, www.notewinebar.com, 4:30pm-9:30pm Tues., 4:30pm-10pm Wed.-Fri., 5pm-10pm Sat., 10:30am-9pm Sun., under $40 dinner, under $25 brunch) combines the romance of a French bistro with some urban edge. For dinner you can enjoy braised oxtail and bone marrow ragu over cavatelli, while brunch allows you to dig into fried chicken over biscuits and gravy. The friendly spot utilizes black tablecloths, mod lighting, and a little outdoor dining area with twinkly lights.

Elementary Coffee Co. (1233 N. 3rd St., 7am-6pm Thurs.-Fri., 7am-4pm Sat., under $10) caters to the weekend crowd inside Broad Street Market. There are tons of books to read and plenty of natural light in this wood-centric café.

Little Amps Coffee Roasters (1836 Green St., 717/695-4882, 7am-4pm Mon.-Fri., 8am-4pm Sat.-Sun., under $10) is a chill hangout. Brick walls, sweet pastries, nitro cold brew, and funky seating options abound.

Downtown

Second Street between Market and North Streets is known as Restaurant Row.

Café Fresco (215 N. 2nd St., 717/236-2599, www.cafefresco.com, 7am-midnight Mon.-Fri., 10am-1am Sun., under $50 dinner, under $20 lunch, under $10 breakfast) serves up exceptional Asian fusion with an extensive menu, featuring items like Mongolian-glazed short rib or a Sriracha panko salmon with a yuzo-dill crème fraiche. At night, the large space feels a little clubby, with cool neon lights. By day Café Fresco is a different story: a full-on coffee-and-breakfast café catering to the capital city's busy workforce. Grab an egg sandwich or baked oatmeal and take a seat outside.

Bacco Pizzeria and Wine Bar (20 N. 2nd St., 717/234-7508, www.baccopizzeriawinebar.com, 11am-11pm Mon.-Thurs., 11am-2am Fri., noon-2am Sat., under $40) mixes traditional Italian fare and plenty of small plates with a diverse wine list. They also have a deep brick-oven pizza menu, but there's nothing extreme here, just perfect plays on Italian specialties like the tomato, mozzarella, artichoke, prosciutto di perma, onions, and wild mushroom on the Quattro gusti. This is a lovely date-night option.

A ridiculous list of 100 draft beers is where the eye goes first at **Federal Taphouse** (234 N. 2nd St., 717/525-8077, www.federaltaphouse.com, 11:30am-2am Mon.-Fri., 11am-2am Sat., 10:30am-2am Sun., under $40). One of several Pennsylvania locations, this Federal Taphouse is a big, family-friendly dining hall. The menu has American favorites, tacos, sandwiches, and wood-fired pizza … really anything that goes well with a beer. The beer list changes all the time.

A little off 2nd Street is ★ **Home 231** (231 North St., 717/232-4663, www.home231.com, 11am-2pm and 5pm-10pm Mon.-Fri., 5pm-10pm Sat., 9am-2pm Sun., under $50 dinner, under $25 lunch and brunch), arguably the best dining experience in the city. A skinny entrance with a cool wood bar space leads to a larger dining room with cute lime-green booths. The mood is jovial and the food is from-scratch and with love: chili-glazed octopus fresh with white beans; a Cornish hen brined in molasses and served with a walnut gremolata; and for brunch … doughnuts. Yum.

You haven't had Mediterranean like **Bricco** (31 S. 3rd St., 717/724-0222, www.briccopa.com, 5pm-10pm Mon.-Sat., 4:30pm-9pm Sun., under $50). Amid a family-friendly atmosphere, Bricco juggles serving formal Italian dishes like Tuscan chicken and classic oysters, and crafting bubbly, savory pizza with ingredients like mushrooms from Kennett Square, the capital of fungi about 80 miles (129 km) southeast.

Accommodations

Under $100

The **Howard Johnson Inn** (473 Eisenhower Blvd., 717/409-5274, $40-100) is staggeringly inexpensive and has everything you'd need, from Wi-Fi to an outdoor pool to even an airport shuttle, as it's about 8 miles (12.9 km) from the airport. The **Best Western Plus Harrisburg East** (1344 Eisenhower Blvd., 717/985-1600, $50-100) is 4 miles (6.4 km) from the airport and has free parking, free breakfast, and a hot tub.

$100-150

City House Bed & Breakfast (915 N. Front St., 717/903-2489, $125-180) is a brick building seconds from the Susquehanna River and close to downtown attractions. Most rooms have fireplaces, while all have king beds and combine country charm with a buttoned-up early 20th-century aesthetic.

As far as chains, the **Quality Inn** (525 S. Front St., 717/233-1611, $80-160) is right downtown and includes microwaves and refrigerators in every room. The **Staybridge Suites** (920 Wildwood Park Dr., 717/233-3304, $120-180) is in the north end of the city, so it's removed from hustle and bustle. The rooms at **Candlewood Suites** (413 Port View Dr., 717/561-9400, $80-150) are a few too many shades of brown, but they're inoffensive and have desks and ample space, plus there's a fitness center here. The **La Quinta Inn & Suites** (990 Eisenhower Blvd., 717/939-8000, $70-170) is nothing out of the ordinary but it is a quick, 6-mile (9.7-km) drive to the airport. A swift five minutes from the airport, the **Holiday Inn Harrisburg East** (815 S. Eisenhower Blvd., Middletown, 717/939-1600, $120-180) has an in-house restaurant, outdoor seating, and a contemporary feel.

$150-250

The Manor on Front (2917 N. Front St., 717/884-9596, $120-240) offers several rooms in an early 20th-century brick house with waterfront views. The tasteful rooms have period furniture and beautiful patterned rugs. Guests rave about breakfast, with items including fresh fruit and pastries.

The big chains in this group include the **Hilton Harrisburg** (1 N. 2nd St., 717/233-6000, $180-260), which is just a 0.4-mile (0.6-km) walk from the Pennsylvania State Capitol and three blocks from the Susquehanna riverfront. The **Residence Inn by Marriott** (4480 Lewis Rd., 717/561-1900, $130-220) has free parking and indoor and outdoor pools. The **Courtyard by Marriott** (725 Eisenhower Blvd., 717/558-8544, $180-220) offers contemporary rooms and a bistro for light dining options. The **Hampton Inn & Suites at Harrisburg North** (30 Capital Dr., 717/540-0900, $150-220) is off US-22 in a quieter part of the city.

Information and Services

Visit Hershey & Harrisburg (3211 N. Front St., 717/231-7788) is the major spot for information about the capital region.

PA-849: Duncannon

To reach **Duncannon** (pop. 1,493), take US-22 north from Harrisburg to the Clarks Ferry Bridge; after crossing, turn onto PA-849 (N. Market Street) as you enter the borough. This is a small borough across the Susquehanna River and 15 miles (24 km) north of Harrisburg. It's also one of the very few communities in which the Appalachian Trail runs along its streets, making it essential for this trip.

The trail comes off the mountain by the river, then rides along the Susquehanna on Market Street. This is where hikers can take a rest, whether on a bed or at a campground, and fill up on burgers and beer at one of the local watering holes. When finished in town, AT hikers continue on Market Street, cross the Clarks Ferry Bridge, and head back toward the woods.

Duncannon is quintessentially working class and community minded, demonstrated by how it welcomes the AT hiking community. There's an annual AT festival, plus all the eateries and bars welcome the business, even if the inconvenient odor hovers in the room.

Duncannon Appalachian Trail Festival

The community comes out to play and celebrate the trail with the annual **Duncannon Appalachian Trail Festival** (High St. between Cumberland and Ann Sts., June, www.duncannonatc.org, free), typically scheduled for around the time that thru-hikers might pass into town. Clubs lead morning hikes at local spots, while the festival proper includes live music, kids' crafts and face painting, food, a wildlife show, and a raffle.

Hiking

Hawk Rock Trail

Distance: 2 miles (3.2 km)

Duration: 1-1.5 hours

Elevation gain: 750 feet (229 m)

Difficulty: Moderate

Trailhead: Inn Road south of Little Boston Road (40.381463, -77.029488)

This hike is basically the opposite route of the northbound thru-hiker arrival in Duncannon, and it's yet another example of Rocksylvania at play. Park in a gravel lot off Inn Road, which is accessible from Market Street just after crossing under US-11. From there take a short walk up Inn to the Appalachian Trail crossing and follow the white blazes into the woods. Quickly the trail gets rocky, and you'll need to take care stepping up as you climb 700 feet (213 m) or so. After about 30 minutes, the climbing stops and you'll be at Hawk Rock Overlook, an outcrop leading to views of Duncannon and the bordering Susquehanna River. For those wanting a second view, stay on the AT until you reach a crest. Look left to see an unmarked trail; in about 0.5 mile (0.8 km), this will lead you to Cove Mountain, which has a more dramatic vista. Either way, you're good to turn around and head back down the cliff and into town.

Food and Accommodations

At ★ **Goodies Restaurant** (6 N. Market St., 717/834-6300, under $10), you'll probably sit at the long counter with some regulars, be called "sugar," and maybe encounter some Appalachian Trail hikers testing their stomachs with "the pancake challenge." It requires eating a ridiculous number of pancakes that increases by one each time another person conquers the feat. Consume 'em all and the pancakes are free. This bare-bones diner is homely, kind as all get out, and serves sausage and gravy and chipped beef.

Sorrento Pizza (104 N. Market St., 717/834-5167, 11am-10:30pm Sun.-Thurs., 11am-11:30pm Fri.-Sat., under $25) is a family establishment broken into two seating areas: a standard pizza shop and a more formal sit-down lounge, though casual attire is more than welcome. The menu also offers pasta, sandwiches, and salads.

A popular bar in town is **The Pub** (101 N. Market St., 717/834-5420, 11am-2am Mon.-Sat., 11am-5:30pm Sun., under $20). Nachos, pub fries, wings, and a burger topped with mayonnaise are regular standouts at this light-wood-toned sports bar that has fun, amiable crowds.

When approaching Duncannon, hikers have been just about instructed to stop at the **Doyle Hotel** (7 N. Market St., 717/834-6789, 11am-9pm Mon.-Sat., noon-8pm Sun., under $20), a really good restaurant and crummy overnight stay for hikers, run by Pat and Vickey Kelly. The downstairs bar and restaurant is lovingly known as a dive, but it's a vibrant little hub with cold beer and juicy burgers. The Kellys know their clientele: Appalachian Trail ephemera is sprinkled throughout the space, and bartenders are known to be quite friendly to the hikers. As for the hotel upstairs, it's been providing beds for guests on and off since 1803, and the age often shows. While the Kellys have renovated some rooms, some hikers haven't been happy with conditions, which include leaks, cobwebs, and moldy bathroom areas. For an alternative lodging option, try the **Red Carpet Inn** (3270 Susquehanna Trail, 717/834-3320, $50-80), whose rooms are just as good as a chain motor lodge.

Hummelstown

Traffic is frequently high in **Hummelstown** (4,520), as it sits between Harrisburg and Hershey, just 11 miles (17.7 km) east of the capital on US-322. Thus there are quite a few small country gift shops on or near Main Street, plus small sandwich shops and basic American diners hoping to catch hungry bellies wary of the crowds in Chocolate Town, U.S.A.

Those wanting to visit Hummelstown from Harrisburg can do so via **Capital Area Transit** (bus stop Hummelstown Park and Ride, 9-1 W. 2nd St., Mon.-Sat.), which also connects to Hershey.

Indian Echo Caverns at Echo Dell (368 Middletown Rd., 717/566-8131, www.indianechocaverns.com, 10am-4pm daily, 9am-5pm summer, $18 adults, $16 seniors, $10 ages 2-11) is one of several popular caverns found in northern and central Pennsylvania, also known as a third-grade field trip for Philadelphia school students. It's also a great family trip and a changeup from the usual sightseeing. You can take a 45-minute tour of a cave carved from limestone that dates back some 440 million years. The cave keeps a temperature of about 52°F (11°C), so have a light layer handy.

Echo Dell's gift shop includes Native American jewelry and pottery, plus toys, minerals, and clothing. An on-site petting zoo houses a couple of goats, plus hens and rabbits. Kids can search for rare gemstones at the Gem Mill Junction and stretch out a bit at the site's playground.

After visiting the caverns, have a bite inside a 19th-century former hotel. **The Warwick Hotel** (12 W. Main St., 717/566-9124, 11am-10pm Tues., 11am-midnight Wed.-Sat., 4pm-10pm Sun., under $35), or the Wick as it's called today, was the Cross Keys circa 1800, then took on other names before becoming the New Warwick in 1926. Today it houses a cool bar made of Pittsburgh Corning, multiple small rooms reminiscent of a former hotel lobby, and some outdoor tables. Its Wick salad is odd: yummy greens and veggies topped by fries and mozzarella cheese. You do you, Wick.

Hershey

From Hummelstown it's a quick 4.3-mile (6.9-km) drive east on US-322 to **Hershey** (pop. 14,257), a word you've absolutely heard before. This is "Chocolate Town, U.S.A.," also known as "The Sweetest Place on Earth," or our own little slice of Willy Wonka's factory.

The name comes from Milton S. Hershey, a Pennsylvania Mennonite who, in 1900, acquired some land with the mission of starting a dairy farm. The milk from his cows would be the basis for his then far-reaching concept: chocolate candies that could be mass-produced and available to the general public.

The chocolatier's brilliant idea led to a global empire, the Hershey Company, which manufactures the iconic Hershey's Chocolate Bar, plus Hershey's Kisses, Reese's Peanut Butter Cups, and Jolly Ranchers. Hershey's farm, meanwhile, expanded so much that he built a massive chocolate production facility and founded a community around it, calling it Hershey. While Hershey is certainly a working community with local businesses and restaurants, its major thoroughfare is Chocolate Avenue, and lights along the median are shaped like Kisses.

Getting There and Around

From Hummelstown, Hershey is just a 4.3-mile (6.9-km) ride east on US-322 and 422. (Be sure to bear onto PA-422 instead of staying on PA-322 before Penn State Health Milton S. Hershey Medical Center).

Staying in Harrisburg and don't want to drive to Hershey (or vice versa)? **Capital Area Transit** (Mon.-Sat.) has multiple bus stops in Hershey, including

Pennsylvania and Pretzels

Oh, does Pennsylvania love its pretzels. In Philadelphia, schools historically reserved time each day for students to purchase a soft pretzel. On its city streets, vendors standing in medians hawk soft pretzels, sometimes up to a dozen in a giant brown paper bag. But it's not just Philly who has pretzel on the brain: Hard pretzels were first produced at the Sturgis Bakery in Lititz, 24 miles (39 km) southeast of Hershey. So how did this yeasty treat become so popular, and so synonymous with the Keystone State?

You can thank the Pennsylvania Dutch, immigrants from southern Germany who almost completely settled in Pennsylvania between the mid-1700s and early 1800s. They made the pretzels privately, and they were always soft, but it wasn't until Julius Sturgis that the hard pretzel took off. He distributed his pretzels and donated hundreds to Union soldiers during the Civil War. The hard pretzels became extremely popular; to this day, they're high sellers in snack aisles across the country, perfect with beer, soda pop, and lazy weekend days.

A couple of places of note for your pretzel enjoyment:

- **Julius Sturgis Pretzel Bakery** (219 E. Main St., Lititz, www.juliussturgis.com, 10am-4pm Mon.-Fri., 9am-5pm Sat.) is open for tours, and yes, it's still in production. You can also buy Sturgis products online.

- **Martin's Pretzel Bakery** (1229 Diamond St., Akron, 717/859-1272, www.martinespretzelspa.com, 6am-6pm Mon.-Fri., 6am-2pm Sat.) is 29.7 miles (48 km) southeast of Hershey and makes all of its pretzels by hand. Visit them and see how it's done, then buy some of their goodies.

the Hershey Hotel, Tanger Outlets, and Hersheypark.

Sights

The Hershey Story

Pay your respects to Milton Hershey at **The Hershey Story** (63 W. Chocolate Ave., 717/534-8939, www.hersheystory.org, 9am-7pm daily summer, 9am-5pm daily winter), a museum devoted to the history of sweet, sweet chocolate candy. Begin with a rundown of Mr. Hershey's life, starting as a middle-class kid dropping in and out of jobs and ending as a philanthropist who put all of his earnings back into the community he founded. Then learn about the evolution of both mass-produced chocolate and the marketing of chocolate to the working American. There's a rotating special exhibit that looks at a key aspect of the Hershey story, but people get a kick out of the **Chocolate Lab** (times vary), where kids and family members can learn how to make chocolate. Of course, chocolate tastings ($6, $10) are available, in which participants receive a flight of warm drinking chocolates from around the world. Kids who participate make hot chocolate.

★ Hershey Gardens

The story of **Hershey Gardens** (170 Hotel Rd., 717/534-3492, 9am-4pm daily Jan., 9am-5pm daily Feb.-Memorial Day and Labor Day-Dec., 9am-6pm daily summer, $12.50 adults, $11.50 seniors, $9 ages 3-12 summer, $10 adults, $9 seniors, $8 ages 3-12 winter) starts in 1937, when Milton Hershey asked for "a nice garden of roses." It's now a 23-acre splendor overlooking the town and featuring 11 themed gardens and a butterfly atrium. It makes for a great hour or two of strolling post-lunch.

There are more than 3,500 roses of 275 varieties in the main rose garden, while a seasonal display garden blossoms with 20,000 tulips of red, yellow, and purple in the spring, and sunset-splattered chrysanthemums in the fall. Hershey Gardens

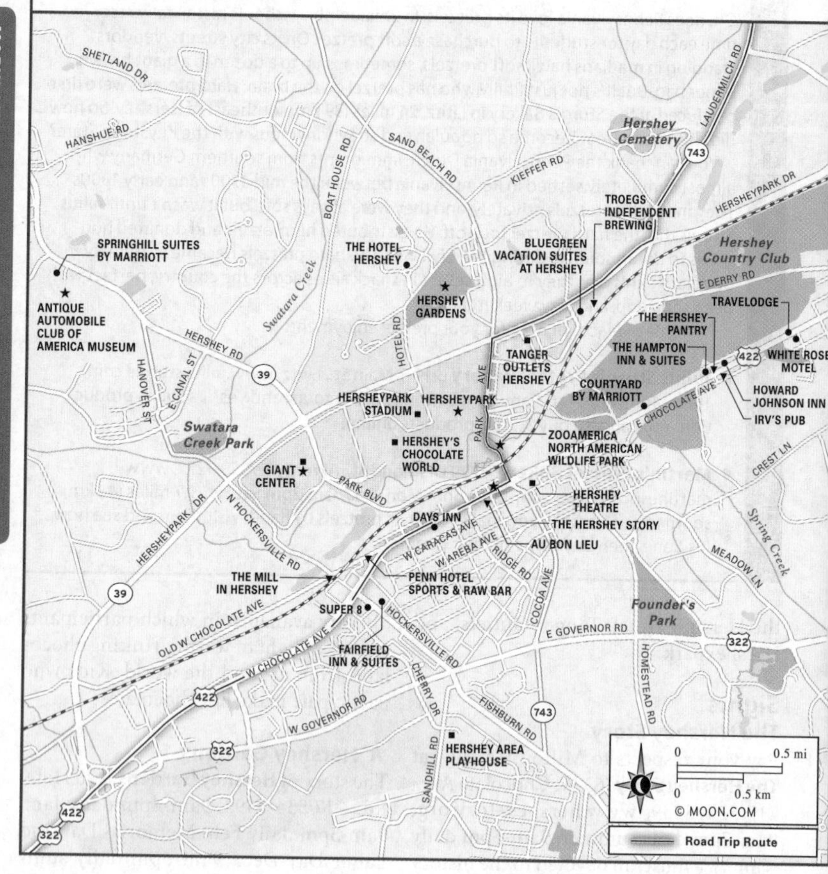

hosts frequent events, like a scavenger hunt where the prize is—you guessed it—candy.

Hersheypark

It's a ritual for most Pennsylvanians to at some point in their lives visit the one and only amusement park in America devoted to branded chocolate candies. **Hersheypark** (100 Hersheypark Dr., 800/437-7439, hours vary by day, Mar.-Sept., also Halloween and Christmas seasons, $67 adults, $45 ages 3-8 and seniors, $29 ages 70 and older; prices are seasonal) is a fun family day with several dozen rides including 13 roller coasters, plus water activities, places to eat, and daily shows. If you can get past seeing an oversized Hershey's chocolate bar or pack of Reese's Peanut Butter Cups attempting to mingle with families, you'll experience a pretty good amusement park.

Famous rides include the 75 mph (121 kph) Skyrush, the biggest and baddest coaster in the park, and the wooden, double-tracked Lightning Racer. The Hershey Triple Tower showcases three tower drops, the tallest sending people to the ground from 189 feet (58 m) up. There's also a substantial gaming area with standard amusements, plus two arcades with video games, crane machines, Skee-Ball, and more. The water rides, including slides, pools, and a lazy river, are in a separate area called the Boardwalk. Weekdays are less packed than weekends, but make no mistake, whenever you come between starting in May, you'll be among crowds. It's best to come in spring.

ZooAmerica North American Wildlife Park

If you have small children and you're seeking a break from Hersheypark, **ZooAmerica North American Wildlife Park** (201 Park Ave., 717/534-3900, 10am-4:30pm daily, $11.50 adults, $9.50 ages 3-8 and seniors, free ages 2 and under) is next door and does the trick—just don't expect the zoo experience of your life. The animal domiciles are cramped, but this place has North American species, from bald eagles to black bears to mountain lions. There are two snack bars in the park, plus a gift shop.

Antique Automobile Club of America Museum

Maybe you need to step away from chocolate for a few hours. Understandable. That's what the **Antique Automobile Club of America Museum** (161 Museum Dr., 717/566-7100, 9am-5pm daily, $12 adults, $11 seniors, $9 ages 4-12) is for. Car enthusiasts are the target demographic, but everyone visiting will find something appealing here. Antique collectors will love the Historic Vehicle Association's ongoing exhibit at the museum, showcasing a changing cast of significant cars from the early days of the automobile. Past exhibits include restored 1950s and 1960s Corvettes, cars and motorcycles

Top to bottom: Doyle Hotel in Duncannon; Hershey's Chocolate World; Mad Elf is a popular beer made at Troegs Independent Brewing in Hershey.

unearthed from garages and barns, and the original prototype of the DeLorean from *Back to the Future*. But just in case you forget where you are, also on view is the Kissmobile Cruiser, a 12-foot-tall and 26-foot-long vehicle in the shape of three Hershey's Kisses.

Recreation

Hiking

From Hershey you can pick up the **Horse-Shoe Trail** (trail crossing near 140 Washington Ave., www.hstrail.com), a 148-mile (238-km) trail that connects the Appalachian Trail near Stony Mountain with Valley Forge, site of a major Revolutionary War encampment 25 miles (40 km) northwest of Philadelphia. The trail is moderate to strenuous, especially closer to the AT and as it enters Berks County south of Reading.

Spectator Sports

Starting every fall, **Giant Center** (550 W. Hersheypark Dr., 717/534-3911, $20-32) plays host to the Hershey Bears, a minor league ice hockey club dating back to 1938 and owned by a subsidiary of the Hershey Company. Currently the Bears service the Washington Capitals, but they've been a feeder team for more than a half-dozen clubs since their inception. The level of play is quite good, with many of the players either past or future National Hockey League talent, and for the price, it's a bargain for a fun night out.

Entertainment and Events

Nightlife

Have you tried Mad Elf? **Troegs Independent Brewing** (200 East Hersheypark Dr., 717/534-1297, 11am-9pm Sun.-Wed., 11am-10pm Thurs.-Sat., under $25) produces the Christmastime favorite, a spiced-up, high-alcohol-content beer perfect for snuggling up in the winter. That said, Troegs has beer for all seasons, and you can try a whole lot of them in its massive brewery and taproom. Take a self-guided tour of the brewery, then enter the large beer hall for a drink. Snacks available include pretzels, poutine, corn dogs, oysters, and sandwiches. This is one of the liveliest and coolest breweries in America, and it makes darn good beer.

Penn Hotel Sports & Raw Bar (600 Old West Chocolate Ave., 717/298-1461, www.thepennhotel.com, 11am-2am daily, under $20) is more laid-back but still has some ambitious menu offerings. It does oysters, flatbread pizzas, and a terrific thing called Old-School Penn Fries: cheddar jack, jalapenos, bacon, and sweet peppers, with ranch dressing and "happy" sauces. The bar of the Penn Hotel is pretty fun, with 23 televisions, shuffleboard, darts, and games like Golden Tee.

Performing Arts

When the Bears aren't playing, the 10,500-seat **Giant Center** (550 W. Hersheypark Dr., 717/534-3911) hosts concerts, primarily featuring country music stars, and performances like Disney on Ice.

Opening in 1939, **Hersheypark Stadium** (100 W. Hersheypark Dr., 717/534-3911, www.hersheyentertainment.com) hosts a slew of outdoor concerts each year, bringing in acts like Kendrick Lamar, Journey, and the Zac Brown Band. In the 1980s it hosted REO Speedwagon, Aerosmith, and David Bowie. Because it's built like a football stadium, it's a funny setup for concerts, with grandstand seating pretty far away on either side of a large field, where patrons sit or stand. The field faces the stage.

Hershey Theatre (15 E. Caracas Ave., 717/534-3405, www.hersheyentertainment.com) is a marvel. Commissioned by Milton Hershey and built during the Great Depression (a time when Hershey built the biggest structures in his community), its lobby floors are made of polished Italian lava rock, and its inner foyer resembles St. Mark's Cathedral in Venice. The theater hosts touring musicals and acclaimed regional and national musicians.

The community stars at the **Hershey Area Playhouse** (830 Cherry Dr., 717/533-8525, www.hersheyareaplayhouse.com, $10-25). Little-known plays and popular musicals both find a home here, where actors in the community take on roles in a black-box setting. It's good, wholesome fun for an affordable price.

Shopping

Hershey's family-friendly attractions are a good match for outlet shopping, thus **Tanger Outlets Hershey** (46 Outlet Sq., 717/520-1236, www.tangeroutlet.com/hershey, 9am-9pm Mon.-Sat., 10am-7pm Sun.) is well traveled, especially during the warmer tourism-happy months. There is plenty of accessories and apparel to be had here, plus specialty stores like a Disney Outlet.

More appropriate for the locale, **Hershey's Chocolate World** (101 Chocolate World Way, 717/534-4900, www.hersheys.com, 9am-5pm Sun.-Fri., 9am-7pm Sat.) is the emporium your sweet little heart desires. One of six Chocolate World locations around the world (others include Times Square, Las Vegas, and Dubai), here you can learn how to make chocolate, get a simulated factory tour, watch a 4-D chocolate mystery, chow on café fare, and yeah, buy as much chocolate as you can possibly fit into your car.

Food

The Mill in Hershey (810 Old West Chocolate Ave., 717/256-9965, www.themillinhershey.com, 11am-10pm Mon.-Thurs., 11am-midnight Fri.-Sat., 10am-3pm Sun., under $50 dinner, under $25 lunch and brunch) takes the mill concept and takes it to 11. In a place with old timber, exposed brick, and exposed stone (a trifecta!), New American is obviously the cuisine of choice. A low and slow brisket has a smoky black-pepper barbecue sauce, and you need to try the citrus polenta with the Maryland crab cakes.

Irv's Pub (814 E. Chocolate Ave., 717/298-6476, www.irvspub.com, 11am-10pm Tues.-Thurs., 11am-midnight Fri.-Sat., 10am-9pm Sun., under $40 dinner, under $25 lunch and brunch) sounds like a dive, but it's a clean, contemporary gastropub serving elevated New American fare. I'd share a couple of small plates like tater tot nachos and smoked trout pate, and pair them with one of Irv's many craft beers or specialty cocktails.

Get fresh crepes at **Au Bon Lieu** (110 W. Chocolate Ave., 717/533-4074, 10am-8pm Sun.-Thurs., 10am-10pm Fri.-Sat., under $15), which boasts 96 different varieties on the menu. The downside is that the crepes are sometimes presented on paper plates, and there's frequently one person behind the counter making the treats, so time can drag while waiting. But the crepes are really delicious. Pick your battles.

A superb breakfast experience, **The Hershey Pantry** (801 E. Chocolate Ave., 717/533-7505, www.hersheypantry.com, 6:30am-9pm Mon.-Sat., under $40 dinner, under $20 lunch, breakfast, and brunch) is a contemporary urban diner known for its egg sandwich on a pretzel roll (apt for this part of the country) and its Italian-stuffed French toast, in which you take a bite and cream cheese oozes out. Lunch and dinner are also served, and the menu leans New American with some Italian flashes. The Pantry also hosts an afternoon tea ($20) that includes a scone with cream, a cup of soup, tea sandwiches, desserts, and a choice of tea. Outdoor seating is available.

Accommodations

If you're seeking an accommodation in Hershey during the summer, plan early and expect higher prices. Rates increase by about 50-60 percent from the winter to spring, and then another 50-60 percent from spring to summer. Fall rates typically reflect spring rates. Below are typical rates for lodging in the midsummer months, when thru-hikers tend to come through the area and when travel traffic is its highest.

Under $100

A longtime favorite of Hershey visitors, the ★ **White Rose Motel** (1060 E. Chocolate Ave., 717/533-9876, $60-100) is affordable, clean, run by a kind and knowledgeable elderly couple, and the runaway best deal in this destination town. Accommodations include above-average motor-lodge-style rooms and two self-contained **cottages** ($270) that are really very cute single-family brick houses. An outdoor pool is on the premises.

$150-250

Many of the usual suspects are in Hershey, most of them 1 mile (1.6 km) from the main attractions, including the **Fairfield Inn & Suites** (651 W. Areba Ave., 717/520-5240, $140-240), the **Courtyard by Marriott** (515 E. Chocolate Ave., 717/533-1750, $125-350, the **Hampton Inn & Suites** (749 E. Chocolate Ave., 717/533-8400, $130-200), the **Travelodge** (1043 E. Chocolate Ave., 717/533-5179, $130-250), the **Super 8** (210 Hockersville Rd., 717/508-7629, $200-250), and the **Days Inn** (350 W. Chocolate Ave., 717/534-2162, $80-160).

Part of the Ascend Resort Collection, **Bluegreen Vacation Suites at Hershey** (176 E. Hersheypark Dr., $150-280) is a toned-down club resort hotel perfect for small families looking to explore the area for more than a weekend. Suites have kitchens and ample sitting space, while guests can use barbecue grills, hang out in the screened-in gazebo, and play in the game room or indoor pool.

Over $250

One of the structures Milton Hershey commissioned during the Great Depression to boost his community's workforce, ★ **The Hotel Hershey** (100 Hotel Rd., 717/533-2171, www.thehotelhershey.com, $250-500) is out of this world. This five-star resort hotel and spa is worth a splurge. Its exterior has Mediterranean flair, including dual winding staircases leading to a Spanish patio with gabled pavilions. Inside is a jaw-dropping lobby with sandstone walls, tile floors, and a fountain. The gardens are immaculate, too. In short, you're staying over at a billionaire's house, but only for a couple hundred clams. Rooms are calming and spacious with plenty of furniture. The hotel offers complimentary valet and shuttle service to Hershey attractions. Beds have Egyptian cotton linens, and baths carry products from the attached spa. As for the spa (717/520-5888, open daily), it offers regular massage, facial, and wet treatments, plus soaking tubs and hydrotherapy baths, an inhalation room, steam rooms, and salons. Sit poolside and rent a cabana with a flat-screen TV, or dine at one of the hotel's four restaurants.

A few chains really bump up their rates during high season. The **Howard Johnson Inn** (845 E. Chocolate Ave., 717/533-9157, $230-320) and **SpringHill Suites by Marriott** (115 Museum Dr., 717/583-2222, $280-350) are among them.

Information and Services

Visit Hershey & Harrisburg (3211 N. Front St., 717/231-7788) is the major spot for information about the capital region. **Hershey's Chocolate World** (101 Chocolate World Way, 717/534-4900, www.hersheys.com, 9am-5pm Sun.-Fri., 9am-7pm Sat.) can tell you anything about Hershey attractions related to the chocolatier, which means almost all of them.

Grantville

Want to stay somewhere unique and distinctive in the Harrisburg-Hershey area while avoiding the crowds of the Harrisburg-Hershey area? Take PA-743 north from Hershey 7.6 miles (12.2 km) to the unincorporated community of **Grantville** (pop. 3,604), home to the ★ **Red Umbrella Bed & Breakfast** (9866 Jonestown Rd., 717/315-6276, $100-160). Inside this renovated 1845 Federal home are three rooms, one with a bubble massage tub and each decorated in simple Victorian-style finery, from balloon-style curtains to patterned rugs. A quiet common room has a fireplace. As for the name, the owners were inspired by paintings by Lancaster artist Liz Hess that featured red umbrellas. They struck a deal with Hess to display her paintings on the walls of the B&B's rooms, and most of those paintings are also available for purchase.

PA-443: Memorial Lake State Park

All that chocolate may have you sluggish, so stretch your legs at **Memorial Lake State Park** (18 Boundary Rd., 717/865-6470, sunrise-sunset), a peaceful patch of land surrounded by Fort Indiantown Gap, home to the Pennsylvania Army and Air National Guard.

To get here from Grantville, turn around on US-22 for 0.5 mile (0.8 km), then turn north onto Bow Creek Road until you hit the junction with PA-443. Head east on PA-443 for 4.5 miles (7.2 km) until you reach Memorial Lake State Park.

Hiking

Memorial Lake State Park has 2 miles (3.2 km) of trails fit for even the most amateur hiker. Take the **Lakeside Trail** (0.2 mi/0.3 km, easy), where numerous benches provide an opportunity to reflect on the serene view. The **Overlook Trail** (0.6 mi/1 km, easy) gives visitors the best view of the lake, as it runs atop the dam that controls water fed from Memorial Lake to Indiantown Run.

Fishing and Boating

The lake is also used for fishing, with bass, northern pike, and yellow perch common. Ice fishing is also permitted, but not in a separate area reserved in the winter for ice-skating.

You can rent a canoe, kayak, paddleboat, or rowboat by the lake through **Green Way Outdoors Boat Rental** (Boundary Rd., 717/865-8000, 10am-5pm Sat.-Sun. spring and fall, 10am-6pm Wed.-Sun. summer, $15-18 per hour). Motorboats are permitted with registration, while nonmotorized craft must have either registration or a launch permit.

Pine Grove

Go 13.6 miles (21.9 km) east from Grantville on US-22 to its intersection with PA-343; head north on PA-343, then PA-645 a total of 8.5 miles (13.7 km) to **Pine Grove** (pop. 2,108), a supply stop for some thru-hikers on the Appalachian Trail. Hikers can get to Pine Grove by walking or hailing a ride north on PA-645, which merges with PA-343 just before the trail crossing. Pine Grove is a residential community with ample fast-casual restaurants and a couple of highway hotels. It's a good place to catch a bite or grab a nap, if necessary.

Sweet Arrow Lake County Park

Pine Grove and Washington Townships share **Sweet Arrow Lake County Park** (108 Clubhouse Rd., 570/527-2505). The lake was originally a water supply for the Union Canal, but since being purchased by the municipalities it has been accessible to fishers and boaters. A dam controlling water releases from the lake creates a small waterfall that's viewable on an easy hike. There's also an 18-hole disc golf course at the park, and you can rent discs if you forgot to bring them or just want to try it out ($20 for three).

Hiking

The park has seven trails, all relatively short with the longest just 2 miles (3.2 km). That's the **Big Dam Trail** (easy), which is named for a former dam on site and loops beside Upper Little Swatara Creek. Discover an old schoolhouse while on this trail. The other popular walk is the **Waterfall Trail** (0.4 mi/0.6 km one-way, easy), which starts at the waterfall parking lot and leads to the falls before meeting up with a boardwalk. It gets slippery on the boardwalk.

Fishing and Boating

With a Pennsylvania fishing license, you can cast in Sweet Arrow Lake, where trout, bass, pickerel, catfish, and carp are in supply. Ice fishing is also permitted when the lake freezes, as is ice-skating. You can rent a canoe or kayak from the park's **clubhouse** (108 Clubhouse Rd., 570/345-8952, 11am-6pm Sat.-Sun. summer, $10/hour) if you're wanting to have some fun on the lake.

Food

Pine Grove has just a few family-friendly restaurants, but all of them are very inexpensive and great for a quick hike refill, headlined by **Do's Pizza** (122 S. Tulpehocken St., 570/345-4041, 11am-9pm Mon. and Wed.-Thurs., 11am-10pm Fri.-Sat., under $15). The usual pizza suspects are here, but get a cheesesteak. They also have Philly-style variations like pizza steak and chicken cheesesteak.

I wonder if anyone has ever played human checkers on the red-and-black floor of **O'Neals Pub** (112 S. Tulpehocken St., 570/915-6093, 4pm-9pm Tues., 11am-midnight Wed.-Sat., under $30)? It isn't hard to imagine, because people seem to enjoy their time at this popular drinks-first, food-later bar. Get some pub fries or Irish nachos here, plus quesadillas and burgers, wings and fish, pasta and asparagus fries, even.

Accommodations

A few chain hotels hang out near the I-81 ramp 2 miles (3.2 km) from downtown. There's the **Hampton Inn** (481 Suedberg Rd., 570/345-4505, $100-130) and the always-reliable **Comfort Inn** (433 Suedberg Rd., 570/345-8031, $60-130).

Pottsville

From Pine Grove, take PA-125 north to PA-209 for about 10 miles (16 km) until you hit **Pottsville** (pop. 14,324), the county seat of Schuylkill County (pronounced *sku-kul*)

The town was originally a major coal mining hub, thanks to a hunter named Necho Allen. According to legend, Allen was camping overnight at Broad Mountain in 1790 and made a fire so he could keep warm while sleeping. The fire spread to a coal outcropping, igniting the mass and unwittingly making this part of the world much richer. Pottsville became an important coal industry center, and the city also expanded with textile manufacturing and brewing, the latter thanks to D. G. Yuengling & Son. By the early 20th century Pottsville was a hopping party of a big city, complete with an NFL franchise. But those mining and manufacturing jobs dwindled over the last several decades.

But with mountains nearby, new restaurants pushing boundaries, and a rich working-class history, Pottsville still draws people to live and work. For hikers, it's a potential zero day for grub and relaxation…and maybe a beer or three.

D. G. Yuengling & Son Brewery

The story of America's oldest brewery starts in 1829, when German immigrant David G. Yuengling moved to Pottsville, still a coal-mining hub, and began brewing under the moniker Eagle Brewery. It would take nearly 50 years for the name change to **D. G. Yuengling & Son Brewery** (Mahantongo St. and S. 5th St., 570/628-4890, www.yuengling.com, 9am-4pm Mon.-Fri., 10am-3pm Sat., free), which people know today as simply Yuengling. Or, if you're from eastern Pennsylvania, you typically just ask a bartender for a "lager," which denotes Yuengling Traditional Lager. You can see and taste that, plus other beers in the catalog of this five-generation family brewery, on a tour of its Pottsville facility. Five tours are held each day; closed-toe shoes are required.

Across the street from the brewery is a gift shop and tasting room, in which tour participants can swig old favorites and whatever's special to the facility. The gift shop is filled with Yuengling merchandise like apparel, books, bar tools, and small gifts, plus Pennsylvania products.

Jerry's Classic Cars and Collectibles Museum

The unique nostalgia trip of **Jerry's Classic Cars and Collectibles Museum** (394 Centre St., 570/628-2266, www.jerrysmuseum.com, noon-5pm Fri.-Sun. May-Oct., $10 adults, $8 seniors and ages 6-12) is something to behold, especially for people who either grew up in the 1950s and 60s or simply love retro. Jerry and Janet Enders run this museum set in an old car dealership, and cars on display have included a 1964 Plymouth Belvedere 426 Wedge and 1972 Volkswagen. Retro ephemera fills the museum, and you can literally get lost in the memories of vintage kitchen products and gas station signage. Gas stations and snack bars have been somehow re-created here, too. Museum items change regularly.

Entertainment and Events

Nightlife

Small bars with regulars? That's Pottsville. You'll get that and a pool table at **Rumors** (661 N. Centre St., 570/622-8687, 6pm-2am Mon.-Sat., under $20), plus steak, burgers, and bar food. There's live music, too. **Strikers Pub** is the bar inside Strike Zone Alleys (2501 West End Ave., 570/622-8741, under $20), so there's an overflow bowling crowd, plus live music, wings and things, and special events like karaoke. Then there's **Woody's Bar & Backyard Paradise** (204 Peacock St., 570/516-9681, 5pm-2am Thurs.-Mon., under $20), a funny bar in that the bar itself isn't the attraction. There are no windows inside, so head outside to the backyard where there's yard games and a fire pit.

Performing Arts

Small but feisty and community oriented, the **Majestic Theater** (209 N. Centre St., 570/628-4647, www.majestictheater.net) hosts more than 50 events each year in its 224-seat venue. Its in-house troupe Majestic Players crank out several plays and musicals each year, including two children's shows.

Shopping

Local artisans show off their pottery at **Mud & Maker** (6 S. Centre St., 484/650-2745, noon-6pm Thurs.-Fri. Mar.-Dec.), which doubles as a studio. Artisans make their wares at the shop, then sell them both at the store and craft shows. Mud & Maker hosts workshops starting in the spring.

Food

Wheel (201 W. Market St., 570/622-2700, www.wheelrestaurantpottsville.com, 11am-9pm Mon.-Sat., 11am-3pm Sun., under $15), short for "wheel of cheese," is the hottest grilled cheese restaurant in town. Diners can fill out a sheet on which they create their own special grilled cheese sandwich. Soups (including tomato, of course) are available, as well as fatty bites and ice cream. Brick walls, high-tops, and a long bar invite a fun time.

Put some tomato with that cheese at **Roma Pizza** (116 W. Market St., 570/628-5551, www.romapizzapottsville.com, 10am-10pm daily, under $20), considered by many tops in the local pizza game. Roma serves wood-fired pizza, plus New York-style pies, salads, burgers, pasta, Italian dishes, and sandwiches. It has a clean and thoughtful wood-paneled dining room, plus old-school booths and a bar.

The longtime favorite in Pottsville is **Ruby's Kitchen** (212 S. 2nd St., 570/581-8772, 10am-4pm Mon.-Fri., under $15), a lunch counter for the midday crowd serving up mouthwatering fare like a chicken salad croissant and cheesesteak. A clean environment, fast service, and good lunches mean it's the most consistently beloved place in the city.

Enjoy dinner in a beautiful stone room at the **Greystone Restaurant** (315 N. Centre St., 570/628-4220, www.thegstone.com, 5pm-9pm Tues.-Wed., 5pm-10pm Thurs.-Sat., under $50), whose menu changes regularly but hovers around gourmet meat and fish, plus starters like escargot and carpaccio of filet mignon. There's outdoor patio seating, too.

The vintage sign marking **Blu Tavern Restaurant** (1323 Bunting St., 570/544-8019, 4pm-9pm Tues.-Sat., 10am-2pm and 4pm-9pm Sun., under $35 dinner, $15 brunch) is inviting enough. Inside is Italian comfort food perfect for a big family dinner.

Accommodations

Speak with Allyson Chryst, innkeeper of ★ **The Maid's Quarters Bed, Breakfast and Tearoom** (402 S. Centre St., 484/223-9497, www.themaidsquartersbedandbreakfast.com, $100-150), and you'll quickly learn about her passion for running a bed-and-breakfast. The young innkeeper has

Top to bottom: D. G. Yuengling & Son Brewery; downtown Jim Thorpe; the Asa Packer Mansion in Jim Thorpe.

wanted to run a B&B since age 18, and she does a fine job of it with the Maid's Quarters. There are three rooms, including a spacious maid's suite with a kitchenette, inside this narrow 1829 stone home. Rooms are decorated in a kindly Victorian manner, though not overdone, with splashes of pastel and minimal furniture. The inn hosts a brunch on the second Sunday of each month ($15-20), and the tearoom opens for special occasions.

There's little in the way of chains here, but there's the **Ramada** (101 S. Progress Ave., 570/622-4600, $90-130), which is a suitable place to rest. **Blu Tavern** (1323 Bunting St., 570/544-8019, $50-65) has two motel rooms for rent. Both are bare bones but have air-conditioning, refrigerator, and coffee pot.

PA-61: The Pinnacle

Few scenic vistas on the Appalachian Trail get the press that **The Pinnacle** receives. Arguably the top overlook in Rocksylvania, the Pinnacle atop Blue Mountain affords views that stretch out beyond the Lehigh Valley.

Also, because of the press it gets, the Pinnacle is typically slammed. You have to get to the parking lot early, before 9am at least to avoid being shut out of a parking spot. The best route from Pottsville is a 20.7-mile (33.3-km) trip south on PA-61 through Port Clinton. (AT hikers pass near Port Clinton through Eckville, an unincorporated community known for its six-person shelter, a small white house with green trim.) As you enter Hamburg, turn left on Mountain Avenue and take that to Reservoir Road, where you turn left.

★ The Pinnacle via Pulpit Rock

Distance: 8.7 miles (14 km)
Duration: 5 hours
Elevation gain: 1,300 feet (396 m)
Difficulty: Moderate
Trailhead: 400 Reservoir Road, Hamburg (40.583101, -75.941668)

The Pinnacle is one of the best single hike experiences on the entire AT. A blue-blazed gravel trail past a yellow gate will lead you to the Appalachian Trail, which you'll follow to the right. After crossing a bridge, turn right on the AT, then in another 0.25 mile (0.4 km) turn right again. Don't get sidetracked after this; just stay on the white-blazed AT through the woods and spot the sign leading you toward Pulpit Rock and the Pinnacle.

From here it's a tough climb on rocky terrain called Blue Rocks, with some scrambling, to Pulpit Rock. Stop here and take in a clear view, but remember, this isn't the big one. The climb continues. The trail can be hard to spot at this point, so stay relatively straight and look for white blazes as you ascend. The 2-mile (3.2-km) climb ends as you pass a yellow-blazed trail. Another 0.4 mile (0.6 km) up is a blue-blazed spur trail pointing you to the Pinnacle. There's also a cairn here that embarrasses all other cairns. The blue trail leads you to the Pinnacle, which you can't miss. On a clear day you can, you know, see forever.

When finished, head back to the AT and continue as it widens as a woods road. Reach a large clearing and spot the blue-blazed trail to your left. That takes you down through a rhododendron forest toward the peaceful Hamburg Reservoir. Walk along the reservoir and through a gate until you reach the bridge. You'll spot the gravel road to the parking lot from there.

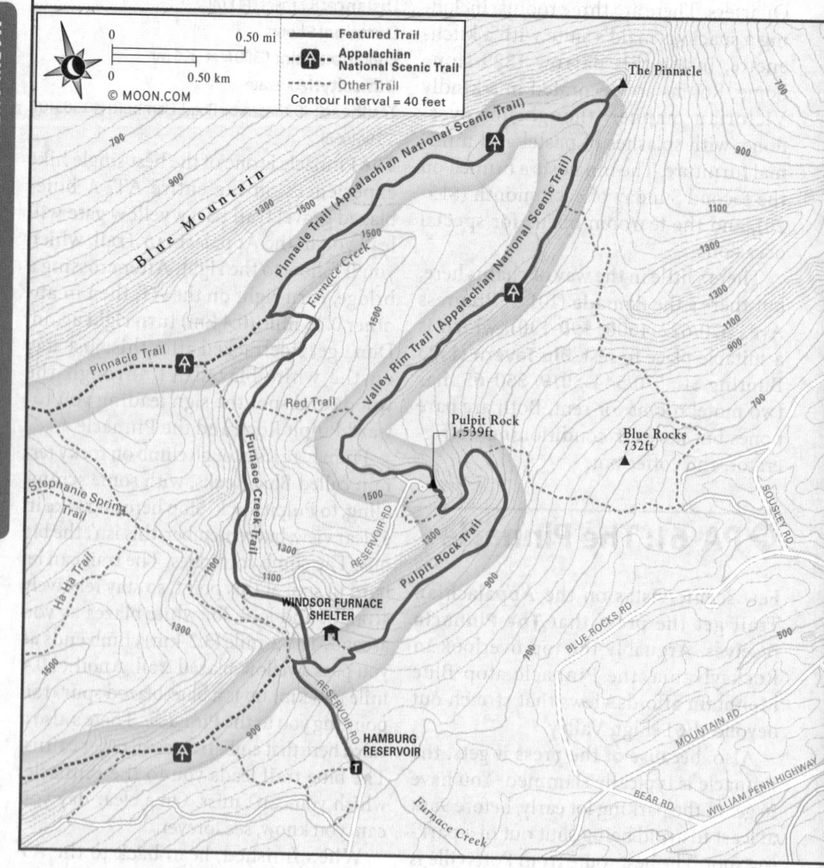

Tamaqua

Drive 15.8 miles (25.4 km) north (east) on US-209 to **Tamaqua** (pop. 7,107), a cute stopover, and another one of those communities with an old train car just resting there, ripe for photographs. There's reason for this, of course: The borough was a railroad hub, home to a grandiose Victorian-style station built in 1874 to facilitate Philadelphia & Reading Railroad passengers shuttling to and from coal country. As coal mining declined and the highway system made the automobile the most convenient method for visiting the area, the railroad and station became less important.

Luckily some passionate residents saved the train station in 1992, listing it in the National Register of Historic Places and restoring the structure for modern use. Today it's home to **Tamaqua Station Restaurant** (18 N. Railroad St., 570/668-3800, 11am-9pm Tues.-Sat., 10am-8pm Sun., under $50), which uses the station's layout of disparate rooms to its advantage. A narrow bar area has some booths, while a couple of other dining rooms are a bit quieter. It seems the whole town could be here for dinner some nights, enjoying fish, pasta, and tender meat dishes. The restaurant lobby tells the story of Tamaqua's railroad past through newspaper clippings and memorabilia. A neighboring gift shop has local history books, wood cutouts, caps, and mugs.

As far as the railroad itself, trains still run via the Reading & Northern Railroad, so be careful when crossing the tracks at the pedestrian walkway.

PA-309: Bake Oven Knob

From Tamaqua, take PA-309 south to an intersection with Mosserville and Mountain Roads. Turn left onto Mountain Road, which becomes Bake Oven Road, a steep slog that takes you to a parking area. You'll have company on this quick hike leading you to Bake Oven Knob, which isn't quite the Pinnacle but still brings it home with two spectacular views.

Bake Oven Knob

Distance: 0.8 mile (1.3 km)
Duration: 0.5-1 hour
Elevation gain: 40 feet (12 m)
Difficulty: Easy
Trailhead: Appalachian Trail crossing at Bake Oven Road (40.744586, -75.738302)

This popular hike is quick and easy, but since we're in Rocksylvania, you have to battle with collections of jagged terrain. You'll start easy enough on the AT, but after a short walk you'll encounter an incline of rocks. Step carefully, and when you're past it, you'll reach a clearing with a graffiti-sprayed rock announcing your location. This is Bake Oven Knob, with views to the west and east available from this 1,550-foot (472-m) perch. You can simply turn back or continue north on the AT, but doing so means staying on the extremely rocky Kittatinny Ridge, where you must step carefully. The **Bake Oven Knob Shelter** is 0.5 mile (0.8 km) from Bake Oven Knob, and that shelter is something else. There are whispers the shelter, which isn't in the best shape and looks like a food stand, is haunted. Hikers have given reports of shadowy figures and abnormal noises, which is strange because nature is nothing if not abnormal noises.

PA-309: Andreas

When the Appalachian Trail meets PA-309 11.5 miles (18.5 km) south of Tamaqua, **Blue Mountain Summit** (2520 W. Penn Pike, Andreas, 570/386-2003, www.bluemountainsummit.com, noon-9pm Thurs. and Sat., noon-10pm Fri., noon-8pm Sun., under $30) is right there for hikers to grab a bite, drink a beer, and even stay overnight. But you may have to meet Ken.

Here's the deal: New ownership has taken over Blue Mountain Summit, but Ken, the former owner of the restaurant and inn, could still be hanging around (he says he won't be hanging around, but others are dubious). Ken is a character who comes off as volatile, but is ultimately genial, and meeting him gives you a story you can tell people for years. Whether or not Ken is around, come here, because the food is good and the vibes are chill. Favorites include the ahi tuna burger and wings. There's a good bar, too.

The on-site **Blue Mountain Summit Bed & Breakfast** ($90-130) includes three rooms described as rustic but are more or less comparable to motor lodge quarters.

Pennsylvania's Folk Heroes

- **Jim Thorpe:** Arguably the finest athlete in American history, Thorpe moved from his Oklahoma Sac and Fox Nation to Pennsylvania to attend Carlisle Indian Industrial School, which ran as a pseudo social engineering experiment aimed at assimilating Native Americans into white Euro-American culture. Thorpe excelled, especially as a sports star. He won Olympic gold medals in the pentathlon and decathlon in 1912, then played baseball for the New York Giants and football for the Canton Bulldogs. He later became immortalized in the Pennsylvania town that took his name.

- **Daniel Boone:** Yup, Kentucky isn't big enough to hold Boone. The family of the pioneer who explored the Bluegrass State moved from England to Pennsylvania in 1713 to join William Penn and his Quakers in the New World. Daniel was born near Reading, about 75 minutes south of Lansford. He lived there from his birth until age 15; his **homestead** (400 Daniel Boone Rd., Birdsboro, 610/582-4900, www.danielboonehomestead.org, 10am-4pm Tues.-Sat., noon-4pm Sun.) is a tourist attraction.

- **David "Robber" Lewis:** Carlisle resident David Lewis was known in the early 19th century as the "Robin Hood of Pennsylvania." The highwayman Lewis and his band of criminals reportedly robbed from the rich—using a network of caves to pull off their capers—and gave to the poor, straight out of Robin Hood's playbook. In 1820 a posse captured Lewis, shooting him before sending him to jail. He died there at age 30.

Lansford: No. 9 Coal Mine and Museum

It's just a 5.3-mile (8.5-km) drive north (east) on US-209 from Tamaqua to **Lansford** (pop. 3,767), which is in Carbon County and is next to Coaldale, just in case you forgot this section of Pennsylvania is the coal region. Lansford's population grew as anthracite coal mining expanded in the 19th and early 20th century, peaking in the 1920s and 30s. The history of Lansford's roaring old days, and of the mining in this area, is illuminated at the **No. 9 Coal Mine and Museum** (9 Dock St., 570/645-7074, 10am-4pm Fri.-Sun. May-Labor Day, 10am-4pm Sat.-Sun. Labor Day-Oct., $10 adults, $6.50 ages 5-10).

The museum is at the site of the No. 9 mine, which produced 90,000 tons of coal per year starting in 1858 and operated until 1972. On guided tours, visitors can ride the train 1,600 feet (488 m) into the mountain, where the miners hospital is set up. Visitors can also see the original 900-foot (274-m) elevator shaft that took miners down into the earth. Just be sure to wear comfortable, closed-toe shoes and a warm layer, as the mine's temperature is typically in the low to mid-50s. Historical items, replicas, and paintings are also on display, and there's a gift shop with books, coal memorabilia, and clothing.

★ Jim Thorpe

There are more than a few American towns given the designation "Little Switzerland" or "The Switzerland of America," so I'll be diplomatic in calling **Jim Thorpe** (pop. 4,607) a seriously gorgeous little town that comes out of nowhere. While driving north (east) almost 10 miles (16 km) from Lansford on US-209, you'll meet a series of curves alongside the Lehigh River. A bridge extends over the river into a more residential part of town once called East Mauch Chunk, but stay on US-209 as it dumps you into

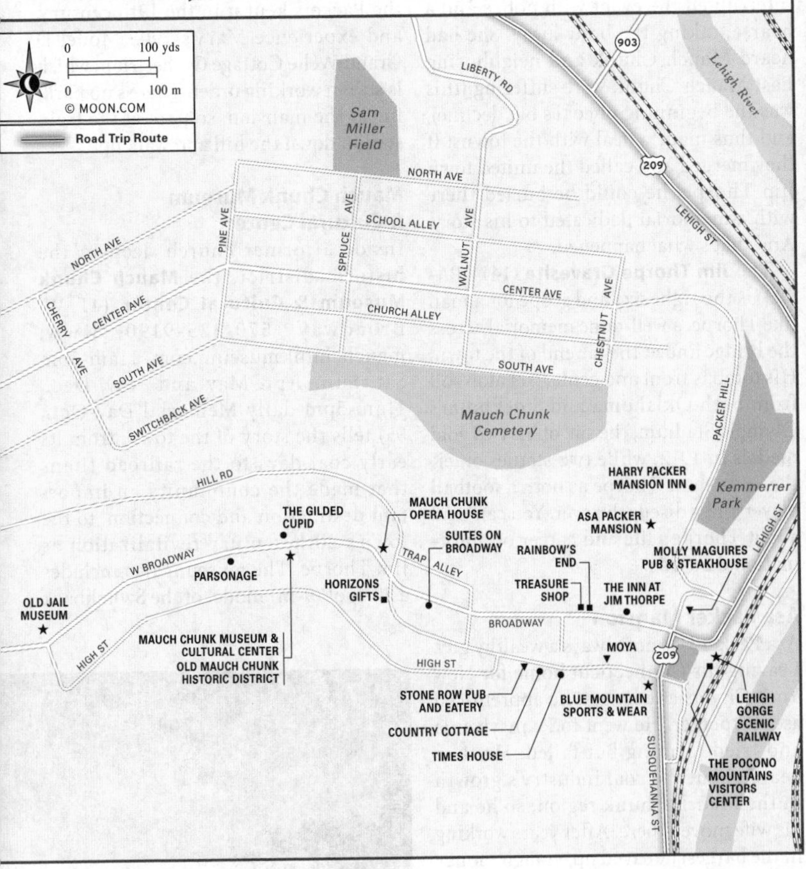

the town's **Old Mauch Chunk Historic District.**

The Old Mauch Chunk Historic District definitely feels Swiss, with cozy narrow streets, tiny buildings made of stone, and a rugged warmth that feels both mountainous and chic. The nearby railroad station still hosts regular rides for visitors, commanding the center of town with plenty of activity on weekends. Museums focused on the town's history, plus mammoth cliff-top manors once owned by the titans of the state's railroad industry, make Jim Thorpe an eye-catching town worth an overnight stay.

Sights

Jim Thorpe Gravesite

First, some background. Mauch Chunk is the former name of the town, meaning "sleeping bear" in the language of local Native Americans. It came to be named after Jim Thorpe thanks to his widow, Patricia, who was upset after Oklahoma denied to give Jim a memorial after his death in 1953. So, according to the story, Thorpe's children and tribal members were performing a traditional Native American burial for him when Patricia interrupted the event with police and a hearse, taking the body away. She had heard Mauch Chunk and neighboring East Mauch Chunk were suffering (this was the beginning of coal's big decline), and thus made a deal with the towns: If they merged and called the united town Jim Thorpe, he could be buried there with a memorial dedicated to his story. And that's what happened.

The **Jim Thorpe Gravesite** (1414 PA-903) is the right size and scope for a man like Thorpe, a well-done memorial across the bridge and at the far end of the town. His tomb is front and center, set atop soil from both Oklahoma and Stockholm's Olympic Stadium, the site of his two gold medals in 1912, while two statues on either side show Thorpe as both a football player and a discus thrower. You can read about Thorpe's life and career on informational boards.

Asa Packer Mansion

Asa Packer was not always a wealthy guy. Leaving his Connecticut home for New York City as a teenager, he apprenticed as a carpenter. He went to Pennsylvania and tried farming but failed. He then heard about the coal industry's growth in the Mauch Chunk region, so he and his wife moved there. After years working in the barges, he saved up enough money to buy the Delaware, Lehigh, Schuylkill and Susquehanna Railroad, after which he expanded it and made millions. In 1861 he moved into an Italianate villa close to the heart of Mauch Chunk. The **Asa Packer Mansion** (37 Packer Hill Ave., 570/325-3229, www.asapackermansion.com, 11am-4pm Sat.-Sun. Apr.-May, 11am-4pm daily Memorial Day-Oct., $10 adults, $9 seniors, $6 students, $3 ages five and younger) stayed in the family until 1912, when his daughter Mary Packer Cummings transferred the mansion to Mauch Chunk. In 1956 the mansion opened to the public.

Visitors can tour the immaculately preserved house, which is decorated as the Packers kept it in the 19th century, and experience Mary's 1905 Model D Grand Welte Cottage Orchestrion, which is still in working order. There's no parking at the mansion, so park at the train station down the hill and walk up.

Mauch Chunk Museum & Cultural Center

Inside a former church deep in the historic district, the **Mauch Chunk Museum & Cultural Center** (41 W. Broadway, 570/325-9190, www.mauchchunkmuseum.com, 11am-5pm Sat.-Sun. Apr.-May and Nov.-Dec., 11am-5pm daily Memorial Day-Oct., $5) tells the story of the town, from its early coal days to the railroad titans that made the community an important destination and connection, to the town's 20th-century revitalization as Jim Thorpe. The museum also includes a 30-foot (9-m) model of the Switchback

Gravity Railroad, which used gravity to transport coal to Mauch Chunk, then to the Lehigh Canal, in the way a roller coaster works.

Old Jail Museum

The former Carbon County Jail is now the **Old Jail Museum** (128 W. Broadway, 570/325-5259, www.theoldjailmuseum.com, tours noon-4:15pm Thurs.-Tues. summer, noon-4:15pm Sat.-Sun. Sept.-Oct., $5-7). Renovated by the local couple who purchased the nearly 150-year-old fortress-style structure in 1995, the museum has 27 cells and a solitary confinement dungeon. It was the site of the circa 1876 hanging of Irish coal miners suspected as members of the secret working-class society the Molly Maguires. In one cell, a handprint from one of those workers allegedly remains. The museum has a small parking lot; in a pinch you can park behind the train station off Susquehanna Street and walk along Broadway to get there.

Lehigh Gorge Scenic Railway

Watch as the mountains pass by and the river winds with you on the **Lehigh Gorge Scenic Railway** (1 Susquehanna St., 570/325-8485, www.lgsry.com, 11am, 1pm, and 3pm Sat.-Sun. Mar.-May, daily June-Nov., days vary by season, $14-19 adults, $9-10 ages 3-12). This mega-popular attraction sends visitors into Lehigh Gorge State Park and up to the old ghost town of Penn Haven, sometimes in circa 1917 train cars. Trips are narrated, giving passengers the stories of the Pennsylvania coal region. Cyclists can load their bikes on the gondola car of the summertime open-air train, get off the train at Penn Haven, and bike back to Jim Thorpe. The railroad hosts special events like Easter Bunny rides and the ever-packed Santa Claus and winter character train rides.

Hiking

Close to downtown Jim Thorpe is the south entrance to **Lehigh Gorge State**

Lehigh Gorge Scenic Railway

Park (301-319 Main St., 570/443-0400), a 4,548-acre parcel cut by the Lehigh River. It provides outstanding white-water rafting opportunities and access to Glen Onoko Falls.

Glen Onoko Falls

Distance: 4.1 miles (6.6 km)
Duration: 3 hours
Elevation gain: 1,000 feet (305 m)
Difficulty: Difficult
Trailhead: D&L Trail parking lot at Lehigh Gorge State Park (40.881116, -75.762934)

If you want to go up these falls you have to do some serious scrambling, and it may get wet, so be extremely cautious. Signs say to hike "at your own risk," so you know this means business. Simply put, follow the orange blazes to a trail deep among rhododendrons. Get in there, then start navigating rocks, climbing and watching your steps. It won't take long to get up. You'll get to see three main falls here. A chain prevents people from going too far out on a lookout between the second and third falls. Atop the third falls, look for the fire ring, but continue going up rocks until the orange blazes return. In 0.5 mile (0.8 km) the trail brings you to a fantastic lookout over Jim Thorpe. Continue on the orange blazes back down the mountain.

Winding alongside a railroad corridor, the **Lehigh Gorge Trail** is a 26-mile (42-km) portion of the longer D&L Trail, which is 165 miles (265 km). This mostly dirt trail is used by hikers and bicyclists, and in the winter by cross-country skiers. The **Switchback Railroad Trail** (North Ave. near Pine Ave.) loops 18 miles (29 km) of crushed stone, starting in Jim Thorpe and heading to Summit Hill before coming back, tracing the old Switchback Gravity Railroad.

Recreation

Rent a kayak and take a shuttle to the Lehigh River through **Blue Mountain Sports & Wear** (34 Susquehanna St., 570/325-4421, 9:30am-6pm Sun.-Thurs., 9:30am-8pm Fri.-Sat., $60 full trip, $25 shuttle only).

Jim Thorpe River Adventures (1 Adventure Lane, 570/325-2570, 8am-6pm daily, $51 adults, $45 ages 6-17) will get you all set up for white-water rafting in the Lehigh. Its introductory adventure takes passengers from Jim Thorpe south to Bowmanstown, about 10 miles (16 km). Its "Big Time" trip takes passengers through 20 rapids over 12.8 miles (20.6 km).

Bicycling is big in Jim Thorpe, but so is everything else, which is why **Blue Mountain Sports & Wear** (34 Susquehanna St., 570/325-4421, 9:30am-6pm Sun.-Thurs., 9:30am-8pm Fri.-Sat.) exists. You can rent a bike here, then hop on the store's shuttle and start an excursion ($10/hour rental, $33-40/hour rental and shuttle). Bike repairs are done here, bike gear is available, and hiking gear also in stock.

Entertainment and Events

Nightlife

Union Publick House (212 Center St., 570/325-8100, www.unionpublickhouse.com, 4pm-2am Mon.-Thurs., noon-2am Fri.-Sat., 11am-2am Sun., under $30) calls itself the only dive in town, and that's probably not a stretch. Besides serving sandwiches, salads, burgers, and a late-night menu, Union has a good beer list catering to both beer snobs and traditional drinkers. The stone walls are cool, as are the jukebox and pool table. Cash only.

You can order a pound of peel-and-eat Old Bay shrimp at **Molly Maguires Pub & Steakhouse** (5 Hazard Sq., 570/325-4563, 11am-1:30am daily, under $30), the Irish standby in a homely space with outdoor deck. Food runs the American gamut: burgers and such. It hosts a mix of locals and people just visiting.

Performing Arts

The rich folks in old Mauch Chunk lived back on Broadway in what's now the "Switzerland" area of town. The neighborhood is home to the **Mauch Chunk Opera House** (14 W. Broadway, 570/325-0249, www.mcohjt.com), a small but pretty concert hall built in 1881 as a stopover for vaudeville performers heading from Philadelphia and New York City to the West. The opera house hosts plenty of shows each year, featuring regional touring groups, classic rock artists, and tribute bands.

Festivals

Oh does Jim Thorpe ever get packed during the **Fall Foliage Festival** (three weekends in Oct., www.jimthorpe.org). Visitors descend on the town for three weekends of live music at the opera house plus three other locations, while artisans display their wares at Josiah White Park. There are drink tastings and a scarecrow contest, as well.

Shopping

Jim Thorpe has more than a few small gift stores, including the Irish emporium **Rainbow's End** (46 Broadway, 570/325-9150, 10am-5pm daily); **Country Cottage** (37 Race St., 570/325-3836, 11am-5pm Sun.-Mon. and Wed.-Fri., 10am-6pm Sat.), which sells homemade jams and pickles; the bumper sticker madness that is **Horizons Gifts** (105 Race St., 570/325-2079, 11am-5pm Wed.-Mon.); and **Treasure Shop** (44 Broadway, 570/325-8380, noon-4pm Tues.-Sat.), which also specializes in Irish gifts but has Jim Thorpe souvenirs and other items.

Food

Stone Row Pub and Eatery (45 Race St., 570/732-0465, www.stoneroweatery.com, 11:30am-8pm Mon., 11:30am-10pm Thurs., 11:30am-11pm Fri.-Sat., 11:30am-6pm Sun., under $25), prefers farm-to-table and from-scratch whenever possible with burgers, pasta, and protein bowls. You might never know you're inside an 1880s stone building with Stone Row's contemporary beige décor.

★ **Moya** (24 Race St., 570/325-8530, 5pm-9pm Mon.-Tues. and Thurs., 5pm-10pm Fri.-Sat., 5pm-8pm Sun., under $50) is the date-night choice. It's hard to see what's happening inside this small brick building in the historic district, but the walls are a neon red, there are few tables and a bar, and the menu is tight. Trust chef Heriberto Yunda, who works with bold flavors to bring new life to traditional gourmet fare like lamb shank and beef short ribs.

Calm and warm orange and gold feel like a touch of **Tuscany at Trattoria 903** (874 PA-903, 570/732-4452, www.trattoria903.com, 11am-9pm Sun. and Tues.-Thurs., 11am-10pm Fri.-Sat., under $30). Traditional Italian fare like penne alla bolognaise are on the menu with veal, chicken, and nothing Americanized.

Just want a sub (or a hoagie, as many call it around these parts)? **Tommy's Subs** (72 W. 4th St., 570/325-4030, 9am-9pm daily, under $15) does the trick. Inexpensive and no-frills, Tommy's offers up a pretty good facsimile of the Philly cheesesteak. Try the funnel fries, too. Grab a slice at **Gaetano's Pizza** (200 North St., 570/325-9411, 10:30am-10pm Sun.-Thurs., 10:30am-11pm Fri.-Sat., under $20), a neighborhood joint with a black-and-white design aesthetic.

Accommodations

$100-150

Jim Thorpe is a destination town, so there are plenty of options for lodging. For the most part you have your pick of bed-and-breakfasts, but the first place you'll stumble upon is **The Inn at Jim Thorpe** (24 Broadway, 800/329-2599, $90-200). Built in 1849, the main inn has 44 tastefully decorated and simple rooms, part Victorian and part contemporary. Suites have Jacuzzis and fireplaces. The inn also owns two separate properties, 55 Broadway and 44 West Broadway; 55 Broadway includes a shared porch, while 44 Broadway is set in a renovated Victorian that has a kitchen and dining area for groups.

$150-250

The cozy **Suites on Broadway** (97 Broadway, 570/325-3540, www.suitesonbroadway.com, $150-245) makes one feel at home with three suites plus a loft, each with balcony access. The three suites have kitchens.

The Gilded Cupid (40 W. Broadway, 570/325-5453, www.gildedcupid.com, $175-200) has three rooms available, each decorated with wallpaper and with a whole lot of fun items and pieces of furniture, from lamps with statuettes to brass beds. There's common garden for reflection and conversation, and a homemade breakfast is served daily.

You'll get breakfast in your room at ★ **Times House** (25 Race St., 267/934-9393, $139-255) the former home of the *Times News* newspaper. That's right: Instead of a sit-down or a race to the lobby, a continental breakfast is set for you upon your arrival; you eat on fine china. The gorgeous rooms mix early 20th-century-style furniture and light shades of neutral colors.

Over $250

Built in 1874, the **Harry Packer Mansion Inn** (19 Packer Hill Ave., 570/325-8566, www.murdermansion.com, $195-375) was the Italianate home of Asa Packer's son, presented to him as a wedding gift. The lovely common rooms project country opulence with plenty of carved wood, while mansion suites and rooms may have fireplaces and antique furniture in sitting areas. A nearby carriage house dates to 1861 and has multiple accommodations, decorated as country guest rooms. The inn hosts wine classes and murder mystery dinners, in which events are based on historical tales.

An 1844 brick house turned B&B, **Parsonage** (61 W. Broadway, 570/325-4462, $110-265) is a pretty cool piece of real estate with gardens and plenty of art. The four rooms are all bright and bursting with character, like the Elinor Room with plenty of knickknacks on the walls and furniture. The Parsonage serves a gourmet breakfast it calls "coal cracker spa cuisine," which means farm-fresh produce. Guests rave about the breakfasts.

Information and Services

The **Pocono Mountains Visitors Center** (2 Lehigh Ave., 570/325-3673, 9:30am-5:30pm daily) can help with information on the sights and sounds of Jim Thorpe.

Lehighton

You'll reach **Lehighton** (pop. 5,276) by driving 4.7 miles (7.6 km) on US-209 north from Jim Thorpe. Driving down North 1st Street in Lehighton, you can imagine how the thoroughfare looked some 70 years ago, at the height of the town's population. This business center of Carbon County was the home of a Lehigh Valley Railroad repair facility, bringing in thousands of jobs. Kids grew up on the porches of their homes, while their parents worked in the small businesses that dot North 1st. These days it's a little different, especially since the railroad shut down operations, but Lehighton is still the largest borough in the county and a business center. The county's economic development commission is here, as are quite a few law firms, a couple of good restaurants, and a wildly popular butcher shop.

Food

The big wooden place with the A-frame red roof is the **Red Castle Brewpub** (80 E. Bridge St., 570/732-0020, 11am-8pm Tues.-Sat., noon-8pm Sun., under $30). Red Castle brews its own stuff—a rarity for Carbon County—though it also serves a bevy of local and state craft offerings. Maybe the most intriguing thing about Red Castle is its menu, which is heavy on Polish fare like haluski (sautéed cabbage and imported noodles) and pierogis served with either ranch, sour cream, or blue cheese. All the Polish delicacies are cooked by the owner's 100 percent Polish mother. If you want an alternative, fries, chicken fingers, burgers, and cheesesteaks are also on board. There's outdoor seating.

You'll see billboards for **Bonnie & Clyde Pub and Grill** (111 N. 1st St., 610-377-0777, www.bonnieandclydepubandgrill.com, 11:30am-10pm Sun.-Mon., 11:30am-11pm Tues.-Sat., hours vary by season, under $35) and think it's a tourist trap, but this neat place actually opened in 2016 and is worthy of a stop. It has a 1930s aesthetic of tin ceilings, whiskey barrels, Gatsby-lite booth treatments, and wanted posters. Order crab cakes served with roasted red pepper mayo or a creole pot of andouille sausage and seafood. The draft list is 36 deep with heavy Pennsylvania focus.

Looking for lunch meat heaven? ★ **Heintzelman Meat Market** (124 Mahoning Dr. E., 610/377-5233) is at least near the gates. Here you'll get an education on Pennsylvania's many amazing meats, most of them being some variation of bologna. For instance, ring bologna is a link of bologna found in the general Pennsylvania Dutch area, and if you're at Heintzelman, you can order it. You can also order the infamous scrapple, along with hamburger meat, steaks, and oh, Lebanon bologna. This smoked and semi-fermented beef bologna is a treat originating from nearby Lebanon County (Annville area), and it goes perfect with yellow mustard.

Top to bottom: Glen Onoko Falls in Jim Thorpe; The Bagel Experience in Brodheadsville; a sign for the Appalachian Trail in Wind Gap.

Beltzville State Park

Along US-209, just 5 miles (8 km) north from Lehighton, **Beltzville State Park** (2950 Pohopoco Dr., 610/377-0045, 8am-sunset daily) is home to Beltzville Lake. The park was developed after the U.S. Army Corps of Engineers dammed Pohopoco Creek to create the lake. The lake is the star of the park, with boaters and anglers using it regularly. There are 15 miles (24 km) of trails at the park, with the hikes spread out around the lake. You can also take a dip from the **525-foot-long sand beach** (8am-sunset summer), with nearby refreshment stand. The only permitted mountain biking in the park is on the 2.5-mile (4-km) Christman Trail.

Hiking

Wild Creek Falls Trail

Distance: 5.5 miles (8.8 km)
Duration: 3 hours
Elevation gain: 55 feet (17 m)
Difficulty: Easy
Trailhead: Christman Trailhead at Pohopoco Drive (40.889133, -75.569440)

This level and smooth hike is a peaceful respite from the rocks that plague Appalachian Trail hikers following the white blazes. Start by following the yellow markers of the Christman Trail for 2.5 miles (4 km), passing streams in the forest. You'll reach an intersection with the Falls Trail and cross a bridge over Wild Creek. Stay left to check out Wild Creek Falls, about 15 feet (4.6 m) in height but a beauty, thanks to its dual streams. When finished, continue on the Falls Trail to loop back to the bridge, then head back on the Christman.

Fishing and Boating

Fishing is permitted at the lake, where trout, striped bass, walleye, muskellunge, and perch swim about. Pohopoco Creek is filled with trout and also ready for anglers. Ice fishing also permitted on the lake. In all cases, state registration is required.

Most recreational boats are permitted on the lake, and the park enforces a maximum speed of 45 mph (72 kph). Motorboats must have current registration, while nonpowered boats have to either have registration or a launch permit. Water-skiing also permitted.

Paddleboards are available to rent through **Beltzville Stand Up Paddle** (Preacher's Camp Dr., 570/269-2440, noon-7pm Mon.-Thurs., 10am-7:30pm Fri.-Sun., $15 per hour). Stand Up Paddle also offers classes and exercise programs for paddleboard, including yoga. Kayaks, stand-up boards, rowboats, and pontoons are also available to rent.

Brodheadsville

After a 10.8-mile (17.4-km) drive on US-209 north you'll hit **Brodheadsville** (pop. 1,800). Now, ask a local twentysomething what to do in Brodheadsville and the answer is simple: "Not much."

Food

Still, he recommended one place: **The Bagel Experience** (West End Plaza Suite 113, 1421 US-209, 610/681-4703, 6am-3pm Mon.-Sat., 6am-2pm Sun., under $10). The owner of the Bagel Experience is originally from Queens, New York, and that kind of cachet helps when you're opening a bagel place out in the Pennsylvania countryside. What also helps is that it smells positively glorious upon entering, even late in the day. All bagels, muffins, and Danish are homemade. Cold cuts and cream cheeses are just waiting to be placed on the bread. The one downfall is there's nowhere to sit, so just wrap up the bagel and eat it at the top of a mountain.

Mai Thai (1457 US-209, 570/801-7822, 11am-9pm Sun. and Tues.-Thurs., 11am-10pm Fri.-Sat., under $20 dinner, under $15 lunch) serves all the standard Thai favorites, including pad thai, drunken noodles, and all kinds of curries in a large, open dining room.

Sciota: Eddie's Toy Museum

It's a 4.5-mile (7.2-km) drive on US-209 North from Brodheadsville to **Sciota** (pop. 1,028), which saves plenty of time if you opt to visit **Eddie's Toy Museum and Store** (1 Fenner Ave., 570/402-0243, 10am-5pm Tues.-Sun. May-Dec., $10). This is a private museum, owned by Ed Stanat, a former racecar driver who's been collecting toys and NASCAR memorabilia for decades. The result is a literal compendium, with somewhere around 23,000 items in the museum. The staggering nostalgia trip includes action figures, Coca-Cola branded items, trucks and cars of all kinds, lunch boxes, and so, so much more. Call ahead to ensure that the museum is open.

PA-33: Wind Gap

For the next detour, turn onto PA-33 south from US-209 and drive another 7 miles (11.3 km) to **Wind Gap** (pop. 2,720). Long stretches of the Appalachian Trail in northeastern Pennsylvania are well confined and don't cross any roads—but then the trail hits PA-33. A large parking area appears. A mobile home park is across the way. That's your welcome to this trail community where hikers can fill up and take a quick breather.

Entertainment and Events

For more than 30 years, the **Wind Gap Bluegrass Festival** (AFBA Mountain View Park, 206 East Mountain Rd., May, www.windgapbluegrass.com) has brought thousands of music lovers to the small borough. The festival welcomes a couple dozen bluegrass bands and soloists over four days, plus offers workshops, a bluegrass academy, an open stage for bands not scheduled to perform, and screenings of bluegrass-themed films. The festival offers free camping if you purchase a ticket for the full weekend.

You can't miss the marquee with the word "Gap" on top. **Gap Theatre** (47 S. Broadway, 610/863-3094) provides a change of pace. This 1947 theater has one screen that shows first-run films, plus hosts frequent events.

Food and Nightlife

Hikers walking into town will take North Broadway south from the trail crossing and find **Scorecard Sports Bar & Grill** (130 N. Broadway, 610/863-5269, www.scorecardbar.com, 4pm-2am Mon.-Fri., noon-2am Sat.-Sun., under $20), a big sports bar good for wings, burgers, sandwiches, and pizza. Hikers might like the Dick Butkus, consisting of two burgers, cheddar, onion rings, and barbecue sauce. Scorecard hosts live music and bar events such as trivia nights.

Small but bursting with charm, ★ **Café on Broadway** (21 S. Broadway, 610/881-4261, www.cafeonbroadwaypa.com, 11am-7pm Tues.-Fri., 9am-3pm Sat., under $20) is the best bet for homespun, hiker-friendly food. The McGarry family owns and runs the place, and it's likely you'll see mom Joyce and daughter Alyssa doing literally everything from sandwiches to burgers to eggs to cookies. Watch the McGarrys do their thing while they chat with locals and generally have a good time. Go for the pastrami cheesesteak, which includes spinach, pepperoncini, and muenster. Wash it down with a milk shake.

Ice cream is found at **Sweet Nanny's Candies and Ice Cream Creamery** (101 S. Broadway, 484/538-6571, noon-9pm Mon.-Thurs., noon-10pm Fri.-Sun., under $10). Have some homemade ice cream, chocolate candies, fudge, or chocolate-covered bananas inside this bright and vibrant little corner shop.

Stroudsburg

Driving north (east) 9.7 miles (15.6 km) from Wind Gap on US-209, the signs begin to take over the space between road and tree. Everywhere you look it's another advertisement for some kitschy Poconos "resort" wanting you and your partner to get away from it all. Maybe the beautiful couple on the billboard is soaking tastefully in a hot tub, their eyes twinkling, champagne flutes tilted ever so slightly. Farm stands, golf clubs, and luxury condominiums promise serenity by the mountains in this long-time getaway destination, and the Poconos remain popular with East Coast families and retirees.

The gateway to the Poconos is **Stroudsburg** (pop. 5,416), which with its neighboring borough **East Stroudsburg** (pop. 10,189) make up a lively hub. Some of that is due to **East Stroudsburg University** (200 Prospect St.), a state university and Division II school that pulls in more than 7,000 students annually. Thus the area has a few fun bars and a pretty good music venue. But really, the area's recent growth (at least from 1991 to 2000) is because of an influx of former New York City residents seeking a quieter community to raise families. The area, a great place to stretch the legs, have a good meal, and catch a show, is accessible to New York (two hours via I-80) but even more accessible to the Appalachian Trail (20 minutes).

Sights

Frazetta Art Museum

The niece of Frank Frazetta told me there's something I'll recognize at the **Frazetta Art Museum** (141 Museum Lane, East Stroudsburg, 570/242-6180, www.frazettamuseum.com, 10am-4pm Thurs.-Sun., $15). Well, I recognized Conan the Barbarian, that's for sure. Frazetta is one of the most revered names in 20th-century art; his chilling work has graced the covers of sci-fi movie posters, comic books, and rock and metal albums. He's also the man whose Conan is the one we most associate with the fantasy hero.

The museum displays a considerable number of original work by Frazetta, including the original "Death Dealer," seen on the first Molly Hatchet album. The facility is inside Frazetta's estate, a beautiful Italianate home on a large property with a pond. When driving up, be wary of the narrow dirt road and don't pull into the nearby private residences. There's a gift shop on premises.

Schisler Museum of Wildlife & Natural History

Opened to the public in April 2016, the **Schisler Museum of Wildlife & Natural History** (Hoeffner Sci-Tech Center, Normal St. and Ransberry Ave., East Stroudsburg, 570/422-2705, 10am-3pm Tues.-Sat. Sept.-May., $6 adults, $4 ages 3-17 and seniors) is down in the basement of an ESU building, so it could be confusing, but the small bit of uncertainty is worth it when you arrive. Walk into the Hoeffner building and go straight down the steps to check out this museum devoted to the ecology of northeastern Pennsylvania.

Arthur and Fannie Greene Schisler, ESU alumni, donated taxidermic mounts to the college to display for the public, leading to this museum, which showcases representations of locations across the world, including the arctic, parts of Africa, and the "Verdant East," which looks closely at the local area. You'll see a black bear, bobcat, and ruffed grouse in the Verdant East, and a polar bear, arctic fox, and snow goose in the "Frozen North." Neighboring the museum is the McNunn Planetarium, which shows a rotating roster of films about space.

Hiking

Levee Loop Trail

Distance: 5 miles (8 km)
Duration: 2.5 hours

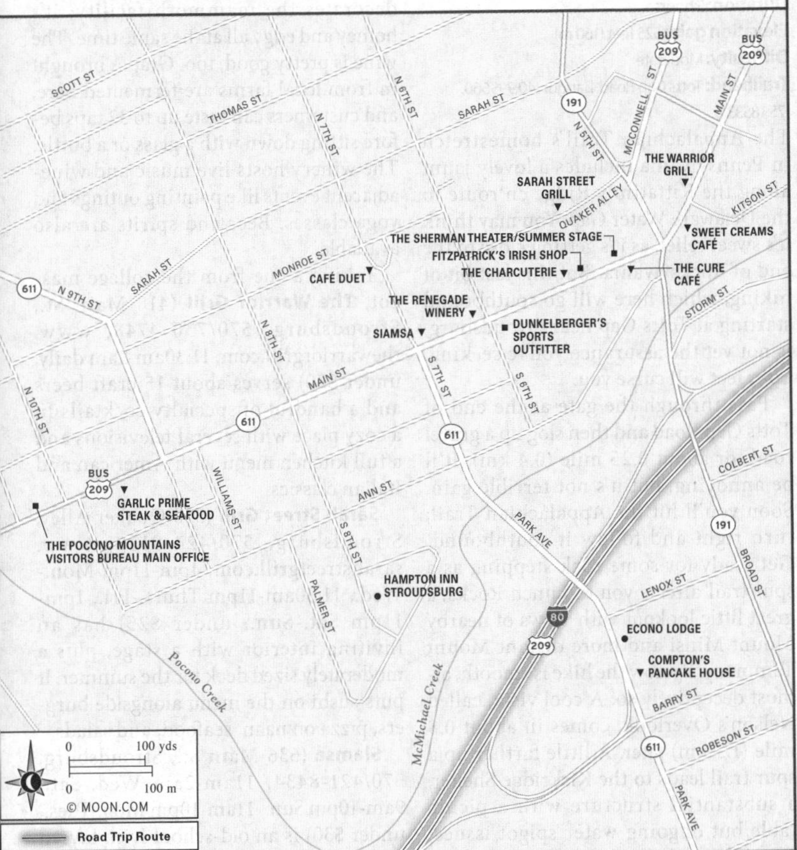

Elevation gain: N/A
Difficulty: Easy
Trailhead: Dansbury Park, East Stroudsburg (40.995660, -75.185332)

The Levee Loop Trail is a nice 5-mile (8-km) walk or bike ride on gravel, paved roadway, and hard dirt. Pick it up by heading out to Day Street and, walking toward Washington Street, turning right on a dirt trail that leads to the trailhead. You'll be at the top of a levee that keeps the creek from flooding into Stroudsburg and East Stroudsburg. Follow the eastern leg of the trail as it walks along the creek, then enter Yetter Park. You'll reach an intersection with Mill Creek Road; be careful as you walk on the road, which you'll use to cross the creek to the other side. Turn left onto Stokes Mill Road and follow that until you see a dirt trail. Take that until you reach Creekview Park; you'll bear left and walk the park's perimeter. That'll spill you onto Fables Fit, a dirt road, which you'll stay on until the trail veers to the left. From there it's an easy walk to Washington Street, where you'll turn left, head back over the creek, and meet up with the trailhead.

Totts Gap to Wolf Rocks

Distance: 8.7 miles (14 km)
Duration: 5 hours
Elevation gain: 525 feet (160 m)
Difficulty: Moderate
Trailhead: Totts Gap Road, Bangor (40.995660, -75.185332)

The Appalachian Trail's homestretch in Pennsylvania includes a lovely jaunt along the Kittatinny Ridge en route to the Delaware Water Gap. You may think it's sweet relief, as it's getting close to the end of Rocksylvania. But this last bit of hiking, which here will go southbound starting at Totts Gap near Stroudsburg, is not yet the assurance you're seeking. Your feet will curse you.

Pass through the gate at the end of Totts Gap Road and then slog up a gravel road for about 0.25 mile (0.4 km). It'll be annoying, but it's not terrible gain. Soon you'll hit the Appalachian Trail; turn right and follow it southbound. Get ready for some rock stepping as a spur trail directs you to Lunch Rocks, a great little lookout with views of nearby Mount Minsi and more distant Mount Tammany. By now the hike is smooth, almost deceptively so. A cool vista, called Nelson's Overlook, comes in about 0.8 mile (1.3 km) later. A little farther up a spur trail leads to the Kirkridge Shelter, a substantial structure with a picnic table but ongoing water spigot issues. Continuing, the trail passes Fox Gap and then, Wolf Rocks, one big hulking mass of stone that you'll have to tackle. After that, however, comes the pretty view of the Pocono Mountains. Take it in, hang out, and then turn around and head northbound on the AT to the trailhead.

Entertainment and Events

Nightlife

You'll understand what "urban winery" means when you visit **The Renegade Winery** (600 Main St., Stroudsburg, 570/350-2638, www.therenegadewinery.com, 11am-9pm Mon.-Wed., 11am-11pm Thurs., 11am-midnight Fri.-Sat., 11am-7pm Sun., under $20). Aged wood and comfortable living room furniture decorates the mammoth facility; it's homey and edgy all at the same time. The wine is pretty good, too. Grapes brought in from local farms are fermented here, and customers can taste up to 32 taps before sitting down with a glass or a bottle. The winery hosts live music and wine-adjacent events like painting outings and yoga classes. Beer and spirits are also available.

Taking a cue from the college mascot, **The Warrior Grill** (418 Main St., Stroudsburg, 570/730-4748, www.thewarriorgrill.com, 11:30am-2am daily, under $30) serves about 15 craft beers and a handful of specialty cocktails in a cozy place with several televisions and a full kitchen menu with American and Italian classics.

Sarah Street Grill (550 Quaker Alley, Stroudsburg, 570/424-9120, www.sarahstreetgrill.com, 4pm-11pm Mon.-Wed., 11:30am-11pm Thurs.-Fri., 1pm-11pm Sat.-Sun., under $25) has an inviting interior with a stage, plus a moderately sized deck for the summer. It puts sushi on the menu alongside burgers, pizza on naan, seafood, and salads.

Siamsa (636 Main St., Stroudsburg, 570/421-8434, 11am-2am Wed.-Sat., 9am-10pm Sun., 11am-10pm Mon.-Tues., under $30) is an old-school Irish tavern and dining room occupying elegant digs. It's popular among locals and visitors. There are sandwiches and Irish fare for lunch, Guinness and steak for dinner. Outdoor seating is available.

Rudy's Tavern (90 Washington St., East Stroudsburg, 570/424-1131, 7am-2am Mon.-Sat., 11am-midnight Sun., under $20) is a classic dive with a jukebox, plenty of cold beer, stirring regulars, and the Super, a hot dog wrapped in bacon and cheese.

Performing Arts

The Sherman Theater (524 Main St., Stroudsburg, 570/420-2808, www.

shermantheater.com) is active in bringing in fresh talent, pulling in national touring acts especially popular with the college crowd. Recent acts include Fetty Wap and Judah & the Lion. The theater, capacity 1,800, hosts an annual beer fest, kids' shows, and open mics, plus **Summer Stage,** a mobile outdoor concert venue that drops national touring acts into locations across northeastern Pennsylvania.

Festivals

The city's annual **Stroudsfest** (Main St., Stroudsburg, Labor Day weekend) brings out dozens of food and craft vendors, plus local musicians who play on multiple stages. Families, ESU students, and even New Yorkers heading out for the weekend all converge for this one-day event.

Shopping

The Poconos are an unexpected haven for Irish Americans. According to the owner of **Fitzpatrick's Irish Shop** (538 Main St., Stroudsburg, 570/424-5455, 10am-5:30pm Tues.-Sat.), scores of Irish Americans have been moving out to the Stroudsburg area for nearly 20 years. Fitzpatrick's is a place they can reconnect with their roots, a shop filled with Irish collectibles like charms, flags, glassware, and religious items.

For hikers, **Dunkelberger's Sports Outfitter** (585 Main St., Stroudsburg, 570/421-7950, 9am-6pm Mon.-Sat., 10am-5pm Sun.) has camping supplies, all-weather gear, and hiking boots.

Food

You'll be overwhelmed by the scent of piping breakfasts in the small dining room of **The Cure Café** (517 Main St., Stroudsburg, 570/664-2888, 7:30am-2:30pm Wed.-Mon., under $20). This bright and cheery spot is the place to be for breakfast, specializing in frittatas and build-your-own omelets. It's also looking out for AT hikers with the Hungry Hiker: two eggs, toast, home fries, meat choice, and two pancakes.

Also in the running for breakfast supremacy is **Compton's Pancake House** (110 Park Ave., Stroudsburg, 570/424-6909, www.comptonspancakehouse.com, 6am-4pm daily, under $20), a relaxed diner with all the goodies, including pigs-in-a-blanket and luscious cream caramel cheesecake pancakes. You can also order chicken and waffles until 2pm.

Not to be forgotten, **Café Duet** (35 N. 7th St., Stroudsburg, 570/431-3442, 8am-5pm Mon.-Fri., 8am-3pm Sat., 9am-2pm Sun., under $20) whips up breakfast sandwiches, baked eggs, and avocado toast with coffee. Light lunch fare is also available, including a delectable melted brie sandwich. It's quaint and quiet with a small garden seating area.

Few restaurants are more devoted to their niche than **The Charcuterie** (548 Main St., Stroudsburg, 11am-3pm Mon.-Tues., 11am-9pm Wed.-Sat., 10:30am-2pm Sun., under $40). Bring your own bottle of wine or beer to this eatery that's all about meats and cheeses, of which they have a great selection. Opt for "petit" charcuterie plates or "grand" platters like the Local, which includes capocollo and soppressata, plus four kinds of local cheese. You can build your own platters or order sandwiches, such as the Vampire Slayer grilled cheese with chilis and a bacon onion sauce. There's fondue, too!

The lights are dimmed at **Garlic Prime Steak & Seafood** (907 Main St., Stroudsburg, 570/476-6555, 4pm-9pm Sun.-Mon., 4pm-10pm Tues.-Thurs., 4pm-midnight Fri.-Sat., under $60), which puts the emphasis on the garlic (pronounced gar-leek). New American dishes like day-boat scallops include a corn and potato hash black garlic puree, or maybe you'd like garlic short rib sliders. This is definitely more expensive than the average restaurant in the area. There's an extensive wine list, and live music on the weekends.

Rootin Tootin Hot Dogs (1232 W. Main St., Stroudsburg, 570/517-7126, www.rootintootinhotdogs.com, 10:30am-8pm

Mon.-Sat., 11am-8pm, under $10) is a cute, low-slung red house with a cuter vintage-inspired interior: red checkerboard floor, booths, a working jukebox playing rotating classic pop hits, and a countertop made from a 130-year-old ash tree. They also host an outdoor **sock hop** on Saturday nights in the summer (4pm-8pm). As for the hot dogs, the Rootin' Tootin' is topped with pulled beef chili, and the Straight Shootin' is topped with homemade cheese sauce. Smashed potatoes, floats, and ice cream sandwiches are also on the menu.

Sweet Creams Café (429 Main St., Stroudsburg, 570/421-7929, 11:30am-5pm Tues.-Thurs., 11:30am-9pm Fri.-.Sat., noon-5pm Sun., under $20) does sundaes, a killer fudge cake, gourmet hot chocolate, and more in its pleasant brick nook. Non-ice cream foods include salads and stuffed potatoes. Get the Potato Monte Verde with avocado, artichoke hearts, Swiss, and vegetables.

Accommodations

You'll have to head up into the mountains for the resorts; here in Stroudsburg you'll get chain hotels. They include the **Hampton Inn Stroudsburg** (114 S. 8th St., Stroudsburg, 570/424-0400, $100-200), **Staybridge Suites Stroudsburg** (561 Independence Rd., East Stroudsburg, 570/420-2828, $100-180), and the **Holiday Inn Express & Suites** (1863 W. Main St., Stroudsburg, 570/872-9040, $150-220).

Lower-priced options include the **Budget Inn & Suites** (320 Greentree Dr., East Stroudsburg, 570/424-5451, $60-120) and the **Econo Lodge** (10 Park Ave., Stroudsburg, 570/424-1771, $60-110).

Information and Services

The **Pocono Mountains Visitors Bureau Main Office** (1004 W. Main St.,

Top to Bottom: Frazetta Art Museum in Stroudsburg; Tumbling Waters at Delaware Water Gap National Recreation Area; a roadside market in Delaware Water Gap.

Stroudsburg, 570/421-5791, 8:30am-5pm Mon.-Fri.) can help with information on the Stroudsburg area.

Delaware Water Gap

From Stroudsburg, drive 4.9 miles (7.9 km) south on PA-611 to **Delaware Water Gap** (pop. 709), a small haven for thru-hikers finally finished with Rocksylvania and needing some time to rest their hooves. The entire community here is built to welcome hikers and other outdoors-loving tourists, so it's a must-visit when you're hopping on and off the Appalachian Trail in Pennsylvania. The oldest hostel on the AT, Church of the Mountain Hostel (opened in 1976), is located here.

Edge of the Woods Outfitters (110 Main St., 570/421-6681, www.watergapadventure.com, 10am-6pm daily) is a necessary stop for thru-hikers needing any sort of gear (like new hiking boots after Rocksylvania took you down). It also accepts mail drops, provides shuttles with advance notice, offers bike rentals, and runs kayak, pedalboard, and paddleboard tours on the Delaware ($40-42).

Food and Accommodations

The **Village Farmer and Bakery** (13 Broad St., 570/476-9440, 8am-8pm daily, under $15) satisfies hunger pangs with hot dogs, a French toast sausage, egg sandwiches, and pies, pies, and more pies. On summer weekends, the Village Farmer unleashes its meat master, who grills up succulent barbecue outdoors. The pulled pork drips and the turkey legs are mouthwatering. Creek-side seating is available.

Hikers may spring for a pie from **Doughboys of the Poconos** (124 Main St., 570/421-1900, 11am-10pm Mon.-Thurs., 11am-11pm Fri.-Sat., 11am-9pm Sun., under $20). The pizzas are cheesy as all get out, and better yet, Doughboys carries a hefty selection of beer and wine.

The Deer Head Inn (5 Main St., 570/424-2000, www.deerheadinn.com, $90-180) offers several basic but airy rooms, some overlooking Main Street, in a massive Victorian with a porch and balcony. Its **restaurant** (5:30pm-9:30pm Thurs.-Sat., 4pm-8pm Sun., Monday hours vary, under $50) has formal fare like ahi tuna and New York strip, but it serves light fare until 10pm, including quesadillas and burgers.

Delaware Water Gap National Recreation Area (Pennsylvania)

The Appalachian Trail crosses I-80 and drops hikers onto New Jersey's side of the **Delaware Water Gap National Recreation Area** (1978 River Rd., Bushkill, PA, 570/426-2452), but there's a wealth of hiking and recreation opportunities in the Pennsylvania stretch.

Getting There and Around

To enter the park from Delaware Water Gap, take Broad Street to River Road, and follow that 3.8 miles (6.1 km) to Hialeah, the south trailhead of the McDade Recreational Trail. River Road runs alongside the Delaware for a bit before tailing off around Bushkill, park headquarters and a small community with a deli and a campground. River Road is typically closed in the winter, but call the park ahead of time to confirm its status.

The best way to get around the park is by US-209, which enters the park just before Bushkill and runs 20 miles (32 km) north to Milford. From US-209 in New Jersey, you can cross the Delaware River into Pennsylvania via the **Dingmans Ferry Bridge** (PA-739, $1) or the **Milford-Montague Toll Bridge** (US-206, $1).

Hiking

Tumbling Waters Trail

Distance: 3 miles (4.8 km)
Duration: 1.5-2 hours

Elevation gain: 254 feet (77 m)
Difficulty: Easy
Trailhead: Pocono Environmental Education Center (538 Emery Rd., Dingmans Ferry)

Jam-packed into 3 miles (4.8 km), Tumbling Water Trail is perfect for a quick taste of the Water Gap, providing vistas, a solid ascent and descent, and of course, a fantastic waterfall. It's part of the network of trails starting at the Pocono Environmental Education Center (PEEC), and it's the best one.

From the parking lot, looking at the PEEC, walk along the right side and go back toward the cabins. You'll see the Tumbling Waters trailhead to the right; turn in and begin an easy hike following orange blazes through the forest. After a while the forest descends and leaves you at a crossing with Brisco Mountain Road. Cross the road and continue following orange until you reach a ridge. Before turning right, look behind you and check out the stone chimney, part of a house that once stood on the property. After the turn, you'll start descending, and toward the bottom of the hill you'll find "steps" dug into the dirt. At the bottom of the hill turn right and you'll see the entrance to a series of switchbacks with a railing. Head down that trail, and as you go, you'll begin to hear the rushing, or tumbling, waters. Tumbling Waters is a pleasant cascade with two falls. You can walk close to the falls (which are beneath you) and catch some views, but be careful.

Head back up the switchbacks until you reach the main trail, then go left to finish the hike. You'll pass through pine and birch, then Pickerel Pond and some marshy areas, before the trail leaves the woods across the road from the PEEC.

Raymondskill Creek Trail

Distance: 0.6 mile (1 km)
Duration: 0.5 hours
Elevation gain: 178 feet (54 km)
Difficulty: Moderate
Trailhead: Raymondskill Road (41.290291,-74.840466)

A short hike with one steep section takes you to the tallest waterfall in Pennsylvania, Raymondskill Falls. The waterfall trail comes in just across from the parking area. Very quickly the Cliff Trail comes in from the right; turn onto it to visit Tri-State Rock, just 0.3 mile (0.5 km) down the trail. From there you'll get an overlook of New Jersey and New York while standing in Pennsylvania. Now back to the waterfall trail: You'll first find the upper falls overlook, which will give you a sense of the height. Continue to the middle falls overlook, where a spur can take you down to the creek. But again, waterfall. Stay on the trail and head to the lower viewing area. When finished, head back up that steep ground.

Recreation

West of the Delaware River, the **McDade Recreational Trail** (31 mi/50 km, moderate) spans nearly the entire length of the park, offering opportunities to hike, bike, and cross-country ski past beautiful river views, through both farmland and forest. Most trailheads are just a few miles apart, with the southern trailhead at **Hialeah** (River Rd. after Shawnee Church Rd.) and the northern trailhead at **Milford Beach** (Milford Beach Rd. off US-209).

There are two swimming beaches on the Pennsylvania side of the park. **Smithfield Beach** (River Rd., 2 mi/3.2 km north of Hialeah) is grassy with picnic areas and a boat launch, plus access to the recreational trail. **Milford Beach** (Milford Beach Rd. off US-209) is also grassy with picnic areas, a boat launch, and recreational trail access.

Boating is permitted on the Delaware from the Gap; all boats must be registered. Speed limit is 10 mph (16 kph) April-September and 35 mph (56 kph) October-March. There are multiple boat launches on the Pennsylvania side, including Bushkill boat launch (US-209, 9 mi/14.5 km north of Hialeah), Smithfield Beach (River Rd., 2 mi/3.2 km north of Hialeah), and Milford Beach (Milford

Beach Rd. off US-209). Rent canoes, kayaks, or rafts from **Kittatinny Canoes** (2130 PA-739, Dingmans Ferry, 800/356-2852, $40-48), or hop in a tube ($27).

Food and Accommodations

Stock up on wares at **Roost Deli and Market** (3251 US-209, Bushkill, 570/588-7062, www.theroostdeli.com, 6am-5pm Tues.-Thurs., 6am-7pm Fri., 7am-7pm Sat., 7am-5pm Sun., under $10). Part convenience store, part deli, and part restaurant, Roost has even the hungriest hikers covered. Breakfast includes omelets and sandwiches with Taylor ham (a cured pork product known as pork roll in south Jersey and Pennsylvania). Lunch and dinner means burgers, sandwiches, hot hoagies, and salads.

Dingmans Campground (1006 US-209, Dingmans Ferry, 570/828-1551, Apr.-Nov., $40-52) can facilitate up to 40 people at its primitive sites. **Rivers Bend Group Campground** (Flatbrookville, 570/426-2452, Apr.-Nov., reservations required) has five campground areas near a cliff overlooking the Delaware.

Information and Services

The **park headquarters** (1978 River Rd., Bushkill, 570/426-2452, 8:30am-4:30pm daily) is 12 miles (19.3 km) north of Kittatinny Point and the Appalachian trailhead.

New Jersey,
New York, and
Connecticut

New York, New Jersey, and Connecticut

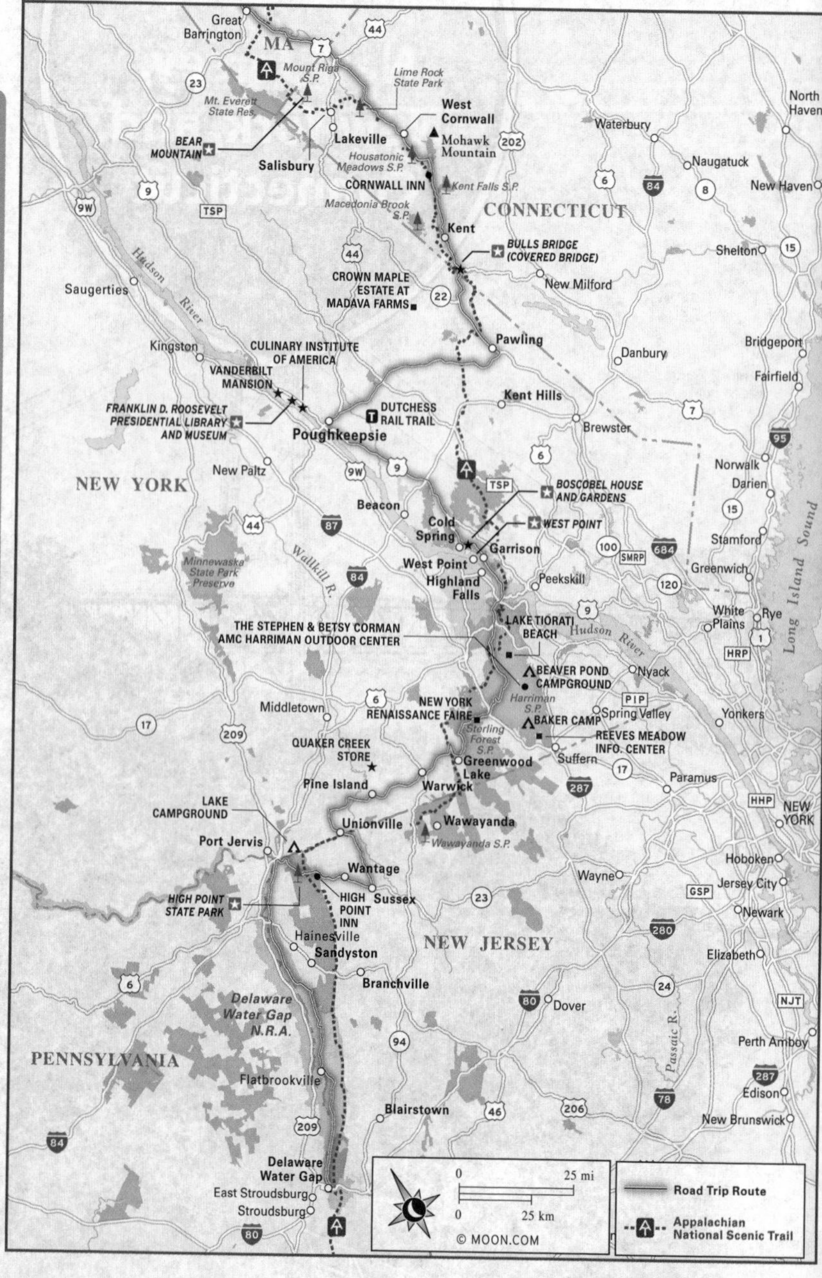

Highlights

★ **High Point State Park:** At 1,803 feet (550 m), the highest point in New Jersey is an obelisk with an observation deck that provides sweeping views of the region (page 278).

★ **Bear Mountain:** The first Appalachian Trail markers were posted on this quintessential New York peak overlooking the mighty Hudson River (page 290).

★ **West Point:** Whether you're taking a tour, attending a football game, or seeing a concert performance with booming fireworks overhead, patriotism isn't hard to find at the majestic campus of one of America's five military service academies (page 295).

★ **Boscobel House & Gardens:** An early 19th-century Federal house sits among charming gardens and offers a world-class view of the Hudson River and West Point. In summer it hosts a phenomenal Shakespeare company (page 300).

★ **Franklin D. Roosevelt Presidential Library & Museum:** Roosevelt set in motion the tradition of presidential libraries and museums with this complex on his family property overlooking the Hudson River (page 310).

★ **Bull's Bridge:** As the Housatonic River rushes underneath, cars facing opposite directions oblige traffic laws at this 19th-century covered bridge, one of two of its kind still in operation in Connecticut (page 317).

The view from atop Bear Mountain in New York, with the Hudson River wriggling below and the Manhattan skyline far beyond, reminds you of the importance of the Appalachian Trail.

When forester Benton MacKaye dreamed up the Appalachian Trail in 1921, he imagined stressed city dwellers setting aside their lives for a weekend, maybe longer, and reconnecting with the wild nature that wasn't so far from their compact apartments. Inspired by MacKaye's plan, the current-day New York-New Jersey Trail Conference set the first miles of what would become America's greatest walking path on Bear Mountain, a destination for hikers that's just 50 miles (80 km) north of New York City but a world away from hectic urban life.

The idea of escaping the city is the overarching theme in the tristate area of New Jersey, New York, and Connecticut. From the Delaware Water Gap in western New Jersey to the undisturbed communities of northwestern Connecticut, this stretch of the Appalachian Trail mixes bucolic splendor with a dash of urbane living. Pricey farm-to-table restaurants stand on the same block as the independent hardware store that's been around for 75 years. Chic boutiques share Main Street with cozy diners that still produce the best eggs in town. In short, travelers can have their kale and eat it, too.

That means plenty of the destinations in this region of the AT are perfect day-trip suggestions. Blairsville is a quirky outpost with a funky history. Warwick and Kent typify quaint Americana with art and shopping options. And Beacon and Poughkeepsie have a wealth of sightseeing and foodie options. The AT passes through it all at relatively low elevation, rising on small mountains and big hills from which views are almost always arresting.

No matter what view you choose, you'll likely be joined by someone at the summit, because everyone visiting this region seems to be seeking their own little escape.

Planning Your Time

Two questions will determine how long you should stay in New Jersey, New York, and Connecticut: Are you hiking, and when are you visiting? If your answer is "yes" and "in the fall," plan on a full week with numerous moderate to strenuous hikes, day trips to some of the cooler small towns and cities, and at least one full day visiting the historic sites in the Poughkeepsie area. If you're hiking in the summer you can cut out two days, a day trip, and a hike. If you're not hiking, no matter when you visit, plan on at least three days to visit the historic spots, take a day trip to a Main Street, and do a little driving in the hills along the Hudson River.

The best way to explore the area is to make Beacon or Poughkeepsie your home base, the former if you want a boutique experience and the latter if you want something more affordable. Warwick and Kent also have solid options for overnight stays. From either Beacon or Poughkeepsie you can take a bunch of day trips, spending up to three hours total traveling to and from the farthest destinations, Blairstown and Salisbury.

Just like nearly everywhere else along the Appalachian Trail, when you travel here will have a hand in the total experience. Summer is busy, as folks drive from New York City to visit and hike the area, but October is high season. Plan on being among crowds if you're in New York or Connecticut during an October weekend. In fact, October is a good time to visit New Jersey, because the crowds are smaller but the foliage is still great.

Best AT Hikes

Compared to the rest of the Appalachian Trail, New Jersey, New York, and Connecticut are a walk in the park for hikers, as there are no peaks taller than 3,000 feet (915 m) here. Still, there's a surprising number of steep trails in this area, and for a region less than 100 miles (162 km) from New York City, the wild vegetation is welcome. You may never realize how close you are to city life.

- ♦ **Mount Tammany Loop Trail (3.5 mi/5.6 km, Delaware Water Gap National Recreation Area, New Jersey):** Though the ascent includes an arduous climb up a rocky trail, the payoff—a clean view of the Delaware River—justifies it. You'll join the AT at the end of the hike (page 271).
- ♦ **Sunrise Mountain (8.5 mi/13.7 km, Stokes State Forest, New Jersey):** The jewel of Stokes State Forest is a peak along the Kittatinny Ridge with a neat stone shelter. The AT rides the ridge and continues up to High Point (page 277).
- ♦ **Cat Rocks Pawling Trail (5 mi/8 km, Warwick, New York):** You can't go wrong on the AT in the Warwick and Greenwood Lake areas, but Cat Rocks provides a fun bunch of scrambling. You're on the AT for the entirety of this up-and-back (page 315).
- ♦ **Bear Mountain Loop (4 mi/6.4 km, Bear Mountain State Park, New York):** There will be crowds, but there also will be a great fire tower, possible views of Manhattan, and an amazing rock staircase. You're on the AT much of the time here (page 290).
- ♦ **Bear Mountain Loop (6.7 mi/10.8 km, Mount Riga State Park, Connecticut):** The tallest peak in Connecticut offers a moderate summiting opportunity with low-grade rock scrambling (page 323).

Getting There

This portion of the trip begins where I-80 crosses the Delaware River at **Delaware Water Gap National Recreation Area** and ends in the northwest corner of Connecticut in **Salisbury.** It may seem like a big stretch, but the drive is just **145 miles** (233 km) and can take a highway driver three hours to accomplish. For a starting point that isn't the middle of an interstate, either the **Kittatinny Point Visitors Center** or **East Stroudsburg, Pennsylvania** (5 mi/8 km west of the visitors center), work just fine.

Car

Starting at the Delaware Water Gap, take Old Mine Road to exit the park, then hook up with **US-206**, riding **River Road** up to **NJ-23**. Take **NJ-23** south to **NJ-284** north to the **Pine Island Turnpike,** which becomes **CR-1A** and heads into Warwick. Connect to **NY-17A**, which enters Harriman State Park and runs into **Seven Lakes Drive,** which heads north to **US-6.** After crossing the Bear Mountain Bridge, turn onto **NY-9D** until it merges with **NY-9** in Poughkeepsie. Then turn onto **NY-55** and take that into Connecticut. Finally, take **CT-7** north to the junction with **CT-112.** A short drive on that road leads to **CT-41,** which will finish the route.

That's a lot of roads, but it forgoes the various major highways that can cause a headache during rush hour. Of course, in this region, most every road will be a headache during rush hour. Beware of driving any of the major highways going to New York City between 7:30am and

Best Restaurants

★ **Blairstown Diner, Blairstown, New Jersey:** Dine at an old-school New Jersey diner with a hearty breakfast and a place in movie history (page 275).

★ **Bellvale Farms Creamery, Warwick, New York:** Get in line for a memorable farm-fresh ice cream cone at this scenic outpost next to the AT (page 285).

★ **The Grange, Warwick, New York:** Tucked away in an old post office, this Warwick spot is quintessential farm-to-table (page 285).

★ **Kitchen Sink Food & Drink, Beacon, New York:** Don't miss fried chicken night every Monday at this cozy and warm eatery (page 308).

★ **Kingsley Tavern, Kent, Connecticut:** Spins on farm-to-table highlight a vast menu with popular weekend brunch service (page 319).

★ **RSVP, Cornwall, Connecticut:** The space is tiny and it's challenging to secure a reservation, but this is an ultra-intriguing French-dining experience (page 321).

9:30am, and away from the city between 4pm and 7pm on weekdays. On summer weekends, reverse that warning. Also, Bear Mountain State Park in New York is a likely traffic jam every weekend in October.

As for those highways, **I-80** runs across the southern end of the Delaware Water Gap and into Manhattan, while **I-84** comes in at the northern end of the Water Gap and runs through to Connecticut. South to north, **I-287** carries traffic through the New Jersey and New York suburbs, and **I-87** is the New York Thruway, a toll road that parallels the Hudson River for a while. Other major arteries include **I-95,** which is the toll-required New Jersey Turnpike in that state, and the Garden State Parkway, also toll-required, which ends at a junction with **I-287** in New York. Speed limits on interstates are typically between 55 and 65 mph (86-105 kph), while on state and county roads expect plenty of variation. Be mindful that when driving into small towns and villages, the speed limit may dramatically reduce to as low as 25 mph (40 kph).

The major travel hub for both ends of the route is, of course, New York City. To reach the Delaware Water Gap from New York City, hop on I-80 west from the George Washington Bridge; it's a 71-mile (114-km) drive taking about 90 minutes without traffic. US-46, the shortest signed, non-spur U.S. highway, runs parallel to I-80 and provides a scenic route, and NJ-23 can also get you from New York City to the Water Gap. Both will add another hour to your drive.

Air

For New Jersey and New York, plus most of Connecticut, the three major New York City area airports operated by the Port Authority of New York and New Jersey have the most options for flying the friendly skies**. John F. Kennedy International Airport** (JFK Expy. and S. Cargo Rd., Jamaica, NY, 718/244-4444, www.panynj.gov/airports/jfk, JFK) has eight terminals, from which 70 airlines operate daily. **LaGuardia Airport** (LaGuardia Rd., Flushing, NY, 718/533-3400, www.laguardiaairport.com, LGA) offers nonstop flights to 64 locations. **Newark Liberty International Airport** (3 Brewster Rd., Newark, NJ, 973/961-6000, www.panynj.gov/airports/newark-liberty, EWR) is the most accessible of the

Best Accommodations

★ **Mohican Outdoor Center, Delaware Water Gap National Recreation Area, New Jersey:** Set up shop in a cabin and take a dip in the center's Catfish Pond (page 273).

★ **Bear Mountain Inn, Bear Mountain State Park, New York:** There's plenty of history at this extensively renovated Adirondack-style hotel with comfortable, bright rooms (page 294).

★ **Thayer Hotel, West Point, New York:** Rest like a Joint Chief. This stone hotel dating to the 19th century has rooms accented in red, white, and blue (page 298).

★ **The Roundhouse, Beacon, New York:** Stay among weekenders up from New York City at this ultra-cool boutique with a waterfall (page 308).

★ **The Inn at Kent Falls, Kent, Connecticut:** Charming and very Connecticut, this bed-and-breakfast has a range of interesting rooms (page 320).

★ **White Hart Restaurant & Inn, Salisbury, Connecticut:** An 1806 New England country inn boasts an understated allure and fine lounge areas (page 323).

airports for this guide's route, providing relatively smooth access to I-95, plus I-280, which connects to I-80. Newark has three terminals and is a hub for United (800/864-8331).

The closest airport to northwestern Connecticut is **Albany International Airport** (Albany Shaker Rd., Colonie, NY, 518/242-2200, www.albanyairport.com, ALB), which has 55 daily commercial arrivals and is accessible via I-90 from US-7 north.

Also part of the Port Authority network, and just a 20-minute drive from Beacon, **Stewart International Airport** (1180 1st St., New Windsor, NY, 845/838-8200, www.panynj.gov/airports-stewart, SWF) is home to Allegiant (702/505-8888), American Airlines (800/433-7300), Delta (800/221-1212), JetBlue (800/538-2583), and Norwegian Air (800/357-4159). **Westchester County Airport** (240 Airport Rd., White Plains, NY, 914/995-4860, www.whiteplainsairport.com, HPN) is an hour southeast of Beacon and is served by American Airlines, Cape Air (800/227-3247), Delta, JetBlue, and United.

Train

There's no direct train service to either the Delaware Water Gap or Salisbury, Connecticut, but New York City's **Metro-North Railroad** (212/532-4900, www.mta.info), whose central hub is **Grand Central Terminal** (89 E. 42nd St., New York, NY, 212/340-2583, www.grandcentralterminal.com), extends to numerous destinations at or near the route. The Hudson Line stops in Garrison, Cold Spring, Beacon, and Poughkeepsie, and also services a Breakneck Ridge stop during weekends and holidays only. The Harlem Line stops in Pawling and Dover Plains, and at the weekends-and-holidays-only Appalachian Trail platform, the only train station on the AT.

Accessible from **New York Penn Station** (34th St. and 7th Ave., New York, NY), **NJ Transit** (973/275-5555, www.njtransit.com) operates the Port Jervis Line, which provides access to Tuxedo and Harriman (both near Harriman State Park) and Port Jervis. Connections for this line have to be made at the Secaucus Junction station.

Bus

From New York City, **Short Line** (845/610-2600, www.web.coachusa.com/shortline) runs passenger lines to the tourist-friendly Bear Mountain and West Point.

In New Jersey, the **Skylands Connect Bus** (973/579-0480, Mon.-Fri.) operates before and during normal business hours and provides connections from Sussex to neighboring towns.

Fuel and Services

The small towns and cities in this region each have at least one gas station. You won't find any close to the Delaware Water Gap or any state park or forest. US-206 is the best bet in New Jersey for a fill-up, though it's a full-service state and, if the attendant also wipes your windshield, a tip is appreciated. Also, New Jersey's gas prices are historically lower than those in New York and Connecticut. Warwick has a few stations, and both NY-9 and NY-55 in Poughkeepsie have plenty.

Dial 511 for reports on road conditions in New Jersey and New York. The toll-free number in New Jersey is 866/511-6538 and in New York it's 888/465-1169. In Connecticut, call 911 if your vehicle is disabled and you need assistance.

For emergency assistance, call 911.

Delaware Water Gap National Recreation Area (New Jersey)

Despite being the most densely populated state in America, New Jersey is still very much known as the "Garden State." That's because, despite the crush of people living in the vicinity of New York City and Philadelphia, the state has abundant farms and forestland. Much of northwestern New Jersey has the latter, plus the state's tallest mountains, and for this it has been deemed the Skylands Region by the New Jersey Division of Travel & Tourism. The Skylands is anchored primarily by the state's portion of **Delaware Water Gap National Recreation Area** (1978 River Rd., Bushkill, PA, 570/426-2452).

New Jersey's part of the Water Gap includes Mount Tammany, Worthington State Park, the historic Millbrook Village, Buttermilk Falls, and Old Mine Road. Then there's Kittatinny Mountain, which is actually a long ridge and not one peak. Kittatinny leaves the park and continues through Stokes State Forest and High Point State Park. The Appalachian Trail follows Kittatinny as part of the Ridge and Valley province of the Appalachian Mountains.

Getting There and Around

The New Jersey side of the Water Gap is accessible from Pennsylvania by crossing I-80 at the south end of the park, crossing a toll bridge on CR-560 from Dingmans Ferry, Pennsylvania, or crossing US-206 at the north end of the park. A few roads in New Jersey lead into the park, including NJ-602 west, which heads into Millbrook Village; Gaisler Road, which leads to the Mohican Outdoor Center; CR-640 west, which runs to the Peters Valley School of Craft; CR-560 west, which provides access to Dingmans Ferry; and Jager Road, which connects Hainesville to Old Mine Road.

Old Mine Road, one of the oldest continuously used roads in America, is the best way up the park, stretching the length of the park and continuing into Port Jervis, New York. At 15 mph (24 kph), it's meant to be enjoyed as a scenic drive, so be patient. Those parking at Turtle Beach or Watergate will be charged a vehicle fee of $10 for up to eight people.

The River Runner shuttle bus primarily drives the Pennsylvania side of the park but it does drop off and pick up visitors at **Kittatinny Point Visitor Center** (1 I-80, Columbia, 908/496-4458) on Saturdays, Sundays, and holidays from Memorial Day weekend to Labor Day weekend. Northbound buses run from Kittatinny Point at 7am, 9am, and then every hour until 2pm and 4pm. Southbound buses arrive at Kittatinny Point at 10:47am, then on the hour starting 12:34pm and ending at 4:34pm. There are also buses at 5:47pm and 7:34pm.

Sights

Millbrook Village

After the construction of a gristmill in 1832, the village of **Millbrook** (Old Mine Rd. and Millbrook Flatbrook Rd., Hardwick, 41.073467, -74.962762, 908-841-9531) slowly began to take shape, peaking with 75 residents and nearly 20 major structures in 1875. The village declined into the early 20th century, and by mid-century was populated only by retirees and vacationers. The proposed Tocks Island Dam would've potentially washed out the village, so historical advocates and the National Park Service moved some of the village buildings to higher ground. Today, what remains is not unlike a larger version of a child's toy village: several original structures or replications and placards that tell the story of life in the hamlet.

The Millbrook Village Society presents multiple events each year, highlighted by **Millbrook Days** (Sept.), a celebration of 19th-century life with demonstrations, music and crafting.

Buttermilk Falls

The cascading **Buttermilk Falls,** at about 200 feet (61 m), is the tallest in New Jersey. It's accessible from Mountain Road off Route 615, which breaks off Old Mine Road about 2 miles (3.2 km) north of Millbrook Village. You can walk stone steps to the top of Buttermilk Falls; afterward, you can take the 1.4-mile (2.3-km) Buttermilk Falls Trail out to the Appalachian Trail.

Hiking

Mount Tammany Loop Trail

Distance: 3.5 miles (5.6 km)
Duration: 2-2.5 hours
Elevation gain: 1,201 feet (366 m)
Difficulty: Strenuous
Trailhead: Parking lot off I-80 in Columbia (40.971786, -75.125616)

Start at the Mount Tammany parking lot and walk toward the entrance where, to your left, you'll find the trail blazed with red dots. This steep 1.2-mile (1.9-km) trail of rocks, dirt, and sand is considered the toughest in the Water Gap, so you'll certainly feel accomplished when finished. Before the summit you'll reach a viewpoint overlooking the Delaware River, with Mount Minsi across the way and a highway far beneath. Continue on Red Dot Trail until the summit of Mount Tammany, which isn't clearly marked but comes at an intersection with the Blue Blaze Trail. That goes another 1.2 miles (1.9 km) down before meeting up with the Dunnfield Creek Trail at a picturesque waterfall and bridge. Turn left to follow the Dunnfield Creek Trail another 0.5 mile (0.8 km) through hemlock and mixed hardwood until it hits the Appalachian Trail. Let those white blazes take you back to the parking lot.

Buttermilk Falls Trail

Distance: 2.8 miles (4.5 km)
Duration: 2 hours
Elevation gain: 1,104 feet (336 m)
Difficulty: Strenuous
Trailhead: Parking lot off Mountain Road at Buttermilk Falls (41.137330, -74.889069)

Buttermilk Falls is the tallest waterfall in New Jersey at about 200 feet (61 m), but you'll scale another 900 feet (274 m) in a little more than a mile (1.6 km) on this blue-blazed trail. That means tired feet, but it also means hooking up with Kittatinny Ridge and the Appalachian Trail. Once you hit the white blazes of the AT, make your way back down a quick descent, or turn right on the trail to meet up with the orange-blazed Crater Lake Trail, which loops around the titular lake. (The Crater Lake extension adds another 2.5 mi/4 km to the hike.) Then head back the way you came.

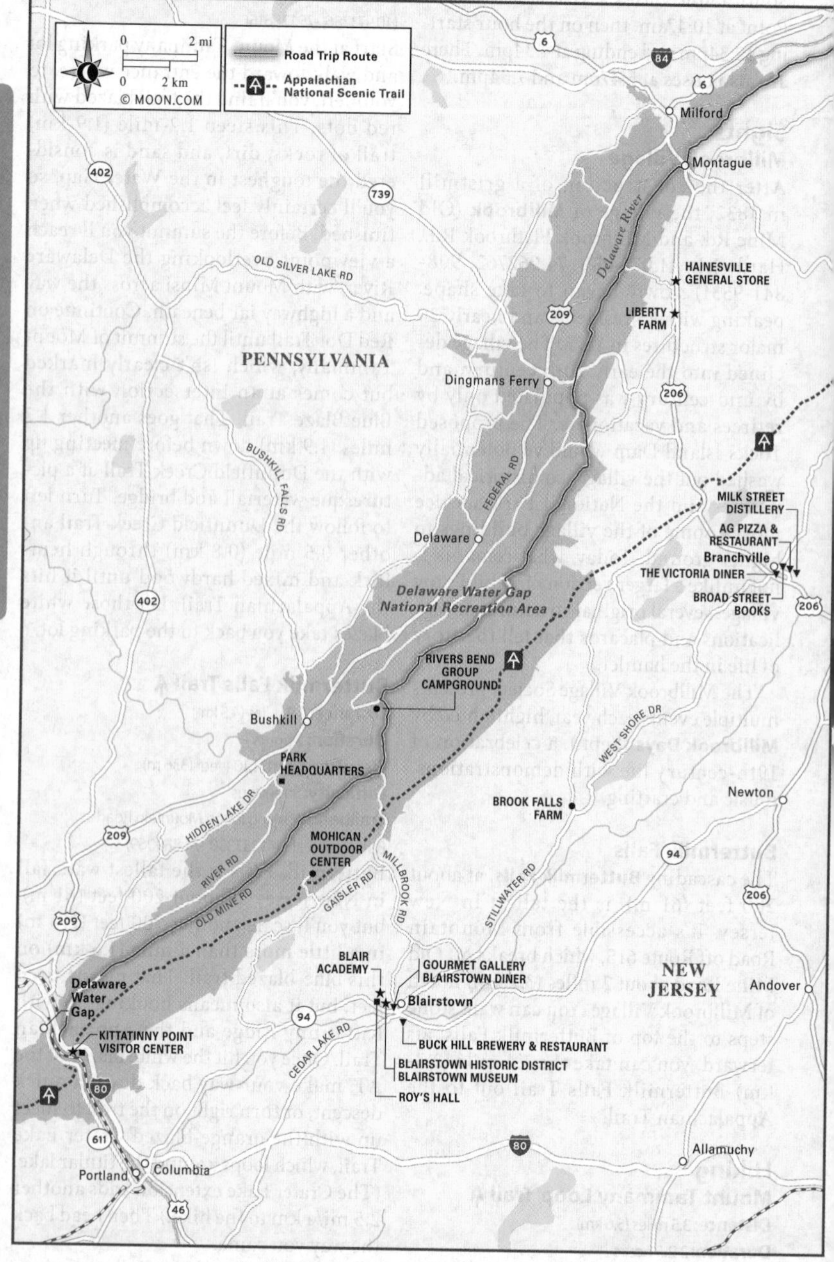

Delaware Water Gap National Recreation Area
0
2 mi
0
2 km
© MOON.COM
Road Trip Route
Appalachian National Scenic Trail
PENNSYLVANIA
NEW JERSEY
Milford
Montague
Delaware River
HAINESVILLE GENERAL STORE
LIBERTY FARM
Dingmans Ferry
Delaware
Delaware Water Gap National Recreation Area
RIVERS BEND GROUP CAMPGROUND
Bushkill
PARK HEADQUARTERS
MOHICAN OUTDOOR CENTER
BLAIR ACADEMY
GOURMET GALLERY
BLAIRSTOWN DINER
Blairstown
BUCK HILL BREWERY & RESTAURANT
BLAIRSTOWN HISTORIC DISTRICT
BLAIRSTOWN MUSEUM
ROY'S HALL
Delaware Water Gap
KITTATINNY POINT VISITOR CENTER
Portland
Columbia
MILK STREET DISTILLERY
AG PIZZA & RESTAURANT
Branchville
THE VICTORIA DINER
BROAD STREET BOOKS
BROOK FALLS FARM
Newton
Andover
Allamuchy
OLD SILVER LAKE RD
BUSHKILL FALLS RD
FEDERAL RD
HIDDEN LAKE DR
RIVER RD
OLD MINE RD
GAISLER RD
MILLBROOK RD
STILLWATER RD
WEST SHORE DR
CEDAR LAKE RD
6
84
402
739
209
206
94
80
611
46

Food and Accommodations

Worthington State Forest Campground (HC 2 Box 2, Old Mine Rd., Columbia, 855/607-3075, Apr.-Dec., $20-25) requires reservations and includes 69 tent and trailer sites, plus a group campsite.

For an indoor experience, the ★ **Mohican Outdoor Center** (50 Camp Mohican Rd., Blairstown, 908/362-5670, $20-50) has bunkrooms, self-service cabins, and a stocked kitchen. Mohican also offers tent sites, runs weekly activities, and offers kayak and canoe rentals on Catfish Pond, which is on the property. There's also a shop in the center, plus a kitchen serving sandwiches and some hot food.

Information and Services

The **Kittatinny Point Visitor Center** (1 I-80, Columbia, 908/496-4458, 9am-5pm Fri.-Tues. Memorial Day weekend-Labor Day, 9am-5pm Sat.-Sun. Sept.) is the lone visitors center on the New Jersey side of the park. The **park headquarters** (1978 River Rd., Bushkill, PA, 570/426-2452, 8:30am-4:30pm daily) is 12 miles (19.3 km) north of Kittatinny Point.

NJ-94: Blairstown

In the early 1820s, John Insley Blair opened a general store in the small New Jersey community of Butt's Bridge. About 50 years later, he was considered one of the wealthiest men in America, valued at between $50 million and $70 million at his death in 1899. Butt's Bridge became **Blairstown** (pop. 5,967) during his lifetime, and while the small New Jersey township stands as a testament to his entrepreneurship, it's most known today for being the place where a vengeance-seeking mother slashed some teens at a campground.

Top to bottom: Mount Tammany and the Delaware Water Gap; Millbrook Village; Buttermilk Falls.

Yep—Blairstown is the setting and filming location for the 1980 cult classic *Friday the 13th*, a real point of pride for the townspeople. Because much of the downtown is relatively unchanged after 40 years, Blairstown feels a bit like the kind of place where some great spooky tragedy took place years before. That said, it's a perfectly lovely and safe little town, and has among the most dining and entertainment options of any community in northwestern New Jersey. Thus, especially if you're spending a few days at Delaware Water Gap, Blairstown makes a great place for a bite or a half-day change of pace from being in the woods.

Getting There

Blairstown is accessible from I-80 on NJ-94, and also from Delaware Water Gap via a 7.3-mile (11.7-km) drive south on Blair-Millbrook Road.

Sights

The Richardson Romanesque buildings of **Blair Academy** (2 Park St., 908/362-6121, www.blair.edu) give some 19th-century color to the community. The private coeducational boarding school sits on 463 acres in Blairstown, and owns many historic structures, including **The Old Mill** (14 Main St.), whose street-level archways are instantly recognizable to fans of *Friday the 13th*. The mill is part of the **Blairstown Historic District,** the community's commercial center. The **Blairstown Museum** (26 Main St., 973/934-2548, www.blairstownmuseum.com, 10am-5pm Fri.-Sat., free) provides a fulfilling introduction to the town.

Entertainment

Roy's Hall (30 Main St., 908/362-1399, www.royshall.org) is a great place to catch a concert or movie after a day of hiking or touring the town. The distinctive 1913

view of Mount Minsi from the Mount Tammany Loop Trail

blue building on Main Street hosts musicians who typically tour the Northeast, and every time the 13th lands on a Friday, there's a screening of the film that put the town on the map.

Food

After re-creating the opening scene of *Friday the 13th,* in which the soon-to-be-killed counselor Annie walks Main Street, head into the **Gourmet Gallery** (31 Main St., 908/362-0051, www.gourmetgallerycafe.com, 9am-4pm Mon.-Thurs., 9am-7pm Fri.-Sat., under $15) for a panini or salad at the café; dinner is served on the weekend. Café seating is available on the inviting front porch.

Old-fashioned diner food is served at the ★ **Blairstown Diner** (53 Rte. 94, 908/362-6070, 6am-7pm Mon.-Fri., 7am-3pm Sat.-Sun., under $25), another location in *Friday the 13th.* Cinematic history is definitely part of the draw here, but the vintage Jersey diner feel make it really worth it. Tin walls, a marble counter, and constant chatter provide a good backdrop for delicious egg dishes and classic early dinner specials like chicken scampi and ribeye steak.

Buck Hill Brewery & Restaurant (45 Route 94, 908/854-5300, www.buckhillbrewery.com, 11am-10pm Sun.-Thurs., 11am-2am Fri.-Sat., under $30) is not a movie location, but it is an expansive food-and-drink spot with two levels of seating and an outdoor patio space with heaters and lawn games. Buck Hill brews its own beer, offering a range of options to suit every type of customer. Food is elevated American fare like short ribs and strip steak.

Accommodations

While there's scarce lodging in the area besides the passing campground, 8 miles (12.9 km) north of Blairstown, up Route 521, is **Brook Falls Farm** (902 Middleview Rd., Newton, 973/692-6019, www.brookfallsfarm.com, $200-250), a historic barn restored to a country cottage, with a hot tub, private grills, and a nearby waterfall.

Branchville

Once a rail hub and part of the Sussex Railroad, **Branchville** (pop. 841) is sleepy but surprising. You could spend more than just a morning in this town, whether perusing books at a quaint bookstore or enjoying a craft cocktail or two.

For hikers wanting a nice kick after a long day working the legs, **Milk Street Distillery** (1 Milk St., 973/948-0178, www.milkstreetdistillery.com, 4pm-8pm Fri., 1pm-7pm Sat., 1pm-6pm Sun., under $15) produces clear spirits and mixes them into cocktails at the bar. **The Victoria Diner** (250 US-206, 973/948-0322, 6am-9pm Mon.-Sat., 6am-3pm Sun., under $25) is a classic diner known for filling breakfasts, and **AG Pizza & Restaurant** (3 Mill St., 973/948-2875, 10am-10pm daily, under $20) serves up bar-style cheese pizzas among a host of other pies.

Branchville's corner bookstore is the independent, family-run **Broad Street Books** (1 Mill St., 862/268-5184, www.broad-street-books.com, 10am-6pm Tues.-Sat., 10am-3pm Sun.), with wooden shelves filled to the brim and a deep selection. More impressive, however, is its staggering CD haul, rivaling any great record store's vinyl collection.

Getting There

Take Millbrook Road to Birch Ridge Road, then bear left onto Shannon Road. That'll turn into Old School House Road, which you'll take until it hits Fairview Lake Road. Turn left, and take that road as it veers right as Owassa Road. Owassa Road will drop you onto Mount Benevolence Road in Crandon Lakes; turn left, then follow the road onto the Owassa Turnpike. That parallels the Appalachian Trail and runs into US-206. Turn right and you'll find yourself in the borough of Branchville.

Stokes State Forest

Six miles (9.7 km) north of Branchville is an underrated gem in the New Jersey Skylands. **Stokes State Forest** (1 Coursen Rd., Branchville, 973/948-3820, $5-20 vehicle entrance fee Memorial Day weekend-Labor Day weekend) is home to the impressive Sunrise Mountain, part of the Kittatinny Ridge, and **Tillman Ravine Natural Area,** a 525-acre hemlock forest whose rushing waters invite a peaceful connection with nature. The Appalachian Trail runs through the park, tracing the ridge for 9.3 miles (15 km).

The park has a network of trails, all toward its northeastern end, while Tillman Ravine sits at the far southwestern end. US-206 cuts the park in half and provides access to Stony Lake and Sunrise Mountain Road, which leads to the summit of Sunrise Mountain. Stony Lake is a popular day-use area with picnicking, fishing, and a **swimming beach** (open

Stokes State Forest

Memorial Day weekend-Labor Day) with horseshoe pits; bring your own horseshoes and spikes.

Hiking

Sunrise Mountain

Distance: 8.5 miles (13.7 km)
Duration: 4 hours
Elevation gain: N/A
Difficulty: Strenuous
Trailhead: Stony Lake parking lot off Coursen Road (41.202264, -74.773499)

Sunrise Mountain is the second-highest peak in New Jersey's section of the Appalachian Trail, and it provides a fine challenge for those warming up for more adventurous hikes up north.

This hike starts by following the red-blazed Swenson Trail, which plods up and down for a bit before meeting the red-and-brown Cartwright Trail. This is when the hike really gets going, as you burn the legs up rocky terrain until you reach the Kittatinny Ridge. You'll hit the AT and turn right, staying on the ridge and ending at the viewing area. Cars can get here, so there's a parking lot, but just smile at the visitors as you continue on the AT for about 2.5 miles (4 km), past the Sunrise Mountain stone shelter and through mountain laurel and some open air. Turn right on the brown-blazed Stony Brook Trail to descend the ridge; take that and the green Tower Trail back to the Swenson Trail and parking lot.

Sandyston

Just 5 miles (8 km) north of the Stokes State Forest entrance, the rural township of **Sandyston** (pop. 1,998) includes a decent sliver of Delaware Water Gap National Recreation Area, plus part of Stokes. Sandyston is the kind of place where people know one another, but in recent years city dwellers wanting a quieter, more rural changeup have been settling amid the township's hills and farms. US-206 is the major highway running through the township, providing access to most everything, including the parks.

Since 2015, Raj Sinha has given folks a reason to wander through his **Liberty Farm** (101 County Rd. 645, 973/219-6356, http://sussexcountysunflowermaze.com, mid-Aug.-mid Sept., $10). Also on the farm is the **Sussex County Sunflower Maze,** where kids and adults get to walk through a field of black-oil sunflowers. Visitors can also pick their own sunflowers, but not the ones in the maze.

The township convenes for food and provisions at the **Hainesville General Store** (283 Rte. 206 South, 973/948-4280, www.hainesvillegeneralstore.com, 5am-6pm Mon.-Fri., 6am-5pm Sat., 7am-3pm Sun., under $15), which has been in operation since 1883 but for the past 23 years has been run by Megan and Bob Horst. In a rustic house that feels like a grandmother's kitchen, the Horsts sell everything from quick bites and candy to used DVDs. The stars, however, are the sandwiches and state-fair-winning pies.

For the former, try the moist chicken Palermo, and for the latter, you really can't go wrong. If you're in a bind, just pick apple.

US-6: Port Jervis, New York, to Tri-State Rock

Drive 15 miles (24.1 km) north on US-206 to **Port Jervis** (pop. 8,828), a city of geographical importance. New Jersey, New York, and Pennsylvania intersect in the Delaware River, and to honor this intersection there's a rock that looks like a giant tackle box beside the river here. **Tri-State Rock** (Laurel Grove Cemetery, Montague Township, NY, 845/858-4000, 8am-4pm daily) is at the point of a peninsula that's also home to Laurel Grove Cemetery. Take the main cemetery road out to the monument.

★ High Point State Park

High Point State Park (1840 NJ-23, Sussex, 973/875-4800, 8am-8pm daily) is home to—that's right—the highest point in New Jersey. It's a manageable 1,803 feet (550 m) that manages to really test your mettle.

A hiker in Connecticut confessed to me that she's deathly afraid of heights. She can hike mountains no problem; it's man-made structures that give her anxiety. I really understood this after climbing up **High Point Monument,** a 220-foot (67-m) obelisk that marks the state's highest point.

The first several of the 219 stairs at High Point are part of a spiral staircase. Then you reach a landing and begin a nerve-wracking climb inside the slowly narrowing walls of the obelisk. If people are coming down when you're going up, you can cut the tension with a butter knife. At the top is a small room with three accessible and smudgy windows, providing 270-degree views of New Jersey, New York, and Pennsylvania. It can get stuffy at the top, so breathe a lot and don't spend the day up there.

While the monument is the star of High Point State Park, the park features a substantial network of trails that run along brooks, wind around lakes, and tour marshlands. Nine miles (14.5 km) of the Appalachian Trail run through the park, which is home to three AT shelters: the Mashipacong Shelter (off Deckertown Road, Sussex), the Rutherford Shelter, and High Point Shelter. All accommodate overnight hikers, though they shouldn't be overcrowded. A campground and day-use area are also in the park.

Getting There and Around

River Road in New Jersey never meets up with NJ-23, so you'll have to enter Port Jervis and take US-6 east to reach NJ-23, which sends you toward the park. NJ-23 is the major road through the park, running west to east and providing parking access for Steenykill Lake, Lake Marcia, the Appalachian Trail, and the road to High Point Monument. Deckertown Turnpike (CR-650) runs through the south side of park and offers AT access, plus a connection to Sawmill Road and Park Ridge Road, which stretch up through the park. Old Mashipacong Road from the west provides another access point.

There's a vehicle-use fee at the park of $5-20 from Memorial Day weekend to Labor Day.

Hiking

High Point Trail

Distance: 4 miles (6.4 km)
Duration: 2-2.5 hours
Elevation gain: 300 feet (91 m)
Difficulty: Moderate
Trailhead: Appalachian Trail parking lot off NJ-23, 0.1 mile/0.2 kilometer south of visitors center (41.302695, -74.667507)

If you'd prefer to hike rather than drive to the obelisk, you're in luck. The beginning of this hike involves walking a busy state highway, but you'll quickly find yourself deep in the narrow fantasia of the Appalachian Trail.

Park 0.2 miles (0.3 km) south of the High Point visitors center and walk north on Route 23 until, across the street to the right, you see the Appalachian Trail marker leading you into the woods. (For an alternative start from the parking lot, follow the AT connector trail away from NJ-23, which will run into the red-blazed Iris Trail. Turn right to meet up with the AT and reach the NJ-23 crossing.) A simple 1.4-mile (2.3-km) hike on the AT awaits. There's a wooden observation deck toward the end, from which you'll get an unobstructed view of the monument. After that the AT runs into the Monument Trail, signified by red and green blazes. You'll take that trail, which crosses the road to High Point and quickly ascends some steep, rocky ground until, voila, the monument is on your right. From there, you can choose to walk inside and climb to the top of the monument.

If you want to drive, take Scenic Drive from NJ-23 at the High Point State Park Office 1.2 miles (1.9 km) to Monument Road. Take that one mile (1.6 km) up to a turnoff, on which you'll make the final climb to the monument.

Cedar Swamp Trail

Distance: 2 miles (3.2 km)
Duration: 1-1.5 hours
Elevation gain: 150 feet (46 m)
Difficulty: Easy
Trailhead: Parking lot past Lake Marcia (41.320016, -74.666148)

A glacier retreating some 15,000 years ago created this wetland, which at 1,500 feet (457 m) above sea level is a unique

Top to bottom: High Point Monument; Cedar Swamp Trail; Stairway to Heaven trail at Wawayanda State Park.

sight with its mossy ground, evergreen white cedars, and spruce trees. To get there, drive along the west side of Lake Marcia and make your third left onto an access road leading to a parking area. From there, follow the purple Cedar Swamp Trail to a fork. Turn left and follow the mossy trail around the marsh. You'll soon step onto a boardwalk taking you across the marsh past rhododendrons and berries. Continue on the purple-blazed trail, turning right at a bench, and you'll get yourself back to the parking lot.

Recreation

The park's Lake Marcia has a lifeguard-protected **swimming beach** (10am-6pm Memorial Day weekend-Labor Day).

Boats may be launched at Sawmill and Steenykill Lakes, and fishing is permitted in all lakes and streams. The state stocks the waters with trout and largemouth bass, among other species.

Accommodations and Camping

High Point Country Inn (1328 NJ-23, Wantage, 973/702-1860, www.highpointmountainmotel.com, $80-120) combines no-fuss motel amenities with a mountain lodge look. The location makes it perfect for park visitors, and the staff is known to be courteous and responsive. It may also be called High Point Mountain Motel online.

The park's **Sawmill Lake Campground** (973/875-4800, Apr.-Oct., $20) has 50 tent sites, two group campsites, and two cabins outfitted with electricity and woodstoves. Nearby flush toilets, picnic tables, and fire rings make life further enjoyable.

Information and Services

The **High Point State Park Visitor Center** (1840 NJ-23, Sussex, 973/875-4800, 8am-4pm Mon.-Thurs., 8am-8pm Fri., 9am-5pm Sat.-Sun.) is across NJ-23 from the Appalachian Trail's approach to the monument.

Sussex and Wantage

Drive south on NJ-23 for 10 miles to reach **Sussex** (pop. 2,130), one of New Jersey's "doughnut towns," which are independent communities surrounded on all sides, like a doughnut hole, by another township. Sussex, surrounded by **Wantage** (pop. 11,358), a small but relatively active community.

Sights

Sussex has a cute Main Street with a couple of shops and an art gallery. Check out **Ward-Nasse Gallery** (35 Main St., 973/875-1987, www.wardnasse.org, 11am-6pm Tues.-Sat., 1pm-6pm Sun.), an import from New York City displaying a range of works from modern artists in and around the tristate area.

You'll also want to check out the **Daughters of the American Revolution Van Bunschooten Museum** (1097 NJ-23, 973/875-7634, 1pm-4pm second and fourth Sun. May-Oct.), a Dutch Colonial house from 1787 that offers a step back in time with period antiques filling a relatively untouched structure.

Food and Accommodations

Taco of the Town (54 Main St., 973/875-9892, 11:30am-9pm Wed.-Thurs., 11:30am-10pm Fri., noon-10pm Sat., noon-8:30pm Sun., under $20) is one of the few places to serve anything resembling Mexican in the area. Despite the sight of a bar at the restaurant, there's no alcohol served, so BYOB. For a formal dinner somewhere between Greek and Italian, **The Green Olive** (1 Libertyville Rd., 973/702-1011, 11am-10pm daily, under $40) is the place. An expansive bar serves pub grub, and there's a downstairs bar that feels much more like a basement dive.

Speaking of dives, the **Airport Pub** (65 CR-639, 973/702-1215, www.airportpub.com, 11am-2am daily, under $15) is the best kind. When visiting, the long,

NEW JERSEY, NEW YORK, AND CONNECTICUT

winding bar could've fit a dozen of my closest friends, while the Touch Tunes jukebox and Hawaiian leis made me feel like coming here past 11pm would've been a hoot. There are plenty of food specials and live music every weekend. The people are chatty and fun, too.

Unionville: Wits End Tavern

From Sussex, drive north on NJ-284 for 7.5 long and lonely miles (12.1 km) to **Unionville** (pop. 612), a tiny outpost that's smack on the AT. There's little to do here, but there is the **Wits End Tavern** (92 NY-284, 845/726-3956, noon-2am Sun.-Thurs., noon-4am Fri.-Sat., under $20), a straight-up beer-and-shots spot with surprisingly delicious burgers and inexpensive platters. It's a regular stop for thru-hikers, who can charge phones and relax for a moment before heading back on the trail.

Pine Island

From Unionville, it's another 6.2 miles (10 km) to **Pine Island** (pop. 1,267). Take the NY-284 south, turn left on State Line Road, and then another left on Liberty Corners Road. Now, don't be fooled by the name: Pine Island is in no way an island, but it used to be...sort of. The nearby Wallkill River used to overflow and flood the area, but higher-elevation areas remained above water and became temporary islands—thus the name. The ground in Pine Island can be very fertile thanks to those centuries of saturation, and the result is rich black soil that's now farmed for, among other things, really delicious onions.

Quaker Creek Store

The agricultural bounty of the area has branded it the Black Dirt Region, and in recent years, local restaurants and beverage producers have taken advantage of this unique ecosystem. One such place is the **Quaker Creek Store** (767 Pulaski Hwy., Goshen, 845/258-4570, www.quakercreekstore.com, 7am-6pm Mon.-Fri., 7am-4pm Sat., under $20). Though it's technically located in Goshen, it's defined by its Pine Island, Black Dirt bounty. This family-run business does justice to Polish delicacies like pierogi (you must order the sautéed onion and mashed potato pierogi) and smoked kielbasa. Also a general store, Quaker Creek has drinks, candy, and whatever else is needed to complete that picnic you're about to enjoy down the road.

Warwick Valley Winery

This area is also home to arguably the most trafficked winery in the Hudson Valley. **Warwick Valley Winery** (114 Little York Rd., 845/258-4858, www.wvwinery.com, 11am-6pm daily, under $30) offers tastings and take-home purchases of its wine, its house-made Black Dirt Distillery spirits, and its well-known Doc's Draft hard ciders. A word to the wise: Get here early. Once the doors open, folks will flood the joint and day-drink away.

The winery has a café on-site, offering grilled meats, pizza, sandwiches and appetizers, but to avoid waiting in line your best bet is to pack a picnic and head right for the booze. Purchase a bottle of wine or cider (or both) and head for the grass, where you can open and sip away. During the summer and fall the winery will present live music (typically guys with guitars), and a few times a year it'll hold miniature music festivals celebrating artists like the Grateful Dead and Johnny Cash.

Pine Island Brewing Company

The **Pine Island Brewing Company** (682 County Rd. 1B, 845/288-2646, www.pineislandbeer.com, 4pm-8pm Thurs.-Fri., 1pm-7pm Sat., 1pm-5pm Sun., under $20) has a rotating lineup of beer available in its sparse, postindustrial taproom and beer garden. The popular beer here is Pine Island Big Brown, a 10.8 percent ABV monster perfect for cooler days.

NJ-517: Wawayanda State Park

From Pine Island, it's a 10.8-mile (17.4 km) drive south on county roads 26, 517, and 515, then through Highland Lakes, to visit **Wawayanda State Park** (885 Warwick Tpk., Hewitt, NJ, 973/853-4462, $5-20 vehicle entrance fee Memorial Day weekend-Labor Day), at the edge of New Jersey's Skylands region. The park is named for the Lenape word meaning "winding water." It's also accurate to call this wild, wild land, because Wawayanda feels like a secret park whose presence is whispered among devoted adventurers. The park has one mega-popular trail and otherwise relatively quiet paths that crawl up rock and through overgrown forest. There's also a 20-mile (32-km) stretch of the Appalachian Trail in the park, and, just to note, a higher-than-zero-percent probability you'll come across a bear den.

The centerpiece of the park is Wawayanda Lake, surrounded by picnic tables, while the Cherry Ridge Trail leads folks from the West Milford area over to Highland Lakes, a community of pricy lakefront properties. There's also a group campsite by Wawayanda Lake.

Hiking

Stairway to Heaven to Pinwheel Vista

Distance: 7.5 miles (12 km)
Duration: 4 hours
Elevation gain: 850 feet (259 m)
Difficulty: Strenuous
Trailhead: Route 517 by Carol Drive, Glenwood, NJ (41.236406, -74.480427)

This is a mega-popular trail, swarmed every summer weekend with high school cross-country stars, area tourists, and the occasional local hustling to get past everyone. Oh, and thru-hikers, since this is on the Appalachian Trail.

For the best and most thorough experience, start outside the park, in the parking area off Route 517, and begin hiking east on the AT. The first section is winding boardwalk, and it's pretty awesome. It reaches an even-more-awesome suspension footbridge over the Pochuck Creek, and then the real hike begins as you enter the state park. You'll climb the strenuous Stairway to Heaven, a long and zigging set of rock steps, to the top of Wawayanda Mountain. The top is known as Pinwheel Vista, a 360-degree view of the area that on clear days includes High Point Monument. Your return trip is the way you came.

Fishing and Boating

Fishing and boating is permitted on Wawayanda Lake. The **boathouse** (Wawayanda Lake Day Use Area, 973/764-1030, 9am-5pm daily, rentals under $30 per hour) at the lake offers canoe and paddleboat rentals.

Warwick

From the eastern end of Wawayanda State Park, at Wawayanda Road, it's a 5-mile (8-km) drive north up the Warwick Turnpike to **Warwick** (pop. 32,065).

You know those lists that tout the best small towns in America? Warwick is always angling to be on those lists. The charming village, which recently celebrated its 250th birthday, is draped in colonial décor and home to creative types who wanted out of New York City. It's also one of the few villages in its area teeming with teenagers and young adults, so the coffee shops and bars are typically hopping. There are also a bunch of good restaurants and markets here, so foodies can enjoy themselves as well.

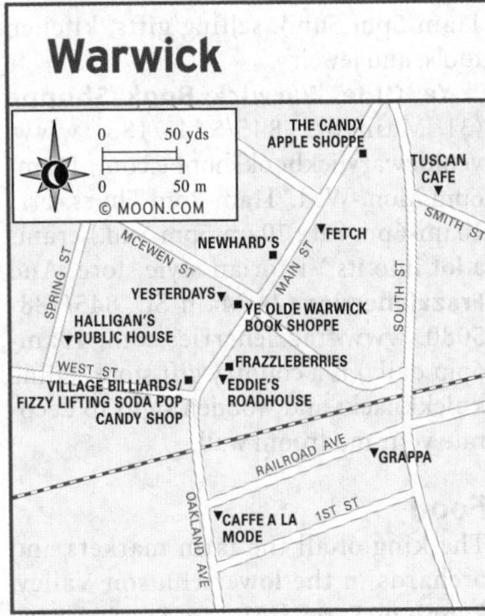

Hiking

For those looking to summit **Mount Peter,** the hike is accessible from the Appalachian Trail at its Route 17A crossing. From the parking area at Mount Peter Ski Area, cross Route 17A and hike into the woods until a blue-blazed connector trail comes in on the left. Turn left onto the trail to reach the **Mount Peter Hawk Watch,** one of the top places in the Northeast to scout these swooping birds of prey.

Bellvale Mountain Trail

Distance: 7.5 miles (12 km)
Duration: 4 hours
Elevation gain: 987 feet (301 m)
Difficulty: Strenuous
Trailhead: Route 17A and Striper Road (41.244104, -74.286587)

The Appalachian trailhead at Route 17A offers hikers options, one of which is this trip southwest along the Bellvale Mountain ridge. It unwraps splendid views of Greenwood Lake during a moderate ramble up and down rugged terrain. Start by following the trail on the side of the parking area, which will immediately enter the woods near the summit of Mount Peter. You'll follow the white-blazed AT as it rides the ridge, providing a few vistas of Greenwood Lake to the east. There's some rise and fall along the way, plus gentle rock scrambling (nothing unmanageable), as you travel 3.7 miles (6 km) to the summit of Bellvale Mountain (1,300 ft/396 m). Once there, turn around and head back the way you came.

Cat Rocks Trail

Distance: 5 miles (8 km)
Duration: 2.5-3 hours
Elevation gain: 100 feet (30 m)
Difficulty: Moderate
Trailhead: Route 17A and Striper Road (41.244104, -74.286587)

A bonus for summer visitors of the Route 17A trailhead is "Bud" Whitt, who sells hot dogs out of a stand and is a godsend for many hungry thru-hikers. Put a pin in it as you start your northbound hike to Cat Rocks Trail. Cross Route 17A on the AT and enter the woods. The blue-blazed connector trail to the hawk watch will come in to the left, so take it if you'd like, but either way, you're taking the AT another 2 miles (3.2 km) or so uphill, then downhill.

Eventually you'll reach a junction with another blue trail, this one an alternate to avoid Eastern Pinnacles, the fun rock scramble that provides great views of Sterling Forest. If it's dry, stay on the AT and do the scramble, using all fours in places. After a pause from scrambling, you'll reach Cat Rocks and do more scrambling. If it's hot and dry here, beware of rattlesnakes.

When the scrambling ends, head downhill, cross a stream, and follow a blue-blazed side trail to the Wildcat Shelter, which regularly houses thru-hikers and will provide a turnaround. If it's wet at all, please consider the blue-blazed side trail at Eastern Pinnacles and Cat Rocks. Follow the AT back toward the smell of frankfurter.

Entertainment and Events

Nightlife

Warwick has some well-trod watering

holes. **Halligan's Public House** (22 West St., 845/986-2914, 11:30am-10pm Sun.-Thurs., 11:30am-11pm Fri.-Sat.) has a red façade indicative of an old-school Irish pub, but it's decidedly more of a standard bar with dining tables inside.

Yesterdays (29 Main St., 845/986-1904, 11:30am-10pm Sun.-Thurs., 11:30am-11:30pm Fri.-Sat.) is a bit more throwback and has a deeper food menu.

For a changeup, **Village Billiards** (17 Main St., 845/544-7750, 4pm-midnight Mon.-Thurs., 4pm-1am Fri., 1pm-1am Sat., 1pm-midnight Sun.) is a spruced-up, 2nd-floor pool hall with a solid bar.

Festivals and Events

For one fall day, Warwick becomes the center of the apple universe with its **Applefest** (Oct.). More than 200 vendors line Main Street while visitors sip cider and eat fair goodies like funnel cake and kettle corn. There's an apple pie-baking contest and farmers market ongoing during the festival.

More spread out, the village's **Warwick Summer Arts Festival** (July, www.warwicksummerarts.com) showcases the area's wealth of dancers, musicians, and visual artists.

And the **Hudson Valley Jazz Festival** (Aug., www.hudsonvalleyjazzfest.org) is based in Warwick and typically features a variety of talented players.

Shopping

Much of the shopping in Warwick reflects the village's vintage mid-century romance. There are two sweets and soda pop shops on Main Street, **Fizzy Lifting Soda Pop Candy Shop** (17 Main St., 845/544-7400, 11am-6pm Sun.-Thurs., 11am-7pm Fri.-Sat.) and **The Candy Apple Shoppe** (60 Main St., 845/544-1844, 11am-6pm Tues.-Fri., 10am-6pm Sat., 10am-5pm Sun.).

There's an honest-to-goodness independent department store in **Newhard's** (39 Main St., 845/986-4544, www.newhards.com, 10am-6pm Mon.-Sat., 11am-5pm Sun.), selling gifts, kitchen tools, and jewelry.

Ye Olde Warwick Book Shoppe (31 Main St., 845/544-7183, www.yeoldewarwickbookshoppe.com, 11am-6pm Mon.-Wed., 11am-8pm Thurs.-Fri., 10am-6pm Sat., 10am-5pm Sun.) crams a lot into its Victorian-style store. And **Frazzleberries** (24 Main St., 845/988-5080, www.frazzleberries.com, 10am-6pm daily) is a country gift store selling knickknacks and wooden signs to decorate your mudroom wall.

Food

The king of all the farm markets and orchards in the lower Hudson Valley, **Pennings Farm** (161 Rte. 94, 845/986-1059, www.penningsfarmmarket.com, 9am-7pm daily, under $30) operates a market filled with locally grown produce and foodstuffs, a pub and grill where the food is farm-fresh, an ice cream stand, an orchard, a cidery, a beer garden, and a garden center. In essence, you can spend

an entire day at Pennings. Just remember that October (and mid-to-late September) is when everyone else will be at Pennings, so plan accordingly.

Just south from the Appalachian Trail crossing at Route 17A is ★ **Bellvale Farms Creamery** (1390 Rte. 17A, 845/988-1818, www.bellvalefarms.com, noon-8pm Mon.-Wed., noon-9pm Thurs.-Sun., under $15), which has next-level ice cream. Special flavors include Bellvale Bog (tons of chocolate, brownie, and fudge) and Great White Way (white chocolate with dark chocolate chunks and raspberry swirl). Lines are typically long, but ice cream can be enjoyed on benches overlooking the vast Warwick Valley.

★ **The Grange** (1 Ryerson Rd., 845/986-1170, noon-8pm Mon. and Thurs., noon-9pm Tues., noon-3:30pm and 5pm-9pm Sat., noon-6pm Sun., under $40) received a vaunted "excellent" review in the *New York Times,* which immediately makes it a tough reservation. But if you want true-blue northeastern farm-to-table, the Grange is a great choice that isn't going to break the bank. Located in an old post office building, it's got a casual, homey atmosphere that provides a nice backdrop for delicious local fare, from fresh pasta to flat iron steak on top of the best mashed potatoes you've ever had.

If you can't score a reservation at the Grange, Warwick has a plethora of restaurants sourcing from the Black Dirt region and using the farm-to-table blueprint. **Grappa** (22 Railroad Ave., 845/987-7373, noon-10pm Mon.-Thurs., noon-11pm Fri.-Sat., noon-9pm Sun., under $50) is a popular spot for date nights and locals looking for nice Italian, possibly outside on the vast front patio area. With a deep wine list, Grappa is also an excellent after-dinner drink spot.

Eddie's Roadhouse (18 Main St., 845/986-7623, noon-midnight Tues.-Sun., under $40) is another popular spot in the village thanks to its brick facing, open-air front, laid-back pub fare, meaty entrees,

Bellvale Farms Creamery in Warwick

and solid beer selection focusing on regional choices.

The **Iron Forge Inn** (38 Iron Forge Rd., 845/986-3411, 6pm-10pm Thurs.-Fri., 5pm-10pm Sat., 11am-1:30pm and 3pm-8pm Sun., under $40) changes its limited menu often and begs a longer, formal meal in its dining room. For those wanting something more casual, the Iron Forge taproom is a gem, a cool basement lair serving rustic plates by a fireplace.

You may walk out of **Fetch** (48 Main St., 845/987-8200, 11am-10pm Sun.-Thurs., 11am-11pm Fri.-Sat., under $40) with both a doggie bag and a doggie. A partnership with the local pet shelter makes Fetch the go-to for dog lovers, with photos of adoption-ready dogs covering the walls. The food, elevated pub grub (including a near-authentic Philly cheesesteak), is worthy of a tail wag.

Warwick may be small, but it packs a punch with its coffee shops and cafes. The perky and punky **Tuscan Café** (5 South St., 845/987-2050, 7am-5pm Mon.-Wed., 7am-10pm Thurs., 7am-6pm Fri., 8am-6pm Sat.-Sun., under $20) has plenty of vegan options, plus a modest seating area and frequent concerts. **Caffe a la Mode** (1 Oakland Ave., 845/986-1223, 6am-8pm daily, under $20) has the vibe of a high school hangout, plus porch seating and milk shakes. For a French fix, **Jean-Claude's Patisserie** (25 Elm St., 845/986-8900, www.jeanclaudesbakery.com, 8am-6pm Wed.-Sat., 8am-3pm Sun., under $15) adds cakes, baguettes, and more to the coffee experience. It's in a well-hidden shopping mall behind the Burger King.

Accommodations

Despite the dining and tourism dollars coming into the village, Warwick has few choices for overnight lodging. Relatively spacious rooms are available at the **Warwick Motel & Suites** (1 Overlook Dr., 845/986-6656, $90-170), which is an otherwise basic stay that serves free bagels and coffee in the morning.

Liz and Terry operate **Ashford Cottage Bed & Breakfast** (26 Oakland Ave., 845/258-7167, www.ashfordcottage.com, $160-200), a restored house with one room and two suites dressed in Victorian finery. The property includes an outdoor pool and gazebo.

Just a minute's drive from the center of the village, the **Warwick Valley Bed and Breakfast** (24 Maple Ave., 845/987-7255, www.wvbendandbreakfast.com, $144-229) has seven distinct rooms, ranging from the spacious French-inspired Provincial to the cozy Loft.

Greenwood Lake

An 8-mile (12.9-km) drive east on NY-17A from Warwick, **Greenwood Lake** (pop. 3,514) is an extremely miniature version of one of central New York's Finger Lakes, but it's much more accessible for New York City residents, so in the summer its namesake village tends to be busy. It's been that way for a century, boasting visitors like baseball legend Babe Ruth and actress Greta Garbo.

The village is concentrated primarily in a peninsula at the head of the lake, while NY-210 and Teneyke Avenue run alongside the lake's west and east sides, respectively, meeting back up near West Milford, New Jersey. The lake provides recreation aplenty and splendid vistas, with a few local restaurants taking advantage with back porches overlooking the water. But despite the lakeside-property cache of the village, Greenwood Lake is solidly blue-collar. Most residents enjoy a good drink and a speedboat ride on the lake (not at the same time, of course).

Recreation

When there's a giant lake outside, you may be tempted to play in it, and that's what residents of Greenwood Lake like to do most. **Skip's Dockside Marina** (63 Teneyke Ave., 845/477-8410, $20-25) rents out kayaks and canoes, and can fix what's wrong with your small vessel, while **Jersey Paddle Boards** (622 Jersey Ave., 845/554-0787, Fri.-Sun., $25-35) is your place for paddleboards, plus kayaks and tandem kayaks. It's also smack between the Breezy Point Inn and the Helm, so afterward you can chow down.

Greenwood Lake was smart in putting a park at the head of its lake. **Thomas P. Morahan Waterfront Park** (Windermere Ave. at the lake) has a small beach with on-duty lifeguard in the summer ($10 when lifeguard is on duty, 11am-7pm Memorial Day weekend-Labor Day), plus a small concert stage, picnic area, and playground.

Food and Accommodations

The Breezy Point Inn (620 Jersey Ave., 845/477-8100, breezypointinn.com, $100) is one of those places with a patio, and it also has four no-frills rooms for lodging, each with two double beds and one single bed. Its restaurant offers mostly German fare like schnitzel and sauerbraten, plus beer (some of it German) and wine.

A few minutes down the road and closer to the village is **The Helm** (649 Jersey Ave., 845/477-3073, http://thehelmny.com, noon-10pm Thurs., noon-midnight Fri.-Sat., 11am-9pm Sun., under $40), positioning itself as the old-world meat-and-drink spot a sailor might visit after a long week at sea. Smoky and savory meals are served in a cool wood-flavored dining room. There's a smoker around back, and the Bloody Helm is a brunch necessity.

Sterling Forest State Park

You'll need to drive 10.5 miles (16.9 km) along winding NY-17A to CR-84 to reach **Sterling Forest State Park** (116 Old Forge Rd., Tuxedo, 845/351-5907). Luscious and arguably wilder than any other parkland in southeastern New York, the 21,935-acre park is an underappreciated wonderland in between the getaways of Warwick and Greenwood Lake and the vast Harriman State Park. Hawks soar overhead and black bears are common in the woods. The Appalachian Trail runs through the park on its way to Harriman and Bear Mountain, while the New York-New Jersey Trail Conference maintains several other trails in the park's interior.

Hiking

Fire Tower Trail

Distance: 4 miles (6.4 km)
Duration: 2-2.5 hours
Elevation gain: 685 feet (209 m)
Difficulty: Moderate
Trailhead: U.S. Sen. Frank Lautenberg Visitor Center (41.19853, -74.25538)

Sterling Iron Works, a sophisticated plant dating to the 1730s, produced in 1778 a 770-link chain that spanned the Hudson River from West Point to Constitution Island to aid the Continental Army in blocking British ships from sailing upriver. The remnants of the plant can be seen on this trail, following the blue-blazed Sterling Lake Loop Trail from the visitors center. After passing that, plus ruins of an old church, you'll reach a sign marking the Bare Rock and Fire Tower Connector Trails. Follow the orange-blazed Bare Rock Trail up a woods road until meeting the blue-on-white Sterling Ridge Trail.

Turn left onto the Sterling Ridge Trail and, after a mile (1.6 km), you'll approach the Sterling Forest Fire Tower. From atop you get a bird's eye view of the state park, plus the Catskills to the north. Continue down another woods road on the red-blazed Fire Tower Trail until hitting a junction with a red-triangle trail. Follow the triangles until the trail hooks up with the Sterling Lake Loop Trail, the original blue blazes from early in the hike. Turn right and head to the finish line.

Sterling Valley Loop Trail

Distance: 5.9 miles (9.5 km)
Duration: 2.5-3 hours

Elevation gain: 1,217 feet (371 m)
Difficulty: Moderate
Trailhead: Route 17A parking area (41.230821, -74.260743)

For a true Sterling Forest experience, the Sterling Valley Loop Trail provides a secluded treasure for hikers wanting a little woodsy action. Start at the parking area off NY-17A and go north on the yellow-blazed trail, paralleling the road for the first few minutes before retreating into the deeper woods. Soon you'll be moving quickly downhill on rocky terrain before landing at a stream. You'll cross the stream a few times before ending up alongside it for roughly 2 miles (3.2 km). That creek flows into Sterling Lake, which will emerge ahead of you as you reach a junction with the Sterling Lake Trail. Follow the yellow-and-blue-blazed combination trail as it hugs the lake, offering stellar fire tower views. After a mile (1.6 km) around the lake the yellow Sterling Valley trail turns right, back away from the lake. Follow that as you start back uphill, on more rocky terrain, toward the parking area.

Bear Mountain State Park and Harriman State Park

Even to me, a former resident of this area, it's still hard to imagine that this wealth of parkland is just 45 miles (72 km) north of Midtown Manhattan. The big city is so close that you can see the Manhattan skyline from the summit of Bear Mountain, which is also the historical origin of the Appalachian Trail. Yup, this is the oldest operating section of the trail, created as a way to escape city life and get back to nature—and you certainly will do so when traversing these two lovely state parks.

Bear Mountain State Park (3006 Seven Lakes Dr., Bear Mountain, 845/786-2701) is smaller than Harriman at 5,205 acres, but it has the main attractions: the titular mountain and the gorgeous Bear Mountain Bridge, a suspension bridge that serves as an introduction to this wild, woodsy enterprise.

At 47,527 acres, **Harriman State Park** (Johnsontown Rd., Sloatsburg, 845/947-2444) is a wonderland, and it feels a lot like a national park in its scope and layout. With a network of accessible mountains and ridges, multiple lakes and beaches, over 200 miles (320 km) of trail (including the AT and New York's Long Path), and plenty of camping areas and nuggets of history sprinkled throughout, Harriman has it all.

Getting There and Around

Harriman State Park

From Sterling Forest State Park it's a 14-mile (22.5 km) drive on CR-84 and NY-17A east to Harriman State Park. Because of its size, there are numerous access points for Harriman State Park, with vehicle use fees collected only at the major lakes (Tiorati, Welch,

Silvermine, Kanawauke) during summer. The Palisades Interstate Parkway runs through the east side of the park; take the Seven Lakes Road exit to enter the park. The Lake Welch access road from the Palisades is only open in season. Seven Lakes Road comes out of the park on the west side at NY-17. US-6, which runs across the northern end of the park, provides parking access for the Long Path, which connects with many trails inside the park.

A shuttle bus, which leaves the Tuxedo Metro-North train station just after 10:45am each Saturday and Sunday in the summer and fall, heads into the park and stops at Lake Welch, Kanawauke Circle, Reeves Meadow Visitors Center, and the AT, among other locations.

If you want a one-time drive through Harriman, **Seven Lakes Road** (Palisades Interstate Parkway to Route 17) is the best way to go. It winds through the center of the park and provides access to, you guessed it, seven lakes.

Bear Mountain State Park

From Harriman, drive 14 miles on NY-17 north and US-6 east to Bear Mountain State Park, which hugs the Hudson River, leaving few access points for visitors. The main entrance is off a traffic circle uniting US-9W (the Palisades Interstate Parkway) with US-6 and US-202, which come over the Hudson on the Bear Mountain Bridge.

You can park at Bear Mountain State Park, paying the $10 vehicle use fee on weekends and holidays, plus weekdays from mid-June to Labor Day weekend (fees not collected before 8am). From the massive parking lot you can access most of the trails, plus the park's many amenities.

Sights

Bear Mountain Bridge

You can walk, cycle, or drive across the gorgeous **Bear Mountain Bridge,** suspended above the Hudson River. That bridge carries everything from local

Bear Mountain Bridge

commuters and residents to city-dwelling tourists seeking a weekend retreat to cyclists and Appalachian Trail hikers, because the trail is literally on the bridge. To me, Bear Mountain Bridge is the single most symbolic image of the Hudson Valley, a historic, man-made connection to nature.

Trailside Museums & Zoo

Inside the four granite buildings of the **Trailside Museums & Zoo** (Seven Lakes Dr., Tomkins Cove, 10am-4:30pm daily, $1 suggested donation), children learn about the animals, geology, and history of the park and the Hudson Valley. Animals on display include turtles, snakes, and fish. After meeting the animals up close, children can take a ride on them ... sort of: Bear Mountain has a **carousel** ($1 per child), on which kids can ride animals like black bears, wild turkeys, and foxes. Painted nature scenes further make this merry-go-round a unique piece of Hudson Valley history.

★ Bear Mountain

You've made it: The Appalachian Trail was born right here at **Bear Mountain,** the 1,289-foot (393-m) rise known previously as "Bear Hill" and "Bread Tray Mountain." There's no actual bread tray on the top of the mountain, but there's a parking lot, as drivers can take Perkins Memorial Drive up to the summit. At the summit you'll get a postcard-worthy view of the Hudson River to the east, and to the southwest the High Point Monument in New Jersey. Plus, it's arguably the one spot on the AT where hikers can spot the New York City skyline. **Perkins Memorial Fire Tower** (Apr.-Nov.), a sturdy brick structure at the summit, provides more splendid views. During weekends in the summer and fall the mountain is pretty packed, with drivers clogging up the roadway and parking all over the place.

You don't have to drive to reach the summit of Bear Mountain, of course. Both the AT and the Major Welch Trail run to the peak; you'll want to descend on the AT, if only to walk the more than 800 stone steps placed on the mountain by the New York-New Jersey Trail Conference and other groups.

Hiking

Bear Mountain Loop ⍋

Distance: 4 miles (6.4 km)
Duration: 3 hours
Elevation gain: 1,100 feet (335 m)
Difficulty: Moderate
Trailhead: Major Welch Trail at Hessian Lake (41.31791, -73.99396)

One of the more popular hikes in New York, the Bear Mountain Loop (via the Major Welch Trail and the AT) is a steep but rewarding walk to the top of Bear Mountain, followed by a marvelous jaunt down stone steps. You'll likely be joined by other hikers and tourists on this one.

From the trailhead begin on the red-circle-on-white Major Welch, which is on dirt trail, stone, and paved road at varying times. The ascent takes you through mountain laurel and pine trees until you climb more stone and finally hit an intersection with the Appalachian Trail. Turn left onto the AT until it reaches the summit and fire tower. Enjoy the view and smile at the tourists who drove up here.

Continue on the white-blazed AT for the descent, which will first take you on dirt and old paved road, until you begin the walk down the more than 800 stone steps laid by volunteers. This is an awesome walk—maybe you'll feel your heart swell up with appreciation for trail volunteers and angels. At the end of the descent you'll stay on the AT until it meets up with the Bear Mountain Inn. Then you'll just go back to the parking lot, while the rest of the AT continues toward the Bear Mountain Bridge.

1777E / Doodletown Bridle Path Loop

Distance: 5 miles (8 km)
Duration: 3 hours

Bear Mountain Loop

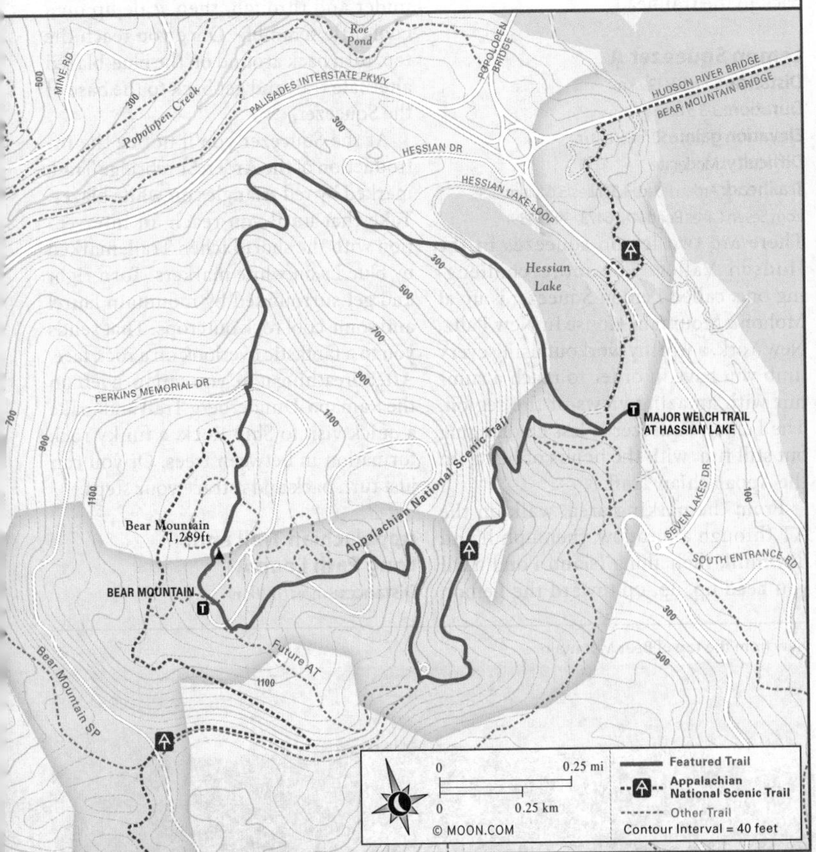

Elevation gain: N/A
Difficulty: Easy
Trailhead: Route 9W (41.300786, -73.985924)

Settled in the 1760s, Doodletown was a mining and logging community that peaked in population in the 1940s, with about 300 people living deep inside an area that's now part of Bear Mountain State Park. Today Doodletown is ghost town, but hikers are encouraged to walk through its roads and glimpse the old structures, which include churches and houses. Signage throughout the ghost town informs visitors of the community's history, and there's a "walking tour" sign of Doodletown if you want to hit all the sites.

Watch for the "Doodletown" sign across Route 9W and head left, following the sign up Doodletown Road. You'll soon reach the 1777E Trail, which you'll follow to a T intersection. Turn right, then left at the church site onto Pleasant Valley Road. You're now in Doodletown, which you can explore as you wish. Just make sure you hop on the Bridle Path, a wide road that runs level before narrowing. Stay on the Bridle Path until you see an intersection with a "2." That's the

1777E trail again; turn right and follow that back to Doodletown Road, then go back to the trailhead.

Lemon Squeezer

Distance: 5.7 miles (9.2 km)
Duration: 3-3.5 hours
Elevation gain: 650 feet (198 m)
Difficulty: Moderate
Trailhead: Arden Road, 3.5 miles/5.6 kilometers from Seven Lakes Road (41.26473, -74.15439)

There are two lemon squeezes in the Hudson Valley. The more challenging one, called Lemon Squeeze, is up at Mohonk Mountain House in New Paltz, New York, a worthy workout using every limb you have in order to reach a summit with amazing views of the region. The Lemon Squeezer is less challenging but still fun, with the bonus of being on the Appalachian Trail.

From the parking area, walk on the AT through a meadow, then uphill and downhill, then along Island Pond until you head up, up, up toward the Lemon Squeezer. You'll know it when you see it: a mass of boulder that you have to squeeze under and through, then scale up on a cool little scramble. Once you reach the top, turn back around on the blue-blazed alternate trail and get back to the base of the Squeezer.

At the Squeezer you'll notice the introduction of the Arden Surebridge Trail, marked by red triangles on white blazes. Take that until you reach an intersection with the short Lichen Trail, marked by blue Ls on white markers. Turn right and get surrounded by mountain laurel and some cool rock outcrops. That sends you to a fantastic overlook on a rock face. After breathing it in, you can turn left on the Ramapo-Dunderberg Trail and make a quick visit to Ship Rock, a funky rock formation in between trees. Or you can just turn back and retrace your steps.

Appalachian Trail and Long Path Loop

Distance: 8 miles (12.9 km)

view from the top of Bear Mountain

Duration: 4 hours
Elevation gain: N/A
Difficulty: Strenuous
Trailhead: Seven Lakes Road at Merritt Bank (41.290198, -74.073858)

Ask 10 people for their favorite Harriman trail, and chances are good that every answer will be different. With so many trails, historic sites, lakes, and campgrounds, the park has something for everyone. This hike, which includes part of the AT and the Long Path, New York's longest single trail, gives you a taste of rugged parkland, ridge walking, and some lake views.

From the parking area at Merritt Bank, walk north up Seven Lakes Road about 0.7 mile (1.1 km) to an intersection with the yellow-blazed Menomine Trail. Turn right onto the Menomine and take that down toward Silvermine Lake. Continue on the Menomine to the William Brien Memorial Shelter, indicating the AT is pretty close. Once you reach the AT, turn right to follow that, with the Ramapo-Dunderberg Trail hanging with you. Soon the trails will break off, and you'll stay on the Ramapo-Dunderberg Trail. That'll cross Seven Lakes Drive and soon meet up with the AT, but you'll stay straight on an unmarked grass road until you reach the aqua-blazed Long Path. Turn right onto the Long Path. For a good while you'll be walking some ridge with a little up and down and plenty of mountain views.

The Long Path will meet up with the Menomine Trail, and you'll turn right to get back on that to Seven Lakes Road. Then go back down to the parking area.

Recreation

The **Bear Mountain Ice Rink** (Seven Lakes Dr., Tomkins Cove, 10am-11:30am Mon.-Tues., 8am-9:30pm Fri., 10am-9:30pm Sat., 10am-7:30pm Sun., $2-10) is outdoors and has a clear view of Bear Mountain. The rink offers 90-minute sessions and sells food and soft drinks.

The **Bear Mountain Pool** (NY-9W, 0.1 mi/0.2 km north of Seven Lakes Dr., 845/786-2701, 10am-5:30pm Mon.-Fri., 11am-6:30pm Sat.-Sun. June-Sept., $2) is perfect for cooling off after a hike up the mountain.

Two of Harriman's lakes have beaches: **Lake Tiorati Beach** and **Lake Welch Beach.** They're open year-round, though swimming hours vary. The swimming season usually runs Memorial Day weekend to Labor Day weekend, and while there's always swimming on weekends and holidays, weekday hours run mid-June to mid-August. Beaches will open for swimming around 10am or 11am and close before 7pm.

Fishing is permitted at most of Harriman's lakes and ponds, though the park requires a New York State fishing license. Those are available at sporting goods stores. **Lake Kanawauke** offers a wealth of largemouth bass, while **Lake Askoti** has good trout fishing. Boating is allowed on select lakes and ponds; permits go on sale in March.

Trail Tale

What does it take to reroute the most trafficked section of the Appalachian Trail? Try 700 volunteers, some paid workers, cranes, human strength, and $1 million.

In 2000 the **New York-New Jersey Trail Conference** began planning a stone staircase designed to descend Bear Mountain, repairing a trail that had been worn down by decades of hiker traffic. Volunteers and workers started in 2006 by splitting 1,000-pound slabs of native granite into 800 steps. Then they laid them into place, taking the utmost care in their placement and position. In 2010 the work was finished and the new trail was unveiled. Meandering downhill, sometimes with switchbacks and protected by boulders, the staircase is a lovely reminder of the work done, largely by volunteers, to protect and enhance everyone's enjoyment of the trail.

You can take the stone staircase up or down, depending on how you start your Bear Mountain adventure. The best way to appreciate it is to descend it, so take the **Major Welch Trail** up to the AT.

Food and Accommodations

The ★ **Bear Mountain Inn** (3020 Seven Lakes Dr., Tomkins Cove, 845/786-2731, $200-400) is a 1915 stone structure that has hosted President Franklin D. Roosevelt and the Brooklyn Dodgers, who trained at Bear Mountain during World War II. A beautiful Adirondack-style facility renovated extensively from 2005 to 2011, it holds queen rooms and king suites with a warm, rustic feel. The inn is home to **Restaurant 1915 and Blue Roof Tapas Bar** (11am-8pm Mon.-Tues., 11am-9pm Wed.-Sun.), which serves classic, rustic offerings like grilled venison and trout—at prices that reflect the restaurant's existence as the only fine-dining establishment in either park.

Camping

Where did the modern concept of the group camp originate? Right in Harriman State Park, where the Palisades Interstate Parks Commission built group camps to welcome poor city dwellers more than 100 years ago. While most of the group camps are meant for children escaping the city or homeless shelters, the **Stephen & Betsy Corman AMC Harriman Outdoor Center** (200 Breakneck Rd., Haverstraw, 603/466-2727, $18-125) is open to the public and has family cabins, tent platforms, and three-sided shelters. There is a dining hall and meeting space on the premises.

For those looking to rough it just a little, **Beaver Pond Campgrounds** (700 Kanawaukee Rd., Stony Point, 845/947-2792, Apr.-Oct., $15-30) has tent and trailer sites, plus hot showers, laundry facilities, and a dumping station. For those wanting it a little less rough, **Baker Camp** (Seven Lakes Dr., 845/429-5400, $60-100) by Lake Sebago has midsize and large cabins available for groups up to six. The cabins have bedrooms, electricity, a front room and porch, plus meals cooked by a chef. Baker Camp also provides boat rentals. There's a two-night minimum for stays.

There are also several **lean-to shelters** in Harriman, including two on the Appalachian Trail (Fingerboard, William Brien Memorial). Those are free; just remember to practice lean-to etiquette.

Information and Services

The **Bear Mountain State Park Office** (3006 Seven Lakes Dr., 845/786-2701) is near the inn and carousel. The **Reeves Meadow Information Center** (54 Seven Lakes Dr., Sloatsburg, 845/753-5122) serves as the visitors center at Harriman State Park.

★ NY-9W: West Point

Few American sites match their location as well as the **United States Military Academy,** or **West Point** (NY-218, 2 mi/3.2 km north of NY-9W). Anchoring a sharp curve above the Hudson River, it is both a fortress and a reminder of the country's military strength. Home to approximately 4,300 cadets, West Point has been training and shaping U.S. Army soldiers and officers since being established in 1802, and its majestic campus is a highly trafficked tourist attraction.

Getting There and Around

Take the 9-mile (14.5 km) drive north on US-9W to reach West Point from Bear Mountain State Park. Or, **Short Line** (845/610-2600, $15) offers daily bus service from Times Square in Manhattan to the **West Point Visitors Center** (2107 New South Post Rd., 845/938-2638, 9am-4:45pm daily). If you're not driving, you have to take the bus, as there are only two ways in.

West Point has an elevated security presence, so don't expect to just waltz right onto campus. Always plan your West Point trip with plenty of time to be cleared and get situated. If you're looking to visit West Point without a ticket to a public event, you'll have to fill out a West Point Local Area Credential at the **Visitor Control Center** (2107 New South Post Rd., 6am-6pm Mon.-Fri.). Have identification ready. Those with tickets to events such as sporting events, concerts, cadet reviews, and graduation can drive to the **Thayer Gate** (Thayer Rd. at New South Post Rd.) or the **Stony Lonesome Gate** (Stony Lonesome Rd. off Route 9W). At both gates, cars will be checked, and all adults ages 17 and older must have valid photo identification.

There are numerous parking lots on campus, including the Buffalo Soldier Field lot close to the Thayer Gate, and the Clinton Field, East, and Doubleday Field lots up by the Plain and Trophy Point. The lots by the Field allow for the easiest access to the central part of campus.

West Point operates guided bus tours of campus, which leave from the West Point Visitors Center. All riders age 17 and older must have valid photo identification. There's also an on-campus shuttle bus called the **CPA Express** (7am-6pm Mon.-Fri.), which runs from the northern parking lots down to the Buffalo Soldier Field lot by the Thayer Gate. The public is permitted on this bus, but those on official business will get priority.

Sights

Most of the buildings at West Point are constructed of black and gray granite and in the Gothic Revival architectural style. Chief among these structures is the **Cadet Chapel** (722 Derussy Rd.), constructed in the early 20th century. A little less imposing, the **West Point Museum** (2110 New South Post Rd., West Point, 845/938-3590, 10:30am-4:15pm daily, free) showcases some of the institute's 60,000 historical artifacts while offering a worthy tour of American military history. Some showstopping pieces include George Washington's pistols, Napoleon's sword, and a gold-plated pistol owned by Adolf Hitler.

The campus includes a multitude of **monuments** honoring influential members of the institution and military heroes, including Col. Sylvanus Thayer, the superintendent from 1817 to 1833 and the man responsible for the curriculum that is taught to this day. The Thayer Monument, along with the Eisenhower Monument, MacArthur Monument, Kosciuszko Monument, Sedgwick Monument, and Washington Monument, are on **The Plain** (Doubleday Rd. and Washington Rd.), the flat central ground that once comprised the entire campus.

Arguably the standout monument is the **Battle Monument,** a Tuscan column and granite base recognizing the efforts of Army servicemen who died for the

Union in the Civil War. That monument, plus various captured artillery from American wars, rests at **Trophy Point** (117 Washington Rd.), a scenic overlook providing a second-to-none view of the Hudson River and valley beyond.

Thayer and George Armstrong Custer are among those buried at the **West Point Cemetery** (329 Washington Rd., 7am-7pm daily), designed to be the "final salute" to those who dedicated their lives to military service. West Point provides a brochure indicating locations of notable gravesites.

Recreation

You can get a history lesson while your tee shot plunges into a hazard at **West Point Golf Course** (732 Victor Constant Rd., 845/938-2435, 7am-dusk Tues.-Fri., 6:30am-dusk Sat.-Sun. and holidays, $19-78), a public course designed by Robert Trent Jones where each tee marker tells a story from American military history. Cadets and active military receive discounted greens fees.

In the winter, **Victor Constant Ski Area** (732 Victor Constant Rd., 845/938-8810, 3pm-9pm Mon.-Fri., 9am-7pm Sat., 9am-5pm Sun.) provides clean, snowy fun with awesome river views. Constant has three main trails and a race trail that veers through forest, plus a bunny slope and ski lodge. Passes and rentals are available.

Spectator Sports

West Point is also home to the Division I FBS Army West Point Black Knights football team, one of the oldest programs in America. While not the national champion they were from 1944 to 1946, the Black Knights still can pose a threat to rivals like Notre Dame, Air Force, and of course, Navy. West Point plays home games at **Michie Stadium** (700 Mills Rd., 877/849-2769), which dates to 1924 and remains one of the coolest venues in sports, if only for the spectacular upper-deck view of the Hudson River and mountains, especially on a fall day.

Army's men's basketball plays its games at **Christl Arena** (600 Thayer Rd.), a funky yellow fieldhouse, and competes in the Division I Patriot League. The women also play at Christl and in the Patriot League, and historically they've fared much better in regular-season competition.

Entertainment and Nightlife

Cadets get their share of entertainment at **Eisenhower Hall Theatre** (655 Pitcher Rd., 845/938-4159, www.ikehall.com), a 4,433-capacity venue with two balconies that pulls in national touring musicals, the occasional country music star, and comedians over a season that runs from fall to spring.

During the warmer months, Trophy Point gets a workout, as it's home to a stage that typically plays host to the **West Point Concert Band** (www.westpointband.army.mil). This collection of musicians puts on concerts throughout the summer months, peaking with the West Point Independence Day Celebration, as rousing and patriotic an evening as you'll ever witness. Folks get to West Point early in the afternoon to picnic on the grass overlooking the stage (and the Hudson River). The band starts playing as the sun begins to set, and once it's dark, fireworks and cannons join the band as it runs through songs like "Stars and Stripes Forever."

In recent years a couple of bands have joined the West Point Concert Band in celebrating heritage and history. The Benny Havens Band, named after an infamous nearby tavern owner, is a modern-day cover band with a military twist and a big ol' horn section. They play at Trophy Point during the summer, along with the Hellcats, an old-fashioned military band with bugles, piccolos, and drums.

If you want to take the edge off like an old cadet, the **Benny Havens Pub & Restaurant** (295 Main St., Highland Falls) is still around to close off the evening.

Hudson Highlands

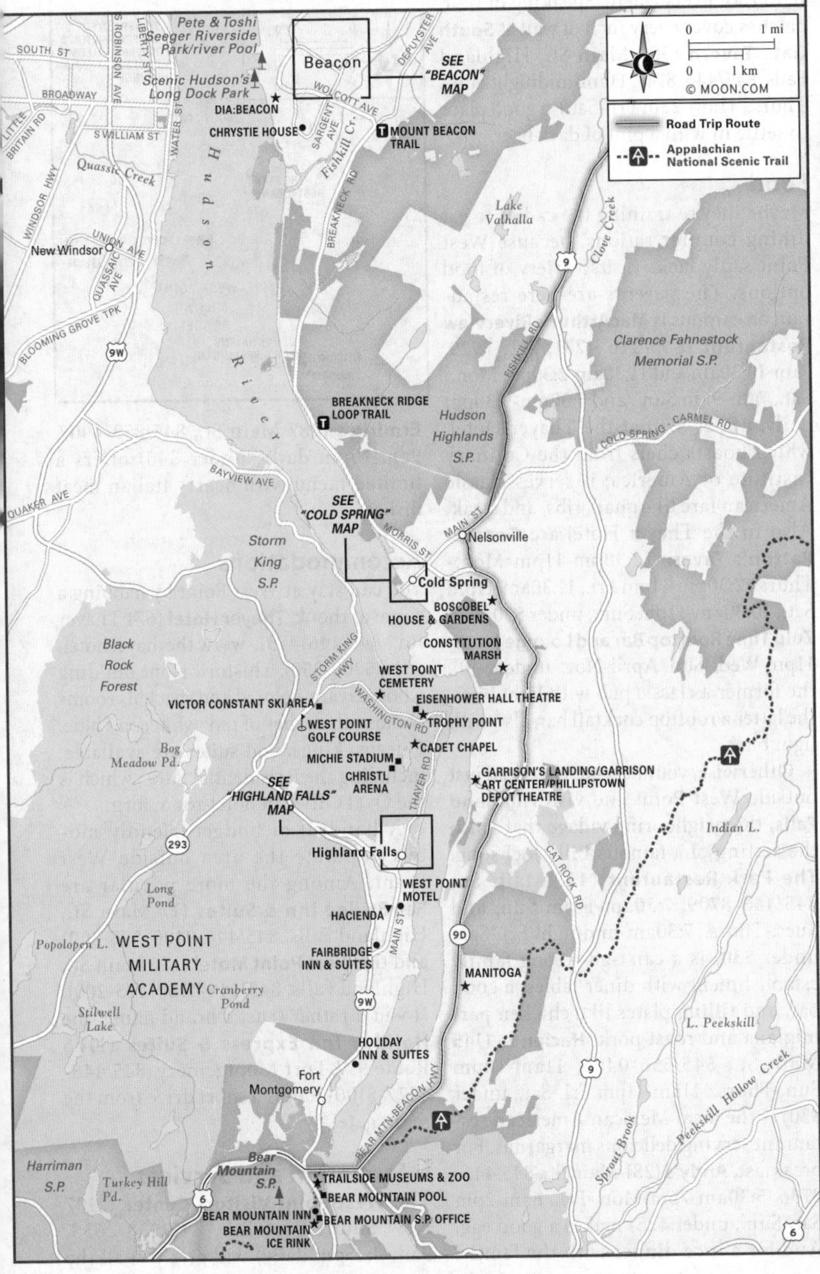

The distinctly local watering hole has a no-nonsense vibe, plus photos and Irish flair everywhere. Speaking of flair, patches cover every inch of wall at **South Gate Tavern** (509 Main St., Highland Falls, 845/446-8747, 11am-midnight Sun.-Thurs., 11am-2am Fri.-Sat.), a good place to settle in with a pint of dark beer.

Food

Maybe they're training the cadets to eat dining-counter rations, because West Point sadly lacks in its variety of food options. The parents-are-here restaurant on campus is **MacArthur's Riverview Restaurant** (845/446-4731, ext. 7929, 7am-10:30am and 11:30am-2:30pm Mon.-Sat., 7am-9am Sun., and 5:30pm-9:30pm daily, under $70) at the Thayer Hotel, which boasts chefs from the Culinary Institute of America; it serves classic American fare like quail, ribs, and steak. Also in the Thayer Hotel are **General Patton's Tavern** (2:30pm-11pm Mon.-Thurs., 2:30pm-11pm Fri., 11:30am-11pm Sat., 10:30am-11pm Sun., under $30) and **Zulu Time Rooftop Bar and Lounge** (4pm-11pm Wed.-Sun. April-Nov., under $30), the former a classic pub with light bites, the latter a rooftop cocktail bar, also with light bites.

Otherwise, your best bet is to head just outside West Point and visit **Highland Falls,** the neighboring village that's also the setting of a famous Billy Joel song. **The Park Restaurant** (451 Main St., 845/446-8709, 7:30am-11pm Sun. and Tues.-Thurs., 7:30am-midnight Fri.-Sat., under $30) is a can't-go-wrong family establishment with diner tables, a good bar, and filling plates like chicken parmigiana and roast pork. **Hacienda** (145 Main St., 845/556-0406, 11am-10pm Sun.-Thurs., 11am-11pm Fri.-Sat., under $30) is the local Mexican American restaurant serving delicious margaritas. For breakfast, **Andy's** (281 Main St., 845/446-8736, 5:30am-7pm Mon.-Fri., 6am-2pm Sat.-Sun., under $25) makes a good egg. And for a nice dinner with the family,

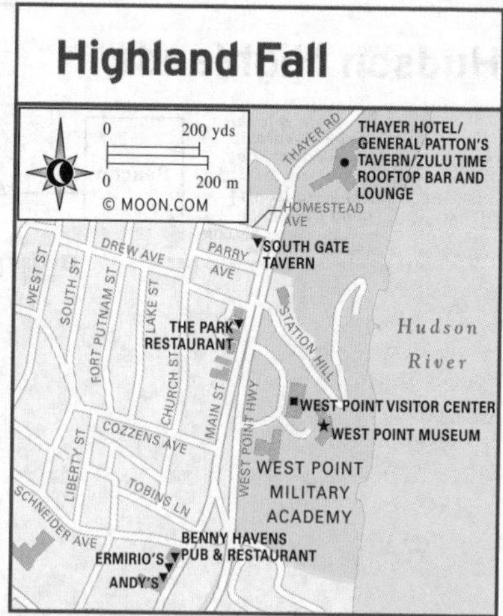

Ermirio's (287 Main St., 845/859-4907, 9am-10pm daily, under $40) offers a limited menu with hearty Italian meat dishes.

Accommodations

You can stay at West Point by nabbing a room at the ★ **Thayer Hotel** (674 Thayer Rd., 845/446-4731, www.thethayerhotel.com, $200-350), a historic stone building whose cream-colored and spacious rooms come with dashes of red, white, and blue. Queens, kings, and suites are available, including the Presidential Suite, which is the Oval Office in hotel-room form.

A handful of budget-friendly motels populate the area outside West Point. Among the more popular are **FairBridge Inn & Suites** (17 Main St., Highland Falls, 845/446-9400, $75-200) and the **West Point Motel** (156 Main St., Highland Falls, 845/446-4180, $75-200). If you'd rather trust a brand name, the **Holiday Inn Express & Suites** (1106 Route 9W, Fort Montgomery, 845/446-4277, $100-200) is a short drive from the main gate.

Information and Services

The **West Point Visitors Center** (2107 New South Post Rd., 845/938-2638, 9am-4:45pm daily) will give you all the information you need about getting in and out promptly and, subsequently, enjoying your visit.

Anthony's Nose

Drive US-6 east from the Bear Mountain traffic circle, and the clouds may drift apart for a few cherished seconds and impart an impressive vista. The Bear Mountain Bridge, a marvel built in 1924 that serves as the AT's Hudson River crossing, offers impeccable views up and down the mighty Hudson while nearly running square into a hill. The top of this hill is **Anthony's Nose,** accessed by an easy-to-moderate hike partially on the AT.

Know that if you go on weekends, you're bound to be enjoying the view with a couple dozen picnicking and selfie-snapping hikers.

Anthony's Nose

Distance: 2.6 miles (4.2 km)
Duration: 2.5 hours
Elevation change: 800 feet (244 m)
Difficulty: Moderate
Trailhead: NY-9D, 0.5 mile/0.8 kilometer north of Bear Mountain Bridge (41.322627, -73.975948)

Anthony's Nose is a popular hike for tourists to the Hudson Valley. Much of that is due to the view. But first, start the hike at the trailhead along NY-9D, where you'll be following the white blazes of the Appalachian Trail up a well-maintained path of stone steps. Because the ascent is quick (nearly 800 ft/244 m in just 0.6 mi/1 km), inexperienced hikers will find the climb deceptively challenging, and they'll be slower up (and down).

Follow the white AT blazes through the generally wooded area to a flat road with two options. The AT hikers will continue to the left, but you'll go right, following the blue blazes of the Camp Smith Trail, named after an active military reservation a few miles down the trail. The Camp Smith Trail continues for 0.7 mile (1.1 km) before it splits left, while a clearing emerges to the right. Head right to find yourself atop the nose (the rock formation that juts out just beneath you), with impeccable views of the Hudson River, Bear Mountain Bridge, and Bear Mountain State Park. It's the best perch in the valley.

Garrison

Just 5 miles (8 km) north from the Anthony's Nose trailhead, **Garrison** (pop. 4,402) is the quintessential Hudson River hamlet (New York-speak for an unincorporated community), with old, historic buildings and a small arts community. Garrison's Landing, the town's riverside historic district, offers the best views of West Point. The name Garrison comes from 2nd Lt. Isaac Garrison, who fought in the American Revolution.

Garrison's Landing

Garrison's Landing (Lower Station Rd. at Black Diamond Hill) is a collection of mid-19th-century buildings mostly in the Carpenter Gothic style. Previous tenants of these buildings included the Garrison and West Point Ferry Company, but these days the district is an arts destination. The **Garrison Art Center** (23 Garrisons Landing, 845/424-3960, www.garrisonartcenter.org, 10am-5pm Tues.-Sun.) is here, along with the **Phillipstown Depot Theatre** (10 Garrisons Landing, 845/424-3900, www.phillipstowndepottheatre.org), which specializes in black-box stage shows. You may recognize some of the buildings from the 1968 film version of *Hello, Dolly!*

Manitoga & the Russel Wright Design Center

With his signature branding the undersides of millions of dinnerware pieces, industrial designer Russel Wright influenced a generation of American home

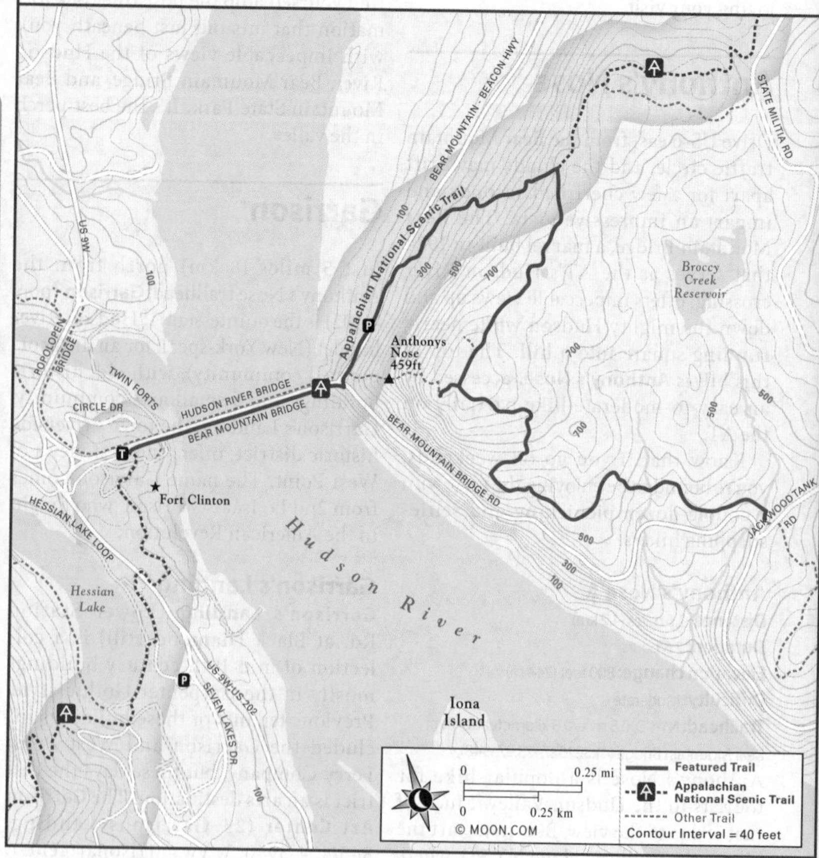

design. His American Modern line of ceramics emphasized simplicity and practicality, evident at his enchanting estate **Manitoga** (584 NY-9D, 845/424-3812, www.visitmanitoga.org, tours 11am and 1:30pm June-Nov.). Anchored by the circa 1960 home Dragon Rock, its interior decorated by Wright, Manitoga features a 30-foot (9-m) waterfall, quarry pool, and landscaped gardens and hiking trails that reveal themselves organically to emphasize a spiritual connection with nature. It's astonishing that, more than 50 years after it was constructed, Manitoga represents an aesthetic that defines the modern Hudson Valley.

★ Boscobel House & Gardens

An awesome aspect of the Hudson Valley is how 20th-century modernity can live coherently alongside early American relics. Such is the case in Garrison, where a short drive from Manitoga leads to the sprawling **Boscobel House & Gardens** (1601 NY-9D, 845/265-3638, www.boscobel.org, 9:30am-5pm Wed.-Mon. April-Oct., 9:30am-4pm Wed.-Mon. Nov.-Dec.). A stately Federal-style house built between 1804 and 1808 sits on a 60-acre plot with gardens and woodlands; tours are offered of the house, which is filled with period furniture.

The site is worthy of a lazy afternoon, especially with a good book or companion, if only to enjoy the view alone. Boscobel's front lawn overlooks the Hudson River at one of its bends, showcasing layers of mountains, jigsaw marshland, and one of the area's better views of West Point.

The best way to enjoy the view is with a homemade picnic before a show by the **Hudson Valley Shakespeare Festival** (845/265-9575, www.hvshakespeare.org, season June-Sept.), which hosts its performances on the lawn under a tent. HVSF typically features three shows: one Shakespeare done traditionally, one Shakespeare done with a twist, and one non-Shakespeare.

Cold Spring

Just a few years ago travelers from New York City would bypass **Cold Spring** (pop. 1,983) to visit the more metropolitan Beacon, with its flashy restaurants and Patagonia-draped citizenry. Lately, however, this cool village just 2.7 miles (4.3 km) upriver from Garrison has become the talk of the region.

Having one of those iconic main streets the best Hudson River communities are known for, Cold Spring begins like an all-American small town (you'll see old drugstore signage, a doll-repair shop, and quite a few antiques galleries) but slowly becomes a shopping haven for upper-middle-class Manhattanites and Brooklynites. More succinctly: You can buy local honey to spread on your artisan bread here.

Top to bottom: Boscobel House & Gardens; Constitution Marsh Audubon Center and Sanctuary; view from Breakneck Ridge.

Sights

The Chapel Restoration

Literally feet from the Hudson River, **The Chapel Restoration** (45 Market St., 845/25-5537, chapelrestoration.org) is a Greek Revival gathering place built in 1833 that has no religious affiliation. Thus, it's used by many as a setting for ceremonies and celebrations, and also hosts a Sunday chamber music series, readings, and sporadic Americana and folk concerts.

Constitution Marsh Audubon Center and Sanctuary

You may think that all the views of the Hudson River become old hat for people living in the Hudson Valley, but oh, that is not the case at all. Even the longest-tenured residents of this winding wonderland can't help but exhale softly while standing on the boardwalk at **Constitution Marsh Audubon Center and Sanctuary** (127 Warren Landing Rd., 845/265-2601, grounds 9am-6pm daily, nature center 9am-5pm Tues.-Sun.). Just don't attempt to go during a busy time (and don't bring pets), because you won't be able to visit.

On NY-9D north between Garrison and Cold Spring, turn left on Beverly Warren Road, then left on Indian Brook Road, then right on Warren Landing Road—and hope that one of the Audubon Center's seven public parking spaces are available. If not, don't park, because your car will be towed. If you are able to park, walk into the Audubon Center and Sanctuary area and take the brief 1.2-mile (1.9-km) hike up and down rock formations to Constitution Marsh, an open boardwalk out on the Hudson River. There's ample room here to contemplate while the birds fly about and the morning (or late afternoon) rolls on.

Shopping

Find that local honey and other provisions at the **Cold Spring General Store** (61 Main St., 845/809-5522, 10am-5pm

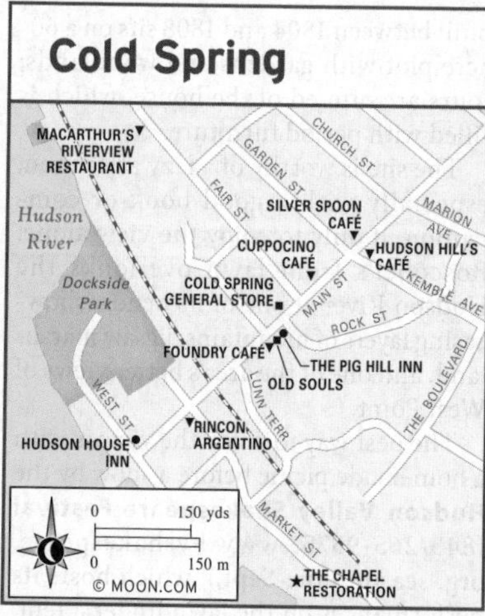

Mon.-Thurs., 10am-6pm Fri.-Sun.), which carries a solid state-centric beer selection that includes a rotating trio of taps for growler fills. Next door is **Old Souls** (63 Main St., 845/809-5886, 10am-6pm daily), an outdoors depot where you can find a Yeti cooler along with helpful trail guides.

Food

Cold Spring has a bunch of down-home morning spots, including **Cupoccino Café** (92 Main St., 845/809-5574, 6am-9pm Mon.-Fri., 8am-10pm Sat., 8am-9pm Sun., under $15), the casual farm-to-table **Silver Spoon Café** (124 Main St., 8:30am-9:30pm Mon.-Thurs., 8am-11pm Fri.-Sat., 8am-9:30pm Sun., under $25), and the easygoing **Foundry Café** (55 Main St., 845/265-4504, 6:30am-3pm Mon.-Tues. and Thurs.-Fri., 8am-5pm Sat.-Sun., under $25), but go under the train tracks to **Rincon Argentino** (21 Main St., 914/482-4795, 9am-7pm Wed.-Sun., under $15) for a phenomenal empanada and conversation with the sweet co-owner.

The best meal in a town with pretty good meals is **Hudson Hil's Café** (129-131 Main St., 845/265-9471, 8am-4pm Wed.-Mon. under $30), which sees considerable lines for brunch, so get there early.

Washington Irving's Legacy

Born in New York City, Washington Irving is one of America's most iconic scribes, able to pen short tales that to this day strike fear into the hearts of readers. His most famous works include "The Legend of Sleepy Hollow" and "Rip Van Winkle." He spent much of his life in the Hudson Valley north of the big city, and you can spend a half day or more visiting sites that maintain Irving's legacy.

- **Sunnyside** (3 W. Sunnyside Lane, Irvington, 914/591-8763, tours 10:30am-3:30pm Mon.-Fri., 10am-3pm Sat.-Sun.) was Irving's cottage-like home in his later years, combining Scottish and Spanish architecture. Set against the Hudson River, it's a stunning example of a house where nature and structure live in harmony.
- **Sleepy Hollow Cemetery** (540 N. Broadway, Sleepy Hollow, 914/631-0081, 8am-4:30pm Mon.-Fri., 8:30am-4:30pm Sat.-Sun.) is Irving's final resting place. It wasn't always called Sleepy Hollow, however. Tarrytown is the larger village, which included the neighborhood of North Tarrytown. In 1996 North Tarrytown split and became its own village, called Sleepy Hollow, in part to take advantage of its literary cache. Oh, and the cemetery is a spooky one, raised on a hill and neighboring the Old Dutch Church.
- **Phillipsburg Manor** (381 N. Broadway, Sleepy Hollow, 914/366-6900, 10am-4:30pm Wed.-Fri., 10am-5pm Sat.-Sun.) stands as a reminder of 18th-century slavery. An old gristmill tells the story of one of the slaves and includes an activity center. In October, the property is home to Horseman's Hollow (Oct., $20-25), a mayhem-filled haunted house where Irving's tales come alive.

Hudson House (2 Main St., 845/265-9355, www.hudsonhouseinn.com, 11:30am-3:30pm daily, 5pm-9pm Mon.-Thurs., 5pm-10pm Fri.-Sat., 3:30pm-8pm Sun., under $40) fires up classic American surf and turf dishes.

Accommodations

Cold Spring is home to a few very nice inns. **The Pig Hill Inn** (73 Main St., 845/265-9247, www.pighillinn.com, $150-250) is a bed-and-breakfast inside an 1825 brick building with understated Victorian-style rooms. Breakfasts are served in a conservatory with views of a garden, or, in the summer, out on the terrace with the flowers.

The **Hudson House Inn** (2 Main St., 845/265-9355, www.hudsonhouseinn.com, $170-260) stands tall at the corner of Main Street and the Cold Spring waterfront. You can nab one of the inn's balcony suites or rooms, which overlook the waterfront and the Hudson River.

Breakneck Ridge

It's a quick 2.2-mile (3.5-km) jaunt north up NY-9D to what has been called the most popular day-hiking trail in America. **Breakneck Ridge** may be just that, considering Metro-North trains from New York City stop at the trailhead a few times each weekend during the warm season. Off those trains come packs of eager, mostly young visitors wearing tank tops, headbands, and yoga pants, prepared to tackle a strenuous 2-mile (3.2-km) rock scramble leading to pretty fantastic Hudson River views. (Note: Check to make sure the trail is open before setting out, as repairs have been ongoing.)

Breakneck Ridge Loop Trail

Distance: 4 miles (6.4 km)
Duration: 3-3.5 hours
Elevation gain: 1,442 feet (440 m)
Difficulty: Strenuous
Trailhead: Route NY-9D, 2 miles/3.2 kilometers north of Cold Spring (41.447809, -73.980861)

Want a challenging and rewarding rock scramble that won't take up the whole day? Welcome to Breakneck Ridge, headlined by a half-mile (0.8-km) scramble that taxes you and, a few times, makes you think about your positioning. Don't try Breakneck Ridge if it's wet, and for the most enjoyable experience, visit the ridge really early on a weekend morning (before the trains arrive) or anytime on a weekday. This place gets crowded, and you'd rather not patiently wait for other hikers scrambling ahead of you.

Park just beyond a tunnel off the side of NY-9D north, then walk to the trailhead, which is at the southbound side at the tunnel. Follow the white blazes of the Breakneck Trail as it immediately takes you up rocky terrain. Soon you'll reach a classic viewpoint with the river and Storm King Mountain in front of you, but the worst is to come. Right away you'll start negotiating larger rocks and boulders while following the white blazes. Then, about 0.25 mile (0.4 km) up, you'll reach another viewpoint, but ahead of you is even harder climbing.

The next 0.25 mile (0.4 km) up is a technical rock scramble where you'll want to use all fours at times, especially if you're shorter than five feet eight. An alternative route (marked with Xs) allows for an easier ascent. Either way, you'll end up atop the ridge, and following the white blazes, you'll go up and down a bit for another half mile (0.8 km). Stay on the white trail until you reach the red-blazed Breakneck Bypass Trail. Turn left and follow the red blazes along the ridge, then down, until they meet up with the yellow-blazed Wilkinson Memorial Trail. Turn left there and follow the Wilkinson back out to NY-9D. Turn left to head back to your car.

Beacon

Continue north on NY-9D about 5 miles (8 km) to **Beacon** (pop. 15,541). Historically, New York City residents travel north to the Hudson Valley every warm season to get away from the grit and grime of urbanity. There are other popular destinations (Rhinebeck, Woodstock, Hudson, Tarrytown), but in recent years, Beacon has become the hot spot for weekenders and day-trippers alike. Plus, young families and New York City expats populate Beacon, so the city has a known progressive and artistic streak. With its long Main Street filled with shops, restaurants, and funky boutique businesses, plus ample recreation opportunities and a world-class art museum, Beacon is well worth full exploration.

There are several public lots in the city that are free on the weekends, with the most accessible being the lot at Church and North Chestnut Streets in the middle of the city's downtown.

Sights

Dia:Beacon

Opening in 2003 in an old warehouse along the Hudson River, **Dia:Beacon** (3 Beekman St., 845/440-0100, 11am-6pm Thurs.-Mon. Apr.-Oct., 11am-4pm Thurs.-Mon. Nov.-Dec., 11am-4pm Fri.-Mon. Jan.-Mar., $12-15) is a renowned contemporary art museum whose presence helped spur Beacon's renaissance as an essential destination. Its collection, spanning from the 1960s to today, is rife with abstract installations that will either have you thoroughly engaged or shaking your head in befuddlement. Either way, the building's soothing vibe, clean lines, and open floor plan lead many a visitor to get lost in the experience. The most popular exhibits are Richard Serra's trio of massive ellipses (watch kids run in these) and a gallery of 1978-1979 work by Andy Warhol.

Bannerman Castle

The historic **Bannerman Castle** may resemble some fascinating military base, but it's actually one guy's clever business idea. Francis Bannerman VI needed a storage facility for his expanding Brooklyn-based military surplus business, so in 1900 he purchased Pollepel Island out in the middle of the Hudson River and built a giant castle and other buildings to house his munitions. No longer a place for weaponry, the island is now a tourist attraction, its castle deteriorating from neglect (and munition explosions in 1920). These days folks can visit the island via boat thanks to **Bannerman Castle Trust Inc.** (www.bannermancastle.org) and via kayak through **Storm King Adventure Tours** (www.stormkingadventuretours.com).

Hiking

Mount Beacon Trail

Distance: 4.4 miles (7.1 km)
Duration: 3 hours
Elevation gain: 1,561 feet (476 m)
Difficulty: Moderate
Trailhead: Intersection of NY-9D and Howland Avenue (41.493605, -73.959793)

As Beacon is seemingly made for day and weekend tourists, Mount Beacon is of course a perfect little hike most people can bang out before breakfast (or dinner). In recent years nonprofit organizations have cleared good trails and cleaned up messes on the mountain, so the hike is easy to follow. But it also has a sneaky gain in elevation.

Park in the lot at the trailhead, and if it's full, there's overflow on Howland Avenue. Follow the red-blazed Casino Trail, past ruins of what was once the steepest railway in the world, to a large staircase. That leads to an uphill climb, still on the Casino Trail, through rocky terrain until you hit the top of the railway. Nearby is the former casino, the source of the trail's name.

Continue on the Casino Trail up the mountain, through more rocky terrain, until you reach an intersection with a white-blazed trail. Head right onto that trail, and it's a quick final ascent to the top, home to an old fire tower with outrageous 360-degree views. When you're finished taking it all in, reverse your steps on the white and red trails back to your car.

Recreation

Legendary folk musician Pete Seeger and his wife, Toshi, lived in Beacon, and after their deaths the city park on the Hudson River was named in their honor. The **Pete and Toshi Seeger Riverfront Park** (123 Red Flynn Dr.) has picnic space, basketball courts, and a **River Pool** (noon-6pm Tues.-Sun. July-Labor Day) that's very Beacon: a large ring with an underwater net, suitable for a maximum of 20 swimmers.

A quick walk from Riverfront Park is **Scenic Hudson's Long Dock Park** (Long Dock Rd.), home base for kayak tours on the Hudson River. Rent a kayak from **Mountain Top Outfitters** (144 Main St., 845/831-1997, 11am-6pm daily late May-Sept., $20-50).

Spectator Sports

Two miles (3.2 km) up NY-9D from downtown Beacon, in Wappingers Falls, is **Dutchess Stadium** (1500 Route 9D, 845/838-0094), home to the Hudson Valley Renegades minor-league baseball team, whose season runs June-September. The short-season single-A affiliate of the Tampa Bay Rays has featured stars like Evan Longoria and Josh Hamilton. The stadium also hosts concerts and college baseball.

Entertainment and Nightlife

Moving from Pawling in 2014, the **Towne Crier Café** (379 Main St., 845/855-1300, http://townecrier.com, 4pm-9:30pm Mon.-Thurs., 4pm-10:30pm Fri., 10am-10:30pm Sat., 10am-9:30pm Sun.) is the big live spot in the city, with music every night but Tuesdays (when it's closed).

Beacon

Acts are mostly world music, folk, classic rock, and blues. Dinner and weekend brunch are also available.

Stepping into **Dogwood** (47 E. Main St., 845/202-7500, http://dogwoodbar.com, 5pm-midnight Mon.-Thurs., 4pm-2am Fri., 3pm-2am Sat., 3pm-midnight Sun.) is like stepping into a Gen-Xer's favorite hang. This no-frills bar is where you'll hear about a neighbor's political campaign and that hilarious pub crawl a week before. On weekends, live music varies from rock trios to jazz to Beastie Boys covers played by kids. It's also known for burgers and a hearty chicken pot pie in the winter.

There isn't a lot of signage drawing you to the **Hudson Valley Brewery** (2 Churchill St., 845/218-9156, 5pm-10pm Thurs.-Fri., 2pm-10pm Sat.-Sun.), but the beer will certainly bring you back. Championing the New England IPA wave and other fruity flavors, the brewery is an essential stop for anyone passionate about craft beer. There's a small tap area, barrels for hanging out, and crowlers to take home. There's also a few tables outside, if you can snag them in time.

Shopping

Art Galleries

Beacon has a nice pick of contemporary art galleries along Main Street, starting with **Beacon Artist Union** (506 Main St., 845/440-7584, www.baugallery.com, 3pm-8pm Fri., noon-6pm Sat.-Sun.), a central location for local artists. **Marion Royael Gallery** (159 Main St., 727/244-5535, 1pm-7pm Thurs.-Sun.) is home to a couple of Florida expats who brought major contacts and dynamic pieces to the city.

Minimalist-designed **Matteawan Gallery** (436 Main St., 845/440-7901, www.matteawan.com, noon-5pm Sat.-Sun.) isn't afraid to bend rules with abstracts by emerging mid-career artists. Artists run **Catalyst Gallery** (137 Main St., 845/204-3844), which rotates exhibitions fairly quickly and will do everything from paintings and photographs to live performance and fiction readings.

The Hudson River School of painting, a genre in which artists like Thomas Cole documented the beauty of the Hudson Valley, inspired the most famous landscape artists in present-day America. A few galleries in Beacon keep the spirit of this genre alive, headed by **Riverwinds Gallery** (172 Main St., 845/838-2880, www.riverwindsgallery.com, noon-6pm Wed.-Mon.), which also has pottery and small gifts. The gallery of **Beacon Institute for Rivers and Estuaries** (199 Main St. 845/838-1600, www.bire.org, 11am-3pm Sat.) focuses more on the river itself with its exhibits, but gives quite a history lesson.

Other Shops

With its open glassblowing studio, **Hudson Beach Glass** (162 Main St., 845/440-0068, www.hudsonbeachglass.com, 10am-6pm daily) is an easy way to spend up to an hour. Just be careful walking through the shop, which

Top to bottom: Dia:Beacon; Bannerman Castle; Walkway Over the Hudson in Poughkeepsie.

displays tasteful dishware, pottery, gifts, and jewelry. **Dream in Plastic** (177 Main St., 845/632-3383, http://dreaminplastic.com, 11am-5pm Sun.-Mon. and Wed., 11am-7pm Thurs.-Sat.) has everything from avocado patches to cat mugs (also, anything cats).

Beacon also has plenty of small clothing boutiques, including the twee consignment **Blackbird Attic** (442 Main St., 845/418-4840, noon-6pm Thurs.-Sat., noon-5pm Sun.-Mon.), and the ultra-hip **Vintage: Beacon** (478 Main St., 845/202-7172, http://vintagebeacon.com, 11am-6pm Wed.-Sun.), where you can get a cute dress, Prada bag, and stylish leather jacket in one purchase. For hikers, the beloved **Mountain Tops Outfitters** (144 Main St., 845/831-1997, 11am-6pm daily) has clothes and backpacking and climbing gear, and runs the kayak tours at Long Dock Park.

Food

The first establishment most people see on Main Street from the train station, **Bank Square Coffeehouse** (129 Main St., 845/440-7165, 6am-10pm Mon.-Fri., 7am-10pm Sat.-Sun., under $15) is quintessential Beacon: a seating area with random furniture, good coffee, beer on tap, and, on the wall outside, a mural of a Garbage Pail Kids trading card. There are some great baked goods and a few lunch items from nearby eateries.

One of the many great farm-to-table restaurants in the Hudson Valley, the cozy ★ **Kitchen Sink Food & Drink** (157 Main St., 845/765-0240, 5pm-9pm Mon. and Wed.-Thurs., 5pm-10pm Fri.-Sat., 11am-2pm and 5pm-8:30pm Sun., under $50) changes its menu periodically but loves duck, cheese, and seafood. It's also open for brunch Sunday. Monday is fried chicken with all the fixins.

A popular lunch spot in Beacon, the comfy **Homespun Foods** (232 Main St., 845/831-5096, 8am-5pm daily, under $25) has fresh sandwiches and salads, plus an array of pastries including Mt. Beacon, a raspberry oat bar perfect for a summit indulgence on Mount Beacon. When the weather's nice, Homespun opens its backyard seating area.

For something down-home but less gourmet, local favorite **Yankee Clipper Diner** (397 Main St., 845/440-0021, 6am-10pm daily, under $25) is a railcar-inspired diner smack in the middle of Main Street, serving up the usual diner fare with booths and counter service. Beer, wine, and cocktails area available, as is a classic vanilla malt and New York-style egg cream.

While new restaurants pop up frequently in Beacon, **Max's on Main** (246 Main St., 845/838-6297, 11:30am-midnight Mon.-Wed., 11:30am-1am Thurs., 11:30am-2am Fri.-Sat., noon-midnight Sun., under $30) is among the city's culinary stalwarts. Go for its friendly vibe and funkily-named steak entrees, such as the Treasure of Steak Madre. There's a decent but narrow bar area with plenty of TVs for sporting events.

Accommodations

The boutique and family-owned ★ **Roundhouse** (2 E. Main St., 845/765-8369, www.roundhousebeacon.com, $200-350) is a converted mill property overlooking a creek and roaring waterfall. Its airy guest rooms and suites are quite chic: white walls, mid-century modern furniture, and ultramodern appliances. There's a complimentary hot breakfast. Reserve way in advance for summer and especially fall.

The **Beacon Hotel** (424 Main St., 845/765-2208, http://beaconhotelhudsonvalley.com, $250-650) is the newer kid in town, though the brick building has been around since 1877. Overlooking Main Street, each of its rooms has a bay window for quiet contemplation. Rooms are minimalist and spacious, bringing a dash of Manhattan 90 minutes upstate. One guest room is a four-sleeper called Hiker's Haven, but its price is meant for those hiking in style, and not necessarily those roughing it.

Like its fellow lodging spots in the city, **The Inn and Spa at Beacon** (151 Main St., 845/205-2900, $200-300) is a meticulously designed boutique hotel with soft gray walls, hardwood floors, and large windows. When the weather's cooperating, breakfast (Belgian waffles) is served on the roof. The spa provides massage treatments, body treatments, facial treatments, facial enhancements, and yoga.

Just outside of the downtown, **Chrystie House** (300 South Ave., 845/765-0251, www.new.chrystiehouse.com, $175-250) is a restored Federal mansion offering elegance in its four rooms. Part of what once was a Hudson River estate, the inn provides a splendid garden with a gingko tree and dwarf horse chestnut trees.

Poughkeepsie

You may just know it for its funny name, but **Poughkeepsie** (pop. 32,736), the largest city in the Hudson Valley and on this section of the trip, is worth exploring.

A place known for its mills, breweries, and rail presence in the 19th century, Poughkeepsie has endured a roller coaster of changes in recent decades. Once home to IBM's main plant, the city has since shifted into a hub for small manufacturing, thanks to an influx of New York City expats searching for a place to settle. You'll find plenty of signs of new life here, with once-abandoned mill buildings turning into apartments and businesses that produce metal designs and craft beer.

What helps sustain Poughkeepsie, however, is tourism, and there are some top-notch sights in the city and vicinity, including a presidential library, the world's longest pedestrian footbridge, and educational institutions that double as landmarks.

Getting There and Around

Poughkeepsie is a 17-mile (27.4-km) drive up US-9 from Beacon. It once functioned as a hub for rail activity, but these days the only train presence is that of commuter vessels shooting folks to the city, generally from points south. The **Poughkeepsie Train Station** (41 Main St., 800/872-7245) is centrally located and serves both the **Metro-North Railroad** (www.mta.info) and **Amtrak** (www.amtrak.com) on its Adirondack, Empire Service, and Ethan Allen Express lines.

Some of the major sights are 5 miles (8 km) north in Hyde Park, so you'll want wheels to get up there. Plus, if you're hoping to hike a bit, walking will only get you to the Dutchess Rail Trail—which is great, but there aren't summits. NY-9 runs along the Hudson River as the main north-south artery, while NY-44 and NY-55 hang together before separating outside the city limits. I-87 is a 20-minute drive over the river and west of the city, while I-84 is closer to 30 minutes south, down NY-9.

If you're trying to cut down on your own gas, the city's **Loop Bus System** (845/473-8424) includes several routes that wind throughout the city, hitting all major tourist attractions and even extending to Pawling.

Sights

Walkway Over the Hudson

So, you want a view without climbing a bunch of rocks, huh? Dating to the late 19th century as the Poughkeepsie-Highland Railroad Bridge and reopened for foot traffic only in 2010, the marvelous **Walkway Over the Hudson** (61 Parker Ave., 845/454-9649, www.walkway.org) is the longest pedestrian footbridge in the world, spanning 1.28 miles (2.1 km) from Poughkeepsie to the Town of Highland in neighboring Ulster County. Providing unparalleled views up and down the Hudson River, the bridge teems with visitors daily, from folks taking selfies to residents out for a run or bike ride.

One Day in Poughkeepsie

Morning

Start your day with a filling breakfast and coffee at the **Poughkeepsie Grind.** Be sure to pick up a pastry for noshing. Then get to the **Franklin D. Roosevelt Presidential Library & Museum** when it opens so you can spend a few hours perusing the grounds without losing too much of the day. After taking in the exhibits, stop at the **Vanderbilt Mansion,** but, instead of touring the home, lay out a picnic blanket and enjoy your snack while taking in a Hudson River view.

Afternoon

Head into Poughkeepsie and walk the 4.4-mile (7.1-km) **Walkway Loop Trail** through the city, over the Mid-Hudson Bridge, along the river, and over the **Walkway Over the Hudson.** After enjoying the spectacular views, grab a midafternoon beer at **Mill House Brewing Co.** If you're not the beer-drinking kind, step off the Walkway and grab a bite at **Lola's.**

Evening

If there's a show that evening at the **Bardavon 1869 Opera House,** buy tickets and enjoy the performance. If not, head down to the waterfront and take a leisurely walk along **Victor C. Waryas Park** before sitting down for dinner at the **Artist's Palate.** Postdinner drinks are three blocks away at **Schatzi's Pub,** and if you're still thirsty, walk another four blocks to **Noah's Ark.**

Accessible from a metered parking lot along Parker Avenue, the walkway has food and merchandise vendors, portable toilets, and an elevator providing ground-level access. It's also run by New York State Parks, and both park rangers and volunteers are eager to offer assistance and tell a story about the history of the bridge.

Those wanting to continue walking can go either west or east on the **Hudson Valley Rail Trail** or **Dutchess Rail Trail,** rail lines paved for public access over the last two decades, or take the 4.4-mile (7.1-km) **Walkway Loop Trail,** which runs back over the Hudson on the Mid-Hudson Bridge and winds through Little Italy in Poughkeepsie.

★ Franklin D. Roosevelt Presidential Library & Museum

The **Franklin D. Roosevelt Presidential Library & Museum** (4079 Albany Post Rd., Hyde Park, 845/486-7770, www.fdrlibrary.org, 9am-6pm daily Apr.-Oct., 9am-5pm daily Nov.-Mar., $18) is worth a day trip to Hyde Park. Before his presidency Roosevelt decided to donate all his political documents to the government, and later he planned a facility set on 16 acres of family land to host the records. Today the property includes the Dutch Colonial-style library, Roosevelt's childhood home Springwood, and the museum built in 1941.

The museum is a stunning look at early 20th-century American history from the Great Depression to the end of World War II, presented in rotating and permanent exhibits. Among the highlights here are audio clips from Roosevelt's famous "Fireside Chats" and important addresses in American history.

Vanderbilt Mansion

Also up the road in Hyde Park, the **Vanderbilt Mansion** (81 Vanderbilt Park Rd., Hyde Park, 845/229-7770, sunrise-sunset daily, grounds free, tours $10) is a quintessential Gilded Age landmark. The 54-room mansion built between 1896 and 1899 was the home of the Vanderbilt family until 1938. The National Park Service runs tours every hour from May to October, and every two hours from November to April.

Along with the mansion are meticulous gardens in an Italian symmetrical style, and lawns that overlook the Hudson. You can almost picture the well-coifed folks enjoying tea while watching sunset; you too can take in these views, as the grounds are open for all to stroll. Bring a picnic if you'd like.

Culinary Institute of America

The chefs in charge of many of the best restaurants in America cut their teeth (figuratively, not with a knife) at the **Culinary Institute of America** (1946 Campus Dr., Hyde Park, 845/452-9600, www.ciachef.edu, 8:30am-5pm Mon.-Sat.). Visitors can tour the school, plus eat at its three restaurants highlighting American, French, and Italian cuisines, along with a café and bakery. The students prepare and serve all the meals at CIA, promising diners a unique experience with every visit. The restaurants tend to be booked solid in the fall, so call way ahead of time to secure your table.

Vassar College

The stately 1861-built Main Building that anchors **Vassar College** (124 Raymond Ave., 845/437-7000, www.vassar.edu) once housed the entire institution. That made sense for Vassar's first class, which had a few dozen students, but times are different, and the nearly 2,500 students at this Seven Sisters liberal arts college now enjoy a 1,000-acre campus with landmarks, an ecological preserve, and an arboretum.

The highlights at Vassar include that Main Building, which along with the college observatory is a National Historic Landmark, and the ecological preserve, which houses the Vassar Farm. There, visitors can hike nine trails, bike eight

Top to bottom: Franklin D. Roosevelt Presidential Library & Museum; Vanderbilt Mansion; Culinary Institute of America.

of them, walk the community gardens, and check out the member-supported Poughkeepsie Farm Project.

Vassar is also home to the **Frances Lehman Loeb Art Center** (845/437-5237, www.fllac.vassar.edu, 10am-5pm Tues.-Sat., 1pm-5pm Sun.), which includes 21,000 works, among them a substantial collection of Hudson River School paintings.

Mid-Hudson Children's Museum

A bright yellow modern-day castle for kids, the **Mid-Hudson Children's Museum** (75 N. Water St., 845/471-0589, www.mhcm.org, 9:30am-5pm Tues.-Sat., 11am-5pm Sun., $9) offers four distinct exhibits that combine education and active play. Oh, and there's the Hyde Park Mastodon, a 12-foot-tall (3.7-m) replica of a real mastodon unearthed nearby, which is interactive for kid play.

Recreation

Hiking

The movement to turn former railroads into walkable trails has seen traction in the Hudson Valley. One of those trails, the **Dutchess Rail Trail** (www.dutchessrailtrail.com), starts at the Walkway Over the Hudson and winds through the eastern end of the city, moving into rural areas as it snakes south toward East Fishkill. The entire trail is 13 miles (21 km).

Parks

Poughkeepsie has a few nice parks offering a range of amenities. **Spratt Park** (165 Wilbur Blvd., 845/451-4100) has a public pool, ballfields, and tennis courts. **College Hill Park** (North Clinton St. and NY-9G) includes a columned structure used for staging events and a nine-hole golf course. **Morgan Lake Park** (51 Creek Rd., 845/418-0016) provides fishing and a connection to the Dutchess Rail Trail.

For those wanting a view, **Victor C. Waryas Park** (1 Main St.) is set against the Hudson River and has benches, a pavilion, and space to sit on the grass on a sunny day. Boat launch access and a skate park are also available.

Spectator Sports

Marist College (3399 NY-9, 845/575-3000, www.marist.edu), which is a self-contained campus, has a Division I FCS team in the Pioneer Football League's Red Foxes. They play their games at **Leonidoff Field,** right beside the campus's main entrance. The Marist women's basketball team frequently qualifies for the NCAA Tournament, while the men's team hasn't reached the "Big Dance" since 1987. Both play in the Metro Atlantic Athletic Conference and run the floor at **McCann Arena,** which is to the left after you enter the campus.

Ice-Skating

The **McCann Ice Arena** (14 Civic Center Plaza, http://midhudsonciviccenter.org, $10 regular admission) hosts public skating on Friday nights and weekend afternoons.

Entertainment and Events

Nightlife

Schatzi's Pub (202 Main St., 845/454-1179, www.iloveschatzis.com, 3pm-2am Mon.-Fri., noon-2am Sat., 11am-2am Sun.) will be your favorite bar if you frequent Poughkeepsie. This brick-clad pub and beer garden features both German fare and the fun hoppy stuff, along with a huge pub-centric menu.

Want a bike ride and a drink? **Backstreet Pub** (103 Parker Ave., 845/242-0542, noon-10pm Tues.-Sun.) offers bike rentals for $5 an hour, a good option since it's right next to the Walkway Over the Hudson. After your ride, return the bike and buy a drink.

The chill, fresh, **Noah's Ark** (135 Mill St., 845/486-9295, 4pm-4am Mon.-Sat.) sheds the pretension and offers happy hour specials, darts, and a pool table. It's also open until nearly dawn, which is rare north of New York City.

The Poughkeepsie waterfront is a notorious haven for thirsty twentysomethings (it's where Snooki from *Jersey Shore* partied before *Jersey Shore*), but it's hard to beat the river views, even when sipping an overpriced vodka cocktail. For that very experience you have the well-established **Shadows on the Hudson** (176 Rinaldi Blvd., 845/486-9500, www.shadowsonthehudson.com, 11:30am-9pm Mon.-Thurs., 11:30am-10pm Fri., 11:30am-2am Sat., 10:45am-9pm Sun.), with its slinky neon bar and leather seating. Then there's **Mahoney's Pub** (35 Main St., 845/471-7026, www.mahoneysirishpub.com, 11am-4am daily), a two-level nightly party that gets really rowdy around St. Patrick's Day.

For something quieter, **Nic L Inn Wine Cellar on the Hudson** (135 N. Water St., 845/452-5649, http://nickelinn.com, 4pm-9pm Sun. and Tues., noon-9pm Wed.-Thurs., noon-10pm Fri.-Sat.) features a robust list of local, French, Italian, and Napa Valley varieties. On a budget? Bottles in the cellar's Twenty Nine Dollar Barrel are perfect to split. There's lunch, dinner, and cocktails also.

Breweries

A relative hike from downtown Poughkeepsie, **Blue Collar Brewery** (40 Cottage St., 845/454-2739, www.thebluecollarbrewery.com, 3pm-10pm Mon.-Thurs., noon-midnight Fri.-Sat., noon-10pm Sun., under $20) really doubles down on its moniker. Inside a brick industrial building, Blue Collar serves decent representations of tried-and-true beer styles with elevated pub grub.

You'll find just about everything at **Mill House Brewing Co.** (289 Mill St., 845/485-2739, www.millhousebrewing.com, 11:30am-9pm Mon.-Thurs., 11:30am-10:30pm Sat., 11am-9pm Sun., under $30), a brewery and brewpub serving 14 of its brews at any time, from a cucumber cream ale to a wee heavy Scotch ale. It also has vast space for dining, where you'll find the usual bar bites alongside entrees, pizzas, and an extensive selection of sausages.

Performing Arts

At night the brilliant marquee of the **Bardavon 1869 Opera House** (35 Market St., 845/473-2072, www.bardavon.org) lights up and ties the city to the 19th century. Like many venues of its time, the Bardavon went through its share of ups and downs, but over the last few decades has been a place to hear live music, watch theater, and chuckle with big-time comedians. Its season runs from fall to spring.

For a more "intimate" experience, the **Chance Theater** (6 Crannell St., 845/471-1966, www.thechancetheater.com) is a historic performing-arts house whose recent history was written during the punk era. The Ramones, the Police, and other bratty bands played on the Chance stage in their young years, and these days hungry rockers pull in crowds on weekends.

While preserving Victorian-age buildings donated by members of the esteemed Vassar family, the **Cunneen-Hackett Arts Center** (9-12 Vassar St., 845/486-4571, www.cunneen-hackett.org) hosts community theater, dance, and music, and runs visual arts exhibits out of both buildings.

Family shows and slightly larger performances take place at the **Mid-Hudson Civic Center** (14 Civic Center Plaza, http://midhudsonciviccenter.org).

Festivals and Events

Poughkeepsie has a substantial Oaxacan community, and every year it celebrates **La Guelaguetza** (Victor C. Waryas Park, 1 Main St., Aug.), a festival with music and dance, Mexican food, and craft vendors. The city also throws a luminescent holiday fete with **Celebration of Lights** (Main St., Dec.). This annual tree lighting, parade, and fireworks display brings thousands out to the downtown each year.

Shopping

Despite being the largest city in the Hudson Valley, Poughkeepsie isn't known for its extensive Main Street shopping experience. Much of the action is out on NY-9, headlined by the **Poughkeepsie Galleria** (2001 NY-9, 845/297-7600, www.poughkeepsiegalleriamall.com, 10am-9:30pm Mon.-Sat., 11am-6pm Sun.). The Galleria has anchor stores like Sears, JCPenney, and Target, plus your usual collection of mall regulars. A stone's throw to the south is the **Shoppes at South Hills** (838 NY-9, 914/304-5659), an outdoor shopping mall.

Food

You can see **Lola's** (131 Washington St., 845/471-8555, www.lolascafeandcatering.com, 10am-5pm Mon.-Fri., 10am-4pm Sat., under $20) from the Poughkeepsie entrance to the Walkway Over the Hudson, so you have no excuse if you're hungry. Lola's, which really loves chalkboards, serves sandwiches, wraps, salads, and soup, but its vegetarian bowls are where it's at. You can add chicken or shrimp if you so choose.

Also part of the New American trend, the **Artist's Palate** (307 Main St., 845/483-8074, 11am-2:30pm Mon.-Fri., 5pm-9pm Mon.-Thurs., 5pm-10pm Fri.-Sat., under $40) sources from local farmers and brings dishes like Hudson Valley duck and seared scallops to its comfortable and chic spot that resembles the Manhattan restaurant you've been dying to try.

Poughkeepsie has plenty of pizza to choose from, but favorites include **Gino's** (706 Main St., 845/454-2525, 11am-11pm Tues.-Sun., under $20), **Emiliano's** (111 Main St., 845/473-1414, 11am-11pm Mon.-Sat., noon-10pm Sun., under $20), **Bacio** (7 Collegeview Ave., 845/486-8080, 11am-11pm Mon.-Sat., noon-10pm Sun., under $20), and **DD's Pizza** (300 Hooker Ave., 845/452-1754, 11:30am-9:30pm Mon.-Sat., under $20).

Your cash goes a long way at **Nelly's** (400 Main St., 845/486-5166, 8am-9pm daily, under $15), an unassuming Dominican lunch counter packing pork, stewed goat, and rice into tin containers. Good Mexican can be found at **Mole Mole** (357 Hooker Ave., 845/452-2850, 11am-10pm Mon.-Fri., 9am-10pm Sat., 9am-9pm Sun., under $20), which serves margaritas in a colorful green interior. And for bright and fresh Jamaican, there's **Golden Crust Caribbean Bakery & Grill** (700 Main St., 845/485-5262, 9am-8pm Mon.-Sat., under $20) and **Pat's Kitchen** (453 Main St., 845/471-4264, 8am-9pm Mon.-Thurs., 9am-10pm Fri.-Sat., under $20).

The Crafted Kup (44 Raymond Ave., 845/483-7070, 7am-7pm Mon.-Wed. and Fri., 7am-9pm Thurs., 8am-6pm Sat.-Sun., under $15) has a small staircase to a raised level with comfortable seating; the Vassar kids give it a workout. **North River Roasters** (8 Cherry St., 8am-4pm Mon.-Fri., 10am-2pm Sun., under $15), keeps a counter inside the Poughkeepsie Underwear Factory, but that doesn't mean you should visit in your skivvies. They do coffee in a remodeled manufacturing building here. Finally, **The Poughkeepsie Grind** (107 Main St., 845/345-9588, 6am-4pm Mon.-Fri., 8am-4pm Sat., under $15) serves up your Saturday-morning coffee and breakfast sandwich.

Accommodations

Despite the influx of young energy in Poughkeepsie, the city remains barren of boutique hotels and funky inns. Instead, most of the lodging you'll find in the city is just south of downtown along the NY-9 corridor. There, you'll get the **Hampton Inn & Suites** (2361 NY-9, 845/463-7500, $175-220), **Residence Inn by Marriott** (2525 NY-9, 845/463-4343, $180-260), **Courtyard by Marriott** (2641 NY-9, 845/485-6336, $120-280), and **Holiday Inn Express** (2750 NY-9, 845/473-1151, $180-270).

There is, however, one independent hotel in the city: the **Poughkeepsie Grand Hotel** (40 Civic Center Plaza,

845/485-5300, http://pokgrand.com, $150-250). The Grand has bright, comfortable rooms, plus a restaurant with burgers, salads, a bar, and more. It's a little pricier than the chains during normal circumstances, but it's the only hotel right smack in the thick of it.

Information and Services

Dutchess Tourism (3 Neptune Rd., 845/463-4000, www.dutchesstourism.com, 8am-5pm Mon.-Fri.) offers the most extensive travel information about Poughkeepsie.

Pawling

Pawling (pop. 2,347), a 21-mile (33.8-km) drive east on NY-55 from Poughkeepsie, is pretty accessible for AT hikers. Not only is the town center a 2.5-mile (4-km) walk from the trail, but there's a train station serving thru-hikers in Pawling. The only train station on the AT, it provides a connection to New York City, making Pawling a good place to start or finish a section-hike or even a long day hike.

Hikers will routinely stop in town, and when they do, they'll find an inviting, close-knit community clanging glasses in local pubs and chatting about their workdays in markets.

Sights

The only railroad station physically on the Appalachian Trail is the **AT Metro-North station** (NY-22, 2.8 mi/4.5 km north of NY-55, http://mta.info), where passengers can board a train headed for Grand Central Terminal in New York City. The train is part of Metro-North's Harlem Line; it arrives in Midtown Manhattan two hours after leaving Pawling. Trains leave Pawling only a few times each day, and typically in the afternoon; arrivals are typically in the morning.

Smack in the middle of the Appalachian Trail, the **Dover Oak** (West Dover Rd. at AT trail crossing) is the biggest white oak tree in New York, standing 114 feet (35 m) tall and springing branches like tendrils to the sky. Park on the side of the road by the oak; you can't miss it. A nice hike to Pawling's version of Cat Rocks starts here.

Hiking

Cat Rocks Pawling Trail

Distance: 7 miles (11.3 km)
Duration: 4 hours
Elevation gain: 900 feet (274 m)
Difficulty: Moderate
Trailhead: Appalachian Trail Metro-North Station (41.59297, -73.58766)

This fun hike will get you lost in an otherwise trafficked area of Pawling, climaxing with a rewarding overlook. Start at the AT train station and head west (or south on the AT, away from NY-22), crossing the railroad tracks and entering the woods. You'll stay on the AT, beginning a moderate ascent that leads you to the Dover Oak. Admire the old tree and then cross the street to finish the ascent. One mile (1.6 km) after the oak, the trail flattens and an unmarked trail to the right tempts you to Cat Rocks. Sit out and enjoy, then come back the way you came on the AT.

Recreation

Adjacent to the village border is **Lakeside Park** (2 Lakeside Dr., $5-15 for swimming), land that used to house a conference center but now features 280 acres of trails, sports fields and courts, a playground, and a lake with canoeing, kayaking, swimming, and a beach. The trails meander around Green Mountain Lake, through the woods, and up to a lookout.

Nightlife

You might not see a Hall & Oates reunion at **Daryl's House** (130 Rte. 22, 845/289-0185, http://darylshouseclub.com, 3:30pm-11pm Wed., 3:30pm-midnight Thurs.-Fri., 11am-noon Sat., 11am-11pm Sun.), owned by blue-eyed soul singer

Daryl Hall, but a mix of other regionally and nationally famous musicians play inside this rustic and intimate venue. The food is also pretty good for a music venue.

Sean, the owner of **O'Connor's Public House** (6 Broad St., 845/289-0666, 11am-3am daily), is likely to snare you in a quick conversation with his lovely Irish lilt when you visit his dark, boldly decorated bar. The Guinness is good, the people delightful, and there's a pool table. Just around the corner is the **Pawling Tavern** (42 Charles Colman Blvd., 845/855-9141, 11am-4am daily), which is as local as it gets with wood tones, live music, and good drink specials.

Food and Accommodations

Dominating half a block in the commercial center of Pawling, **McKinney & Doyle Fine Foods** (10 Charles Coleman Blvd., 845/855-3875, http://mckinneyanddoyle.com, 6:30am-7pm Mon., 6:30am-9pm Tues.-Thurs., 6:30am-9:30pm Fri., 7am-9:30pm Sat., 7am-9pm Sun., under $50) is inviting and, to be honest, massive. A brick-walled bar is a happening spot for specialty cocktails, while diners may chomp on pricey Hudson Valley brook trout in the dining room. The bakery serves Danish, rolls, and muffins. Brunch is available in the dining room.

One of the essential stops for any Appalachian Trail hiker, **Tony's Deli** (841 Rte. 22, 845/855-9540, 3:30am-midnight Mon.-Fri., 4am-midnight Sat., 5am-midnight Sun., under $20) is nothing if not accommodating to the weary traveler. Tony's boasts hefty sandwiches, but its hiker's menu includes, among other feats of fortitude, the ever-popular Ultimate Cowboy Burger: two quarter-pound patties, double bacon, onion rings, jack cheese, and barbecue sauce on a roll. Tony's also has plenty of convenience store fare, plus outdoor tent space for hikers at $2 per person.

The bed-and-breakfast in town is the **Pawling House** (105 W. Main St., 845/855-3851, http://pawlinghouse.com, $175-250), a gem of an overnight stay a few minutes from the village center. Rooms are decked in neat, simple New England colonial style, breakfast is hot and delicious, and service is superb.

Kent

New England's charm follows you as you cross into Connecticut. From Pawling, drive 15 miles (24.1 km) north up NY-55 until it becomes CR-22, cross a famous covered bridge, and head north on US-7 to **Kent** (pop. 2,979).

Walking the charming Main Street of this town, maybe with a cup of coffee, you might think you're visiting a small town inhabited by fast-talking, whip-smart folks just trying to make something out of life. That's because Kent is similar to Stars Hollow, the setting of the television show *The Gilmore Girls*. This isn't just my observation: Devoted *Gilmore Girls* fans have traveled to Kent to compare the two towns, and Kent has bought in, hosting the Gilmore Girls Fan Fest every October.

If a cult television show about people in a quintessential New England town isn't your thing, that's OK: Kent will impress with its landmarks, quality restaurants and quaint inns, and great state parks.

Sights

Eric Sloane Museum and Kent Furnace

The **Eric Sloane Museum and Kent Furnace** (31 US-7, 860/927-3849, 10am-4pm Fri.-Sun. May-Oct., $5-8) is a quirky museum, showcasing both Connecticut's manufacturing muscle and the works of a regionally famous mid-20th-century painter and author. Eric Sloane, the painter and author, amassed quite a collection of hand tools, many produced by the Connecticut manufacturing company Stanley Works (now Stanley Black & Decker). Sloane kept his studio in a Stanley building that was donated to the state in 1969. Thus, to preserve both the legacies of Sloane and Stanley, the museum was born. Paintings, writings, and tools can all be found here, along with an iron furnace that produced pig iron in the mid-to-late 19th century.

★ Bull's Bridge

If there's anything more quintessential New England than the covered bridge, I've yet to find it. Connecticut only has two in operation: the West Cornwall Covered Bridge (we'll get there soon), and Bridge No. 4453, or, more eloquently, **Bull's Bridge** (Bulls Bridge Rd. and US-7).

The first span at this location over the Housatonic River was built by Jacob and Isaac Bull in 1760 and was used for transporting pig iron or iron ore, depending on which history book you consult. Also, legend states George Washington himself crossed the first bridge during the Revolution.

The current bridge was built in 1842 and is in the National Register of Historic Places. It's made of timber in the Town lattice design patented by Ithiel Town and featuring latticed trusses. And, like other covered bridges in New England, the rickety wooden floorboard of the bridge sounds only slightly dangerous when crossing. Be on the lookout, because the bridge will show up without warning when traveling east into Connecticut. Bull's Bridge Road is one lane at the bridge, so practice safe waiting and driving before crossing.

Recreation

Caleb's Peak & St. John's Ledges

Distance: 4 miles (6.4 km)
Duration: 2.5-3 hours
Elevation gain: 1,132 feet (345 m)
Difficulty: Moderate
Trailhead: River Road (41.766339, -73.443204)

Like a choose-your-own-adventure book in reverse, the hike to Caleb's Peak and St. John's Ledges can start at a variety of places. One option is along Skiff Mountain Road at the Appalachian Trail entrance; for this hike, start at River Road and begin hiking back in the direction you drove in, following the white blazes of the AT. After about a half mile (0.8 km) you'll find another opening where the AT heads right, into the woods. Follow the AT.

That's what you're doing the entire time, up a relatively challenging 0.5-mile (0.8-km) rock scramble, with some rock stairs and some trickier parts, until you reach a ridge. Stay on that ridge until you see, to your left, a sign for St. John's Ledges, a nice spot for photos overlooking the Housatonic River. From there, continue on the AT until reaching Caleb's Peak, which offers a second view and a larger area for picnicking. Your best bet is to turn around and follow the AT back to your car; if you'd like, you can continue on the AT down the mountain to Skiff Mountain Road, but you're still going to have to turn around.

Kent Falls State Park

The star of **Kent Falls State Park** (462 Kent-Cornwall Rd., 860/424-3200, 8am-7pm summer, 8am-sunset winter, $9 state residents, $15 nonresidents on weekends) is the cascading **Kent Falls,** the tallest waterfall in Connecticut at 250 feet (76 m), which helps transport water on the Falls Brook to the Housatonic. Because the falls are close to the parking area, it's a scenic spot to enjoy a picnic or barbecue, and families come in droves on warm weekends to enjoy. Thus, the parking lot can fill quickly, and if so, rangers don't let cars in until 10 cars leave.

Hiking

There are two true trails at **Kent Falls State Park,** and their loop is exactly one mile (1.6 km) in length. Start on the red Kent Falls Trail, accessible from the parking lot, and walk uphill 0.1 mile (0.2 km) until a yellow-blazed trail enters from the left. Turn onto the yellow as it ambles upriver, then sharply cuts and comes back toward the brook. It'll intersect again with the red trail, and this time make a right to head downhill toward the falls and parking lot.

Fishing

Kent Falls State Park is a designated trout park, which means its water is stocked with trout before opening day of the season (6am on the second Saturday in April), and novices are especially encouraged to try their hand at catching some fish. Note that anglers can only keep up to two fish per day in these trout parks.

Macedonia Brook State Park

Covering 2,302 acres of wildland, **Macedonia Brook State Park** (159 Macedonia Brook Rd., 860/927-4100) is pound for pound one of the best hiking experiences in New England. Its main road and namesake brook runs up the middle of the park like a spine, while surrounding it are quick-rising mountains with ridges perfect for moderately experienced hikers. There are a few trails ascending these mountains, but a longer loop trail, described below, gives you the full experience in a few hours.

The park has a campground, picnic shelters, and pit toilets; it charges $14-24 for overnight camping.

Macedonia Ridge Trail Loop

Distance: 6.2 miles (10 km)
Duration: 4-4.5 hours
Elevation gain: 1,706 feet (520 m)
Difficulty: Strenuous
Trailhead: Weber Road, 0.25 mile/0.4 kilometer after intersection with Macedonia Brook Road (41.76781, -73.49536)

A difficult but constantly rewarding hike providing views of the Taconics and Catskills, the Macedonia Ridge Trail is the main route for the park with some outstanding scrambling opportunities and plenty of up and down. You can start from the south or north, but to get the best reward at the finish, follow the blue trail east from the parking lot. Staying on blue the entire time, the first 3 miles (4.8

Macedonia Brook State Park

km) will include a quick climb and a difficult, all-fours scramble downhill.

Once you reach the crossing with Macedonia Brook Road, continue on the blue trail as it heads back uphill on rugged terrain to the western ridge. Here you'll get those lovely views of the Taconics and Catskills. Continue here, finishing on steep terrain, until you find yourself back at the parking lot.

Festivals and Events

The popular **Gilmore Girls Fan Fest** (Oct., www.girlmoregirlsfanfest.com, $250) includes appearances and signings by actors who took part in the series, trivia contests, improvisational shows, panels, and cocktail and wine tastings. Don't miss the mother-daughter fashion show and costume contest—the ultimate in Gilmore-related events.

Kent hosts an annual **Gingerbread Festival** (Dec., www.kentctgingerbreadfest.com), in which residents put to the test their knowledge of structural integrity by way of sweet bread. The town chamber of commerce offers a gingerbread map and a riddle to solve for folks wanting to take the gingerbread walk.

Shopping

Your first stop in Kent should be **Annie Bananie General Store** (5 Bridge St., 860/927-3377, www.anniebananieicecream.com, 9am-6pm Mon.-Sat., 10am-5pm Sun.), an all-in-one depot for hikers, tourists, and anyone who wants a summertime treat. You may just meet Annie herself, whose store sells apparel, hiking and outdoor equipment, and locally made foods and crafts. She also serves Annie Bananie's ice cream (courtesy of SoHo Creamery of Great Barrington, Massachusetts), plus grilled cheese, hot dogs, and free popcorn from her old-fashioned stand. For Appalachian Trail hikers she provides shuttles and serves as a post office location.

What's real-life Stars Hollow without an independent bookstore? **House of Books** (10 N. Main St., 860/927-4104, www.houseofbooksct.com, 10am-5:30pm daily) has the feel of a small-town gathering place with regular readings and events, plus trail maps for hikers. House of Books is part of **Kent Barns** (www.kentbarnsct.com), an extensive shopping and dining center off Main Street with buildings that aren't barns so much as postmodern interpretations of barns. There's an eclectic collection of businesses here, from architects and financial advisors to art galleries like **Ober Gallery** (6 Main St., 860/927-5030, www.obergallery.com, noon-5pm Sat., 1pm-4pm Sun.), which showcases contemporary pieces.

Food

Like other towns in this stretch of the Hudson and Housatonic Valleys, Kent specializes in New American farm-to-table variations. Tops in class is the ★ **Kingsley Tavern** (14 N. Main St., 860/592-0261, www.kingsleytavern.com,

4pm-9pm Wed.-Thurs., 4pm-9:30pm Fri., 11:30am-3pm and 5pm-9:30pm Sat., 11:30am-8pm Sun., under $40), a classic gastro-style dining room with modest front porch seating. Go for cozy comfort fare like a shrimp-and-grits brunch or jerk chicken meatloaf dinner.

Down by Bull's Bridge is the aptly named **Bull's Bridge Inn** (333 Kent Rd., 860/927-1000, http://bullsbridge.com, 5pm-9pm Mon.-Thurs., 5pm-9:30pm Fri., noon-9:30pm Sat., noon-9pm Sun., under $40), a classic, all-American steak-and-seafood tavern set in a large colonial house with wood paneling and dining chairs. It's a solid introduction to New England life and cuisine.

For no-nonsense service at a laminate-and-booth joint, try **The Villager** (28 N. Main St., 860/927-1555, www.villagerkent.com, 7am-4pm Wed.-Mon., 7am-3:30pm and 5pm-9:30pm Tues., under $30), serving up a good mix of diner fare, from fluffy French toast to huevos rancheros, plus a Tuesday-night Mexican dinner. There's ample seating outside the front door. **J. P. Gifford Market & Catering Company** (12 N. Main St., 860/592-0200, www.jpgifford.com, 6:30am-6pm Mon.-Sat., 7am-3pm Sun., under $20) is really popular with folks on the go. On a weekend afternoon, be prepared to stand in line a few minutes before ordering one of its renowned sandwiches, like the Catsmo Smokehouse smoked salmon on a bagel. The bare-bones facility has long tables, a tile floor, and takeaway counters.

Get your coffee at **Kent Coffee & Chocolate Co.** (45 N. Main St., 860/927-1445, 6am-8pm Sun.-Thurs., 6am-9pm Fri.-Sat., under $10), known for the brew and the bright energy of the staff.

Accommodations

When staying in Kent you're paying for Kent. ★ **The Inn at Kent Falls** (107 Kent Cornwall Rd., 860/927-3197, www.theinnatkentfalls.com, $230-400) ensures this with a meticulously Stars Hollow-esque presentation. Rooms are charming and fit every traveler, and suites run a range of styles from the traditional (the Lakes Suite has a claw-foot tub) to the unusual (the funky attic-space Gables Suite). An outdoor pool and gardens make the inn feel like a fun estate in which to meander around.

The Starbuck Inn (88 N. Main St., 860/927-1788, www.starbuckinn.com, $200-300) offers old English treats like afternoon tea and sherry, plus complimentary breakfast. Owner Peter is kind, the inn is unassuming, and the stay is comfortable. Channeling the Revolutionary history of the area, the **Fife 'N Drum Inn** (53 Main St., 860/927-3509, www.fifendrum.com, $160-250) is more affordable than the usual bed-and-breakfasts. You get what you ask for in the 12 rooms—the Goldenrod room is colored goldenrod, and the Victorian room is quite Victorian. A downstairs gift shop sells clothing and trinkets, and the **Fife 'N Drum Restaurant** across the parking lot has basic steak and seafood for elevated prices.

Information and Services

Right off Main Street is the **Kent Chamber of Commerce board** (Railroad St.), a handy spot to grab maps and acquire information about the village. For AT hikers, Kent offers a public toilet and shower ($2 for four minutes) right next to the board.

Housatonic Meadows State Park

From Kent, drive 10.7 miles (17.2 km) north up US-7. Providing great fishing access to the Housatonic River, **Housatonic Meadows State Park** (90 US-7, Sharon, 860/672-6772) is a prickly paradise providing an enrapturing getaway from the white-tooth charm of Kent.

Hiking

Pine Knob Loop Trail

Distance: 2.5 miles (4 km)
Duration: 1.5-2 hours
Elevation gain: 1,160 feet (354 m)
Difficulty: Moderate
Trailhead: US-7 (41.83316, -73.38375)

The Appalachian Trail never actually enters Housatonic Meadows State Park; it instead stays in Housatonic State Forest. So your job here is to get there, and then leave it, via the Pine Knob Loop Trail, which is short but tougher than you think, cutting through some brushy forest to a couple of viewpoints. From the trailhead, turn left on the blue trail and start a clinical ascent with the Hatch Brook to your left. After 0.6 mile (1 km), you'll reach the AT junction and turn right to follow that for 0.75 mile (1.2 km). Continue on rocky terrain until the blue trail heads right, leaving the AT. Follow the blue trail to the right and start climbing on even rockier terrain until you reach Pine Knob. Among scores of pines, admire one last view before beginning an arduous descent down some formidable rocks. Back at the bottom, finish the loop on the blue trail to hook back up with the parking lot.

Accommodations

A rustic experience is promised at **Housatonic Meadows State Park Campground** (860/672-6772, $17-60), where overnighters can put up a tent or stay in a small cabin without a bathroom. Showers are available on-site.

West Cornwall

A 2.7-mile (4.3-km) drive up US-7 from Housatonic Meadows State Park, **West Cornwall** (pop. 998) is home to the second covered bridge still in operation in Connecticut. The **West Cornwall Covered Bridge** (CT-128 at US-7), which spans 172 feet (52 m), crosses the Housatonic River with one traffic lane. History dates it to approximately 1864, and despite floods and hurricane-strength winds, this bridge painted a barn-door red has stood the test of time. Walk along Lower River Road to find a small green patch for photo opportunities and a bench; a short trail has been created for folks who want to walk to the riverbed and get a better view.

Food

Try to get a reservation at a restaurant named ★ **RSVP** (7 Railroad St., 860/672-7787, http://rsvp-restaurant.com, 7pm-11pm Fri.-Sat., 6pm-10pm Sun., $110 prix-fixe). This shoebox of a French BYOB kitchen, operated fully by a chef and his partner, does one dinner seating an evening with a prix-fixe menu of five courses. Some of the finest cooking in the French bistro style is happening here. Also, bring cash or check, because RSVP doesn't take credit cards.

The **Cornwall Country Market** (25 US-7, Cornwall Bridge, 860/619-8199, 6am-5pm Mon.-Fri., 7am-5pm Sat.-Sun., under $15) is where the action is in the Cornwall area. A busy stopover for travelers, locals, and hikers, the market has a deli counter, grab-and-go food, a porch, and outdoor picnic tables by the parking lot.

Accommodations

On US-7 you'll find lodging possibilities at the **Cornwall Inn** (270 US-7, Cornwall Bridge, 860/672-6884, www.cornwallinn.com, $150-300), which features four classic and unobtrusive bed-and-breakfast rooms, and **The Amselhaus** (6 Rug Rd., Cornwall Bridge, 860/248-3155, www.theamselhaus.com, $200-300), a large colonial farmhouse with a front porch and two substantial suites. Each suite has a living room, kitchen, and formal dining room, plus 2nd-floor bedrooms. For something more budget friendly, the **Hitching Post Country Motel** (45 US-7, Cornwall Bridge, 860/672-6219, $55-150) is a standard here-for-the-night, side-of-the-road motel.

Lakeville

Continue on US-7 about six miles (9.7 km) until a turnoff for CT-112. Turn west onto that road as it runs into the small town of **Lakeville** (pop. 928). As a neighboring Salisbury village resident put it: "Lakeville has the gas station." Well, it does have a bit more than that, including an understated New England vibe, quite a few dining options, and the nation's oldest road-racing venue.

Lime Rock Park

While the main roads meander around Wononskopomuc Lake, much of the energy here surrounds **Lime Rock Park** (60 White Hollow Rd., 860/435-5000, www.limerock.com), the nation's oldest continuously operating road-racing venue and a treasure among the racing community. Hosting scores of championship motorsport road races since opening in 1956, Lime Rock is no-frills (bring a blanket because there's only grass, no grandstands), so if you want a throwback racing experience, this is it.

Food

Diners in Lakeville prefer **The Boathouse** (349 Main St., 860/435-2111, www.theboathouseatlakeville.com, 11am-9pm Sun.-Thurs., 11am-11pm Fri.-Sat., under $40), complete with sailboat replicas on shelves, a giant boathouse mural behind the bar, fireplaces, and ribs, steaks, and, get this, sushi. For a nightcap, the lively **Black Rabbit** (2 Ethan Allen St., 860/596-4227, www.blackrabbitbarandgrille.com, 11:30am-9pm Mon. and Wed.-Thurs., 11:30am-9:30pm Fri.-Sat., 11am-8pm Sun., under $30) has a semi-local beer selection behind its L-shaped bar, plus superb burgers with greasy buns.

Salisbury

A 2-mile (3.2-km) drive north on US-44 leads to the **Town of Salisbury** (pop. 3,741), which has a bit more going for it. There's hiking, including the tallest peak in Connecticut, plus a couple of places to eat out, the **Salisbury General Store and Pharmacy** (20 Main St., 860/435-9388, 8am-6pm Mon.-Fri., 8am-5pm Sat., 8am-4pm Sun.), and a Main Street made for lazy sauntering. The village sees more than a few weekenders escaping New York City, as well as a celebrity or two (one of their names rhymes with "feral sleep"). Keep your eyes peeled.

Mount Riga State Park

At 276 acres, **Mount Riga State Park** (CT-41, 4 mi/6.4 km north of US-44, 860/424-3000) is a blip compared to the enormous state forests and parks surrounding it, but it packs a wallop with **Bear Mountain,** the tallest peak in the state. (Note: Mount Frissell, whose summit is in Massachusetts, has the highest point in Connecticut, and people will remind you of this.)

There's camping permitted in the park, with tent space available at the **Paradise Lane Campground** off the Paradise Lane Trail. The Riga shelter on the AT is 1.8 miles (2.9 km) south of the junction with the Undermountain Trail and 2.7 miles (4.3 km) south of the Bear Mountain summit. According to thru-hikers, sunrises at the Riga shelter are splendid.

Hiking

Bear Mountain Loop

Distance: 6.7 miles (10.8 km)
Duration: 3-4 hours
Elevation gain: 1,430 feet (436 m)
Difficulty: Strenuous
Trailhead: CT-41 in Salisbury (42.034880, -73.433588)

Connecticut's Bear Mountain is a great morale booster and introduction to bigger beasts. Inexperienced hikers can summit Bear and think "Wow, that wasn't so bad!" Soon enough they may even find themselves hiking Mount Washington in New Hampshire.

From the trailhead, start on the blue-blazed Undermountain Trail until you see a split for the Paradise Lane Trail. Take that up the mountain until you reach a connection to the Appalachian Trail. Make a left to take the AT up to the summit. (For an added bonus, go right on the AT just 0.2 mi/0.3 km down to the picturesque Sages Ravine.) Ascending on the AT includes an easy-to-moderate scramble where hands may be used. After the scramble, the walk at tree line to the summit is moderate. There's a 130-year-old stone pyramid at the summit one can climb to get the best views of the valley below. When finished taking it in, continue on the AT until it hits the Undermountain Trail again. Turn left, then right at the Paradise Lane junction to return to your car.

Food and Accommodations

Holding a relative monopoly in the Salisbury coffee and ice cream game, **Sweet William's** (17 Main St., 860/435-3005, www.sweet-williams.com, 8am-5pm Sun., 7am-5pm Mon.-Thurs., 7am-6pm Fri.-Sat., under $15) is a clean, cozy, and beige café serving pastries (get the cream scones), coffee, and coffee merchandise. Next door is its **desserts and scoop shop** (19 Main St., 860/435-8889, 9am-5pm Sun., 10am-5pm Mon.-Thurs., 9am-6pm Fri.-Sat., under $15), which bakes homemade pies, cakes, cupcakes, and cheesecakes, and offers ice cream via Jane's in the Hudson Valley of New York.

Also in the village, **Country Bistro** (10 Academy St., 860/435-9420, 8am-4pm daily, 5pm-9pm Fri.-Sat., under $50) mixes French bistro-style weekend dinners with generous breakfast service. The cozy spot is owned by a longtime gardening and cookbook author.

For something more reflective of quintessential New England, the ★ **White Hart Restaurant & Inn** (15 Under Mountain Rd., 860/435-0030, 11am-3pm and 5pm-8:30pm Sun., 5pm-9pm Mon. and Wed.-Thurs., 5pm-9:30pm Fri.-Sat., under $50) pulls British-inspired farm-to-table into a dining room that makes you feel like you're having a special meal. For casual diners who want to enjoy a burger, pint, and laugh, the dimly lit, very British taproom is just as special. White Hart also operates a 16-room inn ($250-450), and the rooms, with four-poster beds, leather footrests, and picture windows, showcase clean New England elegance. Also onsite is a Connecticut-chic takeaway café and general store called Provisions.

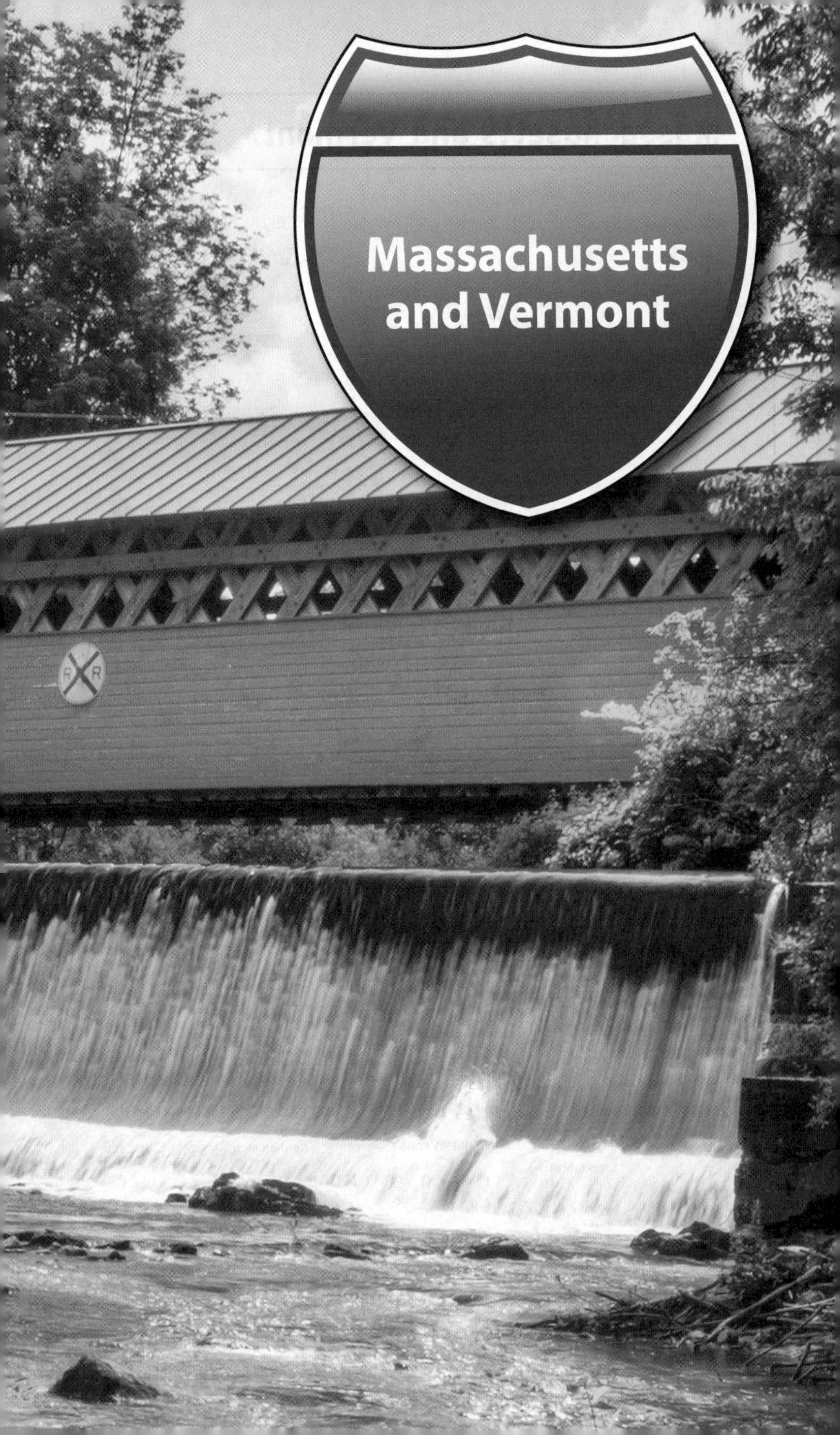
Massachusetts
and Vermont
RXR

Massachusetts and Vermont

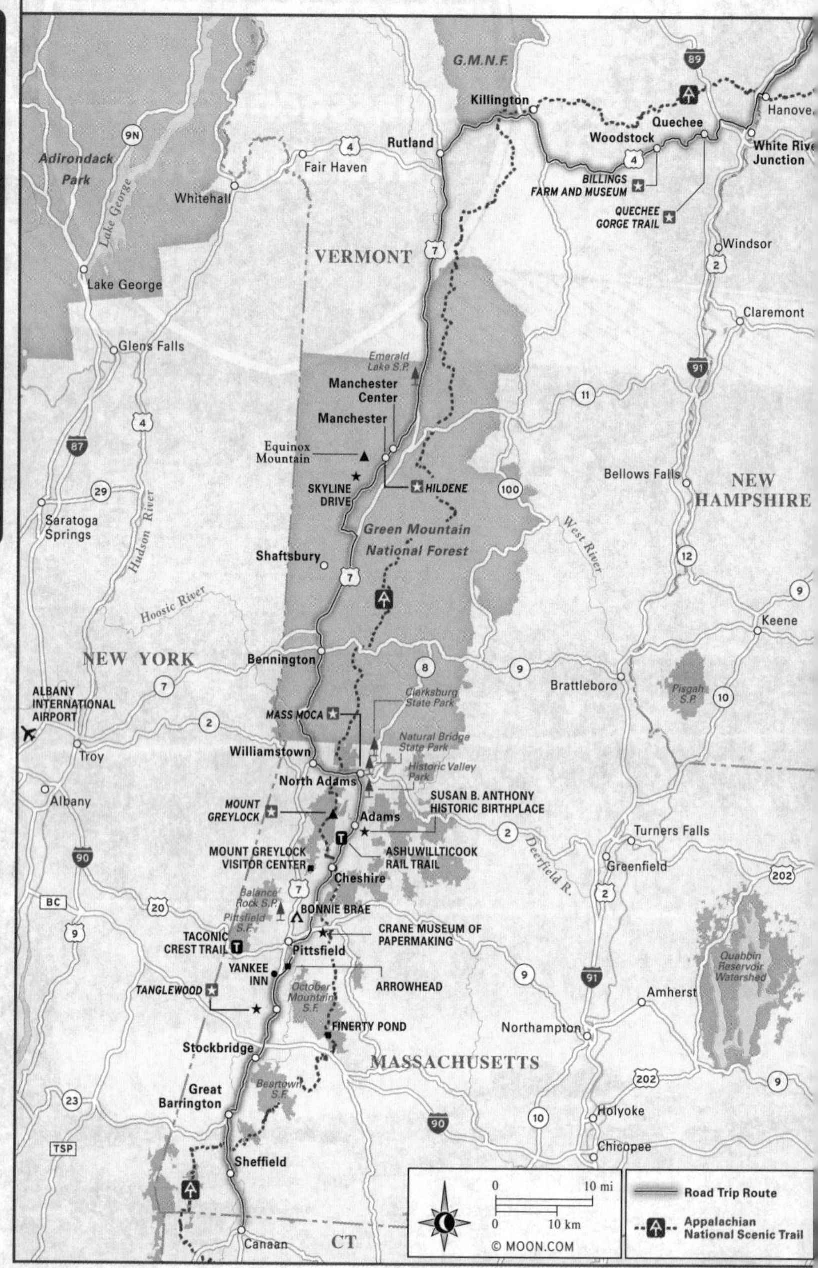

Highlights

★ **Tanglewood Music Center:** The summer home of the Boston Symphony Orchestra is also one of the finest outdoor amphitheaters for enjoying music under the stars (page 342).

★ **Mount Greylock:** This AT summit is the highest peak in Massachusetts. It also inspired Herman Melville and J.K. Rowling (page 352).

★ **Mass MoCA:** Comprising more than two dozen brick warehouses, this mecca for contemporary art provides a full day of fun (page 354).

★ **Hildene:** Abraham Lincoln's son made this gorgeous site his home; today it includes a working farm and plenty of nature trails (page 365).

★ **Billings Farm and Museum:** This working 1890s farmhouse and creamery makes a fantastic family-friendly destination (page 380).

★ **Quechee Gorge Trail:** Make your way down this moderate path into the Grand Canyon of Vermont and take a refreshing dip in the Ottauquechee River (page 382).

Best AT Hikes

There's enough variation in this area of the Appalachian Trail to satisfy every type of hiker. Take a short walk to view a significant waterfall, or prepare for a strenuous climb up one of the highest peaks in southern New England.

- **Race Brook Falls to Mount Everett (4.8 mi/7.7 km, Sheffield, Massachusetts):** Climb beside a waterfall until you reach the AT, then continue with an uphill trek to the summit of this popular peak in the Taconics (page 335).
- **East Mountain Trail (2.8 mi/4.5 km, Great Barrington, Massachusetts):** Skip the crowds and take to this overlooked mountain in the Berkshires. If you want a longer hike, continue to Ice Gulch and a famous lean-to (page 336).
- **Mount Greylock Summit (6.2 mi/10 km, New Ashford, Massachusetts):** Anyone hoping to hike the AT in Massachusetts needs to knock out the tough but rewarding Mount Greylock; do it with this moderate-to-strenuous gain of 1,070 feet (326 m) (page 352).
- **Killington Peak (7.2 mi/11.6 km, Killington, Vermont):** Skip the resort walk and instead take the Bucklin Trail to the AT while getting a taste of cabin life (page 373).
- **Thundering Brook Falls (1 mi/1.6 km, Killington, Vermont):** The first wheel-chair-accessible portion of the AT in Vermont heads to a fun waterfall in the quiet of Killington's municipal center (page 374).

Quintessential New England towns bustling with activity rest beneath the colorful mountain ridges of Massachusetts and Vermont, where the hiking grows more challenging.

That said, these states don't pose the same obstacles as their neighbors to the north. Even amateur hikers can finish the most difficult trails in this stretch before retreating to a small village inn for a nosh and craft cocktail. They'll be surrounded by tourists seeking a country escape with gourmet restaurants and an artistic spirit, found primarily in the Massachusetts towns of Great Barrington, Lenox, and North Adams, and the Vermont towns of Manchester Center and Woodstock.

History also plays a vital role in the tourism of these areas. Two museums pay homage to illustrator Norman Rockwell, while visitors can sit in the very houses that inspired the greatest works of Robert Frost and Herman Melville. Battle sites and monuments remind us of America's hard-fought infancy, and both the childhood home of Susan B. Anthony and adult home of Abraham Lincoln's son put the longer struggle for equality into perspective.

The Appalachian Trail meets with Vermont's famous Long Trail and stays with it for more than 90 miles (145 km) to the popular ski resort town of Killington. From there the trail turns east toward New Hampshire, briefly leaving the mountains and coasting along a deep green valley. It's here that Vermont shows off its brilliant fall hues, sparkling in gold and orange, while passing dairy farms and crossing narrow streams.

Best Restaurants

★ **The Bistro Box, Great Barrington, Massachusetts:** This side-of-the-road joint makes phenomenal burgers and pub fare, plus it has an outdoor game area (page 337).

★ **Nudel, Lenox, Massachusetts:** This narrow space is constantly buzzing, and the American-centric gastro menu changes all the time (page 344).

★ **Blue Benn Diner, Bennington, Vermont:** Get your fill of omelets, pancakes, and meatloaf inside an old train car (page 363).

★ **Up For Breakfast, Manchester Center, Vermont:** Wait on the staircase for a table at this busy breakfast spot. The pancakes do not disappoint (page 368).

★ **Silver Fork, Manchester Center, Vermont:** It's hard to get a reservation, but the fusion of American and Caribbean is totally worth the effort (page 368).

★ **Tuckerbox, White River Junction, Vermont:** Turkish delights with eggplant and lamb pair well with killer coffee and native spirits (page 385).

Planning Your Time

Much like the New York metropolitan area (and, really, much of this part of the world), fall is a busy season. If you can't live without peeping the leaves of Massachusetts and Vermont, plan on requiring more patience than at other times of the year. Try not to come during Columbus Day weekend, as crowds are the biggest and hotel rooms are the most expensive. As an alternative, the weekend after Columbus Day typically has good foliage.

Whether or not you're coming in the fall, plan on a five-day trip to explore the 160 miles (260 km) of Massachusetts and Vermont. You should spend half the trip in Massachusetts, starting in Sheffield or Great Barrington and making Pittsfield a solid base camp because of its central location along US-7 and flexibility of lodging options. In Vermont, either Rutland or Killington makes for a good overnight stop, and White River Junction and Norwich are solid endpoints because of their highway access. If you have less time, be sure to stop in Great Barrington, North Adams, Manchester Center, and Woodstock, the classic New England towns with the most dining and recreation options.

If you're looking to rough it, camp out in Massachusetts at October Mountain State Forest and explore the Berkshires before tackling Mount Greylock. A good long weekend is all you'll need there. While in Vermont, there are plenty of cheap lodging options in Rutland and Killington, but you can also take the Appalachian Trail and Long Trail from Bennington, camping at shelters along the way before stopping at the Inn at Long Trail in Killington. Plan on at least a week for that 90-mile (145-km) trip.

Getting There

Car is the only way to reach Mount Washington State Forest, which is accessible from Connecticut at **CT-41** (becoming MA-41). Travelers from the west can reach the park from **NY/MA-23.** A busier route to the east is **US-7,** which is the primary thoroughfare for this section of the trip.

Car

As the Appalachian Trail leaves the crowded suburbs of the New York

Best Accommodations

★ **Race Brook Lodge, Sheffield, Massachusetts:** You're bound to make a new friend or two on this huge campus with modern farmhouse rooms (page 336).

★ **Red Lion Inn, Stockbridge, Massachusetts:** This historic 18th-century inn with massive front porch is the definitive Berkshires lodging experience (page 341).

★ **Hotel on North, Pittsfield, Massachusetts:** The whimsy winks at you at this millennial-focused boutique hotel in the heart of Pittsfield (page 350).

★ **The Porches Inn, North Adams, Massachusetts:** Pair your eclectic Mass MoCA experience with a stay at this distinctive boutique (page 357).

★ **Safford Mills Inn and Café, Bennington, Vermont:** Skip the traditional bed-and-breakfast experience for this inn with complimentary drinks and dessert (page 364).

★ **The Equinox Golf Resort & Spa, Manchester, Vermont:** A destination hotel if there ever was one in this area, the Equinox provides access to hiking, a full-service spa, and an 18-hole golf course (page 369).

★ **Inn at Long Trail, Killington, Vermont:** Friendly to hikers and positioned next to an AT entrance, it has everything you need for recharging, including a cool pub (page 377).

metropolitan area, highways fade from sight, leaving only wide state routes where traffic is confined to one lane in each direction. The main route is **US-7,** which continues north from Connecticut toward Vermont and becomes the main artery through a number of Massachusetts towns. The speed limit will decrease quickly as it hits these communities, so be prepared to slow from 55 mph to 25 mph. After Pittsfield turn onto **MA-8,** which runs east of Mount Greylock and passes through Adams and North Adams. Turn west onto **MA-2** to hook back up with **US-7** and take that until an intersection with **VT-7A** in Bennington. VT-7A crosses into Manchester and Manchester Center before merging with **US-7** on a higher-speed route. In Rutland US-7 meets **US-4.** Take that east, passing Killington, Woodstock, and White River Junction. There, connect with **US-5,** turning north to Norwich.

Major highways in this region of the AT include **I-90,** also called the Massachusetts Turnpike (or Mass Pike) and running west to east through Stockbridge and Lee, and **I-91,** which shoots south to north along the Vermont-New Hampshire border and offers access to White River Junction and Norwich. It intersects with **I-89,** which comes in from the northwest and continues southeast toward Concord, New Hampshire.

Air

Western Massachusetts and southern Vermont aren't hubs for air travel. In fact, there are no commercial airports in western Massachusetts, and the closest is **Albany International Airport** (Albany Shaker Rd., Colonie, NY, 518/242-2200, www.albanyairport.com, ALB), which has 55 daily commercial arrivals and is accessible via I-90 from US-7 north. Albany provides bus service to Vermont via **Vermont Translines** (www.vttranslines.com).

Accessing Vermont is slightly easier: **Rutland-Southern Vermont Regional Airport** (1002 Airport Rd., North Clarendon, 802/786-8881, www.flyrutlandvt.com) provides daily access to Boston via Cape Air (800/227-3247). Take **The Bus** (www.thebus.com) from the airport to the city of Rutland, or to Manchester or Killington. Cape Air also services **Lebanon Municipal Airport** (5 Airpark Rd., West Lebanon, NH, 603/298-8878, www.lebanonnh.gov), which is a 3-mile (4.8-km) drive east of White River Junction. Cape Air at Lebanon flies passengers to and from Boston and White Plains, New York. Lebanon offers rental cars and bus service through **Advance Transit** (www.advancetransit.com), which takes passengers to White River Junction and Norwich.

Train

Amtrak (102 Railroad Row, 800/872-7245, www.amtrak.com) runs to White River Junction on the Vermonter line, which offers access south to New York, Philadelphia, and Washington DC.

Bus

You can take a **Peter Pan bus** (800/343-999, www.peterpanbus.com) from Albany, Boston, or Port Authority Bus Terminal in New York to Sheffield (105 Main St.); Peter Pan also stops in most towns along US-7 in Massachusetts. There is a **Greyhound connection in White River Junction** (44 Sykes Mountain Ave., 802/295-3011, www.greyhound.com) at the other end of the route. Travelers there can head to Boston, Montreal, or Hartford, Connecticut.

In Massachusetts, the **Berkshire Regional Transit Authority** (1 Columbus Ave., Pittsfield, 413/499-2782, www.berkshirerta.com, Mon.-Sat.) provides six-day-a-week service connecting Pittsfield to North Adams to the north, and Pittsfield to Lee to the south. From North Adams a shuttle takes passengers to Williamstown, while from Lee another route heads south to Great Barrington. BRTA also has a North Adams loop route.

You can do the entire Vermont route via **Vermont Translines** (844/888-7267, www.vttranslines.com, daily). With connection to Albany, the bus system hits Bennington, Manchester, and Rutland on the **North-South Vermont Bus Route,** and Rutland, Killington, Woodstock, and White River Junction on the **East-West Vermont Bus Route.** Its **Vermont Shires Connector** line starts at Albany International Airport and picks up passengers at both the Albany Greyhound Bus Terminal and Rensselaer Amtrak Station en route to Bennington and Manchester Center.

For a more regional experience, the **Marble Valley Regional Transit District** (102 West St., Rutland, 802/747-3502, www.thebus.com, daily) offers the Bus, white-and-red buses with a funky text logo. Routes emanate in Rutland and connect passengers to Killington to the east and Manchester to the south.

Fuel and Services

Because you're staying on major federal and state routes, you're never far from a gas station. Each town has at least one, with the larger towns and cities offering multiple options.

Dial 511 for reports on road conditions when in Massachusetts and Vermont. For emergency assistance, call 911.

Mount Washington State Forest and Bash Bish Falls

The intersection of eastern New York, southwestern Massachusetts, and northwestern Connecticut is a giant swath of wild forest that, thanks to the work of devoted volunteers and state officials, boasts an impressive network of trails leading to tempting peaks. In Massachusetts, this land includes **Mount Washington State Forest** and **Bash Bish Falls State Park,** along with the nearby Mount Everett State Reservation, which holds a section of the Appalachian Trail.

Bash Bish Falls gets the attention around here, seeing as it's the tallest waterfall in Massachusetts and highly accessible for anyone driving into the area. But while Bash Bish Falls State Park is just 424 acres and exists primarily for the waterfall, Mount Washington State Forest is more than 10 times larger and provides enough exploration for overnight hikers.

Getting There and Around

The rural CT-41, also known as Under Mountain Road, becomes MA-41 at the state border and snakes up the southwest corner of the state. It's an 8-mile (12.9-km) drive on MA-41 from the border to an intersection with Mount Washington Road. Turn left and take that toward the park. Go left at the fork with East Street and follow East for 3.2 miles (5.1 km) until an intersection with Cross Road. Turn right on Cross and then right again on West Street, following that to Falls Road. Turn there to enter Bash Bish Falls State Park.

For Mount Washington State Forest, go back the way you came on West Street and turn back onto Cross Road, taking that to East Street. Turn right onto East and the main parking area and forest headquarters will be on your left, as well as the trailhead for the Alander Mountain Trail. If you're not confident in your car's capabilities, know that portions of West Street aren't paved. To avoid the rocks, East Street, accessible from Mount Washington Road, is another option to reach forest headquarters. Overnight parking is permitted only at headquarters.

Sights

Having three brothers, I understand the feeling of being second (or third, or fourth) fiddle. Thus, I feel sympathy for whichever of the twin falls at **Bash Bish Falls** is producing less water. This varies, as the roaring Bash Bish Brook tumbles and cascades en route to a jutting boulder that splits the brook and creates the sibling rivalry. Regardless of your emotional attachment to the falls, you'll find Bash Bish a dramatic scene worthy of an entire series of photos. Keep in mind, however, that if you visit the falls in early summer, you'll be shooing people away from your field of vision. The falls are less crowded in early spring, and if ice has thawed, the falls will be rocking. Swimming and jumping aren't permitted at Bash Bish, and visitors to the falls have been seriously injured or killed in accidents there.

Hiking

Bash Bish Falls Trail

Distance: 1 mile (1.6 km)
Duration: 30 minutes
Elevation gain: 350 feet (107 m)
Difficulty: Easy to moderate
Trailhead: Upper falls parking lot for Bash Bish Falls (42.115043, -73.491467)

A hike made for waterfall tourists who want to feel adventurous, this 1-mile (1.6-km) romp down to the base of the falls and back up is slightly taxing but extremely manageable for just about everyone. From the parking area, follow the blue-blazed trail down some steep, rocky grade until your ears are filled with white noise. That'll be the falls appearing out of the clearing. After taking some time

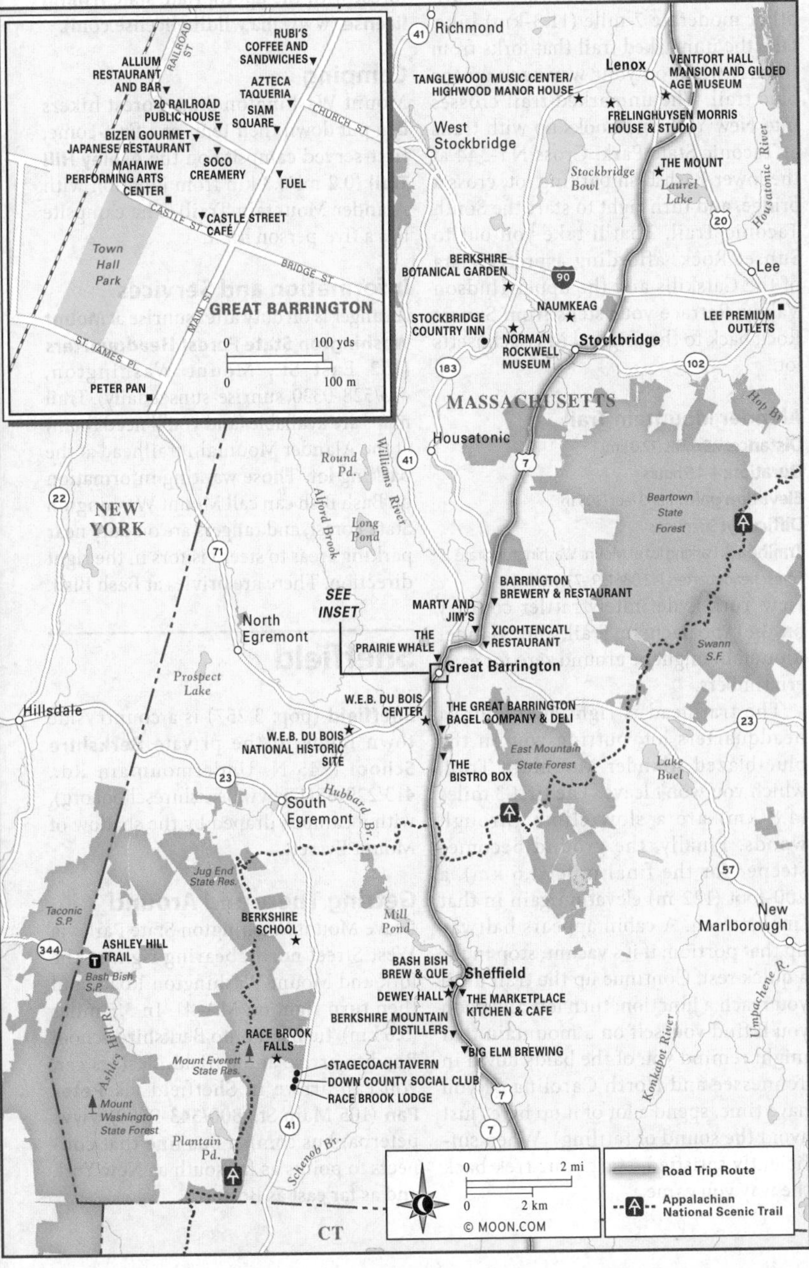
Mount Washington to Lenox
RUBI'S COFFEE AND SANDWICHES
ALLIUM RESTAURANT AND BAR
RAILROAD ST
AZTECA TAQUERIA
20 RAILROAD PUBLIC HOUSE
SIAM SQUARE
CHURCH ST
BIZEN GOURMET JAPANESE RESTAURANT
SOCO CREAMERY
MAHAIWE PERFORMING ARTS CENTER
FUEL
CASTLE ST
CASTLE STREET CAFÉ
Town Hall Park
BRIDGE ST
MAIN ST
GREAT BARRINGTON
ST JAMES PL
PETER PAN
100 yds
100 m
Richmond
Lenox
VENTFORT HALL MANSION AND GILDED AGE MUSEUM
TANGLEWOOD MUSIC CENTER/ HIGHWOOD MANOR HOUSE
FRELINGHUYSEN MORRIS HOUSE & STUDIO
West Stockbridge
Stockbridge Bowl
THE MOUNT
Laurel Lake
Housatonic River
BERKSHIRE BOTANICAL GARDEN
Lee
NAUMKEAG
LEE PREMIUM OUTLETS
STOCKBRIDGE COUNTRY INN
NORMAN ROCKWELL MUSEUM
Stockbridge
MASSACHUSETTS
Hop Br.
Housatonic
Round Pd.
Alford Brook
Williams River
Beartown State Forest
NEW YORK
Long Pond
BARRINGTON BREWERY & RESTAURANT
SEE INSET
MARTY AND JIM'S
North Egremont
THE PRAIRIE WHALE
XICOHTENCATL RESTAURANT
Swann S.F.
Great Barrington
Prospect Lake
Hillsdale
W.E.B. DU BOIS CENTER
THE GREAT BARRINGTON BAGEL COMPANY & DELI
W.E.B. DU BOIS NATIONAL HISTORIC SITE
East Mountain State Forest
THE BISTRO BOX
Lake Buel
South Egremont
Hubbard Br.
Jug End State Res.
Taconic S.P.
Mill Pond
New Marlborough
BERKSHIRE SCHOOL
ASHLEY HILL TRAIL
Bash Bish S.P.
BASH BISH BREW & QUE
Sheffield
DEWEY HALL
THE MARKETPLACE KITCHEN & CAFE
Umpachene R.
BERKSHIRE MOUNTAIN DISTILLERS
RACE BROOK FALLS
Konkapot River
BIG ELM BREWING
Ashley Hill R.
Mount Everett State Res.
STAGECOACH TAVERN
DOWN COUNTY SOCIAL CLUB
RACE BROOK LODGE
Mount Washington State Forest
Plantain Pd.
Schenob Br.
2 mi
2 km
© MOON.COM
Road Trip Route
Appalachian National Scenic Trail
CT

to admire Bash Bish, head back up the blue trail.

For the really adventurous, and another moderate 7-mile (11.3-km) hike, take the unmarked trail that forks from the left when on your way back up the blue trail. The unmarked trail crosses into New York and hooks up with trails at Taconic State Park. Cross NY-344 at the lower Bash Bish parking lot, cross a bridge, and turn right to start the South Taconic Trail. That'll take you out to Sunset Rock, affording a pretty vista of the Catskills and the upper Hudson Valley. Retrace your steps from Sunset Rock back to the original Massachusetts lot.

Alander Mountain Trail

Distance: 7.5 miles (12.0 km)
Duration: 4-4.5 hours
Elevation gain: 1,000 feet (305 m)
Difficulty: Strenuous
Trailhead: Parking lot at Mount Washington State Forest headquarters (42.086159, -73.462114)

New York is definitely rattler country on the Appalachian Trail, and Alander Mountain might be ground zero for eastern timbers.

The trailhead is right at the forest headquarters lot, putting you on the blue-blazed Alander Mountain Trail, which you won't leave. The first 3 miles (4.8 km) are a slow climb through woods. Finally, the ground becomes steeper for the final mile (1.6 km), a 400-foot (122-m) elevation gain in that final stretch. A cabin appears halfway up that portion; if it's vacant, stop in for a quick rest. Continue up the trail until you reach a junction; turn left and soon you'll find yourself on a mountain that might remind you of the balds down in Tennessee and North Carolina. If you have time, spend a lot of it up here (just avoid the sound of rattling). When sufficiently satisfied, start your trek back the way you came.

Fishing

Freshwater fishing is permitted in the forest with the appropriate state **fishing license** (www.ma.wildlifelicense.com).

Camping

Mount Washington State Forest hikers can put down their tents at a first-come, first-served campsite on the **Ashley Hill Trail** (0.2 mi/0.3 km from junction with Alander Mountain Trail). The campsite has a five-person limit.

Information and Services

A ranger is on duty after sunrise at **Mount Washington State Forest Headquarters** (162 East St., Mount Washington, 413/528-0330, sunrise-sunset daily). Trail maps are available (and you'll need them) at the Alander Mountain trailhead at the parking lot. Those wanting information on Bash Bish can call Mount Washington State Forest, and rangers are on duty near parking areas to steer visitors in the right direction. There are privies at Bash Bish.

Sheffield

Sheffield (pop. 3,257) is a countryside town home to the private **Berkshire School** (245 N. Undermountain Rd., 413/229-8511, www.berkshireschool.org), with a campus draped by the shadow of Mount Everett.

Getting There and Around

Leave Mount Washington State Park via West Street north, bearing right at the fork and Mount Washington Road, and then turn right on MA-41. In 3.5 miles (5.6 km), turn left onto Berkshire School Road to arrive at Sheffield. Besides car, you can arrive in Sheffield via **Peter Pan** (105 Main St., 800/343-9999, www.peterpanbus.com), a bus line that connects to points as far south as New York and as far east as Boston.

Sights

It's unusual that a historic space in the Northeast has had just one use its entire life, but that's the story with **Dewey Hall** (91 Main St., 413/229-2357, www.deweyhall.com). Built in the 1880s to honor the life of Unitarian minister Rev. Orville Dewey, the commanding fieldstone and marble structure was meant to be a community gathering space, hosting meetings and cultural events. When I walked into Dewey on a Saturday morning in the fall, a community group was using the space to host a meeting.

Hiking

Race Brook Falls is actually five waterfalls ambling down a long hill that you can climb. Part of **Mount Everett State Reservation** (143 East St., Mount Washington), the falls are accessible from a parking area off MA-41. Take Berkshire School Road west from US-7 until the intersection with MA-41; turn left and drive 2 miles (3.2 km) to the parking area.

Race Brook Falls to Mount Everett

Distance: 4.8 miles (7.7 km)
Duration: 4-5 hours
Elevation gain: 1,800 feet (549 m)
Difficulty: Strenuous
Trailhead: Parking area off MA-41 (42.089800, -73.411097)

The Race Brook Trail starts at the parking area and soon meets up with Race Brook. A trail to the right appears 0.8 mile (1.3 km) in; detour that way to glimpse the lower falls, then head back to the main trail, which begins an ascent to a second fork. Turn right here, then left, and you'll reach the second, third, and fourth falls. At a junction, go left and find the fifth falls. You can continue farther to reach the Appalachian Trail, which after a 1.8-mile (2.9-km) walk north (to the right) reaches a scenic viewpoint at the summit of Mount Everett.

Top to bottom: Bish Bash Falls; Dewey Hall; Great Barrington.

Breweries

A local brew can be had at **Big Elm Brewing** (65 Silver St., 413/229-2348, www.bigelmbeer.com, noon-6pm Thurs.-Sat., under $20), where a couple who met at Pennsylvania's Victory Brewing Company concocts session-friendly ales. There are free tours on Saturdays, plus pints and cans to go.

Complete your Sheffield craft crawl at **Berkshire Mountain Distillers** (356 Main St., 413/229-0219, www.berkshiremountaindistillers.com, noon-4pm Mon.-Thurs., noon-5pm Fri. and Sun., 11am-5pm Sat., under $20), an original in the local spirits movement making bourbon, gin, rum, vodka, and whiskey. Distillery tours ($10) are conducted at noon Friday and Saturday.

Food and Accommodations

Schoolchildren and professionals alike may be found at **The Marketplace Kitchen and Café** (18 Elm Ct., 413/248-5040, www.marketplacekitchen.com, 7am-7pm Mon.-Sat., 9am-4pm Sun., under $20), where the smell of fresh-cut bacon and baked goods will draw anyone into this beige, unassuming café offering healthy options.

For something indulgent, **Bash Bish Brew & Que** (113 Main St., 413/248-1187, www.bashbishbrewnque.com, 5pm-9pm Mon. and Wed., noon-9pm Thurs., noon-9:30pm Fri.-Sun., under $40) slathers Carolina-style barbecue sauce on dishes like pulled pork and brisket. They also do pizza, and an order of loaded fries is sure to pair well with your beer.

As an introduction to the Berkshires, the **Ramblewood Inn** (400 S. Undermountain Rd., 413/229-3363, www.ramblewood-inn.com, $130-225) fits the bill. Not only are rooms named after the mountains you'll need to summit while in the area, but this log-cabin chalet features homey rooms with frilly touches. Its Taconic and Washington rooms share a bathroom. For families with children age eight or older, the inn has a two-room efficiency suite with full kitchen.

One mile (1.6 km) south, ★ **Race Brook Lodge** (864 S. Undermountain Rd., 413/229-2916, www.rblodge.com, $100-350) is an expansive facility with 32 rooms across six buildings. The rooms are decidedly less frilly, a perfect balance of modern amenities and farmhouse chic. Its **Stagecoach Tavern** (854 S. Undermountain Rd., 413/229-8585, 5pm-9pm Thurs.-Sun.) serves up a farm-to-table menu that changes by the week, and its on-site concert venue the **Down County Social Club** is a warm place to hear foot-stompin' rock, folk, and bluegrass.

MA-183: East Mountain State Forest

As the Appalachian Trail lumbers through the Berkshires toward the miniscule town of **Tyringham** (pop. 327), it reaches the shoulder of East Mountain in **East Mountain State Forest.**

Hiking

East Mountain Trail

Distance: 2.8 miles (4.5 km)
Duration: 3 hours
Elevation gain: 720 feet (219 m)
Difficulty: Strenuous
Trailhead: Parking area off MA-41 (42.089800, -73.411097)

Nowhere near as popular as Mount Everett and Mount Greylock, East Mountain is a gem of a find, a knock-it-out climb with a challenge. Starting at the Appalachian Trail crossing at Home Road, head east (north on the trail) into dense forest and begin an arduous hour of hiking. You're doing a little more than 700 feet (213 m) in just 1.4 miles (2.3 km) of frequently rugged, rocky ground. When you level out, you'll get fantastic views of the Taconics.

For a larger challenge, continue on the AT to Ice Gulch. You'll pass the well-kept **Tom Leonard lean-to shelter.** Just beyond that is the impressive gulch that often has sheets of ice, even in summer. Head back the way you came on the AT for a 7-mile (11.3-km) up-and-back.

Great Barrington

Just 6.4 miles (10.3 km) north from Sheffield, US-7 opens up to a wide thoroughfare in the heart of **Great Barrington** (pop. 7,104). This charming town checks off all the boxes: cute, white-trimmed boutiques, three-fork farm-to-table hideaways for fashionably dressed weekenders, and surprisingly stunning views of mountains that peek over the brick buildings that line Main Street. Weekends in the summer and especially the fall find Great Barrington crowded with jovial tourists excited to drink in the Berkshires. As with many of these Massachusetts towns, recreation is linked to hiking the mountains nearby, with **Monument Mountain** getting the most play by far.

Getting There and Around

The **Peter Pan** (362 Main St., 800/343-9999, www.peterpanbus.com) line stops in Great Barrington and connects to points as far south as New York and as far east as Boston. The **Berkshire Regional Transit Authority** (413/499-2782, www.berkshirerta.com, Mon.-Sat.) runs on US-7 and continues north to Lee.

Sights

Born in Great Barrington in 1868, civil rights pioneer W. E. B. DuBois is memorialized at the **W. E. B. DuBois National Historic Site** (612 S. Egremont Rd., 413/717-6259, www.duboisnhs.org, tours 11am, 1pm, 2pm Saturdays June 30-Sept. 1, free). In the summer, docents lead walks on an interpretive trail at the site of his boyhood home. Nearby, the **DuBois Center at Great Barrington** (684 S. Main St., 413/644-9595) exhibits documents written by DuBois while educating about social justice and equity. It abuts the Mahaiwe Cemetery, the final resting place for the DuBois family, though W. E. B. himself is buried in Ghana.

Performing Arts

Like many theaters in small towns across the Northeast, the **Mahaiwe Performing Arts Center** (14 Castle St., 413/528-0100, www.mahaiwe.org) transformed from performing house to movie theater before finding itself on the edge of closure and, subsequently, being saved and reopening as a performing house. The Mahaiwe hosts national acts like the Beach Boys and live Metropolitan Opera feeds.

Food and Nightlife

American

People wait in line for hours to get grub from ★ **The Bistro Box** (937 S. Main St., 413/717-5958, www.thebistrobox.rocks, 11am-4pm Sun.-Tues., 11am-7pm Thurs.-Sat., under $25). The scent of fatty meat from the back of this roadside food truck is enough of an incentive to do so. Sourcing from local farms, Bistro Box cooks up pub fare, sandwiches, burgers, hot dogs, and ice cream floats. Customers can enjoy their meals at the eatery's vast garden with picnic tables and lawn games. Bistro Box is open until it's too cold to run the truck.

If you like ample patio seating, a worn-in dining room with elegant bar area, and New American fare with innovative cocktails, head to **The Prairie Whale** (178 Main St., 413/528-5050, 5pm-10pm Mon. and Thurs.-Fri., 11am-3pm and 5pm-10pm Sat.-Sun., under $30 brunch, under $60 dinner). This comfortable spot isn't afraid to serve rib eye with foie gras butter next to old-fashioned fried chicken and corn bread.

In line with the thrown-together chic character of the town, **Allium Restaurant and Bar** (42-44 Railroad St., 413/528-2118, www.alliumberkshires.com, 5pm-9:30pm Sun.-Thurs., 5pm-1am Fri.-Sat., under $50) does farm-to-table in a space befitting Manhattan with urban rusticity and an open kitchen. Shared plates like fish tacos sit alongside bigger stuff like good ol' roast chicken.

The pre- and post-theater crowd might be found at **Castle Street Café** (10 Castle St., 413/528-5244, www.castlestreetcafe.com, 5pm-9:30pm Sun.-Mon. and Wed.-Thurs., 5pm-10:30pm Fri.-Sat., under $50), a moody hardwood joint specializing in big-ticket bistro classics like crab cake and mushroom risotto.

Joining the brick-and-chestnut vibe of the local farm-to-table scene, **20 Railroad Public House** (20 Railroad St., 413/528-9345, www.20railroadpublichouse.com, 5pm-10pm Mon.-Fri. and 11:30am-3pm, 5pm-10pm Sat.-Sun., under $30 brunch, under $50 dinner) tries fun dishes like ramen bowls, fried chicken biscuits, and poutine, and keeps an exciting, rotating beer list.

Marty and Jim's (109 Stockbridge Rd., 413/528-9720, www.martyandjims.com, 11am-9pm Mon.-Sat., noon-6pm Sun., under $15) is a bare-bones, lime-tinged local favorite for a hearty sandwich with a side of dill pickles.

English-style brews meet a weathered, down-home aesthetic at **Barrington Brewery & Restaurant** (420 Stockbridge Rd., 413/528-8282, www.barringtonbrewery.net, 11:30am-9:30pm Mon.-Thurs., 11:30am-10pm Fri.-Sat., 11:30am-9pm Sun.). In fact, the beer is so traditional that you may not believe the brewery is nearly completely solar powered. The restaurant offers ribs, sausages, and other beer-friendly fare.

Asian

The popular **Bizen Gourmet Japanese Restaurant and Sushi Bar** (17 Railroad St., 413/528-4343, noon-9:30pm Mon.-Fri., noon-10pm Sat.-Sun., under $30) is an expansive space with massive lunch and dinner menus. Around the corner, **Siam Square** (290 Main St., 413/644-9119, www.siamsqaures.com, 11:30am-10pm Mon.-Fri., noon-11pm Sat., noon-10pm Sun., under $30) has great Thai curry dishes.

Mexican

The mole poblano is one of the many authentic specialties at **Xicohtencatl Restaurant** (50 Stockbridge Rd., 413/528-2002, www.xicohmexicano.com, 4pm-9pm Sun.-Thurs., noon-10:30pm Fri.-Sat., under $20), a warm, bold-colored Mexican restaurant emphasizing spice. Outdoor seating is available.

Casual

The bagels are hot and fresh at the **Great Barrington Bagel Company & Deli** (777 Main St., 413/528-9055, www.gbbagel.com, 6:30am-4pm Mon.-Fri., 7am-4:30pm Sat., 7:30am-4pm Sun., under $20). Line up and order your favorite bagel sandwich, or just pile on the lox. Tables are typically taken quickly at **Fuel Coffee Shop** (293 Main St., 413/528-5505, www.fuelgreatbarrington.com, 7am-6pm Mon.-Tues., 7am-10pm Wed.-Sat., 8am-6pm Sun., under $15 breakfast, under $25 lunch, under $35 dinner), a homey, industrial-chic café with the usual brunch suspects, burgers and pad thai for dinner, and strong coffee. Finally, **Rubi's Coffee and Sandwiches** (264 Main St., 413/528-0488, www.rubiners.com, 7am-6pm Mon.-Fri., 8am-6pm Sat., 8am-5pm Sun., under $20) is distinctively turtleneck-sharp with a fireplace and exposed brick facing. It does cheese really well, so line up for a grilled cheese sandwich.

Ice Cream

I have tasted ice cream nirvana, and it's Dirty Chocolate. Ice cream junkies have to hit the primary location for ★ **SoCo Creamery** (5 Railroad St., 413/644-9866, www.sococreamery.com, noon-9pm Sun.-Thurs., noon-10pm Fri.-Sat., under $10), the region's top draw for the sweet stuff, and try its signature multilayered chocolate flavor. SoCo serves a bunch of great styles in its checkerboard, moo-cow shop, but Dirty Chocolate is worthy of placement in my imagined Ice Cream Hall of Fame.

Monument Mountain

The open-space preserve of **Monument Mountain,** just 4.1 miles (6.6 km) north of Great Barrington and reached via US-7, is managed by the Trustees of Reservations, a land-conservation nonprofit established more than 100 years ago. Its major attraction is Squaw Peak, a collection of rocks surrounded by pine trees and boasting a 360-degree view of Berkshire County. Most people who hike Monument Mountain do so to reach Squaw Peak, and because the area is well preserved and advertised, it gets pretty busy.

As for the name? "The mountain where the hapless maiden died is called the Mountain of the Monument," wrote William Cullen Bryant in his poem "Monument Mountain." This 1815 poem tells the story of a woman's alleged suicide by jumping from Squaw Peak. Years later it would be a picnicking spot for Nathaniel Hawthorne and Herman Melville, a place that allegedly inspired Melville's *Moby-Dick*. History, beauty, and wild legend are just some of the reasons Monument Mountain remains very popular.

Monument Mountain Trail

Distance: 2.9 miles (4.7 km)
Duration: 2 hours
Elevation gain: 720 feet (219 m)
Difficulty: Moderate
Trailhead: US-7, 4.1 miles/6.6 kilometers north of Great Barrington (42.242869, -73.335200)

Monument Mountain gets plenty of foot traffic during the warmer months, something that the Trustees of Reservations has figured out: There's a $5 parking fee at the trailhead lot. Take it from me, however: You will get your money's worth at Monument Mountain.

From the trailhead you can choose between the 1.5-mile (2.4-km) Indian Monument Trail and the 0.83-mile (1.3-km) Hickey Trail. The former is less strenuous but takes slightly more time. The latter quickly ascends a steep grade, with irregular hikers stopping periodically for water and a breath. Both trails run into the red-blazed Squaw Peak Trail, which runs along the summit of Monument Mountain. The best views are at a distinctive rock outcrop that offers views of nearby hills and valleys. Light scrambling gets you to the money spot. You can go back the way you came or continue the loop; either way, the total distance comes in at less than 3 miles (4.8 km).

Stockbridge

The warehouse-sized tour bus is a regular mode of transportation for folks visiting **Stockbridge** (pop. 1,947), which is home to well-trod historical sites and arguably the most famous inn of the Berkshires. Fall is especially busy here, as the leaf peepers descend on Stockbridge for long weekends of walking, dining, and learning a bit about Norman Rockwell. But no fall event may be more celebrated in Stockbridge than the arrest of a couple of young hoodlums who threw garbage down a cliff after a Thanksgiving meal at a local diner. OK, that's the fictional story of "Alice's Restaurant," the popular song by Arlo Guthrie. But Guthrie was spot-on: Stockbridge is a town of freshly cleaned sidewalks and gentle gossip. It looks great on a postcard.

Getting There and Around

The **Peter Pan** (approx. 35 Main St., 800/343-9999, www.peterpanbus.com) line stops in Stockbridge and offers connection points as far south as New York and as far east as Boston. The **Berkshire**

Regional Transit Authority (413/499-2782, www.berkshirerta.com, Mon.-Sat.) runs on US-7 and continues north to Lee.

Sights

Naumkeag

Designed to be a summer getaway for Joseph Choate's family in the 1800s, **Naumkeag** (5 Prospect Hill Rd., 413/298-8138, 10am-5pm daily in summer, 10am-5pm weekends Apr.-May, 11am-4pm weekends Oct.-Nov., $15 adults, free ages 12 and younger) is a 44-room country estate sitting on 48 acres and symbolizing the Gilded Age's impact on the Berkshires. While the house with its numerous gabled roofs is impressive and boasts original furniture, the property's gardens get more of the acclaim. Curated by landscape architect Fletcher Steele and family member Mabel Choate, the gardens are surprising, with curved pathways and colorful posts and benches. A must-see is the Blue Steps, whose arched railings and fountains create an inviting yet regal pathway.

Norman Rockwell Museum

Showcasing more than 700 paintings, drawings, and studies by the master, the **Norman Rockwell Museum** (9 Glendale Rd., 413/298-4100, www.nrm.org, 10am-5pm daily May-Oct., 10am-4pm weekdays and 10am-5pm weekends Nov.-Apr., $10-20 adults, children free) has the world's largest catalog of Rockwell's works. Inside the stately white structure, visitors can peruse a deep collection of *Saturday Evening Post* covers and see up close Rockwell's Four Freedoms paintings, which symbolize American values in the mid-20th century.

On the museum grounds is the Stockbridge studio Rockwell used until his death in 1978, open for visitors from May to October. The museum moved the structure from its original location to a rolling hillside that overlooks the Housatonic River valley. The grounds,

view from Monument Mountain

which are dotted by sculptures by Rockwell's son Peter, can be explored by visitors. The Terrace Café is part of the museum and is open during the high summer season.

Berkshire Botanical Garden

Over 15 acres and with thousands of native floral species, the **Berkshire Botanical Garden** (5 W. Stockbridge Rd., 413/298-3926, www.berkshirebotanical.org, 9am-5pm daily summer, $12-15) offers hours of wandering enjoyment. Its defining event is the fall **Harvest Festival** (Oct.), which pulls in about 15,000 visitors over two weekend days.

Food

There's surprisingly slim pickings in Stockbridge. **Once Upon a Table** (36 Main St., 413/298-3870, www.onceuponatablebistro.com, 11:30am-3pm and 5pm-8pm Sun.-Thurs., 11:30am-3pm and 5pm-8:30pm Fri.-Sat., lunch under $30, dinner under $60) is most prominent, serving classic northeastern dishes like roasted duck and rainbow trout in a cozy, beige bistro setting. **Stockbridge Coffee & Tea** (6 Elm St., 413/931-7044, www.stockbridgecoffeeandtea.com, 7am-5pm daily, under $10) is good for a jolt while also providing baked goods and quiches. Its small, gently used bookstore specializes in fiction and philosophy. For grab-and-go or counter service, try the **Elm Street Market** (4 Elm St., 413/298-3634, www.elmstreetmarket.com, 6am-7pm daily, breakfast under $12, lunch under $15), which puts together a solid breakfast sandwich and, for lunch, features the Senator, a roast beef-and-horseradish mayo sando.

Accommodations

From the front porch of the massive ★ **Red Lion Inn** (30 Main St., 413/298-5545, www.redlioninn.com, $125-250), you can breathe in centuries of history. The structure dates back to 1773, and while fires destroyed some parts and ownership has made changes, the inn still offers a window into New England's past. The Lincoln Table at the center of the lobby was first placed at the inn during the 19th century. The inn's 137 teapots also date to the 1800s. The property's 125 rooms, with everything from doubles and twins to queens and kings, are decorated in American Victorian finery reflective of the mid-19th century.

Downstairs the Red Lion Inn is a whirl of activity, mostly centered on the main dining room, where chefs cook up the special native turkey and bake warm apple pie. The Widow Bingham Tavern is more casual, offering the dining room menu plus a few pub-style additions, a full bar, and brick walls decorated with framed photographs and wicker baskets. Outside the inn and down the stairs, the discrete Lion's Den is a cheery hangout with a bar menu and nightly live music.

The circa 1856 Federal house that's now the **Stockbridge Country Inn** (26 Glendale Rd., 413/298-4015, www.

stockbridgecountryinn.com, $229-349) offers eight rooms and suites decorated with pretty patterned wallpaper, four-poster beds, and Victorian-style furniture. The inn serves a full breakfast that may include pancakes, steel-cut oatmeal, or bacon and eggs. Breakfast can be enjoyed on the porch in warmer months, and the inn also has a heated pool.

There are five rooms at **1862 Seasons on Main** (47 Main St., 413/298-5419, www.seasonsonmain.com, $189-395), called Spring, Summer, Fall, Winter, and All Seasons. Creativity aside, these Victorian-style rooms are a bit busier and homelier than at the Country Inn, but still comfortable. Breakfast is served daily, and the inn has an ice cream social nightly.

Lenox

Take US-7 6.6 miles (10.6 km) north from Stockbridge, or MA-20 a short 4 miles (6.4 km) from Lee, to reach **Lenox** (pop. 5,025), where the buttoned-down shirts are just a little crisper. This is a big-money town, full of highly rated restaurants with long waits and stately colonial homes with vast front lawns. It's also home to **Tanglewood Music Center,** a premier entertainment venue attracting plenty of summer tourism.

Getting There and Around

The **Peter Pan** (5 Walker St., 800/343-9999, www.peterpanbus.com) line stops in Lenox and offers connection points as far south as New York and as far east as Boston. The **Berkshire Regional Transit Authority** (413/499-2782, www.berkshirerta.com, Mon.-Sat.) stops on Walker Street on a route between Pittsfield and Great Barrington.

Sights

Ventfort Hall Mansion and Gilded Age Museum

Get the full Gilded Age education at **Ventfort Hall Mansion and Gilded Age Museum** (104 Walker St., 413/637-3206, www.gildedage.org, 10am-4pm Mon.-Sat., 10am-3pm Sun., $7-18), which is both a period estate built in the late 19th century and a comprehensive venue for understanding the importance of this era of American history.

The estate, finished in 1893 as a summer home for cousins turned lovers George and Sarah Morgan (sister of J. P. Morgan), is made of brick and brownstone and offers views of Monument Mountain. After being saved by locals, Ventfort Hall became a museum of the Gilded Age, with the first floor open to the public and showcasing rotating exhibits on the wealthy socialites of the early 20th century. Frequent events include lectures, concerts, and dinner parties.

★ Tanglewood Music Center

Drawing in hundreds of thousands of visitors annually, the open-air amphitheater

of **Tanglewood Music Center** (297 West St., 413/637-5180, www.bso.org, seasonal) is the centerpiece of entertainment in the Berkshires. Tanglewood (located in both Lenox and Stockbridge) was founded in 1940 as a training ground for orchestral performers under the guidance of the acclaimed Boston Symphony Orchestra. With fellowships and concerts, Tanglewood to this day remains a place where gifted young musicians grow with guidance from masters, but it's also a place where folkies, rock stars, jazz vocalists, and actors play for typically sold-out crowds enjoying a cool summer evening.

Big events happen at the Koussevitzky Music Shed, with acts ranging from Broadway superstar Audra McDonald to music legend James Taylor (he's there practically every year) to live broadcasts of *A Prairie Home Companion*. Boston University orchestral students perform at Tanglewood after an intense summer in the Berkshires, and of course, the BSO performs during the summer.

Besides concession stands and an on-site beer garden, Tanglewood features the Tanglewood Café and Grill for made-to-order foods, and the buffet-only **Highwood Manor House** (413/637-4486, dinner Fri.-Sat. and brunch Sun. during season, $65 dinner, $45 brunch, reservations required).

Frelinghuysen Morris House & Studio

Situated in an area filled with Gilded Age enormity, the **Frelinghuysen Morris House & Studio** (92 Hawthorne St., 413/637-0166, www.frelinghuysen.org, 10am-3pm Thurs.-Sun. June-Oct., $7.50-15) is a breath of contemporary air. Modeled after the white-walled European studios of the early 20th century, the Frelinghuysen Morris studio is clean and emphasizes light and space. Its adjoining house, built later, showcases mid-century modern furniture and a clean layout. Art by Pablo Picasso, among other modern masters, can be

the Tanglewood Music Center

found in the house, which hosts tours when open.

The Mount

Edith Wharton broke out from a socialite existence and became one of America's first great female writers during the early 20th century. Early in her career, she bought land in Lenox and designed **The Mount** (2 Plunkett St., 413/551-5111, www.edithwharton.org, 11am-4pm Sat.-Sun., $10-18), a sprawling estate with Italian gardens, that reflects her talents as a writer, designer, gardener, and hostess.

Visitors can walk the grounds and through the house. There are guided house tours year-round and garden tours during the warmer months, and in the fall there's a ghost tour. Private library tours ($150 for two people) are also offered, and the Mount also features exhibits on early 20th-century Lenox and World War I.

Food and Nightlife

If you're looking for a superior meal in the Berkshires, hone in on Lenox, and especially Church Street. I'll start with ★ **Nudel** (37 Church St., 413/551-7183, www.nudelrestaurant.com, 5pm-9pm Sun.-Thurs., 5pm-9:30pm Fri.-Sat., small plates $12, large plates $26, reservations suggested), a shoebox with an open kitchen concentrating on small plates and whatever's fresh from the farms. The menu changes all the time, but you'll typically find out where exactly the ingredients originated.

Alta (35 Church St., 413/637-0003, www.altawinebar.com, 11:30am-2:30pm lunch daily, 5pm-9pm dinner Sun.-Thurs., 5pm-10pm dinner Fri.-Sat., lunch around $25, dinner around $40, reservations suggested) features Mediterranean, mixing French, Italian, and Greek, sometimes in one dish, and has a robust wine list. Alta has a farmhouse-chic dining room and covered patio that's typically bustling for dinner.

You could double down on French at **Bistro Zinc** (56 Church St., 413/637-8800, www.bistrozinc.com, 11:30am-3pm lunch daily, 5:30pm-10pm dinner daily, lunch around $20, dinner around $40, reservations suggested), which does trout meuniere and boeuf bourguignon in a large, bright bistro space with large windows and shutters.

For something slightly more casual, **Firefly Gastropub** (71 Church St., 413/637-2700, www.fireflylenox.com, 5pm-9:30pm Wed.-Sun., around $40) combines classed-up pub grub like wings and nachos with surf and turf in a lounge-like setting. The restaurant's circular bar is a highlight.

Just around the corner from Church Street, **Brava** (27 Housatonic St., 413/637-9171, www.bravalenox.com, 5pm-1am daily, around $40) gets packed on weekend nights, and that's noticeable because it's tiny. But its staggering beer and wine lists pull people in, and they'll stay for tapas aplenty, inventive cheese and charcuterie plates, and craft pizzas.

More locals may be found at the **Olde Heritage Tavern** (12 Housatonic St., 413/637-0884, 11:30am-9pm Sun.-Thurs., 11:30am-10pm Fri.-Sat., bar open until 12:30am, around $25), where the bar scene is hoppin' and the food includes steaks, salmon, sandwiches, and easy grub like fried pickles and a basket of pub fries.

Accommodations

Inside a colonial with large front porch, the **Birchwood Inn** (7 Hubbard St., 800/524-1646, www.birchwood-inn.com, $209-399) is peak Berkshire bed-and-breakfast. Large rooms, most outfitted with cute wallpaper and complementary rugs, hold queens and kings with Victorian furnishings.

For fewer frills than a Berkshire boutique hotel, the **Yankee Inn** (461 Pittsfield Rd., 413/499-3700, www.yankeeinn.com, $86-200) is a converted motor lodge of two renovated buildings. The Main Building includes the hotel's three fireplace suites, furnished with king canopy beds, as well a cocktail lounge and indoor pool. For warm-weather travelers there's also a heated outdoor pool. The South Building feels more like a motel, but the more economical rooms here have also been renovated.

A roaring fireplace in a classy lounge sets the stage at the **Kemble Inn** (2 Kemble St., 413/637-4113, $150-300), a Gilded Age mansion turned luxury hotel with an attached restaurant, **Table Six Restaurant** (www.tablesixrestaurant.com, 5pm-9pm Fri.-Sun. dinner, 11:30am-2:30pm Sun. brunch, under $50 dinner, under $30 brunch).

With rooms in three buildings dating back at least 150 years, the **Cornell Inn** (203 Main St., 413/637-4800, www.cornellbb.com, $140-250) delivers on the New England charm. Its rooms are quirky, combining Victorian with country with motor lodge, and often smaller, but for the price they are relatively good options.

October Mountain State Forest

From the center of Lenox, take Walker Street southeast and cross the Housatonic River, then make a sharp left onto Willow Hill Road to reach the entrance of **October Mountain State Forest** (317 Woodland Rd., Lee, 413/243-1778), the largest state forest in Massachusetts at 16,500 acres. The Appalachian Trail enters the forest after crossing I-90 and runs through its eastern end. There's one AT shelter in the forest, the October Mountain Shelter, coming after a relatively arduous run of climbs among some of the state's taller peaks, including Becket Mountain (2,200 ft/671 m) and Walling Mountain (2,220 ft/677 m).

But what about the titular mountain? October Mountain stands at 1,948 feet (594 m) and was coined by author Herman Melville, who enjoyed the fall view of the plateau from his home. But the most interesting hike here isn't of a mountain, but of Finerty Pond, which is a nice place for AT hikers to cool off before hitting the shelter.

Hiking

Finerty Pond via Appalachian Trail

Distance: 5.5 miles (8.9 km)
Duration: 3 hours
Elevation gain: 740 feet (226 m)
Difficulty: Moderate
Trailhead: Parking lot on MA-20

This is a straight-ahead lumber up the AT, with elevation rising quickly from the parking lot (you'll gain about 700 ft/213 m in 1.3 mi/2.1 km) before reaching a ridge. Both Beckett and Walling Mountains peak by this ridge, so you'll be about 2,200 feet (671 m) up at this point. After about 2 miles (3.2 km) you'll begin descending gradually off the ridge, quickly reaching Finerty Pond. The AT hugs the southern shore of the pond before retreating into the woods. In summer you'll see plenty of mountain laurel pondside. After taking in the view and maybe a dip, turn around on the AT. For extra work, continue on the AT another 5 miles (8 km) to reach the shelter; either way, go back to your car on the AT.

Recreation

There's a substantial population of bass swimming about at the October Mountain Reservoir, and fishing is permitted in the ponds and brooks across the forest. The forest also permits ATV riding, as there's a fair number of multi-use trails large enough to handle bigger toys. Those who dislike the noise of dirt bikes, may wish to stay away, but for those who love ripping it up, the forest's muddy terrain makes for a tempting challenge.

Camping

The **campground** ($17, May-Oct.), which is a 0.2-mile (0.3-km) jaunt from the forest headquarters, has 47 campsites with pets permitted. There are flush toilets on-site, plus accommodations for both RVs and tents.

Pittsfield

Defining **Pittsfield** (pop. 42,591) is difficult, especially considering who you ask. Longtime and former residents are likely to bemoan the Berkshires' largest city as a boring, gray blot that still feels the sting of General Electric's exodus over the last many decades. But step inside a trendy hotel or dimly lit resto and you'll get a different story: Pittsfield is coming back. It's the new frontier for younger city dwellers looking for a challenging place to settle down or invest in a new business. There's plenty of new development in the downtown, but there are still a lot of shuttered buildings and low- to middle-income housing a short walk from big-money theaters and hipster cafes. It's definitely not boring, but it's also definitely not Brooklyn.

Pittsfield also may be the birthplace of baseball. The earliest known reference to baseball was found in a city bylaw authored in 1791, a document available through the **Berkshire Athenaeum** (1 Wendell Ave., 413/499-9480, www.pittsfieldlibrary.org, 9am-9pm Mon.-Thurs., 9am-5pm Fri., 10am-5pm Sat.), the circa 1876 public library of the city.

Getting There and Around

Pittsfield is at the intersection of US-7 and MA-9, but the closest interstate access is south in Lee, where I-90 can be picked up.

Pittsfield has a major bus station, the Joseph Scelsi Intermodal Transportation Center (1 Columbus Ave.). There you can hop on a **Peter Pan** (800/343-9999, www.peterpanbus.com) bus, which runs up and down US-7. Peter Pan provides routes to Albany, Boston, and New York City. For regional access, the **Berkshire Regional Transit Authority** (413/499-2782, www.berkshirerta.com, Mon.-Sat.) has routes that run south to Lee, then Great Barrington, and north to North Adams, then Williamstown.

Sights

A window in the 2nd-floor library at **Arrowhead** (780 Holmes Rd., 413/442-1793, www.mobydick.org, 10am-5pm daily May-Oct., free) offers an unobstructed view of Mount Greylock, which to Herman Melville was shaped like a whale. That inspired his *Moby-Dick,* the great American novel. Melville's former residence is now home to the Berkshire Historical Society, which has restored much of the house to its circa 1850 look and hosts a single guided tour every Saturday and Sunday ($8-15); otherwise you can tour on your own.

Arrowhead is also part of the **Melville Trail,** which isn't an actual walking trail, but a collection of sights connected to the author. Among them are Mount Greylock, October Mountain State Forest, and Monument Mountain.

There's a little bit for everyone at the **Berkshire Museum** (39 South St., 413/443-7171, www.berkshiremuseum.org, 10am-5pm Mon.-Sat., noon-5pm Sun., $6-13), which crams a range of disciplines into one Greek-influenced structure. There's a collection of fossils, rocks, and minerals, a deep dive into local wildlife called *Berkshire Backyard,* an aquarium, and a wealth of fine art, including Norman Rockwell paintings, that was the subject of a 2017 controversy (the museum wanted to sell the art to solve budgetary problems but received enormous pushback from the collecting world). Check out the Feigenbaum Hall of Innovation, which showcases creations and milestones related to the Berkshires, from the precursor to the transformer to the rope tow gripper. Daily events at the museum include film screenings, children's workshops, and artist talks.

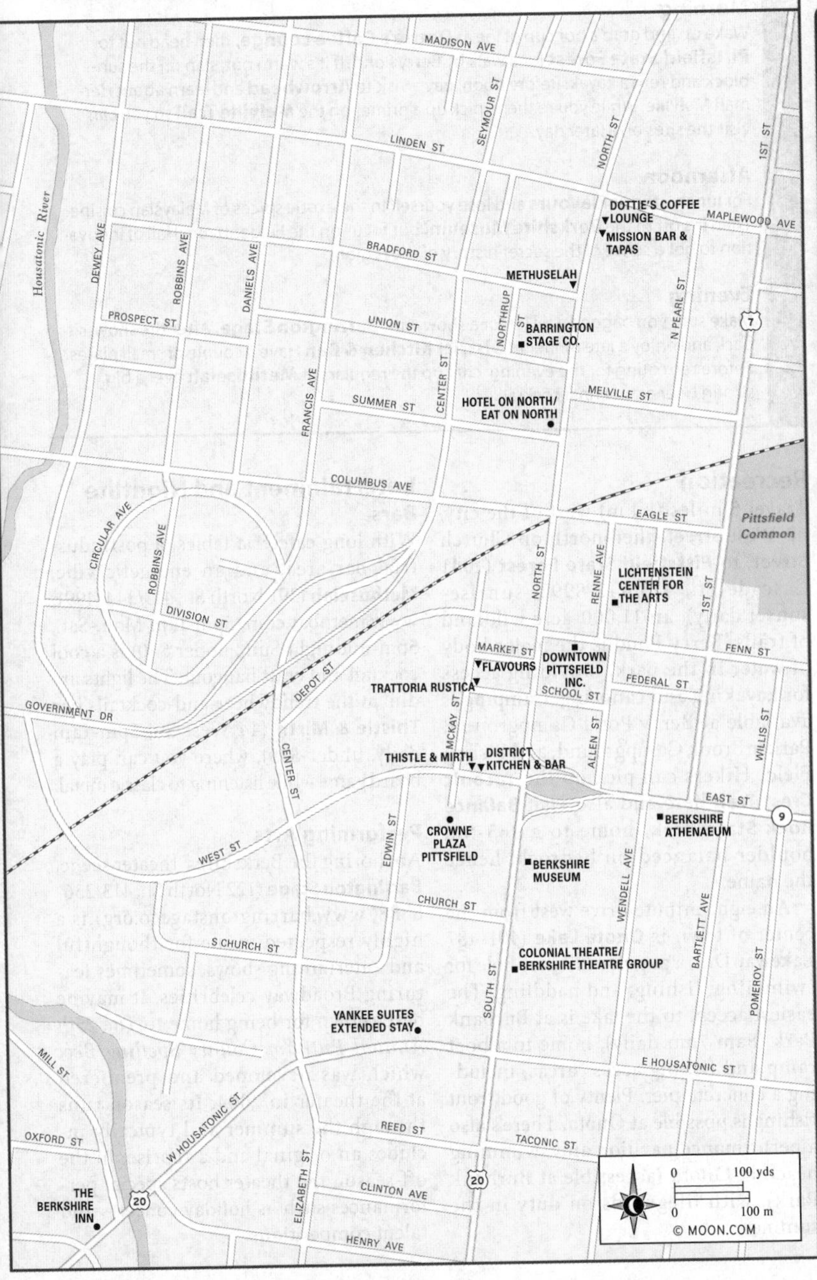
Pittsfield
MADISON AVE
SEYMOUR ST
NORTH ST
1ST ST
LINDEN ST
Housatonic River
DOTTIE'S COFFEE LOUNGE
MISSION BAR & TAPAS
MAPLEWOOD AVE
DEWEY AVE
ROBBINS AVE
DANIELS AVE
BRADFORD ST
METHUSELAH
N PEARL ST
NORTHRUP ST
7
PROSPECT ST
UNION ST
BARRINGTON STAGE CO.
CENTER ST
FRANCIS AVE
SUMMER ST
HOTEL ON NORTH/ EAT ON NORTH
MELVILLE ST
COLUMBUS AVE
EAGLE ST
Pittsfield Common
CIRCULAR AVE
ROBBINS AVE
NORTH ST
RENNE AVE
LICHTENSTEIN CENTER FOR THE ARTS
1ST ST
DIVISION ST
MARKET ST
FENN ST
FLAVOURS
DOWNTOWN PITTSFIELD INC.
DEPOT ST
TRATTORIA RUSTICA
FEDERAL ST
SCHOOL ST
GOVERNMENT DR
MCKAY ST
ALLEN ST
WILLIS ST
THISTLE & MIRTH
DISTRICT KITCHEN & BAR
CENTER ST
EAST ST
9
EDWIN ST
CROWNE PLAZA PITTSFIELD
BERKSHIRE ATHENAEUM
WEST ST
BERKSHIRE MUSEUM
WENDELL AVE
BARTLETT AVE
CHURCH ST
S CHURCH ST
COLONIAL THEATRE/ BERKSHIRE THEATRE GROUP
SOUTH ST
POMEROY ST
YANKEE SUITES EXTENDED STAY
MILL ST
E HOUSATONIC ST
W HOUSATONIC ST
OXFORD ST
REED ST
TACONIC ST
ELIZABETH ST
20
CLINTON AVE
THE BERKSHIRE INN
20
HENRY AVE
0
100 yds
0
100 m
© MOON.COM

One Day in Pittsfield

Morning

Wake up and grab a hot cup of joe at **Dottie's Coffee Lounge,** then head out to **Pittsfield State Forest** for a walk by Berry Pond. If it's warm out, slap on the sunblock and rent a kayak. Before noon, pay a visit to **Arrowhead** and learn about Herman Melville. While you're there, pick up a primer on the **Melville Trail** so you can visit the sites on a later day.

Afternoon

For lunch, stop at **Flavours** and lose yourself in the exotic spices of Malaysian cuisine. Then it's off to the **Berkshire Museum,** but focus on the Feigenbaum Hall of Innovation to get a sense of the secret history of the region.

Evening

Make sure you bagged a ticket for a show with **Barrington Stage.** After the show, sit back and enjoy a late dinner at **District Kitchen & Bar.** Have a couple of small plates. Before retreating for the evening, chat up the regulars at **Methuselah** over a big, strong beer or one final cocktail.

Recreation

Travel 5 miles (8 km) west of the city, up West Street, then north on Church Street, to **Pittsfield State Forest** (1041 Cascade St., 413/442-8992, sunrise-sunset daily), an 11,000-acre wildland of trails. Berry Pond is the major body of water in the park, providing access for kayaking and canoeing. Camping is available at Berry Pond Campground, Parker Brook Campground, and Bishop Field. Hikers can pick up the **Taconic Crest Trail** here and also visit **Balance Rock State Park,** home to a 165-ton boulder balanced on bedrock, hence the name.

An eight-minute drive west from the center of town is **Onota Lake** (401-487 Lakeway Dr.), a popular 617-acre hole for swimming, fishing, and paddling. The easiest access to the lake is at Burbank Park (8am-7pm daily), home to a boat ramp and fishing access areas, including a concrete pier. Plenty of good trout fishing is possible at Onota. There's also a performance pavilion and swimming beach at Onota (accessible at Burbank Park), with lifeguards on duty in the summer.

Entertainment and Nightlife

Bars

With long cafeteria tables, a postindustrial bar area, and an energetic vibe, **Methuselah** (391 North St., 413/344-4991, www.methbar.com, 5pm-1am Mon.-Sat., 5pm-midnight Sun., under $40) is a cool cocktail and craft hangout. The lights are dim at the trendy beer-and-cocktails bar **Thistle & Mirth** (44 West St., 5pm-1am daily, under $25), where you can play a board game while listening to classic metal.

Performing Arts

Anchoring the Berkshires' theater scene, **Barrington Stage** (122 North St., 413/236-8888, www.barringtonstageco.org) is a highly respected venue for thoughtful and entertaining shows, sometimes featuring Broadway celebrities. It may be best known for being home to *The 25th Annual Putnam County Spelling Bee,* which was developed and premiered at the theater in 2004. Its season runs through the summer and typically includes an original and a reprise; in the off-season the theater hosts special performances such as holiday concerts and talent competitions.

Boasting stupendous balconies and an ornate frame around the stage, the **Colonial Theatre** is home to the **Berkshire Theatre Group** (111 South St., 413/997-4444, berkshiretheatregroup.org). It also hosts tribute band concerts, live shows for families, and performers like David Sedaris. The city community arts center is the **Lichtenstein Center for the Arts** (28 Renne Ave., 413/499-9348, 11am-4pm Wed.-Sat.), which keeps a gallery space for a revolving show, plus features musical performances and readings.

Festivals and Events

The **10x10 Upstreet Arts Festival** (Feb., www.discoverpittsfield.com) showcases the finest in Pittsfield's arts scene through a collaboration with Barrington Stage. Everything during the festival is done in sets of 10, from 10 new plays showcased to 10 new artists getting a spotlight at a specific venue, to a big 10-minute firework show. The event happens over, you guessed it, 10 days.

Food

The seasonal menu movement has moved into Pittsfield, headlined by **District Kitchen & Bar** (40 West St., 413/442-0303, 4pm-midnight daily, under $50), which offers a menu of smalls, mids, and bigs. Smoked brisket sandwiches and duck noodle soup are among the highlights in this uber-industrial space with a small bar and a community table.

Get your wood-fired pizza at **Roasted Garlic** (483 W. Housatonic St., 413/499-9910, www.theroastedgarlic.com, 11:30am-9pm Mon.-Thurs., 11:30am-10pm Fri.-Sat., noon-8pm Sun., under $30), which boasts a convivial bar area and plentiful dining space.

Mission Bar & Tapas (438 North St., 413/499-1736, 5pm-midnight Mon.-Thurs., noon-midnight Fri.-Sat., under $40) may reflect a Spanish vibe with its cool lighting and playful jazz nearly every night, but food choices are routinely American with offerings like fried chicken and truffle-parmesan fries.

For the most unique and rewarding dining experience in Pittsfield, try **Flavours** (75 North St., 413/443-3188, www.flavoursintheberkshires.com, 11:30am-9pm Tues.-Fri., 4pm-9pm Sat., hours vary by season, under $30), which serves authentic Malaysian-Chinese cuisine in a dining room with red walls and island décor.

Trattoria Rustica (27 McKay St., 413/499-1192, www.trattoria-rustica.com, 5pm-9pm Wed.-Mon., under $50) is exactly where you'd want to sit back with a bottle of red and a hearty dish of *vitello alla Siciliana*. The brick and stone interior provides a warm, elegant Italian-garden backdrop.

The best coffee in town is at **Dottie's Coffee Lounge** (444 North St., 413/443-1792, 7am-6pm Mon.-Fri., 8am-6pm Sat., 9am-3pm Sun., under $20), which offers breakfast fare, sandwiches, and a variety of breads in a funky space with living room furniture. And **Sarah's Cheesecake & Café** (180 Elm St., 413/443-6678, 7am-3pm Mon.-Wed., 7am-6pm Thurs.-Fri., 8am-3pm Sat., under $20) does cakes for all occasions, but the cheesecakes are worthy of a stop. They also do sandwiches and coffee.

Accommodations

Under $100

Pittsfield has the most diverse budget lodging options in the Berkshires. **The Berkshire Inn** (150 W. Housatonic St., 413/443-3000, www.theberkshireinn.com, $50-100) is a no-fuss motor inn where the help is kind and the rooms are spacious. There's an outdoor pool, too.

$100-150

The White Horse Inn (378 South St., 413/442-2512, www.whitehorsebb.com, $115-260) has eight rooms that are charming and decidedly contemporary, and with nothing smaller than a queen bed. Folks spending more than two nights in the Berkshires can't go wrong with the **Yankee Suites Extended Stay** (20 W. Housatonic St., 413/629-2141, $100-200), which offers suite-style, pet-friendly accommodations with kitchens and near-modern appliances including laundry facilities. Only in town for a night? The **Crowne Plaza Pittsfield** (1 West St., 413/499-2000, $90-200) does the job, as it's right in downtown Pittsfield and has decent if uninspiring rooms.

$150-250

Proof that a younger clientele is visiting Pittsfield, ★ **Hotel on North** (297 North St., 413/358-4741, www.hotelonnorth.com, $149-319) is the trendy boutique hotel marrying 19th-century brick with 21st-century digital accessibility. Rooms showcase Victorian-style seating next to Swedish-inspired desks. Guests seeking some whimsy can sip drinks and kiss in an original birdcage elevator next to the hotel's restaurant, **Eat on North** (413/553-4210, 7am-11pm daily, breakfast and lunch under $25, dinner under $40), which has one of the only raw bars in western Massachusetts. Hours can vary.

Camping

Those keeping it simple can find a place to rest at the **Bonnie Brae Campground** (108 Broadway, 413/442-3754, www.bonniebraecampground.com, $30-100). RV and tent camping is available, plus there are cabins for rent. Flush toilets are on-site, and a dog-walking path surrounds the campground.

Information and Services

Downtown Pittsfield Inc. (413/443-6501, www.downtownpittsfieldinc.com) is the main advocate for tourism in Pittsfield.

MA-8A: Crane Museum of Papermaking

Interested in the history of American papermaking, threading all the way back to the Revolution? Ever wonder who makes the paper of American currency? The **Crane Museum of Papermaking** (W. Housatonic St., Dalton, 413/684-6380, www.crane.com, 1pm-5pm Mon.-Fri. June-Oct., 1pm-5pm Tues.-Thurs. Nov.-May) tells the story of a lost American art form, and yes, Crane is the official paper of the U.S. dollar. The museum is inside Crane's Old Stone Mill, an 1844 structure that kept the machinery that helped produce Crane's unique stock. Take US-8 east 4.3 miles (6.9 km) from Pittsfield to reach the museum.

Cheshire: Ashuwillticook Rail Trail

From Pittsfield, turn onto MA-8 east and continue 10.5 miles (16.9 km) beside the Cheshire Reservoir until an intersection with Church Street. Turn there and continue to Railroad Street, where you'll turn into the parking area for the **Ashuwillticook Rail Trail** (Railroad St., Cheshire, 6am-9pm daily), an 11.2-mile (18-km) rail-trail that runs south to Lanesborough and north to Adams. Its name translating to the Native American phrase "the pleasant river between the hills," this 10-foot-wide (3-m) trail is perfect for cycling, in-line skating, a brisk walk, or a long-distance run.

Adams: Susan B. Anthony Birthplace

Six miles (9.7 km) up MA-8 is Adams, birthplace of iconic activist Susan B. Anthony. Her **historic birthplace** (67 East Rd., 413/743-7121, www.susanbanthonybirthplace.com, 10am-4pm Thurs.-Mon., $3-6 adults, ages 6 and younger free) is an otherwise unassuming yellow building off a narrow road in this town. There, you can learn about her Quaker upbringing, her struggle to bring equal rights to women, and her relationships with other historical figures like Sojourner Truth and Frederick Douglass. There's a shop on-site, plus an outdoor play area where the house's bunnies hang out.

Mount Greylock State Reservation

It inspired Herman Melville to write *Moby-Dick,* and J.K. Rowling made it the dwelling of the wizards of Ilvermorny in her Harry Potter world. Welcome to **Mount Greylock,** the 3,491-foot (1,064-m) peak that towers over all of Massachusetts. The Appalachian Trail summits the mountain on its way north, passing through a subalpine paradise worthy of the literary power that has given it greater life.

Mount Greylock is part of **Mount Greylock State Reservation,** an old-growth forest with stands of red spruce more than 150 years old. The reservation contains over 70 miles (110 km) of trails for hiking and mountain biking in the summer or cross-country skiing, snowshoeing, and snowmobiling in winter.

Rockwell and Notch Roads, which wind through the reservation's forested land, are really scenic drives in the fall

Top to bottom: Ashuwillticook Rail Trail; Susan B. Anthony Birthplace; Natural Bridge State Park.

(and can get quite congested). Sperry Road dead-ends at Stony Ledge, a beautiful picnic spot with a spectacular view of the park's streambeds, forest, and Greylock's summit.

Getting There and Around

From MA-8 there are numerous access points into the reservation, but to reach the summit by car, take US-7 north to North Main Street in Lanesborough. At an intersection with Greylock Road, turn and then enter the reservation on Rockwell Road. Rockwell takes passengers up to the summit.

Note that Rockwell Road starting at the Jones Nose trailhead is **closed** from November to June annually, as is North Adams Road, so winter adventurers have to park at Jones Nose trailhead if they want to hike Greylock. Luckily, that's an AT entrance and it can take you right to the top.

★ Mount Greylock Summit

Distance: 6.2 miles (10 km)
Duration: 4-5 hours
Elevation gain: 1,070 feet (326 m)
Difficulty: Moderate
Trailhead: Campground parking lot at Rockwell Road (42.620022, -73.199383)

There are quite a few hikes in and around Mount Greylock, but this summit hike provides a relatively direct route and is manageable in a couple of hours. Start at the Campground Trail from the parking lot, which will take you across Sperry Road. Continue onto the Hopper Trail, which was built in 1830 as a horse trail by Williams College students to aid the school's president, who could no longer hike up Greylock on his own. That'll take you another 1.4 miles (2.3 km) up wondrous country, especially in the fall, until you intersect with the Appalachian Trail and begin a 1.1-mile (1.6-km) summit ascent amid spruce and wispy grass. You'll soon be atop Greylock, where you'll find the **Massachusetts Veterans War Memorial Tower,** a 92-foot-tall (28 m) stylized granite tower that you can climb up to get a stunning 360-degree view across New England and eastern New York State. Head back the way you came.

Food and Accommodations

Bascom Lodge

In the mid-1930s, volunteers from the Civilian Conservation Corps built **Bascom Lodge** (917/680-0079, www.bascomlodge.net, Sat.-Sun. May, Tues.-Sun. June, daily July-Oct., $35-150), a stupendous arts and crafts lodge that occupies the summit of Mount Greylock. Rustic and simple by design, the lodge accommodates all kinds of travelers but makes a point to help Appalachian Trail hikers. AT hikers can rent a bunk for $35, while private rooms are available starting at $125.

The on-site **restaurant** (8am-10am daily breakfast, 11am-4:30pm daily lunch, 7pm daily dinner, under $15 lunch, prix fixe dinner) at the lodge is also open during the summer, serving locally grown ingredients like a half chicken and potatoes. Dinner is one seating at 7pm.

Camping

There's one primitive campground (Sperry Road, 413/499-4262, www.reserveamerica.com, free) with 18 tent sites and 9 group sites. Reservations are required Memorial Day-Columbus Day; campsites are first-come, first-serve the rest of the year.

Information and Services

The **Mount Greylock Visitor Center** (30 Rockwell Rd., 413/499-4262, 9am-4:30pm daily summer, 9am-4pm Sat.-Sun winter) has all the trail maps you need, plus an exhibit on the history of the mountain.

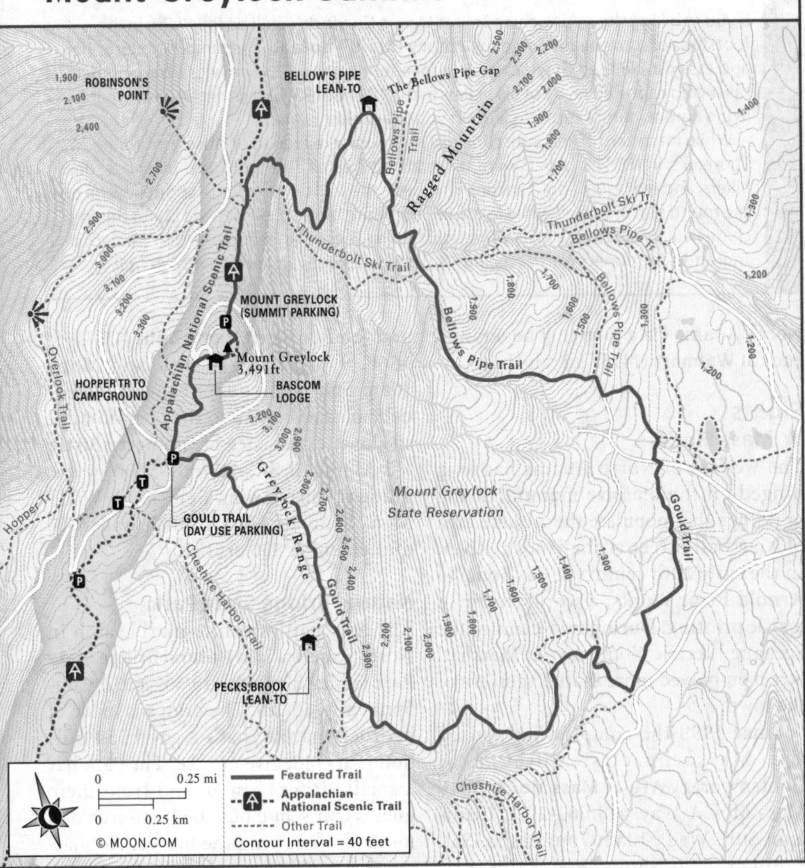

North Adams

Every view of **North Adams** (pop. 13,708), accessible via MA-8 just 6 miles (9.7 km) north of Adams, seemingly shows a few church steeples, the Berkshires, and more than several brick industrial buildings. Once a bustling community for textile workers, North Adams has transformed itself in recent years to a celebrated arts community with a progressive, dialed-in spirit. As more than one resident put it, Appalachian Trail hikers will be given free tickets to local sights, just so they can enjoy what the town has to offer without worry. And some of those hikers find their way back to North Adams later in life, and for good.

Getting There and Around

The **Peter Pan** (70 Main St., 800/343-9999, www.peterpanbus.com) line stops in North Adams and offers connection points as far south as New York and as far east as Boston. The **Berkshire Regional Transit Authority** (413/499-2782, www.berkshirerta.com, Mon.-Sat.) serves

Trail Tale

If you're hiking the Appalachian Trail at Mount Greylock, you'll be following in the footsteps of some heady company. **Henry David Thoreau,** the famous philosopher and essayist, climbed Greylock in 1844 for a sunrise view. Thoreau was a transcendentalist who captured many of his beliefs in the 1854 book *Walden*. In it he wrote that living among nature could, in fact, lift you to a higher plane.

While many thru-hikers subscribe to a philosophy related to or closely mirroring Thoreau's, in 1854 his beliefs were still relatively fresh. These days, thru-hikers, section hikers, and really just about anyone who hikes the trail tends to write about how he or she found him or herself while following the white blazes. Recent texts about this include Paul V. Stutzman's *Hiking Through: Finding Peace and Freedom on the Appalachian Trail* and Scott Jurek's *North: Finding My Way While Running the Appalachian Trail.*

North Adams via a loop that begins and ends at **Walmart** (1415 Curran Hwy.).

Sights

★ Mass MoCA

The welfare of North Adams has long hinged on the massive manufacturing buildings that populate the 24-acre area of Marshall Street at the Hoosic River. In the early 20th century it was home to Arnold Print Works, a world leader in textile printing. During mid-century the Sprague Electric Company on Marshall Street employed more than 20 percent of the town.

Since 1999 the complex has housed the Massachusetts Museum of Contemporary Art, or **Mass MoCA** (1040 Mass MoCA Way, 413/662-2111, 10am-6pm Sun.-Wed., 10am-7pm Thurs.-Sat. summer, 11am-5pm Wed.-Mon. off-season, $8-20, age 6 and younger free). Because of its vast exhibition space, hip character, and fun campus, Mass MoCA is a must-visit spot for any art fan and a major driver of tourism to the artsy North Adams community.

Throughout the complex's 26 buildings you'll find art in every space, from a walkway brought to life by the human voice to small coins in random corners of the museum. These and other wild discoveries fit nicely with major exhibits like line drawings by revered conceptual artist Sol LeWitt. Mass MoCA also has four dining options, including the grab-and-go café **Lickety Split** (413/346-4560, 9am-5pm Wed.-Sat. and Mon., 10am-5pm Sun., under $15) with some delicious ice cream, to the farm-to-table sit-down experience of **Gramercy Bistro** (87 Marshall St., 413/663-5300, www.gramercybistro.com, 5pm-11pm Wed.-Mon., 11am-2pm Sun. brunch, under $50 dinner, under $30 brunch).

Natural Bridge State Park

The only natural white-marble arch in North America is at **Natural Bridge State Park** (1 McAuley Rd., 413/663-6392, 9am-5pm daily, $5-10). The bridge is made of bedrock marble that's a good 550 million years old, give or take. The park has a small visitors center, and from there guests can scope out the least-crowded method of viewing the bridge. No matter what you'll be among tourists wanting to snap pictures at the bridge, so be patient as you walk along the well-marked boardwalk guarded by gates. Besides the bridge, highlights here include an abandoned marble quarry you can explore, and a dramatically positioned marble dam. The fee is for parking, but you can park outside the park and walk a mile (1.6 km) up to the entrance.

Berkshire Art Museum

While it may not get the ink earned by the mammoth Mass MoCA, the **Berkshire Art Museum** (159 E. Main St., 413/664-9550, http://bamuseum.org, noon-5pm

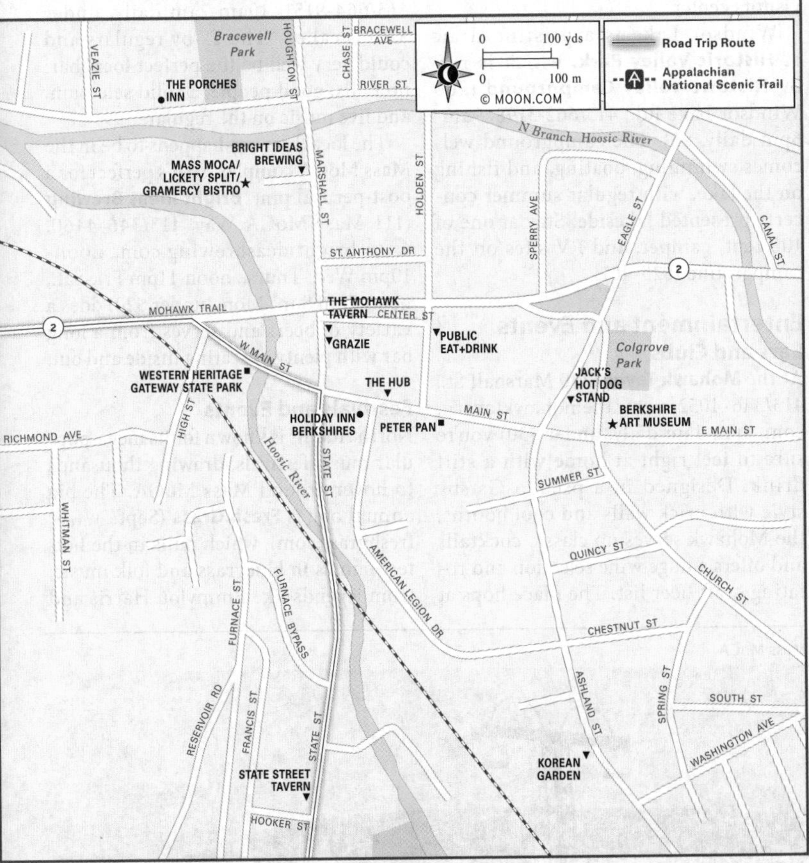

Wed.-Sun., donations suggested) is wild in its own right. The museum is mostly composed of the work of Eric Rudd, a local sculptor and mixed-media artist who isn't afraid to expand his creativity. Walk into the museum and you might be astounded by the ultramodern pieces fit into this church sanctuary.

Recreation

Between 1851 and 1875, workers constructed the Hoosac Tunnel, a nearly 5-mile-long (8-km) cavity through Hoosac Mountain that allowed for rail transport. Drilling problems were abundant, and on October 17, 1867, an explosion inside the tunnel's central shaft sent sharp tools and a large structure down to the bottom where workers were busy. Several workers died; in all, nearly 200 people perished while working on the tunnel, which ultimately cost an unfathomable-for-its-time $21 million. The history of the tunnel construction is captured at **Western Gateway Heritage State Park** (115 State St., No. 4, 413/663-6312, 10am-4pm Thurs.-Mon., free), a former railroad yard on eight acres. The park features self-guided hikes that take visitors into town; pick up a brochure at the visitors center.

Windsor Lake is a pristine draw at **Historic Valley Park,** which is run by **Historic Valley Campground** (200 Windsor Lake Rd., 413/662-3198, 9am-6pm daily, $5). The campground welcomes swimming, boating, and fishing on the lake, with regular summer concerts presented lakeside. Stay at one of 100 tent, camper, and RV sites on the campground ($25-40).

Entertainment and Events

Bars and Clubs

At the **Mohawk Tavern** (30 Marshall St., 413/346-4052, www.themohawktavern.com, 4pm-1am daily, under $30) you're sure to feel right at home with a stiff drink. Designed in a pseudo-Gatsby style with brick walls and cool booths, the Mohawk serves up classic cocktails and offers a huge wine selection and rotating craft beer list. The place hops at night. For something a bit more lived-in, the **State Street Tavern** (167 State St., 413/664-9151, 10am-2am daily, under $20) is called "The T" by regulars and could very well be the perfect local bar: no frills, good people, a solid selection, and live music on the regular.

The local brewery happens to be in the Mass MoCA complex, so it's perfect for a post-perusal pint. **Bright Ideas Brewing** (111 Mass MoCA Way, 413/346-4460, www.brightideasbrewing.com, noon-10pm Wed.-Thurs., noon-11pm Fri.-Sat., noon-7pm Sun.-Mon., under $20) does a variety of beers and serves from a long bar with plenty of seating inside and out.

Festivals and Events

North Adams is known for its mega-popular music festivals, drawing thousands to hover around Mass MoCA. The big annual one is **Fresh Grass** (Sept., www.freshgrass.com), which pulls in the hottest names in bluegrass and folk music, from legends like Emmylou Harris and

Mass MoCA

Bela Fleck to today's hottest names, like Sarah Jarosz and Brandi Carlile. Every two years, the rock band Wilco curates its own festival in North Adams, called the **Solid Sound Festival** (June every odd year, www.solidsoundfestival.com). Artists including Television, Real Estate, Yo La Tengo and, of course, Wilco, have played the grounds of Mass MoCA, while comedians and storytellers perform and foodies revel in artisan delights.

Food

Sister restaurant to Pittsfield's District Kitchen & Bar, **Public Eat+Drink** (34 Holden St., 413/664-4444, www.publiceatanddrink.com, 4pm-midnight Mon.-Wed., 11:30am-midnight Thurs.-Sun., lunch under $30, dinner under $50) specializes in elevated American fare with fun twists inside a fixed-up industrial space with high ceilings and brick walls.

It's more playful inside **The Hub** (55 Main St., 413/662-2500, 11:30am-9pm Sun.-Thurs., 11:30am-9:30pm Fri.-Sat., under $25), which cooks up diner staples like quesadillas, BLTs, and meatloaf.

Sticking with the diner theme but for breakfast, **Renee's Diner** (780 Massachusetts Ave., 413/664-2070, 7am-2pm Mon.-Sat., 7am-1pm Sun., under $15) is inexpensive and steady with specialties including a Frosted Flakes-coated French toast and hangover staple the Garbage Plate. Also for breakfast, the cozy **Brewhaha** (20 Marshall St., 413/664-2020, 7am-5pm Thurs.-Tues., under $20) is known for Belgian waffles and eggs cooked by the same husband-and-wife team that opened the place. For lunch it has a big salad worthy of Elaine Benes's approval.

There's great Korean food at **Korean Garden** (139 Ashland St., 413/346-4097, 11am-9:30pm Sun. and Tues.-Thurs., 11am-10pm Fri.-Sat., under $40), which offers lunch specials like bibimbap and assorted dumplings.

For classic Italian there's **Grazie** (26 Marshall St., 413/664-0044, www.graziena.com, 4pm-10pm Wed.-Mon., under $50), which puts home-style pasta and meat dishes on white tablecloth, but it's generally casual here.

Much more casual is **Jack's Hot Dog Stand** (12 Eagle St., 413/664-9006, 10am-7pm Mon.-Sat., under $5), a local staple since 1917 where you can grab a cheeseburger for under $2 (bacon is $0.30 extra). There's very little counter space available.

Accommodations

There's little in the way of lodging in North Adams. The chic and pricey choice is ★ **The Porches Inn** (231 River St., 413/664-0400, www.porches.com, $250-450), which is owned by the folks behind Hotel on North in Pittsfield and the Red Lion Inn in Great Barrington and offers 47 distinct rooms in an old row of Victorian houses across from Mass MoCA. No two rooms are alike here, with each offering some dash of whimsy, whether it's a colorful rug or unique leather chair. The Porches has a heated outdoor swimming pool and lobby bar, plus complimentary breakfast.

The other option in North Adams is the **Holiday Inn Berkshires** (40 Main St., 413/663-6500, $130-180), whose basic rooms won't make you feel fuzzy like the Porches, but hey, it's half the price.

Information and Services

Few municipal websites offer as much information on their locales as that of North Adams (www.northadams-ma.gov).

Clarksburg State Park

A well-kept wilderness 3.2 miles (5.1 km) north of North Adams via Franklin Street and Middle Road, **Clarksburg State Park** (1199 Middle Rd., 413/664-8345) has 368 acres of forest for hiking, plus Mausert's Pond, which is open in the summer for swimming, kayaking, and canoeing. It has a **campground** ($17-27) with 45 sites for tents and RVs.

Hiking

Mausert's Pond Trail

Distance: 3 miles (4.8 km)
Duration: 1.5 hours
Elevation gain: 90 feet (27 m)
Difficulty: Easy
Trailhead: Day-use area parking lot (42.737368, -73.075604)

Take a nice walk around this 45-acre man-made pond that was once, according to legend, a meadow where locals raced horses. Start from the day-use area parking lot. Turn right from the parking lot, facing the pond, and take up the trail as it begins winding around. You'll ascend only lightly before coming back down near the campground. Hook up with the Shoreline Trail and hug the pond before coming back to the main road and the parking lot.

Williamstown

A brisk 5.2-mile (8.4-km) drive west on MA-2 from North Adams brings you to **Williamstown** (pop. 7,754), which is known primarily as the home of **Williams College** (880 Main St., www.williams.edu) and the Clark Art Institute. If you need to know what kind of town we're talking about here, the Williams College mascot is Ephelia the Purple Cow (possibly named for the purplish hue of the Berkshires behind the grazing cows of the nearby farmland). Williamstown is creative and kooky, liberal and laid-back, home to renowned arts institutions.

Sights

Clark Art Institute

Some of the finest pieces by 19th- and early 20th-century artists like John Singer Sargent and Winslow Homer, plus work by Renoir, Monet, and Degas, can be found at **Clark Art Institute** (225 South

St., 413/458-2303, www.clarkart.edu, 10am-5pm daily July-Aug., 10am-5pm Tues.-Sun. Sept.-June, $20 adults, free for students and children younger than 18), shorthand for the Clark Art Institute, which is known for its renowned art museum of American and European classics. The main museum building includes dozens of rooms tastefully filled with impressionist art, sculpture, decorative arts, and famous portraiture like Gilbert Stuart's circa 1797 turn at George Washington.

Along with the main building, the Clark includes an expansive 140-acre campus with walking trails. **Lunder Center at Stone Hill,** a modern building seamlessly blending with the hillside, houses two galleries and offers gorgeous views of the countryside.

Williams College Museum of Art

At the heart of Williams College is the **Williams College Museum of Art** (15 Lawrence Hall Dr., No. 2, www.wcma.williams.edu, 10am-5pm Fri.-Tues., 10am-8pm Thurs., free), a small but exciting repository that acts as both art museum and educational tool. Museum officials and faculty partner to curate exhibits. Visitors can tackle the museum in a quick hour-long stroll, but it's worth it to stop and gaze at pieces like Sol LeWitt's brilliant wall painting that envelops the atrium.

Festivals and Events

For more than 60 years the **Williamstown Theatre Festival** (June-Aug., www.wtfestival.org) has shined the spotlight on the town, filling summer evenings with exciting and intrepid small shows by Emmy and Tony nominees and winners.

Food

Popular with students, family members, and just about anyone driving through, **Tunnel City Coffee** (100 Spring St., No. 102, 413/458-5010, www.tunnelcitycoffee.com, 6am-6pm daily, under $10) is the

Clark Art Institute

premier coffee shop of northwestern Massachusetts. Pick a morning and the yellow-walled café with plenty of seating will be packed with laptop workers and those seeking a few moments of actual human contact.

Good Indian food can be had, and quickly, at **Spice Root** (23 Spring St., 413/458-5200, www.spiceroot.com, 11:30am-2:30pm lunch Tues.-Sun., 5pm-10pm dinner Tues.-Sun., under $40). The weekday lunch buffet (11:30am-2:30pm Tues.-Fri., $10.95) is a popular option.

It's mostly Italian, but there's certainly some variety mixed in, at **Cozy Corner** (850 Simonds Rd., 413/458-3854, www.cozycornerrestaurantma.com, 5pm-10pm Mon., 11am-10pm Tues.-Fri., 11:30am-10pm Sat., noon-10pm Sun., under $15 lunch, under $30 dinner). Student favorites like the Steak & Cheese Bomb make it a worthy lunch spot.

Bennington

US-7 crosses into Vermont and deposits travelers into the Shires, the tourism-focused term that describes the area from the southwestern border of the state up to Manchester. The Green Mountain National Forest wraps around the towns of Bennington and Manchester, which anchor this area as a haven for travelers looking to hike, climb, fish, hunt, ski, and snowboard. And look for pottery. There is plenty of pottery around these parts. Along with the dishes, **Bennington** (pop. 15,431) is home to the small liberal arts school **Bennington College,** a handful of shops and restaurants, plus several historical monuments and sites.

The Appalachian Trail enters Vermont in the national forest about 13 miles (21 km) southeast of Bennington, where it's aligned with the Long Trail, Vermont's 273-mile (440-km) foot route that stretches up to the state's northern border with Canada. The adjoined AT and Long Trail close in on Bennington at Stage Coach Road, 4.8 miles (7.7 km) from the center of town, then again at the Molly Stark Trail (VT-9), also about 4.8 miles (7.7 km) from the town center. The Molly Stark Trail follows the route taken by American general John Stark and his troops after the Revolutionary War Battle of Bennington on August 16, 1777. And while it's called the Battle of Bennington, and there's a monument to it in town, the battle actually took place in nearby Walloomsac, New York.

Getting There and Around

You can hop on a bus with **Vermont Translines** (844/888-7267, www.vttranslines.com, daily), taking you north toward Rutland on **North-South Vermont Bus Route.**

Sights

Bennington Battle Monument

President Benjamin Harrison presided over the unveiling of the **Bennington Battle Monument** (15 Monument Cir., 802/447-0550, 9am-5pm mid-Apr.-Oct., free), a 306-foot (93-m) obelisk standing in the middle of an open field 1.5 miles (2.4 km) northwest of the town center. Constructed from blue-gray magnesium limestone, it was completed in 1891 and stands behind a statue of Gen. John Stark. Visitors can take an elevator to the top when the monument is open, and on August 16 each year, officials commemorate the anniversary of the Battle of Bennington with a ceremony and the firing of the Molly Stark Cannon, reputedly the oldest active cannon in the world and residing regularly in New Boston, New Hampshire.

Park-McCullough House

So where did President Benjamin Harrison stay while dedicating the Bennington Battle Monument? The **Park-McCullough House** (1 Park St., 802/442-5441, www.parkmccullough.org, 10am-2pm Fri.-Sat., noon-4pm Sun. summer, $15 adults, $12 seniors, $8 ages

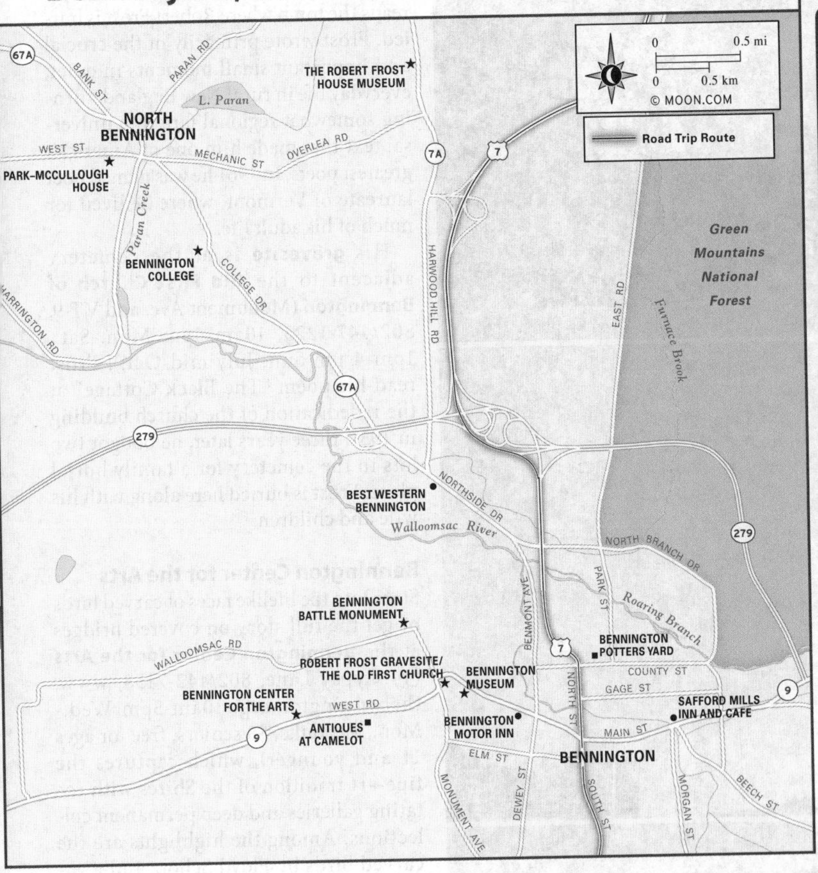

8-17, free ages 7 and younger), which was constructed in 1865 as the home of lawyer Trenor W. Park and his family. Park's daughter Eliza took over the house after her father's death, and she and husband John G. McCullough, also a lawyer, renovated the house and hosted President Harrison in 1891. The 35-room estate is not a Gilded Age house, but a Victorian-era mansion surrounded by 200 acres of farmland. Today visitors can take guided tours of the house, whose furnishings reflect New England life primarily of the 1800s

The house hosts frequent chamber music and folk concerts, though the schedule is always changing. It's also home to **Living Room Theatre,** a professional theater company that uses the house as its personal stage and, sometimes, items from the house collection as props. And, if you're in the area during summer and want to try something totally different, the house hosts a **croquet league** (6pm Thurs. June-Aug.), which includes a cash bar. There's no dress code, but if you want to be authentic, wear white.

Top to bottom: Williams College Museum of Art; Bennington Battle Monument; Bennington Museum.

Robert Frost Gravesite

"I had a lover's quarrel with the world," reads the tomb where Robert Frost is buried. Frost wrote primarily of the crucial and important small moments in quiet, everyday life in rural New England, turning somewhat regional fare into universal text that made him one of America's greatest poets. In 1961 he was named poet laureate of Vermont, where he lived for much of his adult life.

His **gravesite** is at the cemetery adjacent to the **Old First Church of Bennington** (Monument Ave. and VT-9, 802/447-1223, 10am-4pm Mon.-Sat., 1pm-4 pm Sun. July-mid-Oct.). Frost read his poem "The Black Cottage" at the rededication of the church building in 1937; three years later, he bought two lots in the cemetery for a family burial place. Frost is buried here along with his wife and children.

Bennington Center for the Arts

Stare into the lifelike faces of carved birds or get the full story on covered bridges at the **Bennington Center for the Arts** (44 Gypsy Lane, 802/442-7158, www.thebennington.org, 10am-5pm Wed.-Mon., $9 adults, $8 seniors, free for ages 11 and younger), which captures the fine-art tradition of the Shires with rotating galleries and deep permanent collections. Among the highlights are the carved birds by Floyd Scholz and a variety of Navajo rugs as part of the center's Native American art collection. The Covered Bridge Museum includes videos, interactive displays, and a toy railroad that passes through several replica bridges. You could spend an hour or more just reading the vast amount of information about these historic structures.

Bennington Museum

Spending much of her life in the

Bennington area, Anna Mary Robertson Moses started painting folk art at age 78. An unprecedented 33-year career followed, during which Anna became Grandma Moses, a leading 20th-century artist of bucolic outdoor scenes. The **Bennington Museum** (75 Main St., 802/447-1571, www.benningtonmuseum.org, 10am-5pm daily June-Oct., 10am-5pm Thurs.-Tues. Nov.-May, $10 adults, $9 seniors and students, free ages 17 and younger) boasts the world's largest collection of Grandma Moses's work, shown in a permanent exhibit that rotates featured paintings. The museum also exhibits items from Vermont during both the Gilded Age and the early 19th century. If you want a historical primer on southern Vermont, this is the destination.

Hiking

Bald Mountain and White Rocks

Distance: 7 miles (11.3 km)
Duration: 4-5 hours
Elevation gain: 2,160 feet (658 m)
Difficulty: Moderate
Trailhead: North Branch Street at power line crossing (42.889757, -73.180606)

First things first: Bald Mountain isn't bald. There are trees up there, and if you hike here in the summer, you'll have an obstructed view. The better view is from White Rocks. There's limited parking by the trailhead, but if you can park, hop out and start following the blue blazes as they enter the woods. You'll pass under a highway at the funky "Free Expression Tunnel" before heading back into the woods and climbing. You'll cross a few streams, feel the burn on switchbacks, and, after 2.6 miles (4.2 km), reach White Rocks, a shoulder of Bald Mountain that provides a splendid view of the town. It's another mile (1.6 km) to the summit of Bald Mountain, and you'll have to turn left on the West Ridge Trail to get there. Follow those blue blazes back to the base and your car.

Shopping

Antiques at Camelot

Even those well accustomed to endless, barn-style antique centers will shake their heads in awe at **Antiques at Camelot** (66 Colgate Heights, 802/447-0039, www.antiquesatcamelot.com, 9:30am-5:30pm daily), Vermont's largest antique center. The restored barn of 18,000 square feet has multiple levels (some literally coming out of nowhere) where mid-century furniture sits next to military collectibles and vintage Beatles toys. It's easy to stop in here for a minute only to find yourself lost an hour later.

Bennington Potters

During the 18th century Bennington was revered for its stoneware. In 1948, the tradition of creating artistic goods by hand returned to the town with the founding of **Bennington Potters** by David Gil. Today, Bennington Potters' various artisans work together to create works at its facility in town, and pieces are available for purchase in store and online.

The **Bennington Potters Yard** includes the **pottery works** (324 County St., 800/205-8033, 9:30am-6pm Mon.-Sat., 10am-5pm Sun., free), which is open for public tours and offers a full education in pottery making. Visitors watch potters take to each piece along a hands-on assembly line, while potters explain the concepts of forming, fishing, and glazing. Also in the Potters Yard are a 1922 feed mill and a 19th-century one-room schoolhouse, whose interiors showcase ceramics, housewares, and other items for sale. Back in town, **Bennington Potters North** (127 College St., 802/863-2221, 10am-6pm Mon.-Sat., 11am-5pm Sun.) is a renovated brick factory also acting as a showroom.

Food and Nightlife

Some diners *look* like vintage railcars, but the ★ **Blue Benn Diner** (314 North St., 802/442-5140, 6am-5pm Mon.-Tues., 6am-8pm Wed.-Fri., 6am-4pm Sat.,

7am-4pm Sun., under $15 breakfast, under $20 lunch and dinner) is the real thing. The car was placed in Bennington in 1948 and has been whipping up a variety of omelets, pancakes, sandwiches, and dinner entrees ever since. Seating is limited (it's a railcar, remember), so on a weekend morning you'll likely have to wait in line for a seat.

If you don't want the line, **Papa Pete's of Bennington** (1104 Woodford Rd., 802/681-0181, 7am-2pm Mon.-Tues. and Thurs., 7am-3pm Fri.-Sun., under $20) is slightly pricier for breakfast, but it's also home of the 14-inch pancake.

Lil' Britain (116 North St., 802/442-2447, 11:30am-8pm Tues.-Sat., under $20) has authentic British grub like sausage rolls, fish-and-chips, Heinz baked beans, and bangers and mash.

Want a beer? **Madison Brewing Company Pub & Restaurant** (428 Main St., 802/442-7397, www.madisonbrewingco.com, 11:30am-9pm Sun.-Thurs., 11:30am-10pm Fri.-Sat., under $25) has a large dining room with high ceilings and a clear view of its tanks. There are plenty of TVs playing sports throughout the day and night. Madison brews a variety of styles, cooks up basic pub and American fare, and has a small bar area with some stools nearby. You can take home its beer, too.

It'll be quieter at **Northshire Brewery** (108 County St., 802/681-0201, www.northshirebrewery.org, 1pm-6pm Thurs.-Fri., 10am-6pm Sat., under $15), which is open three days a week. It features the easy-drinking Equinox Pilsner, named after the nearby peak. A tasting of four beers is an inexpensive $5.

Accommodations

There are plenty of cheap options for a night's rest in Bennington. The best bets include the **Bennington Motor Inn** (143 Main St., 802/442-5479, $60-100), the diamond-in-the-rough **Paradise Inn** (141 Main St., 802/442-8351, $60-110), and **Best Western Bennington** (220 Northside Drive, 802/442-6311, $89-129), each of which are just fine.

For something more reflective of New England living, and for a wonderful twist on the traditional bed-and-breakfast, the ★ **Safford Mills Inn and Café** (722 Main St., 802/681-7646, $155-255) offers three unique rooms dressed in understated colonial finery, inside a circa 1762 house. As for the twist: The Safford doesn't serve breakfast; instead, it runs an evening **café** (5pm-9pm Thurs., 5pm-10pm Fri.-Sat.) with craft cocktails, wine, beer, appetizers, and dessert. If you stay overnight, the café items, including drinks, are included free.

Shaftsbury: Robert Frost Stone House Museum

The small town of **Shaftsbury** (pop. 3,590) is known primarily for being the home of Robert Frost for much of the poet's adult life. The **Robert Frost Stone House Museum** (121 VT-7A, 802/447-6200, 11am-5pm Wed.-Sun. May 1-Nov. 1, $10 adults, $6 seniors and students, $5 ages 17 and younger, free ages 9 and younger) is where Frost composed one of his most famous poems, "Stopping by Woods on a Snowy Evening," and an exhibit here examines the details and importance of that work. The house is operated by Bennington College.

Mount Equinox

The tallest peak in the Taconic Range, **Mount Equinox** towers over the Shires at 3,840 feet (1,170 m), providing a dramatic summit view of the Green Mountains to the north, central Vermont to the east, the Taconics to the west, and the Adirondacks to the south. There are two ways to experience the summit: A pricy trip on Skyline Drive, which zags up the mountain, from the comfort of your hatchback, or a challenging and leg-burning hike where you gain nearly 3,000 feet (915 m) of elevation. At the top is a parking area and the **Saint Bruno Scenic Viewing Center** (Skyline Dr., Manchester Center, 802/362-1115, 9am-4:30pm daily May-Oct.), which acts as both the mountain visitors center and a facility for the Carthusian Order of monks. They love visitors and have a gift shop.

Skyline Drive

Most people who choose to experience Mount Equinox do so on the 5.2-mile (8.4-km) **Skyline Drive** (9am-4pm daily, $15 car and driver, $12 motorcycle and driver, $5 each additional car passenger, free for ages 9 and younger), the oldest privately owned paved toll road in America. Skyline Drive slithers 3,248 feet (990 m) on a steep incline to the summit, which has a large parking area, viewing center, and six picnic areas. Cars enter at the tollhouse.

Hiking

Mount Equinox Trail

Distance: 7 miles (11.3 km)
Duration: 3.5-4.5 hours
Elevation gain: 2,840 feet (866 m)
Difficulty: Strenuous
Trailhead: Parking lot at West Union Street (43.162459, -73.082286)

It's a constant, unending slog of a hike, but the summit views of the surrounding Green Mountains are glorious if you can muster on.

Start your Mount Equinox journey at a moderate parking area at the end of West Union Street. Past a red gate starts the Red Gate Trail, whose red blazes will take you to an intersection with the blue-blazed Blue Summit Trail. That's your only path until the top, a 3.1-mile (5-km) walk covering 2,800 feet (853 m) of elevation, and it's steep with few areas to stand level. You'll get a break halfway up the trail thanks to a wooden bench. From the bench a sign leads to a spring, which is really a pipe. After the rest, and viewing the pipe, continue up the mountain until a junction with a path for Lookout Rock. Stay on the Blue Summit Trail, which will lead you to the Skyline Drive parking area and visitors center.

Go back the way you came and be especially careful if the ground is the least bit wet—the trail is loose rock and gets slippery fast. Hiking poles are valuable on Mount Equinox.

Manchester and Manchester Center

From the toll road at Mount Equinox it's a 4.2-mile (6.8-km) drive up VT-7A into **Manchester** (pop. 4,391), the quieter of two locales that share the same name. Manchester is home to the Equinox, a resort and golf club that pulls in plenty of tourists seeking the finest in summer relaxation. Another 1.2 miles (1.9 km) north from Manchester is **Manchester Center,** a community within the town of Manchester that includes the commercial center, plus a popular outlet shopping center. These towns are also popular in the fall for leaf-peeping and in the winter for skiing.

Manchester and Manchester Center keep the character of the Shires strong, with kind, well-read folks that are happy to tell you about their fine bookstore over a glass of wine.

Getting There and Around

You can hop on a bus with **Vermont Translines** (844/888-7267, www.vttranslines.com, daily), taking you north toward Rutland on **North-South Vermont Bus Route.** You can also take the Bus via **Marble Valley Regional Transit** (802/747-3502, www.thebus.com, daily), which heads north to Rutland.

★ Hildene

The long road that leads to **Hildene** (1005 Hildene Rd., Manchester, 802/362-1788,

www.hildene.org, 9:30am-4:30pm daily, $20 adults, $5 youth, free ages 5 and younger) allows this estate, the summer home of Abraham Lincoln's son Robert Todd Lincoln, to stand apart in nature. The word "Hildene," in fact, means "hill with valley and stream," leading one to imagine that the home was meant to be its own presence amid the wild Vermont countryside.

While it is a stunning house in its own right, a 1905 Georgian Revival structure surrounded by perfectly manicured gardens and overlooking a sweeping vista of the Battenkill Valley, Hildene isn't just a summer house recalling some age-old time in American history. The 400-acre estate includes a working farm with a solar-powered goat dairy and cheese-making facility, 12 miles (19.3 km) of walking trails, an observatory, and meadows that include farmhouses and a one-room schoolhouse. Guests can tour much of this area, having full access to the trails and farm.

Hildene runs a variety of educational programs during the year and uses the history of the home and its owner to offer reflections on American life yesterday and today. Lincoln was the president of the Pullman Company, which manufactured railroad cars and employed a large number of African American workers as porters. While porters often worked in undesirable conditions, they belonged to a union and received higher wages than many black workers of the era. Hildene tells the story of the Pullman porters in an exhibit called *Many Voices,* which is accompanied by a 1903 Pullman Palace Car known as Sunbeam.

The gardens, farm, trails, and history surrounding the house are enough reason to visit Hildene, but guests are also up close with Lincoln family furniture in

Top to bottom: Robert Frost Stone House Museum; along the hike to Mount Equinox's summit; Hildene in Manchester.

the main house. The highlight is a 1908 pipe organ.

Orvis and the American Museum of Fly Fishing

Anglers from across the world know the name **Orvis** (4180 Main St., Manchester Center, 802/362-3750, www.orvis.com, 10am-6pm Mon.-Fri., 9am-6pm Sat., 10am-5pm Sun.), and they visit the fly-fishing brand's headquarters in Manchester the way baseball fans head to Cooperstown, New York. The Orvis complex is vast, headlined by the two-level flagship store. Along with the deep selection of gear and apparel, the store has an active pond regularly stocked with trout.

The Orvis campus includes the Orvis Rod Shop, Orvis Fly Fishing School, and **American Museum of Fly Fishing** (4070 Main St., Manchester Center, 802/362-3300, www.amff.org, 10am-4pm Tues.-Sun., free). Set in an 1800s farmhouse, the museum boasts a large collection of angling items and rotates exhibits focusing on the history of the sport and the influence it's had on American life.

Hiking

Lye Brook Falls Trail

Distance: 4.6 miles (7.4 km)

Duration: 2.5-3 hours

Elevation gain: 870 feet (265 m)

Difficulty: Moderate

Trailhead: Lye Brook Falls Access Road (43.158833, -73.041046)

Venture into the Green Mountain wilderness and to an awesome little waterfall on this moderate hike with one necessary bit of caution: it gets slippery on the rocks. From the trailhead, follow the Lye Brook Falls Trail as it goes up those slippery rocks, then ease yourself while it levels off. Continue up a steady and infrequently steep trail for another 1.6 miles (2.6 km) or so before descending. After 2.3 miles (3.7 km) total you'll reach the falls, which have close to a 150-foot (46-m) drop. When finished, head back the way you came.

The Golf Club at Equinox

Part of the Equinox's blanket coverage of Manchester, the **Golf Club at Equinox** (108 Union St., Manchester, 802/362-7870, www.playequinox.com, $59-149 May-Oct., $39-109 off-peak) is a well-maintained 18-hole, par-71 course built in 1926 and renovated in 1991. It offers splendid mountain views, tree-lined fairways, and moderately sloping greens. The **Dormy Grill** (11:30am-3pm daily) offers snacks and drinks.

Nightlife

It gets quiet early in Manchester and Manchester Center, but there are a couple of places to go for a late-night bite and beer. **Mulligan's Pub & Restaurant** (3912 Main St., Manchester Center, 802/362-3663, 11:30am-midnight daily, under $25) is part family dining room, part sports bar with old-fashioned green bar lamps and a convivial atmosphere. **The Perfect Wife Restaurant & Tavern** (2594 Depot St., Manchester Center, 802/362-2817, 4pm-10pm Mon.-Sat., under $40) is a dinner spot with a happening bar area cheekily called **The Other Woman.** A greenhouse next to the tavern fills up when it's warmer outside, and there are heat lamps for cooler nights.

Shopping

The hub is the **Manchester Designer Outlets** (97 Depot St., Manchester Center, 802/362-3736, www.manchesterdesigneroutlets.com, 10am-6pm daily), home to 44 designer brands including Ann Taylor, J Crew, and Vineyard Vines.

On a more local front, hikers of all stripes should stop by **The Mountain Goat** (4886 Main St., Manchester Center, 802/362-5159, www.mountaingoat.com, 10am-6pm Mon.-Sat., 10am-5pm Sun.), which not only carries plenty of outdoor clothing, shoes, and gear, but staffs a friendly and accommodating crew that knows all the tricks and tips for hikers. Looking for a place to stay? Need a ride to a trailhead? They can help.

You can find a good book, and a great place to read it, at **Northshire Bookstore** (4869 Main St., Manchester Center, 802/362-2200, www.northshire.com, 10am-7pm Sun.-Thurs., 10am-9pm Fri.-Sat.), whose spacious upstairs hangout area includes café-style tables and counters made for laptops.

Food

Breakfast

Not only is ★ **Up For Breakfast** (4935 Main St., Manchester Center, 802/362-4202, under $20) a great name for a breakfast restaurant, it's also completely accurate: You have to walk up a flight of narrow stairs to reach this 2nd-floor eatery. Often that flight of stairs includes about a dozen or so patiently waiting patrons, because Up For Breakfast is a tiny place serving up superb meals and is perfect for a post-hike refill. If you get a seat at the tight counter, order the Hungry Hiker, a specialty for AT hikers that includes two eggs, sausage, bacon, potatoes, and pancakes (opt for blueberry pancakes). The Wild Turkey Hash is another favorite, combining runny eggs with turkey hash, veggies, and cubed potatoes. Hungry yet? Make sure you bring cash.

If you'd rather chew on some sugary carbs, **Mrs. Murphy's Donuts** (374 Depot St., Manchester Center, 802/362-1874, 5am-6pm Mon.-Fri., 5am-4pm Sat., 5am-2pm Sun.) is can't-miss material. Go early to this quaint diner with a snaking counter to have your pick at a wider selection. Muffins and breakfast sandwiches are also served, but come on, you're here for doughnuts.

Spiral Press Café (1 Bonnet St., 802/362-9944, 7:30am-7pm Mon.-Sat., 8am-7pm Sun., under $20) serves coffee, pastries, and sandwiches.

American

The toughest table in town is at the ★ **Silver Fork** (4201 Main St., Manchester Center, 802/768-8444, www.thesilverforkvt.com, 5pm-9:30pm Mon.-Sat., under $75). Why? For one, there are six tables in this cozy spot, but more importantly, the food never disappoints. The Silver Fork specializes in New American with Spanish and Caribbean twists, so you'll be wise to order both the crab cake and the *mofongo*. Thirty minutes before you want to eat dessert, order the Caribbean bread pudding soufflé. You'll float to the clouds.

Snag a reservation for a weekend-night dinner at the **Copper Grouse** (3835 Main St., Manchester, 802/362-0176, www.coppergrouse.com, 7am-10am breakfast daily, 10am-2pm brunch Sun., 11am-2pm lunch Mon.-Sat., 5pm-9pm dinner Sun.-Thurs., 5pm-10pm dinner Fri.-Sat., under $20 breakfast, under $30 lunch, under $60 dinner), the restaurant attached to the Taconic Hotel. Leather chairs and black walls make this dining room fitting for romantic or celebratory meals, while the New American, Vermont-centric menu features beef tenderloin and a local charcuterie plate.

Established in the 18th century, the **Marsh Tavern** (3567 Main St., Manchester, 802/362-4700, 11:30am-11:30pm daily, under $40) at the Equinox fills up quickly with guests wanting to drink in the history at this stately dining room. Main tavern fare includes crab cakes, shepherd's pie, and a local cheddar-and-ale fondue.

Italian

If fine dining isn't your forte, **Al Ducci's Italian Pantry** (133 Elm St., Manchester Center, 802/362-4449, www.alduccis.com, 10am-4pm Sun.-Mon., 8am-6pm Tues.-Sat., under $20) has all the rations you need, especially if you've just descended a mountain. You can order a prosciutto and mozzarella sandwich with two-year-old ham. That's living.

For an alternative and more of a family sit-down atmosphere, **Christos' Pizza and Pasta** (4931 Main St., Manchester Center, 802/362-2408, www.christospizzaandpasta.com, 11am-10pm Sun.-Thurs., 11am-11pm Fri.-Sat., under $25) combines Italian and Greek specialties, sometimes in the same dish. There are plenty of topping options for pizzas and combination options for pasta dishes.

Accommodations

An institution in Manchester, ★ **The Equinox Golf Resort & Spa** (3567 Main St., Manchester, 802/362-4700, www.equinoxresort.com, $199-599 offseason and weekdays in-season, $499-999 weekends in-season) started as an inn in the mid-1800s, and since 1972 has been a luxury resort for tourists with a few bones. It also commands a considerable portion of the village: Equinox's other lodging properties in Manchester include the **Charles Orvis Inn** and the **1811 House,** and it also runs the **Golf Club at Equinox** (108 Union St., Manchester). In total the Equinox owns 17 buildings of varying styles.

The main hotel building has 200 rooms that include spacious guest rooms and suites with modern twists on 19th-century furnishings. The Charles Orvis Inn has similar rooms to the main hotel, but the 1811 House has decidedly more antiquated rooms with creaking hardwood. Guests can eat at a traditional hotel dining space, the Marsh Tavern (serving lunch and dinner), or at the Chop House, a reservations-first, steak-later spot arranged like a fancy living room with white tablecloths and fireplaces. Sit around a fire pit at the Falcon Bar, which serves adult drinks with tapas. And sometimes an actual falconer shows up with a bird. No joke. There's also a standalone spa at the resort and an indoor swimming pool.

The expensive lodging options aren't restricted to the Equinox. **The Reluctant Panther Inn & Restaurant** (39 West Rd., Manchester, 802/362-2568, www.reluctantpanther.com, $179-599) has 20 rooms across three buildings, each with a sitting area and sleeping area, a fireplace, and modern amenities like flat-screen televisions and Wi-Fi. **The Inn at Manchester** (3967 Main St., Manchester Center, 800/273-1793, www.innatmanchester.com, $155-315) also owns three buildings and showcases a variety of room shapes and styles. Some have fireplaces and porches. The rooms at **Palmer House Resort** (5383 Main St., Manchester Center, 802/362-3600, $185-325) are crisp and relatively basic compared to the other inns, but this place has a nine-hole golf course, indoor and outdoor swimming pools, a fishing pond, and a barbecue pit. And people-watching is the order of the day at the **Taconic Hotel** (3835 Main St., Manchester Center, 802/362-0147, $140-480), which features an expansive wraparound porch with a fire pit and restaurant seating for the **Copper Grouse.** Inside, the Taconic is a supermodern boutique combining country coziness with the West Elm catalog. The Taconic also has a bicycle loaner program, should you want to tour the town on two wheels.

A bit more affordable, the **Stamford Motel** (6458 Main St., Manchester Center, 802/362-2342, $80-135) is a good option if you need to watch the wallet. There are a few ground rules here, including $20 for each additional person who stays in your room and a $60 charge if you want to bring your pet, but the rooms are tidy and the staff gets high praise. Another good choice is the **Brittany Motel** (1056 Main St., Manchester, 802/362-1033, $79-140), which offers a stunning view of Mount Equinox plus everything you'd need out of a standard motel, but with more spacious rooms. No pets allowed here.

Emerald Lake State Park

Take VT-7A until it runs back into US-7 and follow that road north to **Emerald Lake State Park** (65 Emerald Lake Lane, East Dorset, 802/362-1655, 10am-sunset), just 9 miles (14.5 km) north of Manchester. This 908-acre park is best for swimming and hiking, with plenty of wilderness to get lost in (just bring a compass, please). Park visitors will find the remnants of old quarry sites, the reminders of Dorset's thriving early 19th-century marble industry.

Rich Woods Trail System

The park is known for the **Rich Woods Trail System,** a combination of trails totaling 3 miles (4.8 km) in a loop on the west end of the park. A trailhead is south of the recycling center at campground A. Swimming is permitted at Emerald Lake in summer. Fishing of smallmouth bass, bullhead, panfish, perch, and pike can be enjoyed there, too. You can also rent out kayaks, canoes, and paddleboats ($10-20/hour).

Camping

There are 66 **tent and RV sites** ($18-20) at Emerald Lake State Park, plus 37 **lean-to sites** ($25-27).

Rutland

Like Pittsfield in Massachusetts, **Rutland** (pop. 17,292) is a larger city still finding itself among otherwise tourist-happy locations. The downtown has some abandoned buildings and can get pretty quiet, but there's enough hiking and sightseeing here to keep folks busy. Locals may call it "Rut-Vegas," which is a common moniker for almost any city in Vermont. Basically, it's a sarcastic way of calling a place "the big city."

Getting There and Around

The **Marble Valley Regional Transit Center** (102 West St., 802/747-3502, www.thebus.com, daily) is where you can grab the Bus, which will connect you to Killington to the east and Manchester to the south. You can also hop on a bus with **Vermont Translines** (844/888-7267, www.vttranslines.com, daily), taking you north or south via US-7, or east toward White River Junction.

Sights

Norman Rockwell Museum

Whereas the Norman Rockwell Museum in Stockbridge, Massachusetts, resembles a big-city museum with partitioned galleries featuring original pieces, interactive exhibits, and an information desk, Rutland's **Norman Rockwell Museum** (654 US-4, 802/773-6095, www.normanrockwellvt.com, 9am-5pm daily, $10) is mainly one giant room that showcases a collection of *Saturday Evening Post* covers that would make an *Antiques Roadshow* dealer blush. If you want to see a bunch of magazine covers arranged in a logical order, this is certainly the place for you. Otherwise there's little else that's interesting, sans an illustration done by Rockwell detailing the fire that destroyed his studio, which he allegedly drew the very night of the fire. Prints, figurines, plates, and more are available for purchase in the large gift shop.

Recreation

Pine Hill Park (2 Oak St., 9am-6pm daily, www.pinehillpark.org) is a 300-acre park maintained for hiking, walking, and biking. The biking is a big deal, with 16

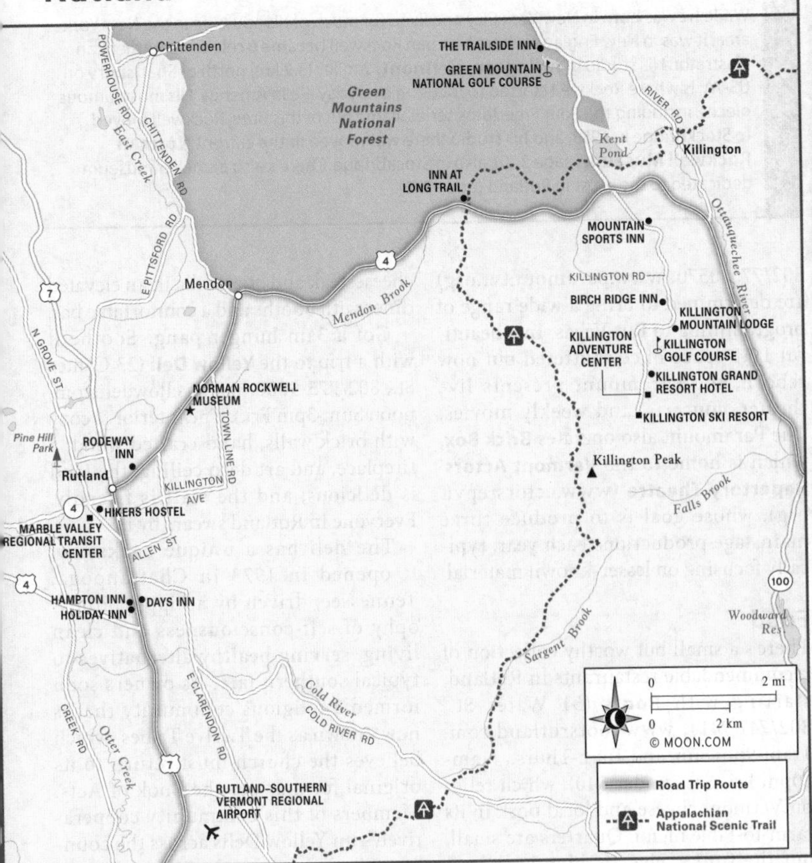

miles (26 km) of single track available for mountain bikers. The list of trails is extensive, with names like Jersey Turnpike and Sore Elbow.

Entertainment and Events

Nightlife

While Vermont is known as a craft beer hub, the southwestern swath of the state is still figuring things out. But **Hop'n Moose** (41 Center St., 802/775-7063, www.hopnmoose.com, 4pm-10pm Tues.-Thurs., noon-11pm Fri.-Sat., noon-8pm Sun., under $25) has been around since 2014. Offering a full lunch and dinner menu, Hop'n Moose goes for a variety of beer inside its sports-bar-style haunt with plenty of hockey memorabilia on the walls. If you plan on returning a bunch of times, join Hop'n Moose's **Mug Club** ($50), which gets you half-off starters Tuesdays and Wednesdays, plus a free mug, T-shirt, bumper sticker, and pint glass.

Performing Arts

The funky and fresh people behind the **Paramount Theater** (30 Center St.,

Norman Rockwell's New England Legacy

While he was born in New York City and lived for much of his adult life in the New York area, it was in New England where Norman Rockwell became a celebrated American illustrator. His studio in **Arlington, Vermont,** 2 miles (3.2 km) north of Shaftsbury on US-7A, is where Rockwell started to focus on everyday life in America. His most famous pieces, including the Four Freedoms series, came out of this time. Rockwell moved to Stockbridge in 1953, and his studio there was moved to the current **Norman Rockwell Museum** (page 340), also in Stockbridge. There's also a smaller museum dedicated to the artist in Rutland (page 370).

802/775-0570, www.paramountvt.org) are determined to bring a wide range of programming to Rut-Vegas. In a beautiful 1913 space once shuttered but now reborn, the Paramount presents live theater, concerts, and weekly movies. The Paramount also operates **Brick Box,** which is home to the **Vermont Actors' Repertory Theatre** (www.actorsrepvt.org), whose goal is to produce three mainstage productions each year, typically focusing on lesser-known material.

Food

There's a small but worthy collection of recommendable restaurants in Rutland, starting with **Roots** (51 Wales St., 802/747-7414, www.rootsrutland.com, 11am-9pm Sun. and Tues.-Thurs., 11am-10pm Fri.-Sat., under $40), which relies on Vermont cheese and local pork in its farm-to-table menu. Quarters are small, but the funky, electric-blue backdrop makes for a unique experience.

Just a block away and around the corner, **Little Harry's** (121 West St., 802/747-4848, www.littleharrys.com, 5pm-10pm daily, under $40) does whatever it feels like doing, and does it well. The menu is varied in this lively, exotic-toned dining room with bar, from chicken parmesan to jerk chicken to mushroom strudel to pad thai.

It's no-muss, no-fuss over at **Kelvan's** (128 Merchants Row, 802/775-1550, 11am-9pm Wed.-Thurs., 11am-10pm Fri., 11am-9:30pm Sat., under $25), which offers standard pub fare like a Philly cheesesteak and quesadilla in an elevated diner with booths and a comfortable bar.

Got a 3am hunger pang? Soothe it with a trip to the **Yellow Deli** (23 Center St., 802/775-9800, www.yellowdeli.com, noon Sun.-3pm Fri.). The interior is cozy with brick walls, hand-crafted wood, a fireplace, and art deco ceiling; the food is delicious; and the staff is friendly. Everyone in Rutland swears by it.

The deli has a unique backstory. It opened in 1973 in Chattanooga, Tennessee, driven by a hippie philosophy of self-consciousness and clean living, serving healthy alternatives to typical southern fare. Its owners soon formed a religious community that is now known as the Twelve Tribes, which believes the church must return to its original form as per the Book of Acts. Members of this community cooperatively run Yellow Delis across the country. They also run the **Hikers Hostel** chain, which are typically in areas near major hiking trails.

Accommodations

Under $100

Rutland has two speeds when it comes to accommodations: cheap and slightly less cheap. The usual motor inn suspects are here and provide basic places to lay your head. They include a **Rodeway Inn** (115 Woodstock Ave., 802/779-0036, $69-129) east of the city center, another **Rodeway Inn** (138 N. Main St., 802/775-2575, $69-129) 0.5 mile (0.8 km) north from the city center, a renovated **Comfort Inn** (19 Allen

St., 802/775-2200, $89-139), and a **Days Inn** (401 US-7, 802/282-4985, $65-125).

Then there's the **Hikers Hostel** (23 Center St., 802/683-9378, www.hikershostel.org, donations and work accepted); your decision to stay there may very well hinge on how you feel around people in a very tight, small religious community described by many as a "cult." Hikers Hostel operates above the Yellow Deli and is reportedly clean, comfortable, and filled with nice people. You may have to do a little work around the house as payment, but hey, helping prepare dinner ain't so bad, right?

$100-200

Close to the intersection of US-4 and US-7 are the two moderately priced hotels: the **Hampton Inn** (47 Farrell Rd., 802/773-9066, $129-189) and the **Holiday Inn** (476 Holiday Dr., 802/775-1911, $100-180). Both have indoor pools, while the Holiday Inn has a bar and restaurant.

Killington

The Appalachian Trail and Long Trail brush past the summit of **Killington Peak,** which at 4,241 feet (1,293 m) is the second-highest peak in Vermont. That mountain is the very reason that the otherwise tiny town of **Killington** (pop. 811) turns into one of Vermont's largest cities during the winter.

Hundreds of thousands annually visit Killington Ski Resort, which occupies the mountain, plus nearby peaks, and is the largest ski area east of the Mississippi River. The resort dominates the town, with its massive hotel and golf course providing the introduction for the huge ski area above, comprising 155 trails and a collection of lodging, drinking, and dining establishments. Surrounding the resort are various restaurants, bars, and accommodations, most of which are either rough-and-tumble or country cozy. Note: In Killington things are either "on the mountain" or "off the mountain." The former refers to anything on the resort, while the latter is the surrounding area where locals hang.

During the summer traffic is quieter, though the resort is turning into a year-round enterprise thanks to the addition of mountain biking trails. But mountain biking doesn't have the draw of skiing here; if you come in summer, you'll be able to find a comfortable room and hike to your heart's content. And the hiking here is good: The AT to Killington Peak is challenging, while up the trail hikers pass Thundering Brook Falls Trail and enjoy beer and an overnight stay at one of the trail's most beloved inns.

Getting There and Around

Marble Valley Regional Transit (802/747-3502, www.thebus.com, daily) offers the Bus, which will connect you to Rutland to the west. You can also hop on a bus with **Vermont Translines** (844/888-7267, www.vttranslines.com, daily), taking you west to Rutland or east toward White River Junction.

Hiking

Killington Peak

Distance: 7.2 miles (11.6 km)
Duration: 5-6 hours
Elevation gain: 2,441 feet (744 m)
Difficulty: Strenuous
Trailhead: Brewers Corner at Wheelerville Road (43.619265, -72.876919)

The quickest way to the top of Killington Peak is via the Flume Trail at Killington Resort, which follows the K-1 Express Gondola for a direct but arduous climb. But this hike here keeps you out of the resort traffic.

Start at the Bucklin trailhead and follow the blue blazes. You'll be beside Brewers Brook for the first mile (1.6 km) of the trek, but soon the trail will climb and get more strenuous. Finally, you'll reach an intersection with the Appalachian Trail and Long Trail; turn right and follow the AT and LT until the Killington Spur comes in. You'll follow that to the summit, using all fours on a relatively challenging scramble. At the summit you'll be able to spot the Adirondack, Green, Taconic, and White Mountains.

When finished, head down the Killington Spur until you reach the intersection with the Appalachian Trail and Long Trail. Close by is Coopers Cabin, a cozy stone structure that's a popular overnight stay for hikers. After checking out Coopers Cabin, follow the AT and LT back to the Bucklin Trail and finish up.

Thundering Brook Falls

Distance: 1 mile (1.6 km)
Duration: 30 minutes
Elevation gain: N/A
Difficulty: Easy
Trailhead: River Road north of Thundering Brook Road (43.680620, -72.782237)

If you're seeking a quick jaunt to a pretty little waterfall, it doesn't get any better than the trail to Thundering Brook Falls. Even better, it's a wheelchair-accessible hike, allowing everyone to enjoy this natural site. From the parking area off River Road, follow the Appalachian Trail south along a 900-foot (274-m) boardwalk built by the Green Mountain Club. The boardwalk snakes around flora until it reaches a viewing area for the falls. The more ambitious can venture up to get other views of the falls, with four drops in total at about 120 feet (37 m) in height.

Recreation

Killington Ski Resort

Winter sports enthusiasts consider Killington the ultimate New England destination for skiing and snowboarding. The popular **Killington Ski Resort** (4763 Killington Rd., 800/734-9435, www.killington.com, $59-69 adults, $33-39 ages 6 and younger) is open from October to May most years, making for one of the longest ski seasons in North America. It also has become a regular venue for the

view from Killington Peak

Audi FIS Women's Ski World Cup, akin to the LPGA Tour in golf.

Killington boasts 155 trails totaling 73 miles (118 km), many of them shooting down from Killington Peak, Bear Mountain, Sunrise Mountain, Skye Peak, Snowdon Mountain, and Ramshead Mountain. The longest ski trail east of the Mississippi is here, the 6.2-mile (10-km) Juggernaut, which cradles the shoulder of Killington Peak before zipping down to Sunrise. While the most difficult trails start at Killington Peak, there are a variety of beginner trails down-mountain, along with a learn-to-ski area.

For trained enthusiasts seeking the maximum Killington experience, the onsite K-1 Lodge is the best starting point for a day of skiing, with the quickest access to the hardest trails. Beginners should hang at the Snowshed, which has daily tours for experienced novices and higher at 10am and 11am. If you're not ready for that, you can also do a Mountain Orientation session, which starts at 9am daily at the trail guide sign atop the K-1 Express Gondola.

Killington Adventure Center and Mountain Bike Park

When the snow melts, Killington Ski Resort becomes **Killington Adventure Center and Mountain Bike Park.** The **Adventure Center** (4763 Killington Rd., 800/734-9435, www.killington.com, $59-69 adults, $33-39 ages 6 and younger) takes over the Snowshed area of the resort, with an alpine coaster, ropes course, zip line, and trampoline jump among the various extreme activities. Mountain biking enthusiasts have many of the ski trails to themselves during the warmer months at the **Mountain Bike Park** (4763 Killington Rd., 800/734-9435, www.killington.com, $20-159 adults, $20-119 ages 18 and younger). Bikes, helmets, shoes, and protection are all available for rent.

Golf

If you have an aversion to the slopes, you can always take on the sloping fairways of **Killington Golf Course** (227 E. Mountain Rd., 802/422-6700, www.killington.com, $40-65 18 holes, $20-40 9 holes), the resort's par-72 public course. About 7 miles (11.3 km) up the road, **Green Mountain National Golf Course** (476 Barrows-Towne Rd., 802/422-4653, www.gmngc.com, $68-90 late-June-closing, $49-70 opening-late-June) offers a mighty challenge surrounded by verdant hills. The view from the 16th tee box is especially gorgeous.

Nightlife

Don't want to drive? Call the **Barrel Rider** (802/422-7433, free), a shuttle that can take you to and from your lodging.

At the first sign of frosty air in Killington, locals will begin preparations for party season. Most eyes will cast toward the **Pickle Barrel Nightclub** (1741 Killington Rd., 802/422-3035, www.picklebarrelnightclub.com), a stalwart

with a main concert stage, multiple dancing areas, and a convivial atmosphere. It hosts concerts most weekend nights but be warned: There's typically a cover charge of around $20.

Next door, sister bar **Jax Food & Games** (1667 Killington Rd., 802/422-5334, www.jaxfoodandgames.com, 3pm-2am daily, under $25) is a spirited bar with pub menu, local beer, plenty of televisions including a huge projection screen, and arcade games. Hikers should know Jax serves food up to last call and is up the stairs from **Scrub-a-Dub-Pub,** a laundry with a full bar and pool tables.

Whether you stay at the Inn at Long Trail or not, you must stop in **McGrath's Irish Pub** (709 US-4, 802/775-7181, www.innatlongtrail.com, under $20) for a pint of Guinness and one of the bar's many Irish whiskeys. There's always some sort of Irish music playing on weekends here, and if you can, snag a seat on the pub's boulder (yes, you can sit on a real boulder, plus a second boulder runs from the pub to the neighboring Rosemary's Restaurant). And don't leave McGrath's until you spend a minute in the small entranceway littered by postcards and photographs from thankful AT thru- and section hikers. I guarantee you'll tear up a little, and it won't be because of the whiskey.

Food

On the mountain, nothing beats **Ledgewood Yurt** (Northbrook Tr., 866/809-9147, www.killington.com, 11am-2pm lunch Sat.-Sun. Jan.-April, under $30), which is, you guessed it, a yurt. Inside, white tablecloths and candlelight accompany hearty fare like lamb and potatoes and smoked pork brisket. The Yurt hosts family dinner nights ($65 per person) during December and

Top to bottom: upper section of Thundering Brook Falls; Killington Ski Resort; Billings Farm & Museum in Woodstock.

February vacations, and five-course adult dinner excursions the entire year ($129, Sat. Apr.-Dec., varying weekdays Dec. 31-Mar.), both of which include sleigh rides to the yurt. Book dinners at least two weeks in advance.

There's an abundance of dining options off the mountain, and a select few rise above the crop. Try **The Garlic** (1724 Killington Rd., 802/422-5055, 5pm-10pm Sun.-Thurs., 4pm-10pm Fri.-Sat., under $40) if you want small plates to pair with a martini or glass of wine.

Large windows showcase the pond and illuminate the modern-rustic space at the **Foundry at Summit Pond** (63 Summit Path, 802/422-5335, 3pm-10pm Mon.-Thurs., 3pm-11pm Fri., 11am-11pm Sat., 11am-10pm Sun., under $30 lunch, under $50 dinner). The Foundry specializes in land and sea fare and features a brunch with chicken and waffles.

It only makes sense that **Choices Restaurant** (2820 Killington Rd., 802/422-4030, 5pm-9pm Sun.-Tues., 5pm-10pm Thurs., 5pm-11pm Fri.-Sat., under $50 dinner) serves everything from nachos to fettucine to Asian shrimp. The casual spot is a longtime favorite, staying busy nightly because of its solid reputation. Sunday brunch (under $30) is offered December to April.

If you want the definitive Killington experience, the **Wobbly Barn** (2229 Killington Rd., 802/422-6171, www.wobblybarn.com, under $75) is the place. Skiers, tourists, and locals congregate at this institution, opened in 1963, for dinner, drinks, and partying. Purists should opt for steak, but the Wobbly also has plenty of fish and vegetable selections. The Wobbly tells guests to arrive before 6pm or after 9pm on weekends for a calm dinner experience. And if you need a ride there, the Wobbly has its own Wobbly Wagon, which runs up and down Killington Road whenever it's open. That's especially valuable if you're staying out late and enjoying a few drinks.

Accommodations

The town books up pretty quickly starting in October.

On the mountain, the **Killington Grand Resort Hotel** (228 E. Mountain Rd., 802/422-5001, www.killington.com, $200-550, varies by season) is the facility that towers over all, a three-star accommodation resembling a mountain chalet. Rooms are basic, with studios and suites that include full kitchens. Amenities include a café with Starbucks coffee, the Killington Grand Spa, a game room and health club, and bar and lounge areas.

At a lower price point, the **Killington Mountain Lodge** (2617 Killington Rd., 802/422-4302, www.killingtonmountainlodge.com, $120-275, varies by season) offers the same basic rooms as the Grand Resort Hotel with clean, unassuming décor. Dip yourself in the outdoor hot tub or hang out by the fire pit.

The cozy **Birch Ridge Inn** (37 Butler Rd., 802/422-4293, www.birchridge.com, $120-250, varies by season) has 10 guest rooms ranging from your mother's spare bedroom to a French provincial room with four-poster bed. Some rooms have fireplaces and whirlpool tubs.

The top draw for hikers is the ★ **Inn at Long Trail** (709 US-4, 802/775-7181, www.innatlongtrail.com, $120-580 mid-Dec.-March, $90-145 April-mid-Dec.), just steps from the Appalachian Trail and Long Trail and commanding a sizable property along the highway. Choose from the pricier fireplace suite, a whirlpool room, or a standard country bedroom with basic amenities. Rosemary's Restaurant and McGrath's Irish Pub are on-site.

Rustic and simple, **Mountain Sports Inn** (813 Killington Rd., 802/422-3315, www.mountainsportsinn.com, $78-285, varies by season) is a step up from motor lodges with circa 1990s accommodations. There's an indoor hot tub and sauna on-site.

Rustic and full of small touches like

Vermont's Beloved Breweries

Vermont is known for beer. In fact, there are multiple beer trails in the state, taking folks around cities like Brattleboro, Burlington, and Middlebury. But the southern part of the state has few trails, because it has few breweries. While people go nuts for upstate spots like Hill Farmstead and the Alchemist, there are a few places to shout out down south. They include:

- **Long Trail Brewing Co.** (5520 US-4, Bridgewater Corners, 802/672-5011, www.longtrail.com, 10am-7pm daily, under $30) is a longtime stalwart in Vermont, hanging between Killington and Woodstock since 1995. The brewery takes its name from the famed Vermont Long Trail, and its beer names are lovingly inspired by the outdoors (Green Blaze IPA, Double Bag).
- **Foley Brothers Brewing** (79 Stone Mill Dam Rd., Brandon, 802/465-8413, www.foleybrothersbrewing.com, 11am-5pm Wed.-Sat., 11am-4pm Sun., under $20) is the kind of small-batch brewery that makes Vermont a brewing capital. Four beers are regularly on tap at this brewery just 16 miles (26 km) north from Rutland on US-7.
- **Northshire Brewery** (108 County St., Bennington, 802/681-0201, www.northshirebrewery.org, 1pm-6pm Thurs.-Fri., 10am-6pm Sat., under $15) features the easy-drinking Equinox Pilsner, named after the nearby peak. A tasting of four beers is an inexpensive $5.
- **Madison Brewing Company Pub & Restaurant** (428 Main St., Bennington 802/442-7397, www.madisonbrewingco.com, 11:30am-9pm Sun.-Thurs., 11:30am-10pm Fri.-Sat., under $25) brews a variety of styles, cooks up basic pub and American fare, and has both a large dining room and a small bar area with some stools nearby.

handcrafted headboards and fluffy towels, **The Trailside Inn** (115 Coffeehouse Rd., 802/422-8800, www.trailsidevt.com, $80-220, varies by season) has plenty of options, including bunk rooms, a two-story private barn, and a loft apartment designed for groups and families.

Woodstock

Roughly 20 miles (32 km) east on US-4 from Killington, the Vermont land evens out just enough. The Shire country fades behind you as the road curves elegantly. Soon the traffic slows, which means another small town is upon you. And with its boutique stores, genteel character, and an open green that abuts a luxury inn, **Woodstock** (pop. 3,048) is one heck of a small town. It's a scenic nook of pep surrounded by rolling farmland. While the Appalachian Trail rests a good 10 miles (16 km) north of the town center, hikers may pop down from the quiet to engage in some weekend tourism.

Getting There and Around

There's bus service to Killington and Rutland to the west, and White River Junction to the east, via **Vermont Translines** (844/888-7267, www.vttranslines.com, daily).

Sights

Marsh-Billings-Rockefeller National Historic Park

It makes complete sense that a house and grounds so focused on stewardship and preserving history is known by three different family names. The history of the **Marsh-Billings-Rockefeller National**

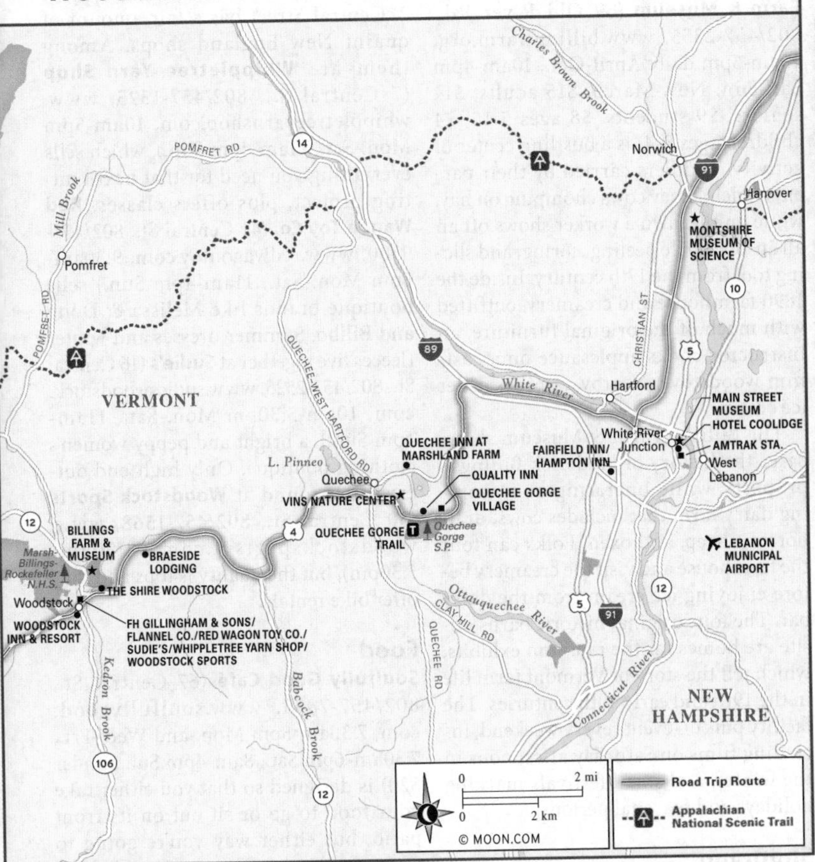

Historic Park (54 Elm St., 802/457-3368, 10am-5pm daily, tours $8 adults, $4 seniors and age 15 and younger) starts with Charles Marsh, a Vermont lawyer who built the main house on 246 acres. Marsh's son George helped spur the modern conservation movement with his 1864 book *Man and Nature; or the Physical Geography as Modified by Human Behavior.* Around this time the house was purchased by Frederick Billings, a railroad magnate who began farming on the property. His granddaughter Mary French Rockefeller took over the house later; she and her husband gave the property to the federal government, which soon turned it into a national historic park.

Now at more than 600 acres, the property is filled with carriage roads and hiking trails that are shaded by trees planted as early as the late 19th century. The mansion, an example of Queen Anne architecture thanks to its various triangular pediments and painted sash windows, can be toured with a fee, but reservations are recommended. Otherwise visitors are permitted to walk the grounds and picnic.

★ Billings Farm & Museum

On a late summer Sunday, the **Billings Farm & Museum** (69 Old River Rd., 802/457-2355, www.billingsfarm.org, 10am-5pm daily April-Oct., 10am-4pm Sat.-Sun. Nov.-March, $15 adults, $14 seniors, $9 students, $8 ages 5-15, $4 children ages 3-4) is a bustling center of activity. Toddlers carried by their parents touch Jersey cows chomping on hay, while on the lawn a worker shows off an all-in-one apple peeling, coring, and slicing tool from the 17th century. Inside the 1890 farmhouse and creamery, outfitted with much of the original furniture, an instructor cooks applesauce on a cast-iron woodstove. Nearby, families order ice cream.

The Billings Farm & Museum showcases the history of Frederick Billings's property while operating as a working dairy farm that includes cows, draft horses, sheep, and oxen. Folks can tour the farmhouse and visit the creamery before enjoying ice cream from the dairy bar. The four original historic barns on-site are homes for the museum exhibits, which tell the story of Vermont farm life in the 19th and early 20th centuries. The facility puts on events every weekend, including films on Saturday afternoons in the winter, and small festivals marking holidays and seasonal periods.

Shopping

Seven rooms of shopping await you at **F.H. Gillingham & Sons** (16 Elm St., 802/457-2100, 8:30am-6:30pm Mon.-Sat., 10am-5pm Sun.), the ultimate general store, which opened in 1886. Its inventory is vast, from local foods like Billings Farm cheese to sweaters, coffee mugs, children's jigsaw puzzles, and motorcycle belts. And that's just scratching the surface. Just across the street, the **Vermont Flannel Co.** (13 Elm St., 802/457-4111, www.vermontflannel.com, 9am-6pm Mon.-Thurs., 9am-7pm Fri.-Sat., 10am-5pm Sun.) doesn't mince words: there is a serious amount of flannel here. The shirts, pajamas, scarves, and blankets are all cuddle-worthy.

Central Street has a fair amount of quaint New England shops. Among them are **Whippletree Yarn Shop** (7 Central St., 802/457-1325, www.whippletreeyarnshop.com, 10am-5pm Mon.-Sat., 11am-4pm Sun.), which sells everything you need for that next knitting project, plus offers classes. **Red Wagon Toy Co.** (41 Central St., 802/457-9300, www.redwagontoy.com, 9:30am-5pm Mon.-Sat., 11am-4pm Sun.) sells boutique brands like Melissa & Doug and Bilibo. Summer dresses and winter fleeces live together at **Sudie's** (16 Central St., 802/457-2525, www.sudieswoodstock.com, 10am-5:30pm Mon.-Sat., 11am-4pm Sun.), a bright and peppy women's clothing boutique. Only high-end outerwear is found at **Woodstock Sports** (30 Central St., 802/457-1568, www.woodstocksportsvt.com, 8:30am-5:30pm), but the quality is tops and they offer bike rentals.

Food

Soulfully Good Café (67 Central St., 802/457-7395, www.soulfullygood.com, 7:30am-5pm Mon. and Wed.-Fri., 7:30am-6pm Sat., 8am-4pm Sun., under $20) is designed so that you either take your food to go or sit out on its front patio, but either way you're going to want to take some time to enjoy this food. Exceptional sandwiches are highlighted by the buttermilk fried chicken salad sandwich, served on a croissant.

On a warm day you'll find scores of people seated outside **Mon Vert Café** (28 Central St., 802/457-7143, www.monvertcafe.com, 7:30am-5pm Mon.-Thurs., 7:30am-5:30pm Fri.-Sat., 8am-5pm Sun., under $20), a popular coffee spot that serves up eggs, toasts, and filling sandwiches and salads.

Totally worth it is **Worthy Kitchen** (442 Woodstock Rd., 802/457-7281, www.worthyvermont.com, 4pm-9pm Mon.-Thurs., 4pm-10pm Fri., 11:30am-10pm

Sat., 11:30am-9pm Sun., under $30), an evolution of Worthy Burger, which is up the road in Royalton. Worthy Kitchen has the famous burger, plus poutine, salads, wings, and fries. Oh, and a killer craft beer list that's always changing and focuses on Vermont breweries. There's a very friendly vibe here.

For a classic sit-down meal, **The Prince & the Pauper** (24 Elm St., 802/457-1818, www.princeandthepauper.com, 5:30pm-8:30pm Sun.-Thurs., 5:30pm-9pm Fri.-Sat., under $100) has been the high-class go-to spot since 1974. They have a bistro menu every day but Saturday, but you might want to opt for the prix fixe menu, which could offer veal Normandy, filet mignon, or Atlantic swordfish. Wooden booths and white tablecloths make for a fine combination of rustic and gourmet. No jacket is required here, but the restaurant frowns on any cell phone use.

Up the road from the town green is **Angkor Wat** (61 Pleasant St., 802/457-9029, www.angkorwatcom, 4pm-9pm Tues.-Sun., under $30), which is housed in simple digs and serves Thai and Cambodian cuisine with an emphasis on healthy options. The crispy Cambodian chicken and steak are top draws, marinated in lemongrass, coconut, and lime leaf. BYOB.

Accommodations

Positioned near the town green and commanding eyes and attention, the stately and impressive **Woodstock Inn & Resort** (14 The Green, 802/332-6853, www.woodstockinn.com, $200-450) has four-star rooms like the Tavern Porch, which includes a closed-in sunroom. Even the hotel's basic double room has a bathroom with subway tile and Vermont marble. A 10,000-square-foot spa has 10 treatment rooms and locally sourced products. Pack your finest gingham shirts for a stay here.

A little more modest, **The Shire Woodstock** (46 Pleasant St., 802/457-2211, www.shirewoodstock.com, $115-200) offers exceptional accommodations with views of the Ottauquechee River. Some of the lightly touched New England-style rooms have fireplaces. Guests can spend some lazy time lounging in rocking chairs on the wraparound porch.

The rooms at the motor lodge-lite **The Braeside Lodging** (908 East Woodstock Rd., 802/457-1366, www.braesidemotel.com, $118-178, varies by season) are decorated in a style one might call "New England on a budget." It's simple and tasteful.

Quechee

Only 7.3 miles (11.7 km) east of Woodstock, and in the town of Hanover, is the village community of **Quechee** (pop. 656), known primarily for **Quechee Gorge,** the deepest gorge in Vermont with a riverbed 165 feet (50 m) below an overlook at US-4. The village itself is a short distance off US-4, accessible by turning left onto Waterman Hill Road and crossing a covered bridge over the Ottauquechee River. The village is narrow and angular, catering mainly to visitors of the village's higher-crust restaurants and inns. Otherwise, back near the gorge, you're in for a heck of a tourist shopping experience.

Sights

The 47-acre **VINS Nature Center** (149 Nature Way, 802/359-5000, www.vinsweb.org, 10am-5pm daily mid-April-Oct., 10am-4pm daily Nov.-mid-Apr., $15 adults, $14 seniors, $13 ages 4-17), short for Vermont Institute of Natural Science, focuses on avian rehabilitation and education. You can spot the many birds at VINS on its mile of nature trails. Special events include daily raptor feeding and demonstrations, allowing guests to get up close to these birds of prey. Since it can get pretty cold and snowy in Vermont, VINS also has an indoor forest exhibit that features a 16-foot (4.8-m) model tree that visitors can climb into, plus other opportunities to touch nature and learn about porcupines, foxes, leaves, and insects.

Shopping

You can't miss **Quechee Gorge Village** (5573 Woodstock Rd., 802/295-1550, 10am-5pm daily). No, really, it's impossible to miss it. Along US-4 is this vast indoor mall in which stores run into one another like a caterpillar. The village is anchored on one end by **Cabot Quechee Store,** whose large sampler table is regularly mobbed by tourists wanting to snack on cubes of sriracha cheddar. On the other end is the **Vermont Antique Mall,** which has more than 450 booths filled with finds. In between you can find yarn and clothing at the **Vermont Alpaca Store,** a true-to-life blacksmith at the **Green Mountain Fire & Hammer Blacksmith Shop,** and upstairs, the **Vermont Toy Museum and Toy Store** ($3/person, $5/family), which is floor-to-ceiling toys, board games, and other fun nostalgia trips.

Food

Simon Pearce is a popular glassware and pottery company with stores across the Northeast, but Quechee is home to the **Simon Pearce Restaurant** (1760 Quechee Main St., 802/295-1470, 11:30am-2:45pm lunch Mon.-Sat., 10:30am-2:45pm lunch Sun., 5:30pm-9pm dinner daily, under $30 lunch, under $50 dinner), where farm-to-table and craft cocktails blend with a workshop, display areas, and a gift shop. The open restaurant, outfitted in brick and light woods and pretty busy at all times, is exactly where you'd take Mom for Mother's Day.

Similarly, **The Parker House** (1792 Quechee Main St., 802/295-6077, www.theparkerhouseinn.com, 5pm-9pm Tues.-Sat., under $60) has porch seating for its decidedly New England menu of meat and fish. Just be warned that if you want to split an entrée, they charge $4 for the inconvenience.

Accommodations

The quintessential Quechee experience can be had from the **Quechee Inn at Marshland Farm** (1119 Quechee Main St., 802/295-3133, $130-180), which sprinkles in a bunch of country touches like quilts, lace over four-poster beds, and wide-planked pine floors. Budget travelers can find solace in the presence of the **Quality Inn** (5817 Woodstock Rd., 802/295-7600, $70-150). You'll get decent rooms here, plus an indoor pool and a gym.

Quechee State Park

Some 13,000 years ago work (by glaciers) began on Quechee Gorge. It is now the highlight of **Quechee State Park** (5800 Woodstock Rd., Hartford, 802/295-2990, 10am-sunset daily mid-May-mid-Oct.), which covers the space once owned by the A. G. Dewey Company. That company processed wool, including material worn by the New York Yankees and Boston Red Sox baseball teams. The mill closed in 1952, and the site became a park shortly afterward.

There are a few trails at the park, one heading to the gorge to the south and another to Dewey's Mill Pond at the northern end. Despite the park's relatively small size, it keeps a campground with 45 tent and trailer sites, plus seven lean-to shelters. This makes Quechee State Park a solid base camp for hiking and traveling in the Woodstock area.

Hiking

★ Quechee Gorge Trail

Distance: 1 mile (1.6 km)
Duration: 30 minutes
Elevation gain: N/A
Difficulty: Easy
Trailhead: Quechee Gorge Visitor Center

Get a down-low view of the Quechee Gorge Bridge before hopping into the gorge itself, experiencing a slice of Vermont's Grand Canyon. From the visitors center walk downstairs and out the

Quechee Gorge Trail

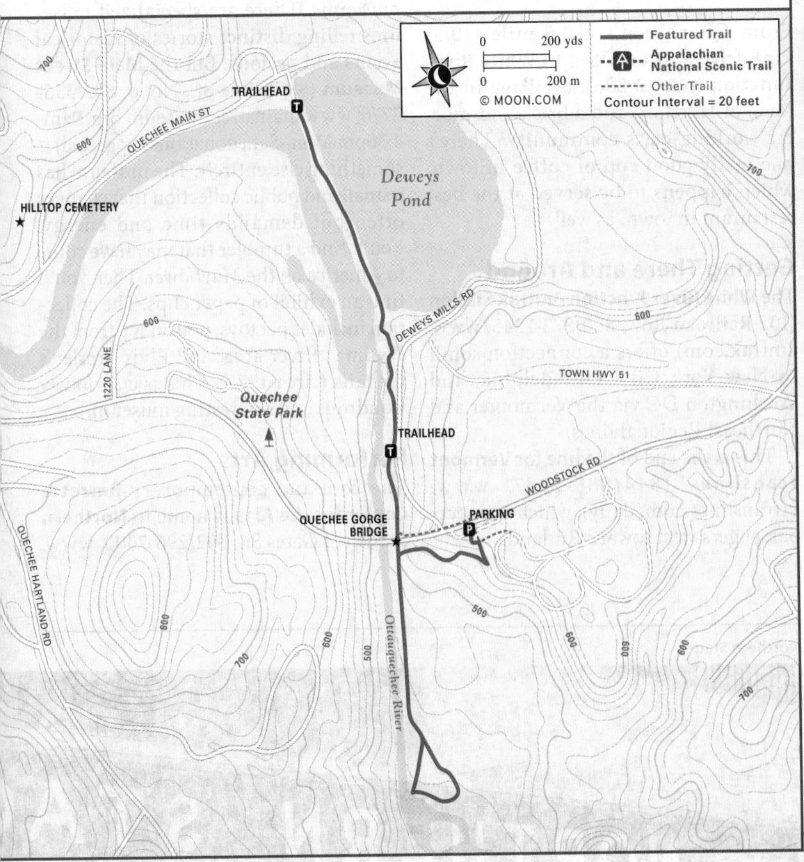

door, following the signs for the Gorge Trail as it meanders on switchbacks. You'll soon reach a T-intersection, and in front of you is the bridge. Take your photos there, and then head left, downhill, toward the gorge. It's a 0.25-mile (0.4-km) walk to where you can step out onto the riverbed. Take more photos, maybe take a swim—just don't mess with the rocks. Head back up the trail toward the bridge and the visitors center.

Accommodations

Quechee State Park has 47 **tent and trailer sites** ($18-20) and seven **lean-to shelters** ($25-27), plus two restrooms with flush toilets and coin-operated showers. Quechee only permits stays of two nights or more.

White River Junction

From Quechee it's a 6.5-mile (10.5-km) drive east on US-4 to **White River Junction** (pop. 2,286), a village in the town of Hartford and a brick-and-mortar working-class community. There's one really good cup of coffee in town, which happens to be served at the best restaurant in town, as well.

Getting There and Around

The **White River Junction Amtrak Station** (102 Railroad Row, 800/872-7245, www.amtrak.com) offers a connection south to New York City, Philadelphia, and Washington DC via the Vermonter and Northeast Regional lines.

This is the end of the line for **Vermont Translines** (844/888-7267, www.vttranslines.com, daily), which connects passengers west toward Rutland.

Main Street Museum

There are art museums. There are science museums. There are specialized museums telling distinct stories of historical events and periods. But the **Main Street Museum** (58 Bridge St., No. 6, 802/356-2776, www.mainstreetmuseum.org, 9am-4:30pm Mon.-Sat., donations suggested) is something else entirely. The museum has a small and public collection that changes often but demands time and energy. You'll find a tumbler that may have come to America on the *Mayflower.* Then you'll find an exhibit of paper clips. The collection includes pet toys, poison ivy from the Potomac River area, and Elvis Presley's toenails (circa 1972). This is a seriously wondrous and interesting museum.

Performing Arts

The cool and contemporary **Barrette Center for the Arts** is home to **Northern Stage** (74 Gates St., 802/296-7000, www.

Northern Stage

northernstage.org), an Actor's Equity theater group. The center seats 240 for intimate performances of six mainstage productions during the winter months, plus new works with an annual festival in January.

Food

★ **Tuckerbox** (1 S. Main St., 802/359-4041, www.tuckerboxvermont.com, 7am-3pm Mon.-Sat. breakfast and lunch, 9am-3pm Sun. breakfast and lunch, 5pm-9pm Tues.-Thurs. and Sun. dinner, 5pm-10pm Fri.-Sat. dinner, under $15 breakfast and lunch, under $50 dinner) has left no *tas* (stone) unturned with the Turkish menu, offering traditional Mediterranean breakfast dishes (for example, soft-boiled egg, olives, cheese, tomato, cucumber, and toast) and serving kebabs and earthenware casseroles for dinner. For a drink in this cool, pastel-walled, postindustrial space, Tuckerbox has traditional Turkish raki. Caution: It's really strong.

The hip **Elixir** (188 S. Main St., 802/281-7009, 4:30pm-9pm Tues.-Sat., under $40) sets up shop in an old freight house, so there's plenty of exposed brick and all hardwood floors, plus leather seating for the "just a drink" crowd. The cuisine is fun gourmet, from risotto cakes to cocoa-dusted filet mignon and potatoes.

Accommodations

Anchoring the downtown of White River Junction, the **Hotel Coolidge** (39 S. Main St., 802/295-3118, www.hotelcoolidge.com, $120-240) has every traveler covered. Most rooms are simple and economical, varying from basic queens to linked rooms to an entire wing devoted to extended-stay visitors. At the intersection of Interstates 89 and 91 are the **Fairfield Inn & Suites** (102 Ballardvale Dr., 802/291-9911, $100-170), the **Hampton Inn** (104 Ballardvale Dr., 802/296-2800, $100-160), and the **Comfort Inn** (56 Ralph Lehman Dr., 802/295-3051, $90-150), each offering basic to moderate accommodations.

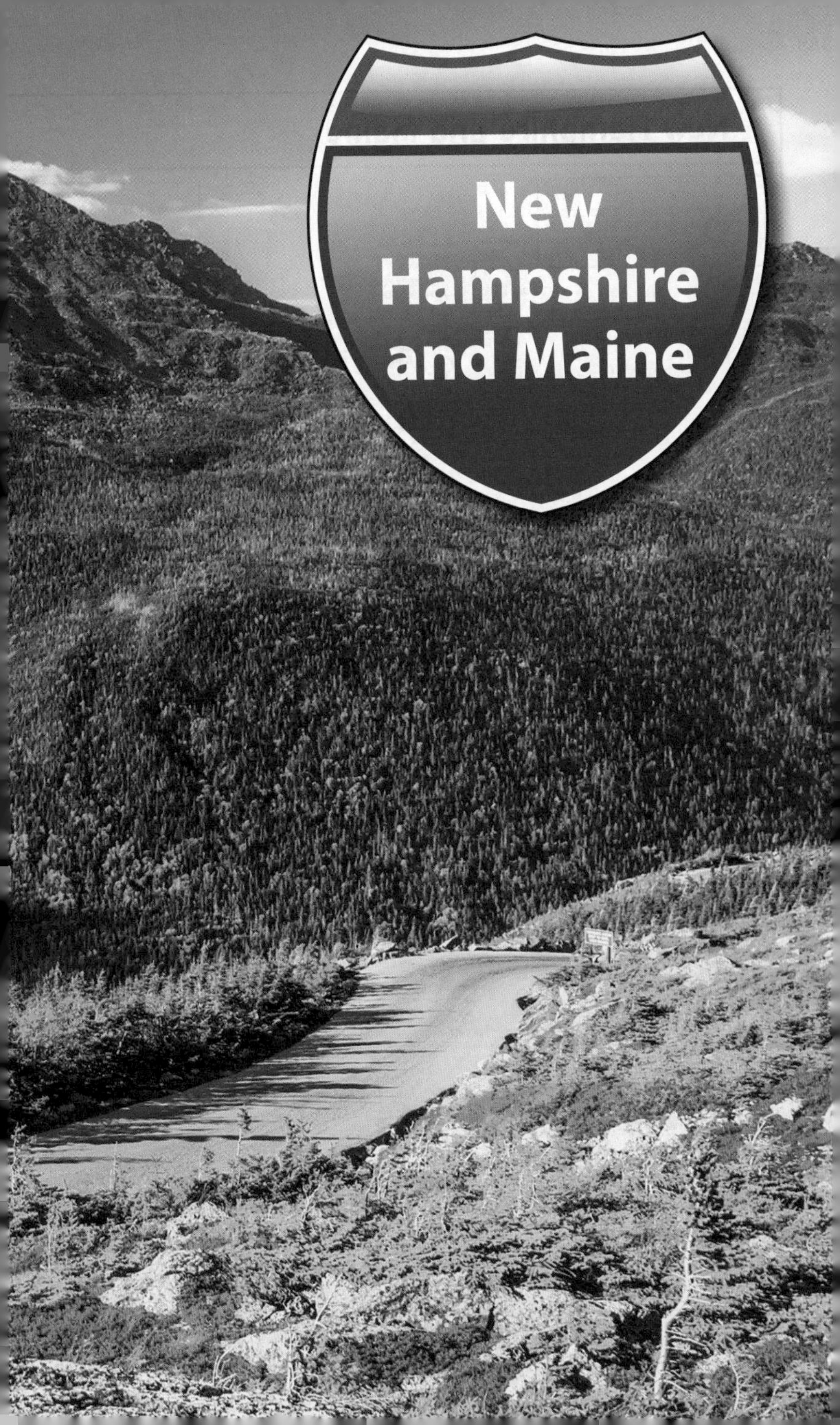
New
Hampshire
and Maine

New Hampshire and Maine

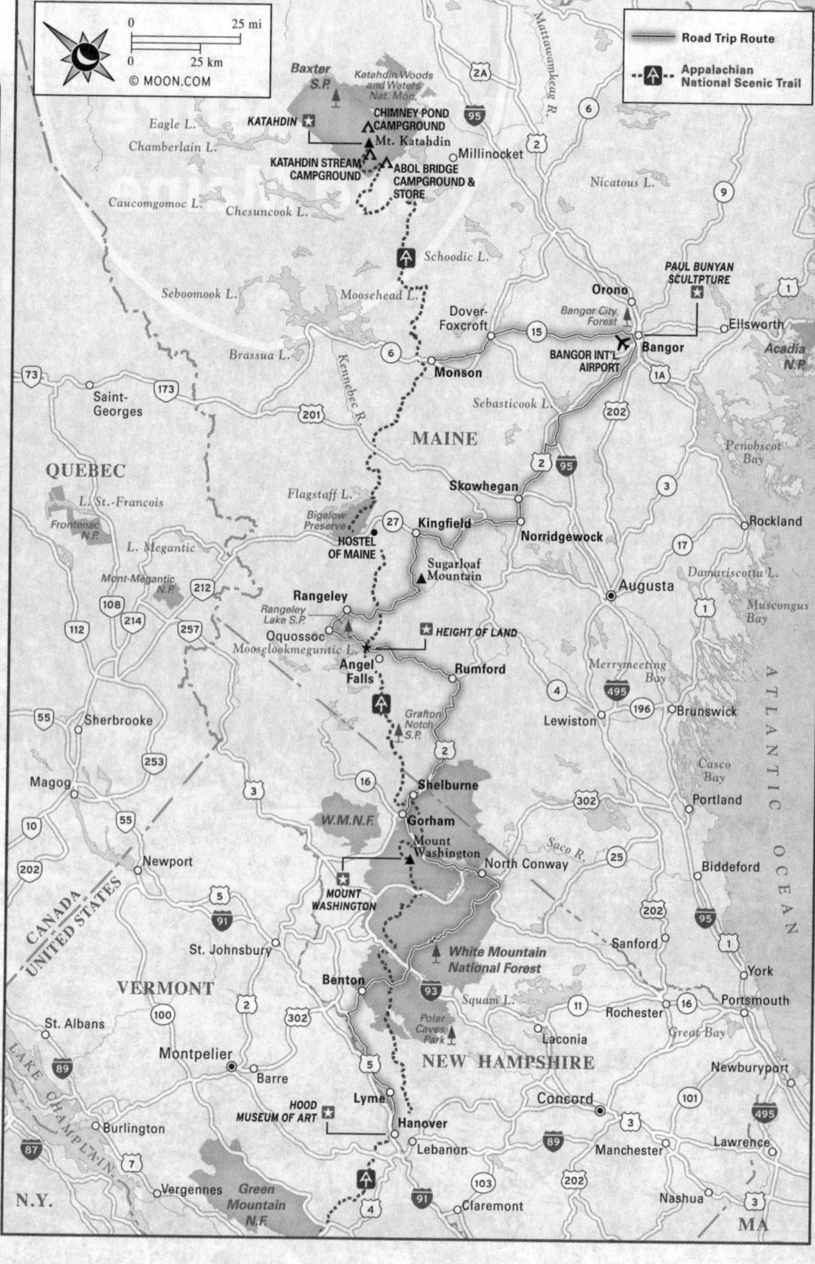

Highlights

★ **Hood Museum of Art:** See everything from 9th-century stone reliefs to works by Georgia O'Keeffe at this acclaimed Dartmouth University exhibit space in Hanover (page 395).

★ **Mount Washington:** If you feel worthy of its magnitude, hike the tallest mountain in the White Mountain National Forest—and all of the Northeast (page 401).

★ **Angel Falls:** Skip and scramble to reach this gorgeous 90-foot (27-m) waterfall that resembles an angel (page 411).

★ **Height of Land:** This pull-off in Rangeley is as breathtaking as it gets: a bird's-eye view of solitary Maine wilderness, lakes and all (page 413).

★ **Katahdin:** This iconic peak marks the northern end of the Appalachian Trail. Admire it from afar or make the strenuous climb if you dare (page 421).

★ **Paul Bunyan Sculpture:** As kitschy as it is, this oversized woodsman in Bangor is the personification of Maine: wild, artistic, historical, and proud (page 424).

Jagged, merciless peaks haunt hikers as they tirelessly move toward the northern terminus of the Appalachian Trail in this otherwise quaint, quirky paradise where outdoor enthusiasts and artistic minds merge.

New Hampshire and Maine, or northern New England, poses the greatest challenge for folks wanting to hike the trail. The road starts innocently enough in the Ivy League town of Hanover, but quickly the journey ascends multiple high peaks as it enters the White Mountains. Here the trees are plentiful: birch and beech species stretching high into the clouds, along with pines that perfume the forests where black bears and deer are common. The highest peaks here may even carry snow in the spring and fall, and that certainly applies for Mount Washington, which at 6,243 feet (1,903 m) demands care and patience from everyone who approaches its mighty cone.

Much of the northern New England road along the Appalachian Trail twists through untamed forests and quiet stretches where, every dozen miles or so, a town sprouts, and it may have just one restaurant, one motel, and one quirky sight. Among the largest towns along the way are Gorham, which provides a meaty introduction to Mount Washington and White Mountain National Forest; Rangeley, a lakeside town with glorious vistas and a down-to-earth vibe; and Skowhegan, far south from the AT but characterized by its artistic spirit. Smaller stops like Lyme, Shelburne, Norridgewock, and Monson prove either essential hiking destinations or whimsical pauses amid a grand journey through nature's cloak.

The AT ends with one final gut punch for hikers: the 100-Mile Wilderness, where civilization is a work of fiction, and the push to the summit of Katahdin, a beauty that anchors Baxter State Park. It's atop that mountain where hundreds each year pop champagne, hug longtime friends who were previously complete strangers, and crouch into themselves for moments of joyous reflection amid sometimes tremendous pain. For those staying closer to the road, the trip ends in Bangor, a quirky city that epitomizes Maine and proves similar to places like Asheville, North Carolina; Roanoke, Virginia; Poughkeepsie, New York; and North Adams, Massachusetts. These are the beating hearts of the East, towns and cities that have evolved through struggle and crafted their own unique beauty along the way.

For those seeking a rustic vacation away from the usual and rich in spirit, northern New England is the perfect landscape to discover. It may not be flooded with national park tourism, and it may stretch into an endless swath of untouched vegetation, but that's just the type of world Benton MacKaye wanted to show Americans when he first dreamed of a single walking path that could connect us to nature.

Planning Your Time

Depending on whether you want to hike some of the Appalachian Trail closer to the northern terminus in Maine, the northern New England section of this trip can vary from 300 to 450 miles (480-725 km). If you want to drive the basic route along US-2 in Maine, you'll want to spend at least five days in this area, with two spent in the White Mountain National Forest area, two spent driving and hiking through Maine, and one spent either in Hanover or Bangor. But if you're itching to hike some AT in the Maine wilderness, give yourself at least one week to truly bask in the beauty and challenge of this stretch.

Both Hanover and Bangor are fine

Best AT Hikes

Northern New England features arguably the roughest and most difficult terrain on the entire Appalachian Trail. Rocky trails, steep ascents and descents, scrambling approaches that demand the use of metal rungs, and unexpected weather patterns make this area often unforgiving for even the most experienced hikers. It rains a lot in Maine, especially in the summer, so the trail can be muddy and cold more often than not. Amateurs can certainly take on New Hampshire and Maine, but timing and preparation is always important.

- **Mount Moosilauke (7.5 mi/12.5 km, Benton):** Grab on to metal rungs and pull yourself up this difficult daylong adventure to summit a 4,802-foot (1,464-m) peak on the way to Mount Washington (page 398).
- **Mount Washington Summit (8.5 mi/13.7 km, White Mountain National Forest):** An extremely challenging hike that forces all hikers to prepare for the worst; still, the best is a glorious view and a feeling you've conquered a beast (page 404).
- **Sugarloaf Mountain (5.8 mi/9.3 km, Carrabassett Valley):** For a full view of Maine wilderness from more than 4,200 feet (1,280 m) up, take on this tough ascent that includes seriously rocky ground (page 416).

starting points for this drive, considering they're the largest communities and serve as bookends. Hanover is accessible from I-91, which connects to western Massachusetts, while Bangor is reached from I-95, which runs the entirety of the Eastern Seaboard. Bangor International Airport can connect you to cities along the East Coast, plus Chicago.

The small towns with more than one accommodation are best for overnight stays. Think about stopping in North Conway, Lincoln, or Gorham while in the White Mountains, and consider a stay in Rangeley for a quintessential Maine experience. Skowhegan is another possible rest stop. Know that it'll be difficult to make a reservation in Hanover during mid-June and early September. And for those wanting to hike Baxter State Park, note that after October 15 the park is only open sunrise to sunset and Katahdin may be inaccessible because of weather. AT thru-hikers have to hurry to finish by this date, so don't find yourself amid the crowds if you can help it.

Otherwise, if you're a novice hiker, be extremely careful about taking on this area, and don't bet on hiking between October and May. It will snow, and visibility will be near or at zero. During the summer it rains frequently, so bring plenty of extra clothing, and don't wear cotton while on the trails. Also, late spring and early summer is a heavy bug season—it's not as fun out there.

Getting There

It's a short drive on VT-10A, across the Connecticut River, from Norwich, Vermont, to Hanover, New Hampshire. Those coming to Hanover from the north or south are likely to drive I-91 to VT-10A, although from the south you could also drive I-89 to US-4, and then go north on NH-10.

Greyhound (3 Main St., 800/231-2222, www.greyhound.com) services Hanover and connects passengers to Boston, while **Dartmouth Coach** (603/448-2800, www.dartmouthcoach.com) also runs buses to Beantown, plus New York City.

Best Restaurants

★ **Lou's Restaurant and Bakery, Hanover:** Cooks at this historic destination sling hash and flip eggs all day for a typically packed dining room taking in a classic New England experience (page 396).

★ **Ariana's Restaurant, Lyme:** It may be a well-worn term, but farm-to-table is done right at this rustic spot inside the Lyme Inn (page 397).

★ **The Sunrise Shack, Glen:** Seriously good breakfasts, from packed omelets to hearty bowls, await hikers and other adventurers (page 406).

★ **The Shed, Rangeley:** This Maine-friendly barbecue joint that's popular among locals isn't afraid to put its spin on brisket and ribs (page 415).

★ **Kel Mat Café, Skowhegan:** Sandwiches, from the classic to the kooky, are the name of the game at this laid-back favorite (page 418).

★ **The Fiddlehead, Bangor:** Just about everything is sourced meticulously at this revered destination for romantic meals (page 428).

Car

From Hanover, you'll drive north on **US-5,** then east on **NH-116** into White Mountain National Forest. Several roads cut through the forest, including **NH-112** and **US-302.** Leaving the forest north of Mount Washington, take **US-2** east into Maine. There are detours up **ME-17** to Rangeley, up **ME-27** to Kingfield and Sugarloaf Mountain, and up **ME-150** and **ME-6** to Monson, but you can stay on US-2 all the way to Bangor. Major north-south highways through this area include **I-91,** which runs through Hanover and south to Springfield, Massachusetts; **I-93,** which connects Boston to the White Mountains; and **I-95,** which runs through Bangor and threads south into Boston, the New York City area, and major points along the East Coast.

Air

The closest passenger airport to Hanover and White Mountain National Forest is **Manchester-Boston Regional Airport** (1 Airport Rd., Manchester, NH, 603/624-6539, www.flymanchester.com, MHT). **American Airlines** (800/433-7300), **Delta Airlines** (800/221-1212), **Southwest Airlines** (800/435-9792), and **United Airlines** (800/864-8331) all fly out of this airport, servicing cities like Washington DC, Chicago, Detroit, Philadelphia, and the New York City area. It's about an 80-mile (129-km) drive on I-89 north from the airport to Hanover. Multiple rental car agencies are located at the airport, and shuttle services may transport passengers to Hanover and locations north and east, including Maine.

Bangor International Airport (287 Godfrey Blvd., Bangor, 207/992-4600, www.flybangor.com, BGR) is home to **American Airlines** (800/433-7300), **Allegiant** (702/505-8888), **Delta Airlines** (800/221-1212), and **United Airlines** (800/864-8331). You can get to New York, Philadelphia, Chicago, Washington, DC, Houston, the Tampa Bay area, Orlando, Fort Lauderdale, Charlotte, and Atlanta from Bangor. Multiple rental car agencies are located at the airport, and taxis and buses also stop there. **God's Country Shuttle Service** (207/480-5222, www.godscountryshuttle.com) takes passengers between the airport and Baxter State Park.

Best Accommodations

★ **Hanover Inn, Hanover:** On the Dartmouth campus is this century-old hotel with queens and king beds in its splendid guest rooms, and many fine amenities (page 396).

★ **Breakfast on the Connecticut, Lyme:** As the name suggests, this riverside bed-and-breakfast serves winning meals and offers relatively inexpensive rooms (page 397).

★ **Riverbank Motel, Lincoln:** This extremely affordable spot includes rooms with kitchenettes and queen beds, something you don't find every day (page 407).

★ **Rattle River Lodge and Hostel, Shelburne:** Once out of the White Mountains, hikers will find this community-focused accommodation very inviting (page 409).

★ **Loon Lodge Inn, Rangeley:** Get a view of the lake in a rustic, wood-walled guestroom at this modestly priced hotel (page 416).

★ **Shaw's Hiker Hostel, Monson:** In the last trail town heading north, this laid-back spot has cozy rooms and gets hikers charged up for the final push (page 419).

Bus

Amtrak (www.amtrak.com) services Bangor through **Concord Coach Lines** (1039 Union St., 800/639-3317, www.concordcoachlines.com); typically, there are two daily buses heading south to Portland and three daily buses coming north from Portland. Greyhound has a station in **Hanover** (3 Main St., 800/231-2222, www.greyhound.com).

Fuel and Services

Always remember to fill up in major cities and towns, especially during this drive, which for long stretches will be without any sign of a gas station. Your best bets for gasoline are in Hanover, the towns surrounding White Mountain National Forest, Rangeley, Skowhegan, and Bangor. Gas prices in both New Hampshire and Maine are typically right at or just below the national average.

Hanover

Sitting on the Connecticut River and serving as a crisp welcome to New Hampshire, **Hanover** (pop. 11,620) is quintessential New England. Its Main Street is a postcard filled with buttoned-up small shops, while the main attraction has been and will be Dartmouth College. And though on a breezy fall morning or blooming spring afternoon you'll spot plenty of rushing Ivy Leaguers and proud parents on the street, the summer is when you'll catch Appalachian Trail hikers stopping for a bite and a quick rest. The trail runs through the town, hooking up with a number of smaller trails as it works east toward the White Mountains.

Getting There and Around

Cross the Connecticut River at Wheelock Street and find yourself immediately ensconced in the elm-lined treasure that is Hanover. Wheelock Street (named for the founder of Dartmouth College) cuts through the town west to east, passing the Dartmouth campus and providing a connection with Main Street and Lyme Road, which combine as NH-10, leading south to nearby Lebanon and north toward White Mountain National Forest.

You can reach Hanover by bus via

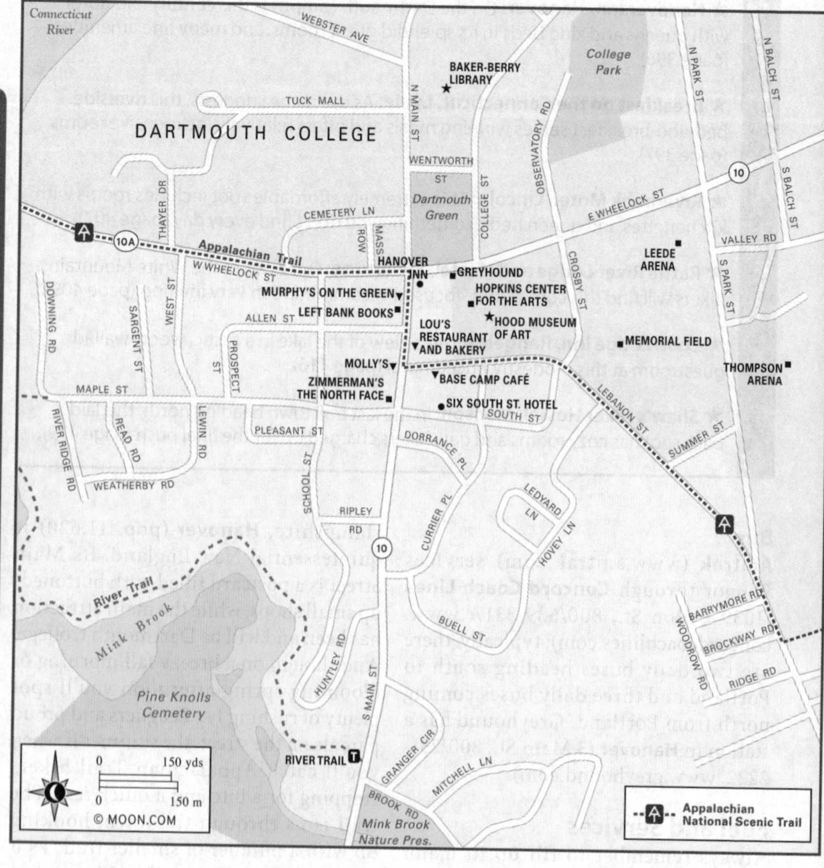

Greyhound (3 N. Main St., 800/231-2222), which operates a bus stop in town but no ticket office. **Dartmouth Coach** (800/637-0123, www.dartmouthcoach.com) shuttles folks to and from both Boston and New York City.

When in town, **Advance Transit** (www.advancetransit.com) operates four lines that connect Hanover to nearby locations like Hartford, Lebanon, and Norwich.

Sights

Dartmouth College

Anchoring Hanover is **Dartmouth College** (603/646-1110, www.dartmouth.edu), an Ivy League school founded in 1769 and educating more than 6,000 students. The college is centered on the Green (Wheelock and Main Sts.), a picturesque field used for college activities, rallies, and celebrations.

The college is home to the **Baker-Berry Library** (6025 S. Main St., 603/646-2560), where down in the lower level you can view *The Epic of American Civilization,* the iconic, stirring fresco mural by Jose Clemente Orozco. Dartmouth shows off collected and gifted documents with various exhibits at the library, while cozy seating and a whimsical spirit reside in the Theodor Seuss Geisel Room, named for a famous Dartmouth alum better known as Dr. Seuss.

★ Hood Museum of Art

A depository for Dartmouth's collection of art, including Native American, European, African, and Melanesian pieces, the **Hood Museum of Art** (6 E. Wheelock St., 603/646-2808, www.hoodmuseum.dartmouth.edu, 10am-5pm Tues. and Thurs.-Sat., 10am-9pm Wed., noon-5pm Sun., free) is coming off a major $50 million renovation that included the addition of new galleries. Be among the first to walk into the new-look Hood, home to works by Claude Lorrain, Georgia O'Keefe, Luca Giordano, and Rockwell Kent. The crown jewel of the collection, however, are 9th-century BCE Assyrian stone reliefs. The museum hosts regular events, from creative workshops to openings of rotating exhibits.

Hiking

Hanover has an expansive trail network; the majority of local trails run fewer than 3 miles (4.8 km) and grade as easy, and most of them are closed to bicycles and motorized vehicles. Tops among them are the **River Trail** (South Main St. at Brook Road, 1.1 mi/1.8 km), which winds alongside the Mink Brook to the Connecticut River; and the **Fred Harris Trail** (Goose Pond Road, Lyme, 3.8 mi/6.1 km), an old AT section that is now overgrown in spots.

Spectator Sports

Take in some Ivy League action in Hanover via the Dartmouth Big Green. The men's and women's basketball teams both play at **Leede Arena** (16 E. Wheelock St., www.dartmouthsports.com), an old-school fieldhouse built in the 1980s. The men's team is historically bad (not making the NCAA Tournament since 1959), while the women have fared much better (seven NCAA tournament bids since 1983).

The Dartmouth football team, which competes in the second-level FCS, plays at **Memorial Field** (4 Crosby St., www.dartmouthsports.com). And the men's and women's ice hockey teams, both Division I squads, play at **Thompson Arena** (4 Summer St., www.dartmouthsports.com). The men's team hasn't come close to a national championship in nearly 40 years, while the women have proven wildly successful with four Frozen Four appearances since 2001.

Performing Arts

Called "the Hop," the **Hopkins Center for the Arts** (4 Wheelock St., 603/646-2422, www.hop.dartmouth.edu) may look, to you, like a miniature version of Lincoln Center in New York City. If so, keen eye, because the Hop was designed by Wallace K. Harrison, the man who later designed, you guessed it, Lincoln Center in New York City. The Hop includes five performance and meeting spaces and plays host to the college's drama and music departments. For visitors, it's home to everything from world music concerts to modern dance recitals to showings of classic cinema.

Shopping

Hikers can stop in **Zimmerman's The North Face** (63 Main St., 603/643-6863, 10am-6pm Mon.-Sat., noon-5pm Sun.) for outerwear, help, and advice. Those thru-hiking the AT have been able to drop off packages here.

An eclectic living room is the setting at **Left Bank Books** (9 Main St., 603/643-4479, www.leftbankbookshanover.com, 9:30am-5pm Mon.-Sat., 11:30am-3:30pm Sun.), which is more of a book-centric vintage store than a full-service trendy bookseller. You can always find something you didn't think you needed here.

Food

Dartmouth College & Downtown

The most famous spot in town is ★ **Lou's Restaurant and Bakery** (30 S. Main St., 603/643-3321, www.lousrestaurant.com, 6am-3pm Mon.-Fri., 7am-3pm Sat.-Sun., under $20), which for more than 60 years has fed Hanover all-day breakfast and classic diner-style lunches like grilled Reubens and BLTs. The wait can build up at Lou's, especially when school is in session, but the spirited service and historical charm are worth it.

Hang out with the *smaht* kids at **Molly's** (43 S. Main St., 603/643-2570, www.mollysrestaurant.com, 11:30am-10pm Sun.-Thurs., 11:30am-midnight Fri.-Sat., under $30), an active restaurant and bar where townies, visitors, students, and teachers all congregate over savory pizza and dirt-cheap margaritas.

Another haunt with pretty good food and books seemingly everywhere, **Murphy's on the Green** (11 S. Main St., 603/643-4075, www.murphysonthegreen.com, 11am-11pm Mon.-Thurs., 4pm-11pm Fri.-Sat., 11am-10pm Sun., under $50) features selections from across the gastronomical map. Try anything with lobster, like the mac and cheese or the lobster meatballs in penne pasta.

Hungry hikers who want to feel like they've just scaled Everest will be happy to find **Base Camp Café** (3 Lebanon St., 603/643-2007, www.basecampcafenh.com, 11am-9pm Sun.-Thurs., 11am-10pm Fri.-Sat., under $20), which takes its cue from the Nepalese cooking tradition. Base Camp is famous for *momos,* or steamy dumplings, while entrees bathing in curry, spiced with chilies, or pan-grilled with vegetables are often gluten-free and vegan friendly.

Lebanon

Few things beat a time-tested delicatessen, which makes **Marsh Brothers Deli at the Little Store** (55 School St., 603/727-9329, 7am-7pm Mon.-Fri., 7am-8pm Sat., 7am-5pm Sun., under $15) a must-visit if you're in the Upper Valley area. Folks clamor for the made-to-order sandwiches, primarily the Cubano, while Marsh Brothers also cooks up a mean burger and, for a treat, mouth-watering donuts with a special tang.

Jonesin' for authentic Cambodian grub? **Phnom Penh Sandwich Station** (1 High St., 603/678-8179, www.phnompenhsandwiches.com, 11am-9pm Mon.-Sat., under $15) keeps a focused menu of four lunch and dinner staples: a pickled sandwich, Jasmine rice stir-fry, pad thai, and fried rice stir-fry. Just add protein. The modest digs from this former food truck are good for ordering out.

West Lebanon

The Upper Valley has some decent diners. **The Four Aces Diner** (23 Bridge St., 603/298-5515, www.4acesdiner.com, 6am-3pm Mon.-Sat., 7am-3pm Sun., under $30) is a favorite with regulars and tourists alike, another place where the line winds out the door. Folks rave about the corned beef hash, but you might just find yourself staring in awe at the beauty of this vintage railcar.

Accommodations

$100-150

The rooms at the **Sunset Motor Inn** (305 N. Main St., West Lebanon, 603/298-8721, www.sunsetinnnh.com, $80-150) are all over the place, from motor lodge chic to something pretty close to the Holiday Inn. This is a basic, one-night-stay kind of place with continental breakfast, proving a solid and inexpensive option.

You'll have a decent stay at **The Baymont by Wyndham** (45 Airport Rd., West Lebanon, 603/298-8888, $100-150), which features a swimming pool and basic rooms on par with any middle-of-the-road hotel.

$150-250

Right in the heart of Dartmouth, the ★ **Hanover Inn** (2 E. Wheelock

St., Hanover, 603/643-4300, www.hanoverinn.com, $180-350) has been in operation since the turn of the century, though its roots extend to the late 18th century as a home for Dartmouth steward Gen. Ebenezer Brewster. The hotel is fully updated, with an on-site restaurant and bar, complimentary Wi-Fi, a fitness center, and room service. Moreover, its rooms are of gorgeous simplicity, dressed handsomely in Dartmouth green. The prices are high here, but you get everything you pay for, down to the bellman and dry cleaning services.

Just as popular with parents, **Six South St. Hotel** (6 South St., Hanover, 603/643-0600, www.sixsouth.com, $170-300) is a snazzy boutique with contemporary amenities like a cocktail lounge, fitness room, high-definition televisions, and valet parking. Rooms are boldly decorated with patterns ahoy, from clovers on wallpaper to static noise on bedspreads, making for a modern mishmash that experience-seeking travelers should enjoy.

Chains you can rely on in the area include the **Courtyard by Marriott** (10 Morgan Dr., Lebanon, 603/643-5600, $150-250) and the **Hilton Garden Inn** (35 N. Labombard Rd., Lebanon, 603/448-3300, $160-300).

Lyme

Take NH-10 an easy 15 miles (24 km) north from Hanover, through unperturbed country roads lined by verdant birch and sycamore trees, into **Lyme** (pop. 1,716), a town along the Connecticut River that serves visitors to Dartmouth, fall leaf peepers, and the occasional hiker needing an overnight stop.

During its early days as Grant's Tavern, the **Lyme Inn** (1 Market St., 603/795-4824, www.thelymeinn.com, $150-400) served tired 19th-century stagecoach travelers. The methods used to reach the inn have improved, as have the amenities, which at this historic accommodation include Italian marble bathrooms and flat-screen televisions, plus fireplaces in some of the rooms. There are five suites at the inn, plus nine standard rooms with all kinds of bedding options. Because Lyme is a hot destination, especially during October weekends and graduation time, the inn can be pricier than your typical middle-of-the-road lodging experience.

At the inn is a better-than-middle-of-the-road dining experience: ★ **Ariana's Restaurant** (1 Market St., 603/795-4824, www.arianasrestaurant.com, 5pm-8pm Thurs.-Mon., under $50). Here, chef Martin works with ingredients acquired from local farms and producers in executing a menu that reflects both the Granite State and unexpected innovation. The restaurant has two dining rooms worthy of the term "elegant rusticity."

Up the road a bit, but still in Lyme, is ★ **Breakfast on the Connecticut** (651 River Rd., 603/353-4444, www.breakfastonthect.com, $99-400), which offers single rooms, suites, and a guesthouse option on a quaint property tucked back from the highway and sitting a stone's throw from the river. While the rooms are designed in a rather dated, grandmotherly fashion, they're clean and comfortable. Some rooms have Jacuzzi tubs, while a hot breakfast every morning really earns this inn its reputation.

NH-25: Polar Caves Park

For the opportunity to explore just why New Hampshire is called the Granite State, take NH-25A east to NH-25 east along the southern edge of the White Mountains to **Polar Caves Park** (705 Rumney Rte. 25, Rumney, 603/536-1888, 10am-5pm spring and fall, 9am-6pm daily summer, $19.50 adults, $14.50 ages 4-12, free age 3 and younger). The center of attention here are nine granite caves formed during the last ice age, which visitors can get close to on walking trails that fit through narrow crevices.

Of course, getting to the caves is part of the fun. Polar Caves Park has mapped out a real labyrinth for visitors, taking them around a duck pond, through a "kissing bridge," and into a rock garden before getting to the main attraction. Kids of most ages can enjoy the climbing wall and rappel line, while everyone can get into the mining sluice to search for gold... or at least some fun stones.

Mount Moosilauke

From Lyme it's a 38-mile (61-km) drive to the town of Benton, where you'll find Mount Moosilauke. You'll have to head north on NH-10 for 22 miles (35 km) before venturing into the White Mountains via NH-116 east. That soon merges with NH-112, which you'll stay on for the remainder of the ride as it twists and turns into the lush greenery of the New Hampshire woods. You'll feel lost in a bouquet of pine trees that are best appreciated under a clear blue sky. The road parallels Stark Falls Brook and rides along Kinsman Notch, a passage between Moosilauke and the Kinsman Ridge that is best captured from nearby Beaver Pond.

Hiking

Mount Moosilauke A

Distance: 7.5 miles (12 km)

Duration: 6-7 hours

Elevation gain: 3,100 feet (945 m)

Difficulty: Strenuous

Trailhead: Beaver Brook (44.040841, -71.791816)

You can summit this 4,802-foot (1,464-m) peak via the Appalachian Trail southbound, which follows a number of trails that had previously been set for climbing the mountain. But be warned: This is one of the tougher single hikes along the trail, a beast of more than 3,000 feet (915 m) of elevation gain that includes potentially slippery metal rungs and steps, not to mention a lot of rocks.

The early part of the hike, accessed from the Beaver Brook trailhead, is heebie-jeebies territory, trekking on steep wood stairs and grasping on to rungs to work your way up. You'll catch the splendid 1,000-foot (305-m) Beaver Brook Cascades before reaching Beaver Brook Shelter, which should be utilized if the weather is threatening. After that, continue on the AT south as it makes a hard right. Now you'll be closing in on an alpine paradise where visibility can be tricky. Weather can change quickly up here, so if there's any worry, find shelter.

When reaching the summit, take it all in: The view includes the rest of the White Mountains, naturally, plus Vermont and the Adirondack line in New York. You'll head back the way you came, but again, be careful, especially in the steep sections.

Lost River Gorge and Boulder Caves

Not even a minute south of the Beaver Brook trailhead, and still on NH-112, is **Lost River Gorge and Boulder Caves** (1712 Lost River Rd., North Woodstock, 603/745-8031, www.lostrivergorge.com, 9am-5pm daily May-June and Sept.-Oct., 9am-6pm daily July-Aug., $21 adults, $17 ages 4-12, free ages 3 and younger). Like Polar Caves Park, Lost River Gorge and Boulder Caves originates from ice age glacier shifting and debris. It was first discovered, according to legend, by brothers who frequently navigated these dangerous slips and holes in the earth.

You can practically do a choose-your-own adventure experience here, as Lost River Gorge includes about a dozen boulder formations, each of varying size. Guests should dress for scrambling if they want to really get into it, otherwise there's plenty of beautiful scenery to behold by standing 300 feet (91 m) below

Remembering the Old Man of the Mountain

About 12,000 years ago, granite bedrock at what is now Cannon Mountain, New Hampshire, thawed in such a way that it formed what resembled the profile of a man's face. First publicly seen and recorded in 1805, the "Old Man of the Mountain" soon became an icon of New Hampshire. Wrote Daniel Webster, renowned senator and former secretary of state: "Up in the mountains of New Hampshire, God Almighty has hung out a sign to show that there He makes men." Yes, New Hampshire residents think pretty strongly of the Old Man of the Mountain.

Because the Old Man was a granite formation, continued thawing was inevitable. Cracks formed, and despite state work to fix the profile, it collapsed completely in May 2003. In one night, the Old Man of the Mountain had vanished.

Today, however, you can view the Old Man of the Mountain once again. The **Old Man of the Mountain Memorial** (Tramway Dr. at US-3, Franconia) is a touching and simply stated viewing area of Cannon Mountain. There, visitors can fit their feet in marked ground (measured to align with their height) and gaze at the mountain through a "steel profiler." The profilers are long poles topped by relief that, when viewed at the right position, creates the profile of the Old Man, allowing the visitors to see exactly what it looked like before May 2003.

and gazing at the rock walls, mountains, and pathways. The venue also features—of course—a mining sluice, which is in addition to the admission fee.

White Mountain National Forest

You may wonder why **White Mountain National Forest** (71 White Mountain Dr., Campton, 603/536-6100) isn't a national park. Primarily, it's because the logging industry utilizes a small but essential chunk of the land purchased by the government more than 100 years ago. That falls in line with the conservation mission that drives the U.S. Forest Service. If the designated White Mountain area was a national park, it would be completely preserved, thus eliminating what makes it important to industry in New England.

That said, most of White Mountain National Forest plays like a national park, including visitors centers, a scenic drive that captures the wild beauty of the location, and of course, two big honkin' tourist attractions that are made for bumper stickers. In fact, if you don't see one "This car climbed Mt. Washington" bumper sticker during your time in New England, you're doing it all wrong.

The forest is home to said mountain, the tallest in the Northeast and arguably the most iconic summit both east of the Mississippi and on the entire Appalachian Trail. Standing at 6,288 feet (1,917 m), it towers above the typical 1,500-foot (457-m) hills of the New York and New Jersey highlands, rises past the 3,500-foot (1,067-m) middle children that populate the Virginia Blue Ridge and Green Mountains, and soars over the 4,500-foot (1,372-m) beasts that top parts of North Carolina and Maine. Still, Mount Washington isn't the highest point on the AT (that honor belongs to Clingmans Dome), but in a snowy northern climate standing a mere 330 miles (530 km) from the end of the journey, it's one of the most imposing and deliciously challenging sights any hiker will meet. Also, tourists love driving their cars to the top.

Getting There and Around

If you're on NH-112 in the Mount Moosilauke area you're already in the national forest, driving the Kancamagus Highway, a National Scenic Byway that

White Mountains

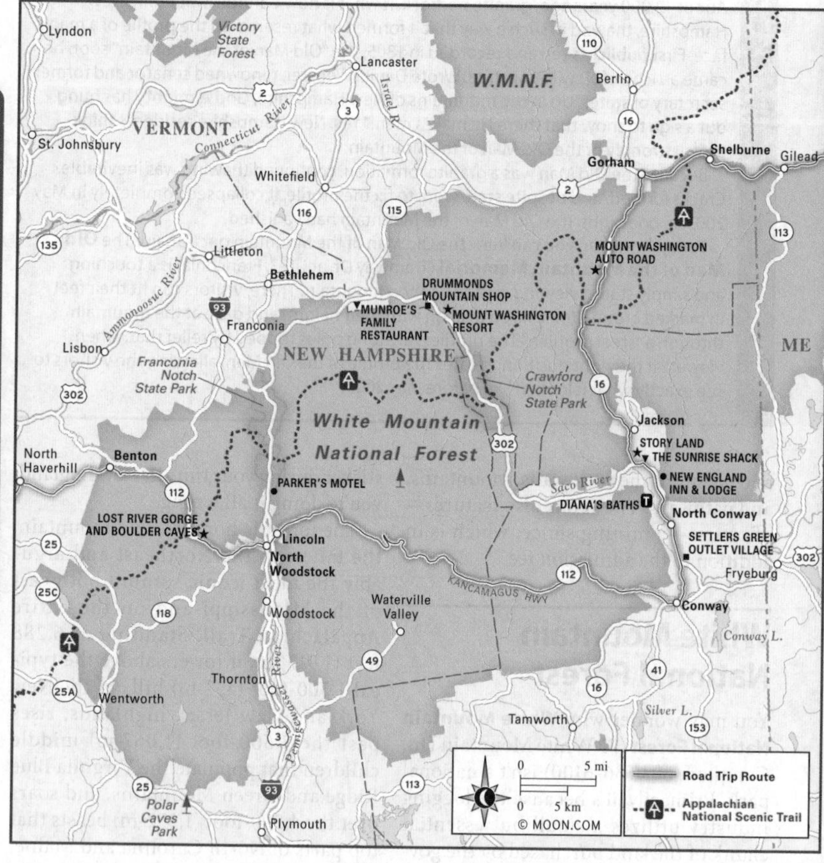

cuts through the woods in between the most prominent mountain ranges. If you think of the park as a square (it's not quite that shape but it'll do), the Kancamagus runs along the southern portion of the square from west to east. I-93 and US-3 run through the western end north to south, providing easy access to Woodstock and Franconia Notch, home to that other major tourist attraction, the former site of the Old Man of the Mountain.

Take US-3 north to US-2, which rides the north end of the forest and hits Gorham and Shelburne, popular stops for tourists wanting to climb Mount Washington. NH-16, known as the White Mountain Highway, connects Gorham to Bartlett, then Conway, another popular lodging and shopping destination. US-302, which runs parallel to NH-112 but closer north to Mount Washington, is another popular way to drive across the forest.

Like other national forests, White Mountain is free to enter, but **passes** ($5 daily, $30-40 annual) are needed for those who want access to trailheads and day-use areas. Driving a car is the best way to see the whole forest, but those who'd rather not drive can take Concord Coach (www.concordcoachlines.com, $30-50), a bus line that connects Boston to towns inside the forest (Conway, Franconia, Gorham, Jackson, Lincoln, North Conway, Pinkham Notch). But then, if you want to move around the park, you'll have to rely on hiking, cycling, or ride-sharing.

★ Mount Washington

The crown jewel of the Presidential Ridge of the White Mountains, Mount Washington is one of the greatest tests of hiking endurance and skill in America. Its height and status as a meeting place for storm fronts and high winds make for dangerous, volatile weather conditions from November to April. If you're planning on hiking the summit, you'll need to be experienced and prepared. If you make it up there, you'll be rewarded with a beautiful perch that, on a clear day, offers views as far north as Canada and as far east as the Atlantic Ocean.

You can also enjoy the view without the stress by simply driving the car to the top. The **Mount Washington Auto Road** (1 Mount Washington Auto Road, Gorham, hours vary May-Oct., $31 car and driver, $17 motorcycle and operator, $9 adult passenger, $7 ages 5-12 passenger, free ages 5 and younger) provides access to the summit via a 7.6-mile (12.2-km) ascent lasting about 30 minutes; the descent can take up to 45 minutes. Once on the road, cars can stop at designated turnoffs (and may want to, as the drive is at about a 12 percent grade), and folks can even get out and hike from a turnoff. Overnight parking is allowed at the turnoffs, but drivers must alert the tollgate upon entering.

At the summit is the Sherman Adams Visitor Center, which includes a cafeteria

Top to bottom: Mount Washington; Mount Washington Resort; Diana's Baths.

One Day in the White Mountains

Morning

Well, you're going to want to hike. Head out to **Arethusa Falls** to get a glimpse of pure beauty, then head east on US-302 and grab the best breakfast in town at the **Sunrise Shack.** After that big breakfast, work it off at **Diana's Baths.** Tour the waterfalls and take a quick dip to cool down.

Afternoon

With exercise out of your system, it's time to see the sights. Hop in the car and head up the **Mount Washington Auto Road** to reach the summit of the Northeast's highest peak. After milling around at the **Sherman Adams Visitor Center** and **Summit Stage Office,** carefully drive down the mountain and head into Gorham. Grab a late lunch and a pint at **Mr. Pizza.**

Evening

Head back toward North Conway, because it's time to do a little predinner shopping. Visit **Settlers Green Outlet Village** to score some gifts and stock up for winter. End your day with dinner and some whiskey at **Deacon Street,** or if you want a few beers, hike on over to **May Kelly's Cottage.**

and gift shop. The Summit Stage Office (which is chained to the ground) is open for visitors, a place to pay homage to the highest wind speed ever observed by a human (231 mph/372 kph in 1934). Those paying for the Auto Road also get free admission to the Extreme Mt. Washington Museum at the Mount Washington Observatory, which has interactive displays showing visitors the mountain's conditions during the harsh winter. Also, if you pay for the Auto Road, you get that bumper sticker informing the world that you drove a car up to the top of Mount Washington.

Guided tours (www.mtwashingtonautoroad.com) to the summit are available for those who don't want to drive, and they include stories and facts about the mountain. A **hiker shuttle** (available most days during the summer, $31 adults, $26 seniors and military, $13 ages 5-12) transports folks to the summit from three locations in the forest (AMC Pinkham Notch Visitor Center, Great Gulf trailhead, Auto Road base). Reservations are not accepted for the shuttle, which can't promise rides down the mountain.

Bretton Woods Canopy Tour

First off, what is Bretton Woods? It's a place where, in 1944, the United States, Canada, European allies, Japan, and

Australia agreed on a monetary order for transactions between independent states, which lasted until 1971. But, OK, what is Bretton Woods? It was first a parcel of land in a plantation owned by Sir Thomas Wentworth of Bretton Hall in England. Within the town of Carroll, it's now a recreation area that's home to a ski resort and the Mount Washington Resort, a grand hotel that opened in 1902 and plays host to thousands of tourists each week.

Visitors from near and far can ride high above Bretton Woods on a canopy tour at the **Mount Washington Resort** (99 Ski Area Rd., Bretton Woods, 603/278-4947, www.brettonwoods.com, $90-120). Guides orient visitors on safety procedures and equipment and then bring them up to nine zip lines over Rosebrook Canyon, ranging in length from 120 to 830 feet (37-253 m). There are three rappels and tree platforms up to 70 feet (21 m) high, and zip line speeds can get up to 30 mph (48 kph). Participants must be age 12 and older.

Story Land

In the middle of the White Mountains is a land of make believe. **Story Land** (850 NH-16, Glen, www.storylandnh.com, 9:30am-6pm daily summer, 9:30am-5pm weekends spring and fall, $30-55) was created by a husband and wife who built a village inspired by dolls they purchased from a German woman. Since opening in 1954, the park has expanded with family-friendly amusement rides like roller coasters, raft rides, and swan boats, plus character dinners (Cinderella isn't just a Disney princess) and live shows featuring kids favorites like Daniel Tiger. Food options at the park include burgers, summer sandwiches and carnival fare, ice cream, coffee, wraps, and salads, while the venue also has a few gift shops. Oh, and a sluice, because New Hampshire.

Diana's Baths

In the spring, water rushes down Lucy Brook, creating marvelous shows in the waterfalls of **Diana's Baths** (3275 West

the White Mountains in the distance

Side Rd., Bartlett, 603/447-5448, $3). Once home to a sawmill and later protected by the U.S. Forest Service, the waterfalls that make this stunning tourist attraction can really run when the snow has finally melted. In summer Diana's Baths is a popular swimming hole. Play with caution when ambling out on the rocks and ledges.

Hiking

Mount Washington Summit

Distance: 8.5 miles (13.7 km)
Duration: 7-8 hours
Elevation gain: 3,200 feet (975 m)
Difficulty: Strenuous
Trailhead: Pinkham Notch Visitor Center (44.257384, -71.253135)

Don't try to hike to the top of Mount Washington if you haven't yet summited a mountain of more than at least 3,000 feet (915 m). Now, if you have, the best time to try the mountain is between August and the end of September, when temperatures at the top will typically be in the 50s and the chance of snow and ice is minimal. There's still a good chance of cloud cover no matter when you go, so be prepared for rain at any time.

The Tuckerman Ravine Trail, starting at Pinkham Notch Visitor Center, is the most popular way up and down the mountain, and far too many inexperienced tourists in sandals and blue jeans will be out there. You can attempt the harder Boott Spur Trail or the less trafficked Jewell Trail, which parallels the Cog Railroad and makes for an interesting ascent, but I say stick to Tuckerman Ravine—especially if it's your first time. If you do, however, want a little more out of it (and you don't want to constantly navigate around tourists), try veering onto the Lion's Head Trail, which branches off from Tuckerman Ravine at Hermit Lake and works you out a little more with challenging boulders and a narrow, exposed ride to the headwall, which comprises the final mile or so. For the way down, the Tuckerman

Mount Washington Summit

Trail Tale

Time for some **AT stats.** The numbers continue to grow. In 2017, the Appalachian Trail Conservancy reported that 3,839 people started a northbound thru-hike at Springer Mountain in Georgia, nearly 500 more than the number of people that started a northbound hike in 2016, and more than 1,200 more than in 2015. As more people learn about thru-hiking the AT through movies and books, and as training methods improve, those numbers are bound to only grow larger. Still, the same number of people—around 680—tend to finish thru-hikes at Katahdin, at least since 2015.

Those ages 22-32 remain the largest group of long-distance hikers on the trail, according to a survey by TheTrek.co, which also found that the overwhelming majority of these hikers (96 percent) identify as white.

Most thru-hikers heading north tend to begin their journeys between early March and mid-April. Those who go southbound? They're likely to begin at Katahdin around June, which means they'll get to Springer sometime in December. Southbound thru-hikes are considerably tougher than northbound hikes, as the start means the toughest ascents and terrain in Maine, and the finish means sometimes bitterly cold weather from the Great Smoky Mountains to Springer Mountain.

Ravine makes more sense, as you'll have a slightly more level descent, but not by much. That's when you'll get to spend some time at Hermit Lake, home to shelters maintained by the Appalachian Mountain Club. It's also home to HoJo's, the old caretaker's cabin where you can buy some merchandise or a snack.

Arethusa Falls

Distance: 3 miles (4.8 km)
Duration: 2 hours
Elevation gain: 950 feet (290 m)
Difficulty: Moderate
Trailhead: US-302 at Arethusa Falls Road (44.148231, -71.366213)

Within Crawford Notch State Park (which is inside the national forest), Arethusa Falls is a brilliant waterfall dropping 140 feet (43 m) from a granite cliff. Discovered in 1875, the falls are the second tallest in New Hampshire and are easy to access from a parking area and trailhead by US-302. From the parking area, head onto the Arethusa Falls trail, identified by blue blazes. You can peel off onto the Bemis Brook Trail after a few moments, which takes you to two small waterfalls, Bemis Brook and Coliseum. If you do this, continue beyond Coliseum and you'll meet back up with the falls trail.

Just 1 mile (1.6 km) from the fork joining the Bemis Brook and falls trails you'll head down to Arethusa. Along the way you'll trample across two bridges and do a small amount of up and down, but the payoff is absolutely worth it. Arethusa sings in front of your face; you can get pretty close to it, too, if you're careful.

When finished enjoying the mists of the falls, turn around and head back via the falls trail.

Shopping

Nothing says New England vacationing more than outlet shopping. **Settlers Green Outlet Village** (2 Common Ct., North Conway, 888/667-9636, www.settlersgreen.com, 9am-9pm Mon.-Sat., 10am-6pm Sun.) is a tax-free magic land of retail stores, restaurants, and more, from Eddie Bauer, Gap, and Crabtree & Evelyn to Adidas, Eastern Mountain Sports, and Coach.

Drummonds Mountain Shop (2272 US-302, Bretton Woods, 603/278-7547, www.drummondsmountainshop.com, 8am-5pm daily) is a full-service provider of hiking and camping gear, also specializing in bike rentals ($25-45).

Food

North Conway and US-302 South

When you're hanging out in the White Mountains during chilly evenings, only a stiff drink that warms the blood will suffice. **Deacon Street** (32 Seavey St., North Conway, 603/356-9231, 4pm-11pm daily, under $40) is a whiskey bar that offers several dozen styles of bourbon, scotch, blended whiskey, and rye. Food here is the usual American fare, but you'll want in on Deacon's dinner specials, like Thursday night's burger and dollar-beer offer. That's a certified winner.

Up the road is a popular haunt for the North Conway folks: **May Kelly's Cottage** (3002 NH-16, North Conway, 603/356-7005, 4pm-9pm Wed.-Thurs., noon-10pm Fri.-Sat., noon-8pm Sun., under $40). Serving traditional Irish favorites like corned beef and cabbage and calves liver and onions, May Kelly's is a warm, cozy embrace with beer-raisin' locals and gleeful optimism abounding.

Grab some all-day breakfast at **Priscilla's** (2541 NH-16, North Conway, 603/356-0401, 6am-2pm daily, under $25), which offers very basic grub 6am-8am, then breaks out a more involved menu for the rush, including raisin bread French toast and an asparagus melt. Enjoy your meal in a cheery space with bright golden walls.

Also open for breakfast is ★ **The Sunrise Shack** (644 NH-16, Glen, 603/383-7169, 6am-3pm daily, under $20). Don't be deceived by this rustic wood building topped by a sign with the buzzing "Open" notification: This is seriously good food. Hikers will enjoy making a Base Camp Omelet (starting with three eggs), while innovative and inexpensive breakfast bowls fill up just about anyone. Also: beer for breakfast.

Or beer for lunch or dinner. Try **Moat Mountain Smokehouse & Brewing Co.** (3378 NH-16, North Conway, 603/356-6381, www.moatmountain.com, 11:30am-11:45pm daily, under $30) for burgers, nachos, sandwiches, and pizzas, along with—of course—smoked meats. The brewery cranks out a variety of styles for all types of drinkers.

Franconia and US-302 North

Looking for some healthy options in the Franconia area? **Maia Papaya** (2161 Main St., Bethlehem, 603/869-9900, www.themaiapapaya.com, 7am-3pm Mon.-Thurs., 7am-5pm Fri.-Sun., under $15) has you covered. This fun café has some great vegetarian options, including an artichoke melt and pesto melt, plus an Elvis melt with peanut butter and banana. Breakfast has everything from burritos to sandwiches to homemade granola. There's lots of coffee options, too.

For a good old-fashioned meal, head to **Munroe's Family Restaurant** (633 US-3, Twin Mountain, 603/846-5542, 7am-2pm Mon.-Tues., 7am-8pm Wed.-Sun., under $20), which offers big breakfasts including—get this—breakfast tacos. Diner food is served all day in a bustling, fun atmosphere, perfect for a full White Mountains experience.

Lincoln and NH-112

Most of the eating (and lodging) options in the western end of White Mountain National Forest are in Lincoln. The majority are standard fare for a tourist-heavy town, from busy taverns to family-friendly spots that serve burgers, pizza, and big breakfasts. Tops among them is **Black Mtn. Burger Co.** (264 Main St., Lincoln, 603/745-3444, www.blackmtnburger.com, 11:30am-9pm Thurs.-Tues., under $30), which does American grill fare pretty well. Those with some hunger pangs are going to want the Pounder, which is literally a pound of burger meat with whatever cheese you want (within reason).

The **Café Lafayette Dinner Train** (3 Crossing at Riverplace, North Woodstock, 603/745-3500, www.cafelafayettedinnertrain.com, 4pm-9pm Thurs.-Sun., seasonal and hours may vary, $85-100 adults, $65-80 ages 6-11) is a unique opportunity to dine on the rails. As a train runs alongside the Pemigewasset River, diners enjoy a five-course meal that changes seasonally. During the winter the café opens its depot for wine and tapas.

There's pasta, pizza with a variety of toppings, and steak tips at **Rustic River Restaurant** (5 Main St., North Woodstock, 603/745-2110, www.rusticriverrestaurant.com, 11am-10pm Thurs.-Sun., under $30). With a shabby exterior but an eclectic and friendly interior, Rustic River feeds the North Woodstock area quite well.

Accommodations

Under $100

An inexpensive and fantastic option if you're in the Lincoln area, ★ **Riverbank Motel** (183 Connector Rd., Lincoln,

Top to bottom: Arethusa Falls; North Conway; Franconia.

603/745-3374, www.riverbankmotel.com, $50-130) has bright and clean rooms with queen beds and kitchenettes, plus cabins and cottages with more sitting room.

Parker's Motel (750 US-3, Lincoln, 603/745-8341, www.parkersmotel.com, $50-130 winter, $75-150 summer) has dated but perfectly suitable rooms, along with suites that have gas fireplaces for those cold New England nights.

$100-150

Inside a Federal-style home, the **1785 Inn** (3582 NH-16, North Conway, 603/356-9025, www.the1785inn.com, $100-170) keeps the digs relatively subdued. Rooms may have double beds, but there are queens and kings available, along with a condo suite with kitchen and dining area. The inn has a swimming pool and on-site trails.

Another decent and affordable option in the North Conway area is the **North Conway Mountain Inn** (2114 NH-16, North Conway, 603/356-2803, www.northconwaymountaininn.com, $80-160 summer and fall, $70-90 winter and spring). With 34 rooms with either queens or doubles, it makes a good one-night stay for a reasonable price.

$150-250

The garden suites at the **New England Inn & Lodge** (336 NH-16, Intervale, 603/356-5541, www.newenglandinn.com, $110-250) were recently renovated, and they're spacious and clean spaces to spend a weekend. Elsewhere this classic rustic northeastern accommodation has loft suites with Jacuzzi tubs, plus large family-friendly suites with plenty of room to spread out.

Commanding the center of Jackson, **The Wentworth** (1 Carter Notch Rd., Jackson, 800/637-0013, www.thewentworth.com, $120-400) offers a quiet, midlevel hotel where rooms have doubles and queens, and suites include private whirlpool tubs or outdoor hot tubs. Rooms and suites are dressed in muted pastel colors—a bit dated, but they are well cared for and perfect for a weekend in the country.

Gorham

From Franconia, it's a 39-mile (63-km) drive east via NH-115 and US-2 to **Gorham** (pop. 2,626), a crucial point of interest for hikers leaving White Mountain National Forest and a tourist spot for those spending considerable time in the area. A longtime railroad town, Gorham is a blue-collar community that sees plenty of Mount Washington traffic in the summer, meaning a few decent restaurants and accommodations.

Gorham Moose Tours

Once you enter the White Mountains area you'll start seeing signs for moose crossings. While you won't always see one lumbering down the street like in the opening to *Northern Exposure*, you'll have opportunities to head into the woods and find one in its natural habitat. **Gorham Moose Tours** (69 Main St., 603/466-3103, www.gorhammoosetours.org, $30 adults, $20 ages 5-12, $10 age 4 and younger) runs 3-4-hour sightseeing adventures at night and has a success rate between 93 and 99 percent. That means you're more than likely to see at least one moose on a tour. The tours begin at the information booth in front of Gorham Town Common.

Food

You'll see a lot of Gorham at **Mr. Pizza** (160 Main St., 603/466-5573, www.mrpizzanh.com, 11am-11pm Sun.-Thurs., 11am-midnight Fri.-Sat., under $20), a friendly, homey restaurant with outdoor seating, booths, a modest bar area, and inexpensive pizza, sandwiches, and beer.

Not so much upscale as refreshingly fine, **Libby's Bistro** (111 Main St., 603/466-5330, www.libbysbistro.org, 5pm-10pm Fri.-Sat., under $40) combines home-style favorites like burgers and pasta with ethnic dishes like Thai green curry and Middle Eastern fried chicken. Hang in the comfy bistro with brick walls and mismatched furniture (but tablecloths) or have a seat at the neighboring and more casual **Saalt Bar** (5pm-10pm Wed.-Sun.).

Dine on authentic Italian at **Nonna's Kitchen** (19 Exchange St., 603/915-9203, www.nonnasgorham.com, 4pm-9pm Wed.-Sun., under $40). Nonna's is the kind of place where you can have fulfilling chicken, veal, fish, or pasta, plus a glass of wine, and not spend more than $30. You may want to spend more, though, because this is very good homemade food. You'll feel at home in this cute little yellow house with tin walls and wood tables.

Accommodations

The **Top Notch Inn** (265 Main St., 800/228-5496, www.topnotchinn.com, $120-170) is the best place to stay in Gorham, on par with any nice, family-friendly hotel. Kings, queens, doubles, and even cottages are available here. The hotel has a pool and hot tub.

A step down and more like a traditional motor lodge, the **Gorham Motor Inn** (324 Main St., 603/466-3381, www.gorhammotorinn.com, $100-150) has kings, queens, and doubles in basic spaces. An outdoor pool and Wi-Fi are among the amenities.

It may look like a large condominium complex, but the **Royalty Inn** (130 Main St., 603/466-3312, www.royaltyinn.com, $90-120 Jan.-mid-June, $120-150 mid-June-Oct.) is your standard one-night stay where you can drop your bags. It has older and grungier digs, but it's right in town and there are two pools on-site.

Shelburne

It's a mere 5.7-mile (9.2-km) drive east on US-2 to **Shelburne** (pop. 372), a dinky New Hampshire town that's important because it greets Appalachian Trail hikers exiting the exhilarating heights of Mount Moriah and the White Mountains. This crucial stopover helps a tired hiker rest before venturing into the wild unknown of Maine.

★ **Rattle River Lodge and Hostel** (592 US-2, 603/466-5049, www.rattleriverhostel.com, $35-120) awaits some of those weary hikers with fantastic amenities and spacious rooms. The lodge has private rooms, a few with private bathrooms, plus two seven-person dorm rooms with bunk beds. But the highlight of Rattle River is the large kitchen and dining room, which can seat up to 15, and a living space with a fireplace. It's a good place for hikers to recharge while in the White Mountains, or, for northbound thru-hikers, to share a few memories before the final push in Maine.

ME-26: Grafton Notch State Park

While the Appalachian Trail heads northeast from the Shelburne area, drivers have to plug onward east on US-2 to cross into Maine, the final frontier on the AT. From Shelburne, via US-2 and then ME-26, it's a 31-mile (50-km) jaunt to **Grafton Notch State Park** (ME-26, Newry, 207/824-2912), a fine introduction to "Vacationland" that includes a classic Maine peak with a difficult sidetrack just begging you to indulge.

Old Speck Mountain ain't no speck. Topping out at 4,170 feet (1,271 m), it's the tallest mountain in the Mahoosuc Range, a branch of the White Mountains straddling the New Hampshire-Maine border.

A smaller and accessible mountain in the Mahoosuc Range with two distinct peaks, **Baldplate Mountain** is one of the first climbs for Appalachian Trail hikers in Maine. The trail tramples along both the West Peak (3,662 feet/1116.2 m) and East Peak (3,812 feet/1161.9 m).

Hiking

Old Speck Mountain

Distance: 7.5 miles (12 km)
Duration: 4 hours
Elevation gain: 2,550 feet (777 m)
Difficulty: Strenuous
Trailhead: Parking area off ME-26 at Grafton Notch, Newry (44.590557, -70.946125)

The Old Speck Trail, accessible from ME-26, also happens to be the Appalachian Trail south. So, from the parking area, follow those white blazes south. You'll have the option to take the side trail known as the Eyebrow, a fun challenge that ascends steeply to a viewpoint (as if you're climbing up an eyebrow). To get there you'll have to work with steel rungs and ladders. If you choose the Eyebrow, you'll give yourself a sufficient warm-up (and it really works as a standalone hike) for the rest of Old Speck. You'll find yourself back with the AT after a mile (1.6 km) or so, and if you don't choose it you're hiking about the same distance, but in woods. The choice is yours.

The AT continues south as the Old Speck Trail, crossing Cascade Brook and rising through the woods to great views of Grafton Notch. After a little more than 2 miles (3.2 km) you'll reach a spur trail, which you'll want to take the rest of the way to the summit. Up there is a fire tower where you can watch falcons and check out superb views of the Mahoosuc, plus the White Mountains and out to the Rumford area. When done at the summit, head down on the AT (it's best you don't try the Eyebrow on the descent).

Baldplate Mountain

Distance: 5.8 miles (9.3 km)
Duration: 4 hours
Elevation gain: 2,200 feet (670.6 m)
Difficulty: Strenuous
Trailhead: Parking area off ME-26 at Grafton Notch, Newry (44.590557, -70.946125)

This hike starts at Grafton Notch, where ME-26 slices through the range, and climbs to the West Peak. There's plenty of elevation gain, with a little bit of danger, in this tough hike on the Appalachian Trail. From the trailhead at ME-26 you'll stay on the AT north for 2.9 miles (4.7 km), and the beginning is relatively easy. For the first 1.9 miles (3.1 km) you'll climb a rugged dirt trail in lonesome woods crossing the Bear River and a few streams. After a mile (1.6 km) on this trail you can veer onto a blue-blazed spur to Table Rock, a perch that offers a straight view of Old Speck.

Back on the AT, a little farther up you'll reach stone steps that travel steeply up to the Baldplate Lean-To. Once you reach the lean-to, which is frequented by AT thru-hikers, section hikers, and all sorts of Maine travelers, take a breather and prepare. After the lean-to, the AT continues north for a mile (1.6 km) on a seriously steep grade where you'll find yourself watching for slick spots.

After the toughest part comes the summit, which provides views of Old Speck behind you, East Peak and the last of the Mahoosuc ahead of you, plus smaller hills pushing out toward the Rangeley area. If you so choose, you can continue another mile (1.6 km) to East Peak; it's flat for the first 0.7 mile (1.1 km), then it gets a little rocky and steep. When finished, turn around and head down the AT south, but be careful when descending—it'll go fast.

Rumford

Drive south on ME-26 until it connects with US-2. Turn left to head east on US-2 and drive 16 miles (26 km) to **Rumford** (pop. 5,711), a former mill town whose position on the Androscoggin River proved conducive to paper production. Now the water is a tourist attraction, led by Rumford Falls, accessible by the Rumford Falls Trail.

Hiking

Rumford Falls Trail

Distance: 1.6 miles (2.6 km)

Duration: 1-2 hours
Elevation gain: 250 feet (76 m)
Difficulty: Easy
Trailhead: US-2 and ME-108 (44.544917, -70.543373)

This basic loop starts on a sidewalk from the intersection of US-2 and ME-108. From the visitors center head west on US-2 toward the river. Cross the river and continue along the road for another 0.5 mile (0.8 km). Then, at South Rumford Road, turn left and cross the river once more. You'll see a dam down the river, which you'll be getting closer to in just a moment. Turn left once over the bridge and take a gravel road along the river toward the waterfall. The falls themselves are spread out and drop a little more than 100 feet (30 m) over granite. Continue on the trail back up toward the parking area to finish the loop.

Accommodations

Want a room in Rumford? The **Hotel Rumford** (65 Canal St., 207/364-3621, www.hotelrumford.com, $60-90) is steady as she goes. Look for the sign featuring the old-school Pat Patriot mascot and you'll be home. The Hotel Rumford has three distinct rooms, each extremely basic and good for a cheap night with free Wi-Fi.

★ Angel Falls

It's a heck of a drive up ME-17 west from Rumford to Township D, home to **Angel Falls.** It snows more than a bit up in these parts, and since traffic isn't necessarily at New York City levels, roads aren't patched up as quickly. You'll bounce, you'll swerve, and you'll keep one eye locked on the side of the road because you never know when a moose may appear. But after 17 miles (27 km) up the winding state route, you'll turn left onto Houshton

Top to bottom: Grafton Notch State Park; Rumford; Rangeley Lake State Park.

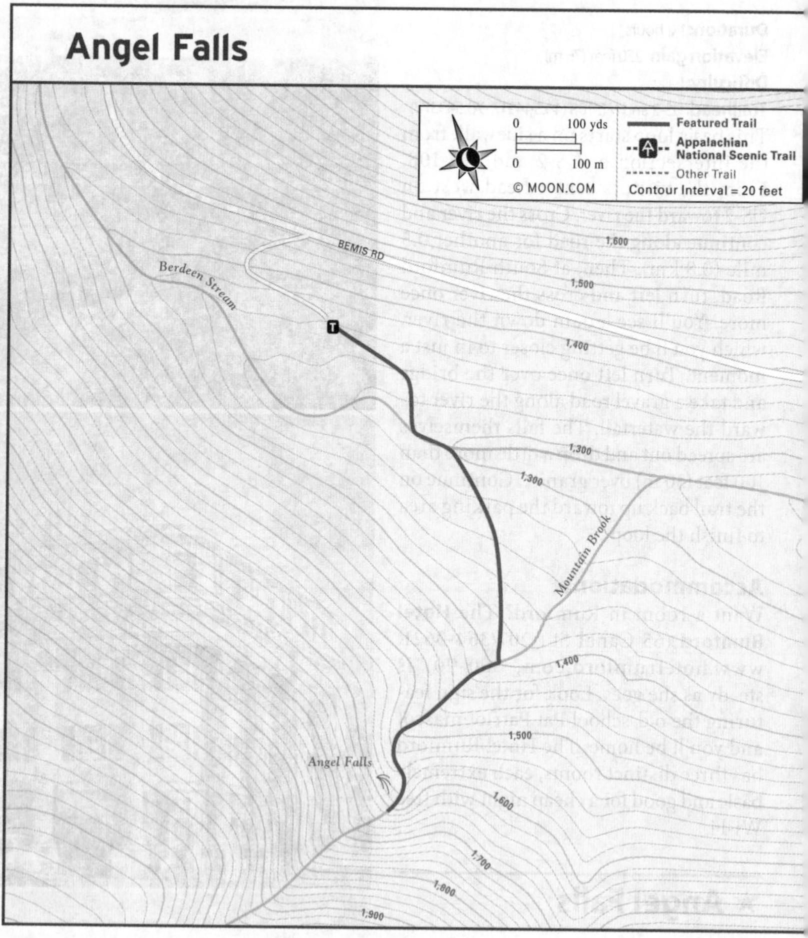

Angel Falls

0 100 yds
0 100 m
© MOON.COM
Featured Trail
Appalachian National Scenic Trail
Other Trail
Contour Interval = 20 feet
BEMIS RD
Berdeen Stream
Mountain Brook
Angel Falls
1,300
1,400
1,500
1,600
1,700
1,800
1,900

Road, then right on Bemis Road to reach the falls.

Hiking

Angel Falls Trail

Distance: 1.6 miles (2.6 km)
Duration: 1-2 hours
Elevation gain: 200 feet (61 m)
Difficulty: Easy
Trailhead: Bemis Road at logging road (44.788519, -70.704502)

Angel Falls plunges about 90 feet (27 m) over a dramatic shelf, and, when the flow is just right, looks like an angel. It's a simple 0.8-mile (1.3 km) hike to the falls, accessible from a logging road that comes in 3.2 miles (5.1 km) down Bemis Road. Keep watch for red blazes and stay with them while on your hike; you'll scramble some rocks and cross the Berdeen Stream three times to reach the falls, which provide a show-stopping scene. The most challenging time to hike to Angel Falls is in early or mid-spring, when the water rushes voluminously and the trail is a little tougher to access. It requires extreme care, but the payoff is worth it.

Rangeley

Drive the winding ME-17 another 28 miles (45 km) north from Angel Falls to **Rangeley** (pop. 1,168), the epitome of Maine's "Vacationland" moniker. A longtime industry town where logging thrived in the 19th century, Rangeley by the early 20th century became a popular destination for big-city tourists seeking cool mountain air and robust fly-fishing and boat-fishing opportunities. The trout are plentiful out here, found in Rangeley Lake, a 6,300-acre body of water that's as blue as it gets in the East. The lake, plus the views from the nearby mountains, make Rangeley a picturesque place to spend a little time and make some memories. For AT hikers it's a little out of the way, but still worthy, if they have time to take a zero day here.

Sights

Wilhelm Reich Museum

A pioneer of sexual liberation and, in his time, a controversial psychoanalyst, Wilhelm Reich authored works like *The Mass Psychology of Fascism* and *The Sexual Revolution*. He also introduced to America the orgone box, which he claimed could cure cancerous tumors before it was banned by the U.S. government. Later Reich purchased land near Rangeley, and there built a cabin, then a laboratory and observatory, calling the property Orgonon. Today the property is the **Wilhelm Reich Museum** (19 Orgonon Cir., Dodge Pond Rd., 207/864-3443, www.wilhelmreichtrust.org, 1pm-5pm Wed.-Sun. July-Aug., 1pm-5pm Sat. Sept., $8 adults, free ages 12 and younger), which offers a half-hour documentary video, exhibits on Reich's work, and a look at his inventions. Cottages are available to rent on the property, and visitors can walk on its system of trails.

Rangeley Lake State Park

Camp by Rangeley Lake at **Rangeley Lake State Park** (1 State Park Rd., 207/864-3858), which offers swimming and fishing for salmon and trout. The campground (207/624-9950, www.campwithme.com, $20-30) has 50 sites on the lakefront, each with views of Saddleback Mountain. There's a two-night minimum at reserved sites and a two-week maximum stay altogether.

Rangeley Outdoor Sporting Heritage Museum

A vast collection of fly ties, a 12,000-year-old Native American meat cache, a circa 1910 rustic cabin, and a variety of vintage vessels are among the prized sights at the **Rangeley Outdoor Sporting Heritage Museum** (ME-4 at ME-17, Oquossoc, 207/864-3091, www.rangeleyoutdoormuseum.org, 10am-4pm daily July-Aug., 10am-4pm Wed.-Sun. May-June and Sept.-Oct., $5 adults, free age 12 and younger). The museum tells the story of the great outdoors surrounding Rangeley through these items, plus photographs, old films, and nature art.

★ Height of Land (Rangeley Scenic Byway)

After bouncing about on ME-17 for a few miles, you'll see a beautiful opening in the Maine wilderness. Go ahead, jump out of the car and sop up the scene—a lake that stretches out from your feet to miles beyond. Continue on in the car, careening as the elevation rises quickly and the trees grow smaller, until you finally see two signs: one marked "Scenic Overlook" and the other describing an Appalachian Trail crossing. Out of the car again, you'll see a trail crossing to the right—stone steps coming from the woods—and a scenic overlook to the left: **Height of Land** (ME-17 and Appalachian Trail, Roxbury).

For my money Height of Land is the finest scenic overlook in America. On a crystal-clear day the view stretches for worlds, from Mooselookmeguntic Lake and Toothaker Island in the foreground to the White Mountains and New Hampshire hills well in the back. The view is atop Spruce Mountain (about 2,200 ft/671 m above sea level), a place where tourists clamor during sunset to watch the world slowly transform against a backdrop that hasn't changed in thousands of years. For AT hikers, Height of Land represents the beginning of the true Maine wilderness, a mesmerizing journey through untouched forests of pine and birch where the toughened confront their most imposing challenges. From here the adventure makes all the sense in the world.

Hiking

Saddleback Mountain

Distance: 11 miles (17.7 km)
Duration: 7-8 hours
Elevation gain: 2,200 feet (671 m)
Difficulty: Strenuous
Trailhead: ME-4 9.7 miles/15.6 kilometers south of Rangeley (44.886908, -70.540567)

Standing 4,121 feet (1,256 m), Saddleback Mountain is one of the tallest mountains in Maine, home to the Saddleback Ski Resort, and one of the first true tests for Appalachian Trail hikers in Vacationland. Thru-hikers journeying toward Katahdin must summit Saddleback on the AT, but it's worth it: from the top the view includes Rangeley Lakes and the mountains leading toward the 100-Mile Wilderness. It's yet another reminder of the cruel test that awaits the most ambitious backpackers.

This one is a risky proposition but rewarding for those who stick it out. From the parking area head north on the Appalachian Trail, which means crossing ME-4. Cross the Sandy River 0.1 mile (0.2 km) into the trek, and at 0.5 mile (0.8 km) cross Beech Hill Road. Nearly 2 miles (3.2 km) into the hike you'll reach the Piazza Rock Lean-To, which can support up to eight people. A privy by the shelter welcomes folks with a sign that says, "Your move." There's a reason: Inside the privy, between the two holes for doing business,

Height of Land

is a cribbage board, making this the best privy ever invented. Near the shelter is Piazza Rock itself, a boulder resting far above the floor and inviting the daring to climb.

Past the lean-to you'll reach Ethel Pond, then a bit later, Eddy Pond, which is fed by Cascade Stream. The hike continues another 3 miles (4.8 km) as a strenuous slog in sometimes slippery conditions, but the summit is gorgeous if it's clear out there. You'll head back the same way, this time going south on the AT.

Bald Mountain

Distance: 2.5 miles (4 km)
Duration: 1.5 hours
Elevation gain: 940 feet (287 m)
Difficulty: Moderate
Trailhead: Bald Mountain Road 0.5 mile/0.8 kilometer south of ME-4 (44.955133, -70.790465)

For a more modest hike in the Rangeley area, Bald Mountain sufficiently challenges without becoming an all-day affair. There are moments when the Bald Mountain summit hike plays as challenging, but these are passing moments when you have to scramble a little or take on a couple hundred feet in a short distance. It starts as a quick hike along a blue-blazed trail, but it slowly grows a bit more strenuous. Still, this is an enjoyable side trip that leads to a summit with views of the lakes and Saddleback. Take the same blue-blazed trail back to the base.

Fishing

Fishing is plentiful out in Rangeley. You can go out on the boat and attempt to hook trophy-size landlocked salmon and brook trout in Rangeley Lake, or take it to the rivers if you're fly fishing. Walk-in ponds, like Ledge Pond on the Appalachian Trail, are stocked with brook trout. Of course, if you're fishing at all in Maine, you must carry a valid **fishing license** ($11-25 resident, $11-64 nonresident). They're available in sporting goods stores, convenience stores, and town clerk offices across the state.

Food

★ **The Shed** (2647 Main St., 207/864-2219, www.getshedfaced.com, noon-9pm Mon.-Sat., under $30) offers true-blue 'cue in the form of ribs, pulled pork dinners, and beef brisket. Because it's Maine, they also have fried clams, plus a host of sides to complement your experience. The place isn't so much a shed as it is a quintessential Maine hideout, where inside a contemporary bar setup invites easy evenings with some bones to pick and beers to drink.

The **Gingerbread House Restaurant** (55 Carry Rd., Oquossoc, 207/864-3602, 7am-3pm daily, under $30) thankfully isn't an actual gingerbread house, because think of the winters. This well-appointed house has a comfortable dining room where breakfast visitors typically order the eggs Benedict, and later in the day it's crab cakes, burgers, and ribs.

Accommodations

The pretty, sky-blue **Rangeley Inn & Tavern** (2443 Main St., 207/864-3341, www.therangeleyinn.com, $110-275) goes back to at least the early 20th century, a grand hotel that grew in prominence through the decades. Guest rooms here may have twin beds, queens, or kings, and enough room to relax for a night or two. Suites have fireplaces and tidy living rooms. The inn also takes reservations for its renovated Haley Pond Lodge, where prices are slightly higher for rooms with water views and private decks.

Lakefront living? Get it at ★ **Loon Lodge Inn** (16 Pickford Rd., 207/864-5666, www.loonlodgeme.com, $100-165), which offers doubles, queens, and kings set up in either timber-lined rooms perfect for that romantic, rustic vacation, or calmer lakeside rooms that are arranged for beautiful sunsets. Rooms also have splashes of vintage flair, from iron headboards to an early 20th-century writing desk.

Bring your seafaring dreams to the **Town & Lake Motel** (2668 Main St., 207/864-3755, www.rangeleytownandlake.com, $90-150), which sits on Rangeley Lake and has docks from which guests can launch kayaks and canoes for no charge. Rooms are staggeringly basic, but it's hard to beat the affordability and location. Plus, guests rave about the nice owners, and the local ATV trails are steps away from the motel.

Daggett Rock

From Rangeley, drive 22 miles (35 km) east on ME-4 toward Phillips. Then turn north onto ME-142 and drive another mile (1.6 km). Now stop. Interested in scaling an absurdly large granite boulder that happens to be the 10,000-year-old remains of a glacial retreat? **Daggett Rock,** accessible via a relatively easy 0.3-mile (0.5-km) hike on a level trail, is the boulder, the largest glacial erratic (meaning it was left behind when a glacier skipped town) in Maine, and a popular spot for bouldering aficionados. To get there, take the trail off Wheeler Hill Road, 2.4 miles (3.9 km) east of its intersection with ME-4 in Phillips. There are more than a dozen problems (bouldering sequences) you can take on Daggett, which is split, giving it crevices perfect for climbing.

NH-25: ME-27: Sugarloaf Mountain

Home to the second-largest ski resort east of the Mississippi River and the third-highest peak in Maine, **Sugarloaf Mountain** stands 4,237 feet (1,291 m) high and invites hikers to dig into its arduous terrain and cloud-scraping cone. If you want to tackle Sugarloaf, from Phillips, take ME-142 north to ME-27, then drive another 4.3 miles (6.9 km) south on the narrow, older Caribou Pond Road to the intersection with the Appalachian Trail.

Hiking

Sugarloaf Mountain

Distance: 5.8 miles (9.3 km)
Duration: 4-5 hours
Elevation gain: 2,300 feet (701 m)
Difficulty: Strenuous
Trailhead: Caribou Pond Road 4.3 miles/6.9 kilometers south of ME-27 (45.039145, -70.344820)

Only experienced hikers need apply for Sugarloaf Mountain, whose rocky terrain and often low visibility makes for frequently treacherous trips. If you can get to the trailhead (if not, get as close as you can and stay off the road, then walk it to the AT), you'll take the AT south up a quickly worsening ascent where the ground moves easily and falls can be frequent. A breath-stealing hike up gets better once the Sugarloaf spur trail comes in, and you'll want to take that to the summit, because the AT continues south toward Spaulding Mountain.

The summit of Sugarloaf allows 360-degree views of the Carrabassett Valley, plus Mount Abraham and Crocker Mountain. The AT used to summit Sugarloaf, but now it crosses Crocker because of the ski resort.

Accommodations

Hang out with Justin and Melanie at **Hostel of Maine** (3004 Town Line Rd., Carrabassett Valley, 207/237-0088, www.hostelofmaine.com, $44-185). The couple's impressive timber lodge has private rooms with en suite bathrooms and pine bunk beds, plus a common living room with a fireplace. A continental breakfast is offered every morning.

Kingfield

From Sugarloaf Mountain it's just an 18-mile (29-km) drive down ME-27 South to **Kingfield** (pop. 968), both the gateway to Sugarloaf and a trail town on the Appalachian Trail.

Stanley Museum

In 1897, the twins Francis and Freelan Stanley built their first car. Two years later Freelan and his wife drove a car to the top of Mount Washington. The Stanley name has been linked with New England industry for more than a century, primarily because of those early steam-powered vehicles, but also because of their love of photography and the arts. The Stanley family collection is on display at the **Stanley Museum** (40 School St., 207/265-2729, www.stanleymuseum.org, 11am-4pm Tues.-Fri. Nov.-April, 11am-4pm Tues.-Sun. May-Oct., $4 adults, $3 seniors, $2 ages 12-18, free age 11 and younger), which is set at the birthplace of the Stanley twins. Among the highlights at the museum are several Stanley Steamer cars, dry-plate photography that was part of the family's early riches, violins, and art by sister Chansonetta.

Food and Accommodations

Orange Cat Café (329 Main St., 207/265-2860, www.orangecatcafe.com, 7am-3pm Mon.-Sat., 8am-3pm Sun., under $15) is a popular hangout in Kingfield, a funky, whatever-happens kind of place that has a few good breakfast items, plus salads, sandwiches, and homemade pastries. There's a colorful and quirky interior.

Those needing to stay in Kingfield can shack up at the **Herbert Grand Hotel** (246 Main St., 207/265-2000, www.herbertgrandhotel.com, $75-150). The hotel has been operating for a little more than 100 years and it shows, being a creaky, worn building. But rooms have been outfitted with care, and there seems to be a story for every single one of them. In fact, if you're interested in what could be a haunted hotel that has a past that includes speakeasies, cocaine parties, and a never-ending roulette of owners, the Herbert is your place.

Norridgewock

From Kingfield, take ME-16 16 miles (26 km) southeast, then continue on US-201A another 11 miles (17.7 km) to **Norridgewock** (pop. 3,367), an outpost on the Kennebec River where you should stop for some soft-serve ice cream. **Frederick's Dar I Whip & Homespun Family Restaurant** (120 Mercer Rd., 207/634-4962, 11am-9pm daily summer, under $10) specializes in cool treats after a hot day, but you can also fatten up on lobster rolls, hot dogs, and macaroni and cheese here. For those needing a quick refill before heading into the mountains, Frederick's hits the spot.

Skowhegan

Hop just 6 miles (9.7 km) from Norridgewock up US-2 to **Skowhegan** (pop. 8,302), which rests on the banks of the Kennebec River. The most famous resident of Skowhegan is probably Margaret Chase Smith, the first woman to be elected to both the U.S. House of Representatives and Senate, but the most famous landmark pays homage to the first residents of the area. **The Skowhegan Indian** (65 Madison Ave.) is a 62-foot-tall (19-m) wooden sculpture designed by Bernard Langlais in 1969 and dedicated to the Maine Indians, and it looks like one of those mid-1980s "three-dimensional" cartoons.

You can find more of Langlais' works, such as *Girl With Tail* (a mermaid), by walking through downtown Skowhegan, primarily along Main Street near Water Street. In all there are more than 20 Langlais pieces scattered throughout the town, and they're among the most oddball treasures in modern installation art.

Entertainment and Events

The **Bigelow Brewing Company** (473 Bigelow Hill Rd., 207/399-6262, 3pm-8pm Fri., noon-8pm Sat.) is a community hangout bedecked in wood and surrounded by peaceful environs. Visitors can sip brews while mingling outdoors near a cozy stage setup or by a fountain of beer kegs. Wood-fired pizza is available, too.

For more than 200 years (longer than Maine has been a state), the **Skowhegan State Fair** (www.skowheganstatefair.com, Aug.) has brought scores of eager visitors to this small town to celebrate a heritage built on agriculture and to have fun in the summer sun. Cattle shows, horse pulls, tractor pulls, and a demolition derby are among the highlights. Kids race about the midway, munch on fair food, and take to amusement rides. Each night is capped by a mainstage show, frequently headlined by a local country music band.

Food

Located inside a former bank—which you'll be able to tell from the large vault in the kitchen—the **Bankery** (87 Water St., 207/474-2253, www.thebankery.com, 7:30am-6pm Mon.-Sat., under $20) is a diamond in the rough in Skowhegan, the place to grab coffee and a scone, éclair, or whoopie pie, as you do in Maine.

Heritage House (182 Madison Ave., 207/474-5100, www.hhrestaurant.com, 11:30am-2pm and 5pm-9pm Tues.-Thurs., 11:30am-2pm and 5pm-10pm Fri., 5pm-10pm Sat., 5pm-9pm Mon., under $60) is a throwback to restaurant culture of the 1980s. Big dinners come with a dinner salad, bread and butter, and a choice of starch. A lunch buffet ($9) includes two soup options, a salad bar, fruit, cheese and deli meat, entrees, vegetable, and starch. It's a steal for those looking to fill up in the middle of the day.

Grab something quick at the **Snack Shack** (100 Waterville Rd., 207/474-0550, www.snackshackme.com, 11am-8pm Tues.-Sat., under $20), a family-run, well, shack, with classic roadside shack fare like clam strips and hot dogs, plus lobster rolls, salads, wings, and a bevy of wraps.

For a darn good sandwich, head to the ★ **Kel Mat Café** (147 Madison Ave., 207/474-0200, www.kelmatcafe.com, under $20), which features about 25 of them, from classic roast beef and tuna to the Hawaiian wrap, which includes ham, provolone, chicken, pineapple, and vegetables. The unassuming wood-and-brick-toned digs of the Kel Mat make it a somewhat hip hangout.

ME-15: Monson

As we get farther north and east in Maine, closing in on the 100-Mile Wilderness and Baxter State Park, know that tourism isn't necessarily big business in these parts. If you're coming to a place like **Monson** (pop. 658), chances are you're here to partake in some nature-based physical activity, and chances are even greater you're about to tackle the great 100-Mile Wilderness. Monson is the prelude to the most unforgiving stretch of the Appalachian Trail, so of course it's very hospitable to hikers. They can—and should—stock up here, because once they leave Monson, there really isn't anywhere else to go but forward.

To reach Monson by car, from Skowhegan, go north 36 miles (58 km) on ME-150 to the intersection with ME-6, then go west on ME-6 another 11 miles (17.7 km).

Appalachian Trail Visitor Center

Situated inside the Monson Historical Society building, the **Appalachian Trail Visitor Center** (ME-6 and Water St., 207/573-0163, 8am-11am and 1pm-5pm June-Oct.) is open when the weather is cooperating for hiking, and when thru-hikers are most expected to begin trickling into town. The visitors center offers a rest opportunity, and its staffers can help hikers figure out the best way to survive and thrive in the 100-Mile Wilderness and on Katahdin.

Monson Post Office

The most important U.S. Post Office along the Appalachian Trail just might be the **Monson Post Office** (2 Greenville Rd., 800/275-8777, 9:15am-12:15pm and 1:15pm-4:15pm Mon.-Fri., 7:30am-11:30am Sat.). Obviously, this is where hikers pick up important packages. It's also the last U.S. Post Office on or near the AT.

Food and Accommodations

Gather 'round at **Spring Creek Bar-B-Q** (26 Greenville Rd., 207/997-7025, www.springcreekbar-b-qmaine.com, 11am-7pm Thurs., 11am-8pm Fri.-Sat., 11am-5pm Sun., under $30), a fun joint where owners Mike and Kim keep a positive vibe while serving up pretty darn good 'cue. Offerings include barbecue pork, burgers, potato salad, corn bread, sandwiches of all shapes, and plenty of beer.

For a cozy room before a big hike, check out ★ **Shaw's Hiker Hostel** (17 Pleasant St., 207/997-3597, www.shawshikerhostel.com, $12-60), home to Kimberly and Jarrod, thru-hikers back in 2008. They offer everything from private single and double rooms to bunk houses and tent spaces, or—if you're really on the run—hot showers ($5). Meals are an additional $9, while the staff offers a shuttle service that can head up to Baxter State Park or down to Gorham.

Also in town is the **Lakeshore House** (9 Tenney Hill Rd., 207/997-7069, www.thelakeshorehouse.com, $25-70). The rooms here are pretty standard, but there are a couple of bathrooms, a common area with an impressive VHS collection (ask your parents if you don't know what that means), and a restaurant (11:30am-9pm Tues.-Thurs. and Sun., 11:30am-10pm Fri.-Sat.) that serves common American grub that's made to order.

Gorman and Lyford

For those who want a taste of the 100-Mile Wilderness without having to spend ten days backpacking it, the Appalachian Mountain Club has an option for you.

In **Gorman** and **Lyford,** the Appalachian Mountain Club offers day- and weekend-hiking splendor at the AMC Gorman Chairback Lodge and Cabins (its sister location is in Little Lyford). These two lodges offer accessible hikes to moderately challenging peaks along the 100-Mile Wilderness without having to backpack for over a week or plan months in advance.

From Monson, drive north about 14 miles (22.5 km) on ME-6 to Greenville, where at Pleasant Street, you'll hang a right. Drive on this road, also known as E Road, for a little over 17 miles (27.4 km). It'll be a winding and hardscrabble 45-minute drive. You'll venture into the 100-Mile Wilderness, turning right once you reach Gorman Chairback Camp Road, where it's another couple of miles to the AMC Gorman Chairback Lodge and Cabins.

Staying at the AMC lodges or not, you'll have to pay $14 (cash only) to access the 100-Mile Wilderness trails at the Hedgehog or Katahdin Ironworks checkpoints.

Hiking

Lodge to Lodge Trail

Distance: 6.5 miles (10.5 km)
Duration: 3-3.5 hours
Elevation gain: 875 feet (266.7 m)
Difficulty: Moderate
Trailhead: AMC Gorman Chairback Lodge and Cabins (1 Chairback Road T7, Greenville, 45.461547, -69.316281)

This specific trail heads north from Gorman Chairback to Little Lyford; for an out-and-back to return to Gorman Chairback, it'll be 13 miles (20.9 km) and seven to eight hours total. For this you'll first follow the Gorman Lodge Trail for 1.4 miles (2.3 km), some of it beside Long Pond. Soon you'll begin a slight climb to the Lodge to Lodge Trail, which will connect you to Little Lyford. Turn right onto Little Lodge and take that 1.4 miles (2.3 km) up and down to the crossing with Katahdin Iron Works Road. After the crossing, continue another 2.3 miles (3.7 km) on gently rising and descending trail through pine and spruce forest, and across a stream, until meeting West Branch Pleasant River. You'll hike beside the river until reaching Little Lyford.

Third Mountain Peak

Distance: 5.6 miles (9 km)
Duration: 3-4 hours
Elevation gain: 1,200 feet (365.7 m)
Difficulty: Strenuous
Trailhead: AMC Gorman Chairback Lodge and Cabins (1 Chairback Road T7, Greenville, 45.461547, -69.316281)

Gorman Chairback is close to three major peaks on the Appalachian Trail: Chairback Mountain (2,190 feet/667.5 m), Columbus Mountain (2,342 feet/713.8 m), and Third Mountain (2,069 feet/630.6 m). The experienced and prepared hiker can try tackling all three in one long day (or overnight by accessing the Chairback Gap Shelter on the AT), but those seeking a challenge without a full day's work can make the half-day trek to and from Third Mountain.

Start by taking the Long Pond Trail south from the AMC facility. It's a 0.6-mile (.97-km) hike on relatively level ground, and across a stream, until you reach a left turn to the blue-blazed Third Mountain Trail. That begins a climb of nearly 700 feet (213.4 m) in a mile (1.6 km), though first you'll cross Chairback Mountain Road, which provides parking for those not staying at the AMC lodge. The climb is full of switchbacks and navigates some steep ground. You may have to use your hands on some of the boulders, and you'll definitely have to use them up a ladder closer to the AT. Once you reach the AT, turn left to head north and it's another 0.7 miles (1.1 km) to the peak of Third Mountain. You still have some climbing to do, but it's not as stressful as the ladder. Once you reach the peak, you'll find yourself at Monument Cliff, which offers picturesque views of nearby summits and the vast wilderness ahead.

Accommodations

The **AMC Gorman Chairback Lodge and Cabins** (1 Chairback Rd. T7, Greenville, 207/717-0270, www.outdoors.org, May-Oct. and Jan.-mid-Mar., $39-186 members, $47-225 non-members) offers a perfect, secluded getaway in the woods. Built in 1867, the grounds include a plethora of ponds and streams and the Lyford and Gorman network of trails that connects to the AT. Guests can rest in a co-ed, shared bunkhouse that has 10 bunks and a universal bathroom, or get some privacy in one of 12 cabins. Four deluxe cabins have a queen bedroom, while the standard cabins max out at a full bed. Breakfast and dinner are served family style (at 8am and 6pm sharp), while lunch is made-to-order and packed for your hike. Rates vary by season and will increase deeper into summer, when more hikers are expected around the 100-Mile Wilderness.

About 9 miles (14.5 km) north of Gorman Chairback is **AMC Little Lyford Lodge and Cabins** (15 Moosehead Lake Rd., Greenville, 207/280-0708, www.outdoors.com, May-Oct. and Jan.-mid-Mar., $36-125 members, $44-150 non-members). Little Lyford has a 12-person shared bunkhouse and 10 cabins, each similar to the deluxe cabins at Gorman Chairback. And like at the former, the staff provides a family-style breakfast and dinner at 8am and 6pm sharp, plus to-go lunches. Rates vary by season and will increase deeper into summer.

ME-11: Baxter State Park

"Man is born to die, his works are short-lived. Buildings crumble, monuments decay, wealth vanishes. But Katahdin, in all its glory, forever shall remain the mountain of the people of Maine." Those were the words of Percival P. Baxter, the governor of Maine from 1921 to 1924. He purchased nearly 6,000 acres of land in 1930, then donated it to Maine, his only wish being that the land be kept wild.

And wild it certainly is. **Baxter State Park** (Baxter Park Rd., Millinocket, 207/723-5140, $15/vehicle May-Oct.) is a land of wonder, home to more than 215 miles (345 km) of trails, a wildlife sanctuary, and of course, the mighty Katahdin, the highest peak in Maine. About 60,000 people visit Baxter each year, with more than a few of them finishing the Appalachian Trail there.

Getting There and Around

It's a long one. From ME-6 you'll drive east to ME-11. Turn left in Milo to go north and stay on ME-11 until you reach Millinocket. You'll turn onto Katahdin Avenue, which becomes Millinocket Road, and follow that as it becomes Baxter Park Road and enters Baxter State Park. In all it's about 85 miles (137 km) by car from Monson to Baxter.

Driving on Baxter Park Road and hiking on the AT are the ways in, at least from the southern end of the park. It takes a while to get there and to get around. Only the patient and the willing make this happen.

★ Katahdin

Its name comes from the Penobscot Indians, who gave it the word for "greatest mountain." Katahdin, it can be easily argued, lives up to that name. This granite beast stands 5,267 feet (1,605 m) above sea level and has been home to inspiring hikes since the 17th century. Moose, black bear, and deer are common on the mountain. For hikers, danger is also common. AT hikers will use the Hunt Trail to reach the summit, and that includes metal rungs and some tough boulder climbing. Another trail, Knife Edge, is a 1.1-mile (1.8-km) connector from Pamola that is just 3 feet (1 m) in width, with cliffs at both sides. It's outrageously fun to navigate the sharp cliffs of this trail, but care must be taken: one false step could mean serious injury or death.

Before you plan your hike, it's important to understand that Baxter State Park limits the number of hikers on Katahdin each day. There are three parking lots from which the Katahdin trails depart and most of the spaces in those lots are reserved by hikers in advance. (A limited number of first-come, first-serve spots are handed out when the park opens at 6:00 AM each morning, and people will line up to grab them.) Reservations can be made online or by phone. Maine residents can book a parking spot TK in advance and non-Mainers can reserve their spots two weeks before their hiking date. Weekends are far more competitive and there is no parking allowed on the side of the roads in the park. The booking fee is a reasonable $5 per parking spot.

Mount Katahdin

Distance: 9.5 miles (15.3 km)
Duration: 5-7 hours
Elevation gain: 4,200 feet (1,280 m)
Difficulty: Strenuous
Trailhead: Park Tote Road at the Katahdin Stream Campground (45.885531, -69.000389)

There are a few different trails to reach the iconic Katahdin summit, but this hike follows the official AT route via the Hunt Trail. Start at the Katahdin Stream Campground parking lot by the wooden post with a white blaze. You'll walk west along a dirt path to the start of Hunt Trail, which follows Katahdin Stream and ascends through the woods at a gentle grade. Turn right at the junction for The Owl after 1 mile (1.6 km) and cross the stream on a wooden footbridge. Take note of the outhouse on the other side of the crossing. The trail starts climbing at this point, and you'll be scrambling over some rock stairs for a bit, until the trail emerges from the forest at 2.5 miles (4 km), revealing great views of The Owl, a peak west of Katahdin. The Hunt Trail gets harder at this point; you'll be scaling some huge boulders with the help of metal rungs, challenging your upper body strength to lift yourself up a little more. The trail levels out and reaches Hunt Spur at 2.8 miles (4.5 km). This steep ridge is tough, but the views along it are great, including forests and lakes below and Katahdin in the distance.

The trail reaches the tableland of Katahdin at 3.1 miles (5 km), opening up into an exposed plateau of tundra and rocks. Go left at the junction with the Abol Trail at 3.7 miles (6 km). The trail will curve to the northeast and climb a series of rock steps. At 4.7 (7.6 km) miles, you will arrive at the summit of Mount Katahdin. The payoff beats anything: the Katahdin sandwich board that marks the northern terminus of the Appalachian Trail. You did it.

Katahdin in Baxter State Park

Recreation

You can rent canoes and tubes, or go white-water rafting, via **Abol Bridge Campground** (Golden Rd., Millinocket, 207/447-5803, $25-100), which utilizes the Penobscot River.

Shopping

If you're a northbound hiker who just blew out a boot in the 100-Mile Wilderness, or you're a southbounder who has already suffered a gear casualty, **Abol Bridge Store** (Golden Rd., Millinocket, 207/447-5803, www.abolcampground.com) is a major savior. Positioned at the Abol Bridge that connects the wilderness to Baxter State Park, the store has supplies, but also drinks (alcoholic and nonalcoholic), chips, candy, and other goodies.

Accommodations

The **Abol Bridge Campground** (Golden Rd., Millinocket, 207/447-5803, May-Oct., $25) has tent and RV sites available for hikers between the 100-Mile Wilderness and Baxter State Park. Bathrooms, a shower house, and a beach are on-site, and Abol Bridge includes a hot breakfast with your stay.

The **Katahdin Stream Campground** (207/723-5140, $12-40) has 12 lean-to shelters and nine tent sites. Guests can fish and swim in the stream, too.

For backcountry campers near the trail, **Chimney Pond Campground** (207/723-5140, $12-40) is on the east side of Katahdin and has nine lean-tos and a 10-person bunkhouse. Swimming is permitted in Chimney Pond.

Bangor

Resting beside the Penobscot River far from the Appalachian Trail, **Bangor** (pop. 33,039) is the closest city to the northern terminus, and because it has an airport, it's where many thru-hikers visit when the journey ends and it's time to head back home. The third-largest city in Maine was an important hub for lumbering, especially in the 19th century, and ships left Bangor with lumber bound for cities across the world. When lumbering began to wane, the paper industry started to thrive. Today the city (pronounced "Bang-or") is still home to large-scale paper manufacturing, but it also has diversified with successful health care and tourism industries.

Bangor is a fun day trip with enough kooky sights, including the house of a famous writer and the statue of a famous logger, to keep you busy. About 9 miles (14.5 km) up US-2 is the **University of Maine** (www.umaine.edu), whose presence has helped brighten the city through a cool arts scene.

Getting There and Around

From Skowhegan it's a 55-mile (89-km) drive east on US-2 to Bangor. If you're coming off the Appalachian Trail and Katahdin (via Millinocket), you could

Mount Katahdin

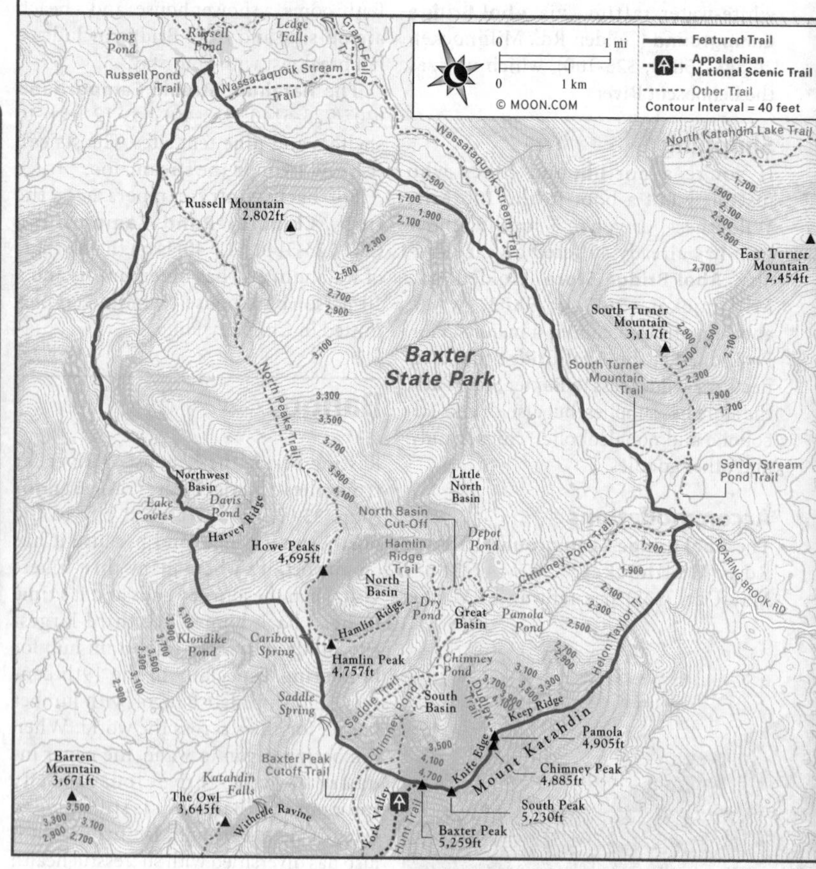

either take the more direct I-95 south, or you can continue on ME-157 to US-2 and drive that south for a slightly more scenic route along the Penobscot. You'll add about 13 miles (21 km) with that detour.

Concord Coach Lines (www.concordcoachlines.com) services Bangor at the **Bangor Transportation Center** (1039 Union St., 800/639-3317, 6:30am-6:30pm daily) and connects passengers to Logan International Airport in Boston. Meanwhile, **Bangor International Airport** (287 Godfrey Blvd., 207/992-4600, www.flybangor.com, BGR) has service to New York City, Philadelphia, Washington DC, Charlotte, Chicago, and cities in Florida through American Airlines, Allegiant, Delta, and United. Most Appalachian Trail shuttle services pick up and take hikers from and to Bangor.

Sights

★ Paul Bunyan Sculpture

There he is: The great symbol of wilderness towering over the streets of Bangor. The **Paul Bunyan Sculpture** (519 Main St.) is an iconic sight, depicting the plaid-wearing frontiersman while clutching an ax and peavey. At 31 feet (9 m) tall and weighing 3,700 pounds (1,680 kg), the fiberglass statue was erected in 1959 and honors a man whose legend may have originated in Bangor, though nobody is quite sure. The man who designed the statue wanted to install a Babe the Blue Ox statue next to Paul, but nothing has yet come of those plans.

Maine Discovery Museum

Kids have the opportunity to engage with a variety of exhibits at the **Maine Discovery Museum** (74 Main St., 207/262-7200, www.mainediscoverymuseum.org, 10am-5pm Mon.-Sat., noon-5pm Sun. summer, 10am-5pm Tues.-Sat., noon-5pm Sun. Sept.-May, $7.50), including an exploration of a tree house, beaver lodge, and man-made river in the *Nature Trails* exhibit. The favorite children's story *Goodnight Moon* comes to life in the *Booktown* exhibit, and *Tradewinds* introduces children to customs from cultures across the world. The museum hosts daily events like story time and craft workshops.

Stephen King's House

Stephen King is arguably the greatest horror writer of the last 50 years, authoring extremely popular works like *Carrie, The Shining, Cujo, Pet Sematary, It, Misery,* and *The Green Mile.* Born in Maine, King has set many of his works in his home state, and he still lives in Bangor today. You can see **his house** (47 W. Broadway) and take a few pictures outside, but he doesn't let in visitors or give tours. And you'll know it's his place: A black gate whose design includes a spider web and two bats stands in front of a deep-red, gothic-style mansion with towers and columns. It's literally an author's version of a haunted house.

Top to bottom: the sign at the top of Katahdin; downtown Bangor; Stephen King's House.

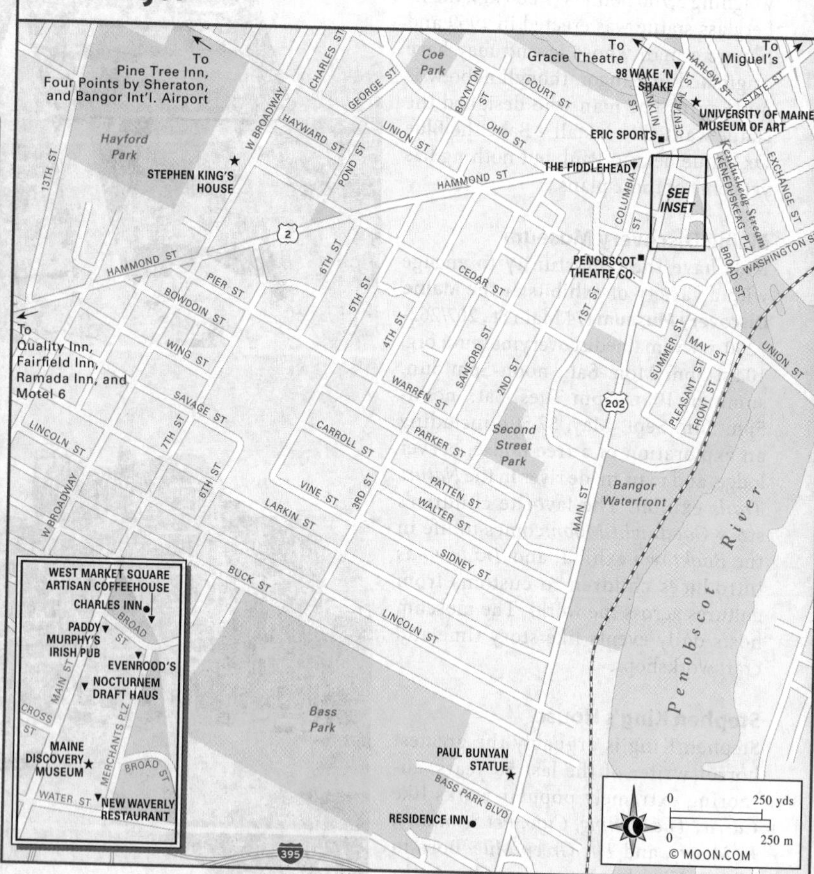

University of Maine Museum of Art

Nestled on the Kenduskeag Stream, the **University of Maine Museum of Art** (40 Harlow St., 207/581-3300, www.umma.maine.edu, 10am-5pm Tues.-Sat., free) showcases modern art primarily from Maine and the East Coast. Its permanent collection includes more than 3,800 works, some from artists like Andy Warhol, Pablo Picasso, and Edward Hopper, while current artists are encouraged to submit their work for review.

Recreation

Parks

Spreading out over 680 acres, the **Bangor City Forest** (Tripp Dr. at Stillwater Ave., 207/992-4490, www.cityforest.bangorinfo.com) has 9 miles (14.5 km) of trails for hiking, running, and biking, plus a boardwalk perfect for viewing wildlife including Canada geese, which arrive in the spring.

Spectator Sports

The biggest show in town? College

One Day in Bangor

Morning

Get in your steps at the **Bangor City Forest,** where you can watch for native birds. After the walk (or run), grab coffee and a light nosh at **West Market Square Artisan Coffeehouse.** Once you've had your fill, start walking through the downtown, along the greenbelt by the Penobscot River, to check out the **Paul Bunyan Sculpture.** Behold Paul in all his Bunyan-ness.

Afternoon

Spend a lazy afternoon at the **University of Maine Museum of Art,** indulging in its vast collection of contemporary art. Now that you're hungry, head to **Nocturnem Draft Haus** for some German fare and a cold pilsner. All that walking has probably made you tired, so grab a nap before the evening begins.

Evening

Be sure you made reservations at **The Fiddlehead** for dinner. Maybe you have a show planned, too? A night with the **Penobscot Theatre** would be just fine. Afterward, have a nightcap at an old Bangor standby, **Paddy Murphy's Irish Pub.**

hockey. The University of Maine Black Bears men's and women's hockey teams play in one of college hockey's most competitive leagues, Hockey East, against storied programs like Boston University and the University of New Hampshire, with whom they have the Border War rivalry. Catch them at **Alfond Arena** (College Ave. and Long Rd., Orono, www.goblackbears.com), a 5,712-seat venue whose paraboloid shape makes it a cozy place to take in a game.

Entertainment and Events

Nightlife

For a slice of Ireland, and a pint and a shot, **Paddy Murphy's Irish Pub** (26 Main St., 207/945-6800, 11am-1am daily, under $20) is the best choice, a jumping little place with a decent food selection of burgers and sandwiches, plus one "Irish" dish (fish-and-chips). There's a lively crowd, frequent live music, and outdoor seating.

Go a little German at **Nocturnem Draft Haus** (56 Main St., 207/907-4380, www.nocturnemdrafthaus.com, 3pm-11pm Mon.-Wed., 3pm-midnight Thurs., 3pm-1am Fri.-Sat., under $30), whose "knosh" menu includes German and French bar favorites like landjäger and curds. As for beer, it changes the taps constantly and features a good variety of both local and imported suds, served up at a long bar by fun folks.

Not so much a dive as it is a well-tread haunt, **New Waverly Restaurant** (36 Merchants Plaza, 207/942-4897, noon-1am daily, under $20) has cold beer, nice people, and a pool table. Seemingly everyone who comes here has a good time.

Performing Arts

Built in 1914 with an exterior of terracotta, the Bangor Opera House combines art deco design with an ornamental old-world exterior. Today it's the home of the **Penobscot Theatre Company** (131 Main St., 207/942-3333, www.penobscottheatre.org), which produces several plays and musicals each year.

A little bit away from the downtown, the **Gracie Theatre** (1 College Circle, 207/941-7888, www.gracietheatre.com) at Husson University was built in 2009, seating 500 inside an acoustically marvelous facility. The theater presents concerts and stand-up shows, plus university theatrical performances.

Festivals and Events

Each year, the **American Folk Festival** (www.americanfolkfestival.com, Aug.) pulls together a vibrant cross-section of the folk music scene. Typically held over a three-day period, the festival also showcases local artisans and crafters, and offers a range of food options.

Shopping

Browse over two floors of antiques and collectibles at the **Antique Marketplace** (65 Main St., 207/941-2111, www.antiquemarketplacecafe.com, 10am-5pm Mon.-Sat., noon-5pm Sun.). The collection encompasses a wide range of goods, including rare books, vinyl records, and estate jewelry.

The Rock & Art Shop (36 Central St., 207/947-2205, www.therockandartshop.com, 10am-6pm Mon.-Thurs., 10am-7pm Fri.-Sat., 10am-4pm Sun.) blends nature, art, and rocks into a unique shopping experience.

Grab hiking gear and clothing at **Epic Sports** (6 Central St., 207/941-5670, www.epicsportsofmaine.com, 10am-6pm daily), which carries all the big outdoor brands.

Food

As good as it gets for localism in Maine, ★ **The Fiddlehead** (84 Hammond St., 207/942-3336, www.thefiddleheadrestaurant.com, 5pm-9pm Tues.-Sun., under $60) procures from local farmers and producers to create memorable New American fare. Brick walls, a solid wine list, and candlelight make this a superb date-night spot, and the food is pretty unforgettable. If you're seeking a perfect dinner to close your Maine adventure, you've picked the right place.

Also in the New American space, and inside a former bank, **Evenrood's** (25 Broad St., 207/941-8800, www.evenroods.com, 11am-9pm Mon.-Fri., 4pm-9pm Sat., 10am-8pm Sun., under $50) specializes in the meats. Go for filet mignon here, or better yet, the 14-ounce rib eye in a red wine demi-glace. There's plenty of local beer on tap in this spacious dining area, which still has the old vault door. Pretty cool.

Sadly, the rest of Bangor is heavy with chain restaurants, but if you want a decent Tex-Mex experience, try **Miguel's** (697 Hogan Rd., 207/942-3002, www.miguelsbangor.com, 11am-10pm Mon.-Sat., 11am-9pm Sun., under $40). Miguel's is especially good when you need a margarita (or two) or you want to sample a tequila flight. The food is fine, from fajitas to enchiladas to tacos, with locally sourced meat and vegetables, naturally.

The **West Market Square Artisan Coffeehouse** (24 Broad St., 207/992-2270, 7am-5pm Mon.-Fri., 8am-5pm Sat., 8am-2pm Sun., under $10) is cutely designed, but let's be honest: the coffee is the star here. West Market offers pastries and quiches, plus dessert goodies, along with some seriously good joe.

For a fun breakfast, head to **98 Wake 'N Shake** (98 Central St., 207/990-0500, 7am-4pm Mon.-Fri., 9am-2pm Sat., under $25). There are simple dishes here, like one egg, two eggs, and three eggs, plus locally roasted coffee, and smoothies. All are served in a sunny little place that was once called Java Joe's.

Accommodations

Under $100

Just looking for a room for the night? You'll be fine at the **Pine Tree Inn** (22 Cleveland St., 207/573-9133, www.pinetreeinnmaine.com, $60-120). I know that isn't the strongest recommendation, but these rooms are bland, like those of a 23-year-old bachelor. Still, they have all the amenities you need, including kitchenettes.

Otherwise, you can opt for a room at the **Motel 6** (1100 Hammond St., 207/947-4253, $60-100), which offers double and queen rooms.

$100-150

There are a few solid chain choices at this price point, including the **Four Points by Sheraton** (308 Godfrey Blvd., 207/947-6721, $120-180), the **Ramada** (357 Odlin Rd., 207/904-2998, $120-180), and the **Quality Inn** (250 Odlin Rd., 207/942-8272, $120-180).

$150-250

The **Charles Inn** (20 Broad St., 207/992-2820, www.thecharlesinn.com, $120-220) is right in the middle of the hubbub, and because it was a recent subject of a *Hotel Impossible* cleanup, it is in much better shape than previously. Still, it's just a decent place to stay for a night. Rooms should be updated a bit and the themes (mostly about famous residents like Stephen King) aren't really necessary. But it's clean and has character, that's for sure.

As for chains, you have the **Fairfield Inn** (300 Odlin Rd., 207/900-0001, $150-200) and **Residence Inn** (22 Bass Park Blvd., 207/433-0800, $150-220), which sits just a few blocks from the Penobscot River and is walking distance from the Paul Bunyan statue.

Essentials

Getting There

Air

The route in this book assumes most visitors will be flying into Atlanta, but there are plenty of airports along the way that allow visitors to meet up with the AT. The following are the biggest airports along the route.

Georgia

Hartsfield-Jackson Atlanta International Airport (800/897-1910, www.atl.com, ATL) is 10 miles (16 km) south of downtown Atlanta and is the world's busiest airport by passenger traffic, serving more than 260,000 passengers daily. It's a hub for **Delta Airlines** (800/221-1212) and focus city for **Frontier Airlines** (801/401-9000), **Southwest Airlines** (800/435-9792), and **Spirit Airlines** (801/401-2222). It also services **Alaska Airlines** (800/252-7522), **American Airlines** (800/433-7300), **Boutique Airlines** (855/268-8478), **JetBlue Airways** (800/538-2583), and **United Airlines** (800/864-8331), plus several international carriers. Hartsfield-Jackson connects to Atlanta's MARTA public transportation system, with trains leaving every 10-15 minutes.

North Carolina

You can fly into **Asheville Regional Airport** (61 Terminal Dr., 1, Fletcher, 828/684-2226, www.flyavl.com, AVL), which serves **Allegiant** (702/505-8888), **American Airlines** (800/535-5225), **Delta** (800/221-1212), **Elite** (877/393-2510), and **United** (800/864-8331). Nonstop destinations include Atlanta, Charlotte, Chicago, Dallas, Newark, New York, and Washington DC, plus multiple Florida stops.

Virginia

Roanoke-Blacksburg Regional Airport (5202 Aviation Dr. NW, 540/362-1999, www.roanokeairport.com, ROA) has service to eastern and midwestern hubs like Atlanta, Philadelphia, Charlotte, and Chicago via Allegiant (702/505-8888), American Airlines (800/433-7300), Delta (800/221-1212), and United (800/864-8331). Rental car companies are stationed at the airport, and there's a bus stop 150 feet (46 m) east of the terminal building for Smart Way (540/982-6622), which runs throughout the Roanoke region.

Pennsylvania

Harrisburg International Airport (1 Terminal Dr., Middletown, 888/235-9442, www.flyhia.com, MDT) is 9 miles (14.5 km) southeast of Harrisburg. It provides nonstop service on Air Canada (888/247-2262), Allegiant (702/505-8888), American Airlines (800/433-7300), Delta (800/221-1212), United (800/864-8331), and Southern Airways Express (800/329-0485) to 13 cities, including Washington DC, Philadelphia, Atlanta, Boston, Charlotte, Chicago, Detroit, Pittsburgh, and Toronto. Many of the hotels along Eisenhower Drive in Harrisburg provide airport shuttle service.

New York

For New Jersey and New York, plus most of Connecticut, the three major New York City area airports operated by the Port Authority of New York and New Jersey have the most options for flying the friendly skies. **John F. Kennedy International Airport** (JFK Expy. and S. Cargo Rd., Jamaica, NY, 718/244-4444, www.panynj.gov/airports/jfk, JFK) has eight terminals, from which 70 airlines operate daily. **LaGuardia Airport** (LaGuardia Rd., Flushing, NY, 718/533-3400, www.laguardiaairport.com, LGA) offers nonstop flights to 64 locations. **Newark Liberty International Airport** (3 Brewster Rd., Newark, NJ, 973/961-6000, www.panynj.gov/airports/newark-liberty, EWR) is the most accessible of the airports for this guide's route, providing relatively smooth access to I-95, plus I-280, which connects to I-80. Newark has three terminals and is a hub for United (800/864-8331).

Maine

Bangor International Airport (287 Godfrey Blvd., Bangor, 207/992-4600, www.flybangor.com, BGR) is home to **American Airlines** (800/433-7300), **Allegiant** (702/505-8888), **Delta Airlines** (800/221-1212), and **United Airlines** (800/864-8331). You can get to New York, Philadelphia, Chicago, Washington, DC, Houston, the Tampa Bay area, Orlando, Fort Lauderdale, Charlotte, and Atlanta from Bangor. Multiple rental car agencies are located at the airport, and taxis and buses also stop there. **God's Country Shuttle Service** (207/480-5222, www.godscountryshuttle.com) takes passengers between the airport and Baxter State Park.

Train

Amtrak (800/872-7245, www.amtrak.com) service is dependable through this region. Amtrak services Atlanta at **Peachtree Station** (1688 Peachtree St. NW, 800/872-7245) via its Crescent line, which connects New Orleans to New York City.

The Crescent line starts in New York City and runs south past Washington DC to **Charlottesville** and Lynchburg. It continues south toward Charlotte, Atlanta, and New Orleans. A branch of Amtrak's Northeast Regional, which starts in Boston, extends into Lynchburg and **Roanoke.** Amtrak's Keystone Service connects New York City to the **Harrisburg Transportation Center** (4th and Chestnut Sts., 800/872-7245, www.amtrak.com) via Philadelphia. Amtrak runs to White River Junction on the Vermonter line, which offers access south to New York, Philadelphia, and Washington DC.

You can take Amtrak or **MARC** (Mon.-Fri., www.mta.maryland.gov) trains to Harpers Ferry and walk to Maryland Heights; a few other locations on this route are also accessible by train. MARC's Brunswick Line travels to Brunswick and Frederick, though only on weekdays.

Bus

You can take a **Greyhound bus** (800/231-2222, www.greyhound.com) to every major city and most of the larger towns near the Appalachian Trail.

In Atlanta, **Greyhound** (6000 N. Terminal Pkwy., 404/765-9598, www.greyhound.com, 8am-1:30pm Mon.-Fri.) has a station at Hartsfield-Jackson airport, and another **downtown** (232 Forsyth St. SW, 404/584-1728, www.greyhound.com, noon-midnight daily). Expect to pay between $20 and $100 for a one-way trip to Atlanta, depending on your place of origin.

Other useful stations in the South include **Asheville** (2 Tunnel Rd., 828/253-8451, www.greyhound.com, 7:30am-4:30pm, 8am-10pm Mon.-Fri., 7:30am-9:30am and 2:30pm-10pm Sat.-Sun.), connecting riders to Washington DC, Atlanta, and other locations; **Johnson City** (137 W. Market St., 423/926-6181, 7:30am-3:30pm, 8am-10pm Mon.-Fri., 7:30am-9:30am and 1:30pm-10pm Sat.-Sun.), with connections to Atlanta, Cincinnati, and other regional destinations; and **Roanoke** (26 Salem Ave. SW, 540/343-5436), Lynchburg (800 Kemper St., 434/846-6614), and Charlottesville (310 W. Main St., 434/295-5131).

In the North, besides the major stations in New York City and Bangor, there are stations in **Frederick,** where service departs from the **MARC station** (100 S. East St., 301/663-3311) and offers connections to Washington DC, Baltimore, Philadelphia, and New York City; **Hanover** (3 Main St., 800/231-2222, www.greyhound.com); and a **connection in White River Junction** (44 Sykes Mountain Ave., 802/295-3011, www.greyhound.com) in Vermont. Travelers there can head to Boston, Montreal, or Hartford, Connecticut.

Car

All of the major car rental agencies are set up at the airports listed above. Because Atlanta is a major hub, you can get there from almost anywhere via a major highway. From Florida, **I-75** runs northwest into the city. Heading west from Charleston, South Carolina? Take **I-26** west to **I-20** west. From northeastern points like Richmond, Virginia, and Charlotte, take **I-85** south. On the other side of the mountains, **I-75** connects Detroit, Cincinnati, and Knoxville, Tennessee, to Atlanta. From Mobile, Alabama, **I-65** runs north to **I-85** north into Atlanta. Finally, from Dallas, take **I-20** east to the city.

Because the Appalachian Trail is a ribbon through America's eastern wilderness, there are more than a few places where you'll have to rely on state and county roads to get from one place to another. The most convenient interstate highways for travelers looking for quicker routes include **I-75,** which connects Atlanta travelers to the Blue Ridge; **I-81,** which runs alongside the Blue Ridge up through Pennsylvania; **I-84,** which cuts across New Jersey and New York to New England; and **I-91,** which runs up the middle of New England to **US-2,** the final stretch through Maine.

Road Rules

Highway Safety

Always observe state speed limits when driving. Maine has a maximum speed limit of 75 mph (120 kph). In Georgia, North Carolina, Tennessee, Virginia, West Virginia, Maryland, Pennsylvania, and New Hampshire the speed limit may reach 70 mph (113 kph). New Jersey, New York, Connecticut, Massachusetts, and Vermont observe maximum speed limits of 65 mph (105 kph). Speed limits typically decrease in metropolitan areas (including in Atlanta, Asheville, Roanoke, Harrisburg, and Poughkeepsie), and local roads through towns and villages will almost certainly carry decreased speed limits.

Road and Weather Conditions

At higher elevations, roads can freeze or be heavily snow-packed, especially between November and April. These mountain roads are also subject to wind and rain damage. Thus, sections of the Blue Ridge Parkway, Skyline Drive in Shenandoah National Park, and other roads inside protected lands will close when conditions are unsafe for driving. Before setting out on your trip, inquire about road conditions with the relevant parks and sites.

High-elevation roads may also be extremely narrow and challenging to navigate. If you feel any trepidation about driving on a road, don't attempt it. If you are driving on a narrow road where traffic moves in both directions, proceed slowly and take note of areas where you can pull off to let oncoming traffic pass.

Wildlife on the Road

While a black bear is unlikely to walk out onto the road (it has happened, though), squirrels, raccoons, and skunks are seen far more often. Still, the biggest wildlife threat to your car is the white-tailed deer, which is common to the entire eastern part of the country and poses the highest risk around sunrise and sunset, and at night when visibility is low. Honk your horn if approaching deer by the road, brake slowly, and never swerve to avoid hitting one.

While in New Hampshire and Maine—especially on state and local roads—be on the lookout for moose. The highest risk occurs in late summer and early fall, during the fall breeding season, and at dusk or night. Drive slowly and use high beams whenever necessary.

Road Etiquette

Like in much of the country, left lanes are used for passing, and traffic should always leave one lane of distance, whenever possible, when emergency vehicles are pulled over. Not every state observes the law of turning on headlights for road workers, but as a general rule, turn them on.

Congestion will be highest in the New York metropolitan area between New Jersey and southern Connecticut, and drivers are known to be stressed and independent-minded at times. Remember to exercise caution and play nice. That said, heavy traffic patterns can occur anywhere, so remember to keep cool when confronting tense situations. Also, if traveling the interstates—especially I-81—you'll be joined by more than a few tractor-trailers who are trying to hit deadlines. If a tractor-trailer driver is trying to pass, let him or her go, and leave a safe distance between you and the cars around you.

Parking

Generally, there is plenty of parking for sights and landmarks along the route. In **Atlanta** you'll have to pay for parking more often than not (meters typically are enforced 7am-7pm Mon.-Sat., \$2/hour; lots \$7-25/hour). There are also meters and designated public parking areas in cities like **Harrisburg** (\$1.50-3/hour), **Asheville** (\$1.50/hour), **Roanoke** (up to \$3/hour), and **Poughkeepsie** (\$1/hour), where equipment is enforced during normal business hours and often on Saturdays.

Maybe more important for hikers is where to park when hitting the trail. Almost every time the Appalachian Trail crosses a road, there will be a **parking area,** typically an enlarged patch of gravel or asphalt. The same holds true for trailheads of well-known hikes. If a parking area looks full, don't try to wedge into it; instead, there may be another smaller parking area or a road pull-off nearby.

Only a few parking areas along the route, typically inside protected, government-maintained land, are accessible by paying a small fee. Usually these fees cover maintenance.

Fuel

As a general rule, fill up the tank before starting a daily drive, or whenever you're below a half tank and you've reached a town or city with at least one gas station. You'll encounter the greatest challenge in the area between **Chattahoochee-Oconee National Forest in Georgia and Asheville, North Carolina,** where stops include Hiawassee, Franklin, and Hot Springs; on the **Blue Ridge Parkway** and **Skyline Drive,** where nearby gas stations might be up to 30 miles east or west of an exit; and in **Maine,** where gas is harder to find north of US-2.

If you're pinching pennies, **avoid filling up too much in Pennsylvania and Connecticut,** where gas prices are historically well higher than the national average. **Tennessee and Virginia tend to have lower gas prices** than the national average.

Motorcycles and Bicycles

Because of the winding, rising-and-falling roads that compose this route, motorcyclists are likely to accompany you on the road. Share the road with these riders, treating them like any other vehicle and keeping safe distances. In the New York metropolitan area there's a good chance you'll be sharing the road with sport bike riders, and sometimes they'll attempt to weave around cars and lane-split on congested highways. Keep watch that a rider isn't coming up your side, even if he or she is practicing illegal riding technique (lane-splitting isn't permitted in any state on this route).

Generally, you won't find too many bicyclists on this route, though mountain bikers will take to higher-elevation areas, and cyclists are always found in cities. As a rule, bicyclists are vehicles sharing the road, so give them room on the outside. When stopped at an intersection next to one making the same turn as you, give him or her the right of way.

Hiking Basics

Trail Rules

While there are no official rules for hiking trails, it's good to know what's around you at all times. First, try not to hike alone. There's safety in numbers, especially in nature. If you're hiking slower than others around you, opt to let hikers pass whenever opportunities arise by stepping slightly off the trail in safe ground. Never stray from a trail, and if you get lost, remain in place and call for help, if possible.

Equipment Checklist

Before you hike, make sure you have:

- Sturdy shoes or boots with good traction
- Water (1-2 liters at minimum)
- Backpack
- Food (granola, fruit, tightly packed meat and cheese)
- Breathable clothing
- Layers for cooler and/or rainy weather (thermal, gloves, jacket, hat, headband, facial stocking, long underwear, high socks)
- Hiking poles
- Compass
- Cooking supplies (if overnight): camping stove, pot, silverware, plates, cups
- Tent, sleeping bag, sleeping pad, or hammock
- Extra plastic bag for trash
- Phone numbers, addresses, contact information of help, local aid
- First-aid kit

Travel Tips

Conduct and Customs

The legal drinking age is **21.** Be prepared to be asked for identification in bars and restaurants when ordering alcohol.

Most states across the country ban **public smoking,** but Tennessee, Virginia, and West Virginia generally allow it, with some exceptions. In Pennsylvania, smoking may be permitted in bars and some restaurants, but on a place-by-place basis.

Traveling with Children

Children are more than welcome on trails, but parents and guardians should be prepared when hiking with kids; always bring extra water, food, and spare clothing. Children without experience on trails should not hike in higher elevations and on tough terrain. And almost any child younger than age 15, sans the ultra-excited born hiker, will get bored of walking through nature at some point.

That means you should plan to keep kids interested during the trip with visits to larger cities with museums and fun attractions. Areas surrounding national parks generally have entertainment for kids, while wildlife centers and park visitors centers can fill in gaps between days spent in the great outdoors.

Consider, also, that kids may get upset tummies when riding through the winding hills of the Appalachians. Have a plan in place, and extra clothes at the ready, in case someone gets sick in the car.

Senior Travelers

Those age 55 and older should be ready to take advantage of discounts when on the road. Have identification ready (drivers license or passport) and inquire any time you visit a museum, art center, attraction, accommodation, or historical site.

Travelers with Disabilities

Organizations along the Appalachian Trail have addressed the need for more access in recent years, but depending on the disability, many sections of the path will be challenging if not impossible to attempt. There are a few wheelchair-accessible portions of the trail, including **Thundering Brook Falls** in Killington, Vermont, and **Bear Mountain** in New York.

Environmental Concerns

The parklands and forests along the route are preserved so future generations can enjoy nature in as pristine a state as possible. Always adhere to **Leave No Trace** (www.LNT.org) principles. Plan ahead and prepare, travel and camp on durable surfaces, dispose of waste properly, leave what you find, minimize campfire impacts, respect wildlife, and be considerate of other visitors. These easy rules can improve the outdoor experience for everyone.

If you pack something in, pack it out, and consider carrying a **trash bag** on trails to pick up after less responsible hikers. If each of us would make this a habit, we could clean up a lot of litter that clutters up our view and is detrimental to the environment. **Dogs** are allowed on some trails throughout our route, though they must be on leash or under physical control at all times. If you have Fido out on the trail or let him use the grassy facilities at an overlook or wayside, be sure to pick up what he's putting down.

As far as wildlife goes, keep a safe distance and don't feed the bears (or anything else). This makes the animal grow accustomed to people and can have a negative impact on its health.

Health and Safety

For emergencies anywhere in the United States, dial **911** on your phone for immediate assistance. When hiking, note the nearest ranger station, medical station, or visitors center, plus the closest community. Before heading out, notify a few people of your planned whereabouts and leave contact information for planned overnight stays, post offices, and drop-off points.

Wilderness Safety

Remember that when outdoors in the wild, you're invading the homes of countless creatures, from the very small to the dangerously large. Don't disrupt the environment by grabbing flora and altering trails, and keep a safe distance from wildlife that may find its way near the trail.

Snakes are common in many areas, especially in dry, warm weather in rocky areas, so watch the ground. If a snake is on the trail, don't try to touch it. You can attempt to go around it while giving a wide berth. If there's no way around, however, maintain distance and wait until it leaves.

Less common are **black bears,** though they inhabit the trail area. They are most active early in the morning and in the evening and may appear if they smell food. Thus, the first rule is to keep food and waste packed away. Second, talk loudly, clap hands, and generally make noise when hiking, as bears tend to avoid commotion.

However, if you see a bear, attempt to quietly and calmly leave. If the bear notices you, talk to it and slowly wave your arms to show you're not a threat. Slowly try to back away from the area. Do not run away, as that may trigger an attack. If a black bear attacks, use pepper spray and fight back with all your might. Do not play dead with a black bear.

Hikers should beware of **ticks,** some of which can transmit Lyme disease. An insect repellent and some thorough body checks (use a partner for more fun) should keep you tick free after a jaunt through the woods. If you do get a bite or if you notice a red circular rash that's similar to a bull's-eye, consult a physician; Lyme disease can be life-threatening in the worst cases. **Spiders** can be a concern in places, namely woodpiles and some of the backcountry shelters. Most are harmless, though the brown recluse is seen from time to time, but more commonly you'll see a black widow spider, easily identifiable by the red hourglass on the female's abdomen.

Along the trails and roadsides, you'll likely encounter **poison ivy, poison oak,** and **poison sumac,** all of which deliver an itchy blister when you come in contact with the oils they secrete. These oils are active for several months, so if you walk through a field of poison ivy, be sure to wash your pants, socks, and boots well, lest you inadvertently get poison ivy a month later. You may also come upon **stinging nettles,** which leave itchy welts akin to mosquito bites; these are harmless and generally go away quickly.

Information and Services

Visas and Officialdom

Visitors from other countries must present a valid **passport** and **visa** issued by a U.S. consular official unless they are citizens of a country eligible for the Visa Waiver Program (such as Canada) in order to enter the United States. For more information on traveling to the United States from a foreign country, visit www.usa.gov.

Money

Obviously, you're paying with the U.S. dollar on this trip. Most locations now accept credit cards or debit cards, but it's wise, especially when hiking, to carry cash in case of an emergency. Be sure to leave tips for service workers when traveling; as a guide, plan to have at least $20 on your person before heading out for the day.

Communications and Media

Magazines

For hikers, especially, consider reading publications such as ***Backpacker*** (www.backpacker.com), ***Outside*** (www.outsideonline.com), and ***Blue Ridge Outdoors*** (www.blueridgeoutdoors.com) for tips and suggested hikes throughout the Appalachian Trail.

Internet Access and Cell Phones

Internet access and smartphone connections may be spotty throughout the trail area, but you should be able to connect in even the smallest towns, especially in the motels and hotels along the way.

Maps and Tourist Information

One of the best resources for exploring a new region is a good map. DeLorme's atlas and gazetteers are indispensable. The detail provided is enough to plan short day hikes or longer expeditions, and they point out everything from trailheads and boat launches to campgrounds, hunting and fishing spots, and back roads of all types. Otherwise, be sure to stop into ranger stations to pick up park maps. For general traveling, consult **AAA** (www.aaa.com) for maps and information for the region.

Suggested Reading

Hiking the AT

Miller, David. *The A.T. Guide Northbound 2017: a Handbook for Hiking the Appalachian Trail.* Jerelyn Press, 2017. The authority on thru-hiking the Appalachian Trail is David "AWOL" Miller, whose guide is updated annually and contains thorough information on elevations, shelter locations, road crossings, hostels, restaurants, mail drop-off points, and more.

History and Culture

Bryson, Bill, and Jackie Aher. *A Walk in the Woods: Rediscovering America on the Appalachian Trail.* Anchor Books, a Division of Random House, Inc, 2016. There are countless memoirs written by thru-hikers after completing a journey on the trail, typically getting extremely personal about the challenges faced and the dreams conquered. These seem to have been born around the time that Bill Bryson's story grew as the popular cultural touchstone about the path. Bryson takes a lot of liberties when describing his walk, so don't think of it as gospel. Instead, it may be worth a snicker or two.

Catte, Elizabeth. *What You Are Getting Wrong about Appalachia*. Belt Publishing, 2018. Catte gives a great look at the modern nuances of the region, which helps to dispel common misconceptions and generalizations.

Joyner, Leanna. *Hiking through History: Civil War Sites on the Appalachian Trail*. Harpers Ferry: Appalachian Trail Conservancy, 2015. Joyner provides a great background of the Civil War history of the trail.

Travel

Jensen, Jamie. *Moon Road Trip USA: Appalachian Trail*. 8th ed., Avalon Travel, 2018. Jensen offers a more general, shorter version of road tripping along the Appalachian Trail.

Internet Resources

AT Organizations

Appalachian Trail Conservancy
www.appalachiantrail.org
The Appalachian Trail Conservancy is the organization that oversees the trail's preservation and maintenance. It's the main advocacy group for trail conservation, and it serves as a conduit for volunteer opportunities and provides information for those interested in hiking the trail. Thru-hikers register with the AT Conservancy before heading out each year so they're counted as official thru-hikers.

Nantahala Hiking Club
www.nantahalahikingclub.org
An organization that helps promote AT preservation and maintenance in Georgia and North Carolina.

Piedmont Appalachian Trail Hikers
www.path-at.org
An organization that helps promote AT preservation and maintenance in southwest Virginia.

Potomac Appalachian Trail Club
www.patc.net
An organization that helps promote AT preservation and maintenance in the mid-Atlantic.

Green Mountain Club
www.greenmountainclub.com
An organization that helps promote AT preservation and maintenance in Vermont.

New York-New Jersey Trail Conference
www.nynjtc.org
An organization that helps promote AT preservation and maintenance in New York and New Jersey.

Appalachian Mountain Club
www.outdoors.org
The Appalachian Mountain Club promotes preservation of the AT and other trails from the mid-Atlantic to Maine.

AT General Information

Appalachian National Scenic Trail
www.nps.gov/appa/index.htm
This is the national park organization's official website for the Appalachian Trail. It offers helpful alerts in effect and resources about how to get involved.

Appalachian Trail Museum
https://www.atmuseum.org/
The website of the Appalachian Trail Museum has an "online museum," which offers a depth of AT information, such as general history, trail stories, and shelter registers and vintage guides.

Outdoor Recreation

Blue Ridge Parkway
www.nps.gov/blri
Details the history of the park and provides real-time road maps that show detours, delays, and closures; downloadable maps that make hiking and planning a trip section-by-section easy; and write-ups on the flora, fauna, and geographical features of the Parkway.

Great Smoky Mountains National Park
www.nps.gov/grsm
An extensive history of the park; details on the flora, fauna, and natural features in the park; and downloadable maps and contact information for rangers and park offices.

Shenandoah National Park
www.nps.gov/shen
Information on trails and park activities as well as Skyline Drive, the flora and fauna, the history, and the landscape. Skyline Drive details include maps of the road and trails, contact information for various waysides and lodges, and links to secure in-park lodging.

State Parks
www.stateparks.org
This website run by the National Association of State Park Directors offers current news and events, resources, and reservation and search tools for state parks in the United States.

United States Forest Service
https://www.fs.fed.us
The official website for the United States Forest Service provides helpful information on national forests, including search tools, maps, and recreation fees and passes.

INDEX

A

Abrams Falls Trail: 78
accessibility: 436-437
accommodations: 36, 113, 189, 269, 330, 393; Asheville 93-94; Atlanta 49-50; Bangor 428-429; Beacon 308-309; Frederick 199-200; Hagerstown 209; Harrisburg 227-228; Hershey 235-236; Pittsfield 349-350; Poughkeepsie 314-315; Roanoke 143; Stroudsburg 258; Warwick 286
Adams: 351
Admiral, The: 15, 92
air travel: 432-433
Alander Mountain Trail: 334
Alliance Theatre: 47
All Saints Episcopal Church: 192
AMC-Berkshire: 22
American Museum of Fly Fishing: 367
Amicalola Falls State Park: 52-53
Andreas: 243
Andy Layne Trail: 134-135
Angel Falls: 389, 411-412
Angel Falls Trail: 412
Angels Rest and Wilburn Valley Overlook: 126
Annapolis Rock: 25, 185, 187, 204-205, 206
Anthony Creek Trail: 77
Anthony's Nose: 299, 300
Anthony, Susan B.: 351
Antietam National Battlefield: 26, 28, 203
Antique Automobile Club of America Museum: 233-234
Appalachian National Scenic Trail: 439
Appalachian Trail and Long Path Loop: 292-293
Appalachian Trail Conservancy: 21, 22, 109, 177, 178-179, 439
Appalachian Trail Museum: 10, 21, 185, 216, 439
Appalachian Trail to Annapolis Rock: 205
Appalachian Trail Visitor Center: 23, 419
Apple Orchard Falls Trail: 146-147
Architecture Trail: 87
Arethusa Falls: 23, 402, 405-406
Ariana's Restaurant: 392, 397
Arkaquah Trail: 55
Arlington: 372
Arrowhead: 346, 348
Artist's Palate: 310, 314
Artsfest: 226
Asa Packer Mansion: 246
Asheville: 8, 15, 25, 34, 84-94, 432, 433, 435
Ashuwillticook Rail Trail: 350
Atlanta: 8, 15, 23, 34, 35, 37-50, 432, 433, 434, 435
Atlanta Botanical Garden: 44
Atlanta Braves: 45
Atlanta Dogwood Festival: 47
Atlanta Dream: 45
Atlanta Falcons: 45
Atlanta Hawks: 45
AT Metro-North Station: 315
Attaboy Beer: 194, 197
Augustoberfest: 208

B

Bake Oven Knob: 26, 243
Baker-Berry Library: 394-395
Baker Park: 196
Bald Mountain: 23, 415
Bald Mountain and White Rocks: 363
Baldplate Mountain: 409, 410
Bangor: 15, 23, 390, 423-429
Bangor City Forest: 426, 427
Bannerman Castle: 305
Bardavon 1869 Opera House: 310, 313
Barrette Center for the Arts: 384-385
Barrington Stage: 348
Bartram Trail: 61
Bascom: Center for the Visual Arts: 59
baseball: 45, 88, 128, 132, 196, 208, 223, 305
Bash Bish Falls Trail: 21, 332-335
Basic City Beer Co.: 17, 20, 154
Basic Park: 153
basketball: 45, 88, 100-101, 128, 395
Battle Monument: 28, 295-296
Baxter State Park: 10, 12, 23, 420-423
Beacon: 21, 25, 266, 304-309
Beacon Artist Union: 307
Beacon Institute for Rivers and Estuaries: 307
Bear Mountain (Connecticut): 18, 26, 322, 323
Bear Mountain (New York): 21, 26, 265, 266, 290, 437
Bear Mountain Bridge: 6, 10, 288, 289-290, 299
Bear Mountain Ice Rink: 293
Bear Mountain Inn: 269, 294
Bear Mountain Loop (Connecticut): 26, 267, 323
Bear Mountain Loop (New York): 26, 267, 290, 291
Bear Mountain Pool: 293
Bear Mountain State Park: 26, 288-294
bears: 156, 437
beer/breweries: 20, 88-89, 140-141, 152, 196-197, 238-239, 281-282, 313, 336, 378
Bell Mountain: 23, 57
Belle Boyd Cottage: 172
Bellvale Farms Creamery: 21, 268, 285
Bellvale Mountain Trail: 283
BeltLine: 44

Beltzville State Park: 252
Bennington: 360-364
Bennington Battle Monument: 360
Bennington Center for the Arts: 362
Bennington Museum: 361-362
Bennington Potters: 363
Berglund Center Coliseum: 141
Berkshire Art Museum: 354-355
Berkshire Athenaeum: 346
Berkshire Botanical Garden: 21, 341
Berkshire Mountain Distillers: 336
Berkshire Museum: 346, 348
Berkshire School: 334
Berkshire Theatre Group: 349
Berryville: 175
bicycling: 435-436; Maryland/Pennsylvania 191, 223, 248; Massachusetts/Vermont 375; Virginia/West Virginia 114-116, 138
Big Bald: 23, 98
Big Dam Trail: 238
Big Dan's BBQ: 17, 104
Big Elm Brewing: 336
Big Meadows: 17, 158, 163-164, 166
Big Meadows Wayside: 166-167
Big Red Trail: 25, 202
Big Run: 160-162
Big Run Loop: 160
Big Walker Lookout: 124
Big Wilson Creek: 120
Billings Farm & Museum: 327, 380
Biltmore Estate: 15, 28, 33, 86-87
Biltmore Winery: 86-87
Biscuit Head: 17, 35, 86, 92
Bistro Box: 329, 337
Black Lantern Inn: 113, 143
Black Locust Trail: 200
Black Mtn. Burger Co.: 23, 407
Blackrock Summit: 17, 158, 160
Blacksburg: 126-131
Blair Academy: 21, 274
Blairstown: 21, 273-275
Blairstown Diner: 21, 268, 275
Blairstown Historic District: 274
Blairstown Museum: 274
Blairsville: 266
Bland: 125
Blood Mountain Shelter: 54
Blue Benn Diner: 329, 363-364
Bluegrass with Blue: 67
Blue Hole Falls: 17, 33, 103-104
Blue Mountain Barrel House: 152
Blue Mountain Brewery: 152
Blue Ridge Mountains: 34
Blue Ridge Parkway: 14, 15, 17, 111, 435, 440
Blue Ridge Summit: 211
Blue Wing Frog: 17, 112, 173
Bluff Mountain Trail: 150
boating: Georgia/North Carolina/Tennessee 62; Maryland/Pennsylvania 217, 237, 238, 252, 260-261; New York/New Jersey/Connecticut 282, 286-287, 293
Bon Paul & Sharky's Hostel: 36, 93
books: 438-439
Boone, Daniel: 244
Boonsboro: 25, 201-203
Boonsboro Museum of History: 201
Boscobel House & Gardens: 265, 300-301
Botanical Gardens at Asheville: 86, 87
Bote Mountain Trail: 77
Boulder Caves: 398-399
Boyd, Belle: 172
Branchville: 275-276
Brasstown Bald: 23, 29, 55-56
Brava: 23, 344
Breakfast on the Connecticut: 393, 397
Breakneck Ridge: 20, 303-304
Breakneck Ridge Loop Trail: 304
Bretton Woods Canopy Tour: 402-403
Brew Ridge Trail: 152
breweries: *see* beer/breweries
Bricco: 222, 227
Brick Box: 372
BRITE Bus: 113
Broad Street Market: 222, 226
Brodheadsville: 252-253
Brooks Hill Loop Trail: 196
Brown, John: 212
Brunswick: 191-192
Brunswick Heritage Museum: 191
Brunswick Main Street: 191
Brunswick Railroad Days: 191
Brushy Mountain Trail: 139
Bryson City: 64, 65-66
Buck Ridge Trail: 216-217
Bull's Bridge: 21, 26, 265, 317
Burgundy Lane Bed & Breakfast: 189, 210
Burial Beer Co.: 15, 86, 88
Bus, The: 331
bus travel: 433; Georgia/North Carolina/Tennessee 37, 41; Maryland/Pennsylvania 188-189, 221; Massachusetts/Vermont 331; New Hampshire/Maine 391, 393; New York/New Jersey/Connecticut 270; Virginia/West Virginia 112
Buttermilk Falls: 271
Buttermilk Falls Trail: 29, 271

C

Cabbagetown: 15, 46, 48-49
Cades Cove Visitor Center: 72

Cadet Chapel: 295
Café Nola: 194, 199
Café on Broadway: 188, 253
Caleb's Peak & St. John's Ledges: 21, 317
Caledonia Public Golf Course: 214
Caledonia State Park: 214
camping: 12; *see* accommodations
C&O Canal Trail: 191
Cannon Mountain: 399
car travel: 13-14, 434-436; Georgia/North Carolina/Tennessee 35-36, 40; Maryland/Pennsylvania 187; Massachusetts/Vermont 329-330; New Hampshire/Maine 391-392; New York/New Jersey/Connecticut 267-268; Virginia/West Virginia 111
Carlisle: 218-220
Carrier Park: 88
Carroll Creek Linear Park: 196
Carroll Creek Promenade: 194
Carvins Cove Natural Reserve: 140
Cashiers: 63
Catalyst Gallery: 307
Catoctin National Recreation Trail: 200
Cat Rocks Pawling Trail: 267, 315
Cat Rocks Trail: 283
Cavender Creek Vineyards: 51-52
Cedar Creek Trail: 147
Cedar Swamp Trail: 279-280
Celebration of Lights: 313
Cellar Door: 194, 197
cell phone service: 438
Centennial Olympic Park: 44
Center for Civil and Human Rights: 28, 43
Center for Puppetry Arts: 33, 41, 42-43
Center in the Square: 17, 136
Central District (Shenandoah National Park): 163-168
Chambersburg: 212-214
Chance Theater: 313
Chapel Restoration: 302
Charles Town: 176-177
Charlotte: 23-25
Charlottesville: 433
Chattahoochee-Oconee National Forest: 23, 53, 435
Chautauqua Festival: 123
Cherokee: 15, 66-69
Cherokee Nation: 66-68
Cheshire: 350
children, traveling with: 436
Chimney Rocks: 211
Chimney Rocks Loop: 211
Christianburg: 131
City Island: 223
Civil Rights Movement: 28
Civil War: 28
Clark Art Institute: 358-359
Clarksburg State Park: 358
Clay Corner Inn: 113, 131
Clermont Lounge: 41, 50
Clingmans Dome: 8, 15, 33, 72-73
Clingmans Dome Visitor Center: 72
Cold Spring: 301-303
College Hill Park: 312
Colonial Theatre: 349
Commonwealth of Virginia's Department of Game & Inland Fisheries: 114
Community Bridge Mural: 21, 185, 194-195
Concord Coach Lines: 424
Connecticut: 10, 263-270, 316-323, 435
Constitution Marsh Audubon Center and Sanctuary: 302
Constitution Park: 153
Crane Museum of Papermaking: 350
Crazy Larry's Hostel: 113, 117
Cube Fest: 129
Culinary Institute of America: 311
Cunneen-Hackett Arts Center: 313
Curate: 35, 86, 92-93
Cure Café, The: 21, 257
currency: 438
cycling: *see* bicycling

D

Daggett Rock: 416
Dahlonega: 25, 50-52
Dahlonega Jam Sessions: 67
Dahlonega Trailfest: 11, 50
Damascus: 17, 22, 110, 111, 113-118
Damascus Brewery: 20, 116
Damascus Trail Days: 11, 114
Dancing Bear Lodge: 36, 80, 81
Dan's Restaurant & Tap House: 25, 202
Dark Hollow Falls: 17, 158, 164
Dartmouth Big Green: 395
Dartmouth Coach: 391, 394
Dartmouth College: 23, 394-395, 396
Daughters of the American Revolution Van Bunschooten Museum: 280
Deacon Street: 402, 406
Deep Creek: 20
deer: 13, 434
Delaware Water Gap: 10, 22, 259
Delaware Water Gap National Recreation Area: 10, 21, 259-261, 267, 270-273
Devils Backbone Basecamp Brewpub: 20, 151-152
Dewey Hall: 335
D. G. Yuengling & Son Brewery: 21, 238-239
Dia:Beacon: 304

Diana's Baths: 403-404
Dickey Ridge Visitor Center: 159
Dickinson College: 218
Dida's Distillery: 173
Dillard: 62
disabilities, tips for travelers with: 436-437
District Kitchen & Bar: 348, 349
dogs: 437
Doodletown Bridle Path Loop: 290-291
Dottie's Coffee Lounge: 348, 349
Double Crown: 86, 89
Dover Oak: 315
Downtown (Atlanta): 46, 48
Dragon's Tooth: 132-133
driving: *see* car travel
DuBois Center at Great Barrington: 337
DuBois, W. E. B.: 337
Due South BBQ: 17, 131
Duncannon: 10, 22, 228-229
Duncannon Appalachian Trail Festival: 11, 228-229
Dutchess Rail Trail: 312

E

EARL, The: 41, 47
East Mountain State Forest: 336-337
East Mountain Trail: 328, 336-337
East Point: 46-47
East Stroudsburg: 10, 21, 26, 254
East Stroudsburg University: 254
East Tennessee State University: 99-100
East Tennessee State University Buccaneers: 100-101
Eddie's Toy Museum: 253
Edith Bolling Wilson Birthplace and Museum: 17, 123
Edward P. Thomas Memorial Pool: 196
Eggleston: 125
Eisenhower Hall Theatre: 296
Elementary Coffee Co.: 222, 226-227
Elizabethton: 17, 103-104
Elizabethton Covered Bridge: 104
Elkwallow Wayside: 158, 171-172
Elm Street Market: 21, 341
Elmwood Park: 139
Emerald Lake State Park: 370
emergencies: 437
entertainment: Asheville 88-91; Atlanta 45-48; Blacksburg 128-129; Frederick 196-197; Hagerstown 208; Harrisburg 224-226; Hershey 234; 248-249; Johnson City 101-102; Poughkeepsie 312-313; Warwick 283-284; Waynesboro 154
environmental issues: 437
Equinox Golf Resort & Spa: 330, 369
Equinox, Mt.: 10, 29, 364-365
equipment: 12-13, 436
Eric Sloane Museum and Kent Furnace: 316-317
Erwin: 99
Evangelical Lutheran Church: 192
events: *see* festivals/events
Everedy Square & Shab Row: 25, 194, 198, 199

F

Fairgrounds Park: 208
Fall Foliage Festival: 249
Fallingwater Cascades Trail: 146
Family Meal: 194, 198
Farmhouse Kitchen & Wares: 158, 162
Farm in Antler Hill Village: 87
Fashion Archives and Museum of Shippensburg University: 214
Fatback Soul Shack: 112, 131
Ferst Center for the Arts: 47
Festival of Christmas Past: 78
festivals/events: 11
Fetch: 21, 286
Fiddlehead, The: 392, 427, 428
Finerty Pond via Appalachian Trail: 345
Firestone's Raw Bar: 194, 199
Fire Tower Trail: 287
fish/fishing: Georgia/North Carolina/Tennessee 62; Maryland/Pennsylvania 200, 211, 217, 237, 238, 252; Massachusetts/Vermont 334, 345; New Hampshire/Maine 415; New York/New Jersey/Connecticut 282, 293, 317; Virginia/West Virginia 114, 120, 122-123, 153, 160-162
Flat Rock Trail System: 211
Flavours: 348, 349
Flip-Flop Festival: 11, 180
flip-flop hiking: 180
Foley Brothers Brewing: 378
food: *see* restaurants
football: 45, 101, 128, 296, 312, 395
Four State Challenge: 179
420 Fest: 48
Fox Theatre: 47
Frances Lehman Loeb Art Center: 312
Francis Scott Key Monument: 196
Franconia: 23, 406-407
Franklin: 8, 15, 22, 59, 63-65
Franklin D. Roosevelt Presidential Library & Museum: 21, 265, 310
Frazetta Art Museum: 254
Fred Harris Trail: 395
Frederick: 8, 21, 25, 192-200, 433
Frederick Coffee Co.: 194, 199
Frederick Festival of the Arts: 197
Frederick History Bicycle Loop: 200
Frederick Keys: 194, 196

Frederick Visitor Center: 200
Frelinghuysen Morris House & Studio: 342-343
French Broad River Greenway: 88
French Broad River Park: 88
Fresh Grass: 11, 356-357
Front Royal: 17, 110-111, 157, 172-175
Frost, Robert: 10, 361, 363
Fuel Coffee Shop: 21, 338

G

Gambrill State Park: 200-201
Gamut Theatre Group: 225-226
Gap Theatre: 253
Garrison: 299-301
Garrison's Landing: 299
gas stations: 14, 435; Georgia/North Carolina/ Tennessee 37; Maryland/Pennsylvania 189; Massachusetts/Vermont 331; New Hampshire/Maine 393; New York/New Jersey/ Connecticut 270; Virginia/West Virginia 113
Gatlinburg: 15, 78-80, 81
Gauntlet Loop: 138-139
gem mines: 59
Georgia: 8, 31-57, 432
Georgia Mountain Fair: 56
Georgia Tech Yellow Jackets: 45
Giant Center: 234
Gilmore Girls Fan Fest: 319
Gingerbread Festival: 319
Gingerbread House Restaurant: 23, 415
Glen Manor Vineyards: 173
Glen Onoko Falls: 21, 248
Gold Museum Historic Site: 50
golf: 208, 214 296, 367, 375
Golf Club at Equinox: 367
Goodies Restaurant: 188, 229
Gorham: 23, 390, 408-409
Gorham Moose Tours: 408
Gorman: 419-421
Grafton Notch State Park: 409-410
Grandin Theatre: 141
Grange, The: 268, 285
Grantville: 237
Great Barrington: 10, 21, 25, 337-339
Greater Lynchburg Transportation Company: 112
Great Lakes to Florida Highway Museum: 123
Great Smoky Mountains National Park: 8, 12, 15, 34, 71-83, 440
Great Smoky Mountains Railroad: 67
Green Mountain Club: 439
Green Mountain National Golf Course: 375
Greenbrier State Park: 25, 202
Greencastle: 210
Greenwood Lake: 286-287
Greyhound: 37, 41, 85, 112, 188, 192, 331, 391, 394, 433
Greylock, Mt.: 10, 18, 26, 327, 328, 346, 351-352, 353, 354

H

Hager House: 208
Hagerstown: 8, 205-210
Hagerstown City Park: 207-208
Hagerstown Greens at Hamilton: 208
Hagerstown Roundhouse Museum: 206-207
Hagerstown Suns: 208
Half-Gallon Challenge: 216
Hamilton Gardens: 23, 56-57
Hands On! Regional Museum: 100
Hanover: 22, 23, 25, 393-397, 433
Hanover Inn: 393, 396-397
Happy Hawg: 23, 58
Harpers Ferry: 21, 110, 112, 177-181
Harpers Ferry-Bolivar Historic Town Foundation: 181
Harpers Ferry Zip Line & Canopy Tours: 180
Harrah's Cherokee Casino Resort: 68
Harriman State Park: 288-294
Harrisburg: 10, 21, 220-228, 433, 435
Harrisburg Midtown Arts Center: 225
Harrisburg Senators: 223
Harry F. Byrd Visitor Center: 159
Hartford: 82
Harvest Festival: 341
Hawg N Dawg: 25, 99
Hawk Rock Overlook: 20, 229
Hawk Rock Trail: 187, 229
health: 437-438
Height of Land: 10, 18, 23, 389, 413-414
Hellcats: 296
Hershey: 230-236
Hershey Area Playhouse: 235
Hershey Bears: 234
Hershey Gardens: 185, 231-232
Hersheypark: 232-233
Hersheypark Stadium: 234
Hershey Story: 231
Hershey's Chocolate World: 235, 236
Hershey Theatre: 234-235
Hessian Barracks: 195
Hialeah: 260
Hiawassee: 22, 23, 56-58
High Knob Nature Center: 200
Highland Falls: 298
Highlands: 62-63, 65, 66
Highlands Plateau Greenway: 59
High Point Monument: 10, 18, 278
High Point State Park: 21, 265, 278-280
High Point Trail: 21, 278-279

High Shoals Falls: 23, 57
hiking: 26, 29, 436; best hikes 26, 29, 34, 111, 187, 267, 328, 391; trail tales 98, 180, 201, 205, 294, 354, 405
Hildene: 327, 365-367
Hillbrook Inn: 113, 176-177
Historic Biltmore Village: 91
Historic Ebenezer Baptist Church: 43
Historic Fire Station No. 6: 43
Historic Valley Park: 356
history: 6, 26, 28, 438-439
Hi-Wire Brewing: 20, 89
Hogback Mountain: 17, 109, 111, 168, 170
Holiday Homecoming: 78
Home Grown: 35, 41, 48-49
Home 231: 21, 188, 227
Hominy Creek Park: 88
Hood College: 192
Hood Museum of Art: 23, 389, 395
Hoosac Tunnel: 355
Hopkins Center for the Arts: 395
horseback riding: 62, 120
Horse Heaven Loop: 120
Horse Pen Trail: 138
Horse-Shoe Trail: 234
Hotel Hershey: 189, 236
Hotel on North: 330, 350
Hot Springs: 17, 22, 23, 95-97
Hot Springs Resort and Spa: 17, 23, 97
Hot Springs Trailfest: 11, 96
Housatonic Meadows State Park: 321
H. Ric Luhrs Performing Arts Center: 214-215
Hudson Beach Glass: 307-308
Hudson Highlands: 297
Hudson River School: 307
Hudson Valley Brewery: 20, 306
Hudson Valley Jazz Festival: 284
Hudson Valley Renegades: 305
Hudson Valley Shakespeare Festival: 301
Hummelstown: 230
Humpback Rocks: 20
Humpback Rocks Trail: 152-153
Hungry Mother State Park: 122
Hussy Mountain Horse Camp: 120

I

ice hockey: 234, 395, 427
ice-skating: 139, 218, 293, 312
Indian Echo Caverns at Echo Dales: 230
Inn at Kent Falls: 269, 320
Inn at Long Trail: 330, 377
Inn Boonsboro: 189, 203
International Peace Fountain: 45
Internet access: 438
Internet resources: 439-440
Iron Horse Station: 23, 97
Iron Mountain Trail: 113, 114
Irving, Washington: 303
itineraries: 15-29; Asheville 86; Atlanta 41; Bangor 427; Frederick 194; Harrisburg 222; Pittsfield 348; Poughkeepsie; Shenandoah National Park 158

J

Jack Brown's Beer and Burger Joint: 17, 141
Jacks Gap: 23
Jacks Gap to Brasstown Bald: 55-56
Jack's Knob Trail: 55
Jackson Hole Trading Post and Gem Mine: 59
Jefferson: 192
Jefferson Rock: 21, 178
Jerry's Classic Cars and Collectibles Museum: 239
Jimmy Carter Presidential Library and Museum: 15, 41-42
Jim Thorpe: 21, 25, 26, 185, 186, 244-250
Jim Thorpe Gravesite: 246
Jim Thorpe River Adventures: 26, 248
John Brown House: 212
Johnson City: 17, 99-103, 433
Julius Sturgis Pretzel Bakery: 231

K

Katahdin: 10, 12, 23, 29, 98, 389, 390, 405, 421-422, 424
kayaking: 248
Kel Mat Café: 392, 418
Kent: 10, 21, 22, 26, 266, 315-320
Kent Falls: 317
Kent Falls State Park: 26, 317-318
Key, Francis Scott: 196
Killington: 373-378
Killington Adventure Center and Mountain Bike Park: 375
Killington Golf Course: 375
Killington Peak: 10, 20, 328, 373-374
Killington Ski Resort: 374-375
King Center: 43
Kingfield: 417
King's Birth House: 43
King's Gourmet Popcorn: 153
Kingsley Tavern: 21, 268, 319-320
King, Stephen: 425
Kipona: 226
Kitchen Sink Food & Drink: 268, 308
Kittatinny Point Visitor Center: 270-271
Krumpe's Do-Nut Shop: 188, 209

L

La Guelaguetza: 313
Lake Askoti: 293

Lake Kanawauke: 293
Lakeside Park: 315
Lakeside Trail: 237
Lake Tiorati Beach: 293
Lakeville: 322
Lake Welch Beach: 293
Lansford: 244
Laughing Heart Lodge: 36, 96-97
Lazy Hiker Brewing Co.: 15, 20, 63
leaf-peeping: 10
Leave No Trace: 437
Lebanon: 396
Lehigh Gorge Scenic Railway: 247
Lehigh Gorge State Park: 247-248
Lehigh Gorge Trail: 248
Lehighton: 250-251
Lemon Squeezer: 292
Lenox: 10, 342-345
Levee Loop Trail: 254-255
Lewis, David "Robber": 244
Lewis Mountain: 164-166
Liberty Farm: 277
Lime Rock Park: 322
Lincoln: 23, 407
Lincoln Highway Memorial Marker: 212-213
Lincoln Theatre: 121
Little Amps Coffee Roasters: 222, 227
Little Chicago Downtown Music & Arts Festival: 102
Little Devils Stairs: 168
Little Five Points: 46, 48
Little Hogback and Hogback Mountain Loop: 111, 168, 170
Little House of Pancakes: 35, 79
Living Room Theatre: 361
Lodge to Lodge Trail: 420
Loft Mountain Campground: 113, 162
Loft Mountain Wayside: 17, 158, 162
Lola's: 310, 314
Long Trail: 328
Long Trail Brewing Co.: 20, 23, 378
Loon Lodge Inn: 393, 416
Loop Bus System: 309
Loop Trail: 21
Lost River Gorge and Boulder Caves: 398-399
Lou's Restaurant and Bakery: 392, 396
Lover's Leap Trail: 17, 25, 96
Lower Hominy: 83
Lucky: 112, 141-142
Lunder Center at Stone Hill: 359
Luray: 17, 110, 167-168
Luray Caverns: 17, 164
Lye Brook Falls Trail: 367
Lyford: 419-421
Lyme: 397
Lynchburg: 147-149
Lyric Theatre: 129

M

Macedonia Brook State Park: 318-319
Macedonia Ridge Trail Loop: 26, 318-319
Madison Brewing Company Pub & Restaurant: 378
Maggie Valley: 69-71
Magnetic Theatre: 90
Mahaiwe Performing Arts Center: 337
Maid's Quarters Bed, Breakfast and Tearoom: 189, 240-241
Main Street Museum: 384
Maine: 10, 387-393, 409-429, 433, 435
Maine Discovery Museum: 425
Majestic Theater: 239
Major Welch Trail: 290, 294
Manchester: 365-370
Manchester Center: 10, 23, 365-370
Manitoga: 299-300
maps: 438
MARC: 112, 177, 188, 191, 192, 433
Marianna Black Library: 67
Marion: 121-122
Marion Royael Gallery: 307
Marist College: 312
Marshall House Inn: 36, 95
Marsh-Billings-Rockefeller National Historic Park: 378-379
Mars Hill: 97
MARTA: 41
Martin Luther King Jr. National Historic Site: 15, 41, 43
Martin's Pretzel Bakery: 231
Maryland: 8-10, 183-210
Maryland Craft Beer Festival: 197
Maryland Ensemble Theatre: 197
Maryland Heights: 18, 21, 29, 185, 189-190
Maryland Heights Trail: 29, 190
Maryland Symphony Orchestra: 208
Maryland Theatre: 208
Mason-Dixon Appalachian Trail Outdoor Festival: 11, 210-211
Mason Ruby & Sapphire Mine: 59
Massachusetts: 10, 325-360
Massanutten Lodge: 166
MASS MoCA: 10, 23, 26, 327, 354
Mast General Store: 28, 91
Matteawan Gallery: 307
Mauch Chunk Museum & Cultural Center: 246-247
Mauch Chunk Opera House: 249
Mausert's Pond Trail: 358
Max Patch: 20, 34, 83-84

May Kelly's Cottage: 402, 406
McAfee Knob: 17, 26, 109, 111, 133, 134
McCann Ice Arena: 312
McDade Recreational Trail: 260
Melville, Herman: 346
Melville Trail: 346, 348
Memorial Lake State Park: 237
Memorial Square: 212
Methuselah: 348
Metro-North Railroad: 269, 309
Michaux State Forest: 211
Mid-Hudson Children's Museum: 312
Mid-Hudson Civic Center: 313
Midtown (Atlanta): 45
Midtown Arts Center: 222, 225
mileposts: 14
Milford Beach: 260
Millbrook Village: 271
Miller House: 206
Millinocket: 23, 421-422
Mill House Brewing Co.: 310, 313
Mill Mountain Park: 139-140
Mill Mountain Zoo: 140
Millworks: 222, 226
Moat Mountain Smokehouse & Brewing Co.: 20, 406
Mohican Outdoor Center: 269, 273
Molly's Knob Loop: 122
money: 438
Monocacy National Battlefield: 194, 196
Monson: 22, 23, 418-419
Monson Post Office: 419
Montford Park Players: 90
Montgomery County Regional Tourism Office: 131
Monument Mountain: 21, 339
Monument Mountain Trail: 339
moose: 14, 408
Moosilauke, Mt.: 18, 391, 398
Morgan Lake Park: 312
Moss Arts Center: 129
motorcycles/motorcycling: 69-70, 435
mountain biking: *see* bicycling
Mountain Crossings at Walasi-yi: 54-55
Mountain Home: 17, 113, 174
Mountain Life Festival: 78
Mountainside Theatre: 68
Mountain Sports Festival: 11, 91
Mount Beacon Trail: 305
Mount Equinox: 10, 29, 364-365
Mount Equinox Trail: 365
Mount Everett State Reservation: 335
Mount Greylock: 10, 18, 26, 327, 328, 346, 351-352, 353, 354
Mount Greylock State Reservation: 351-353
Mount Greylock Summit: 328, 352-353
Mount Katahdin: *see* Katahdin
Mount Moosilauke: 18, 391, 398
Mount Olivet Cemetery: 196
Mount Peter: 283
Mount Peter Hawk Watch: 283
Mount Riga State Park: 322-323
Mount Rogers: 18, 20, 109, 111, 119
Mount Rogers A.T. Club: 22
Mount Rogers National Recreation Area: 119-121
Mount Rogers Summit: 109, 111, 119
Mount Tammany: 10, 21
Mount Tammany Loop Trail: 267, 271
Mount, The: 344
Mount Washington (NH): 10, 20, 23, 390, 391, 401-402, 404-405
Mount Washington Auto Road: 23, 401-402
Mount Washington Resort: 403
Mount Washington State Forest (MA): 332-334
Mount Weather: 175
Moya: 21, 188, 249
Mr. Pizza: 23, 402, 408
Munroe's Family Restaurant: 23, 406-407
Museum of the Cherokee Indian: 15, 33, 66-68
Music Midtown: 47-48
Music of the Mountains: 67, 78

N

Nantahala Brewing Taproom & Brewery: 20, 64
Nantahala Hiking Club: 439
Nantahala National Forest: 8, 15, 59-66
Nantahala Ranger District: 66
National Civil War Museum: 10, 21, 28, 185, 222
National Museum of Civil War Medicine: 194, 195
Natural Bridge State Park: 26, 147, 354
Naumkeag: 28, 340
Neels Gap: 53-55
Neels Gap to Blood Mountain: 34, 53-54
Newfound Gap Road: 15, 73
Newfound Gap to Clingmans Dome: 73, 76
New Hampshire: 10, 387-409
New Jersey: 10, 263-282, 432-433
New York: 10, 263-270, 282-316, 432-433
New York City: 26
New York-New Jersey Trail Conference: 6, 22, 266, 294, 439
Nine Mile: 86, 93
Noah's Ark: 310, 312
Nocturnem Draft Haus: 427
No. 9 Coal Mine and Museum: 244
Norman Rockwell Museum (Rutland): 370
Norman Rockwell Museum (Stockbridge): 340-341, 372
Norridgewock: 417
North Adams: 10, 23, 25, 26, 353-358

North Carolina: 8, 31-37, 59-98, 432
North Conway: 406
Northeast Hiking Trail: 44
Northern District (Shenandoah National Park): 168-172
Northern Stage: 384-385
North Park: 153
Northshire Brewery: 378
North-South Vermont Bus Route: 365
Nudel: 329, 344

O

Oconaluftee Visitor Center: 71-72
October Mountain State Forest: 345-346
Old Edwards Inn and Spa: 36, 66
Old First Church of Bennington: 361
Old Jail Museum: 21, 26, 247
Old Man of the Mountain: 23, 399
Old Mauch Chunk Historic District: 26, 245
Old Mill: 274
Old Mine Road: 270
Old Rag: 17, 164
Old Speck Mountain: 409-410
100-Mile Wilderness: 10
1777E/Doodletown Bridle Path Loop: 290-291
Optimist, The: 41, 49
Orvis: 367
Otter Creek Recreation Area: 149
Otter Creek Trail: 149
Overlook Trail: 237
O. Winston Link Museum: 138

P

packing: 12-13, 436
Paddy Murphy's Irish Pub: 427
Palisades Restaurant: 112, 125
Paramount Theater: 370-371
parking: 435
Park-McCullough House: 360-361
passports: 438
Paul Bunyan Sculpture: 389, 424-425, 427
Pawling: 315-316
Peach House Bed & Breakfast: 36, 49
Peaks of Otter: 17, 143-146
Pearisburg: 125-126
Peggy Lee Hahn Horticulture Garden: 127-128
Pennsylvania: 8-10, 183-189, 210-261, 432, 435
Pennsylvania National Fire Museum: 223
Pennsylvania State Capitol: 222-223
Penobscot Theatre: 427
performing arts: Asheville 90-91; Atlanta 47; Blacksburg 129; Frederick 197; Hagerstown 208; Hershey 234-235; Jim Thorpe 248-249; Poughkeepsie 313; Roanoke 141; Stroudsburg 256-257; Waynesboro 154
Perkins Memorial Fire Tower: 290
Pete and Toshi Seeger Riverfront Park: 305
Peter, Mt.: 283
Peter Pan Bus: 331, 337, 339, 342, 346, 353
Peter's Pancakes and Waffles: 15, 69
pets: 437
Philadelphia: 26
Phillipsburg Manor: 303
Phillipstown Depot Theatre: 299
Piedmont Appalachian Trail Hikers: 439
Piedmont Park: 44
Pigeon Forge: 80, 81
Pine Grove: 237-238
Pine Grove Furnace General Store: 216
Pine Grove Furnace State Park: 10, 21, 216-218
Pine Hill Park: 370-371
Pine Island: 281-282
Pine Island Brewing Company: 281-282
Pine Knob Loop Trail: 321
Pinnacles Overlook: 158, 170-171
Pinnacle, The: 18, 26, 185, 187, 241, 242
Pittsfield: 23, 346-350
Pittsfield State Forest: 348
Plain, The: 295
planning tips: 8-29; Georgia/North Carolina/Tennessee 35; Maryland/Pennsylvania 186; Massachusetts/Vermont 329; New Hampshire/Maine 390-391; New York/New Jersey/Connecticut 266; Virginia/West Virginia 110-113
Point of Honor: 147-148
Point, The: 178
poison ivy (oak and sumac): 438
Polar Caves Park: 397-398
Pole Steeple Trail: 216
Ponce City Market: 33, 43-44
Pop's Grits and Eggs: 35, 70
Porches Inn: 330, 357-358
Porter Beer Bar: 41, 46
Port Jervis: 278
Potomac Appalachian Trail Club: 439
Pottsville: 21, 238-241
Poughkeepsie: 10, 266, 309-315, 435
Poughkeepsie Grind: 310, 314
pretzels: 231
Pride of the Susquehanna: 223
Public Eat+Drink: 26, 357
Punchbowl Mountain Overlook: 150

QR

Quaker Creek Store: 281
Quechee: 381-382
Quechee Gorge: 381
Quechee Gorge Trail: 327, 382-383
Quechee State Park: 382-383

INDEX

Raccoon Run Trail: 214
Race Brook Falls: 29, 335
Race Brook Falls to Mount Everett: 29, 328, 335
Race Brook Lodge: 330, 336
rafting: 248
Rangeley: 10, 23, 25, 390, 413-416
Rangeley Lake State Park: 413
Rangeley Outdoor Sporting Heritage Museum: 413
Rangeley Scenic Byway: 413-414
Ranger Falls Interpretive Trail: 62
Rappahannock Cellars: 173
Rattle River Lodge and Hostel: 393, 409
Raymondskill Creek Trail: 260
Red Castle Brewpub: 26, 250-251
Red Lion Inn: 330, 341
Red Umbrella Bed & Breakfast: 189, 237
Reece Museum: 99-100
Renee's Diner: 26, 357
Renegade Winery: 256
rental cars: 13
restaurants: 35, 112, 188, 268, 329, 392; Asheville 92-93; Atlanta 48-49; Beacon 308; Frederick 198-199; Hagerstown 209; Harrisburg 226-227; Hershey 235; Pittsfield 349; Poughkeepsie 314; Roanoke 141-143; Stroudsburg 257-258; Warwick 284-286
Reynoldstown: 15, 46, 48-49
Rich Woods Trail System: 370
Ridgeview Park: 153
Righteous Room, The: 41, 45
Riprap-Wildcat Ridge Loop: 17, 111, 160
River Arts District: 15, 86, 91
Riverbank Motel: 393, 407-408
Riverfront Park: 223-224
River Pool: 305
Rivers Edge Sports Complex: 139
River Trail: 395
Riverwinds Gallery: 307
road conditions: 14, 434; Georgia/North Carolina/Tennessee 37; Maryland/Pennsylvania 189; Massachusetts/Vermont 331; New York/New Jersey/Connecticut 270; Virginia/West Virginia 113
Roanoke: 17, 25, 110, 136-143, 433, 435
Roanoke Festival in the Park: 141
Roanoke Pinball Museum: 137-138
Roanoke River Greenway: 139
Roanoke Star: 17, 18, 109, 136
Roanoke Visitor Information Center: 143
Robert Frost Gravesite: 361
Robert Frost Stone House Museum: 363
Roberts, Nora: 201, 202
Rockfish Gap: 152, 157
Rockwell, Norman: 10, 340-341, 370, 372
Rocky Top Trail: 15, 18, 33, 76-78
Rogers, Mt.: 18, 20, 109, 111, 119
Roof, The: 44
Rooftop Terrace: 44
Roosevelt, Franklin D.: 310
Rose Creek Mine: 59
Roseland: 151-152
Roundhouse, The: 269, 308
Rouzerville: 210-211
RSVP: 26, 268, 321
Ruby's Kitchen: 21, 240
Rumford: 410-411
Rumford Falls Trail: 410-411
Russel Wright Design Center: 299-300
Rutland: 23, 370-373

S

Saddleback Mountain: 414-415
safety: 434, 437-438
Safford Mills Inn and Café: 330, 364
Saint Bruno Scenic Viewing Center: 365
Salem: 132
Salisbury: 10, 21, 322-323
Sam's Gap to Big Bald: 26, 34, 98
Sanders, Dale: 180
Sandy Hook: 189-190
Sandyston: 277-278
Scenic Hudson's Long Dock Park: 305
Schatzi's Pub: 310, 312
Schifferstadt: 194
Schisler Museum of Wildlife & Natural History: 254
Sciota: 253
seasons: 10
senior travelers, tips for: 436
Settlers Green Outlet Village: 402, 406
Seven Lakes Road: 289
Shady Valley: 105
Shady Valley Cranberry Festival: 105
Shaftsbury: 363
Sharp Top Trail: 144-145
Shaw's Hiker Hostel: 393, 419
Shed, The: 23, 392, 415
Sheffield: 334-336
Shelburne: 409
Shenandoah National Park: 12, 17, 110, 156-172, 440
Sherman Adams Visitor Center: 401-402
Sherman Theater: 256-257
Shippensburg: 214-215
Shippensburg Corn Festival: 215
Shippensburg University: 214
Silver Fork: 329, 368
skiing: 296, 374-375
Skowhegan: 390, 417-418

Skowhegan Indian: 418
Skowhegan State Fair: 11, 418
Skyland: 166
Skyline Cavern: 17, 173
Skyline Drive (Mount Equinox): 365
Skyline Drive (Shenandoah National Park): 14, 15, 111, 158, 435
Skyline Park: 44
SkyView Atlanta: 44
Sleepy Hollow Cemetery: 303
Smart Way Bus: 112, 136
Smithfield Beach: 260
Smithfield Plantation: 128
Smith Mountain Lake: 140
smoking: 436
Smoky Mountain Diner: 25, 97
Snallygaster myth: 205
Soco Falls: 70
Southern District (Shenandoah National Park): 159-163
South Mountain State Park: 204-205
South Street Brewery: 152
Sovereign Remedies: 86, 90
spectator sports: *see* baseball; basketball; football; hockey
speed limits: 434
Spelunkers: 112, 173-174
Spence Field: 77
Spence Field Shelter: 77-78
Splash Valley: 140
Spratt Park: 312
Spring Creek Bar-B-Q: 23, 419
Springer Mountain: 52-53
Springer Mountain Loop: 26, 33, 34, 53
Stairway to Heaven to Pinwheel Vista: 282
stand-up paddleboarding: 252
Stanley Museum: 417
Starr Hill Brewery: 152
state parks: 440
Staunton: 158, 162-163
Sterling Forest State Park: 287-288
Sterling Valley Loop Trail: 287-288
Stockbridge: 10, 21, 339-342
Stokes State Forest: 276-277
Stony Man Mountain: 168-170
Story Land: 403
Stroudsburg: 254-259
Stroudsfest: 257
Sugarlands Visitor Center: 72
Sugarloaf Mountain: 391, 416-417
Summit Stage Office: 402
Sunnyside: 303
Sunrise Mountain: 267, 276, 277
Sunrise Shack: 392, 402, 406
Susan B. Anthony Birthplace: 351
Susquehanna Art Museum: 222, 223
Sussex: 280-281
Sussex County Sunflower Maze: 277
Sweet Arrow Lake County Park: 237-238
Swift Run Gap: 157
swimming: 122, 217, 260, 293
Switchback Railroad Trail: 248

T

Tamaqua: 242-243
Tammany, Mt.: 10, 21, 267, 271
Tanger Outlets Hershey: 235
Tanglewood Music Center: 21, 327, 342-343
Tarrytown: 303
Taubman Museum of Art: 137
Taylors Valley Loop: 120
10x10 Upstreet Arts Festival: 349
Tennessee: 8, 31-37, 71-83, 98-105, 435
Thayer Hotel: 269, 298
theater: 47, 68, 90, 208, 225-226, 234-235
Third Mountain Peak: 420
Thirsty Monk Brewery & Pub: 86, 89
Thomas Morahan Waterfront Park: 287
Thomas Wolfe Memorial: 87
Thoreau, Henry David: 354
Thornton Gap: 157
Thorpe, Jim: 244, 245-246
Three Ridges Overlook: 20, 151
Three Ridges Trail: 151
Three Sisters Vineyards & Winery: 52
thru-hiking: 98
Thundering Brook Falls, 23, 29, 328, 374, 437
Tillman Ravine Natural Area: 276
Times House: 189, 250
Tinker Cliffs: 134-135
Top of Georgia Hiking Center: 36, 58
Topton: 64
Totem Hole Playhouse: 214
Totts Gap to Wolf Rocks: 187, 256
tourist information: 438
Townsend: 80-82
Trailfest, Hot Springs: 11, 96
Trail House: 194, 198
trail magic: 22
Trailside Museums & Zoo: 290
train travel: 138, 315, 433; Georgia/North Carolina/Tennessee 37, 40-41; Massachusetts/Vermont 331; Maryland/Pennsylvania 188, 221, 247; New York/New Jersey/Connecticut 269; Virginia/West Virginia 112
TransAmerica Bicycle Trail: 113, 114
transportation: 432-436
travel tips: 436-437
Triple Crown BBQ: 17, 167
Tri-State Rock: 278

Trophy Point: 296
Trough Trail: 138
T.S. Candler Memorial: 55
Tuckerbox: 329, 385
Tumbling Waters Trail: 21, 29, 259-260
20-Minute Cliff Overlook: 17, 150

UV

Unionville: 281
United States Forest Service: 440
United States Military Academy (West Point): 295-299
University of Maine: 423
University of Maine Museum of Art: 426, 427
University of North Carolina Bulldogs: 88
Unto These Hills: 68
Up for Breakfast: 329, 368
Urban Trail: 87
U.S. Army Heritage and Education Center: 218-219
Vanderbilt Mansion: 28, 310-311
Vassar College: 311-312
Ventfort Hall Mansion and Gilded Age Museum: 342
Vermont: 10, 325-331, 360-385
Vermont Actors' Repertory Theatre: 372
Vermont Institute of Natural Science: 381-382
Vermont Translines: 330, 331, 365, 370, 373, 384
Victor Constant Ski Area: 296
Victor C. Waryas Park: 310, 312
views: 18
VINS Nature Center: 381-382
Virginia: 8, 107-175, 432, 435
Virginia Beer Museum: 17, 109, 172-173
Virginia Creeper Trail: 17, 113, 114
Virginia Museum of Transportation: 138
Virginia Safari Park: 147
Virginia Tech Hokies: 128
Virginia Tech University: 109, 126-128
visas: 438
Visit Hershey & Harrisburg: 236
Volt: 188, 194, 198

WXYZ

Walkway Loop Trail: 310
Walkway Over the Hudson: 309-310
Wantage: 280-281
Ward-Nasse Gallery: 280
Warren Rifles Confederate Museum: 172
Warwick: 21, 25, 26, 266, 282-286
Warwick Summer Arts Festival: 284
Warwick Valley Winery: 281
Wasena Park: 139
Washington County Museum of Fine Arts: 207-208
Washington DC: 25-26
Washington Monument: 201
Washington, Mt.: 10, 20, 23, 390, 391, 401-402, 404-405
Waterfall Trail: 238
waterfalls: 29
Wawayanda Lake: 282
Wawayanda State Park: 282
Wayah Bald: 15, 20, 34, 60-61
Wayah Bald Tower: 60
Wayne Theatre & Ross Performing Arts Center: 154
Waynesboro: 17, 22, 25, 110, 153-155, 210
Waynesboro Heritage Museum: 153
Waynesboro Water Trail: 153
weather: 10, 12, 434
Weaverville: 95
W. E. B. DuBois National Historic Site: 28, 337
Wedge Brewing Company: 15, 86, 89
Weinberg Center for the Arts: 197
Weis Center for the Performing Arts: 218
West Cornwall: 26, 321-322
West Cornwall Covered Bridge: 26, 321
Western Gateway Heritage State Park: 355-356
Western Maryland Blues Fest: 208
West Lebanon: 396
West Market Square Artisan Coffeehouse: 427, 428
West Point: 28, 265, 295-299
West Point Black Knights: 296
West Point Cemetery: 296
West Point Golf Course: 296
West Point Museum: 295
Westside Provisions District: 48
West Virginia: 8, 107-113, 176-181
Weverton Cliffs: 190-191
Weverton Cliffs Trail: 187, 190-191
Wharton, Edith: 344
Wheels Through Time: 69-70
White Duck Taco Shop: 86, 93, 101
White Hall Tavern: 178
White Hart Restaurant & Inn: 21, 269, 323
White Mountain National Forest: 10, 23, 399-408
White River Junction: 384-385, 433
White Rock Falls Trail: 150-151
White Rock Gap: 150-151
White Rose Motel: 189, 236
Whiteside Mountain Trail: 61
Whitetop Laurel Creek: 120
Whitetop Mountain: 118
Whitetop Mountain Summit and Buzzard Rock: 118
Wild Creek Falls Trail: 252
wilderness safety: 437-438
wildlife: 156, 434, 437

Wild Wolf Brewing Company: 152
Wildwood Park: 222, 224
Wildwood Park Loop: 222, 224
Wilhelm Reich Museum: 413
Williams College: 358-359
Williams College Museum of Art: 359
Williamstown: 358-360
Williamstown Theatre Festival: 359
Wilson, Edith Bolling: 123
Wind Gap: 253
Wind Gap Bluegrass Festival: 253
wine/wineries: 173, 256, 281
Wits End Tavern: 281
Wohlfahrt Haus Dinner Theatre: 124
Wolfe, Thomas: 87
Wolf Mountain Vineyards: 52
Woodruff Arts Center: 47
Woodruff Park: 44-45
Woodstock: 10, 23, 378-381
World of Coca-Cola: 43
Wright, Russel: 299-300
Wytheville: 17, 123-124
Yee-Haw Brewing Company: 17, 101
Zeroday Brewing Co.: 20, 222, 224-225
zip-lining: 180
ZooAmerica North American Wildlife Park: 233

LIST OF MAPS

Front Map

Appalachian Trail: 2–3

Discover Appalachian Trial

chapter divisions map: 8

Georgia, North Carolina, and Tennessee

Georgia, North Carolina, and Tennessee: 32
Atlanta: 38–39
Springer Mountain Loop: 54
Nantahala National Forest: 60
Great Smoky Mountains National Park: 74–75
Newfound Gap to Clingmans Dome: 76
Rocky Top Trail: 77
Downtown Asheville: 85
Johnson City: 100

Virginia and West Virginia

Virginia and West Virginia: 108
Damascus to Roanoke: 115
McAfee Knob: 133
Roanoke: 137
Downtown Roanoke: 138
Peaks of Otter to Waynesboro: 144
Shenandoah National Park (Southern District): 161
Shenandoah National Park (Central District): 165
Shenandoah National Park (Northern District): 169
Little Hogback and Hogback Mountain Loop: 170
Harpers Ferry: 178

Maryland and Pennsylvania

Maryland and Pennsylvania: 184
Frederick, MD: 193
Appalachian Trail to Annapolis Rock: 204
Hagerstown: 207
Harrisburg: 221
Hershey, PA: 232
The Pinnacle via Pulpit Rock: 242
Jim Thorpe, PA: 245
Stroudsburg, PA: 255

New Jersey, New York, and Connecticut

New York, New Jersey, and Connecticut: 264
Delaware Water Gap National Recreation Area: 272
Warwick: 283
Bear Mountain Loop: 291
Hudson Highlands: 297
Highland Fall: 298
Anthony's Nose: 300
Cold Spring: 302
Beacon: 306

Massachusetts and Vermont

Massachusetts and Vermont: 326
Mount Washington to Lenox: 333
Pittsfield: 347
Mount Greylock Summit: 353
North Adams: 355
Bennington, Vermont: 361
Manchester: 367
Rutland: 371
Woodstock: 379
Quechee Gorge Trail: 383

New Hampshire and Maine

New Hampshire and Maine: 388
Hanover: 394
White Mountains: 400
Angel Falls: 412
Mount Katahdin: 424
Bangor: 426

PHOTO CREDITS

Title page photo: daveallenphoto | dreamstime.com;

Page 4 © manon ringuette | dreamstime.com; page 5 © kelly vandellen | dreamstime.com; page 7 © (top) Timothy Malcolm; (bottom) teri virbickis | dreamstime.com; page 9 © (top left) Timothy Malcolm; (top right) serge skiba | dreamstime.com; (bottom) Timothy Malcolm; page 11 © larry metayer | dreamstime.com; page 16 © (top left) jon bilous | dreamstime.com; (top right) jon bilous | dreamstime.com; (bottom) Timothy Malcolm; page 18 © Timothy Malcolm; page 19 © (top left) jon bilous | dreamstime.com; (top right) Timothy Malcolm; (bottom) jill lang | dreamstime.com; page 20 © Timothy Malcolm; page 24 © (top left) andrew kazmierski | dreamstime.com; (top right) alpegor | dreamstime.com; (bottom) susan leggett | dreamstime.com; page 27 © (top left) svecchiotti | dreamstime.com; (top right) durdenimages | dreamstime.com; (bottom) Timothy Malcolm; page 28 © Timothy Malcolm; page 30 © jonathan ross | dreamstime.com; page 42 © (top) Timothy Malcolm; (middle) pivariz | dreamstime.com; (bottom) f11photo | dreamstime.com; page 51 © (top) Timothy Malcolm; (middle) kelly vandellen | dreamstime.com; (bottom) Timothy Malcolm; page 56 © leigh ryan | dreamstime.com; page 61 © (top) jon bilous | dreamstime.com; (middle) jill lang | dreamstime.com; (bottom) dean neitman | dreamstime.com; page 68 © (top) Timothy Malcolm; (middle) Timothy Malcolm; (bottom) Timothy Malcolm; page 73 © sean pavone | dreamstime.com; page 84 © (top) maxim sivyi | dreamstime.com; (middle) Timothy Malcolm; (bottom) carol r montoya | dreamstime.com; page 101 © (top) kristie gianopulos | dreamstime.com; (middle) Timothy Malcolm; (bottom) Timothy Malcolm; page 106 © nps; page 117 © anthony heflin | dreamstime.com; page 119 © (top) Timothy Malcolm; (middle) jason ondreicka | dreamstime.com; (bottom) michael papasidero | dreamstime.com; page 127 © (top) Timothy Malcolm; (middle) Timothy Malcolm; (bottom) Timothy Malcolm; page 135 © noel nason | dreamstime.com; page 139 © (top) dbpetersen | dreamstime.com; (middle) larry metayer | dreamstime.com; (bottom) Timothy Malcolm; page 145 © (top) larry metayer | dreamstime.com; (middle) larry metayer | dreamstime.com; (bottom) larry metayer | dreamstime.com; page 148 © sean pavone | dreamstime.com; page 157 © nps/neal lewis; page 163 © (top) jon bilous | dreamstime.com; (middle) nps/katy cain; (bottom) jon bilous | dreamstime.com; page 171 © (top) nps/neal lewis; (middle) Timothy Malcolm; (bottom) Timothy Malcolm; page 179 © (top) Timothy Malcolm; (middle) cvandyke | dreamstime.com; (bottom) Timothy Malcolm; page 182 © svecchiotti | dreamstime.com; page 195 © (top) christian hinkle | dreamstime.com; (middle) jon bilous | dreamstime.com; (bottom) jon bilous | dreamstime.com; page 206 © (top) adam parent | dreamstime.com; (middle) jon bilous | dreamstime.com; (bottom) jon bilous | dreamstime.com; page 212 © jon bilous | dreamstime.com; page 217 © jaymudaliar | dreamstime.com; page 219 © (top) Timothy Malcolm; (middle) Timothy Malcolm; (bottom) Timothy Malcolm; page 224 © jon bilous | dreamstime.com; page 233 © (top) Timothy Malcolm; (middle) angie westre wieand | dreamstime.com; (bottom) Timothy Malcolm; page 240 © (top) Timothy Malcolm; (middle) jon bilous | dreamstime.com; (bottom) Timothy Malcolm; page 247 © jon bilous | dreamstime.com; page 251 © (top) jonathan mauer | dreamstime.com; (middle) Timothy Malcolm; (bottom) Timothy Malcolm; page 258 © (top) Timothy Malcolm; (middle) Timothy Malcolm; (bottom) james kirkikis | dreamstime.com; page 262 © songquan deng | dreamstime.com; page 273 © (top) lfyv75 | dreamstime.com; (middle) jon bilous | dreamstime.com; (bottom) dawn j. benko | dreamstime.com; page 274 © michael ver sprill | dreamstime.com; page 276 © andrew kazmierski | dreamstime.com; page 279 © (top) Timothy Malcolm; (middle) dawn j. benko | dreamstime.com; (bottom) tetyana ohare | dreamstime.com; page 285 © Timothy Malcolm; page 289 © songquan deng | dreamstime.com; page 292 © gary718 | dreamstime.com; page 301 © (top) james kirkikis | dreamstime.com; (middle) harold bonacquist | dreamstime.com; (bottom) Timothy Malcolm; page 307 © (top) Timothy Malcolm; (middle) karen foley | dreamstime.com; (bottom) Timothy Malcolm; page 311 © (top) michael gordon | dreamstime.com; (middle) sphraner | dreamstime.com; (bottom) nancy kennedy | dreamstime.com; page 318 © americanspirit | dreamstime.com; page 324 © colin young | dreamstime.com; page 335 © (top) steveheap | dreamstime.com; (middle) Timothy Malcolm; (bottom) reinout van wagtendonk | dreamstime.com; page 340 © Timothy Malcolm; page 343 © joe benning | dreamstime.com; page 351 © (top) jdwfoto | dreamstime.com; (middle) lei xu | dreamstime.com; (bottom) stuwrtlttle | dreamstime.com; page 356 © Timothy Malcolm; page 359 © sandra foyt | dreamstime.com; page 362 © (top) colin young | dreamstime.com; (middle) Timothy Malcolm;

(bottom) igokapil | dreamstime.com; page 366 © (top) Timothy Malcolm; (middle) Timothy Malcolm; (bottom) lei xu | dreamstime.com; page 374 © heather hubbard | dreamstime.com; page 376 © (top) heather hubbard | dreamstime.com; (middle) 1miro | dreamstime.com; (bottom) Timothy Malcolm; page 386 © richardseeley | dreamstime.com; page 401 © (top) jon bilous | dreamstime.com; (middle) Timothy Malcolm; (bottom) allard1 | dreamstime.com; page 403 © Timothy Malcolm; page 404 © meinzahn | dreamstime.com; page 407 © (top) colin young | dreamstime.com; (middle) iainhamer | dreamstime.com; (bottom) catuncia | dreamstime.com; page 411 © (top) drewthehobbit | dreamstime.com; (middle) Timothy Malcolm; (bottom) Timothy Malcolm; page 414 © Timothy Malcolm; page 422 © lynnemariehale | dreamstime.com; page 425 © (top) bncc369 | dreamstime.com; (middle) wangkun jia | dreamstime.com; (bottom) isabel poulin | dreamstime.com; page 430 © cvandyke | dreamstime.com;

ACKNOWLEDGMENTS

What an incredible experience: Hiking, road-tripping, eating, drinking, and meeting fantastic people, plus driving approximately 3,500 miles and writing nearly 200,000 words. I couldn't have done this without my team at Avalon Travel: Rachel Feldman, Darren Alessi, Albert Angulo, and Nikki Ioakimedes. Their assistance and sharp editing skills made my job a whole lot easier.

I must acknowledge the Appalachian Trail Conservancy for its help and its tireless advocacy for hiking and adventuring. The New York-New Jersey Trail Conference has always been a shining light, and has done a yeoman's job creating and documenting trails. Thanks also to the Appalachian Mountain Club and its chapters, as well as the Green Mountain Club in Vermont. Thanks to hikers I met along the way, the tipsters in small towns and rural areas who were happy to share their knowledge, and the kind folks with free food, cheap motel rooms, and good conversation.

Thanks to John DeSanto, who doesn't realize he turned me onto hiking. Thanks to Peter Wright, who pushed me to be stronger in the wild. A big hand to editors and writers whose assistance has always been invaluable, especially Brenda Gilhooly, Alyssa Sunkin-Strube, Brian Mahoney, Barry Lewis, and John Meo. Also, thanks to Julia and Bruce Malcolm. The long days spent in the car, refusing to use anything but the family-sized Rand McNally U.S. map book, proved crucial to my love of road trips.

Finally, thanks to my wife, Sarah Malcolm, for her unwavering support, and for giving me the opportunity to take multiple road trips—even with an infant at home. Oh, and a quick shoutout to the 2010 Subaru Legacy: I never really liked you, but we did this together. RIP.

From Trips to Remember & Epic Adventure

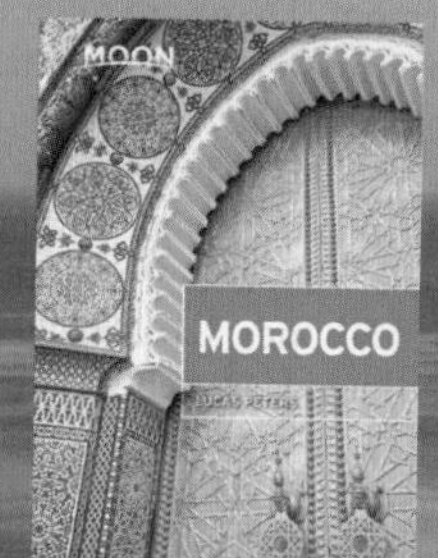

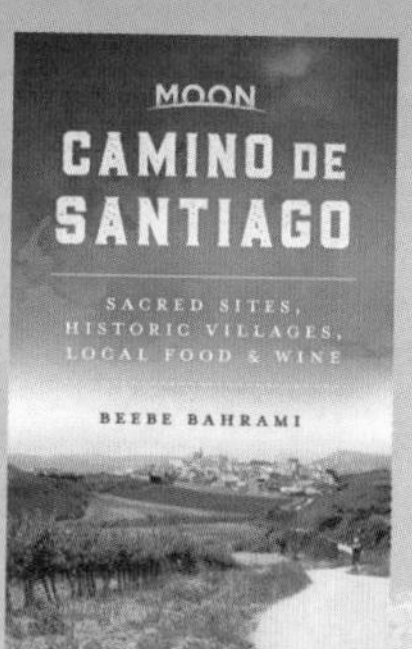

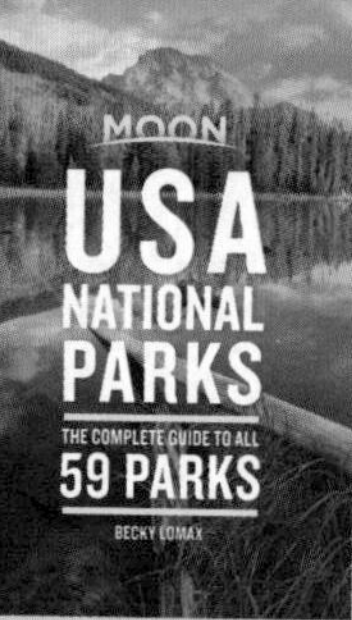

...to Beachy Getaways Around the Globe

HIT THE ROAD WITH MOON!

Inside the pages of our road trip guides you'll find:

- Detailed driving directions including mileages & drive times
- Itineraries for a range of timelines
- Advice on where to sleep, eat, and explore

Stretch your legs and hit the trails with ***Moon Drive & Hike Appalachian Trail.***

MOON.COM | @MOONGUIDES    

Road Trip USA

Covering more than 35,000 miles of blacktop stretching from east to west and north to south, ***Road Trip USA*** takes you deep into the heart of America.

This colorful guide covers the top road trips including historic Route 66 and is packed with maps, photos, illustrations, mile-by-mile highlights, and more!

Find your next adventure with Moon Travel Guides